The China Race

The China Race

Global Competition for Alternative World Orders

FEI-LING WANG

Published by State University of New York Press, Albany

© 2024 State University of New York

All rights reserved

Printed in the United States of America

No part of this book may be used or reproduced in any manner whatsoever without written permission. No part of this book may be stored in a retrieval system or transmitted in any form or by any means including electronic, electrostatic, magnetic tape, mechanical, photocopying, recording, or otherwise without the prior permission in writing of the publisher.

For information, contact State University of New York Press, Albany, NY www.sunypress.edu

Library of Congress Cataloging-in-Publication Data

Name: Wang, Fei-Ling author.
Title: The China race : global competition for alternative world orders / Fei-Ling Wang.
Other titles: Global competition for alternative world orders
Description: Albany, NY : State University of New York Press, [2024] | Includes bibliographical references and index.
Identifiers: LCCN 2023023018 | ISBN 9781438496580 (hardcover : alk. paper) | ISBN 9781438496603 (ebook) | ISBN 9781438496597 (pbk. : alk. paper)
Subjects: LCSH: China—Foreign relations—1976– | Globalization—China. | China—Foreign relations—United States. | United States—Foreign relations—China. | China—Politics and government—1976–
Classification: LCC DS779.47 .W333 2024 | DDC 327.51073—dc23/eng/20220815
LC record available at https://lccn.loc.gov/2023023018

10 9 8 7 6 5 4 3 2 1

For Yvon, Justin, Anna, and Bella
and children everywhere

Contents

LIST OF ILLUSTRATIONS	xi
ACKNOWLEDGMENTS	xiii
INTRODUCTION	1
The China Race	2
Arrangement of the Book	5

CHAPTER 1
The China Race: A Normative Analysis of Global Competition

and World Order	9
The Uncommon Race	11
The Qin-Han Polity and the China Order	14
A Framework of Analysis	17
Three Hypotheses	21
A Contextualization: The China Race versus the Cold War	32
Consequences of Choices	39
Odds of Success of the Options	48
Principles of Normative Assessment	51
A Short Note on Globalization	64
Further Considerations on Preferences and Criteria	67
Issues of Epistemology	71

CHAPTER 2
PRC Foreign Policy: From World Communism to Community

of Common Destiny	77
The Motivation and the Routes	78
World Revolution or Common Destiny: The Core Interest	85

viii | Contents

Omnidirectional Efforts: Nothing Is Small	90
Foreign Policy of and for the Party	93
Cost to the People	97
Impact on the Chinese Nation	105
Service and Disservice	112
The Effects of Beijing's Ventures Abroad	121
Torrents of Bad Coins	125
Deals with PRC Characteristics	133
Time for Engaging in the Race	136

CHAPTER 3

The PRC-USA Rivalry: For Existence and the World	141
An Existential Rivalry	141
The Challenger	145
Aiming High and Globally	148
Further Reflections on PRC Power and Aims	152
The State of Sinology	159
A Study of China Studies	164
Reframing the Paradigms	171
The Reorientation of US China Policy	178
The Anticipated Zigzags	181
The China Race in the United States	186
The Glacier in Motion	192

CHAPTER 4

Contaformation: A Strategy for Managing the China Race	201
The Parameters	202
Contaformation: Components and Objectives	213
The State of the Race	221
Crushing the Party and Quashing the Peculiar Racism	225
Ideas on Racing Well	231
The Worldwide Race	238
The China Race in the PRC	245
Empowering the Chinese People	251
More Tracks and Shortcuts	256
Winning the Race versus Transforming the PRC	260
The Race and Peace: Matrices of Cost	265

Contents | ix

EPILOGUE
The Future of China and the World   275

NOTES   283

WORKS AND SOURCES CITED   339

INDEX   445

Illustrations

Table 2.1	Visa-Free Privileges (Selected Countries, 2020–24)	116
Table 2.2	Visa Fees in Zimbabwe (2010s)	118
Table 2.3	Annual Illicit Financial Outflow via Trade Misinvoicing (2008–17)	133
Table 4.1	Matrices on Desirability, Cost, and Preference	267
Table 4.2	Costs of Two Wars	272

Acknowledgments

This book is the third volume of my rather immodest trilogy on China, which includes *The China Order* (2017) and *The China Record* (2023)—both also published by the SUNY Press.

During the nearly two decades that I have spent working on the trio, I have accumulated countless debts to people too many to be listed here individually. The drafting of this tome was largely done during the COVID-19 pandemic of 2020–23, a period in which I continued to benefit from the always inspiring and rewarding interactions with my colleagues and students at the Georgia Institute of Technology. The following institutions, listed alphabetically, kindly hosted my related research visits over the years: European University Institute, National University of Singapore, National Sun Yat-sen University, National Taiwan University, Sciences Po, Sungkyunkwan University, Tunghai University, US Air Force Academy, University of Macau, University of Tokyo, and Yonsei University. Generous grants from the Fulbright Commission, the Georgia Tech Foundation, the Hitachi Foundation, and the Minerva Initiative helped my research. A Neal Family Grant provided editorial assistance. I received valuable comments when I presented parts of my work at (in addition to the host institutions above): Academia Sinica, American Political Science Association, Auburn University, Council on Foreign Relations, Center for Strategic and International Studies, the Hudson Institute, International Studies Association, Joint University of US Special Forces, Korea University, Ludwig-Maximilians-Universität, National Chengchi University, National Chungcheng University, National Chungshin University, National Tsinghua University, Peking University, Princeton University, Seoul National University, the Strategic Multilayer Assessment Program and other US government programs, Sun Yat-sen xiv | Acknowledgments

University in Guangzhou, US Air Force War College, US Military Academy (West Point), US National War College, Universiti Kebangsaan Malaysia, University of Denver, University of Hawaii, University of Indonesia, University of London, University of Malaya, University of Pennsylvania, University of Tennessee, University of Victoria, and Victoria University. I salute you all from the bottom of my heart.

Dr. Michael Rinella and his team at SUNY Press made this book and its prequels possible. As always, I benefited greatly from the anonymous reviewers. Katherine Thompson and especially Dr. Paul Goldsman edited the manuscript with marvelous expertise and meticulousness. Anthony Xu helped put together the Works and Sources Cited list. Amane Kaneko designed the cover. Of course, I am alone responsible for any imperfections that may remain.

My extended family and my friends are always the great source of love and support that has sustained, expanded, and enriched my life and my work. Words simply cannot describe my eternal gratitude. This book is particularly for my children, who, together with children everywhere, have been the main motivation for me to take the self-assumed responsibility and audacity to complete this project. If this book, and my other writings, allow the kids, old and young, to think in a distant future that I have tried to have some forethought and contemplation, in addition to all those oldster's follies they could certainly and easily giggle over, I am content. Kiddos, y'all are always my proudest accomplishment—be yourselves, try your best, do well, and dream high.

Introduction

In the two prequels to this book, *The China Order: Centralia, World Empire, and the Nature of Chinese Power* (2017) and *The China Record: An Assessment of the People's Republic* (2023), I have attempted to explore the Chinese political tradition and worldviews and assess the record of the People's Republic of China under the Chinese Communist Party (CCP-PRC).[1] As a follow-up, this third volume of my trilogy on China attempts to answer the questions regarding the significance of and how to address the rising power of the CCP-PRC state. In the process, it gives consideration to alternative directions and the organizational optimality of human civilization. The simple message is that humanity faces a grand choice between competing world orders that shape the political organization among and within the nations and countries of the world. The policy references from this book likely will challenge a number of reigning notions and inconvenience significant vested interests. The author is not unaware of the immodest appearance of this book and is anticipating the likely rebuffs. Indeed, unpleasant premonitions of an impending inundation and the demanding efforts needed to steer clear often remain unheard or unheeded until the ship has irreversibly plunged into the abyss, pushed by the combined forces of misplaced intentions and the tyranny of small decisions at critical junctures.[2] An irreparable point of inflection is often not visible without the distance of time and space. As always, counterfactual analysis in hindsight and vindication in retrospect, therefore, rightfully remain delicious but forbidden fruits.[3]

More specifically, this book concerns a defining choice for the direction of human civilization that is unfolding right now: Will humanity continue the evolving Westphalian system with its current variant of the so-called liberal international order (LIO), a decentralized world polity of international relations among sovereign nations and states, or

2 | The China Race

be tempted by world political unification, which will inevitably result in a world empire like the China Order, which centrally ruled the entirety of the whole known world in east Eurasia for many centuries? Proposals and contentions regarding how to order and govern the world differently are neither new nor rare. To politically unite the whole known world is both a "natural" action and an ancient and "universal" ideal.[4] Human history has witnessed both successful and failed world empire–building projects in many "worlds," including the Mesopotamian-Persian world, the Mediterranean-European world, the Indian world, the Sinic world, the Mongolian world, and the Mesoamerican world. Many international systems have existed since the Sumerian city-states in Mesopotamia, largely isolated from each other; most were ended by the imperial power of a "world" empire.[5] In reality, these empires were limited by geography and technology, and only encompassed the whole known worlds of their respective civilizations. Thus, they never really united the polity of the whole of humanity. At present, however, the choice to embrace political unity is genuinely global and probably irreversible, and hence weighted with unprecedented urgency and unparalleled importance. There is the usual risk associated with a consequential choice due to "clouds of vagueness," endless uncertainty and unreason, innate "demands for precision," and path-dependence on "moral certainty."[6] There is also the unusual risk of an aggregate decision that is unprecedentedly holistic in scale and likely irrevocable in course.

The China Race

The grand choice of world order is now strikingly presented in the form of an epic contest, the so-called China Race centered around the PRC-USA rivalry, between the rising power of the CCP-led PRC state and the existing world order of the LIO shaped by the West under the leadership of the United States.[7] The two clashing sides of this global competition represent contrasting ways of ordering nations and states as the principal units of human organization, incompatible norms and rights for the people and divergent modes of government, alternative models of state-society and state-market relationships and socioeconomic development, and distinctive human-nature relationships. Consequently, the China Race is about the fortunes of humanity, as these disparate orders of world politics ultimately result in drastically different optimal-

Introduction | 3

ity of security, tranquility, justice, innovation, and efficiency for all of humankind. It concerns, therefore, shaping or reshaping, and directing or redirecting, human civilization.

The focus of this book is on the political organization of globalizing human civilization facing alternative world orders under competing leaders. Humankind has long approached questions regarding the world order with deliberations to optimize its "historical dynamics," and hence human civilization has not developed entirely adventitiously.[8] In fact, the Westphalian world order, based on national sovereign equality, is itself probably neither "natural" nor inevitable.[9] In 2019 and 2020, groups of eminent American and international experts assembled by the Council on Foreign Relations identified the potential and propensity for another profound—and likely defining and "reordering"—transition of the current world order and its leadership, with decorous and abstruse speculations about the associated uncertainties and possibilities.[10] In 2021, a group of Western scholars of international relations jointly published an attempt to identify the multiple, serious, and in some cases previously overlooked challenges to the existing world order, including the rise of Chinese power, which could transform the LIO "from within and without in unprecedented ways."[11] Some PRC analysts openly argued in 2021 for a pending "great competition [and] vast change centered on the world order of global governance," at a level that had been "unseen in a century" or "the first time in four centuries"; and a senior CCP official in charge of "public diplomacy" publicly declared in 2022 that the PRC "has resolved in desperation to compete with the US and the West in all areas [and] must win that competition."[12] Characteristically, such broad arguments are politely reticent.

This book, however, intends to immodestly and unambiguously outline how the world is facing grand and present choices between alternative world orders, and how to move forward. One path is to continue the world order of the Westphalian system of international relations among sovereign nations, under which humankind continues to compare and compete and, yes, struggle and fight toward an ever more possible future, maximizing optimality aggregately, for all. Another path is to politically unite the Earth into one reign, as epitomized by the China Order: people drift, with the hedonistic elites overly embracing *carpe diem*, and degenerate due to an institutional regression that will seal human civilization into a suboptimal or even disastrous and irreversible repeat of the not-too-distant past.

4 | The China Race

How to navigate the currents of globalization under the Westphalian world order to preserve or undo popular sovereignty *and* liberal democratic rule of law, with old wisdoms and new technologies, appears to be a key challenge for all nations.[13] More specifically, the 18 US government intelligence agencies jointly predicted in March 2021 a world of more competition and confrontation "between China and a Western coalition led by the United States," with "competing visions of the international system and governance that reflect their core interests and ideologies."[14] Across the Pacific, CCP-PRC leader Xi Jinping proclaimed one month later the imperative task of "making a wise choice" for the pressing question of "where should humanity be heading?"[15] He further declared in the United Nations five months later, and repeated to foreign partisans in March 2023, that "the world is once again at the crossroads of history."[16] Mighty minds think alike, albeit from opposing perspectives.

Central to this choice is the leadership of the current international community, which will determine how the world shall be ordered and led—the prize of the China Race between the West, led by the US, and the challenger, the CCP-dominated PRC state.[17] Far more than just an issue of how a nation is governed and behaves, the kleptocracy of the CCP-PRC state represents a viable mode of political governance that is evidently undesirable to the people, but seductive to the ambitious few, as it is increasingly formidable and strident, and thus "threatens global security" and well-being.[18] "Corruption fuels inequality, siphons off a nation's resources, spreads across borders, and generates human suffering. It is nothing less than a national security threat in the 21st century." So declared US president Joe Biden in fall 2021.[19] In December 2021, analysts in the US sounded the alarm that the global race has entered the "decade of maximum danger" and Americans must counter the PRC maximally with "whatever" as "there is no time left to waste" if they want to possibly "avoid an outcome they cannot afford."[20] Almost as if to explicate that "outcome," in fall 2022 and spring 2023, PRC scholars bluntly redeclared an imminent and inevitable "100-year change" of "international governance" from under the Westphalian system to a singular "global governance" of "one Village Earth [. . .] community of common human destiny," so as to redetermine "who governs" and "who are governed."[21]

The China Race has actually been in progress since the creation of the PRC in 1949, but was largely dismissed, assumed or wished away by the United States until the CCP-PRC's recent elevation on the world stage. The outcome of the China Race is in no way guaranteed, as the

Introduction | 5

contest becomes increasingly arduous and costly. Given population size and potential, its many peculiarities, and its long history, China could indeed become a viable, alternative, and even finer world leader, as the British philosopher Bertrand Russell envisioned a century ago.[22] That positive statement of possibility, now seen by many as feasible and even inevitable, only makes it more of an imperative to consider the normative desirability, policy preferences, and conscious actions humanity faces in choosing the leadership and order for the world, as this book contends. Successfully managing the China Race so as to actively shape the future in the best interests of the world, including the Chinese people, is highly probable as long as the Race is approached properly and confronted in time. Humanity has an excellent chance to avoid leaping backward or embracing suboptimal alternatives, with a comprehensive strategy addressing the rising CCP-PRC power that I call *Contaformation*—containment and engagement for the transformation and incorporation of China. A fully engaged and well-run China Race is a grand and global competition that, in and of itself, is natural and critically benefits the health and progress of human civilization.[23]

In the language of the well-established game theory,[24] the China Race (and the PRC-USA competition) appears to approximate a zero-sum game that is asymmetric, noncooperative, and continuous in nature for the CCP regime and the US/Western leadership (and the Westphalian world order itself). But it is essentially a non-zero-sum game that can be cooperative and positive for the world, including the Chinese people. Well played, this global competition could be as beneficial as any other games among nations. An optimal management of the China Race, therefore, means persevering and gaining from the great competition with a secure preservation of the Westphalian world order; an avoidance of a Sino-American war to the fullest extent possible, keeping the "inherently systemic and global war" between the two rivalries at the level of "low intensity," rather than "high intensity conflict" or total war;[25] and a transformed China as a great power devoid of the CCP's mode of governance and pursuits.

Arrangement of the Book

The first part of this book, chapter 1, is a general introduction to the China Race, the epic contest for power, influence, and leadership that will

6 | The China Race

ultimately determine the destiny of human civilization. Being contended in this competition is the post–Cold War version of the Westphalian system, the LIO currently led by the US and its Western allies. Eagerly running in the Race as the challenger is the rising power of the PRC state under the CCP struggling for regime survival. The CCP-PRC has captured China and the Chinese people, extracting resources from the world's largest population (prior to 2024) and second-largest economy, tapping a host of odd allies for political reconfiguration, challenging democratic rule of law, and advancing a political globalism for a safer world for authoritarian governance, at the minimum, and a world empire of either world communism or the China Order, at the maximum. At stake in this existential Race, beyond the survival of two opposing political systems, is the well-being of all humankind, including the Chinese people.

To analyze the China Race and contemplate the rationale and means to manage it well, it is necessary to introduce a few hypotheses, principles, and parameters to support a normative assessment of the contenders. As I have attempted to demonstrate in the two prequels to this book, the CCP-PRC state is a viable and mighty power, but it represents a suboptimal and undesirable alternative to governance of the West as the world leader, and a China Order–style world political centralization as an inferior alternative to the current world order based on the Westphalian system. I will discuss further issues such as globalism and national interests, justice and the common good, power transition in international relations, and why the US remains the least likely destroyer and the last capable defender of the less undesirable Westphalian world order. After a consideration of preference, epistemology, and the meaning of victory, I submit the desirability, imperativeness, and achievability for the whole world, including the Chinese people, of optimally managing the China Race and decisively prevailing in it.

The second part of this book, chapters 2 and 3, addresses what the CCP-PRC has been doing internationally and the impact of Beijing's actions abroad. A central thesis concerns the urgency and peril represented by the PRC challenge. A tight and exploitative control of the world's largest (or second largest after 2023) population in an era favoring the supremacy of equal human rights and globalism has given the CCP powerful machinery for its global pursuits. The unfortunate state of Sinology in the pluralistic West, especially the United States, compounded by the CCP's capable and effective efforts to build its global "united front," has significantly enhanced Beijing's hand. The unscrupulous autocracy thus appears strong, even invincible, in its global race with the US to reshape world politics and rebuild a China Order–like world empire for the whole of humanity.

However strikingly successful in maintaining power and increasingly resourceful in its global ambitions, the CCP-PRC state is nonetheless found to be inherently suboptimal and fragile, with deep flaws and weaknesses both at home and abroad. These deficiencies can be fruitfully and inexpensively exploited by its opponents in the China Race. Beijing's foreign policy has been largely as cost-ineffective as it is undesirable, and as suboptimal as its domestic policies. At an astronomical cost to Chinese life and resources, and with many failures, the CCP-PRC accomplished little to serve the Chinese people or the Chinese nation beyond safeguarding and enriching the ruling elites. The gap and conflict between the regime's pursuits and China's national interests have become ever more apparent, making the cost of the party-state's governance through force and deception ever more exorbitant. With its gross inefficiency and rampant corruption, Beijing heavily depends on the goodwill, naivete, and somnolence of the West, afflicts the Chinese people with depressed living standards and assaults on their rights and freedoms, and faces growing problems such as popular resistance and unfavorable demographics—all of these points are critical targets for a reoriented, concerted, and intelligent effort to slow, constrain, and transform the CCP-PRC state.

Chapter 4 comprises the third and final part of this book, describing and elaborating on the feasibility and desirability of an effective and efficient strategy for managing the China Race, the so-called contaformation, a portmanteau for containment and engagement for the transformation and incorporation of China. After a quick recap of the nature of the China Race and the CCP-PRC state as the systemic challenger, I discuss a strategic approach of firm containment and smart engagement, enabling the world, including the Chinese people, to benefit from the global competition and avoid a tragic repeat of the history of the post-Qin Chinese world. This strategy has three hierarchical aims: to prevent the CCP mode of polity from becoming the new leader of the international community and to stop the alternative world order of political centralization; to avoid a direct war between China and the United States, to the fullest possible extent; and to transform the CCP-PRC state sociopolitically and to fully incorporate China into the international community.

This comprehensive management of the China Race, with well-reasoned objectives and fine-tuned methods, I argue, will enable the West

8 | The China Race

and the world, including the Chinese people, to feasibly and affordably benefit from and ultimately prevail in the China Race at minimal cost and tolerable collateral damage. By enabling and encouraging sociopolitical transformation of the PRC but leaving it mostly to the Chinese people, the conclusion of the China Race could be surprisingly peaceful, rewarding, and speedy in the end.

The epilogue is a brief summary of the book and the whole China trilogy, concluding with speculations on future scenarios for China and the world.

1

The China Race

A Normative Analysis of
Global Competition and World Order

This chapter starts my effort to understand the implications of and the response to the rising power of the People's Republic of China (PRC). It focuses on how and why the world could and should respond to the PRC ruled by the Chinese Communist Party (CCP)—the CCP-PRC state. I outline the China Race, a comprehensive competition between the CCP-PRC state and the West led by the United States, centered around the global PRC-USA rivalry, for the future of the world and human civilization.[1] As I discuss, the PRC is powerfully reviving and pushing a feasible and even appealing alternative to the current world order—the so-called LIO (liberal international order) variant of the Westphalian world order, which has anchored human civilization for centuries. This necessarily challenges the USA, the current leader of the existing world order. In this book, the Westphalian world order is identified, conceptually, as a human-constructed political system with core principles of sovereignty and the sovereign equality of states and, by extension, key norms such as national self-determination and mutual-nonintervention.[2] The LIO has added to the Westphalian system some "liberal values" of consequence such as democratic rule of law, collective security, human equality of freedom and universal human rights, and "free movement of goods and capital."[3]

After a précis about the nature and record of the CCP-PRC state, I seek to address two sets of questions in this chapter. First, is the China

10 | The China Race

Order of world empire for the whole *tianxia* (all under heaven), or a world political unification in general, more desirable for humankind than the Westphalian system of international relations? Is the PRC, as a modified Qin-Han polity of authoritarianism, a viable or even preferable model of governance and socioeconomic development, and hence an equally or even more desirable world leader than the USA? I will attempt to consider how to assess the key alternatives that the rising Chinese power is purportedly presenting to the world: a "Confucian model of *tianxia*" to replace nations states; a "Confucian hybrid regime" of rule by law with the people's will "expressed" through meritocracy to supplant democratic rule of law; Confucian hierarchical ethics to supersede personal rights and freedoms; and a "socialism with Chinese characteristics" (in fact an authoritarian state-capitalism or "partocracy capitalism" or party-capitalism) to replace the "capitalist world order."[4] Second, how should the world, and the Chinese people, respond to the rising power of the CCP-PRC state? How do we interpret China's intentions and actions? Is Beijing's effort to recenter and reorder the world at all feasible or just hyperbole to justify the regime's survival and extraction? What choices are feasible and desirable for the world and the Chinese people in order to manage the China Race? Between the two extreme endings, a hot and total war or a CCP victory, what are the chances, benefits, costs, boundaries, prospects, shortcuts, and pitfalls of the China Race?

To advance the reasons and approaches for how to engage and run the China Race, this chapter aims to frame a principled normative assessment. It will address questions about globalism, justice and the common good, power transition in international relations, and why the PRC has become a formidable challenger while the USA remains the least likely destroyer and most capable protector of the Westphalian world order. This conceptual framework will be used in the rest of this book to analyze and appraise the record and the actions of the CCP-PRC state on the international stage. The party-state is seen as a suboptimal and undesirable but feasible alternative of governance to the West as the world leader, and, as a world leader, Beijing's China Order of world political centralization (under a variety of colorful names) is deemed to be an inferior but seductive alternative to the Westphalian system. This chapter will further consider the issues of preference, epistemology, and the history of the Cold War to set the stage for the detailed discussion later in this book on the strategy of *Contaformation*—containment and engagement for the transformation and incorporation of China—for an optimal management of the China Race for the benefit of the world and the Chinese people.

The Uncommon Race

International competition between great powers, like rivalries or races among nations in general, is common and fully expected under a decentralized world political order. As I will elaborate later, such comparisons and contests are in fact key attributes of a de facto or, better, a de jure world order of political decentralization among the sovereign nations or the international political anarchy (IPA) that have fundamentally enriched and advanced human civilization. Naturally, international competition, especially the so-called great power competition, may sometime end in a singular power concentration and a systemic conquest, building a centralized and uniform world governance and creating a structural transformation or game-change, and extinguishing the practice and ideology of world political decentralization. Such has been the experience of numerous human civilizations, such as those in Mesopotamia, the Sinic world, and Mesoamerica. Since the 17th century, the Westphalian system has legally codified the IPA in Europe as the world order for sovereign nation-states and has evolved and expanded to cover the whole globe. Great power competition with the expense of enormous energy and colossal impact, however, has continued for a variety of reasons, with survival as the most basic motive, and the overthrow of the Westphalian system as a high ambition. Indeed, rounds of great power competition have driven and shaped the evolution of the Westphalian world order, determining the leadership, main character, dominant norms, and main achievements for the international community, through cycles of the rise and fall of nations and rounds of "power transition" among the leading members of the community.[5] So far, the dynamic and ceaseless great power competition and the subsequent power transitions have managed to preserve the basics of the Westphalian world order. Some of the major (usually "rising") contenders did have the conviction and force to attempt a systemic transformation. They, however, have all failed, withered, been voluntarily or involuntarily restrained, or transformed to become contented members of the system.

The China Race between the CCP-PRC state and the US-led West appears to be a rather common great power competition in that

12 | The China Race

it similarly concerns power and leadership, and produces the expected benefits of stimulating contestation, innovative experimentation and focused investment, and risky tensions and costly confrontations, with spillover effects and powerful lessons impacting other nations. Yet, the China Race has been uncommon in many profound ways, mostly because the rising contender, the PRC, is destined to seek a systemic alteration of the world with its deeply held vision of a centralized world political unification, "once in one hundred years" (since World War I) or "unseen in four hundred years" (since the Peace of Westphalia).[6] The China Race has the rare but potent combination of fundamental, institutional, sociopolitical, and ideological incompatibilities between the two competitors, with their unprecedented magnitude, multiplicity, and reach constituting a systemic and viable choice with ultrahigh stakes for world leadership and world order. It represents a uniquely definitive and directional juncture of history, an inflection point, for the fortunes and future of all human civilization.[7] The China Race is not just about who and how to win the game of international competition; it is not just another great power competition to determine relative power and gains; it is about the game of international competition itself—whether the Westphalian world order of political decentralization and sovereign equality among nations will survive.

In fact, the China Race has been in the open ever since the creation of the PRC by the CCP in 1949. Yet, it has been disguised, discounted, dismissed, normalized, assumed off, or wished away several times by the West in the past seven decades.[8] As I will analyze later in this book, the peculiar state of Sinology in the West seems to have been partially but significantly responsible for those disguises and dismissals. Like a spreading underground fire, a surging glacier or tectonic friction, the China Race relentlessly persists and grows to take its natural course, seen or not, increasingly dashing fond wishes and vested interests along the way.

As a senior PRC scholar noted, the extensive cross-Pacific exchanges that have enriched and delighted many since 1979, when Beijing and Washington established full diplomatic relations, perhaps might continue with "an implicit understanding: the United States would not openly attempt to destabilize China's internal order, and in turn, China would not intentionally weaken the U.S.-led international order."[9] Without the overlapping strategic interest of opposing the Soviet Union, however, that "live and let live" PRC-USA relationship, circa 1978–89 and 1998–2010s, is inherently transient and conditional, if not fully fantastical.[10] PRC leaders and analysts have now re-enshrined the Maoist "philosophy and art of struggle" and openly advocated for "dealing with the US by winning the continued struggles."[11] Today, ignoring the China Race is no longer feasible, chiefly because the CCP has changed its strategic calculus to resume and aggressively expand the pursuit of its innate mandate or "mission" for regime security since 2007 at the latest, when it chose Xi Jinping as the heir-apparent. The spectacular "coming-out party" of the 2008 Beijing Olympic Games unmistakably started to signal the rising power and confidence of the party-state, just when the West was being battered by the Great Recession and the long war on international terrorism, which was akin to a severe and persistent allergy. A year later, in January 2010, *China Economic Weekly*, run by the *People's Daily*, the CCP's mouthpiece in Beijing, bluntly published a special issue on China's role in "redesigning a new global order" and pushing for "world transformation."[12] Refusing to change its politics and policies in order to synchronize with the US-led world order and match Chinese socioeconomic changes since the 1980s, the CCP inevitably dictates that the rising PRC power systematically and methodically challenge and replace US leadership and Western values, due to its insatiable drive for power and control, and in order to secure the regime's survival. The "new era" of the PRC under Xi, who, as I have shown in *The China Record*, literally emulates and seeks to outdo Mao Zedong, has intensely reenergized the return of the China Race since 2012.[13] The US and the West subsequently awoke in the 2010s–2020s to face the China Race with a new understanding: the rising Chinese power, with the CCP-PRC state being neither weakened nor transformed, is the systemic challenge and existential threat of the time.[14]

The first step in examining the uncommon China Race is to clarify the organizational and ideological nature of the CCP-PRC as a Qin-Han polity of authoritarianism, and discuss Beijing's innate worldviews and its preordained pursuits of the China Order, a world-empire political order. The structural DNA of the Qin-Han polity determines the profile of the CCP-PRC, which may be said to exhibit a "nucleotide combination" of ACGT: "authoritarianism, consumerism, global ambitions, and technology" with an "ideological mixture—Marxism-Leninism, traditional thought, historical analogy, and economic success."[15] Essentially, authoritarianism-totalitarianism defines the character, capacity, and behavioral patterns of the CCP-PRC state.[16] Without the mandated destiny of the China Order inherent in the Qin-Han polity embodied in the CCP-PRC,

14 | The China Race

which has struggled eternally for regime survival in a fundamentally inhospitable environment, neither the nation of China nor the Chinese people would seem to have the reason and resolve to reorder the post–Cold War Westphalian world order.[17] To preserve its rather "premodern" autocracy, the CCP has forcefully attempted to "rejuvenate" the ideology of the Qin-Han polity and the China Order. It has also wrapped itself in many imported, "modern" ideas and phraseologies: from the Stalinist Marxism that is bankrupt in its homeland, and the rising puffery and fanaticism of globalism that seems to be capturing the post–Cold War world, to the resurrected Nazi-esque ideas of dictator-worship that seem to have inspired many in the PRC to imagine a "Sinocentric *Großraum* (greater space) that spans all of Eurasia—or, perhaps, a Sino-*Reich*."[18] The CCP-PRC party-state is fully invested in its regime security and enjoys considerable advantages in international gaming as a resourceful autocracy in control of a mega country, including among its allies many West-educated agents and apologists.[19] It recruits a motley group of odd partners from all quarters in order to advance its political globalism toward its brand of world governance, and, ultimately, a world empire. The China Race is therefore highly uncommon and consequential, not just regarding the survival of the CCP-PRC political system and the well-being of the West, but also the fortune and fate of all humankind.

The Qin-Han Polity and the China Order

In the two prequels to this book, *The China Order* and *The China Record*, I have attempted to document and assess the CCP-PRC state as a reincarnation of the Chinese Qin-Han polity. The Qin-Han polity, named after two consecutive world empires two millennia ago, was subsequently improved and repeatedly practiced in the Sinic world. It is an imperial political system based on Chinese Legalism coated with Confucianism that mandates a worldwide political centralization or a world empire. It is a premodern (pre-Enlightenment) polity of authoritarianism and even totalitarianism, a centralized governance that rules people in a manner akin to herding livestock, with the unscrupulous use of force and ruse for the benefit of the autocratic regime (often just for a singular ruler).[20] What is unique about this modified Qin-Han polity since 1949, however, is that the CCP-PRC is far from ruling the whole known world, and is still unable to control or hold off the many powerful and more advanced countries, even in pretention. Consequently, the deep incompatibility and intense conflicts the CCP-PRC state has with the current world order necessarily makes this Qin-Han polity, the autocratic party-state based on Legalism coated with pseudo-communism and pseudo-Confucianism,[21] stuck in perpetual and increasing animosity and paranoia, as it must coexist with many other nations it dreads fundamentally but cannot control or prevail over.

Hopelessly outdated and out of place in the post–World War II world, and especially the post–Cold War world, the CCP-PRC state has an acutely inadequate and diminishing political legitimacy in China. It has relied on force and trickery, along with a certain amount of populist appeasement, to centrally rule over a massive and transforming country. This mode of governance may deliver a so-called CCP Optimality, enabling the regime to remain in power, continue enriching itself, and showcase the efficacy of authoritarianism and autocratic state-capitalism or partocracy capitalism. Despite its many blunders and failures, the CCP-PRC state has indeed saved and enriched itself during the past four decades by means of its selective and tactical acceptance of the West-led Westphalian system, pro tempore. For the Chinese people, however, the party-state has produced the horrific China Tragedy and the lasting China Suboptimality, which perpetuate and magnify social discontent and regime insecurity. The CCP has thus been cruelly locked into an endless and exorbitant life-and-death struggle from day one, externally against the existing world order of sovereign nations, and internally against Chinese society, which has been continuously influenced and updated by the outside world, Westernized in many ways, since the 19th century.

Inevitably, like all imperial systems at other places and in other times, the PRC autocracy is destined to seek survival and security through organizing and governing or influencing the whole known world, or effectually pretending to do so. Whenever possible, the party-state struggles for a singular world order of authoritarianism or even totalitarianism, in the same way that Chinese emperors organized and ruled the whole known Chinese world for many centuries. Increasing raw power and expanding centralized control are the CCP's ultimate means and objectives. This world political recentering and reordering in the direction of world empire has been touted at various times and to different audiences as a restoration or rejuvenation of the imperial China Order for the *tianxia* (the whole known world), a grand revolution to build a promised paradise of world socialism and communism, or some

16 | The China Race

eye-catching globalization endeavors catering to a variety of idealists. A world state of the China Order (or with some other label), however, tends to become an authoritarian or even totalitarian world empire, with socioeconomic and cultural performances that are historically suboptimal and often disastrous for the people.[22] Still, world political centralization attracts and excites the ambitious worldwide, many of whom are not necessarily autocrats, Chinese, or Communists. Adding to the PRC's attraction are its sophisticated radical and liberal veneer, humanistic and idealistic appearance, and globalist guise.[23] Its imported Leninist-Stalinist version of Marxism, for one, advocates for an eventual world political unity under the "scientific world outlook" of socialism and communism for a utopian heaven on earth.[24]

Since 1949, the CCP-PRC party-state has commandeered the Chinese people in service of its first and foremost goal of staying in power forever. In the awkward and agonizing disguise of the Chinese nation-state (in fact a remnant of a multination empire), the PRC is mandated or cursed to unscrupulously influence, recenter, and reorder the world in its image, wherever and whenever possible. As I wrote at the end of *The China Record*:

> Unmonitored and unrestrained, the underperforming and undesirable CCP regime has controlled and used one fifth of productive humankind to nonetheless become a suboptimal giant, a formidable contender for power and influence on the world stage, and a viable and even tempting substitute for the current world leadership. [. . .] The CCP-PRC party-state represents an alternative political system that is suboptimal while formidable, undesirable yet feasible, derisory but serious, with many, real and profound consequences for the entire world.

More specifically, in the PRC, the deeply harbored ancient concept of *tianxia yitong* or world unity/unification has now been actively revived, colorfully repackaged, and extensively beautified as a "better" option than the "modern [world] system that emerged in the 17th–19th centuries." It is said to provide a "cultural empire," a "smart democracy" of "*contopia*" (a singular, common state for all) with "a Confucian Improvement or Confucian Optimum—namely a Pareto Improvement for everyone" under a hierarchical oneness of the whole world, to "save us from global chaos."[25] In this way, as a senior CCP official wrote in 2020, humanity may finally resolve the "three-millennia struggle" between "Western/Greek civilization, which values freedom first," and "Eastern/Chinese civilization, which values order first."[26] This "Chinese vision of world order" is seen by some as not too distant from the "Marxist proposition" envisioning a uniform, cosmopolitan or universal world order of socialism and its natural improvement of communism.[27] To an American commentator, Beijing "wants to assimilate" the world, and "the Chinese have acquired the technical means from the West to ruin" the West in so doing.[28] The official version of this grand objective of a revived China Order, with Xi Jinping's personal imprimatur as of 2012, is "the China Dream" of "building a community of common destiny for humanity," which he has repeated constantly ever since.[29] In mid-2021, the CCP's mouthpiece published two frontpage "proclamations" declaring that the Party's "internal DNA" of socialism and communism "has not let China down," and that the CCP-PRC does "not let socialism down [and will] do more to promote world socialism."[30] In the words of Gennady Zyuganov, the longtime chairman of the Communist Party of the Russian Federation, which the CCP proudly published to celebrate its centennial in 2021, the CCP-PRC, "during the dark moment of the world Communist movement, has not only held on but also picked up the banner that was dropped by the brotherly Soviet Communist Party to become the leader of the march toward Communism."[31] A year later, another front-page "proclamation" by the *People's Daily* continued to self-identify the CCP as "the leader directing the future of human society."[32]

A Framework of Analysis

Despite the apparent randomness of highly improbable events with massive impacts, the so-called Black Swans, the world we live in is neither adventitious nor unchangeable, but often shaped by choices and actions under the influence of certain convictions and ideals, especially at the critical junctures that define the world order and the flow of history.[33] Indeed, many human-made world empires or "global empires" of the various "whole known worlds" (or, more precisely, the separate spheres or regions of the globe), desirable or not, have risen and fallen to characterize the history of various human civilizations.[34] Over the past five centuries, a period during which human civilization has experienced revolutionary advances, international competition has led to many rounds

18 | The China Race

of power and leadership transition among the great powers—whose rises and falls in apparent cycles have aggregately improved human polity at both the national and international levels. Yet, so far, the basic Westphalian system, which brews and sanctions international competition, has managed to stay intact. It is thus easy for observers to take it for granted that great power competition is always about the same game, akin to periodical sport contests or business cycles. Financial guru Ray Dalio (cochairman of Bridgewater), for example, has recently portrayed "big cycles" of the rise and decline of empires over 500 years based on financial power, and has forecast that the current world order resembling "the most recent analogous time" of 1930–45 will give way to "the rise of the Chinese empire."[35] To others, the China Race is more about "China vs. democracy: the greatest game," or a worldwide "China challenge to freedom" with an "imperialist" agenda.[36] According to the analysis of a PRC scholar, the rise of China seems to represent another "resentful rise of national power," like that of Germany and Japan before World War II and the Soviet Union, as opposed to an "adaptive rise," rising to deliver revenge, shed shame, seek power, and build an ideal society; as such, a resentful risen power "will certainly disrupt and depose the existing international order" with all of its might.[37]

This book surmises that the China Race certainly includes but also profoundly exceeds the rivalry between two competing political ideologies and two sets of sociopolitical values, broadly branded as communist dictatorship and capitalist democracy, both the products of modern European history. It is not just a simple, cyclical, redistribution of power or the emergence of a new hegemon within the *same* world politics of the past five centuries.[38] It is less a Black Swan from nowhere than a Gray Rhino charging, an "obvious danger" that people are ignoring.[39] Beijing's "strategic plan to conquer Hong Kong," which was unseen, covered up, or wished away by so many for so long until "the fall of Hong Kong" in 2020–21, is but one illustration.[40] The China Race is about the possibility of a systemic reorganization and redirection of human civilization, and thus goes far beyond a mere dethroning of the West as the leader of the international community. It is about a systemic transformation of that community of sovereign nations into a non-Westphalian, hierarchical political centralization of humanity. A world political centralization, displacing and replacing the decentralized Westphalian system, as will be analyzed later, is bound to be a world empire of authoritarianism and totalitarianism like the China Order that once governed the Chinese world in east Eurasia. In the words of a rising CCP analyst and propagandist, the PRC is competing with the US in four areas: model—"who will be the model of development for the nations"; collaboration—"who can unite more nations to solve the world's problems"; dividends—"who can bring more benefits to the world"; and perspectives—"who will lead humanity to higher civilization."[41] As such, the China Race suggests a vital choice for different sociopolitical norms and ideologies at a critical juncture in human history.

It may not be that difficult or unnatural to accept a new and seemingly viable China Order (with or without that exact name) centrally unifying the world, as world empires have emerged and existed for long periods of time in the past, in just about all known worlds of human civilization. Optimal or suboptimal as it may be, as a historical trend, the coming of the China Order may simply be hard to resist, let alone stop, by an affluent and hedonistic society under pluralistic democracy. It may not be wise to risk the wrath of the presumptive leader of one-fifth of humanity, as this could realistically result in open conflict or even world war in the age of weapons of mass destruction. Surely, the Chinese people are fully entitled to aspire to a better life in the "Chinese Dream," a conception imitating the fabled "American Dream" that may overlap with the CCP's China Dream of recentering and reordering the world.[42] Furthermore, those who have believed in and advocated for an alternative to the Westphalian system can handily and often correctly list many downsides and problems and even unethical aspects of the current world order. Besides, at least theoretically, the introduction of an equal but different rival could help to curb possible (some would argue inevitable) American abuses of power and minimize the often outsized and unbidden American impact. After all, Washington could be captured by certain interest groups or narrow-minded ideologues at times to missteer the world. Acknowledging the fact that the PRC is not democratizing, "liberal globalists" might nonetheless hope that, in any event, the rising China would force the US into "a race to the top" rather a race to the bottom under the existing world order, a managed peer competition producing a "performance sweepstake" for the world.[43] Some even envision a chance for "global justice and democratic socialism" to emerge from the running of the China Race.[44]

In fact, many have already started to cheer for the possibility, argue for the inevitability, and hedge their bets on the arrival of a new Chinese world leadership. To some, it is sensible to welcome a brisk

20 | The China Race

transfer of power to Chinese leaders, who would compete to reform and improve the world in many ways.[45] To be sure, like a rising firm or state that has yet to become a monopoly or world empire, the PRC has been quite impressive and competitive in the world economy for about three decades, delivering remarkable albeit mostly still *average* growth, as I have attempted to document in *The China Record*.[46] Such arguments are plentiful in Chinese publications. Notable views in this vein in English include the bold but short-lived proposition of a "Chimerica"—a symbiotic coleadership of the world by the PRC and the USA.[47] A concrete example of action to this end is the extensive and profitable business relationship between Stephen Schwarzman, the leader of the US private equity firm the Blackstone Group, and the PRC, including the critical, "savior" loan of $3 billion from Bank of China to Blackstone in its dark period of 2007–14, and the well-funded Schwarzman College for "creating global leadership for the 21st century" at Beijing's Tsinghua University, which opened in 2016.[48] Unsurprisingly, Blackstone has continued to cheer and "help" the PRC. Its big investment in 2021, the $3 billion acquisition of SOHO China, owned by politically disfavored billionaire developers (Pan Shiyi and Zhang Xin), however, still fizzled out due to Beijing's obstruction.[49]

However, both theory and history undeniably indicate that a monopoly, once established, leads to a systemic and lasting stagnation and suboptimality, as the record of the China Order in the Sinic world abundantly demonstrates.[50] Empirically, the true long-run cost of the exciting rise of a monopoly or world empire—often horrendously expensive—tends to be obscured, blatantly overlooked, or effectively disguised until it is too late. Practically speaking, the rosy pictures and wishful thinking concerning the rising PRC leadership of the world can be effectively countered in two ways, as a combined exposé of the true nature of the China Race. First, as I have attempted to accomplish in the prequels to this book, *The China Order* and *The China Record*, a thorough investigation of the CCP-PRC state unmistakably establishes its record as a suboptimal and often disastrous system of governance and socioeconomic development, thus indicating how abysmally tragic it would be for all of humanity were the indisputably inferior (but still feasible and capable) PRC to replace the qualitatively much less undesirable (but still imperfect and vulnerable) US leadership of the world.

Second, as I will try to demonstrate in this chapter, there is a clear normative preference for the Westphalian world order of nation-states over the alternative of a China Order–like centralized world autocracy. The US is currently in position to be the foremost (though perchance not necessarily the last) shield ensuring the continuation of the Westphalian system, so long as it remains a firm, stable, and domestically molded devotee of the system. There is nothing inevitable or preferable about the PRC winning the China Race, and, with timely adjustments, concerted effort, and proper improvements, the US and the West could still cost-effectively and even peacefully engage and prevail in the China Race, maximizing the best interests of the world, including the Chinese people.

Three Hypotheses

My normative analysis of the China Race rests on a three-fold hypothesis that sets the premises for the rest of this book.

HYPOTHESIS I

The Westphalian system has been proven to be a much less undesirable world order than all other feasible alternatives, including the facile and intoxicating ideal of a unitary world government, whether a world empire like the China Order or the Inca empire; a tyranny of the Nazi or Communist world movement; the Japanese dream of "all the world under a single roof" (*hakkō ichiu*), which led to "ultra-statism";[51] or a "feudal" or even liberal "world democracy," to singularly govern the whole world for the common good.[52] It was the "escape from Rome" and the failures of world empire–building that historically allowed the Europeans to surge ahead to "dominate" and transform the entire world, as the historian Walter Scheidel (and others) argued in 2019. This is, of course, notwithstanding the many imperfections and problems of the Westphalian system, such as its "Westfailure" in managing world financial markets, as the political scientist Susan Strange put it back in the 1990s.[53]

There is a long tradition of nobly and idealistically assuming that there is a recognizable and even measurable "common good" in politics for all, from Aristotle ("the common interest," *to koinei sympheron*), Saint Thomas Aquinas (*bonum commune*), John Locke ("public good of the people"), and Jean-Jacques Rousseau (*le bien commun*) to the contemporary philosopher Jürgen Habermas (common good of "the emancipatory

22 | The China Race

potential of modernity") and the multinational specification of "sustainable development."[54] Non-Western societies have also seen their share of such ideals, from Confucian thought to Islamic teachings.[55] Hindus and Buddhists have held the ideal of a world "without war and conquest" since the Indian emperor Ashoka's *Dharma Edicts.*[56]

My contention is that all those great, inspiring ideals about the common good for all are valid and valuable, but the pursuit and realization of the common good through politics should be mostly handled via community and national endeavors, through the continuous modernization and adjustment of the domestic organization of a given nation or state as the premium unit of human grouping.[57] Beyond the scope of nations and states, the quest for the "common good" for all ought to be balanced with other key (and even more critical) values of human civilization, and never used to justify a world government, assuming that there are no other comparative and competitive human civilizations interacting with our unique human civilization on planet Earth. Attempting to realize the common good for all through the formation and execution of a world government—axiomatically, to govern with a singular and centralized force—will end up producing minimal good and maximum bad for most if not all, as theory and history have both amply instructed us. Like biodiversity, the diversity of human polities and sociocultures, coexisting and competing in a decentralized way with both selection and elimination implied, is decidedly more optimal for the health, evolution, and continuation of human civilization and the human species.[58] It takes a "diversity regime" of national governances, especially the worldwide international order based on comparison and competition, to curate, codify, organize, renew, reinforce, and improve that sociopolitical and cultural diversity and complexity.[59] A sustained reiteration of contests among different social groups, based on their conflicting preferences in the context of international competition and often under the banner of nationalism, is viewed by some economists as central to the rise of modern democracy itself,[60] as the "unnatural" but least undesirable national political system.

A decentralized world polity existed de facto for millennia in various "worlds," but as a codified and legalized international order, it was only created in the 17th century and became a fully globalized norm as recently as the end of World War II (or even the Cold War) just a few decades ago. Contrary to common stereotypes, even an uncodified, de facto (and hence less efficacious) Westphalian system, like the Sumerian city-states in Mesopotamia, the Warring States in the Sinic world, and the classic Hellenic-Roman period and the Middle Ages in the Mediterranean-European world, actually performed better than the world empire alternative, with regard to diversity, dynamism, innovation, and prosperity, especially in the development of "the culture of reason."[61] To approach an optimality in organization with respect to lowering transaction costs and facilitating innovation in both governance and the economy, a complex and constant competition is a dynamism that is far superior to any singular and centralized authority.[62] A codified, de jure international system with its diversity regime, such as the Chanyuan system in east Eurasia, the Peace of Westphalia in west Eurasia, and the globalizing United Nations, is even more desirable. However, the Westphalian world political order is more unnatural than tribal state, autocracy, or world empire. Functionally, of course, it is a necessary but not sufficient condition for human innovation and prosperity, which often are also caused or hampered by other conditions and factors, including sheer luck or misfortune. It is structurally effervescent and unstable, and often precarious, due to its inherent competitive dynamics of innovation and changes in the economy, demography, technology, and ecology, resulting in constant power redistribution or transitions with new paradigms and initiatives. Furthermore, its de jure version has had only a relatively short history of existence for political legitimacy and cultural internalization.

The Westphalian system has been a lively system always under tremendous and increasing pressure from both within and without to change, explode, or decay. It has, fortunately, survived and evolved into its current form, the so-named LIO, thanks to critical steps of enhancement, experiment, and expansion, such as the Peace of Utrecht (1713), the Congress of Vienna (1815), the League of Nations (1920–46), the Kellogg-Briand Pact (1928), and the United Nations (since 1945).[63] The LIO has been in place for many impressive decades with considerable legitimacy but may still be vaguely defined and "bound to fail."[64] To some, the LIO is a "rules-based order," in contrast to "realpolitik."[65] It has further expanded since the end of the Cold War in the 1990s to become the so-called LIO-II, featuring a "post-national liberalism" that has attempted to assume "a significant amount of authority beyond the nation-state" with a "growing liberal intrusiveness of international institutions," such as "humanitarian interventions."[66] I suggest that the LIO in fact relies on sets of rules chiefly made and enforced by the United States and its allies with the underpinning of their particular,

24 | The China Race

and seemingly more desirable, norms and ideals since World War II. Yet it is still but one version of international relations and interactions under the Westphalian system, dynamically shaped, reshaped, challenged, and even undone by the realpolitik of great power competition. It may approximate a global governance to some, but, thankfully, and preferably, is not replacing the Westphalian world order, yet. As already outlined in a number of seminal works, this world order has managed to emerge and continue only through extraordinarily visionary leadership, difficult and oftentimes unglamorous diplomacy, concerted efforts expended over generations, heavy costs and gargantuan sacrifices, and some luck or special "anomaly."[67]

HYPOTHESIS 2

Compared to the past and possible future leading powers under the Westphalian system, the internally super-diverse and politically well-checked-and-balanced United States is, structurally, ideologically, and legally by far the least likely power to overthrow the Westphalian system. The built-in and long-tested sociopolitical principles and constraints in the US, however, are neither static nor guaranteed, subject to constant and various pressures and tensions for changes, corrections, or convalescences that can lead to evolution and improvement, but also could lead to the dysfunction, decline, and even demise of the American power.[68] Like so many other great powers, the US has its share of elites and politicians who dislike or disregard the Westphalian world order, which is, in fact, often inconvenient, unpleasant, and unruly.

The US-led variety of the Westphalian world order, the LIO, naturally exhibits the extensive inequity, arbitrariness, and irrationality associated with any great power politics in a world system featuring international political anarchy. But it is perhaps the only iteration of the Westphalian system since its codification in 1648 to have a leading power that is so unlikely (a near impossibility) to transmute it into its opposite, namely, a world empire. After the Spanish-American War of 1898, the United States "voluntarily" stopped expanding territorially and administratively. The nationalist inspiration of "Manifest Destiny" always lingers in the United States, but this concept long ago transformed from the expansion and conquest of imperialism to a hegemonic leadership and interest-driven partnership in competition, with order and rules, *fair play*, among coequal sovereign nations.[69] The US relationships with its dependents, like Cuba, the Philippines, South Korea, South Vietnam, Taiwan, and recently Iraq and Afghanistan, have amply demonstrated the American observance of the basic Westphalian principles, and hence its abundant experience of frustration and "failures" in those places. This contrasts clearly with what the Soviet Union had done to the dependent states in its camp, and Moscow's imperial "success" until the end of the Soviet Bloc in places like Eastern Europe and Mongolia.

There may be something special about worldviews in the Anglo-American political genealogy. Features like a strong tradition and practice of feudalism and federalism, many autonomous communities and groups in competitive coexistence, and layered decentralization of sociopolitical authority seem to have helped to mitigate the so-called "iron law of oligarchy" in human polity.[70] Perhaps reaffirming how leaders should behave, the British prime minister Boris Johnson conceded in his reluctant resignation speech in July 2022 that "in politics, no one is remotely indispensable, and our brilliant and Darwinian System will produce another leader."[71] Externally, the British Empire was once global-reaching ("on which the sun never sets") but did not act like a world empire—it was at most an "empire project" or an "unfinished empire."[72] In 2016–20, the British decided to exit the European Union, in order to safeguard their sovereignty, countering political regionalization and globalization, as has been argued by some of their most influential leaders since the late 1980s.[73] In 2021, the New Atlantic Charter by the United States and the United Kingdom reaffirmed in contemporary language the same pledge of preserving the Westphalian world order and its values and norms that the two countries had declared 80 years before in the Atlantic Charter of 1941.[74]

Unlike other past top-ranked powers in a de facto or de jure Westphalian system, the United States was a very reluctant leader of the system, only taking on this role after it was literally forced to do so by the Second World War. The US has since had the ability and the opportunity to turn the world into an American world empire perhaps twice—at the end of World War II and at the end of the Cold War—but, instead, has chosen to safeguard the Westphalian system and legalize its operations. Whether nobly or selfishly, it has always vigilantly treasured its own national sovereignty, as well as that of others, above many if not all other international pursuits. For example, the US, due to its concern for American national sovereignty, has readily abandoned or distanced itself from many, often worthy, pieces of international and global governance it initially envisioned, engineered, and financed. Washington has stubbornly stayed out of the League of Nations of 1920, the UNCLOS (United Nations Convention on the Law of the Sea) of 1982, the CBD (Convention on Biological Diversity) of 1992, and the ICC (International Criminal Court) of 1998. The US has been very wary of the global climate control regime, dropping out of the Kyoto Protocol of 1997, and leaving the Paris Agreement of 2016 for two years before rejoining it in 2021. As the lead founder of the United Nations, the US has in the 21st century repeatedly withdrawn or threatened to withdraw from major UN agencies and programs, such as the UNESCO (the UN Educational, Scientific, and Cultural Organization), the UNHRC (the UN United Nations Human Rights Council), and the WHO (the World Health Organization).[75] By 2023, when this book was drafted, some American politicians had repeatedly introduced, over more than two decades, legislation in the US Congress to quit the UN altogether so as to "restore American sovereignty."[76]

Many, including some Americans, have either criticized or praised the US as already a de facto world empire that has often acted to seek rents and enjoy privileges, behaved with impunity as a bully and imperial force, and displayed markedly self-absorbed worldviews.[77] Such a characterization is perhaps not completely erroneous, but it is largely a selective reading of facts and history, often a partisan and even satiric analogy used to articulate policy preferences or historical narratives, commonly with exaggerations of certain deviant and extreme opinions and impulses within a pluralistic and experimenting society. Portrayals of the US as a world empire are also often in service of purposeful policy arguments and deliberate distortions, not to mention blatant propaganda advancing other, hidden agendas.[78] It is commonplace and simplistic to conflate a voluntary or "drafted" leader of peer countries with world government, confuse the provision of public goods such as ad hoc international policing with world governance, and confound the anchoring of the world financial system with global extraction. The US may indeed enjoy substantial and seemingly unfair value-transfers as the issuer of the US dollar, the de facto world currency, among other noteworthy benefits.[79] But to equate that to the extraction or exploitation by a world empire grossly mischaracterizes and embroiders the nature of American foreign relations, and glosses over American sacrifices and contributions to the maintenance and improvement of the LIO and the Westphalian system. Despite its reputation for nationalism and self-interest, the US has enabled great security and prosperity for decades for most if not all sovereign nations, including even system-challenging countries like the PRC.

In 1961, when asked to name his proudest accomplishment as president of the United States during and after World War II, Harry Truman replied, "That we totally defeated our enemies and then brought them back to the community of nations. I would like to think that only America would have done this." And more than four decades later, Henry Kissinger followed up with the observation that "[a]ll of Truman's successors have followed some version of this narrative."[80] In 1963, with American power and position second to none in the world, President John F. Kennedy declared that the United States aimed to "make the world safe for diversity."[81] This American "exceptionalism" seems to have roots in the internal sociopolitical structure and ideological orientation of the US, the grand "American experiment," which can be traced back to Greco-Roman civilization and the post-Enlightenment Judeo-Christian tradition.[82] A key particularity of that structure and orientation can be succinctly summarized as "The 'people,' in the broadest sense, have become an entity to be served rather than used."[83] To be sure, US foreign policy has been affected by the country's dynamic views of its identity in the world and the dangers it faces, and thus subject to variations and overhauls.[84] Thus far, deeply structured and long internalized pluralism, federalism, and checks-and-balances in a system based on democratic rule of law seem to have ensured the American distaste for and vigilance against a centralized, solo political authority, both at home and abroad.

The LIO under the leadership of the United States and its allies is by no means the best international order for everyone, let alone a perfect one. To some (such as the CCP-PRC leaders), the LIO and its generic Westphalian system could be fairly viewed as very undesirable and even detrimental, and the US leadership remains the biggest obstacle to altering it. As a bulwark against CCP ambitions, and for the survival and functioning of the Westphalian system, US/Western leadership is therefore structurally, ideologically, and even legally the least unreliable option. The key to the safety of the Westphalian system seems to lie in the internal composition and foreign policy orientation of its dominant country rather than simple raw power. Indeed, the US-led post–World War II version of the Westphalian system has provided humanity with the longest period of stability in modern history. It has preserved the system's ordering principle for sovereign nations and maintained the longest absence of direct war among the largest and most powerful nations.

The only war directly involving the major countries in the nearly eight decades since 1945 has been that between the USA and the PRC in 1950–53, when Beijing sent troops in the telling disguise of "volunteers" to fight the US-led UN troops in Korea.[85] In perspective, since its codification in the 17th century, the Westphalian system had only one other (and much praised) "long peace," namely, the century after the 1815 Congress of Vienna.[86] But the system during that period was not truly global, and that century still experienced at least 17 direct wars among the largest and most powerful countries of the time, in addition to the countless wars of colonization and decolonization.[87]

Ideally, this already highly advantageous "liberal internationalism" can and should be "reformed" and strengthened further.[88] Scaling back, downsizing, and even leadership change are all fully warranted for the vitality and sustainability of the LIO and the generic Westphalian world order, when needed. Other nations of different geographical, ideological, and ethnic persuasions, including a successfully reformed and reoriented China, could take over world leadership from the US and ensure the survival and functioning of the Westphalian system, less or more liberal, provided that they are similarly or superiorly organized and equipped to equally or better safeguard the key principles of the Westphalian system. But, except for the still unlikely "United States of Europe,"[89] no such nation is even remotely visible at this time.

Despite the countless (often bestselling) predictions about the certain decline and demise of the United States, which have proliferated since its ascendance, the US leadership of the LIO has persisted and expanded.[90] In fact, dire warnings predicting the decay, decline, collapse, and even disappearance of US democracy with its power seem to have been a common concern of many influential Americans of various persuasions, in waves, for many decades since the 1950s.[91] The wild and much-analyzed swings and polarizing disruptions in US domestic politics, as exemplified recently by the election cycles of 2008, 2016, and especially 2020–21, attest to the inertial imperfections and endless trials, but also the solid pluralism, innovative dynamism, remarkable resilience, and renewability of the world's oldest democratic rule of law.[92] Visible and growing resentments and threats to the US leadership in the world are plentiful, however, and have resulted in decades-long tensions in various directions,[93] chief of which is currently the conscious effort by the CCP-PRC, and none of which represent a credible safekeeping much less progress or upgrading of the Westphalian world order. This book submits that the current West/US-led world order can and should prevail in the China Race, thereby fending off serious challenges from illiberal world powers like the PRC, potent domestic threats of extreme populism and infeasible tribalism, and unbridled globalism. Even with its nationalistic tendencies, the United States is likely to "remain the world's sole superpower" and continue the LIO at least in part because liberal ideals are deeply linked "to vital US national interests."[94] The US is currently the lone "can-do" power with the resources needed to anchor the existing world order.[95] Furthermore, it is reported by economists in the 2020s to "remain richer than China for the next 50 years or more" and "riding high" to lead all nations in socioeconomic performance and technological innovation.[96] An overwhelming and increasing majority (65%–98%) in eight representative countries (Brazil, Egypt, Germany, India, Japan, Mexico, Nigeria, and Poland) reportedly prefer the US as the world's leading power over China.[97]

HYPOTHESIS 3

The rising Chinese power under the CCP-PRC state is currently the force most capable of affecting and remaking the Westphalian system. It is now the lone contender that presents a viable and alluring, but suboptimal and undesirable, alternative to the American-Western leadership of the world.[98] Driven by its pursuit of reordering the world for the sake of regime survival, the CCP-PRC state also enshrines the Leninist-Stalinist version of Marxism, which calls for a uniform world socialism and communism. It must be reiterated here that it is the genes of authoritarianism and totalitarianism in the Qin-Han polity, which are now embodied in the CCP-PRC, rather than the rising power of China as a nation or the great aspirations of the Chinese people, that have inevitably and consistently reasoned and resolved to recenter and reorder the world into a China Order–like world empire.

Viewing China as an alternative leader influencing and reordering the world is not new, nor is the deep sense of uncertainty about that possibility and its implications. One century ago, disappointed with the Soviet Union and following a months-long visit to China, the socialist-leaning British aristocrat-philosopher Bertrand Russell outlined the China he saw, including its many problems, such as the so-called "chief defects of the Chinese[:] avarice, cowardice and callousness [and the fact that] all except a very few foreign-educated Chinese will be guilty of corruption."

30 | The China Race

Still, with critical reforms and development, Russell believed that "China by her resources and her population, is capable of being the greatest Power in the world after the United States [and presenting itself] to mankind as a whole new hope in the moment of greatest need." However, he also worried about the nightmarish possibility of an unfortunate combination of China's defective traditions (cultural norms and ideational values) with the power of "progress" (an efficient economy and belligerent military) "to embark upon a career of imperialism."[99] The creation of the PRC, as both John F. Kennedy and Douglas MacArthur foresaw seven decades ago, could be considered as such a "tragic story" with an impact that could last for centuries.[100] Beijing has since unceasingly resisted, reduced, and replaced the US position in its effort to recenter, lead, and reorder the world, and it has acted out in this way more assertively in the 21st century. In the words of the director for China at the US National Security Council right before he joined the government, CCP has had a staged and opportunistically expanding "displacement strategy" of the "long game" to guide Beijing's US policy.[101]

It may be comforting to consider that the West-led world order appears to enjoy a worldwide "distribution of identity," which may weaken Beijing's prospect of taking its place as a new world hegemon through the popularity of its ideology.[102] But, fundamentally, world politics has been mostly shaped by sheer force, which can powerfully arrogate and effectively asphyxiate popular ideals. Though indisputably suboptimal and undesirable, the CCP has a tight control over the world's largest (prior to 2024) population and second-largest economy, from which it can derive enormous power and resources.[103] The skilled unscrupulousness of the PRC autocracy also gives it a paradoxical optimality in the game of international competition and conquest, especially against pluralistic democracies, which are bound by rules, norms, and numerous internal and external checks. As John Adams penned back in 1798: "Our Constitution was made only for a moral and religious People. It is wholly inadequate to the government of any other."[104] With centralized and focused efforts, with Western technology in its possession, but without the framing and constraining Western institutions and norms, the CCP-PRC state has the capacity to acquire the "superiority in applying organized violence" that was key when "the West won the world," over the course of recent centuries.[105] As studies of group psychology and mass movements have demonstrated, a persistent "minority" can often effectively exert great influence on the majority.[106] The concerted efforts by the CCP-controlled

PRC, a minority of humankind, could readily overpower the West and the world at large.

The growing globalization of the world economy, culture, and society may amplify the possibility for the CCP-PRC variant of the China Order–style world governance to replace the US-led LIO, with "visionary policy initiatives [. . . and] mechanisms of global governance," according to some pro-PRC analysts.[107] Globalism, with its "universal" values, which originated and have flourished under the LIO, offers ever more persuasive rationales for a fundamental change to the Westphalian system, often under the appealing banner of pursuing the "common good" or a new "stakeholder capitalism."[108] Such calls seem at times increasingly indisputable, seeking ideals like peace, universally valued and protected equality, and rights for all, and reduction of poverty, epidemics, environmental degradation, and terrorism. "The worst uses" of powerful new technologies like AI (artificial intelligence) may have allowed the CCP-PRC state to rule more effectively and expand its power: "every blip of a citizen's neural activity [is fed] into a government database" enabling a totalitarian social control "by precog algorithms [that] identify [and even incapacitate] dissenters in real time."[109] A world empire under the guise of globalism could emerge with minimal kinetic battles, delivering a nasty surprise to many of us who may naively believe that modern weapons of mass destruction, especially the terror of nuclear weapons, have rendered empire-building futile and obsolete.

Therefore, the pretense of good intentions, utilized by a determined and self-serving political force, combined with actions and inactions by all others, could well pave the road to hell (or heaven, depending on one's standpoint) for the whole world, as with the Qin's unification of the whole known world in east Eurasia over two millennia ago. This situation could prove similar to what happened on the Chinese Mainland more than seven decades ago with the CCP's "unexpected" victory in the Chinese Civil War, leading to China's calamitous great leap backward. The Westphalian system, like the market economic system, which inevitably produces a monopoly to destroy itself from within, harbors resilient and perennial seeds of its own demise. Ironically, the LIO version of the Westphalian system, with its reigning ideals of equal rights for all and the frustrating reality of international inequality, provides unprecedentedly fertile ground and an extremely fostering ecosphere for those seeds to sprout and transform the whole system. The CCP-PRC represents, so far, the only global competitor determined and capable

32 | The China Race

enough to unscrupulously galvanize, hijack, and utilize the transmuting forces to systemically replace the Westphalian world order, perhaps with greater ease and speed than anyone can anticipate. As the further analysis of Beijing's intentions and actions in the rest of this book attempts to substantiate, the CCP-PRC state already appears to be "a rising power with revolutionary aims, poses a significant threat and must be contained or confronted, even if doing so risks war between the great power and its emerging adversary."[110]

A Contextualization: The China Race versus the Cold War

Ideas matter, particularly the kind that propels concerted action with force. The idea of world empire, with its great variety of names—world state, global state, and universal state—and even more diverse justifications, has been prominent among perhaps the most exciting, glorified, and potent ideas that have driven countless great powers, ambitious leaders, and idealistic or selfish individuals throughout human history.[111] The defenders of a decentralized world polity are viewed as "the good guys" not necessarily because they are inherently good (or more democratic or better governed), but because they ensure and practice a continuous competition or contestation that maximizes the chances for all to be good (or more democratic or better governed). The builders of world empire, often admired as heroic leaders, or even charismatic "saviors" or "liberators," would necessarily extinguish the flame of international comparison and competition and accordingly minimize the chances for all to be well and better governed.[112] World empire builders tend to be, in fact, more focused, driven, daring, cunning, and resourceful, but worse at governing the people, and often even bona fide "bad guys." Unlike in Hollywood, however, good guys do not always win, let alone automatically. Like the axiom goes, "good guys finish last." In human history, the less undesirable type of polity and world order—democratic rule of law and the international system of nation-states—has indeed been far less common and much more fragile than autocracy and world empire. Perhaps it is precisely because the good and the better often lose in the real world that Hollywood produces endless tales with happy endings to attract and please the masses.[113]

It may be easy, conceptually, to compare the China Race to the Cold War, the epic, all-encompassing, but largely peaceful rivalry, without a direct or total war, between the West and the East (namely, the Soviet Union–led communist bloc, including the PRC for much of that period), which ended with the victory for the West. There is certainly a great resemblance between the two contests, important for drawing useful lessons from the past, as some see today's PRC as "becoming the Soviet Union."[114] In a way, the China Race may be viewed as the unfinished Cold War, a renewed or enhanced phase of global competition between values and ideas for world order and alternative directions for human civilization, or the choice between totalitarianism and its opponents.[115] In November 2022, after repeating his "global development initiative" and "global security initiative" at the 17th G-20 summit meeting in Bali, Indonesia, the PRC leader Xi Jinping was indeed once again certified by his propaganda machine as "leading the development of the world" with his "China solution" to turn the so-called "Chinese style modernization" into "the new choice for humanity's modernization," thus "pointing out the right [alternative] direction for all the nations."[116] Like the Cold War, the China Race may be appropriately viewed as a "Values War" for the "Holy Trinity of National Security, Long-Term Interests and Values" between the CCP-PRC and its opponents, the "like-minded" democracies in the West and beyond, including "the long-suffering Chinese people."[117]

Once again, the world appears to have been "divided into liberal and illiberal spheres" led by the PRC/Russia and the West, respectively, along the cleavages of politics, ideology, and economic interest.[118] Indeed, two distinct camps have emerged, a new "bipolarity," as illustrated by the two groups of nations confronting each other in the United Nations on the same day, October 6, 2020: Led by Germany, 39 countries made a "Joint Statement on the Human Rights Situation in Xinjiang and the Recent Developments in Hong Kong"; the PRC, "on behalf of 26 countries, criticizes U.S., other Western countries for violating human rights."[119] Similarly, Japan's 27th submission of a Resolution on Nuclear Disarmament was adopted by the UN General Assembly on December 7, 2020 with 150 affirmative votes, including the US, 35 abstentions, and only four negative votes, from China, North Korea, Russia, and Syria.[120] On March 12, 2021, the PRC and 16 other nations, including Cuba, Iran, North Korea, Russia, and Venezuela formed "the Group of Friends,"[121] perhaps in response to the European Union and the upgraded Quad comprising

34 | The China Race

Australia, India, Japan, and the US. Days later, the US, the UK, and Canada formally joined the EU in sanctions against Beijing for its policy in Xinjiang, the first such collective action since 1989.[122] One week later, Beijing signed a 25-year, $400 billion deal with Iran, directly opposing the West.[123] A Chinese political exile, one of the student leaders of the 1989 Tiananmen Uprising, wrote in 2021 that a "new Axis is taking shape among China, Russia, Iran and North Korea" together with their "possible allies like Burma, Venezuela, Cuba and Pakistan."[124] A partnership among the US-sanctioned states of TRICK (Turkey, Russia, Iran, China, and North Korea) appeared in Eurasia in the 2020s.[125]

To leading PRC analysts, and also British and American analysts, the "two close camps" or blocs or alliances, the US (with the West, including South Korea) versus the PRC (with Russia, North Korea, Iran, and perhaps Burma and Afghanistan under Taliban), plus "a vast" and "complex intermediate zone of neutrality" containing most other countries in the "Global South," have already become "the short term pattern and the long term trend" in world politics.[126] In action, as French analysts have noted, there seems to be a "Russification" of Beijing's worldwide "influence operations," as the CCP has copied (with enhancements and improvements) many of Moscow's Cold War techniques.[127] Beijing's actions in Africa, for example, seem to parallel Moscow's during the Cold War.[128] As I will elaborate later in this book, the CCP also seems to have been loyally copying the playbook of the USSR, which fruitfully recruited and utilized many agents, sympathizers, and "useful idiots" before and during the Cold War, in the United States and even highly placed inside the US government, including influential figures like Harry Dexter White, the US official who was a leading architect of the Bretton Woods system.[129] Since early 2022, the PRC has openly maintained a "partnership without limit" with Russia, as the only major country in the world supportive of Moscow's invasion of Ukraine; a year later, in March 2023, the "comprehensive partnership" was reaffirmed to be at "the highest level in history."[130]

The phrase "Cold War," attributed to George Orwell in 1945 and Walter Lippmann and Bernard Baruch in 1947 on the two sides of the Atlantic, aptly described world politics between the late 1940s and early 1990s.[131] Its ending, however desirable, preferable, and foreseeable in hindsight, was neither guaranteed nor inevitable. Many useful lessons can be drawn from that period of history to assist in the conceptualization of the China Race and how to run it well.[132]

The China Race | 35

It is more than worthwhile to recall George F. Kennan (1904–2005), a towering American thinker of the 20th century, who in the late 1940s penetratingly analyzed the sources of conduct of the Soviet Union and framed the foundation for a containment-based strategy for the West to laboriously but eventually win the Cold War.[133] I had the personal good fortune to meet Kennan in the early 1990s, and to sit at his former desk for a brief moment in Fort McNair years later. Kennan's brilliance and insights continue to affect all serious discourse on world politics to this day. Sharing numerous symbols and slogans with the Soviet Union, the CCP-PRC is a similarly mighty and yet fundamentally fragile and undesirable sociopolitical system, aggressively opposing the West both ideologically and normatively, with a gigantic and resourceful but un-innovative and inefficient economy. Moscow and Beijing have both challenged "the free world" with a synthesis of "authoritarianism [that] combines communism and traditional nationalism [with the] quest to construct a worldwide socialist order with [it] at the center."[134] Like the Moscow that Kennan brilliantly analyzed decades ago, the Beijing of today is also deeply under siege and suffers from a chronic sense of insecurity, "impervious to logic of reason, and it is highly sensitive to logic of force," and similarly formidable, opportunistic, "unruly and unreasonable," but manageable, "without recourse to any general military conflict," if handled well as the "greatest task our diplomacy has ever faced and probably greatest it will ever have to face."[135] Similarly, in the words of US secretary of state Antony Blinken, the US should spare no effort this time "to manage the biggest geopolitical test of the 21st century."[136] Just like the Soviets, the CCP may also fail to "bury the West."[137]

The wisdom of a strategy of comprehensive and patient containment rather than a costly rollback still inspires today.[138] In 1992, with extraordinary modesty and humility coupled with a thoughtful suspicion about the military-industrial complex in the US, Kennan credited the peaceful ending of the Cold War to an "inevitable and impending" trend of regime change necessitated by the internal problems and mechanisms of the USSR, not to the external effort and strategy that was often associated with his name. Likely concerned that the euphoria of momentary victory could dangerously reduce alertness to the continuing challenge from the PRC, Kennan cautioned that "[n]obody—no country, no party, no person—'won' the cold war."[139] Kennan indeed had keen insights about China's "corrupting" political culture and "arrogant" worldviews, and thus advised, in the 1950s–60s, to

36 | The China Race

dismiss but "not ignore" the PRC.[140] According to his major biographer, Kennan strongly opposed Nixon's visit to China and the whole "engagement" policy "for all his life"; he would probably comment today on the challenge from the PRC with "I told you so."[141] In hindsight, what he predicted and preferred for the Soviet Empire became a reality mercifully soon, for its demise could have easily taken many painful centuries, as was the fate of the Chinese world empires and the Byzantine Empire. This outcome was rightfully the result of conscious, multidimensional, and persistent efforts to win the Cold War, ranging from comprehensive embargos to arms races, along with proxy wars in place like Korea and Vietnam that were not always easy, pleasant, or inexpensive.[142]

Compared to the Moscow examined by Kennan, the Beijing of today is an even more unscrupulous autocracy with extraordinary extraction ability.[143] The CCP is more than an inflexible ideologue of a twisted European radicalism. Domestically, Beijing faces relatively few explosive confrontations among ethnicities, even though it is clearly still struggling between its imperial tradition of forging a so-called "Chinese nation" (*zhonghua minzu*) and its Stalinist legacy, which mandates "all [56] nationalities (*ge minzu*) to coexist equally."[144] The PRC's deep insecurity and inherent antagonism against the West is mostly determined by the very nature of its Qin-Han polity and the tradition of its China Order *tianxia* ideation, rather than by external invasions, or the "Russian experience" analyzed by Kennan. Perhaps learning from the fall of the Soviet Union, the CCP over the past three decades has increasingly returned to the traditional Qin-Han imperial practice of control through forced assimilation of a singular "community of the Chinese nation," hollowing out the Stalinist pretention of multi-nationality coexistence under the unifying banner of communism. Beijing's linguistic-cultural-religious eradication and assimilation programs in places like Tibet, Xinjiang, and Inner Mongolia have thus intensified, at the cost of now being internationally labeled as "genocide" and "crime against humanity."[145] Yet, such ghastly actions based on the Soviet "lessons" may indeed preempt somewhat a mighty force capable of disintegrating the PRC. The CCP has moved far beyond Stalinist isolation in an era of rising globalist capitalism and has effectively deployed selective engagement to tap into, contaminate, and corrode the sources of power in the West—essentially draining and poisoning the well of its opponents.[146] Unlike the Cold War, the great multilevel "3D chess" game between Beijing and Washington[147] has been ignored, dismissed, and assumed or wished away by the West for too long.

The China Race | 37

Unlike during the Cold War, the significant business entanglement and corporate ties have often easily prompted capitalist movers and shakers in the US, for example, to enduringly "trust" the PRC for the precious cross-Pacific "co-dependence."[148] With a much larger economy and huge international trade, plus the sympathy and support of a strange world-wide amalgamation of authoritarianists, isolationists and capitalists on the right, and liberals, globalists, and socialists-communists on the left, the CCP-PRC has a much greater chance than the USSR to defeat the West and ultimately dominate and reorganize the world, even peacefully.

Therefore, the status-quo defense of just containing the PRC appears neither feasible nor sufficient this time. As some have argued, containment may have already become "not feasible" in the West-PRC competition.[149] To distance and decouple from the PRC is perhaps strategically wise and tactically efficient but could be economically painful and politically costly in Western democracies, where interest groups and disagreements naturally flourish to distract and detract in the absence of a Pearl Harbor-style attack. It is similarly imperative to constrain the CCP-PRC state with minimum costs, ideally through facilitating its own gradual but inevitable ending. It is also uniquely critical to adopt a concerted and comprehensive strategy for the US and its allies to be on the offensive so as to usher in that hopefully destined ending more effectively and efficiently. A more comprehensive strategy, which I call contaformation—containment *and* engagement for transformation *and* incorporation—is needed. It is a multifaceted effort to intelligently benefit from and ultimately prevail in the China Race for the West and the world, including the Chinese people, by countering, constricting, reshaping, and transforming the CCP-PRC power. As a long-time China hand observed, it is for "the United States to lead a global alliance of like-minded states to weaken China abroad and to foster fundamental political change within China."[150]

The idea of contaformation is broader and sharper than the portmanteau *congagement* (containment and engagement), which has been somewhat in use for over two decades.[151] Contaformation is a firm and conscious strategy, rather than a vague and expedient hedging policy. The China Race, the global competition between the CCP-PRC state and the US-led West, implies severe challenges and grave undesirability with a feasible implication for the demise of the existing world order and world peace. Yet, it also has its positive and beneficial aspects as a global competition and contestation between great powers, which is both

38 | The China Race

natural and often healthy to the Westphalian world order and human civilization. The US and its allies must do their utmost to contain the CCP's power and ambition, to stop it from leading and reordering the world, with a sustained, comprehensive containment and an all-in competition through strength, efficiency, and innovation. Over time, the benefits generated by a well-managed global competition will decisively favor the West, more than compensating for the necessary costs and the transient pains. The US-led West should also actively and wisely run the China Race with intelligent and extensive engagement, to work with the Chinese people to unapologetically assist in an institutional and ideological transformation of the CCP-PRC state.[152] It is indeed common to automatically assume that the PRC-USA competition is "zero-sum" and hence unacceptable.[153] For the CCP regime (also for the West-led world order), however, the China Race does have existential impact. The sociopolitical transformation of the PRC likely will result in an ever-fuller and ever more content incorporation of China into the international community, decisively facilitating more positive-sum competition. Containment and engagement are the principle means for attaining firm, well-reasoned objectives. I will elaborate on the conta-formation thinking later in this book.

The four-decade-long engagement with the PRC, or more accurately the lopsided and incomplete "economic engagement" with the CCP-dictated, selective decoupling, has produced extensive and profound but lopsided and deficient changes in China.[154] It has greatly benefited many but failed to alter the PRC's behaviors and worldview, while enriching and strengthening the systemic challenger in Beijing. As Richard Nixon propounded back in 1967, the West must aim "to induce change" in China,[155] thwarting the resourceful "high tech totalitarianism" of the CCP with firm principles and stern force, while consciously preserving the fundamentals of the Westphalian world order and maximizing the benefits of the PRC-USA competition with engagement.[156] In hindsight, Nixon and his team quickly flouted his wise advice and started the "tra-dition" of dropping the requisite companion—the political transformation of the PRC—in a rush to enlist Beijing's perceived indispensable help in dealing with Vietnam and Moscow.[157]

With the principled strategy of transforming the CCP-PRC through a robust containment and the already extensive connections and engage-ment in place, Western leaders will minimize or even avoid the political price of distancing and decoupling with China, while making the insecure CCP regime more fully bear the cost of its self-preservation. The US-led West should engage the PRC with a *full* coupling or a selective coupling-decoupling on the West's terms, rather than allowing the CCP to continue its elective coupling-decoupling in the China Race, without attempting the unnecessary total decoupling or disengagement. The Chinese people, including many if not the majority of the PRC elites, will then face the stark choice between a full Sino-Western relationship (of economic *and* sociopolitical *and* ideological coupling of both competition and cooperation), which has amply proven highly beneficial to most if not all, and the CCP's selfish monopoly of Chinese foreign policy in perpetuity, which features the regime-preserving antagonism against the West and the party-state's self-isolation or selective decoupling from the world.[158] Feeling the sociopolitical heat of economic globalization, for example, the CCP has indeed increased its distance from the world: Beijing openly pushed China into a "dual circulation" in the 2020s, an economic strategy "fit for a new Cold War" of "sustained geopolitical competition with the U.S."; the CCP also prohibited foreign or international schools in China from enrolling PRC citizens, ending a two-decade-long practice that had been very popular with Chinese elites.[159]

Compared to the Cold War, to contaform (contain and transform) the CCP-PRC is a different race, likely broader and more arduous, with many parties and moving targets but also new pathways and many shortcuts. After outlining the many similarities and difference between the USA-PRC and the USA-USSR rivalries, a thoughtful analysis concluded that "the actual Cold War was a mix of isolation and engagement, deterrence and cooperation," so the US "must deter, contain, engage and cooperate with Beijing."[160] The China Race is equally critical as but far more challenging than the Cold War, yet it is still similarly manageable, beneficial, and winnable, peacefully.

Consequences of Choices

To a great extent, the future is ours to make.[161] Normative concerns and desires matter decisively in human history. Facing a multitude of distinct options, the obvious limitations of human ability and eternal scarcity of resources, leaders throughout human history have made concerted efforts to design, construct, or deconstruct their civilizations, with or without adequate deliberation. At a juncture of choices between the revival of

40 | The China Race

the China Order and the continuation of the Westphalian system in the direction of globalizing humanity, a carefully reasoned normative preference is vital. While a world empire like the China Order has empirically shown its historical tenacity for repetition, the Westphalian system, per its structural nature and dynamic attributes, tends to change and mutate, with the inherent risk of self-destruction via replacement by the construction of a world empire. Managing the China Race for the world and the Chinese people requires the effective constraint and transformation of the CCP-PRC state to preserve the current world order, preferably peacefully; it is not about destroying China as a sovereign state, or vilifying the Chinese people and their heritage, or eliminating the dynamic competition and even contestation between China and the US. Strategically, the CCP has the minimal aim of making its authoritarian-totalitarian regime safe in the world through recentering international relations—to have a "hegemony with Chinese character-istics"[162]—and the maximal goal of reordering humanity into a singular world empire with the label of world communism or the China Order or something else. Both objectives are incompatible with the current world order, representing distinctively suboptimal alternatives. Accordingly, an effective containment of the rising Chinese power under the CCP (and the implication of that rise) should be the minimum, while the political transformation of the PRC state and the peaceful incorporation of China the maximum, for an optimal management of the China Race.

As I have attempted to show in *The China Order* and *The China Record*, the CCP-PRC state of a modified Qin-Han polity is a proven suboptimal giant with a masked yet unmistakable record of continual tragedies and suboptimalities. PRC history is filled with immense peace-time losses of life, great destruction of the Chinese environment and antiquities, inferior governance with low sociopolitical tranquility and justice at exorbitant costs, substandard socioeconomic development, massive devastation of culture, and hindrance of people's intellectual development and moral refinement. The PRC has been underperforming disastrously for the Chinese people; a China Order–like world order would likewise fundamentally wrong and fail humankind. The global coronavirus pandemic in 2020–23, COVID-19 caused by the SARS-CoV-2 virus, acrimoniously nicknamed by some the "China Virus" or even the "CCP Virus," seems to be a vivid illustration of this point.[163] Once again, just as has happened so many times before in the Sinic world under the China Order, human life in the whole known world may be massively compromised, this time under the extensive globalization in which the CCP-PRC state has had an increasingly major impact and well-documented abuses.

Based on historical records, structural analyses, and normative appraisals, it is imperative for the US, the West, and the world, including the Chinese people, to prevail in the China Race in a timely manner. In the past, the great "East-West Divergence" and the resultant two records of human civilization were chiefly determined by the two kinds of "world" political processes.[164] Today, the China Race is determining the future of not just a region but of all human civilization. From the perspective of preserving and hopefully also improving the current world order, a victory in the China Race could be conceptually framed as making good decisions about three choices at two-levels.

CHOICE 1 AT THE TOP LEVEL

A world political unification and centralization of the China Order (or world communism or any other name) must be avoided at all cost. This means either the rising Chinese power must be checked, contained, outperformed, weakened, and reduced, or the CCP-PRC state must be transformed and replaced, or both—a goal that is as immensely worthwhile as it is daunting.[165]

A concerted and careful strategy that combines pushes and pulls, and targeted and selective reciprocal tit-for-tat, would be effective and surprisingly peaceful,[166] and would deliberately induce and empower internal changes in the PRC. A smart rethinking and creative but proper exemption of some of the key principles of the Westphalian system, such as sovereign equality and noninterference in domestic affairs, are imperative. The world should not allow Beijing to comfortably hide behind its piecemeal aggressions with the pretention of being reasonable, tolerable, and ignorable. Between the extremes of the Munich Conference and Pearl Harbor, a lot can be done to restrict and transform the CCP-PRC while competing with it. Beijing may be clever in its use of deception and bribery, but its power can be safely and even peacefully contained and drained. Incremental acts of containment and engagement would signal pauses rather than an ending of the China Race. The strategy of seeing "China return to its pre-2013 path—i.e., the pre-Xi strategic status quo"[167]—would be prudent, but far from enough to achieve victory in the China Race. The CCP's Qin-Han polity should be continuously and

42 | The China Race

firmly discredited, delegitimized, and impoverished, so as to facilitate its internal transformation, to reduce and eventually eliminate the chance for this inferior governance to rule the entirety of humanity. Furthermore, the livelihood, rights, and potential of the Chinese people, nearly a fifth of humankind, morally justify concerted efforts to change and improve the Chinese political system. The necessary costs associated with these efforts are extremely tolerable compared to the opportunity cost of risking a redirection of human civilization. The price of containing and transforming the PRC is just the cost of business paid for the maintenance of the Westphalian Peace, especially its current version, the LIO. It is a very fruitful long-term investment for humanity, and especially for the Chinese people.

The key consideration in the effort to manage the China Race optimally is that there should never be a worldwide political unification, and international cooperation must never carry such adornments or move in that direction. In other words, the West must curb the enthusiasm and inhibit the temptation for a full political globalization, even in the name of winning the China Race. International political anarchy featuring US leadership is clearly preferred to PRC leadership of the world, not just because the US represents a proven, relatively superior, and less undesirable way of governance, but also because the US, as the world leader, is much less destructive of the Westphalian world order. When compared to a Han-Chinese world empire, a "world-state" ruled by the US (or any other nation), which may appear to be much less imperial, would still be equally undesirable and disastrous, with perhaps only marginal differences. As a Chinese intellectual exiled in the US put it in 2021, "[A] world government armed with AI and genetic engineering that locks humankind into a given fate without freedom is more frightening than [the threat of human] extinction."[168] The bottom line in managing the China Race means preserving the imperfect but precious (and precarious) world political decentralization and competition. Neither the PRC, nor the USA, nor anyone else should politically unify planet Earth. The only exception to this would be if there were viable and meaningful interplanetary or even intergalactic comparison and competition to effectively substitute for international comparison and competition on Earth—when humankind has established independent and competitive societies on other planets or when competitive extraterrestrials have initiated interactions with Earth.[169] In that case, the so-called "anthropocentric" conceptualization of national sovereignty, especially its utility, may then indeed require some reconsideration.[170] As George Kennan concluded in his famous "Long Telegram" back in 1946, "After all, the greatest danger that can befall us in coping with this problem of Soviet communism [read CCP-PRC world empire here], is that we shall allow ourselves to become like those with whom we are coping."[171]

CHOICE 2

A transformed China without the Qin-Han dictatorship, even if not necessarily a full-blown Western-style liberal democracy, should be welcomed as an important member of the international community. It should be accepted even as a tough competitor that is internally unique, experimental, and suboptimal, so long as Beijing legally, ideologically, and institutionally abandons its ambition for recentering and reordering the world, and is reliably restrained, or both. The China Race itself and particularly those non-system-altering Sino-Western competitions and even contestations would in fact contribute to the aggregate innovation, efficiency, and progress for all. Liberal democratic rule of law may be, so far, the least-bad human polity. But it is unwise to eradicate all illiberal or undemocratic experimentations by trial and error in politics and policies, many of which could at least provide valuable lessons and help to contrast and consolidate the better choices in human civilization. A dissimilar and competitive China, peaceful (or even occasionally unpeaceful) under the Westphalian system, would help in sustaining and energizing the worldwide comparison and competition that have powered human civilization.

The prerequisite and key benchmark for accomplishing this objective is for the Chinese people to have a thorough and deliberative rereading of their own history in a viable marketplace for diverse ideas and open information. The nearly one-fifth of humankind residing in China is obviously entitled to live, compete, advance, and seek freedom and happiness as one country or under the governance of several states, just like many other great peoples, provided that they are no longer intoxicated, hijacked, and used by the CCP autocracy to revive the China Order and reorder the world in its illiberal authoritarian image. Once informed and freed, the Chinese people, whether ethnically Han or non-Han, are fully capable of good governance and self-improvement. They will be able to contribute to human civilization in a profound way, qualitatively and quantitatively much more extensively than what they have ever

44 | The China Race

been able to manage under the Qin-Han polity and the China Order. To achieve a maximal victory in the China Race through sociopolitical transformation of the PRC probably requires the transformation and even the end of the CCP's one-party autocracy, or the "Zhongnanhai Empire." Indeed, as some Chinese believe, the "Chinese people now live better because Mao Zedong is gone; they will live even better without the CCP slavery system altogether."[172] As a Hong Kong–based Chinese philosopher argued, both peace and prosperity in China could be secured with "an orderly transition to democracy."[173] Such a choice, profound to the ending of the China Race in favor of the world and the Chinese people, however, is at a lower level of the Race and should be largely a choice for the Chinese people to make. I will return to this choice later in this book.

CHOICE 3

In running the China Race, the US and its allies should avoid a full-scale, high intensity "total" war with China, to the fullest extent possible. As with the highly desirable objective of transforming and incorporating China, however, this choice of how to run the China Race is at a lower-level and must be subject to the nonnegotiable top-level goal of the preservation of the Westphalian world order led by the US and the West.

Some further considerations regarding the relationship between world order and world peace are in order here. The wish for perpetual peace and equal happiness for all is an ideal, a noble and ancient intention that has and will continue to drive great ideas and works to improve human civilization through national actions and international competition and cooperation. Dante, the author of *Divine Comedy*, argued for a singular world empire to govern the whole globe for lasting peace and happiness, free even from the spiritual world empire led by the Pope.[174] Since then, there has been a long list of influential individuals advancing the ideal of perpetual peace under a supranational and worldwide political unification, including intellectual giants and influential politicians like Charles-Irénée de Saint-Pierre, Jean-Jacques Rousseau, Immanuel Kant, Jeremy Bentham, James Mill, Woodrow Wilson, H. G. Wells, Clarence Streit, and Albert Einstein, and transnational efforts like the UN-affiliated Perpetual Peace Project (since 2008). Many influential ideologies, ranging from Stoicism, Catholicism, Islam, Confucianism, and communism to Fascism, also display the belief that a centralized, uniform human polity would provide more peace and happiness.[175]

Among these, Immanuel Kant's proposal of global government by a "federation of free states," or a legal union of constitutional republics with rule of law as the ultimate form of world polity, providing a perpetual peace so as to maximize freedom/liberty and rights for the people, has remained perhaps the most powerful and persuasive reasoning for world political unity based on his insuperable analysis of pure reason, practical reason, and judgment. Yet, even in Kantian language the argument for world government is more idealistic than scientific. Metaphysically, Kant argued exhaustively that people are bounded in recognizing and reasoning the whole and the ultimate, hence the value supremacy of liberty/freedom, including the sovereignty and independence of both individual morals and nations' own laws and norms.[176]

Kurt Gödel, the great logician and mathematician, proved back in the 1930s the existence of terra incognita, the impossibility of providing and proving consistently all truth even in abstract science. The 20th century political philosopher Karl Popper went to great lengths to refute the fallacy of teleological historicism, and argued for the centrality of uncertainty and the importance of choice in human civilization—changes and improvements through endless and free experimentation and falsification. The psychologist Steven Pinker argued in the 2020s that free, ceaseless, and boundless search, reason, and contest are key to increase the inherently limited human knowledge and rationality.[177] A system sanctioning open and constant exploration and experimentation through competition and construction by trial and error is far superior to a system fixated on any set of theorems or ideals that may appear the best and most persuasive at a given time. An inference of the argument for a decentralized, divided, and competitive human polity beyond nation-states may be envisioned as a remedy to possibly address the Hobbesian "circular reasoning": how to balance the arguments for a sovereign political authority (the Leviathan) with the imperatives of minimizing and optimizing that authority, so as to ensure the diverse and evolving human rights and needs other than order and security.[178]

Some scholars of Constructivism in international relations have argued, "ideally," for the inevitability of "a world state," with its "global monopoly of violence," as the desirable outcome of the evolution from a

46 | The China Race

system of states to a society of states, a world society, a collective security, and finally a world state; in this view, the Westphalian system is regarded as "despotic," undemocratic, and destructive in nature.[179] However, this book contends that a world government or world state, even with the most thoughtful contractual arrangement (a de facto or de jure Rousseauist "social contract") best enforcing the "general will" to maximize freedom for the law-governed units and self-restraining individuals,[180] would still be less optimal than a decentralized polity featuring comparison and competition with contestation, ensuring that human "understanding of the external world" dynamically expands and endlessly improves. World political unity is thus inherently more suboptimal and undesirable than world political decentralization in maximizing reason, goodness, freedom, and peace. Political unity and centralization of public power for order and peace are most meaningfully and efficiently accomplished within and by sovereign nations with, ideally, a well-enforced "social contract" between the state and the people. Beyond that, world political unification would provide very little, if any, extra order and peace, but necessarily inflict heavy costs impacting other critical values, such as efficiency and innovation. To minimize war, a certainly heavy but occasional price of intergroup and international competition, a world government could doubtfully add much beyond the ever-improving national politics and international interactions, and at a grave expense that risks a structural suffocation and even extinguishment of the engine that drives human civilization.

To be sure, the hierarchical monopoly of the use of force or violence by the state is an inherent aspect of human polity, a price or cost for the essential provision of order and security. This does harbor traces of or resemblances of arbitrariness, exclusion, and even despotism, especially regarding international inequality. Democratic rule of law with protected rights for all strives to mitigate that cost internally. But, historically, such a national mitigation has been facilitated and critically maintained by external forces of international competition through comparison and migration and, yes, at times even wars and annexations. Democracy, the "least evil" form of human political authority, can hardly grow, let alone function well, inside a singular human grouping. An "iron law of oligarchy" has been observed to inevitably move political organizations, including liberal democracy, toward autocracy over time.[181] Humans, like other living beings, tend to go authoritarian and totalitarian for power and domination, and "doing evil" to all, even in a functional democracy when there is an unchecked authority, grave uncertainty, serious (often just putative) danger, and real (or manufactured but believed) fear.[182] In practice, without the peer pressure to stimulate it and check it, a singular political authority with the monopoly of force in practice has a much larger, more "natural," and even inevitable tendency toward the tyranny of authoritarianism and totalitarianism than remaining a tight-knit family/clan/tribe, a hedonistic "cosmic-city," a fraternal feudal system, or a functional democracy. After all, as a Chinese historian and an European psychologist have both argued, authoritarian tyranny, undesirable and disastrous in nature, is "a very low-level sociopolitical organization," simple and natural, requiring only animal instincts and the capacity of "dull bureaucrats and technocrats" to function and sustain.[183] Thus, a peerless world state or world-federation, even one starting out with a strong democracy, thus would morph easily, naturally, and almost certainly into a world empire of nondemocracy, contrary to the ahistorical naivete of some idealistic thinkers. Authoritarianism is by no means exclusive to right-wing conservatives, as "liberals" or various "left-wing activists" and socialists are fully capable of pursuing tyrannical and dictatorial power, assaulting liberalism, and ushering in some kind of "confessional state," even through "democratic" processes.[184] As Fredrich Hayek famously argued, a "serfdom" of a coercive "collectivist organization of society" was the same under Fascism and communism, which were both "totalitarian culminations of what had started as democratic socialism."[185]

Empirically, as I have attempted to show in this book and its prequels, the grand wish for world peace cannot be fulfilled via a world government, which is destined to create perpetual stagnation and endless involution with frequent disasters and violent conflicts that are often worse than inter-state wars, as the history of the China Order (and other real and aspirant world empires) has amply instructed us.[186] Pinning one's hopes on the inner qualities of the ruler of a world government, even a group of capable, moral, self-restrained, and well-reasoning leaders of a sovereign federation of constitutional republics, for example, is akin to valuing an enlightened dictator over a messy democracy in politics, a limited number of business geniuses over the competitive market in an economy, or a few superstar scholars over the unrestricted research of the countless members of a competitive academia.

Odds of Success of the Options

The China Race, like any other meaningful race, is neither painless nor costless. It is probably appropriate here to revisit and reconsider some of the post–Cold War norms and idealistic values of the LIO, which has morphed into a postnationalism, with excessive intrusions into nation-states and the resulting intensified "contestations,"[187] which compromise the Westphalian principles. More awareness and remedies are needed regarding "the epistemological challenge of truth subversion" in the LIO, which has led to "blind spots" and faulty policies with global impact, due to group-thinking, and media-monopoly caused by the shrinkage of the competitive market of values and ideas.[188] Managing the China Race optimally for the world may require at times some "race-to-the-bottom" acts of reciprocity, standard in a Westphalian world order, as is necessary for winning any serious fight with ultrahigh stakes. The Australians, for example, in dealing with the CCP influence on their college campuses in 2021, seem to have lifted a page from the CCP's playbook.[189] The current world order indisputably requires constant adjustment and improvement; much could be done to enhance and improve international cooperation for peace, security, equity, transparency, and environmental sustainability, both bilaterally and multilaterally. But no idealistic value should trump the meaningful international (and internal) comparison, choice, and competition that have been a main engine of human civilization. Even a temporary world political unity in the name of worthy global values should be vigilantly watched and actively hedged against, as these good intentions for laudable causes could become intoxicatingly seductive in paving the way to a detrimental world empire.

Therefore, to the world, including the Chinese people, the China Race is first and foremost about a choice to secure the Westphalian world order led by the US and the West. The transformation of China, and cross-Pacific peace, as well as many other noble ideals and great values, are highly worthy objectives but must be considered secondary courses and leverages or shortcuts, in a clear hierarchy. The China Race is tough and comprehensive, featuring arms races and economic races, reciprocal confrontation, the building of alliances, and realignments. There will also be the risk of some armed conflicts. Peace is of supreme value to humanity, but human civilization has progressed through countless, worthy fights or so-called "just wars."[190] Meaningful human endeavors such as investment, construction, and exploration all entail necessary costs, risks, and sacrifices; the critically important China Race is no exception.

The choices considered above, with a clear desirability that has been hopefully well-reasoned, also have a high probability of accomplishment in the China Race. The mighty PRC state may perform quite optimally for a small clique of CCP autocrats and allow Beijing to unscrupulously win certain battles and ventures. However, as I have attempted to demonstrate in *The China Record* and continue to discuss later in this book, the CCP-PRC is essentially a suboptimal polity for the Chinese nation and the Chinese people. It has critical and even fatal flaws centered around the fact that it lacks the Chinese people's consent to rule, which is why Beijing spends much more on internal policing and propaganda than on national defense. The CCP's "Mandate of the People" is a great deception that is in fact easy to shatter. The Chinese economy, while massive, is largely suboptimal, with unrepairable structural inefficiencies and a systemic lack of innovation. It is also geopolitically disadvantaged by the so-called "island chains" facing its only coastline on the Western Pacific, the narrow and foreign-controlled Melaka Strait choking its critical shipping lanes, and its 13,000-mile border (some of which is still contested) with 14 countries, including four nuclear powers and several security allies of the US.[191] Beijing is incapable of militarily projecting hard power beyond its homeland, and much less able to project soft power abroad, even with heavy financial inducements.[192] China is heavily dependent on the international market for critical technology, indispensable parts, raw materials, especially food and fuel, and income in hard currencies. All these issues make it uncomplicated (at least in theory) to push the PRC into becoming a "constrained superpower" focusing on regime security at home instead of pushing outward for territorial expansion.[193] Prevailing in the China Race through taming and transforming the CCP-PRC, therefore, may turn out to be much easier, more peaceful, and sooner than expected.

The very same obsessive, expensive, and debilitating needs of the CCP for its regime security at home mandates its ambitious actions abroad. The PRC is in the China Race for the sake of much more than the usual nationalist competitions under the Westphalian system—settling disputes with peers, pursuing relative power, seeking vanity and wealth, grappling over territory and property, or promoting a particular ideology or faith. Beijing's ambition is uniquely holistic, global, unscrupulous, expensive,

50 | The China Race

and exhausting. It is a ceaseless fight for the security of a passé autocracy around the world, life-or-death and all-or-nothing, akin to a total civil war that will not end until either the whole world is united under one ruler or the CCP dictatorship is gone. The Chinese national power and national interests are in fact just the vehicle, shell, tool, and disguise, not the end, for the CCP, despite its latest investment in Han-Chinese chauvinistic propaganda that redoubles the invention of extensive and growing Chinese nationalist claims in the world.[194] For decades, Beijing has been striving for the leadership and transformation of the world in its image as an imperial Qin-Han polity-based and Leninist-Stalinist communism-labeled authoritarian world empire. The CCP autocracy struggles for that mirage of ultimate security by controlling and even extinguishing the political contention with democratic rule of law, both inside and outside of China. The "inevitable" and "original" global mission of the CCP, professed clearly for decades in a variety of idioms and patois, is far from the genuine Chinese national interest. What serves the CCP often opposes and sacrifices the interests of the Chinese people. It is this remarkable divorce between the Chinese national interests and the CCP rulers' political interests that holds a key to the efficient and peaceful demise of the regime. The West's victory in the China Race is in fact in the fundamental interest of the Chinese people and the Chinese nation.

Inside the CCP-PRC state, many if not most of the political elites are palpably disillusioned with the party's "original" mission for world domination, and have become thoroughly materialistic, cynically pragmatic, and self-servingly duplicitous. They, especially the more enlightened ones, tend to feel content with being left alone to repress and exploit the 1.4 billion Chinese people.[195] CCP officials, including many senior cadres, are now hastily enriching themselves through pervasive corruption and short-term behavior while they can, as I attempted to document in *The China Record*; they are eager to take their families and fortunes abroad, mainly to Western countries, before the CCP ship sinks. Unlike the more "genuine" developmental state in places like Japan and South Korea, the "developmental state" of the CCP-PRC is also a "rapacious regime" and an "ersatz developmental regime."[196] Such a polity systemically enables and singularly encourages widespread corruption by its ruling elites to plunder the nation. Such a decay may hasten the end of the CCP-PRC regime but is largely harmless abroad beyond its corrosive impact on ethics in other nations.

The very few top CCP rulers, however, cannot afford to behave like their deceitful and unreliable cronies—they have the world to lose (brutally) and little better to hope for once the regime comes to an end. The autocratic leader in Beijing is thus basically cursed with three difficult options to choose from: (1) enslave the Party and coerce the Chinese people into a seemingly eternal fight to subjugate the West (particularly the US) at all costs; (2) pursue isolation from the outside world and pretend that the PRC is a self-sufficient heaven on earth, thereby minimizing foreign influence and curbing treacherous defections, though at the risk of technological stagnation, economic failure, and popular resentment; or (3) transform the CCP-PRC political system and worldview so as to fundamentally quell the urge for a world empire in its image.

After jettisoning the Qin-Han polity, performing what is essentially precision surgery or gene therapy to control or remove authoritarianism from the Chinese political DNA, the Chinese people, including their leaders, could enjoy genuine security and prosperity; China could coexist and compete with other nations peacefully and is more than likely to flourish in the Westphalian system upon accepting the system's rules and norms. It might even emerge as a benevolent new leader of the world and a new Mecca for immigrants and imitators.[197] Sadly, Beijing has thus far resolutely rejected and crushed any gestures toward the third option, instead fully choosing a combination of the first two options and sparring with the US for control over the world. The CCP-PRC state thus challenges the current world peace and imperils the future of human civilization, while also sacrificing and endangering the Chinese people, including its elites.

Principles of Normative Assessment

Here, a further discussion of preferences for different political systems and competing world orders is in order, with a proposition of principles to be used in a normative assessment of the China Race. Much has been written about normative preferences in human polity. One of the most well-known articulations of the characteristics of a desirable polity is an expression that emerged during the French Revolution—liberty, equality, fraternity (*liberté, égalité, fraternité*)—which, interestingly, has also been adopted as the national motto of other countries, such as Haiti.[198] An

52 | The China Race

influential work that addresses sociopolitical desirability along these lines is the theory of justice and fairness of John Rawls.[199] Rawls and his supporters developed a "liberal egalitarianism" with clear policy objectives in the mid-20th century, which has dominated the discourse of liberalism in the era of globalization.[200] Rooted in Aristotle, Thomas Hobbes, John Locke, Immanuel Kant, and John Stuart Mill, "liberalism's fundamental premise," argues another theorist, is "the natural freedom and equality of all human beings."[201] Some political philosophers argue for a global "international distributive justice" based on the principle of universal human rights.[202] Others tend to agree to the centrality of equality in justice and fairness but emphasize its religious and political foundations.[203] Economists like Robert Fogle acknowledge "the egalitarian creed that is at the core of American political culture," analyzing "modern egalitarian ethics which raised equality of condition over equality of opportunity," and advancing a "spiritual [or . . .] immaterial equality" for the future.[204] Conservative historians believe "the exalted quest for equality, justice, and fairness" is "eroding our freedoms" for some "predetermined arc of history bending toward [. . .] utopian mandate."[205] The philosopher Robert Nozick offered a strong refutation of distributive justice with a sweeping analysis of political philosophy and ethics, arguing instead for an "entitlement theory of justice," a minimal state, and people's freedom to choose what society and polity to live in.[206] Archaeologists have demonstrated the ubiquity of inequality throughout human history.[207] Armed with insights of the science of genetics, the psychologist Kathryn Harden provocatively but persuasively affirmed the limit of sociopolitical actions in affecting human diversity, inequality, and meritocracy.[208]

Human desires and utility-functions are in fact multifaceted and dynamic, with varied calculus and diverse emphases on various values and objectives. Between the insatiable aggregate of human desires and the inherent scarcity of resources, our values are often incompatible and mutually conflicting. Liberty or the freedom of choice, framed and reasoned through comparison and competition, is surmised to be a key value that enables and maximizes those other worthy human pursuits, including justice and equality. Political philosopher Isaiah Berlin illustratively listed precious human values ranging from freedom or liberty, happiness, "material security, health, knowledge," and "equality, justice, mutual confidence," to public order. But, "liberty is liberty, not equality, or fairness or justice or culture, or human happiness of a quiet conscience." Liberty and equality are not always that compatible or inseparable, contrary to the "foolish and utopian" belief of Marxism.[209] As much as Immanuel Kant insisted on the universality of "the moral law," his "doctrine of virtue" and emphasis on reason seem to grant a centrality to individual liberty, individual virtues, or "internal dispositions of character."[210] Classic thinkers of so-called "conservatism," like David Hume, Edmund Burke, and Joseph de Maistre, also argued long ago for the inherent irrationality and imperfection of human knowledge and human behavior, and thus the need to avoid the rash and the tempting trap of a "perfect" design, a universal right, or a single authority based on *the* reasoning of a specific time, however persuasive and imperative that reasoning may appear.[211]

Without engaging in an unnecessary and lengthy discussion here about the varied and multiple values and the distinct endowment and epistemology among individuals, families, and groups, as well as the optimization of immediate versus long-term interests, "the definition of *acceptable* multiculturalism," and the hierarchical ordering of coexisting values,[212] this book proposes two simple principles as the foundation for a normative analysis of the domestic organization of a nation in general and its political system in particular.[213] A third principle is proposed to assist in an assessment of national politics versus world politics. These principles should provide us a more firm and sensible foundation in assessing and reacting to the rising power of the CCP-PRC state in the China Race.

Principle 1: Effectiveness and Fairness

Although itself not necessary for the organization and operation of a human polity, fairness or justice, including liberty and equality for all, is clearly desirable and preferable, as it benefits and gratifies people (especially the disadvantaged), maximizes human potential, and ensures the cost-effective construction and exercise of public authority. Yet, liberty and equality are not naturally compatible values—they are often in conflict and are not guaranteed. Unjust and unfair political regimes have emerged and existed throughout human history. The foremost value of human politics is in its ability to construct and exercise public authority effectively for a host of human needs and desires. Is a particular political system (an institutional arrangement of the state and its execution of public authority) effective in providing its key utilities? Is it inclusive of most if not all segments of the society and a stable majority,

54 | The China Race

if not all members, while still capable of effective action? The first and central role of the state, as the public authority of a given nation, is to provide order and security for the people and to regulate interpersonal and intergroup interactions.[214] Here, inclusiveness is hypothesized as a better gauge than equality for measuring fairness or justice, as it helps to stabilize and empower a polity by the inexpensive and lasting provision of political legitimacy through participation of most if not all the people.

Fairness or justice is an essential but subjective and often conditional value of politics in any sizable human grouping, especially important to a non-autocratic polity where people's views matter. How to measure and operationalize this value, however, is not straightforward. In 1776, the landmark Declaration of Independence argued eloquently: "We hold these truths to be self-evident, that all men are created equal, that they are endowed by their Creator with certain unalienable Rights, that among these are Life, Liberty and the pursuit of Happiness." In 1789, after winning the American Revolutionary War, the US founders created the Constitution of the United States to "form a more perfect Union, establish Justice, insure domestic Tranquility, provide for the common defence, promote the general Welfare, and secure the Blessings of Liberty to ourselves and our Posterity." In the same year, the revolutionary National Assembly of France approved the Declaration of the Rights of Man, which states as article 1 that "[m]en are born and remain free and equal in rights. Social distinctions may be founded only upon the general good." The immense influence of these visionary and noble ideals notwithstanding, the challenge remains, as it is inherently hard to define fairness or justice as liberty *and* equality *for all*, beyond the less obscure right to life. What is fairness and what is happiness and how does one understand the "general good" for a society? Perhaps there is inherently no perfect answer to those eternal questions, as human beings naturally have their individual endowments and dispositions and thus their multifaceted and competing perspectives and desires, which are often inconsistent and mutually exclusive.

What is most fair, equitable, and just for one is often not so for another or for the collective good of a community and society, and vice versa. Numerous authors have sought to define justice and fairness, from religious leaders to philosophers and everyone in between. In practice, it is mostly the public authority, the state, that decides and ensures justice through adjusting and balancing liberty and equality, among many other competing needs and desires. Political determination varies depending on how the state is organized and run. But even the least deficient political system we know, democratic rule of law with popular sovereignty and universal suffrage, is only capable, so far, of addressing these questions approximately and often unsatisfactorily, let alone perfectly.[215] The cherished systems and popular social ideals supporting equality of opportunity, such as meritocracy for power and reward, could in fact be both "false" and "bad" for many.[216] Good laws, wise and benevolent leaders, and able implementers matter. However, just like democratic rule of law itself, maximum justice or fairness of a human polity through an optimal balancing between liberty and equality is best achieved, adjusted, and ensured through constant and dynamic comparison and competition both internally and externally, which is also the engine for efficiency and innovation that powers human civilization.

Reconciling the competing and even incompatible values of liberty and equality, as the theory of justice has attempted, often leads to an emphasis on the more easily measurable distributive justice (or equality of conditions) as the foundation for a social contract anchoring a more preferred human polity.[217] In practice, fairness and justice are therefore often defined as the maximization of socioeconomic equality, as appraised by an increasingly egalitarian distribution of income and wealth with equal social status and political rights for all. This seemingly self-evident value of equality for all as a measure of fairness of the sociopolitical order has long, deep, and ancient roots in just about all human societies, including Chinese civilization, as illustrated by the advice from none other than Confucius: "[W]orry not about insufficiency, worry about inequality."[218] Pursuing justice through equality has indeed been a powerful and implementable idea that has built and improved but also destroyed many states and civilizations. This credo of morality has been summarized in modern technical language as the principle of *maximin*, namely, the focus on socioeconomic policies that promote "the greatest benefit to the least advantaged members of society."[219]

Countless intellectuals have taken the idea of equality for all as a given. The compassionate and often passionate and appealing critiques of inequality, and the earnest proposals for using public authority and political power to promote or increase equality, beyond the principle of equity or proportionate equality, have inspired and energized but also enraged and led to the slaughter of countless people through rebellion, revolution, and other sociopolitical struggles. Karl Marx and his followers in action for more than a century have left a clear record demonstrating that idealistic efforts toward socioeconomic equality through violent

56 | The China Race

politics and central planning only result in disaster and more inequality.[220] Still, many continue to advocate equality through political means, albeit not all violently. Joseph Schumpeter, among others, cast serious doubts on the "creative destruction" of the inequality-producing capitalism back in the 1940s.[221] A recent paragon of such efforts is the 700-page global bestseller, *Capital in the Twenty-First Century* and its 1,100-page sequel, by the French economic historian Thomas Piketty, as well as his *A Brief History of Equality*.[222]

There is no need to fully discuss the Piketty report on the state and impact of inequality in the world today and how to interpret and assess the role of human polity in inequality. Likewise, a thorough analysis of the practicality and wisdom of the Piketty prescription of "participatory socialism" via periodical reallocation of "conditional" property rights by the state is not relevant here. But the surging enthusiasm for distributive socioeconomic equality around the world, especially among the advantaged and those privileged with liberty, must be recognized as a powerful reflection of the mighty ideological forces of national socialism and political globalization or globalism that are lurking in the wings. In August 2021, Fox News, a right-leaning US media outlet, reported that 59% of registered Democratic voters in the US "favor socialism," up from 40% just a year before.[223] In June 2021, the G7 nations reached a "historical" agreement to impose a 15% global minimum corporate tax. Within a matter of days, this was agreed to, at least verbally, by 130 countries (with 98% of the world's GDP), including China.[224] In light of the analysis in this book, however, major moves like this should be constantly scrutinized and verified, and frequently adjusted. Depending on how it is to be implemented, this "consensus" on global minimum corporate tax could simply represent a multilateral coordination of fiscal policies to revise the obsolete state-market relationship—arguably long overdue in the digital age of high capital mobility; it might help to level the field so companies heavily subsidized by states like the PRC would have to compete less unfairly; it could help in "ending the race to the bottom."[225] It could also be yet another idealistic but counterproductive attempt at a global governance of the economy, with likely abusable, undesirable, and even detrimental consequences.

It is interesting to notice the empirically observed discrepancy between the globalist elites, who tend to worry about worldwide inequality, and the masses and deprived, who tend to crave a decent, locally defined life. The intentional or unintentional mix-up or obscuration of national-community equality and global equality is intriguingly prevalent in the discourses of some of the best-known scholars. Perhaps it is the inherent human morality that values equality for a hardwired sense of pleasure and security, perhaps it is the persuasive utilitarian hypothesis of inequality brewing vices and dreaded political disorder, or perhaps it is just an internalized monodimensional normative view of human polity and human civilization. In this regard, Piketty's "social federalism" and "transnational democracy" "in charge of global public goods (climate, research, etc.) and global fiscal justice" based on "participatory democracy" or "democratic, ecological, and multicultural socialism" are new assonances of the traditional ideal of world government of egalitarian democratic socialism, and equally facile.[226] A specific objective along this line of reasoning seems to be what Bernie Sanders, the self-declared "democratic socialist" politician in the US, has advocated: a global minimum tax *with* a "global minimum wage"; to have a "universal basic income" in the "world of insecurity" so to salvage the declining democracy everywhere.[227] With no need to accept or refute the philosophy of justice and fairness defined by equality, this book instead considers justice and fairness as members of a unit, a nation, mostly in terms of equity, as measured by state effectiveness and institutional inclusiveness. A universal *equalizanda* of egalitarianism across nations, as appealing as it may be in political philosophy and necessarily mandating a certain world government, is viewed as unattainable, unnecessary, and undesirable.

Principle 2: Efficiency and Innovation

Beyond its proportional and distributive justice, a particular political system (an institutional arrangement of the state and its execution of public authority) is assessed based on whether it optimizes the intergroup and interpersonal comparison and competition, with contestation, to dynamically generate maximum innovation and efficiency, minimize aggregate transaction costs, make timely adjustments and adaptations, and consider and test improvements and alternatives. The aggregate cost calculation, naturally, must include the value of inclusiveness, as any human organization (community, nation, state) inevitably produces exclusions at varied aggregate costs.[228] This principle can be viewed as individual and intellectual freedom to choose, compete, and innovate, as Albert Einstein succinctly stated while on the run from Nazi Germany 91 years ago:

58 | The China Race

Without such freedom there would have been no Shakespeare, no Goethe, no Newton, no Faraday, no Pasteur and no Lister. There would be no comfortable houses for the mass of people, no railway, no wireless, no protection against epidemics, no cheap books, no culture and no enjoyment of art at all. There would be no machines to relieve the people from the arduous labour needed for the production of the essential necessities of life. Most people would lead a dull life of slavery just as under the ancient despotisms of Asia. It is only men who are free, who create the inventions and intellectual works which to us moderns make life worth while.[229]

In many ways, optimizing and maximizing efficiency and innovation are more fundamental to the health and betterment of human civilization, as this provides the ever-enlarging foundation for any effective sociopolitical organization, proportional and distributive justice, and the survival and well-being of human life itself. If the right to life comes first in assessing human polity and human civilization, then normatively there is the inevitable conflict, and even trade-off, between the two great values of liberty and equality. To be sure, nations/states and cultures/ civilizations have all long struggled with their dynamic, never-ending, balances between equality and diversity/liberty.[230] For the aggregate good of humankind, the critical freedom (or political security) of choice, competition, and experimentation, and the resultant efficiency and innovation, are more important than—though should not and in fact do not completely displace—the noble ideals of equality for all that emphasize the idea of leaving no one behind.[231]

The indispensable freedom of competition and innovation is provided for and protected by a liberal political power allowing and even encouraging diversity that could theoretically be an enlightened autocracy or a democratic rule of law; historically, the latter has demonstrated overwhelmingly better chances and more stability.[232] Such a polity, however, is costly in terms of popular support, especially in a mass democracy where justice is easily and convincingly defined as equality, since competition necessarily engenders inequality through the creation of winners and losers, even if just temporarily. Of course, serious economic inequality, especially when coexisting with sociopolitical exclusions, is neither necessary nor inevitable for competition, innovation, and efficiency. As I have attempted to show in *The China Record*, the same symptom of high economic inequality in different countries, the PRC versus the US, for example, can have a great variety of causes and consequences. A well-organized and well-governed society in the 21st century, with high efficiency, vibrant innovation, an affluent economy, and an effective distributive safety net could minimize inequality and even eradicate absolute poverty.[233] But the subjective feeling of unfairness and injustice caused by relative socioeconomic inequality or poverty could be just as strong if not stronger than the hostilities between classes in the crude versions of capitalism of the 18th and 19th centuries or in today's less advanced countries.[234] The pursuit of equality tends to supersede or even asphyxiate liberty in a mass democracy, especially with the magnification and exaggeration of sensational electoral politics and mass media. In this situation, the favoring of equality over liberty tends to appear in the form of an excessive welfare state, egalitarian redistribution, radical identity politics, and extreme contravention of evolution based on fitness.[235] An advanced, efficient, and innovative economy would then "equalize" but stagnate and decline, together with the overall living standard and quality of life of the entire nation.

PRINCIPLE 3: NATIONAL OPTIMALITY VERSUS WORLD OPTIMALITY

Effectiveness, fairness, efficiency, and innovation can be viewed nationally to assess a political system, as I have attempted to do with the Chinese state in the prequels to this book, *The China Order* and *The China Record*. They can also be approached globally to consider the fate and future of the entire human civilization, as with the China Race discussed throughout this book. What is considered optimal for one nation may not be optimal for the whole of humankind, just as what is best for one individual or one group or tribe may not be good for a nation. Of the three ideal formations of human grouping, globalism, nationalism, and tribalism,[236] I submit that tribalism is as unmerited as it is infeasible after the Enlightenment and industrialization, while globalism is as undesirable as it is unnecessary; nationalism governed by democratic rule of law in a system of equality of national sovereignties appears to be the least suboptimal way of human organization, while all three groupings may have their places and roles concurrently.

There is the "natural selection" of individual humans as biological beings (and individual identities like tribe/ethnicity/race/nationality and culture/ideology/lifestyle), which seems to have the morality and value

60 | The China Race

of competition for survival and expansion, hardwired by the so-called "selfish gene." There is also the "group selection," which determines the evolution of biosocial groupings (families, societies, and polities of sovereign states and the world order itself), necessitating the ethics and probity for altruistic cooperation and selfless inequality of the individuals and individual subgroups, so as to manage and remove harmful genetic mutations and behavioral deviations before the "deleterious mutation accumulation" suboptimizes and even ruins the overall grouping (and also dooms the individual genes within).[237] Between the two selections, both of which can be "positive" (retaining and reproducing the fitter mutations/variations) and "negative" (reducing and eliminating the unfit mutations/variations), a dynamic balance resulting in a "stabilizing" and "balancing" selection seems critical to the optimal evolution and thriving of the human species and human civilization. Imbalance or dysfunction of the individual and group selections simply drive species into extinction.[238] The worldwide success of ants over the span of 130 million years perhaps illustrates the point well. Instead of the biochemical mechanism of "distributed processes" or "distributed algorithms," which organizes the ants, however, humans rely more on structured institutions (law and governance) and their internalization: the division of labor and the communicated behavioral norms of various cultures and ideologies.[239]

Normative values such as effectiveness and fairness are chiefly defined and assessed at the level of nation/state as the "sovereign" unit of human grouping. Equality, especially distributive equality, and the theoretical maximization of efficiency for all (or for an abstract, singular, world economy) should be viewed as secondary. Practically, the inevitable conflicts of interest and values among people preferably end in orderly national and subnational compromise, redistribution, or suppression, with reform, revolution, or emigration as the safety valves for adjustment. Communal- and national-societies can and should optimize the collective and individual values and interests equitably and inclusively for all members with an evolving "social contract" that organizes people in their division of labor in the group, and with a distributive justice for and obligatory contributions from everyone.[240] Beyond that, the unavoidable conflicts of interest and values among peoples should be maintained and managed, in order to sustain the ceaseless international comparison and competition, with the rise and decline (and reorganization) of states as mostly the consequence of alleviation. Of course, international competition could feasibly end in a world political unification, as the history of world empires in the Chinese world and other "worlds" has demonstrated. As I have hypothesized in this chapter, however, a unified governance above the nations is both suboptimal and detrimental to the best interests and key values of human civilization.

It is obvious that all humankind worldwide should be rated and treated as equal in their basic rights, and that the world economy should maximize its total efficiency and innovation (and the dissemination of income and technology). However, it is submitted here that for the aggregate and dynamic good of all of human civilization and ultimately every human being, institutionalized comparison, choice, and competition among the sovereign nations, based on and reproducing international inequality and differences, are qualitatively more important than the noble ideal of indiscriminate and simultaneous socioeconomic equality and maximum efficiency for *every* human being or *every* human group. To prioritize and maximize justice defined as equality, especially the equality of opportunity and stature for *everyone* before the law, is both ideally imperative and functionally practical within a local community or within a country, where the body politic operates under and for the same common sovereign power. Unlike in the domestic setting, however, the barriers, differences, and "just inequality" among nations is a necessary and highly rewarding price that human civilization must pay to advance and flourish aggregately.[241] A human being bears a multidimensional and multilayered identity in which some aspects are more important than others. National affiliation or citizenship, as the critical group identity in a politically decentralized world, makes international inequality morally and politically the least costly way to sustain the competition and innovation essential to human civilization. An ambitious individual may voice (speak out and participate to act), revolt, or exit (emigrate) for an improved chance in life; an affluent community or society may experiment and adjust its own limits and provisions for the weakest or least "fit" members; a competing state may emulate others and improve for the sake of stability and survival in many ways, including reform, revolution, and realignment. In these ways, a decentralized world polity institutionally, ideologically, and dynamically ensures both fairness and liberty, at the individual, community, and state levels, and thus aggregately optimizes human civilization at the minimal cost.

This principle of normative assessment of world politics presumes that the ultimate guarantor and promotor of less- or least-bad national politics is the institutionalized comparison, choice, and competition

62 | The China Race

among sovereign nations. World politics is inherently different from national politics, and what is politically optimal for a nation may be detrimental to the world. The main provisions and roles of governance are already (or should have been) furnished by a functional state, though with varying degrees of success. National politics already address most if not all human political needs.[242] The normative question is then simply what type of world political order is more conducive to the maximization of effective, inclusive, efficient, and adaptive governance delivered first and foremost by the governments of various nations/countries. Indeed, national "democratic capitalism" has an uncertain fate when facing the countries of "autocratic capitalism" in an era of uneven globalization, in which capital has much greater mobility than other elements of the economy, chiefly human labor.[243] For Western "liberal/democratic capitalism" to improve its chances in fending off the threatening challenge of "state-led political or authoritarian capitalism" represented by the CCP-PRC and its ilk, however, appropriate and conscious choices and actions are imperative.[244] The Westphalian world order remains the key structure ensuring the future for liberal or democratic capitalism, at the highly tolerable cost of a dynamic international inequality that is meaningfully mitigated by international competition and adaptation, redistributive transfers, and migration.

States are monopolies of political power and a world government would be the worst kind of monopoly, even in the name of providing universal and maximum good. Political monopolies tend to pursue and become addicted to maximization of power and ever more control for themselves, unless they are structurally constrained and locked in constant competition with peers for authority, capability, resources, and even existence. External comparison, choice, and competition, through diplomacy, trade, migration, and, yes, conflicts and war, are necessary mechanisms for internal competition and improvement, as they push states to gravitate toward liberal politics that favor and sustain efficiency, innovation, and inclusion, and hence national well-being, stability, competitiveness, and power. A well-run illiberal polity may succeed in acquiring the spurring capability to overpower its competitors with trickery and luck. But, over time, as my examination of the China Suboptimality in *The China Record* illustrated, an autocracy becomes inherently inefficient and stagnant, and thus less competitive, and eternally insecure. Nationally, people, when they are able, should and do experiment with the scenarios of maximum equality for all, even at the expense of liberty and efficiency, maximum efficiency even at the expense of equality and liberty, or an optimal balance among the sets of key values. Such national pursuits are automatically and constantly checked and tested by the comparative and competitive Westphalian world order of international relations. Either the people make timely readjustments or they have the luck of ceaselessly rapid growth to ensure or restore an optimal justice through an equilibrium between liberty and equality; or the particular state declines, fails, and fades, resulting in its people suffering, dying, rebelling, or emigrating with their capital and technology to search for a better polity. With a world political unification, a world empire, or even a world federation of democracies (so far only in theory), there would essentially be one closed system for all humanity, lacking the mechanism of checks and contestation by peer polities, with nowhere to emigrate, experiment, and innovate, and little out-of-system stimuli, resources, and information. Under a singular worldwide public authority, even with the best possible initial equilibrium between liberty and equality, all will end up worse off eventually, due to entropy driven by the energy-dynamics of demography, knowledge, and desires.

Laudable community and national goals like justice and fairness through maximum equality for all would lead to irreversible injustices and endless disasters if attempted uniformly worldwide. The same is true of economic efficiency and innovation, and their dissemination. To prioritize an abstract global equality or world efficiency at the expense of corroding the Westphalian system of division and competition among sovereign nations would end up ruining the ultimate engine for efficiency and innovation for everyone. While inequality is highly suboptimal socially, economically, and politically for a community and a nation, international inequality is much less undesirable, as it is the engine driving competition, a force that is critical to the well-being and vitality of the entirety of human civilization in the long run. It is a necessary and dynamically low price (due to the highly competitive nature of international politics), akin to but even more tolerable than the state as a so-called "necessary evil."[245] In fact, a measured inequality within a nation is not really the top concern for a political system; it is much less a concern internationally beyond the psychological discomfort reflected in the lenses of sensational journalism. It is impractical and cost-ineffective to measure (let alone achieve) worldwide socioeconomic equality. Relative national equality is more than enough to sustain justice and fairness, with revolution and emigration as the safety valves.

64 | The China Race

International inequality remains the main mechanism through which meaningful comparison and competition continuously power human civilization, without most if not all of the undesirable consequences to political legitimacy and effectiveness of governance that national and community inequalities may inflict.

A Short Note on Globalization

The much-cheered process of globalization in recent decades has been a telling case.[246] Economic globalization is perhaps natural and desirable for the pursuit of efficiency and prosperity, and has gained a great deal of momentum under the global peace and stability provided by the US-led LIO. The synergy of a worldwide economic integration and division of labor, the reduced transaction cost due to the ever freer and faster mobility of capital and goods, and the global scale of production and specialization have yielded enormous benefits: more goods at lower prices for more people, easier and higher profits for capitalists (especially financial and technology proprietors), wider and speedier spread of new technology, and significant economic growth in many previously less developed countries.[247] Also, quite naturally, economic globalization evades and even escapes from the sovereign controls and regulations of nation-states, especially so-called "soft" or weak states, which are prone to be influenced or even "captured" by interest groups and political corruption.[248] The globalizing world economy is thus characterized by a spectacular unevenness and incompleteness: an integrating market of capital without an international labor market or common labor and environmental standards. At least two major negative externalities have emerged: the rising inequality due to discrepancies in mobility and standards for capital-technology versus labor; and the often unjust and even illegal schemes between illiberal regimes and shortsighted capitalists in greedy swaps of wealth for power.[249] The mass relocation of jobs (but not laborers) in the developed countries, for example, has greatly intensified political fights for distributive justice, identity politics, and nativism in the West, resulting in profound sociocultural and economic polarization and damage, accompanied by hefty political costs.[250]

A "globalized" anxiety of unbuffered, zero-sum, and uniform class conflict has risen powerfully in both the developed and developing nations; the optics of a "Westfailure"—the inability to manage the irrationalities and imbalances caused by economic globalization under the Westphalian system—has grown ever more dismal.[251] A tiny but remarkably assimilated global elite class has emerged to form a powerful de facto and de jure transnational alliance to undermine the position and power of the non-elites in just about all countries. People, groups, and nations are all geared up to determine what must be done to accompany and "better" manage the mighty globalization, providing fertile ground for many traditional and nontraditional international conflicts: from the resumption of great power politics for power transition and intensified battles for nations' relative gains to asymmetrical struggles like international terrorism and radical extremism.

The rather sad ending of the so-called "first globalization" of the 1870s–1914, which has a great deal in common with the current round of globalization (since the 1940s),[252] perhaps illustrates what a worldwide integration of the economy could and could not do. Great economic exchange and interdependence among nations, contrary to an abundance of wishful thinking, could not ensure world peace, let alone a normatively preferred or bettered world order. Economic globalization nourishes and energizes the ideas, urges, and fantasies for political globalization, providing the irresistible pretenses and unprecedented means for global struggles for power and control akin to a worldwide civil war, resulting in unheard-of levels of death and destruction. Many, such as the rising power of Wilhelm Germany (and later the Nazis and the Japanese militarists), hoped to reach a "justified" worldwide sociopolitical unification through the old-fashioned methods of warring and conquest. Others, like the Leninists (and later the Stalinists and Maoists), resorted to violent revolution at an epic scale to replace the loathsome imperialism, the "inevitable" result of globalized capitalism, with a "scientific" and ideal system of world socialism and communism.[253] Still others, especially between the two world wars, pursued idealist but ultimately failed experiments like the League of Nations and the illegalization of war.[254]

Prompted by the consequences of economic globalization and perhaps also mindful of the fraught history of the early 20th century, many conscientious contemporary global elites understandably advance a sociopolitical globalization in the forms of globalism, global governance, and global distributive justice to deal with a long list of amplified "global" issues, such as environment degradation, refugees, pandemics, terrorism, tax evasion, poverty, and inequality. Influential and well-reasoned ideas that have emerged in recent years, such as "global tax fairness" and universal/global "multi-level basic income," seem to all justify and require centralized and uniform world governance and redistribution.[255] Mostly rejecting the passé idea of world political unification through force, so far, the West-dominated global elites are nonetheless inspiring, energizing, and even demanding a political globalization or world government, which, as I have attempted to demonstrate, is just a nostrum that is worse than the diseases it purports to treat, fundamentally diminishing both global economic efficiency and innovation, and undermining good governance and world peace. Adding to the mounting pressure for nations to race to the bottom, and contributing to the rise of crony capitalism and international kleptocracy, unchecked economic globalization has produced sociopolitical and economic consequences that offset and even roll back the aggregate gains. The dynamism of international comparison and competition itself is twisted and even derailed. And, of course, there are also the rather traditional wannabe world-empire builders; chief among these is the rising power of the CCP-PRC. The China Race, therefore, concerns and will decide what to do about economic globalization: to manage and moderate it under the West-led Westphalian world order or to attempt to "fit" it to a world political unification, the China Order style.

The undesirable externalities of economic globalization could and should be effectively regulated and managed by national governments through unilateral, bilateral, and multilateral actions that will curb the monodimensional, unbridled pursuit of the dreamy world economic efficiency and "naturally" ensure that there will be no total and complete political globalization. In addition to their growing decoupling, derisking, and supply-chain reshoring in the context of the China Race, the European Union, for example, has unilaterally initiated antitrust actions to curb online monopolies, with mixed but promising results.[256] Concerning this development, some have started to dread and sensationalize the coming "split along national lines" and "war with itself" of the globalizing Internet.[257] However, an institutionally and operationally decentralized Internet, ensured by national or multinational anti-monopoly policies, is fundamentally beneficial to humanity, resulting in aggregately more innovation and efficiency. "The era of the global Internet is over [and the US must face] a fragmented Internet," declared a bipartisan CFR (Council on Foreign Relations) report in 2022.[258] "A degree of 'bifurcation' in the U.S. and Chinese tech sectors," however, is probably both inevitable and advisable.[259] Such policies, of course, are qualitatively different from state censorship in places like China and North Korea, which is often instituted under the pretense of resisting "foreign" monopolies but is in fact just information control and obscurantism. The fashionable lamentation over the "collapse of globalization," in fact, seems both premature and misplaced.[260]

Further Considerations on Preferences and Criteria

In addition to the three principles discussed above and my short note on globalization, of course, the list of the desirable, valuable, and important aspects of a national or subnational political system can grow much longer. Beyond the essential provision of order, security, organization, and regulation, and the core values of efficacy, inclusiveness, efficiency, and innovation, many more desirables could certainly be added to compare and more fully evaluate a government. Important attributes of a state's record include social tranquility, economic prosperity and distributive justice, equal and maximum rights and freedom for citizens, people's life expectancy and living standard, disaster prevention and relief, protection of antiquities and the environment, public projects and services, et cetera. Frequently, however, many of the desirables attributable to the state are outcomes and extensions of the essential provisions and core values listed above. I have attempted in the prequels to this book to assess the record of the CCP-PRC state as an alternative political system based on these criteria. There can also be endless specific, transient, and parochial niches and extravagances, both material and psychological, that are important to certain individuals and groups in assessing a polity.

What about international peace? One might wonder if that preference should not be key to a normative assessment of national and world politics. Peace or peacefulness—the lack of war and other violent conflicts, particularly the kind between sovereign nations—are highly prized values of human politics. But I submit that peace is one, but not *the*, essential criterion of a normative assessment of world politics. In contrast to the critical value of international comparison and competition with contestation, of which war is but one usually decisive, often effective, but actually very rare and mostly tool of last resort used by states, peace at any cost is of decidedly less value to human civilization. War happens for complex, often ad hoc, and occasionally just reasons at the international, national, and subnational levels.[261] Empirically, there is a qualitative difference between an international war (other than a

68 | The China Race

system-altering war of world conquest) and a domestic "civil" war, as the latter is almost always far more destructive and deadly, if not more common. In fact, international war, and especially the effort preparing for it under a functional Westphalian system, has been documented as driving great competition and innovations in many fields, ultimately making humankind safer and richer.[262] The goal of "outlawing" international war rightfully remains just an admirable ideal.[263]

Both the Westphalian Order of nation-states and the China Order of world empire can be either peaceful or warring. A world government (as a type of world empire that has existed many times before, or as a "world federation of free states," which has so far remained an idealistic possibility in theory only) has been theorized, wishfully but conceivably and admirably, to reduce the "permitting" effect of international war and thus increase the chances for peace, and possibly even a "perpetual peace."[264] However, as my study, in *The China Order*, of the many Chinese world empires has shown, the world under a singular government is by no means more peaceful; on the contrary, it tends to be more war- and violence-prone, with many ultra-destructive and extremely deadly "world" civil wars and violence, in stark contrast to international wars under a Westphalian-like world order. One failed rebellion in China in the 19th century reportedly killed as many people as all the international wars worldwide in the 19th and 20th centuries combined. In the 20th century alone, many more Chinese died in civil wars and man-made famines than in all China's wars with foreigners.[265] Thus, the existence of war informs little when assessing a world political order, while the proneness to war (either civil war or external war) is clearly a key and central value in assessing a national political system, whose main mission is to provide order and security. For that, there are theories of democracy peace and free-trade peace as well as open-exchange peace.[266] Empirically, the democratic rule of law appears to be more peaceful than other forms of governance, both internally and externally.[267]

One more conceptual issue related to our preferences for political systems is technology, especially revolutionizing technologies and their impact on human organization and governance. Many new and potential technologies are widely touted as transforming the backbone and the basics of human civilization, with literally countless predictions (many of which yield bestsellers) either cheering on or warning of the consequences of these new technologies. For example, new worldviews and world politics may have emerged due to the possibilities of instantaneous communication

The China Race | 69

and same-day transportation (in contrast to the "traditional" size of the world, measured as at least two months by the fastest means of travel). The Internet, especially the Dark Net, and blockchain technology are widely asserted to have completely and irreversibly decentralized and democratized human polity within political globalization.

However, this book adheres to the notion that all technology is fundamentally a product of and confined in its use by human political and economic institutions and norms, as well as human nature and ability. The decisive factor determining the creation, spread, and application of technology (or the lack thereof) in any society is its political system. Systemically and aggregately worldwide, the Westphalian system has been the world order most conducive to technological revolution and dissemination, far more than its alternatives. Technology itself is not yet an independent variable shaping the institutional and operational fundamentals of human civilization. The much-discussed political impact of ICT (information and communication technology) in the PRC has been, at best, very mixed. The fast-developing ICT, including AI (artificial intelligence), seems to have expanded and enhanced, rather than diminished, the CCP's autocratic control of the Chinese people and their minds.[268] There are probably only two scientific and technological breakthroughs that may remake human civilization in fundamental ways: thermonuclear power generation, which may largely end the law of scarcity and thus rewrite human economics; and the full realization of bio- and genetic-engineering, such that we may reconstruct the basic needs, desires, and mental and physical capacities of the human species.[269] Neither of these two technologies, however, is likely to become a reality any time soon, if ever, despite exciting breakthroughs like the one made by the Lawrence Livermore National Laboratory on fusion technology in 2022.[270] Existing norms, institutions, and laws, for example, have already started to significantly restrict and even ban the development of human bio- and genetic-engineering technology. Even the innovation-craving CCP had to stop and jail its American-trained "rogue scientist" after his wanton genetic editing of three human babies.[271]

Given the points I have outlined so far, this book thus advances the normative contention that regards the Westphalian system as the preferred political order for the world beyond individual nations, just as the open market system is preferred for the economy, and democracy with rule of law is preferred for the domestic politics of a nation. A functional system of coexistence of sovereign nations and states, an international political

70 | The China Race

anarchy, or a decentralized world polity, fundamentally and effectively sanctioning and facilitating constant and profound international comparison and competition, is akin to the constant competition among firms in an open market without any single firm monopolizing the whole market. Through trade, diplomacy (including alignment), migrations, exchanges, and sometimes conflicts and war, and even the annexation and annihilation of a state (not to be conflated with genocide), the sovereign units of the international system must fully engage in a constant and fateful comparison, choice, and competition with one another. The "death" of a state or a firm as an entity, which commonly occurs in such competitions, does not mean the eradication of a people, statehood (national sovereignty), or capital, but mostly involves transfer and reorganization. Such structured and sustained international comparison and competition among peers ultimately secures and promotes internal competition and improvement of the units, as well as mitigating and minimizing the inherent costs and irrationality, or the necessary evils of the national state power, which is by nature monopolist, forceful, extractive, and change resistant. A stable, codified, world order of international comparison and competition therefore ensures and optimizes sovereign nations externally, while enabling and impelling the creation, continuation, and refinement of national political systems toward a less-bad polity such as democratic rule of law. Decentralized world polity is also critical to the national and international market economy, because it fundamentally restricts the forces of sociopolitical distortion and monopolistic stagnation.

Either of the two kinds of decentralized world order works well: the codified de jure type—preferred due to its transparency and higher legitimacy, and hence more stability—like the Westphalian system, which has been in place since 1648, and the Chanyuan system in the Sinic world of east Eurasia between the 11th and 14th centuries; or the de facto kind, like the long-running "world" politics in the Mediterranean-European world during the 4th to 17th centuries and the pre-Qin Chinese world. As in the economy, where the best firm necessarily decays into inefficiency and stagnation once it becomes a monopoly, the best state, even a gloriously vibrant democracy, would inevitably decline into bad and disastrous governance of the China Order–like world empire upon becoming the only government for the whole known world.[272]

To be sure, none of the three human institutions—the open market, democratic rule of law, and the Westphalian system—are perfect or "natural." They often exist and function in different places and different times for the sake of different purposes, with great variation in degree, effectiveness, and consequences. It is not that rare for them to underperform, by some measures and on certain issues, compared to their alternatives.[273] They are all constantly under subversive pressures and entropy dynamics and thus are completely breakable and reversible.[274] Liberal democracy, for example, "is hard, counter-intuitive and complicated, and requires self-restraint, reason, and toleration at levels most humans are incapable of," observed an American commentator in 2020.[275] But the open market, democratic rule of law, and the Westphalian system are the least bad for human economic activities, sociopolitical life, and world order respectively. Constant improvement is always desirable and doable, if the politically enabling framework and mechanisms are preserved to dynamically sanction new ideas and actions.[276]

Issues of Epistemology

Key characteristics of autocratic rulers, particularly within the Chinese Qin-Han polity, include tight information control, constant indoctrination of the people, inevitable doubletalk, and extensive hypocrisy. The CCP is especially focused and skilled in the monopoly and suppression of information, deployment of misinformation and deception, and the so-called "United Front" of trickery and bribery for the purpose of divide-and-conquer. Instrumental to its rise and maintenance of power and seizing "the right to define international narratives," has been the CCP's propaganda and censorship machine, which, in size and effect, is second to none in human history.[277] The party-state is clearly masterful in appropriating ideas, slogans, and banners, and creating sophisticated disinformation for its pursuit of power and control, at home and abroad.[278] As the two prequels to this book (and other authors) have tried to elaborate, fake news, counterfeit goods, half-truths, number games involving doctored statistics and visuals, fabricated facts, and even outright lies are commonplace in the PRC.[279] Deceptive statements and deceitful gestures as well as severe punishments for independent reporting and thinking, including prison and even death, are common occurrences there.

Given that, it is legitimate to question what the rising Chinese power is really bringing to the world, beyond Beijing's public gestures and slogans. Could it be that the CCP is in fact not pushing for world domination or rule? Rather, this incredibly self-serving and inherently

72 | The China Race

insecure clique of rulers with bottomless perfidy may simply be interested in controlling and manipulating the Chinese people with its wavering but always grandiose plan for the world in order to justify its power and extraction. All dictators and dictator-wannabes are inherently narcissistic and ultraselfish, regarding their country and even the world as their own property or at their willful disposal for their personal and family pursuits, indulgences, and fantasies, including eternal life through physical immortality or family power and wealth in perpetuity. Most, if not all, Qin-Han rulers of the Chinese empires were clearly exemplary in that regard. The CCP rulers, self-claimed "people's servants," are even more so, though their excesses often go unseen due to skilled propaganda and expansive concealment. They are in it for the mostly free supply of the finest luxury the country and the world can provide (the so-called special provisions or *tegong*), for example, sparing no effort in an attempt to prolong their lifespans to 150 years.[280]

As the logic of authoritarian and totalitarian politics would predict, a dictator inherently needs a great cause or a grand vision to create a perpetual warlike atmosphere. This might be a fight against a hated internal enemy (like the Jews in Nazi Germany, or the "class enemies" in the Stalinist Soviet Bloc and Maoist China), or a mighty external foe (ranging from the unjust and annoying neighbors to the "Western imperialists who always want to annihilate us"), or to fight for ever more "living space," or a purer heaven on earth (a theocratic kingdom or a communist paradise).[281] Might the CCP's majestic talk about constructing a "community for common human destiny," about being "at the center of the world stage," about "leading humanity," and about "building a better and more just world order" be just empty talk and slogans to cover up their true intentions of power grabbing and greedy self-service?[282] Might the CCP leaders, fully aware of their deficiencies and indulging extravagantly in the fruits the existing world order has to offer, be simply using that empty rhetoric (along with ostentatious actions) to enslave and extract from their own people? Might it be that, with their sprinkling of Chinese funds around the world, especially in places like Africa, the CCP is inadvertently assisting the economic development of less developed countries? Might the concern about the CCP's alternative vision for the world be exaggerated? To be sure, even in a functional democracy, overpromises, grandiose slogans, unrealistic ideas, fabrication and exploitation of all sorts of fear and animosity, and absurd rhetoric are commonplace during the heated moments of election campaigns.

The China Race | 73

Without full access to the internal meetings and files of the CCP leadership and genuine interviews with the secretive leaders of the PRC, one can never claim to know 100%, in real time, what is actually on the minds of the CCP-PRC rulers, much less to reveal and convince the world about the intentions and plans of the ever more powerful and resourceful CCP-PRC state. Similarly, up to the summer of 1939, very few in the world were fully persuaded about what Nazi Germany was intending to do; and it was not until after 1945 that the world learned what Nazi Germany was truly capable of doing. Thus, we may never know what the CCP is intending and capable of doing to the world unless there is a postmortem somehow, someday. And, if the CCP were to ultimately prevail in the China Race, there would never be a truthful autopsy, just as in China (including many non-PRC Chinese communities) there is still no good historical account of what the Qin-Han polity meant for the Sinic world over its many centuries—history and folk legends were often deceptively written and spread in imperial China just as they are in today's PRC.[283]

Fortunately, with the new technology and social connectivity we have today, it is not that hard to piece together the simple truths and hard facts mangled by slogans and distortions. As I have attempted to document in this book and its prequels, the nature, record, and activities of the CCP-PRC state are both qualitatively and quantitatively certain and assessable. A multifaceted consideration of all available information is key. Through a process of careful identification and authentication, comparative evaluation, and logical deduction with informed intuition, we can steadily and confidently construct holistic and richly nuanced observations to approximate the truth. The CCP leadership is clearly not simply prattling on about reorganizing the world in its image; since day one, it has been approaching that task forcefully, often with all it has, as its historical mission and as an enduring necessity for the survival of its regime. Equally important, it does not really matter that much what the CCP's "true" intentions are at a given time if we can analyze the facts and the pattern of its actions. As the cliché goes, if something moves, sounds, eats, and excretes like a duck, then with comfortable certainty we should just call it a duck (except for some bioengineering miracle or marvel of robotics). With generations of scholarship and reportage, we already have sufficient evidence to ascertain the CCP's worldviews and action plans. In fact, it seems somewhat paradoxical that the secretive CCP has been quite consistent and candid about what it wants and

74 | The China Race

pursues, if one could just see through the tactical smokescreens, control the urges for wishful thinking, and simply "trust the Communists to be Communist."[284] Indeed, the CCP has always openly enshrined "communism," by definition a uniform worldwide phenomenon, as its ultimate objective—all the way back to the opening paragraphs of its Party Constitution at its start in 1921.[285]

Particularly since the 1990s, the CCP has been flying high the banner of "saving China" for a "great rejuvenation of the Chinese nation/civilization," but has never specified exactly which period of Chinese history is to be revived. An explicit list seems to include the great Han-Chinese world empires of Qin-Han and Sui-Tang and even the Yuan and Qing, the non-Han world empires of the Sinic world.[286] In 2021, a leading PRC scholar of international relations asserted explicitly that the CCP's grand rejuvenation meant the return of the Sinocentric world order of the early-Tang era, when the emperor had the title of Celestial Emperor, Khan of Heaven (*Tengri Qaghan*), or Emperor of *Tianxia*.[287] With the findings I have attempted to present in this book and its two prequels, I am fairly confident about ascertaining how the CCP-PRC state governs at home and acts abroad and worldwide. The question of whether the ultimate aim of these actions is to rejuvenate a Chinese world empire of the past or to create a "new" communist paradise seems largely an irrelevant point of semantic trivia. Even if the PRC is in fact "a declining power," "at the end of China's rise," posing real but different kinds of threats to the international order and world peace that are driven by a desperate struggle for regime survival rather than a confident takeover of the world,[288] the analysis about the China Race in this book would still hold. For Beijing, its regime survival and world domination to recenter and reorder the world are just two points on a continuum.

Finally, things take on their own momentum once they are set in motion. Rhetoric is not exactly policy or action, much less fait accompli, but it can have real consequences for both action and reaction. Lies and fantasy feed, facilitate, and fan themselves over time. Blustering and bluffing can affect and even twist people, including the speaker, after endless and deliberate repetitions and echoes. For example, Nazi Germany might not have wanted the total physical extermination of the Jews from the very beginning, but soon enough the willing executioners of Hitler's directives found the Holocaust to be "necessary" in the overall course of their pursuit. Constantly and consistently speaking

The China Race | 75

of grand schemes without meaningful debate and dissention, however deceptively and hyperbolically intended, can affect and alter the speaker's mind and action, particularly when the speaker is surrounded by those who seek to please their boss through further doubletalk, selective or forged information, self-serving delusions, and shameless sycophancy.[289] For instance, a "headline" article in 2020 by a senior CCP cadre asserted that Xi's idea of a "community of common destiny for humanity" has been "unanimously echoed, supported and accepted by the people of all countries in the world," so Xi is fully qualified and more than ready to be the desperately needed new world leader "to govern the globe" better; days later, another article, written by a senior propagandist, on behalf of the CCP, certified Xi Jinping Thought as the updated and improved "Marxism in the 21st century" and "the China solution" to lead the entire humankind.[290] A democracy with rule of law may also have politicians who trade in fear- and hate-mongering, empty talk, and grandiose slogans, but the opposition, the media, the built-in checks and balances, and the public itself periodically restrict, repudiate, reduce, and replace excessively offending leaders.[291] By contrast, an authoritarian or totalitarian regime must blindly and haplessly follow, to the bitter end, its unchecked and unrestrained "free" and "great" leader, who in turn could easily become a tragic victim, together with the regime and the people, of his own grand but delusional plans, projects, and disorder.

On July 1, 2021, Xi Jinping, the general secretary of the CCP and chairman of the PRC speaking at the Tiananmen Gate in Beijing, repeated the standard party line that he and his comrades were in a mighty and eternal struggle for world peace, since "[we] the Chinese people do not carry any aggressive or hegemonic genes in our blood." In the same officially labeled "important speech," Xi also repeatedly urged his 95 million party members and the 1.4 billion Chinese people in the PRC and anywhere else in the world to maximize PRC strengths in all areas from technology to United Front ventures, "rejuvenate" China back to some unspecified past but definitely prior to 1840, build the military to become "world's best," and "continuously construct a community of common human destiny" to prepare for a "great, once-in-a-century change" in the world, and "push the wheels of history toward bright goals." In October 2022 and March 2023, upon making himself a Mao-like ruler without a term limit, Xi repeated the same grand objective with added phrases: "developing a Chinese way of democracy," "a Chinese style of modernization," and "creating a new mode of human civilization" for

76 | The China Race

the whole world.[292] It may be easy to dismiss the Mao-style rhetoric, the "venting cannon" of hot air,[293] of self-aggrandization and regime-serving propaganda full of arrogance and delusion, illogic and perfidy, and the ignorance of science and facts. It is also plain but critical to see the party-state's concrete plans and specific calls for consequential actions, and treat the ultrahigh stakes in the China Race with the seriousness that they warrant.

2

PRC Foreign Policy

From World Communism to
Community of Common Destiny

External relations have always been critical to China's identity, stability, and power as well as its political, economic, and sociocultural development since the mid-19th century. The Chinese Communist Party-dominated People's Republic of China (CCP-PRC) owes its creation, survival, name, banners, ideology, and policy tools to foreigners. Today, "Beijing's official ideology (Marxism-Leninism), key pillars of political legitimacy (nationalistic rhetoric and state-led development programs), and main provision of technology are all externally sourced."[1] After the failures of Mao Zedong's Great Leap and his pretentious global revolution for a new China Order of the world, the CCP retreated and went low key, switching sides with highly dramatic acrobatics akin to a conditional surrender in the 1970s–80s. This major opponent of the West and the United States was then rescued, accepted, and enriched by its adversary—the US-led Westphalian system of the liberal international order (LIO). Yet, the CCP-PRC state remains fundamentally incompatible with the leaders of the LIO, and has refused to change in pace with the outside world and the rapidly transforming Chinese society. A Qin-Han polity and authoritarian-totalitarian polities in general, are preordained to pursue a world empire in their image to secure what they perceive as their optimal regime security. Ideologically, that innate logic of the CCP-PRC state based on the Confucianism-coated Chinese Legalism actually fits well with the dogma of Marxist-Leninist communism, which

78 | The China Race

deems itself destined to eventually become a whole-world phenomenon and discounts and disregards national divisions and national interests. A Qin-Han polity and a Leninist regime interestingly share the same politics and worldviews of premodernity—world orders of both the China Order and world communism are thus equal in undesirability.[2]

On the world stage, the CCP-PRC state is possessed by the twin forces of the tradition and ideation predisposed in a Qin-Han polity for building a singular empire for the whole known world—the *tianxia* (all under heaven), and the "scientific" and "modern" rationalization of the imported Marxist-Leninist ideology for constructing a world communism. Guided by the China Order mandate and Communism, the CCP has been driven, by its own innate need for political security and survival, to commandeer China for its political interest of recentering and reordering the world rather than behaving like a Chinese nation-state.[3] In practice, the PRC therefore has been in a mighty struggle for the survival and power of the regime, aiming to resist, reduce, and replace the US leadership first, and ultimately to overthrow the Westphalian system whenever and wherever possible.[4] This defining characteristic of the seven decades of PRC foreign policy has oscillated from open hostility and even hot war, to deliberate concealing and hiding, to revived assertiveness and belligerence. In the past decade, the CCP seems to have retaken a global approach, fully resuming its failed course of influencing, leading, recentering, and reordering the world. Like it or not, for Beijing, an epic China Race with the West and the US has always been on to determine the fate and future of the CCP-PRC. It is now also increasingly impacting the fortunes of human civilization, with the grand, directional choice of international leadership and world order.

With an examination of the foreign policy of the PRC and an assessment of its record of performance abroad, this chapter intends to analyze the nature, pattern, strengths, weaknesses, accomplishments, failures, and implications of Beijing's international ventures, with findings that will, hopefully, shed light on why and how to engage in the China Race.

The Motivation and the Routes

The motivation and rationale behind the CCP-PRC's grand strategy of displacing and replacing the United States and recentering and reordering the world is not related to any fundamental conflicts of interest between the Chinese nation and the US/West, or between the Chinese and American/Western peoples, nor to a notion that the Westphalian system, particularly the post–World War II and post–Cold War international order, hampers or contradicts the interests of the Chinese nation and the Chinese people. On the contrary, as I demonstrated in the prequels to this book, the time China has spent under the Westphalian system since the mid-19th century has represented one of the three best eras in the entirety of Chinese history. The West, and the US in particular, have been overwhelmingly and comprehensively beneficial to the progress of the Chinese nation and the improvement of life for the Chinese people. Thanks to the wise decision to remain with the winning sides of both world wars in the 20th century,[5] China achieved a high level of security and international prestige by 1945. As one of the Big Five, China was poised to modernize and empower itself, to become a world leader.

All that changed when the CCP-PRC successfully replaced the similarly organized but decidedly less authoritarian Republic of China under the Kuomintang or Nationalist Party (KMT-ROC). A revived Qin-Han (more Qin than Han) regime, hardcore authoritarian and even totalitarian, brought a great leap backward, a long, tragic detour for Chinese politics, society, and economic development. China's foreign policy reversed and reoriented based on calculations for the survival and power of the CCP regime.[6] Knowing full well that the CCP-PRC represents rebellion against the reigning world norms, Beijing has been seized by a deep sense of insecurity from the beginning and has turned against the benefactors of China. The PRC slid back to the traditional worldview of the Qin-Han imperial polity, wrapped in pseudo-Communist phraseology, and only feels safe and content with a world empire in its image, whatever name and facade that world government may have. To the CCP, as a world-challenging political force, the Chinese nation and the Chinese people are merely captured vehicles and dispensable assets for the maximization of its security, power, and indulgence.

Over the past seven decades, the PRC has vacillated between walling off the country to insulate itself and engaging the outside to challenge and change the current world order and norms. Both tactics are undertaken for the regime's survival and are primarily determined by the leadership's calculus of the international balance of power. From Mao to Deng (including Jiang and Hu) and Xi, the CCP's top leader's sense of ability and needs at a peculiar moment has led to different

80 | The China Race

mixtures and tactics, sometimes dramatically "new" in appearance, to warrant colorful labels such as "revolutionary state," "developmental diplomacy," or "revisionist stakeholder."[7] But the party-state's core interests and main pursuits have been remarkably consistent, as I will elaborate later in this chapter. Maximum control over and extraction from the nearly one-fifth of all humans who live in China have always remained the first and the foremost objectives. The CCP Optimality of autocratic governance, described in *The China Record*, is translated into foreign policy with considerable success in safeguarding the regime against all odds. However, this CCP Optimality inevitably causes the same China Suboptimality in diplomacy as it does in domestic governance and socioeconomic development.[8] Its inferior socioeconomic performance necessarily reduces Beijing and forces it to seek critically needed foreign recognition and resources, especially technology.[9] The political influence of the West, deemed "germs and flies from outside" by the CCP, comes with the international exchange. A frightened CCP then exhaustively tries to control and insulate at home and redouble its effort for influence and alterations abroad. Beijing has been stuck between self-reliance with self-insulation, and beseeching external powers for resources, all accompanied by a deep fear. A bittersweet, love-hate emotion colors the CCP's attitude toward the world, especially the West. The ultimate solution, not surprisingly, is in the DNA of an authoritarian-totalitarian polity: to influence and reorder the whole known world in order to extinguish any meaningful comparison, competition, and challenge to the regime, while allowing for worldwide control and extraction. As some observers put it, "survival and domination are two sides of the same coin for the CCP."[10]

To survive and prosper in the incompatible and inhospitable environment of the US-led LIO, the CCP uses coercion and tricks to equate itself with China and the Chinese people, in a process akin to using a massive human shield. "The West [or American imperialism, or foreigners, or just unspecified 'forces abroad'] never cease to annihilate us [us Chinese or us China]" has been one of the most consistent themes of propaganda in the PRC.[11] Reflecting its deep apprehension regarding regime survival, Beijing ingeniously stirs up the phantom of external threats to the Chinese nation, a spectacular deception in the post–World War II world, to justify and ensure its control of and extraction from the Chinese people, who are actually the real source of the CCP's insecurity.[12] Outside of the PRC, Beijing's often simulated exhibition of paranoia is frequently viewed as a wildly ludicrous gambit. For many, however, this view may consciously and subconsciously rationalize a China policy that attempts to accommodate and appease the PRC, akin to the goodhearted management of a needy and sensitive youth with a fragile ego. In reality, as a PRC scholar observed, the CCP's complex of insecurity and anti-Americanism has been a "nightmare for generations of Chinese" that has driven Chinese foreign policy to oppose the world at great cost and has badly served the Chinese people.[13]

In the same vein, to justify extraction, demand sacrifices, and defend and enrich its authoritarian regime, the CCP has been employing a crude version of political *realism* to view the Westphalian system as a jungle-like struggle for power and survival. "Those who fall behind get beaten" (or the weak/small will be beaten/eaten), a slogan probably first coined by Joseph Stalin in 1931 for essentially the same purposes, has been a consistent propaganda line in the PRC for over seven decades. Sometimes in varied wordsmithery such as "the weak or small can't have diplomacy," this power fetishism and might-makes-right worldview is rooted in China's own tradition of autocratic politics and world-empire imperialism, potently blended in with the flawed official narratives of modern Chinese history, which the prequels to this book, *The China Order* and *The China Record*, have attempted to debunk.[14] Xi Jinping highlights it to his senior cadres in this way: in the world, "the weak get beaten, the poor go hungry, and the mute are cussed."[15] With such a social Darwinism rationalizing incessant life-or-death power struggles and domination by force, the CCP has since 2018 enshrined the phrase "rich and strong state," ahead of all other values and objectives, in its "constitutional oath" for top leaders.[16]

In the 21st century, PRC foreign policy has exhibited another round of big swings with the same consistent aims. First, the CCP was forced to retreat and hide when the regime felt weak and needy, playing very successfully into the West's wishful thinking of incorporating the PRC into the current world order, and rousing the powerful greed of international capitalists. Highly rewarded and enriched, the CCP soon predictably changed course by the time of the Great Recession (2007–9), as it started to sense opportunities to satisfy its always burning urge to reduce and replace the US and to recenter and reorder the world in its image. By that time, the many Western "germs and flies" had come with critically needed Western capital and technology and seemed to have considerably transformed Chinese society and empowered the Chinese people. This greatly heightened the insecurity of the CCP-PRC state, which has always had woefully insufficient political legitimacy. For Beijing, the ratcheted-up China Race between the CCP-PRC and the West/US is not about serving and advancing the interests of China nor about "regional security"; it is about the existence and security of the party-state through acquiring power and the leadership of the world, currently enjoyed by the US, and reshaping the norms of "global governance."[17] Certain academic speculation envisions the PRC as the future "pivot or hub" (*shu niu*) of the world that will simply validate "the China Order as the holographic miniature of the World Order."[18] Such worldviews are poised to remain as the consistent motivation behind Chinese foreign policy, so long as the CCP-PRC state remains a Qin-Han polity of authoritarianism.[19] By 2021, PRC-based journalists concluded that a comprehensive divergence and confrontation between the PRC and the US had become "irreversible."[20]

The CCP seems to have seen and pursued two routes to fulfilling its dream of the China Order to assure its ultimate regime security: takeover and replacement. First, the CCP intends to capture and take over the existing international order, the currently West/US-led LIO, as the new world leader through force, ruse, or alliance, displacing the US and the West in general. As India's former ambassador to China put it, Beijing intends to capture the leadership of the current world order, whatever the current order is at present.[21] On this route, two concurrently usable tracks represent "two paths to global domination" for the CCP-PRC, as identified and analyzed by Hal Brands and Jake Sullivan in 2020. The CCP could engage in traditional expansion and power projection from the Western Pacific to other parts of the world through military and financial means, or it could take the new globalist approach to influence by controlling multilateral institutions and world agendas politically, economically, and diplomatically.[22]

While following the first track, even before they had "liberated" the entire Chinese Mainland, Mao and the CCP planned in 1947 to "liberate" Korea and Vietnam and the whole of East Asia. In November 1949, almost immediately after the founding of the PRC, Mao's deputy, Liu Shaoqi, openly told visiting Asian and Oceania guests that the Maoist revolution was to be exported to the world as "the universal road of liberation and revolution." That expansion plan was reconfigured in 1950, with the rebranding of the PRC as "the center of revolution for East Asia" under Stalin's leadership of world communism.[23] Failed in its foreign ventures but having managed to survive the end of the

Cold War, the CCP-PRC nonetheless continued its traditional approach of expansion, investing heavily in military force and bases in the East and South China Seas and Central and Southeast Asia and beyond, to make "a PLA with world-class capabilities that becomes the dominant military in East Asia."[24] An ambitious recent plan in that vein has been the BRI (Belt and Road Initiative), linking and incorporating China's neighboring countries as well as faraway places. The "nature" of the BRI, as some PRC analysts have candidly asserted, is "to construct a China-centered global network of trade and investment."[25] As such, as seen by US analysts, it "poses a significant challenge to U.S. economic, political, climate change, security, and global health interests."[26] Africa is reported to have become the CCP's "promising testing ground for the export of its political and economic governance concepts."[27]

On the second track of the first route for taking over world leadership, the PRC has attempted to control as many international organizations as possible in order to launch a global propaganda effort, fully leveraging its position as a permanent member of the UN Security Council, its vast pile of hard currencies, and the openness and freedoms of Western societies. Beijing "uses its resources strategically to set the agenda for multilateral engagement," often directly through personnel staffing. In 2020, PRC diplomats became top administrators of four UN agencies, the International Civil Aviation Organization, the International Telecommunication Union, the Food and Agriculture Organization, and the UN Industrial Development Organization, meaning that China had gained the largest number of top positions held by any UN member. It also headed the World Health Organization and Interpol until recently, and aggressively sought (but failed) to head the World Intellectual Property Organization. CCP cadres, now top executives of intergovernmental organizations, have openly declared that they would "undoubtedly defend" and advance Beijing's interests while at their posts.[28] In 2020, for example, with the agreement signed a year prior by two minister-level CCP officials (one PRC head of statistics and one PRC vice-foreign minister, then serving as the UN deputy secretary general), the UN opened its "Global Big Data Center" in the PRC.[29] "Beijing intends to translate the gradual shift in power from West to East at the United Nations," observed the French in fall 2021.[30]

The second route for the CCP's global ambition is replacement—to create and grow an alternative world order to gradually and methodically overshadow, overthrow, and replace the LIO and its parent, the West-

84 | The China Race

phalian system. The PRC has been showering money abroad to export its autocratic way of governance and partocracy-capitalist economic development to any polity that may be interested, especially in Africa and the rest of Global South.[31] Beijing has exported its draconian use of new technologies like AI (artificial intelligence) for surveillance and social control to places like Ethiopia, Malaysia, Mongolia, Pakistan, Sri Lanka, Venezuela, and Zimbabwe.[32] It has poured countless resources into internationalizing its currency, the RMB (the PRC currency, *Renminbi* or the "People's Money"), as a competitor to international hard currencies like the US dollar, the Euro, and the Japanese Yen.[33] Beijing has underwritten and led the formation of various multinational networks, including the umbrella BRI and the China-Africa Forum. Nearly a trillion US dollars has been promised to bankroll and control alternative international financial institutions like the Asian Infrastructure Investment Bank (AIIB), the BRICKS Bank, and the BRI Fund.[34] Though characteristically avoiding the entanglement of alliances—as the CCP has inherited the mentality of a Qin-Han world empire, which fundamentally distrusts and dismisses legal contracting with other countries as peers—Beijing has financed and expanded the Shanghai Cooperation Organization (SCO) since 2001 as a quasi-alliance network, "a major platform for cooperation in Asia, opposing the US-organized camp."[35] In the 2020s, Xi Jinping branded the "ceaselessly expanding" SCO with a "Shanghai Spirit" of "uniting all progressive forces in the world to march forward together as the builder of world peace, contributor to global development, and protector of international order," and specifically "prevent the color revolutions incited by external forces."[36] Displaying a remarkable (if unintended) sense of humor, the PRC, with the world's tightest online censorship, organized a World Internet Conference Organization in 2022 to "collectively build a community of common destiny in cyberspace."[37] In 2023, disdaining The Hague–based Permanent Court of Arbitration (founded in 1899, currently with over 120 members), Beijing founded its Hong Kong–based International Organization for Mediation, together with nine other "friendly countries."[38]

According to four Sinologists with Chinese heritage, the PRC is working toward its version of "institutional revisionism," aiming at "a peaceful transformation of the international order," in opposition to the United States, that could be "hard" or "soft" in style, and with or without an archetypal "power transition."[39] As will be further examined later in this book, with its consistent motivation for regime survival, the

CCP has been pursuing an omnidirectional, all-fronts strategy, trying everything possible to simultaneously pursue both the takeover and the replacement approaches as its comprehensive "China solution" for the world, under the new general banner of "constructing the community of common destiny for humanity."[40]

World Revolution or Common Destiny: The Core Interest

From literally day one of its existence in 1949, the CCP-PRC state has always been at odds with the US and the international order dominated by the Western democratic rule of law. Under the *tianxia* mandate for reconstructing the China Order for the survival and security of his regime, Mao Zedong consistently and unscrupulously pursued his dream of "unifying the whole world" and presiding over "the grand unity of the people of the world," "to create a new world" through his "continued revolution" of global war against anyone in his way—chiefly the US and the West, but also his former boss and benefactor the Soviet Union.[41] Chinese lives and treasure, and international moral principles, including treaty alliances, all meant very little to the CCP, driven by its desire to stay in power forever. Utterly unpopular and isolated from the international community after the Korean War (1950–53), Mao mainly pursued the revolution and replacement strategy rather than the capture and takeover approach.[42] Dreaming of a repeat of his successful violent, rural-based struggle, which had made him the conqueror of China, Mao tried everything to launch global guerrilla warfare and "use the rural [of the poor nations] to encircle and capture the urban [the advanced nations]," and then to conquer and rule the whole world.[43] This undying dream remains on full display in Beijing; one PRC analyst openly fantasized in 2020 that Africa, the global "rural" today, would allow Beijing to build "another China overseas" for its global ambition.[44]

The CCP has squandered untold resources and ruined countless lives in the PRC through bizarre and comical fool's errands, such as national campaigns to dig bomb shelters everywhere, and the Third Front program, which moved the military-industrial complex to remote places in order to mobilize and militarize the whole country so as to "wage wars of annihilation" against phantom foreign invaders.[45] Having failed miserably on most accounts due to the CCP's meager ability and his own incredibly incompetent mismanagement, and facing the possibility of total destruction at the hands of two nuclear superpowers, Mao was forced to resort to old imperial tricks, such as playing one barbarian against another. Still pretending to be somehow leading a world revolution, the CCP reversed its former stance to enter a quasi-alliance with its chief nemesis the United States to alleviate the mortal threat by its equally devious and amoral former comrade the Soviet Union. That dramatic conditional surrender and complete switch of sides in the Cold War extended the life of the CCP-PRC state and has brought great rewards of wealth and legitimacy to Beijing to this day.[46]

However, the CCP-PRC has remained politically intact, having survived the lure and pressure of the post–Cold War world order. As I have demonstrated before, the new Qin-Han political system continued, holding the flag of Mao Zedong Thought and now the banner of Xi Jinping Thought with essentially the same partocracy of governance.[47] Therefore, Chinese foreign policy has also exhibited an expected consistency in safeguarding the CCP regime above all else. The core PRC objective in foreign policy is now described as "state security," cleverly disguised as the rather common "national security" under the Westphalian system, deliberately taking advantage of the vagueness in the Chinese language regarding the distinction between state, country, and nation. The "invented" or contrived notions, such as that the CCP is the guardian of China, the "central state" of an ancient "[Han-]Chinese [nation-]state with a continuous history stretching back millennia," instead of being "a conquered province of a Manchu empire" for centuries,[48] have become seemingly unshakable national creeds. Though this might seem normal and reasonable enough, the CCP concept of "state/national security in totality" means, first and foremost, the survival and security of the one-party autocracy, the so-called "political security."[49] The PRC is much more a "CCP Inc" than a "China Inc."[50] In February of 2023, the then PRC foreign minister, while launching a "global security initiative" to offer a "Chinese solution to break the many security dilemmas" among nations, expanded Beijing's doctrine equating China's national security with CCP's regime security with a rather inauspicious declaration that "there will be no world security if China is not secure."[51] Many PRC citizens and foreigners have been jailed and executed for alleged crimes of endangering national/state security. Almost all of them, in fact, could only be deemed, however remotely, to have been undermining the power and stability of the CCP. A recent example of the PRC's dubious use of national/state security to control and silence political opposition and dissent is its implementation of the State/National Security Law in the Special Administrative Region of Hong Kong, in blatant violation of its legal and international treaty obligations.[52]

With its typical double-talk in vague verbiage, the post-Mao CCP-PRC state has tried to define its core interests of national/state security as beyond any negotiation or compromise. Yet the officially stated core interests are unscrupulously variable and evasive, hiding the main and utterly selfish objective—the eternal and total rule by the CCP in China and beyond. The PRC's list of "core interests" has encompassed huge and ever-changing items, ranging from Taiwan, Tibet, and Xinjiang to the Senkaku (Diaoyu) islets, the artificial islands in the South China Sea (since 2014), and Central Asia.[53] But the core of the core interests has been stable and clear. In 2009, the top PRC diplomat Dai Bingguo told his host, US secretary of state Hillary Clinton, that China had three "core interests" in the following order: to safeguard its political system and state security, to preserve national sovereignty and territorial integrity, and to have a sustainable and stable socioeconomic development.[54] In 2011, the PRC State Council released a white paper listing among the core interests "China's political system established in the Constitution and overall social stability."[55] In 2015 and then again in 2021, a leading Chinese scholar of international relations put it bluntly: "Only if the U.S. respects—and does not challenge—China's basic political system and the rule of the Communist Party, will it be able to persuade China to do the same vis-a-vis America's leadership position in the world," while "[the CCP's] 'socialism with Chinese characteristics' and 'the liberal international order' [led by the US] appear to be increasingly incompatible."[56] In 2020, another senior CCP analyst argued for a preemptive "first use" of force, including nuclear weapons, against any "imminent" threat to those core interests.[57] Also in 2020, the top PRC diplomat Yang Jiechi openly reaffirmed Beijing's "wholistic view of national/state security": "to safeguard the leadership of the CCP and [. . .] to protect the national/ state regime security and institutional security." As a PRC intellectual explained it in 2023, "China's core interest is just the interest of its core [ruler]."[58]

In March 2021, during high-level PRC-USA talks in Anchorage, the Chinese team bluntly declared that "[we] can never tolerate any harm of the ruling position and institutional security of the Chinese Communist Party, and this is the untouchable red line [in Chinese foreign policy]."[59]

Months later, in July 2021 and twice in 2022, the PRC foreign minister repeated that the CCP's unchallenged leadership in China is the first and foremost of Beijing's "three bottom lines" in the "critically important" US-China relationship. Upon closer look, the second and third "bottom lines"—PRC's mode of economic development and its "internal affairs" in places like Hong Kong, Xinjiang, and Taiwan—also appear to be all about the party-state.[60] In September 2021, a senior analyst from CICIR, a major PRC government foreign policy think tank, elaborated on the old consistency and new elasticity and dynamicity of the CCP's "national/state security in totality" (*zongti guojia anquan*), a term that was coined by Xi Jinping: "political security [or] regime security is the foundation of national/state security," and "wherever the state interest expands to, the boundary of state security shall follow up, and [our] work for state security shall cover there too."[61]

The overall course of the PRC's foreign policy has accordingly stayed consistent from Mao to Xi "for security, prosperity, and power," with acrobatics now and then for the purpose of concealing and distracting, especially during the two decades of 1989–2008.[62] The standard official narrative tends to describe a loyal pursuit of the "Five Principles of Peaceful Coexistence"—*Pancha Shila*, which was first jointly proposed by India and the PRC in 1954.[63] The PRC and India have coexisted ever since, but hardly peacefully. The pretention of liberating humanity through a Moscow- or Beijing-led world communist revolution had to be discarded when it became an overly bankrupt enterprise after the Cold War. Fighting for the cause of the Third World against the West became an ever-hollower claim as Beijing profited from its interactions with poorer nations through trade and investment just like the West. Anti-hegemonic posturing to rally support has also faded, as Beijing cannot resist behaving increasingly like a hegemon itself.[64] Colorful and dazzling talk aside, Beijing has always walked with the same aim of meeting the regime's political needs. The "key driver of Chinese diplomacy" always remains "to support the Chinese Communist Party and keep the regime in power."[65]

"The grand unity of all people in the world" is still carved on the wall of Tiananmen, but the inescapable mandate has been repackaged and re-represented several times, from seeking a "new and fairer and more just world order" of multipolarity, to a China-led globalization and multilateralism, to "new great power diplomacy," and finally to the major component of Xi Jinping Thought: the "China solution" to the problems of global governance through the construction of "a [CCP-led] community of common destiny for humanity."[66] The concept of community for a common destiny and organic harmony is not new, and was especially impactful in the 20th century. Nazi Germany, for one, used the notion of *Volksgemeinschaft* (people's community) to justify and promote its nationalist, racist, and imperialist agenda as a totalitarian regime.[67] In CCP lingo, "Community of Common Destiny for Humanity" or "Community of Common Human Destiny" (CCHD) may be inspired by the ancient Chinese ideal of Great Unity or World Harmony.[68] The phrase in Chinese was reportedly coined by an obscure Chinese-Guyanese writer in his 2006 declaration for a short-lived Datong Party or "World Unification Alliance," which aimed for a "peaceful unification of the world by 2030."[69] Probably unaware of the backstory in the Western Hemisphere, the CCP's *People's Daily* first printed the phrase CCHD to advocate for an Asian-Pacific "regional integration" in 2007. During a visit to Japan in 2011, PRC premier Wen Jiabao used the phrase "community of common destiny," which was subsequently repeated in Beijing's *White Paper on China's Peaceful Development*, in September 2011.[70]

Xi Jinping formally formulated CCHD as his grand, overarching, and idealistic innovation for world order after taking over the CCP in 2012.[71] In his 2017 New Year's message, Xi declared that the "Chinese people have always wanted a great world harmony for all under heaven as one family" (*shijie datong, tianxia yijia*). Four years later, he refined the same message as "the Great Way is shared and all under heaven is one family."[72] The phrase was soon written into the CCP Constitution in 2017 and the PRC Constitution in 2018. Eager to please, PRC diplomats managed to insert the phrase into a handful of UN agencies' resolutions in 2017, and then celebrated this as a great triumph of Xi Jinping Thought on the world stage.[73] The PRC foreign minister wrote bluntly that what Beijing seeks is a "new global governance system" to replace the current "US-led" world order, fighting the global "rivalry and contest that will deeply affect the future of humanity and the earth."[74] A senior CCP propagandist disguised as a scholar followed up with the open assertion that Common Destiny simply meant the "rapid rejuvenation of China," to "first become the equal of [. . .] then more powerful than the US," building and leading "a very different [world] order" in one-generation's time to "become the real number one" leader of the world and "put the US [and everyone else] under our management."[75] In April 2021, Xi Jinping officialized this aspiration once again in a public speech phrased

90 | The China Race

in typical CCP vernacular, asserting that his party has been struggling for a full century "for the happiness of the Chinese people, the rejuvenation of the Chinese nation, and the common grand harmony of the world [. . . and] actively promoting the construction of new international relations."[76] Officially, CCHD contains a set of "common human values" or "common values for all humanity" that are superior to and "fundamentally different from the so-called [West-originated] 'universal values.'"[77] In an ingratiating spin by a web-based PRC commentator, the scheme of Common Destiny "contains communism, socialism, and the Chinese thought of grand harmony"; it pleases human instinct, "occupies humanity's moral high ground," and "is the first ever grand design by China for all humankind," which will allow "China to seize the world authority of narratives at the top level," pursue its "revolutionary foreign policy," and lead its "Chinese version of globalization."[78]

Omnidirectional Efforts: Nothing Is Small

Fully aware of the critical importance of external relations, the CCP-PRC has always put great emphasis and attention on its foreign policy, despite its pretension and propaganda about already being the leader of the world. The nature of the Qin-Han style centralized autocracy of the regime structurally determines a secretive micromanagement of Chinese diplomacy by the CCP ruler. The PRC's foreign policy is characterized by tight message control and constant image management. With the blanket silencing of open and meaningful discourse and disagreement, Beijing enjoys a tactical advantage in dealing with foreigners by pretending to have the unanimous support of the Chinese people with a national consensus. The CCP's unscrupulous and unmonitored use of seemingly unlimited resources in a focused way allows for weighty, agile, meticulous, and mesmerizing responses that are often easily mistaken for flexibility and pragmatism, especially by foreign negotiators unfamiliar with the CCP's political culture. Beijing's dazzling inconsistence and elusiveness regarding methods, alliance orientation, and especially rhetoric are often misconstrued as sophistication and wisdom.

Based on Maoist class analysis and united-front tactics, the PRC categorizes and treats foreigners (from individuals to states) with which it interacts as comrades-in-arms, old or new friends/brothers, neutral but hopeful, neutral but hopeless, or enemies. That categorization can change

PRC Foreign Policy | 91

or even totally reverse within a moment, depending on Beijing's demands or whether someone has "hurt the Chinese people's feeling."[79] Like in its domestic politics, the CCP acts externally with very few institutional, legal, or moral constraints. Anything goes when it comes to meeting its main and consistent goal of staying in power forever. Born to be a rebel, the PRC state has always seemed to be an omnidirectional insurgent, seeking no less than revolutionary change to the current world order, to remake it in its image, whenever and wherever possible. "The two aims of the Party are to conquer the whole surface of the earth and to extinguish once and for all the possibility of independent thought," as classically written by George Orwell at the time the PRC was just created.[80]

Zhou Enlai (1898–1976), the PRC's longtime foreign policy tsar and Mao's top manager and executioner, laid down the principles and mechanisms for a highly centralized micromanagement of foreign policy, as summarized by his much-reiterated quote "nothing is small in foreign affairs."[81] As was typical of Qin-Han rulers, Mao and his successors have personally "completely monopolized" PRC foreign policy. They have used meetings with foreign dignitaries to symbolically bolster their political legitimacy and power at home. The reclamation of symbols of China's world stature, such as its permanent seat on the UN Security Council, first obtained by the ROC for China in the mid-1940s, has become perhaps the only selling point of the Maoist CCP-PRC state,[82] which is otherwise increasingly known to many as a nearly total failure. Aside from such symbolic accomplishments, Mao and his successors have frequently relied on token praise by foreigners to demonstrate Beijing's importance and popularity in the world, mostly for domestic consumption. Massive and opaque foreign aid and bribery plus lavish and often ostentatious hospitality, like hosting and paying for extra-luxurious international conferences and visits, in addition to the diplomatic power of its position in places like the UN Security Council, have been important ways to obtain the international recognition that is endlessly craved by the legitimacy-challenged CCP rulers. This use of the Chinese people's money for the ruler's vanity and legitimacy has exploded in recent years as Beijing has felt rich and swung back to more assertive action abroad. Noted examples include the incredible waste of money on the 2008 Beijing Olympics,[83] the 2010 Shanghai World Expo, the 2022 Beijing Winter Olympics, and the many "home court diplomacy" extravaganzas like the hosting of the China-Africa forum and the APEC and G20 summits in the 2010s. In addition to its massive and costly Great Firewall, for control and pro-

92 | The China Race

paganda at home, the CCP-PRC has been making great efforts abroad to push its model of "censorship going global."[84]

With varying degrees of bluntness, Mao and his successors have been fighting the same worldwide war-like struggle for the recognition and leadership of the world. Omnidirectional and acting in ways large and small, Beijing pushes out with a seemingly coordinated and steady course in all directions—nicknamed the "salami-slicing approach"—backed by a so-called "total national mobilization" (*juguo tizhi*), as exemplified by Beijing's ultra-expensive but impressive drive to earn medals in international sports competitions, something the CCP learned from the Soviet Union.[85] Such a total mobilization and concentration of resources regardless of means and cost can indeed be effective in support of its foreign ventures. But the extreme extraction and endless exploitation and the accompanying waste of lives and money are the usual results. Some have estimated, for example, that for every gold medal a PRC athlete won at the Olympic games in the 2010s to glorify the party-state and please the nationalistic crowds, the bill to the Chinese taxpayers was ¥600 million ($93 million), or "the equivalent of the total annual revenue of nine poor counties"—not to mention the countless young Chinese lives twisted and ruined in the process of training those medal-winning human robots.[86]

Costs and lives are literally no object to Beijing in service to its grand ambitions abroad. Direct consequences at home have included the "Great Leap Forward" to great famine, the endless political purges, the economic calamity and the overall China Tragedy, and the lasting China Suboptimality.[87] Whenever possible, Beijing has also directly exported its model of violent revolution to nearly all neighboring countries in Southeast and South Asia and faraway places in Africa and Latin America. "Between 1964 and 1985, China spent between $170 million and $220 million training some 20,000 fighters from at least nineteen African countries."[88] Many PRC citizens actually joined and died in revolutionary rebellions and gruella warfare in Southeast Asia.[89] As at home in the PRC, the CCP cares little about lives in other countries. Mao infamously talked about sacrificing one-third to one-half of all human beings (then numbering 2.9 billion) in a global nuclear war so as "to completely eliminate capitalism and acquire an eternal peace."[90] CCP-inspired and supported insurgencies and rebellions, like the hellish Khmer Rouge in Cambodia and the brutal Shining Path in Peru, have indeed perpetrated inhumane massacres and caused great destruction.[91]

Today, appearing confident and even arrogant, Beijing undertakes "a series of aggressive, bullying, paranoid and weird stunts to try to exert dominance and pressure" via its "tantrum diplomacy," the so-called "wolf warrior diplomacy," costly to both the Chinese and other peoples.[92]

Foreign Policy of and for the Party

Similar and closely related to its political and socioeconomic records at home, the record of Beijing's foreign policy exhibits a peculiar feature: a duality of the CCP Optimality and the China Suboptimality. Instead of "serving the people," as the official motto from Mao to Xi calls for, Chinese foreign policy, just like Chinese domestic policies, mainly serves the party rulers and has done that job reasonably well. The CCP-PRC has managed so far to stay in power, maintaining its partocracy against all forms of internal resistance and external rivalries. The inordinate expense of the China Tragedy and the China Suboptimality at home aside, the CCP regime has enjoyed international security at the enormous and ongoing cost of the interests of the Chinese nation, the Chinese people, and the world at large. Having yet to achieve its goal of either taking over the globe or recentering and reordering the world, the CCP's foreign policy has served, enriched, and strengthened the rulers quite satisfactorily for seven decades. The rebuilding of the China Order of world empire, under whatever name or decoration, is steadily making headway, while China's national interests and the well-being of the Chinese people are poorly protected and served. As a mode of governance for the people, the CCP-PRC state has proved itself inferior and costly compared to other nations, often with disastrous consequences, both on the international stage and at home.

For the CCP's ruling coterie, Beijing's foreign policy has achieved several noteworthy objectives, especially worldwide normalization and recognition for the legitimacy of the regime. Thanks to countless resources expended to purchase and punish, many clever ruses to manipulate, and the effective assistance of numerous willing or inadvertent foreign "useful idiots," who tend to be "vain, narcissistic, highly susceptible to flattery, and greedy,"[93] the CCP-PRC state is now considered by and large just another normal nation-state. Beijing has used hundreds of "foreign experts" in dozens of countries to bolster the legitimacy of its regime at home and for propaganda abroad.[94] The decorative post of "Chairman

94 | The China Race

of the PRC" is mistranslated as President of China; the CCP-PRC state is equated with China as a nation and a country; and the CCP itself is legitimized as just "a ruling party chosen by the Chinese people" decades ago. When Beijing insists on speaking, acting, and demanding on behalf of the nearly one-fifth of humanity under its rule—a highly impressive and powerful position, given the reigning world norms of equality of every human being—few now ask how the CCP got the honor of representing that many people for all those decades.

The CCP cadres, who have all vowed to sacrifice anything and everything for the party leaders and the eventual victory of world communism, have now been received as peer leaders, business partners, respected colleagues, equal diplomats, and even trustworthy friends in nearly every corner of the international community. Beijing's agents and surrogates are now routinely given equal, if not more, attention in the Western media, press, and conference halls. Some of those party bosses and cadres are now heading and influencing international organizations inside and outside of the UN.[95] The profound normalization and legitimacy the West has bestowed both tangibly and intangibly on the CCP, the sworn enemy and self-mandated "burier" of the West, is truly astounding in both its theatrical incongruity and its vital consequences.[96] Over the past three decades, to be sure, the CCP elites have all looked quite Westernized in appearance, fully indulging in the Western lifestyle, with the best goods and services money can buy worldwide. Many of them are phony communist double-talkers—Western educated, and quite well versed in globalist lingo, with their families often having already emigrated to the West. But their professed "original intent and mandated mission," according to the party leaders and theorists, is still the same Leninist-Stalinist-Maoist dream of replacing and subjugating the West, and the United States in particular.[97]

A major, concrete success of CCP-PRC foreign policy over the past three decades has been its deep, extensive, and often open and unfiltered access to Western society, capital, markets, technology, and decision-makers. The PRC has benefited in crucial ways from the same open international trade and financial systems that Beijing has fairly easily and highly rewardingly manipulated and defrauded. Just in the so-called "tax havens," the poorly regulated off-shore capital markets, the PRC has opaquely gained access to huge amounts of foreign capital, "from raising a negligible amount of capital in these markets to accounting for more than half of equity issuance and around a fifth of global corporate bonds outstanding" in the two decades prior to 2023.[98] Always resenting and protesting the US presence around the world, especially in its neighborhood, the PRC has nonetheless enjoyed its free ride on the open, international sea lanes. This open but mostly one-way access has been critical to the rise of the Chinese economy and PRC state power. Imported and pirated Western technology and piles of foreign currency have in turn enabled and empowered PRC foreign policy both diplomatically and militarily. Certainly, this is not the first time the US and the West have critically aided a determined challenger with technology, capital, and markets. In the 1920s–30s, the US provided literally all the technology the Soviet Union needed to industrialize itself.[99]

The explosive growth in the PRC's foreign economic exchange with nearly every country (with the West commanding the lion's share)—at great cost to Chinese workers and the Chinese environment, as I have reported in *The China Record*—has politically benefited the CCP regime in two additional unique and crucial ways beyond its immense acquisition of foreign recognition, technology, and hard currency. First, and critically, foreign trade industries and foreign investment in China have provided decent jobs to many Chinese people, while the capital-burning, state-owned enterprises do not create new jobs at all, and the job-creating native private enterprises are always politically suppressed and financially deprived. Official PRC reports concluded that foreign trade employed over 180 million people in 2019 (23.4% of total PRC employment, or 41% of total nonagricultural employment); and foreign-invested enterprises were five times more effective in creating jobs than the national average, directly employing over 45 million workers with better pay, and at least 100 million indirectly (10% and 23% of the total nonagricultural employment, respectively).[100] In a suboptimal economy that chronically experiences unemployment and underemployment, the political significance of foreign economic exchange to the CCP-PRC state, which needs to provide enough decent jobs or "rice bowls" to people to justify its rule and pacify discontent, is hard to exaggerate.

Second, the massive and rapidly growing capital outflow (whether as legitimate foreign investment or illicit capital flight) and the associated emigration, especially the legal kinds through schooling, work, and investment, have, over the past four decades, intriguingly provided much-needed safety valves for the CCP-PRC state, however inadvertently. The brainy, the audacious, the educated, and the rich—people who are both willing and capable of making political demands—now have a ready and rewarding opportunity to exit should they prefer, thereby significantly reducing pressure on the regime by the endless discontent and dissent. Going abroad and staying there to better their lives, instead of focusing their energy on changing Chinese politics at home, has been a viable choice for ambitious and able young Chinese since the early 1980s. A conservative estimate is that over 11 million PRC citizens permanently emigrated in the three decades prior to 2019.[101] Many if not most of these emigrants would have been potent "troublemakers" for the CCP if they had remained in the heavy-lidded, high-pressure boiler of the repressive regime at home. The lure of profiting from trade and other dealings with people back home in the PRC, together with the privilege and protection of foreign residency or citizenship, further diminish the motivation and rationale for challenging the CCP for many able Chinese who have made it abroad.

Unlike in the past when, with the China Order in place for the whole known world, a Qin-Han polity often had to rely on physical elimination, imprisonment, or internal exile to control discontent (until the day when it was overpowered and overthrown by rebellion), today's PRC state can utilize voluntary or involuntary exile abroad to rid itself of political opponents and critics. Indeed, Beijing has consciously exiled many of its citizens since 1989, often playing the "human rights card" and releasing and expelling political dissidents to placate Western critics.[102] Unlike during the late-Qing and the ROC eras, when overseas Chinese, especially political exiles, had a great impact on Chinese politics, today's overseas Chinese often do not have the will or the ability to significantly influence the politics of their motherland. The foreign-backed political organization and action, including military uprisings, which shaped Chinese politics in the first half of the 20th century and led to the rise of the CCP, simply do not exist today. The CCP leadership has "learned the lesson from history" and has always tightly restricted any foreign-financed sociopolitical activity in the PRC so as to "prevent the possible birth of another CCP."[103] This is why the CCP has been very hostile to foreign-connected NGOs (nongovernmental organizations) and religious groups, which are actually very beneficial to the Chinese people.

The West today respects the equal sovereignty of the PRC much more than imperialist powers like Russia-Soviet Union and Japan respected that of the ROC. The often-tricky distinction between freedom fighters and terrorists is less of an issue today, as the West often categorically defines violent protest as terrorism.[104] Nonviolent actions by Chinese exiles against the CCP are ineffectual and simply dismissible. Beijing's extensive, arbitrary, and even inhumane deprivation of the right of overseas citizens and Chinese-foreigners to visit their ancestral homeland, together with the tight censorship of information and Sino-foreign communication have allowed the CCP to strengthen its control over the Chinese people, even in an era of globalization when so many Chinese are in fact living and traveling abroad. Beijing's extensive infiltration has paralyzed many if not most dissident groups in exile. All this, in addition to the *hukou*(household registration)-based spatial segregation, helps to explain the "puzzle" of why the Chinese elites and middle class, including many of those living abroad, seem uninterested in political democratization, or at least are not very serious about fighting for it.

Cost to the People

The cost of the CCP's foreign policy to the Chinese people has been just as hefty and horrific as its domestic policies. As I have reported in the prequels to this book, tens of millions of Chinese, uncounted and mostly unnamed, perished in the Chinese Civil War of 1946–50, the Great Famine of 1959–63 (1958–65 in many localities), the Cultural Revolution of 1966–77, the countless political campaigns, purges and "harsh strikes" from the 1940s to the 2020s, and the mismanaged or human-made disasters and epidemics of the past decades. The CCP-PRC state often seems to view Chinese lives as worthless and dispensable, both abroad and within its borders. In fact, much of the massive loss of life and resources at home, such as during the Great Famine, has been related to or even directly prompted by Beijing's needs and ventures abroad. The politically optimal Chinese foreign policy, which has served the CCP rulers reasonably well, has been exorbitant and deadly to the Chinese people.

Within just a few decades, the PRC's war dead abroad far outnumbered the total war dead of the United States over more than two centuries. From the heavy losses of life in the Korean War of 1950–53, the Sino-Indian Border War of 1962, the border conflicts with the Soviet Union in 1969, the Vietnam War in the 1960s and 1970s, and the invasion of Vietnam in 1979, and the subsequent decade-long border battles to the deadly border clash with Indian troops in 2020, the PRC has never fully, let alone verifiably, released data on the number of Chinese

98 | The China Race

soldiers killed or injured. Beijing's long history of hiding, neglecting, and dismissing its war casualties is already well documented. Under Xi Jinping's so-called "people-centered new" governance of "strong/great power diplomacy," the PRC still typically hides facts about the loss of Chinese lives at the hands of foreigners. After the overnight Sino-Indian border skirmish on June 15, 2020, which reportedly resulted in the deaths of over 40 Chinese troops and twice that number of Indian deaths, for example, Beijing provided only some mistranslated foreign reports as a source of information for the Chinese people, pretending there were no Chinese casualties. Meanwhile, India released a detailed accounting of the number and identities of all its dead.[105] Eight months later, only in a reportage by the PLA celebrating "the heroism of our new era," were four of the Chinese soldiers killed in the clash mentioned.[106]

When overseas Chinese (many with PRC citizenship) were massacred by the thousands in Indonesia in 1965–66 over some alleged Beijing-sponsored political conspiracy, and then again in 1998 due to simple racial and ethnic hatred, the PRC state lodged protests but did almost nothing to count or assist the victims, not to mention investigating and intervening to punish the perpetrators.[107] This is only a little better than the Chinese emperor centuries ago who, instead of accepting repentance and compensation, actually praised and rewarded the Spanish governor for killing thousands of ethnic Chinese in 1603 in the Philippines, because those Chinese were "traitors" who dared to escape the Ming Empire.[108] In less gruesome instances—the deaths that occurred during the construction of Tazara (the Tanzania-Zambia Railway) in the 1970s; the three dozen Chinese who died in a sealed truck en route to Britain in 2000 (each had paid smugglers $30,000); the scores of Chinese miners, fishermen, and merchants killed by police in "friendly" places like Ghana in 2012, Korea in 2016, and Zambia in 2020—Chinese fatalities are almost always swept under the rug and customarily prohibited from being mentioned and discussed, let alone commemorated in the PRC. Rising power or not, the PRC seems to manifestly disregard Chinese lives abroad just as it does at home.

The financial cost of the CCP's foreign policy to the Chinese people is always kept under wraps. To this day, there is no published government data on how much Beijing has spent overseas during the past seven decades. The very sketchy figures of the PRC budget for diplomacy are highly unreliable and useless. Scholarly works and anecdotal reports have only pieced together a rough picture of the CCP's truly extravagant squandering of the Chinese people's money abroad for its political objectives, with no consent or oversight from the Chinese people. For its political needs for external legitimacy, or even just token support from phony foreign political parties (which are sometimes just foreign intelligence outfits), the CCP-PRC has secretively showered hard-earned hard currency all over the world, especially in the West, even when the Chinese people themselves were terribly short of the hard currency needed to buy basics such as medicine and food from abroad. In serving its ambition to lead a global revolution and oppose and replace the West (and the Soviet Union), significant Chinese aid has gone to states, groups, and individuals that are at odds with the West, apparently including the Taliban of Afghanistan in the 2020s.[109] Massive foreign aid may have even been used to rescue a family member of a top CCP leader who was caught engaging in wrongdoing overseas.[110]

Over the six decades ending in 2009, the CCP reportedly gave an estimated \$36.6 billion to over 110 countries around the world, even in periods when China was enduring poverty and famines and was a major recipient of massive official aid from the West (over \$107 billion during 1979–2003 alone).[111] That sprinkling of money has swelled into a torrent over the past decade as part of the so-called great power diplomacy undertaken by the wealthy-feeling CCP. Starting from a very low level in 2000, PRC foreign aid has exploded, significantly surpassing that of the United States almost every year since 2009; the cumulative total over the past two decades is now estimated to be larger than that of the US, despite the fact that the PRC still has a much lower GDP (especially per capita GDP).[112] For about a decade beginning in 2009, just two PRC state banks (the China Bank of Development and the Export-Import Bank of China) lent more money to developing countries than the World Bank.[113] The snowballing scheme of Xi Jinping's BRI has been allocated up to \$1 trillion (nearly 10 times more than the Marshall Plan in today's dollars) to fund ever-increasing and often highly questionable projects like pipelines and high-speed transportation through the tribal region of Northern Pakistan.[114]

Thus far, the major beneficiaries of the CCP money spigot have been, by far, Russia and other infamous international pariahs like North Korea, Iran, Venezuela, and Zimbabwe, which are mainly noted for their anti-Americanism (and maybe crude oil or mineral deposits). The CCP seems to have consistently pursued its realpolitik of "my enemy's enemy is my friend," with little regard for China's real national interests, not to mention legal and moral principles.[115] The latest addition to the list of beneficiaries seems to be the Taliban regime, following the US departure from Afghanistan.[116] Many funding recipients, countries like Libya and Venezuela, have been major defaulters, resulting in enormous write-offs of the Chinese funds once the local rulers collapse or change. Many of Beijing's well-oiled "friends," such as Albania, have proven fickle and unreliable, sometimes even assuming an anti-Beijing stance. In this regard, the PRC seems to be duplicating the experience of the former Soviet Union, which harshly extracted from the Russian people for its highly cost-ineffective global aid programs in political opposition to the West.[117]

Many if not most of Beijing's beneficiaries in fact have a much higher living standard and per capita GDP than the PRC. The impoverished and even starving Chinese people have often been forced unknowingly to transfer wealth to whomever the CCP deems momentarily useful for its political aim of staying in power. According to a PRC scholar, Beijing's annual aid to North Korea alone has been as high as $6 billion.[118] In a single announcement in 2018, Xi Jinping offered over $60 billion to African nations, mostly as free aid or interest-free loans.[119] Beijing spends lavishly on educational funding, more than all Western European nations combined, to literally bribe nearly any African or Asian student to study in China in order to "internationalize" its colleges for higher rankings.[120] For prestige and propaganda, possibly espionage and recruiting, and perhaps even the desires of cadres to emigrate with their families, Beijing has funded over 120 (decreased to 14 by summer 2022) Confucius Institutes (CIs) plus over 500 Confucius Classrooms in the United States alone since 2004.[121] The number of similar American cultural centers in the PRC, however, is zero, with only four ever permitted by Beijing. In some cities, like New York and Atlanta, three CIs were once set up, competing for the rather small number of students interested in learning the PRC's version of the Chinese language and culture. The CIs, numbering over 480 worldwide in 2020 (down from over 540 in 2018), may be evidence of the CCP's impatient, aggressive, and spare-no-cost campaign to mimic and compete with the so-called soft power or sociocultural influence of the West. In practice, CIs have enabled a certain amount of CCP propaganda overseas, as well as considerable emigration for the connected and chosen few, all at a high cost to the Chinese people. Programs like the CIs—"academic malware" according to American anthropologist Marshall Sahlins[122]—are not cheap. The PRC typically provides start-up funding of $150,000 and an annual operating cost of $100,000–$200,000 for each of the CIs in the US, with some costing much more.[123] For each American student taking a Chinese language class at a CI, Beijing pays the sizable annual amount of $8,000 (while commonly charging the student no tuition or a nominal fee of only $50–$80 for a semester-long course). This contrasts starkly with the annual per-pupil funding in the PRC (elementary through high school), which is officially reported as only $391–$510 (or $1,478–$2,092 by a different accounting method).[124]

In this century, China's massive financial aid and strong support to Russia seem to have been driven by the CCP leadership's political interest, at the great expense of China's national interest. Through opaque deals involving subsidized trade, financial infusions, and aid, Russia has received far more Chinese money than any other country, including Pakistan and North Korea.[125] On February 4, 2022, the CCP reaffirmed its "limitless, ceiling-less, and restriction-less strategic cooperation" with Moscow in a Xi-Putin joint communiqué that proclaimed the two "will jointly improve global governance"; this was followed by massive new funding to Moscow.[126] Very quickly, however, Putin put the PRC in an awkward bind with his much-condemned invasion of Ukraine.[127] Deceived by Moscow or not, Beijing has to either support Putin unconditionally as promised, at the risk of offending the West and most other nations, and particularly Ukraine; or back away from its fresh total pledge to Moscow, costing China immensely in reputation and credibility and offending the Kremlin; or remain maladroitly stuck on the fence, suffering on both sides. Soon enough, Beijing appeared to critically back up Moscow: in May 2022, Russia became the PRC's largest crude oil provider with a jump in quantity of 55% over the previous year and at a price of $126 per barrel, about 10% higher than market rate (Brent and OPEC prices).[128] Months later, the number three official of the CCP leadership openly told his Russian host that Beijing "supports and understands" Moscow's action in Ukraine "to protect its core interests" and has been in "various ways collaborating with" (ceying) the Kremlin.[129] The Chinese treasury and China's national interests, together with the Chinese people living in Ukraine, have been adversely affected by Beijing's camaraderie with a fellow autocracy challenging the reigning world order.[130] As the West starts to historically unite in its policy reassessment and reorientation after the Russo-Ukrainian war, the CCP's collusion with Moscow is costing China in many ways.[131]

102 | The China Race

Other than the remarkable cost-ineffectiveness and manifested selfishness of spending the Chinese people's money for the CCP's procurement of legitimacy and influence abroad, the gargantuan Chinese financial outflow, in the form of various foreign aid expenditures and a "Grand External Propaganda" (*da waixuan*) program (since 2009), has apparently become a popular and discreet way for many party-state officials to embezzle and flee with public funds. High-profile foreign celebrities are hired for propaganda via pricey, questionable intermediaries, for example.[132] The costly effort to cultivate a responsible "great power" image abroad, together with massive, nontransparent spending, appears in fact to be deeply self-contradicting.[133] Very much in sync with the widespread corruption at home, the CCP cadres in charge of the PRC's opaque PRC budget abroad—often assisted by their hungry "white glove" agents and intermediaries (commonly trusted overseas Chinese or foreigners) in under-the-table collusion with key leaders of the recipient countries, especially in places where neither rule of law nor a free press exists—often simply enrich themselves, their families, and cronies, and then emigrate.[134] There has been rich anecdata on fake projects and phony invoices for foreign aid and investment ventures, massive kick-backs and quid-pro-quos between the PRC officials and fund recipients, and illicit money transfers and laundering. The resultant "disappearance" of Chinese public funds on a massive scale is then easily attributed to the unruly foreign recipients. As one PRC blogger noted, Beijing's foreign aid is often a feeding frenzy of "pocketing" the people's money by CCP cadres, who pay officials of "the beggar countries" to "take the blame."[135]

The management of the vast funding appropriated opaquely for foreign aid and external propaganda machines, such as the CIs, seems to be even more corrupt and primed for easier theft of public money than the already unaccountable and irresponsible fiscal policies at home, as reported in *The China Record*, due to the well-guarded tradition of centralization and secrecy regarding anything related to "foreign policy." Outrageous insider contracting, for example, has made the website of CI Headquarters "the most expensive website ever built in history."[136] Beijing also spends massively and opaquely to propagate and disinform on social media platforms like Twitter (now X) that are banned in the PRC.[137] The widespread corruption of the cadres involved has, strangely, led to a substantial vested interest group inside the PRC that pushes for ever more foreign spending, supposedly for the sake of influence, information, and other gains abroad for the regime. The larger, stealthier, and shadier that such spending "has to be," the better it is for this sizable group of CCP elites. This self-interested group functions similarly to the larger interest groups of "stability-maintenance" cadres and birth-control officials, who tend to exaggerate and push for ever more funding for their lines of work, in order to enrich themselves and their cronies with public funds through rampant rent-seeking activities.[138]

The corruption inside the PRC foreign policy agencies, therefore, naturally makes actual influence-purchasing abroad rare and super expensive. One big success of the CCP's activities abroad may have been its influence over Tedros Adhanom, the director-general of the WHO since 2017, who flagrantly defended Beijing in 2020 at the expense of managing the COVID-19 pandemic and protecting the credibility of the WHO. As a leftist revolutionary and later an Ethiopian politician, Tedros Adhanom is alleged to owe Beijing tens of millions of dollars and also his career advances over the years.[139] In 2021–23, however, he was quickly accused in PRC social media as a "traitor," "American puppet," and "China-basher" when he changed his tune to call for more PRC openness in tracing the origin of the virus and reporting on the spread of the disease in China.[140]

Every so often, in the addition to the poorly monitored "free" aid, recipients of Chinese money request debt forgiveness, often with the friendly help and approval of CCP cadres who are likely to have personally benefited handsomely from the lending and then also the write-off. One such round was in June 2020, when Beijing declared the forgiveness or reduction of the massive debts owed by 77 unnamed "developing countries," many of them in Africa.[141] This was perhaps intended to head off the astronomical amount of COVID-19-related compensation demanded by a number of African countries ($200 billion by some Nigerians alone).[142] In other cases, a recipient may simply declare post hoc that the opaque Chinese loans are illegal or unethical and thus not pay them back, as Kenya attempted to do in 2020 on the $4.3 billion star project of the Nairobi-Mombasa Railway. The PRC financed 90% of the project, which had been completed three years before.[143] In the 2020s, the list of countries seeking relief has continued to grow, with new additions like Zambia in 2022.[144] In early 2023, the new PRC foreign minister Qin Gang visited several African countries and reportedly "wrote off debt after debt all the way [he] traveled."[145]

In this way, the still poor (or poorer) Chinese people are forced and duped, anonymously and unwillingly, to constantly transfer huge

104 | The China Race

amounts of wealth they so badly need to better their own lives at home to massive, surreptitiously run, charity-like programs that buy political recognition and influence for Beijing, enrich CCP cadres and their foreign buddies, and build projects that may be of benefit to the people of the recipient countries. Only in 2018 did Beijing set up the China International Development Cooperation Agency to provide some limited transparency.[146] In recent years, a fair amount of private capital has flowed, both legally and illegally, from the PRC to many countries. But, as shall be analyzed later, Beijing suppresses the often more active and profitable nonstate actors in foreign economies just as it does at home.

To many observers, the massive aid and investment from the PRC in places such as Africa look like deliberate "debt traps"—bait for either selfish and evil gains or outright colonialism—since these programs are often established in haste and secrecy, with meager feasibility studies, and scant proper management and oversight, and thus hold little if any prospect of financial returns for China.[147] Others tend to argue, not entirely erroneously, that Beijing's spending sprees in Africa and elsewhere seem benign and "win-win," not really a trap for properties or colonies. Both views, however, are often rather oblivious to what really drives PRC foreign policy in their assessments of Chinese investment.[148] Given the analysis in this book about the motivations behind Beijing's charity abroad, those debt traps may not trap many recipients after all, as they will likely result in write-offs rather than Chinese invasion or occupation, with a happy ending for all: the CCP rulers who get their desired symbolic political support, the corrupt officials of both sides, the contractors and workers who get paid, and the local people at large who do end up with some useful infrastructure and economic growth (although some of those Chinese-built highways are "from nowhere and to nowhere" and are of inconsistent quality).[149] Many BRI megaprojects, such as the $2.7 billion Coca Codo Sinclair dam in Ecuador, "are falling apart" soon after completion.[150] Many if not most Chinese working in Africa, however, seem to experience a life of the usual bitterness, with "aspirations and predicaments," as at home.[151] The only certain losers "trapped" are the powerless and voiceless Chinese people, who are left holding the bag (akin to what has happened with hugely irrational state investments like the excessive high-speed railways in the PRC itself). Worse, while shouldering the exorbitant costs, few if any PRC citizens get to enjoy the projects they overpaid for in foreign countries.

Impact on the Chinese Nation

Chinese foreign policy since 1949 has so far effectively delivered a decent service to safeguard and legitimize the CCP regime abroad. This is arguably a major component of the PRC national interest, especially according to realist observers of international politics, given that the CCP, despite its questionable legitimacy and undesirability, has indeed been ruling China. This achievement, as we have demonstrated, has inflicted staggering losses of life and treasure on the Chinese people. It has also disserved the Chinese nation, often damaging or endangering other key, arguably more basic, components of Chinese national interests, such as territorial integrity, credibility, dignity, freedom and power of the nation, the safety and rights of the citizens, and economic interests.[152] In particular, the CCP has repeatedly and irretrievably damaged China's national credibility and trustworthiness just to safeguard and enrich itself. For example: in order to secure its vital access to the American market through a WTO membership, bypassing US scrutiny, Beijing made grand promises of economic and political reform it did not intend to keep; to silence political critics, it scorned international obligations to strangle Hong Kong and suppress information about a pandemic; to occupy and militarize the disputed South China Sea, it broke pledges to successive US presidents. For its partisan interest, the CCP squanders the world's trust in the PRC to create a dangerous predicament for the Chinese nation.[153]

With its inherent political logic mandating the China Order of world empire and its ideological rationale of Marxist-Leninist world revolution for Communism, the CCP-PRC state is a global rebel in the uncomfortable and painful but necessary disguise of a Chinese nation-state. This structural and normative peculiarity determines and explains the poor service or disservice the PRC foreign policy has provided the Chinese nation and the Chinese people, both of which are routinely exploited and treated as dispensable, despite how often and how hard the CCP has claimed to be *the* Chinese nationalist or patriot. Intentionally challenging and remaking the existing world order has necessarily always made the PRC's foreign policy difficult and costly. The record of the PRC foreign policy in serving and advancing the interests of the Chinese people abroad, beyond the realist, state-centered understanding of national interests, therefore, has been suboptimal and disastrous, very much the same as the overall China Suboptimality at home (as analyzed in the prequel to this book, *The China Record*). Both internally and externally, the hypocrisy of the CCP's ubiquitous slogan of "serving the people" in a supposedly "people's republic" is about the same.[154]

The CCP has a consistent track record of fully and often exclusively pursuing the Party's interest for power or its ideological mission (such as following Moscow's decrees to sacrifice China for world communist revolution). Only a few years after its formation and long before its rise to power in China, the CCP (and its armed rebellion of the "Chinese Soviet Republic") openly acted as Moscow's agent to defend and assist the Soviet Union over bona fide Chinese national interests during the Sino-Soviet War of 1929 in Manchuria. In 1950, just months after its creation, the PRC plunged into the Korean War, which resulted in China being "the only total loser" out of all the parties involved.[155] The CCP has always deeply loathed and opposed the United States, a nation that has massively benefited and critically assisted the Chinese nation since the late-19th century, and treated the Chinese people perhaps the least badly among all the nations since at least the 1940s, even actually assisting and financing the rise of PRC state power. At the same time, the CCP has repeatedly adulated and even worshipped the Soviet Union/Russia as its tutor, buddy, and "natural ally," "with no limits," although Moscow has snatched far more land and treasure from China than any other foreign power over the past two centuries, wreaked bloody havoc in China in the last century, and frequently disparaged and abused the Chinese people to this day.[156] Perhaps this is because, tellingly, in post-Stalin Moscow and post-Mao Beijing, the communist autocrats appear to think and act alike with their similarly organized Leninist political systems.[157] This deliberate misorientation of Chinese foreign policy shows a total divorce and often direct contradiction between the CCP and China/the Chinese people it governs. The state-society or ruler-people relationship in the PRC troublingly resembles the relationship between a clever and powerful kidnapper and the manipulated and brutalized hostages.

The PRC entered the United Nations in 1971, assuming the ROC's position as one of the victorious Big Five post–World War II powers. Five decades later, China remains divided, as the ROC continues to govern in Taiwan. China's international standing is still little more than one of the original G5. It is neither a member of the G7 (or G8), nor a member of the OECD (Organization for Economic Cooperation and Development), the club of developed countries, which includes three East Asian nations (Japan, Singapore, and South Korea). Massive trade and overseas spending plus busy and extravagant international summits and visits have yet to give China much global leadership, influence, or soft power outside its immediate neighborhood and some foreign interest groups, aside from self-aggrandizing propaganda bubbles.[158]

Some possible bias notwithstanding, an Anglo-American research team ranked the PRC in 2015 at the bottom of its list of 30 "global leaders in soft power," after Turkey and Mexico; by 2019, Beijing was ranked 27th out of the 30, behind Greece and Brazil and higher only than Hungary, Turkey, and Russia, while Germany and the US were ranked 3rd and 5th, respectively.[159] A comparative study finds that the Chinese language, despite having the largest number of native speakers in the world, ranks only 27th as a globally important language and 14th as a source of original works translated into other languages, behind many less-spoken languages like Japanese, Polish, Czech, and Norwegian. According to a PRC expert, of the 100 trillion-plus parameters or data used to train the phenomenal AI model ChatGPT, "less then 1% are in Chinese."[160]

Opinion surveys show that many if not most nations have developed ever more negative views about China; this was true even before the COVID-19 pandemic, which originated in China. In 2019, in 34 countries surveyed by the Pew Research Center, people who had unfavorable views of Beijing outnumbered those with favorable views, especially in Western Europe and East and Southeast Asia, where more than half of the population held negative views of China. In late 2020, countries like Australia (81%), Canada (73%), Italy (62%), Japan (86%), and South Korea (75%) all reported the highest rates of disliking China ever recorded. In the US, 73% of Americans held negative views of Beijing, by far the worst impression recorded since the 1970s, up from 55% five years ago. In 14 developed countries, an average of 73% of people held negative views of China. The highly unfavorable views of China continued to be "widespread worldwide" in late-2023 when this book went to print.[161] As a theatrical irony of history, the Maoist Philippine Communist Party, carrying out the longest communist rebellion in the world, reportedly ordered its guerrilla fighters in 2020 to target Chinese firms to defend Filipino national interests.[162] The TV viewership of the opening ceremony of the 2022 Beijing Winter Olympics was reported to be the smallest in history, 55% lower than the 2018 PyeongChang Games in South Korea, and 64% lower than the 2014 Sochi Games in Russia.[163]

After more than six decades of active and expensive diplomacy, out of its 20 neighboring countries, China still has the same two nominally

108 | The China Race

friendly neighbors it had in the 1950s: North Korea, its only treaty ally, and Pakistan, its so-called "all-weather friend." Both have cost Beijing enormously and also have caused various complex issues and problems; neither offers much in the way of perks to PRC citizens, such as visa-free entry. Pyongyang, in particular, reportedly views Beijing as its "biggest" external threat.[164] One senior PRC historian asserted that Beijing "has spent so much blood and all of the nation's resources for so long, yet still failed to even get a pro-China government" in Pyongyang, as the Kim Dynasty has only shrewdly taken advantage of Beijing's preposterous ambition to lead the world communist movement.[165] Still, the CCP seems to firmly view Pyongyang as a "strategic asset" in its "strategic rivalry with the United States."[166] For two decades, the PRC has been the only country in the world burdened with four nuclear powers directly on its border, negatively affecting its national security and freedom of action, not to mention the possible fallout from nuclear exchanges or accidents. Over the decades, the PRC has counted perhaps only one head of state as its lasting friend, King Norodom Sihanouk of Cambodia, who was more like Beijing's overindulged pet.[167] In China today, one sees countless replicas of foreign buildings and even entire towns, with "the White House copied the most often,"[168] but few if any foreign countries have built replicas of Chinese monuments (let alone PRC designs), beyond chinoiserie built over two centuries ago and a few Chinese elements in some amusement parks.

The failure of PRC foreign policy in serving and advancing the Chinese nation is amply demonstrated by the fact that the total territory of today's PRC, though much more tightly and thoroughly united and ruled, is in fact smaller than that of the ROC in 1945, even including Taiwan. Boasting that it valiantly guards "every inch of land left to us by our ancestors,"[169] Beijing has in fact given in to a series of territorial demands by neighbors, starting by reaffirming the ROC's reluctant acceptance of the independence of Outer Mongolia in a secret attachment to the PRC-USSR alliance treaty of 1950.[170] Chinese and foreign scholars concluded that, for the sake of its regime survival and security, the CCP-PRC state has been habitually willing to give away Chinese territory.[171] Territorial concessions made by the PRC, like those to Burma, all seem to serve the CCP's political interests.[172] After winning the border war with India in 1962, Beijing ordered Chinese troops to withdraw after "teaching the Indians a lesson," by returning the land in dispute to India to show some "heavenly goodwill," hoping to be paid back with more later—an idiotic show suitable only for the rule of an ancient Chinese world-empire. Even so, Beijing has maintained that the land in dispute is actually China's, thus protracting a problem over territory between the world's two most populous nations.[173] Always eying opportunities to influence and control South Asia, Mao later (in 1967) personally promised Indian communists all the disputed land in a bid to urge them to violently overthrow the government in New Delhi.[174] A PRC scholar of Cold War diplomacy found that the CCP's political and domestic needs, wrapped up in the language of world revolution, drove the PRC to make territorial concessions in exchange for political and policy support, "almost with no exception every time." The PRC ended up giving away thousands of square kilometers of land (up to 100 percent of the disputed territory in some cases) to nearly all its neighboring countries, including Afghanistan, Burma (Myanmar), Mongolia, Nepal, North Korea, Pakistan, the Soviet Union/Russia, and Vietnam. Yet, those sacrifices of Chinese land were all essentially "counterproductive," even as measured by the CCP's expedient objectives at the time.[175]

Within the Greater China region, Hong Kong and Macau have been critically important to the CCP-PRC in the years of isolation and thereafter, for Beijing's vital access to foreign technology, capital, markets, and luxuries. They were returned to the PRC through special decolonization deals with the United Kingdom and Portugal in 1997 and 1999, respectively. The two special administrative regions were to enjoy autonomy in internal affairs for 50 years. While Beijing has largely pacified and controlled the tiny casino town of Macau through amalgamation and infiltration, the Hong Kong people's resentment and resistance to Beijing's meddling grew significantly beginning almost immediately after the turnover. "The island and the mainland are drifting further apart," even violently.[176] Fewer than half of Hong Kong residents and "almost nobody in Hong Kong under 30 identifies as Chinese" in 2019, after 22 years under the PRC's supposedly special and lenient rule and considerable showering of financial favors.[177] A chain of events in the 2010s has driven the most developed Chinese city, the financial center of Greater China and beyond, to tumble downhill—from Beijing's secret kidnappings of book publishers and business tycoons, to stern repression of popular demonstrations and demands.[178] On July 1, 2020, the CCP, probably having had enough of the inconvenience and uncontrollability of Hong Kong, acted to break its legal treaty with the United Kingdom and trash the Basic Law of Hong Kong by imposing a National/State

110 | The China Race

Security Law on Hong Kong.[179] The CCP abruptly stepped in to rule Hong Kong in largely the same way it has ruled Mainland China for decades. Beijing thus effectively ended Hong Kong's special status and forced pivotal changes to the West's Hong Kong policy. This policy change had a profound impact.[180] The rough and sad ending of the Hong Kong deal, at less than halfway through its planned lifespan, demonstrated not only Beijing's unrestrained and impatient ambition and ultra-thin skin when facing the annoyance of Hong Kong's free press, but also a grand policy failure. This turn of events has resulted in a detrimental blow against Hong Kong, a foreclosure of Chinese sociopolitical diversity and dynamism, and a huge loss to China's national interests, especially its international credibility.[181]

The ROC in Taiwan, the losing party of the Chinese Civil War, has maintained its de facto independence while scoring much higher on political democracy, socioeconomic achievement, and international stature than the PRC. Mainly deterred by the US, Beijing suspended its military "liberation of Taiwan" in 1979, and has showered money and favors on Taiwan in an attempt to woo the Taiwanese into peaceful unification ever since, with the threat of military force always in the background. Deng's "One Country Two Systems" proposal for Taiwan, however, has produced few results, and the apparent breakdown of that design in Hong Kong lately has only doomed this cleverly expedient strategy for cross-strait relations. The pro-independence Democratic Progress Party leader Tsai Ing-wen, who has repeatedly refused the "one China" concept, won her presidential reelection in 2020 despite Beijing's strong opposition, high-pressure intimidation, and concerted sabotage.[182] For its own selfish political interests, the CCP refuses to accept Taiwan as another Chinese state or as a political peer in a possible Chinese federation/confederation, which might be optimal for the Chinese nation but would certainly undermine the party-state's Qin-Han political system. With the apparent and costly failure of its Taiwan policy, and unlikely "to swallow the bitter fruit" of seeing its political opposite and opponent alive and well, the CCP is ratcheting up its rhetoric and preparing for a military invasion, which implies grave and uncertain consequences for the Chinese nation.[183] The Taiwanese people, however, have clearly left Mainland China. From 1992 to 2015, Taiwanese people who identify themselves as "Chinese" basically vanished (from 25.5% to 2.4%, fewer than those who "don't know" who they are), while those who identify themselves as "Taiwanese only" shot up from 17.4% to 67%, or even as high as 83%.

PRC Foreign Policy | 111

This mindset has continued into the 2020s.[184] Insisting it has always been an independent nation since 1912, Taipei would undoubtedly declare its full legal separation from Mainland China the minute the PRC's lethal threat of force was lessened to an acceptable level.[185] In August 2022, to vent anger and save face after US House Speaker Nancy Pelosi visited Taiwan, ignoring its furious protests and intimidation, Beijing dashed to "decouple" China further from the world by firing ballistic missiles into international waters around Taiwan, dismissing the G7's call for calm as "a piece of wastepaper," and cancelling the few remaining collaborations and talks with the US on climate, theater military confidence, repatriation of illegal immigrants, and crime and narcotics control.[186] Months later, in April 2023, US House Speaker Kevin McCarthy met visiting Taiwanese president Tsai Ing-wen in California, ignoring again Beijing's angry protests and threats.[187] Dreading but unable to crush its political contrast, the CCP seems stuck being haunted by Taiwan, but it makes the Chinese nation pay the price for that, exceedingly and endlessly.

There is perhaps one exception to the generally derisory record of PRC foreign policy in terms of serving the Han-Chinese national interest. Since the early 1950s, the CCP has used force and trickery to conquer and colonize the vast, non-Han regions of the former Qing-ROC peripheral attachments: Xinjiang and especially Tibet and, to a lesser extent, the borderlands like Inner Mongolia and Yunnan. For that purpose, the CCP launched a war, or "one sided slaughter" and destruction, against the largely pacifist and basically unarmed Tibetans in 1958–59, followed by systematic repressions and purges over the decades against the Tibetans, Mongolians, and Muslim nationalities. Conditions have been especially dire for the Uyghurs, more than a million of whom have reportedly been detained in vast reeducation camps in Xinjiang since the 2010s.[188] The killings and imprisonment, forced exile and migration, destruction of antiquities, culture and the environment, and the brewing of lasting ethnic and cultural hatreds aside, the CCP did bring those sparsely populated but vast and resource-rich lands, nearly one-sixth to one-third of the total PRC territory, under the direct and centralized control of a Han government for the first time in history. Tremendous costs in blood, resources, and conscience notwithstanding, Han Chinese nationalists may well believe that the CCP-PRC state has expanded their "living space" and opportunities by occupying and controlling those lands.[189] Indeed, in addition to obtaining some key geostrategic positions in the Asian hinterland (particularly on the Tibetan Plateau), the PRC

112 | The China Race

has already extracted a significant amount of wealth from those regions, especially natural resources such as oil, gas, and minerals. Xinjiang, for example, has 41% of the coal, 22% of the oil, and 28% of the gas deposits in China.[190]

The real overall cost-effectiveness of the CCP's policy of conquest and control in those regions, even just financially in an era of a globalized market for raw materials, so far remains a highly guarded secret, but it is likely not good, given that Beijing has had to invest astronomical amounts to pacify the local peoples and buy off the local elites in order to build up and link the regions. For example, Beijing's per capita spending on "maintaining stability" or policing is four times and three times the national average in Tibet and Xinjiang, respectively.[191] Megaprojects with little if any financial returns include the world's highest-altitude railways to Lhasa, which cost $16 million per kilometer ($25.6 million per mile) to build and an undisclosed amount to maintain and operate, and the "world's first desert-encircling railway" in Xinjiang, which envelopes the Taklamakan, China's largest desert (and the world's second-largest mobile desert).[192]

Service and Disservice

In practice, PRC foreign policy exhibits the same distinctive features of hypocrisy, split personality, paranoia, and even schizophrenia that are readily seen in the CCP's domestic policies. Countless PRC ruling elites have either openly or secretively sent their families and their personal wealth to the West (the US in particular), the countries they always officially resent, abhor, smear, and undermine. Massive public funds in hard currency (almost all from the West), earned by the Chinese people through their hard work, are spent opaquely cultivating the officially extolled and even enshrined "friendships" with the likes of Ethiopia, Iran, North Korea, Pakistan, Russia, Venezuela, and Zimbabwe, of which even the occasional online expressions of disapproval are often strictly prohibited. Yet, tellingly, few if any PRC elites have ever emigrated to these places. It seems that the rulers of those "friends of China" are fully aware of the CCP's hypocrisy and have acted similarly. Beyond the rhetorical payback of praising the CCP rulers and some symbolic gestures of support for the beleaguered Beijing in places like the UN Human Rights Commission, the PRC and its citizens do not really enjoy perks or respect in those countries. For instance, Beijing reportedly spent hundreds of billions of dollars in sketchy oil and gas deals to subsidize the financially struggling Kremlin, and constantly sacrificed the rights and interests of PRC citizens in Russia so as to avoid offending the anti-Chinese, xenophobic Russian leaders, all for the sake of the appearance of comradeship with Putin and some Russian military technology. Yet, in an actual test of that "natural and limitless" alliance in practice, Russia has always sold New Delhi military technology more sophisticated than what it sells to Beijing. Immediately after the Sino-Indian boarder clash in June 2020, Russia quickly supported India with more weapon transfers.[193]

Related to the rather effective service to the Party that Chinese foreign policy has provided, PRC ruling elites and their families and cronies have now obtained the considerable reverence, mobility, and worldwide access that the rich and powerful of any country commonly get. To escape the drawbacks of the unpopular and even dreaded PRC citizenship, however, seems key to the new and better life of the PRC elites, as many of them have directly emigrated and hold foreign (overwhelmingly Western) citizenship or residency. As reported in *The China Record*, China's rich and famous are disproportionately running away. "The richer, the more inclined to emigrate," declared a Beijing newspaper in 2014, due to the "deep sense of insecurity" caused by CCP policies at home.[194] Some have chosen an easier way, purchasing inexpensive passports of countries like Dominica, Grenada, St. Kitts and Nevis, and Gambia, for simple or even visa-free travel to the West or a chance at the US green card lottery. Others have obtained their "global citizen" rights and benefits through the backdoor of obtaining the travel papers of Hong Kong and Macau, as the West has made an exception to accept citizens of those locales as peers. While numbering in the millions, PRC elites with elevated stature abroad represent a very tiny minority of the Chinese people. Their new identity and place in the world, however, are often affected by changes in immigration schemes in the West. Many PRC citizens with Hong Kong residency, for example, may have to search for other escape routes again in the 2020s should the West fully end the exceptional treatment extended to the former British colony.[195]

For the ordinary Chinese who cannot get rid of their PRC citizenship, Beijing's foreign policy has largely delivered them poor service or outright disservice abroad. The CCP has managed to create and sustain mistrust, hostility, and even hatred in the world for the Chinese people over the decades. The unscrupulous and devious Party-first and Party-only

114 | The China Race

diplomacy described earlier has cost the Chinese people an immeasurable amount of credibility and goodwill. Beijing's export of its half-baked communist revolution and violence has given the PRC a reputation as an unrepentant international outlaw and subversive element. The CCP's reliance on the use of force-induced fear and conspiracy, bribery, censorship, and propaganda to govern is repulsive to many if not the majority of the elites in other countries, particularly in the West. The chronic lack of the freedoms of speech, press, assembly, and internal migration in the context of the lack of rule of law and rampant corruption, the stubbornly low living standard, and the heavily polluted environment have all made the PRC greatly undesirable and the Chinese people hardly enviable to common people around the world—as has been amply illustrated by the coinciding massive emigration from and the tiny, almost nonexistent immigration to the PRC.[196] Few, if any, non-PRC elites are fond of being subjects of the CCP-PRC state, as easily seen in the countless interviews and observations I have made in more than three dozen countries from the 1990s to the 2020s. To be sure, Beijing still has plenty of fans abroad. Acting as a pampered, cajoled, and usually well-compensated agent or abettor of the CCP regime, while enjoying the protection of the rights and freedoms that a non-PRC citizenship affords, can be addictively tempting, rational, and rewarding to many, even including some humanistic, compassionate, and idealistic foreigners with a distaste for dictators. There is also the real and deep attraction of a rich mega-autocracy to the egoistic, the venturesome, the power- and wealth-hungry, and the aspirant everywhere.

Despite the heavily propagated image of an idealized life in the superior fantasyland of the Centralia, the Chinese nation and the Chinese people today are still commonly treated by peers as a second-class society and "second-class foreigners," especially by the so-called "friends of China" heavily subsidized by the CCP.[197] China's national standing in the world declined dramatically during the first three decades under the CCP-PRC; it rose during the past four decades, but to barely above the standing previously achieved under the KMT-ROC. In 2015 and 2019, Beijing held two "perfect" military parades, to celebrate the 70th anniversaries of the end of World War II and the founding of the PRC, respectively. Other than a swapping of South and North Koreas, the nations represented by the leaders and the VIPs attending the pageantry to watch the goose-stepping marchers with Xi Jinping were almost identical to the precious few international guests of Mao Zedong 60 years ago. No other leaders of Western or major developing countries were present at Tiananmen. In July 2020, when imposing a national/state security law on Hong Kong to effectively end its treaty obligation to the city's autonomy, Beijing mobilized 52 countries to voice support in the UN. They are the same developing or "not-free" countries that have symbolically sided with the PRC over the years due to ideological similarities or financial benefits.[198] One analyst concluded in 2020 that "the ledger is brutally clear. Xi Jinping's regime has no allies of global economic weight or credibility."[199] In 2008, over 70 heads of state or government, including the US president, attended the opening of the Olympic Games in Beijing; in 2022, that list was down to 20, as almost all Western countries announced a diplomatic boycott.[200] So much for the rise of Chinese soft power.

An indubitably revealing fact about the grand failure of Chinese foreign policy in serving its people abroad is simply how unwelcome the PRC passport is around the world. The PRC passport has stubbornly been among the least welcomed passports in the world since 1949. In 2014, PRC citizens had visa-free entry privileges for short-term visits to a paltry nine countries as part of approved tourist groups, and to only three tiny countries (Mauritius, Seychelles, and San Marino, which has no entry port) plus Jeju Island of Korea as individuals.[201] In 2020–21, the ordinary PRC passport had visa-free or visa-on-arrival privileges in 23 countries (including tourist islands like Jeju, Saipan, and Turks and Caicos), and in a total of 49 countries with restrictive requirements. Including the visa privileges granted to government (for official use) and diplomatic passports, the PRC ranked 70th out of 109 (or 143rd out of 200) countries, with 74 countries granting it some visa privileges—behind Taiwan (146), and similar to Lesotho (75) and Malawi (73) in the world popularity contest of passports. In 2023, according to the PRC Foreign Ministry, countries affording visa-free or visa-on-arrival privileges to the ordinary PRC passport actually decreased to only thirteen (see table 2.1).[202]

The welcome afforded to PRC citizens, shockingly and strangely, is far out of balance with China's stature as one of the Big Five permanent members of the UN Security Council, one of the handful of "legit" nuclear powers and active space explorers, the world's largest exporter, the second-largest economy, with the world's largest military (in size, and the second-largest in budget), a great natural endowment, a large and industrious population, and a cultural heritage that is long, rich, and colorful. It is especially embarrassing when compared to Taiwan,

Table 2.1. Visa-Free Privileges (Selected Countries, 2020–24)

Ranking	Country	Visa-Free Countries
1	Japan	191
2	Singapore	190
3	Germany	189
	South Korea	189
6	France	186
7	UK	187
	USA	187
9	Canada	193
11	Poland	181
16	Chile	174
19	Brazil	170
	Hong Kong	170
24	Israel	160
33	Taiwan	146
34	Macao	144
51	Russia	118
56	South Africa	101
69	Lesotho	75
70	**China (PRC)**	**74**
71	Malawi	73
76	Philippines	67
79	Cuba	64
83	Rwanda	60
85	India	58
89	Vietnam	54
93	Laos	50
94	Haiti	49
96	Myanmar	47
103	North Korea	39
108	Iraq	28
109	Afghanistan	26

Source: The Henley Passport Index 2020-Q2 (henleyglobal.com; posted June 4, 2021). By 2024, this ranking remained stable.

which had only 14 countries formally recognizing it diplomatically in 2021 but a passport twice as popular as the PRC's. The causes of the sad global reception of PRC citizens (other than the few rich and powerful elites) are probably multiple but not incomprehensible. The CCP's official line, other than covering up this incongruity, always involves blaming the ever-changing "external forces that want to annihilate us." The misdirected, mismanaged, and often counterproductive use of the PRC's diplomatic resources appears to be a key reason. The overall China Suboptimality of the CCP-PRC polity is the root of the problem. The sociopolitical and psychosomatic impact of CCP governance on the Chinese people's behavior, as evidenced by rampant corruption, the lack of moral compass and honesty, and massive fraudulent activities and fake products, as reported in *The China Record*, also seems to be a direct cause. The verdict by the nations against the PRC's governance and its foreign policy, therefore, seems loud and clear.

The CCP has a long tradition of tight and meticulous message- and image-control based on the "principle of distinguishing between the internal and the external" (*neiwai youbie*)—speaking and acting very differently inside the party-state and inside the PRC than in public and abroad.[203] This prized ploy of "just for domestic consumption" versus "foreigners only" reflects the duality and duplicity of the Confucian-Legalist imperial rulers under the China Order in the past.[204] Within just weeks in 2019–20, for example, a PRC scholar published an article in English in a major US journal asserting that, with a bit more friendliness and rewards, the US could completely lead China to democracy and liberalization. The scholar then turned around and wrote in Chinese on PRC social media laughing at democracy-dreaming "American liberal idiots" and suggested taking full advantage of them to safeguard the party-state.[205] Ruses like this may have hitherto served the party-state well in brainwashing and controlling the Chinese people and placating and recruiting the impactful but often condescending or naive foreigners. In the era of the Internet and massive international travel, however, the ever more numerous discrepancies and contradictions between Beijing's internal and external words and deeds are easily detectable, costing the Chinese people dearly in trust and credibility at home and abroad.

Anecdotally, the ineffectiveness and failure of the CCP-PRC state in serving its citizens abroad is in plain view. Other than one tourist destination (Jeju Island of South Korea), almost none of the PRC's neighbors (not even Hong Kong and Macau, which were "returned" to the PRC over two decades ago) allow PRC citizens to visit visa-free. In

118 | The China Race

Asia, fewer than 10 countries give PRC citizens the convenience of a tourist visa on arrival. In Europe, only five Eastern European countries allow PRC tourists to visit visa-free. In Latin America, even Cuba and Venezuela, Beijing's anti-American friends, refuse to grant Chinese visa-free privileges. In Africa, despite the explosive growth of the Chinese presence there (the PRC is now Africa's largest trade partner and second-largest investor), and with massive and often "no strings attached" aid and undisclosed cash payments, PRC citizens are clearly and routinely treated much worse than most other nationalities. Zimbabwe, for example, has been a major recipient of aid from the PRC since the 1980s—at times up to about one-quarter of Harare's operational budget. Allegedly, Beijing pays under-the-table allowances to many, if not most, senior officials and officers of that country as well. Despite signs and gestures of friendship toward Beijing, including the enthusiastic chanting of "Xi, my brother, friend of Africa" by then-dictator Robert Mugabe in Africa and Beijing,[206] PRC citizens living in Zimbabwe complained bitterly to this author in interviews about abuse and mistreatment by the Zimbabwean government and how PRC diplomats "are not helping us at all" (see table 2.2).[207]

In another of Beijing's friends in Africa, Angola, which does not grant visa-free access to holders of PRC passports, a Chinese national is reported abducted "every two days" in the capital, Luanda, according to the head of PRC consular service there, who readily admitted that

Table 2.2. Visa Fees in Zimbabwe (2010s)

Landing Visa	
US citizen	$30
Russian citizen	$30
Japanese citizen	$30
UK citizen	$55*
EU citizen	$30
Canadian citizen	$75*
Advance Visa (14 days before arrival)**	
PRC citizen	$65–161

* British are treated less favorably, for obvious reasons. Harare dislikes Canadians, because Ottawa froze Robert Mugabe's assets and banned arms transfers to Zimbabwe.
** Zimbabwe finally started to grant PRC citizens landing visas for tourism in fall 2019.
Source: Wang and Elliot (2014, 1023); evisa.gov.zw/regime (posted on June 30, 2021).

he could not do much to help.[208] One influential PRC website polled its readers in 2016–18 regarding the PRC consular services provided to nonofficial Chinese overseas. The long list of answers was littered with complaints about the terrible attitude, utter carelessness, and thorough incompetence of the PRC diplomats serving Chinese citizens. The most-liked answers were: "I have never heard from any [Chinese], not even one, who has ever said anything nice about the [PRC] diplomatic services overseas"; "Never ask for any help from them for anything, because they cannot solve any problem for you, big or small, and you have to endure the terribly bad temper of the jacks-in-office"; "For seasoned Chinese merchants overseas, it is only the last resort to try your luck at the [PRC] embassy and consulate when you are helplessly facing certain death."[209]

Indeed, even when overseas PRC citizens and ethnic Chinese are facing death, the People's Republic has typically been unhelpful and sometimes partially or even directly responsible for the killing, as in the massacres against overseas Chinese in Indonesia in 1965–66 and 1998.[210] Large-scale government actions, including systematic confiscation, massive expulsion, and other abuses against overseas Chinese, including PRC citizens, have occurred in some of Beijing's allies and friends, such as North Korea, Russia, and Vietnam. But the CCP has generally always kept its silence, with perhaps the rare exception of criticizing Hanoi for its massive expulsion of the "boat people" in the late 1970s, due to Beijing's specific geopolitical anti-Soviet Union calculations at the time.[211] The Chinese diaspora is faced with "the ambiguities of ethnicity and diasporic consciousness, and the tension between maintaining one's culture and assimilation."[212] They have traditionally been used extensively by the ROC and now the PRC for the regime's policy purposes in the name of patriotism for the "motherland," especially in Southeast Asia. Yet when those overseas Chinese have been in dire need, Beijing's protection has been painfully inadequate or nonexistent. Unsurprisingly, despite the heavy PRC investment in overseas propaganda and United Front that have led to the conspicuous show of loyalty by a few, only 41% of Chinese-Americans, for example, actually have favorable views of China, while 59%–95% of all other Asian-Americans view their ancestral homelands favorably.[213]

Moreover, while providing substandard service and often outright disservice to PRC citizens abroad, the CCP-PRC state appears to have employed its considerable network, the "united front" of agents, informants, and sympathizers, to monitor, influence, and control Chinese abroad.[214] There is reportedly "increasing cooperation between the Chinese Government, the Chinese Communist Party ('CCP'), the Peoples Liberation Army ('PLA') and the [Chinese] Triads in expanding the criminal activities of organised crime across the world and especially in promoting and expanding Chinese political policies toward Hong Kong, Macau and Taiwan. In many areas, the Triads have played a major role in Chinese economic and political interactions with its neighbours and trading partners, especially in the international trade in dugs [sic], chemical substances and people smuggling."[215] Overseas Chinese have been subject to the carefully calibrated and well-financed propaganda of the CCP, which has dominated Chinese language media and social media platforms abroad.[216] They are routinely "told to serve the motherland," often at the expense of their new homeland, or else labeled and mistreated as "traitors."[217] One report in 2020 listed "600 U.S. Groups linked to Chinese Communist Party influence effort" through the CCP's United Front work: "at least 83 Chinese hometown associations [. . .]; 10 'Chinese Aid Centers' [sic]; 32 [Chinese] Chambers of Commerce; 13 Chinese-language media brands; about half of the 70 associations for Chinese professionals in the US; 38 organizations promoting the 'peaceful reunification' of China and Taiwan; five 'friendship organizations' and 129 other groups [. . . and] 265 Chinese Student and Scholar Associations," including the 30-year-old "Committee of 100," whose membership includes some of the most accomplished Chinese-Americans. Similar "United Front groups" in the UK were estimated in 2023 to be "nearly 400."[218] In 2022, even a Chinese visiting scholar reputed to be a political dissident was indicted for working for the PRC Ministry of State Security to silence critics in the US.[219]

Beyond the US, the CCP is seen by French analysts as engaging in worldwide "influence operations" that include "public opinion, psychological, and legal warfare" and united front ploys to "seduce, subjugate, infiltrate, and coerce" in order to holistically achieve a "Machiavellian moment" of intimidating the world into submission.[220] CCP agents are reported to have secretively abducted wanted dissidents overseas in Australia, Canada, Hong Kong, Macau, Southeast Asia, and New Zealand.[221] There are also cases of PRC citizens punished for criticisms or artistic satires they voiced or posted when abroad.[222] Beijing's effort to rather directly control and influence (and also recruit and intimidate) PRC citizens abroad appears to be extensive and active in the West, very noticeably on college campuses where large numbers of young Chinese from the PRC reside.[223] Demonstrating its power overseas, the CCP announced in 2021 that it had directly developed "all kinds of relations and partnerships" with over 600 political parties in 160 countries "to work together for the construction of the community of common human destiny." In July 2021, over 500 of these political groups took part in an "unprecedented" online summit organized by the CCP to continue the grand mission of constructing that community "for a better world," with the new, more infinite, objective of "taking up the responsibility for people's happiness and humanity's progress."[224]

The Effects of Beijing's Ventures Abroad

Despite all of its failures and blunders at home and abroad, the CCP-PRC state has constantly tried to convince the Chinese people inside and outside the PRC that the bitterness, hardship, and sacrifice they have endured are worthwhile, noble, and necessary for the greater good of themselves and humanity. As the then CCP foreign policy czar Zhou Enlai summarized in 1971, "the Chinese people do not hesitate to bear the greatest national sacrifice"—in that case, to support Hanoi in the Vietnamese War.[225] For the CCP, of course, the endless national sacrifice is always fully justified by its desire to stay in power forever (in order to serve the people, as it claims) and, by extension, its grand endeavor to influence and reorder the world. From Mao to Xi, this consistent PRC foreign policy goal has been dressed up in various ways, sometimes almost totally naked, while at other times adorned agreeably or even fashionably to fit the reigning norms and ideals of the world. In serving the needs and wishes of the CCP ruling elites, the interests of China as a nation and of the Chinese people are fully negotiable and dispensable, and often sacrificed in the name of grand and noble but empty causes. In Beijing, "domestic political process and culture greatly influence the style and formulation of foreign policy" especially when diplomacy remains secretive and monopolized by the ruler.[226]

The highly centralized and secretive nature of its foreign policy, in the overall context of endless indoctrination with CCP narratives of history and the tight control of information,[227] has allowed Beijing to successfully sell its foreign policy to the Chinese people, or so it seems. Within the PRC, Mao and the CCP are commonly considered patriots and humanists who saved, protected, and benefited the Chinese nation.

122 | The China Race

After recording that Mao's true objective for the brutal Great Leap Forward was a "worldwide influence larger than the one satellite [Sputnik] launched by the Soviet Union," even Li Rui, a close but later-purged assistant and a leading critic of Mao, still made great efforts to portray Mao as a leader who was seeking equality and a better life for the Chinese nation and humanity, though in a delusional and wrong way.[228] The CCP's claims of nationalism or patriotism are often packaged together with its official facades of humanitarian egalitarianism, rebellious populism, utopian communism, and revolutionary romanticism to give the rising PRC power the benefit of the doubt as a progressive force in the world. Beijing's intention abroad is evidently for domination and reorganization of the world for the benefit of the regime, something undesirable and disastrous and thus requiring counteraction and containment, as I have attempted to demonstrate. Still, some may reasonably contend that the CCP-PRC state, if constrained from systemically transforming the world (a big if indeed), could be positive or even beneficial to the world through its active foreign ventures, regardless of its motivations, as a manifestation of a key structural virtue of the Westphalian system—to facilitate competition and trial-and-error among the nations. Perhaps the China Tragedy and China Suboptimality, which have characterized the record of governance of the CCP-PRC state at home, could somehow be avoided or diluted in Chinese foreign policy.

To further the examination of the CCP's foreign conduct so as to crystalize the reasons and means for managing the China Race, through a comprehensive strategy of containment and engagement for transformation and incorporation, I continue with an assessment of the international impact of Beijing's foreign policy, along with a discussion of the nature of that policy and its consequences for the Chinese nation and the Chinese people. It is suggested that the PRC's foreign policy, aside from serving the regime's interests of survival and security abroad with chronic disservice for the Chinese people, has been mostly a negative, suboptimal, and even disastrous force internationally since its birth. Just as the Chinese people are greatly wronged while a tiny ruling group has enormously benefited, Beijing's foreign policy has disserved and impaired the people of the nations it has touched, enriching a tiny group of foreigners, mostly "friends of China." Moreover, the PRC has also affected many institutions and norms of the international community in many ways, mostly harmful rather than innocuous. Concerning business activities, political governance, legal matters, human rights, and ethics, the CCP has made a concerted and effective effort to export its values, norms, and conduct.[229] In short, Beijing has brought certain benefits and competition to the world, but also a disproportionately larger amount of trouble and harm.

The major focus of PRC foreign policy since 1949, as reported in this book and its prequels, has been to challenge the West/US-led world order and, for a while, to challenge the Soviet Union for the leadership of the world communist movement. That omnidirectional mission, however, has been carried out opportunistically whenever and wherever it seems possible. Perhaps having learned a lesson from the Korean War, which ended with the PRC as "the only total loser," the CCP, to this day, has been notably cautious about engaging in a direct, kinetic war with either the United States or any other major power. The most impactful action of the PRC's foreign policy, therefore, has been its monetary and material sponsorship and support (sometimes directly with personnel) of nearly any government, group, or individual that is at odds with or claiming to oppose the West, the US, or, at one time, the Soviet Union. The banner for such actions has evolved from anti-colonialism, anti-capitalism, and anti-imperialism to anti-hegemonism and anti-unilateralism. In recent years, massive Chinese funding has also flowed out of the PRC for the specific purpose of grabbing power and leadership in the international financial system and internationalizing the RMB in order to make the People's Money a hard currency.[230]

While Beijing's expensive export of its brand of armed revolution failed miserably, its equally expensive support of various decolonialization and anti-West struggles has fared better. In places like Algeria, Angola, Ghana, Libya, Mozambique, Namibia, Serbia, Sudan, and Zimbabwe, Beijing often enjoys considerable goodwill, personal connections, and influence among the local rulers and elites as a result of its past and ongoing assistance. However, this assistance could hardly be considered cost-effective: those countries have frequently supported Beijing politically on the international stage, but often just symbolically or even erratically. Similarly, the PRC has poured great amounts of resources into the countries that Beijing deems friendly, useful, or simply approachable. At an opaque but likely exorbitant cost, Beijing has given countries like Albania, Cambodia, Ethiopia, Ecuador, Fiji, Kenya, Myanmar, Pakistan, Sri Lanka, and Tanzania considerable infrastructure and significant money. It remains questionable, to be sure, whether the massive funding from Beijing has really helped local socioeconomic and political development,

124 | The China Race

or has actually retarded its natural course. This is especially the case where the supposedly "string-free" PRC aid appears to act as the bad coins that drive the good coins away, stunting or even reversing much-needed sociopolitical and educational progress in the recipient societies. Nevertheless, at least materially, there are obvious signs suggesting that China's national sacrifice, the unmonitored flow of the Chinese people's money to serve the CCP regime, has had various tangible, positive, and beneficial impacts abroad in some countries, especially in terms of infrastructure development, charity donations, and trade.[231]

The picture becomes more complex when more closely analyzed. In many places, such as Albania, Cambodia, Central Africa, DR Congo, Ethiopia, Iran, Iraq, Libya, Serbia, Sudan, Syria, Tanzania, and Zimbabwe, Beijing has been extensively and openly supporting and subsidizing authoritarian regimes or even despotic dictators that are brutal to their own people, sometimes until the very end. One of the most horrific cases was the killing fields in Cambodia under the Beijing-funded and tutored mini-CCP of Pol Pot's Khmer Rouge in the 1970s, which was responsible for what was perhaps the most atrocious massacre in human history proportionate to population size.[232] Even the relatively mild authoritarianism that promoted a modified Maoist socialism in Tanzania, nicknamed the "Little PRC," has evidently failed the people there socioeconomically.[233] Clearly, more detailed studies of the individual countries are needed to assess the full effects of the PRC in each case. The existing literature already suggests a mixed if not a totally negative assessment. A key question to ponder seems to be a counterfactual one: If these regimes did not receive such "stringless" aid and support from Beijing for whatever purposes, might the poor governance, bad policies, and brutal tyrannies end sooner, with less death and destruction?

With significant transfer of wealth and diplomatic support to many countries in the Muslim world, most of which enjoy a higher per capita GDP than the PRC, Beijing has secured a cordial, if not always stable, relationship with the rulers of Central Asian countries, Egypt, Indonesia, Iran, Jordan, Pakistan, Syria, Saudi Arabia, and Turkey. A leading reward for Beijing appears to be these states' deafening silence on the CCP's mistreatment of its Muslim minorities in places like Xinjiang.[234] At this stage, one can only speculate what kind of long-term impact this Beijing-induced and purchased CCP-style moral ambiguity and duplicity may have on the local culture, society, and politics in those countries.

Torrents of Bad Coins

More systematically, a gush of "People's Money" from the PRC in the 21st century, with little to no consent or oversight from the hard-working and bitterness-eating but voiceless Chinese people, has increasingly affected the world economy in general, and the existing international financial system in particular.[235] As I have attempted to report in *The China Record*, Beijing has maintained an extraordinarily high rate of extraction from the Chinese economy to grow its revenue two to four times faster than the growth in China's GDP for the past quarter-century, something a senior PRC official admits to be "unprecedented in history and unparalleled in the world."[236] The PRC state's central control of Chinese GDP is estimated to be as high as 38%, possibly even 47%—far higher than, for example, US federal control of American GDP, which is currently around 10% and has never been above 20%.[237] Beijing also controls the world's largest foreign currency reserve, which itself is about the same as the total US federal spending or four times more than the US defense budget. This huge pile of "real money" gives the CCP a great source of financial power internationally. The wild spending of PRC money overseas has unsurprisingly bought considerable influence for the CCP's rulers abroad while delivering mixed benefits to local populations and an overall disservice to the Chinese economy and the world economy. The full impact of the torrents of RMB, the People's Money, on the institutions and norms of the international community and world financial order seems to have been profound and mostly disagreeable, even downright harmful. As Gresham's Law in economics would predict, the circulation of bad coins tends to drive away good coins to the detriment of the whole market.[238] This seems literally and figuratively the case with regard to the role of the PRC in the world economy.

First, there is the deep problem of structural imbalance in international trade and finance related to the hoarding of foreign (hard) currencies by the PRC state through its excessive pursuit of trade surpluses and its tight control of the domestic capital market. The world-record pile of foreign currency in the hands of the CCP, mostly earned through US trade deficits, hovers around $3 trillion as of 2020, comprising about 26% of the world's total foreign currency reserves.[239] This vast hoard indicates great inefficiency and dislocation in the Chinese economy caused by the CCP's political needs. It is viewed as a major culprit in massive distortions

126 | The China Race

of world trade and liquidity circulation, which have been responsible for global inefficiency and repeated financial crises.[240] PRC trade partners, especially the US and the West in general, do get substantial value in the quick profits from their export of capital and technology, and through the massive import of cheap goods made in China that are deliberately subsidized by the PRC state and help to control inflation. But this has had a serious impact on local job markets in the West, with profound fiscal and sociopolitical consequences.[241] Over time, this politically and unilaterally twisted economic exchange greatly distorts the world market and especially the more open national economies.[242]

The developed countries have consequently experienced massive job losses, especially affecting low- or unskilled workers, who are internationally immobile and often inaccurately see themselves as facing competition from new immigrants and refugees. This has amply manifested in the ground-shifting rise of nativism, populism, and socialism in the West, symbolized by the historic Brexit, the increased American anti-immigration sentiment, and the rise of radicals of both the left and right in the West. At the same time, a small minority of capitalists and technology owners in the West, who are internationally highly mobile, together with the CCP's ruling elites and some Chinese capitalists, have accumulated astronomical wealth very rapidly and disproportionately. This is a classic case, with interesting twists, of the so-called unholy triangle or "triple alliance" described by dependency scholars in places like Latin America.[243] Stark and stubborn socioeconomic inequalities and sociopolitical polarization have ensued around the world, significantly plaguing Western Europe and North America in particular. This is reflected in a surge of enthusiasm in Western academia for criticism of the ills of capital in the 21st century.[244] Upward socioeconomic mobility, class flexibility, and sociopolitical tranquility are all challenged and undermined in the West. Government expenditures increase ceaselessly, while revenue growth stalls, due to the combination of joblessness at home and the legal and illicit mobility of capital abroad. The fiscal problems have ignited and magnified all sorts of sociopolitical, racial, ethnic, communal, and other divides and problems. It may be simplistic and over-deterministic to claim that the CCP-PRC has ruined the Western welfare states, but Beijing has evidently driven its partners, particularly the West, to go low, if not yet racing to the bottom. National political tranquility everywhere and international peace have all been affected.[245]

Second, since 2009 at the latest, in sync with the overall PRC-USA rivalry, Beijing has been forcefully pushing for an internationalization of its currency, the RMB or People's Money. As I have reported in *The China Record*, the PRC state has highly irrational and irresponsible fiscal and monetary policies, though, again, they may still be perfectly rational and even optimal for the CCP rulers.[246] Those policies have created world-record pressures of hyperinflation and gigantic asset bubbles. The circulation of RMB (M2, cash and convertible deposits) in 2021 totaled an astronomical ¥225.6 trillion ($33.76 trillion), more than twice the size of the Chinese GDP and nearly twice as large as the worldwide total US dollar M2 stock. In 2022, the supply of RMB further increased 9.8% and the circulation of M0 (cash) exploded 18.5%, growing two to four times faster than the Chinese GDP.[247] For Beijing, a simple and ideal way to possibly get out of this terrible predicament would quite reasonably be an internationalization of the RMB—namely, to flood the world trade and financial system with the bad coins of the massively overprinted People's Money. If the RMB could have a worldwide circulation like a hard or convertible currency, such as the US dollar, the euro, the Japanese yen, or the pound sterling, then the CCP might defuse the inflation time bomb at home and obtain "game changing" influence over world affairs.[248] A dual goal much advocated in the PRC is to obtain the position of "rule-maker" and grab the international seigniorage that has been enjoyed by the US since at least 1971, when President Richard Nixon ended the fixed peg of the US dollar to gold.[249] According to PRC analysts, turning the RMB into an internationalized "currency of great power" is critical to China's rise, as it would serve "to deeply tie-up the Chinese economy and monetary policy with the world economy" and allow the PRC to seize the leadership of the world financial system from the US and "to harvest the hegemony of the USD," even with the tradeoffs of lower trade surplus, reduced foreign currency reserve, RMB depreciation and fluctuation, and opening the PRC capital market. "Making RMB an international currency has become the necessary condition for world peace," declared a senior PRC official-scholar in 2023.[250]

In pursuit of that holy grail, Beijing has explored all means, including cryptocurrency and block-chain technology, with "Chinese characteristics," to internationalize the RMB digitally. That, however, is likely counterproductive in practice.[251] Block-chain technology decentralizes the money supply, and thus a *real* cryptocurrency based on block-chain would

128 | The China Race

be poised to undermine an autocracy and offer limited, if any, help in internationalizing a national currency. The CCP finally understood that in 2021 and soon started to forcefully "stamp out" all cryptocurrencies, such as Bitcoin.[252] Beijing's much-hyped "Digital RMB" or DECP (digital currency electronic payment) seems to turn the concept of cryptocurrency on its head by using a centralized ledger for the CCP to further its control of the Chinese economy and the Chinese people for more and easier extraction and more nuanced tracking of people's daily lives, probably with little effect on RMB internationalization.[253]

Given the size of the Chinese economy, particularly foreign trade, an internationalization of its currency is perhaps a natural and welcome development. It would be especially beneficial to the Chinese economy and the world economy if the RMB were internationalized through a liberalization of the PRC economy that would end the state monopoly of the banking system and capital market, letting the market determine foreign exchange rates, and abating the excessive pursuit of trade surplus and uneconomical hoarding of foreign currencies.[254] Indeed, many observers both inside and outside the PRC deem this to be the natural and positive next step in reforming the PRC's political economy, one that may also help to right the unbalanced international financial market.[255] However, Beijing's vision of the internationalization of the RMB remains problematic and worrisome.[256] There is little if any genuine liberalization of the Chinese economy accompanying it. Some of the chief economists in the PRC have proposed numerous measures to "accelerate" RMB internationalization, but nothing to touch the core issues.[257] In fact, a strong countertrend over the past decade has pushed to consolidate and expand the state monopoly of the Chinese capital market with more irrational monetary policies. The very brief relaxation of capital market and foreign exchange controls in 2015—mostly intended to persuade the West to include the RMB in the IMF's SDR (special drawing rights), for example, mortified the control freaks in Beijing when the PRC foreign currency reserve shrunk by more than a quarter in less than a year due to the massive outflow of capital, and the Chinese stock market took a nosedive. Extensive and draconian administrative controls (including jailing "the disobedient brokers") quickly resumed and have continued since the IMF granted that inclusion.[258]

In a move nicknamed "turning left with the right-turn signal on," the CCP seems determined to guard its monopoly of the Chinese financial system at all costs and play the same tricks of gaming the international financial system as it has done quite successfully with the WTO and its major trading partners for more than two decades. Beijing only internationalizes the RMB to gain more, not less, political power, in the form of expedient relief rather than systemic reform, and for the main purpose of capturing and overhauling the international financial order "built and dominated by the West."[259] A China-controlled *Tianxia* Currency" of the co-called "World Renmin Yuan" has already been "scientifically designed" by some PRC economists as their fanciful replacement of the USD for "a brighter future of economic globalization."[260] Successful or not, the mighty efforts by the CCP along this line, such as the digital RMB payment system, could still mean serious challenges to the current international financial order led by the US, American foreign policy, and the overall well-being of the US-led West.[261] Foreign observers have even started to sound the alarm that "China is killing the dollar."[262] Indeed, some PRC bloggers have openly cheered for the fantasized "hunt and kill of the USD" in the 2020s so as to "exterminate the United States."[263]

Perhaps as part of the West's wishful thinking and rather generous accommodation of China, Beijing has made headway, most notably through the IMF's inclusion of the RMB in the basket of five currencies for SDR in 2015. As the only nonconvertible (or soft) currency out of the five, the RMB weights an impressive 10.92% in the basket—higher than the yen (8.33%) and pound (8.09%), and behind the dollar (41.73%) and euro (30.93%).[264] That major step by the IMF was "with the understanding that Beijing would continue to make progress" to marketize its monetary policy. However, within less than a year a massive outflow of capital from the PRC had produced a near-panic political reaction by the CCP, which effectively stopped and reversed the reforms required for further internationalization of the RMB.[265] The PRC has significantly lowered its ambition for RMB internationalization, from "to accelerate to accomplish it" in 2014, and "to steadily accomplish it" in 2015, to finally "to cautiously promote it" in 2020 when the 14th Five-Year Plan (2021–25) was made.[266] In the real world of international financial markets and away from the politics and maneuvering in the hallways of international organizations, the RMB still remains an insignificant player, and this will continue as long as Beijing refuses the necessary reforms and liberalization at home. The RMB had a consistently small share of the world's total foreign currency reserves in the 2010s and 2020s (1.8%–2.8%), far behind the USD (59%), euro (21%), yen (5.6%), and pound (4.8%), and just slightly higher than the Canadian and Australian dollars (2.4% and 1.8%, respectively) in 2022.[267] As a "global payment" currency, the RMB's share was only 2.15% by 2023 (declined from 2.7% a year ago), behind the USD (41.89%), euro (36.34%), pound (6.08%), and yen (2.88%).[268] As a PRC analyst observed, the CCP kept inflicting "self-injuries," chiefly the politically driven controls of the PRC capital market and foreign exchange, to make the whole internalization effort cost-ineffective and "self-sabotaged," despite "showy" successes like the IMF's inclusion of the RMB in the SDR basket.[269]

Nevertheless, in the 2020s, senior PRC officials and experts believed that, with sweeping and versatile efforts to strongly and persistently "push for the reform of the international monetary system," "the RMB has already started to gain the character of an international reserve currency" in many ways, allowing Beijing "to get [more real] money from the banknote printing machine instead of digging [deeper] into the pockets of the taxpayers."[270] When in June 2022 the Bank for International Settlements (BIS), after two years of deliberation, announced a RMB liquidity arrangement to provide extra liquidity to Asia-Pacific central banks, PRC analysts cheered for the acceleration of "de-dollarization" and RMB internationalization.[271]

Third, the CCP-PRC has created a multitude of alternative and parallel financial institutions. Given the unchanged political system in the PRC and its partocracy relationship between the state and the economy, the RMB is unlikely to become a trustworthy international currency anytime soon under the existing international financial order dominated by the West (particularly Wall Street and the City of London). The cooling down of Western enthusiasm for incorporating the PRC since the mid-2010s, reflected in Beijing's failure to obtain the market-economy designation from the WTO and the West, has further damped that Chinese dream. Probably fully anticipating that result and in its tradition of omnidirectional efforts, Beijing has attempted to find other routes to world financial power. A key ploy is to create and lead multilateral financial institutions to mimic and replace West-dominated financial institutions, like the World Bank, the Asian Development Bank, and the IMF. With a capital commitment far exceeding $1 trillion, Beijing has founded the AIIB (Asian Infrastructure Investment Bank) and the New Development Bank (BRICS Development Bank) since 2015, and more than 20 BRI-related investments funds, such as the Silk Road Fund, since 2013.[272] To counter the West-led global financial transaction network, the Society for Worldwide Interbank Financial Telecommunication (SWIFT), the PRC launched a Cross-Border Interbank Payment System (CIPS) in 2015, which quickly grew by late 2021 to "1,100 partners covering over 3,400 banks in 200 countries."[273] After SWIFT sanctioned Russia following its invasion of Ukraine in 2022, analysts in Beijing celebrated the opportunity to "expand CIPS" and "accelerate the internationalization of the RMB."[274]

The international capital market could certainly use some fresh competition and more lenders. Thus, Beijing's massive spending on those alternative institutions, though political and self-serving to be sure, is not necessarily bad in and of itself under the Westphalian system. And it is still too early to see what kinds of norms those PRC-led institutions may promote to reshape the world financial system and how the RMB may become internationalized in this way. But, given our knowledge of how the CCP typically governs at home and behaves abroad, the odds are high for the torrent of People's Money flowing through those institutions to be potent but bad coins, intentionally or unwittingly driving the good ones away.[275]

Related to its massive spending on creating its own platforms for international finance, Beijing has also invested heavily in selling the RMB to the world through unilateral actions, leveraging its massive trade volume and its huge pile of foreign currency. A key move has been the heavily subsidized, RMB-priced oil trade market in Shanghai, which by 2020, two years after its setup, had managed to capture 10.5% of global oil futures. Most of that, however, has been the PRC's own massive imports. A Petroyuan or petro-RMB, if it really expands, now with a fixed, Beijing-insured peg to gold, would help to internationalize the People's Money significantly at the expense of the USD, which has been the currency for oil pricing for decades.[276] Beijing has also attempted to bilaterally price the massive quantity of raw materials it imports in RMB, with so far only very limited success. Even the supposedly "limitless" partner Russia still accepts the RMB for only a fraction of its overpriced oil and gas sales to Beijing.

For its pressing needs at home and its burning desires abroad, Beijing has attempted to administratively create "global financial centers" to internationalize the RMB and host international capital. In 2020–21, Beijing once again offered the island of Hainan numerous rights and special permissions to "construct a free port" and a "world center for global trade and finance" by 2025–30. All kinds of businesses on the island seem to have the blessings of the CCP, except those that can be categorized under "six disallowed": those that involve danger to state security, damage to the socialist system, smuggling of goods, prostitution/gambling/narcotics, environmental destruction, and corruption.[277] With that, the chances for the island to become another Hong Kong or Hawaii, as has been the goal since the 1980s, appear to be slim to nonexistent. Under the omnipresent CCP, which must control everything, it is impossible to have that which is required for any real financial hub to succeed: a rule of law that protects property rights and individual freedoms as well as entrusting and enforcing contracts.[278] Similarly, in 2004, Beijing set up a tariff free zone in Shanghai, which was enlarged to become the Shanghai pilot free trade zone in 2013. In 2018–19, the zone was further expanded with yet more "authorized" freedoms to "become a global financial center" in 2020.[279] However, international media soon discovered that, the hype has sputtered in recent years, and even PRC state-owned banks were abandoning it.[280]

Fourth, and finally, and closely related to the rampant corruption inside the PRC that I have documented in *The China Record*,[281] the massive outflow of the People's Money is simply related to capital flight and money laundering. The known and unknown funds flowing out of the PRC have perhaps helped to lower interest rates and enable cheap lending in the West, the most desired destination for Chinese people's money. However beneficial it may be to local financiers, realtors, and borrowers, such funds appear to also threaten to undermine the financial order and corrupt financial institutions in the West and worldwide.[282]

Every year, an estimated tens or even hundreds of billions of dollars run away from the PRC through massive emigration, legal and illegal, to nearly everywhere. The casinos in Macau and the underground banking system in Southern China and Hong Kong were reported to launder PRC money in amounts of at least $10 billion every month in the mid-2010s.[283] Anonymous, offshore shell companies and trade mis-invoicing have been two major modes of illicit capital flight that do not necessarily require the often-arduous emigration of the capital owner (see table 2.3). The leaked Panama Papers of 2016 alone showed that over 30,000 wealthy PRC citizens, including the family members of many top CCP leaders, have moved their wealth out of the country clandestinely through offshore accounts and shell companies in the tax havens since the 1990s.[284] In 2000–2011, $1.08 trillion in capital reportedly fled the PRC "illegally."[285] The illicit outflow of Chinese capital through trade misinvoicing in 2008–17 was estimated by one study as steadily around

Table 2.3. Annual Illicit Financial Outflow via Trade Misinvoicing (2008–17)

Country	Total ($billion)	To Developed Countries ($billion)
China	482.4	323.8
Russia	92.6	62.9
Mexico	81.5	56.8
India	78.0	36.1
Malaysia	64.1	36.7
Poland	53.9	40.9
Brazil	53.2	20.3
Thailand	49.6	28.1
UAE	45.2	17.7
Indonesia	43.4	20.0

Note: Value gaps are used as the proxy to measure trade misinvoicing.
Source: Global Financial Integrity (2020).

$482 billion each year ($324 billion to the 36 developed countries) or about 19.6% of total Chinese foreign trade volume, making the PRC by far the top origin of this mode of capital flight out of the 135 developing countries, equal to the next nine origin countries combined.[286]

Deals with PRC Characteristics

Another consequential aspect of PRC foreign policy is its conduct and style. The post-Mao CCP has worked hard to "connect to the tracks of the world" in some important ways in order to safeguard and enrich the regime; it is all about earning hard currencies (or "real money") and conducting business with "Chinese characteristics," to offer a "China solution" to guide and lead the world.[287] Scholars have analyzed the PRC's mercantilist export-led growth as a "capitalism without democracy" or a "capitalism with Chinese characteristics."[288] With neither the need nor the space to elaborate on these elastic and evolving Chinese characteristics, which the CCP has traditionally used to justify and enhance its policies

134 | The China Race

since Mao, the following items seem of consequence to understanding Beijing's impact on the world, constituting the context and reasons for the China Race.

One remarkable feature of the PRC's way of doing business abroad is deeply rooted in the dark side of Chinese traditional culture, which has been magnified and glorified by the masterfully unscrupulous CCP. The rampant corruption, double-dealing, and outright cheating, and widespread piracy and counterfeiting inside the PRC, as reported in the two prequels to this book, seem to also characterize Chinese activities abroad.[289] Countless cases of the effective use of unethical and illegal practices, such as bribery, infiltration, and espionage by PRC officials and merchants alike, have been widely documented in the United Nations, foreign capitals, and the headquarters of foreign multinational corporations (MNCs).[290] On Wall Street, false financial data about PRC firms may have misled and swindled American investors out of tens of billions for years, as illustrated by the case of Luckin Coffee, one of the latest companies to get caught.[291] A total of 107 PRC firms were delisted from the US stock market in just the few years prior to 2020 on the grounds of accounting and auditing problems; by late 2022, many additional Chinese companies (at least 131 out of the total of 262) were added to list of "companies at risk of delisting" amid the US-PRC tensions in the aftermath of the COVID-19 pandemic.[292] The shocking rate and extent of this expulsion/exodus suggest systematic and intentional forgery and creative accounting in the IPOs (initial public offerings) of PRC companies. The landmark "audit deal" the US reached with China in August 2022, in which Beijing relented in allowing US regulators to access the audit papers of the PRC firms, may help to slow or reverse the delisting trend, while pushing the reform of corporate accounting and auditing in the PRC, with real effects that remains to be seen.[293]

More broadly, a vast flood of counterfeit and substandard products from China has become commonplace in the American and world markets. Having depleted fish stocks at home, PRC fishing fleets have been "plundering marine resources," defying laws and regulations worldwide from the West African coast to the Galapagos Islands, threatening both local economies and ecology.[294]

The mighty corrosive power of money from the PRC has evidently reached US politicians, creating, for example, the "worst corruption scandal in almost a century" in Los Angeles, and sensational fundraising honey traps by PRC agents in several US states.[295] Through a casino operation, some PRC businessmen have "conquered a piece of America" in Saipan with its hallmark practices of bribery and labor abuse.[296] In its own neighborhood, there have been significant corruption outflows to many countries "along China's Belt and Road," with multimillion dollar payoffs to "despots and crooks" like the disgraced Malaysian prime minister Najib Razak.[297] Plenty of anecdata suggest often visible changes in the behavior of many non-PRC accountants, educators, and lawyers after their dealings with PRC customers and counterparts.[298] The CCP's negative impact on freedom of speech, for example, is now visible outside of the PRC; as one American observer commented in mid-2021, "integration with China was supposed to spread our values; it's done the opposite."[299]

Furthermore, as illustrated by the PRC's presence and activities in Africa, Beijing is exporting a model of economic development that characteristically suppresses the private sector, represses labor rights, and disregards the environment.[300] The PRC is viewed by many in recipient countries as benevolent and generous, with its considerable aid, medical teams providing free basic care, and mega state loans and contracts. But Chinese private business abroad is largely on its own, especially the numerous small businesses with few special ties to the CCP cadres in charge of Chinese foreign policy.[301] Beijing eagerly exports its model of state-society and central-local relationships to its beneficiaries, such as its state-capitalist (or partocracy-capitalist) mercantilism for development—partially exemplified by its grand plan to establish 50 of its prized SEZs (special economic zones) abroad, with about one dozen operating in Africa by 2020, proceeding often at the expense of Chinese and local private entrepreneurs.[302] Evidently, however, Beijing is not practicing what it preaches to its "natural" friends: as Africa's largest trade partner, the PRC enjoys double benefits as it continues the classic African-foreign trade pattern of resources for manufactured goods, while enjoying a large and persistent trade surplus with Africa. Almost all of the massive Chinese investment in Africa has been directed at producing for the local markets (with the exception of resources like oil and minerals), rather than for export of labor-intensive manufactured goods back to China—the strategy that should have been prescribed by the so-called "Chinese model" of foreign investment-financed export-led growth, which has critically benefited the PRC economy over the past four decades.[303]

136 | The China Race

Time for Engaging in the Race

With the same set of core interests and international goals, exclusively defined as the power and survival of its autocratic regime, the CCP-PRC state has spent seven decades as a determined and preordained rebel, almost always at odds with and challenging the West/US-led LIO version of the Westphalian world order. Primarily a function of its perception and calculus of the balance of power in the world and colored by the personalities and vision of its top leaders,[304] Beijing's foreign policy has had major ups and downs and twists and turns, with significant double-talk, colorful banners, acrobatic maneuvers, selective coupling, conditional surrenders, and even total reversals, as dazzling distractions, deceptions, and disguises. Structurally, ideologically, and genetically, however, the objective of the CCP's foreign policy has always been to seize global leadership from its political foe, the West and particularly the US, and ultimately recenter and reorder the world in its image. After repeated failures that drove the PRC state to the brink of collapse, the post-Mao CCP leaders raised a new banner in the 1980s to selectively "open" the PRC to the US and the West.[305] Beijing has since successfully employed recycled ideas of the late-Qing empire, pitting barbarians against barbarians and self-strengthening through imitation and importation. The Chinese economy has boomed, and the PRC's state power on the international stage has skyrocketed.

Today, the CCP's rulers seem to continue to struggle with regime insecurity, but feel rich and powerful. With their new confidence comes new impatience. Beijing has simply had enough of the inconvenience and indignity of Deng Xiaoping's hiding and waiting strategy.[306] It has resolutely turned its back on the "prudential," arguably wishful, analysis—that the CCP should start democratization to replace its fleeting "teleological-revolutionary" political legitimacy, at home and abroad, ensure the survival of the PRC regime, and seek China's best interests.[307] Driven by the same innate logic of its Qin-Han polity, while facing mounting, new sociopolitical and economic pressures, the CCP rulers seem to have bet their fortune on a strong dictatorship at home and an aggressive foreign policy abroad—the two actually reinforce each other and appear as two sides of the same coin. "Betting that the West is in irreversible decline," in the face of events like the tumultuous US electoral politics and Brexit, the CCP has become ever more confident over the past decade.[308] The "limitless" partnership with fellow autocrats in places like Moscow has likely reinforced fanciful thinking about a replay of the Cold War, only to be better fought and won this time with Beijing in charge.

Under Xi Jinping's imitation of Mao Zedong, the CCP seems to have resumed the failed Maoist pursuit of its Mandate of Heaven (or Mandate of the People or Mandate of History) for a world revolution under its leadership. PRC foreign policy quickly graduated from using the Western (technology) to serve the Chinese (system) to rejuvenating the Chinese system (of the Qin-Han polity and the China Order), and using it to influence and lead humanity and reorder the world. Under a general umbrella of "China going global,"[309] suavely repackaged and powerfully propagated, the CCP's "great power diplomacy of the new era" so far appears in the form of largely peaceful, polished, "normal" nationalistic appeals, but is unmistakably accompanied by an explosive expansion of military force and a global agenda full of bellicose demands and pursuits. It would seem, however, that the nation of China and the Chinese people are once again being used as a pool of pawns, not the master or the end, of Chinese foreign policy.

Beijing's constant and consistent omnidirectional struggles abroad to safeguard and strengthen the regime have been remarkably effective and even successful. But the Chinese nation and the Chinese people have endured great costs and have been poorly served. The distance and divorce between the political interests of the CCP-PRC state and the interests of the Chinese nation and the Chinese people are very profound and highly exploitable. This has afforded Beijing some disproportionate power on the international stage. A critical way to effectively constrain PRC foreign policy and efficiently transform the CCP regime, however, is also right there readily available in the same place. Like a good rereading of China's history, a transparent account of China's foreign policy would serve to detoxify, motivate, and empower the Chinese people to reshape or even remove the PRC's worldview and diminish Beijing's burning desire to confront, challenge, and replace the existing world order.

The impact of the PRC's active and massive foreign ventures in the world has been highly mixed, featuring the same deep suboptimality and undesirability that have characterized the overall record of the CCP-PRC state. The CCP has emerged as a formidable power that could compete skillfully to advance much further, even reaching the critical point of no return on its way to victory in the China Race, defined narrowly in terms of its political interest rather than China's national interest or

138 | The China Race

the interest of humanity. As has happened in human history numerous times, a suboptimal or even disastrous power with enough concentrated might and wile could fiercely compete with and unexpectedly conquer its richer and preferable peers, and feasibly control and reorder the whole known world. In early 2023, a 19-country survey indeed found that the CCP has been doing a convention-defyingly effective job in selling its model of governance worldwide.[310] Still, as the patterns and records of its domestic and foreign policies reveal, as I have attempted to demonstrate in this book and its two prequels, the legitimacy-, efficiency-, and innovation-challenged CCP-PRC state faces the probability of defeat if its opponents, including the Chinese people, counteract with timeliness and decisiveness.

With a renewed *tianxia* pursuit to unseat the United States and to build the China Order of world empire, the CCP-PRC state has now continued and elevated the China Race for new world leadership and an alternative world order with added energy and intensity. The West's arguably smart and successful geopolitical play of "the China Card" in the 1970s–80s for winning the Cold War has long since run its course. "The China Fantasy" of the "automatic" political transformation of the PRC through open trade, accommodation and friendship, favored by many, including both idealists in the Ivory Towers and capitalists on Wall Street from the mid-1990s to the early 2010s, seems to have faded.[311] Similarly, the benevolent efforts since the late 1990s undertaken in hopes of incorporating the PRC in the current world order as a new and "responsible stakeholder"[312] seemed to have fizzled and backfired by the mid-2010s. The momentous, two-decade-long distraction by international terrorists following the 9/11 attack, which, according to PRC analysts, "saved the CCP" and "shielded China,"[313] has also thankfully abated.[314]

Six decades ago, the legendary Shanghai-based international business tycoon Victor Sassoon lamented that "Chinese [Communists] don't like foreigners and they never have. They do business with us but only to the extent it suits their purposes."[315] Probably feeling the same way, "many CEOs are about to discover—if they haven't already—that the risks of doing business in an increasingly authoritarian China are starting to outweigh the benefits of being there," wrote the CEO of the Connecticut-based Chief Executive Group in April 2021.[316] Worldwide, even before the COVID-19 pandemic, countries "big or small" were already "pushing back against China's overreach and domineering behavior," and confronting "their political differences and economic and security challenges with China."[317] Backlashes against the CCP's "party-state capitalism [. . .] including intensified investment reviews, campaigns to exclude Chinese firms from strategic sectors, and the creation of novel domestic and international institutions to address perceived threats from Chinese actors" seem to have emerged around the world, and particularly in the West.[318] The time has now arrived, hopefully not yet too late, for the West, especially the United States, to focus on fully engaging and optimally managing the China Race.[319]

3

The PRC-USA Rivalry

For Existence and the World

Having attempted to outline Chinese foreign policy under the CCP, I now turn to discuss the epic rivalry between the PRC and the USA, the core element of the China Race between the CCP-PRC state and the West (and the world). This chapter will further consider the rising power of the PRC in relation to the United States and analyze the global nature of the cross-Pacific competition, the state of Sinology in the West and the US in particular, the recent evolution and reorientation of US China policy, and the general state of the China Race.

An Existential Rivalry

As I have alluded to earlier in this book and its two prequels, *The China Order* and *The China Record*, the CCP ruling group has been a world-class master of wordsmithery and the "dark" art of power politics, both internally and externally. As firm believers and well-rewarded practitioners of Chinese Legalism, which relies on force and ruse (and especially deception and manipulation) to succeed and rule, the CCP leaders had locked their attention on the United States as the most powerful nation in the world since even before becoming the rulers of China in 1949. Sometimes bluntly with open hostility, sometimes politely with ambivalent enmity, and sometimes almost hidden with simulated partnership, the CCP has always regarded the US as its top rival and treated it as such; the US is the eternal challenger and a mortal threat to its Qin-Han polity of authoritarian partocracy. The China Race in general and the PRC-USA rivalry in particular have always been about the political and even physical existence of the CCP-PRC state and, by the global and systemic nature of the competition, also about the existence of the US as the world leader and the main embodiment of democratic rule of law.

The CCP's structurally determined and deeply held anti-Americanism may seem irrational, erroneous, and illogical from the perspective of the Chinese people and much of the rest of the world—not to mention China's century-long history of highly beneficial relations with the US. There is not a shred of evidence suggesting the possibility of an American invasion or colonization of China; the cross-Pacific cultural differences and economic frictions are all well within the normal bounds of international relations, and decidedly dwarfed by the highly complementary and enormous benefits for both sides generated by a friendly relationship. Yet from the CCP's standpoint, continued hostility toward and fear of the US are not unjustified, testifying to the distance and even divorce between the political interests of the CCP-PRC state and the national interests of China and the Chinese people. Without a sociopolitical transformation and change of worldview in the PRC, and in the absence of an unlikely, if not impossible, US capitulation that accepts the CCP's way as the model of political governance and accommodates all of Beijing's demands, the very existence of the US political system itself—"the American way of life"—with its power, wealth, and appeal, remains always a genuine and lethal threat to the CCP-PRC autocracy. And, unlike prior to the mid-19th century, it is no longer possible for Beijing to keep or assume away the mighty Western-American power, both the hard and the soft kinds, no matter how hard the CCP tries with censorship, disinformation, and "thought work" or brainwashing. So long as the US keeps being itself, namely, a vibrant contrast and weighty alternative to and an inevitable opposite and mighty critic of illiberal autocracies in the world, especially those with means, whatever Washington and the Americans do or do not do to or for China will not alter Beijing's inborn political calculations. The nation of China is secure and prospers; the CCP regime's fear of being "annihilated" by the US, however, is real. PRC analysts wrote in 2022 that the US "will never accept" the CCP as equal or superior, with its determined pursuit of a "rejuvenation of the Chinese nation," and a "new globalization [with a] community of common destiny of human-ity."[1] According to PRC analysts, the PRC-USA rivalry is therefore "a long and ultimate confrontation" for which "all conflicts are strategic and all *détentes* are just tactical," and both sides are seeking "the total defeat of the opponent."[2] Even a "possible victory of the US and West" "in the race against COVID" would "mean many dire consequences for China [and we] must immediately prepare for that worrisome situation with the most urgency."[3] Easily misidentifying the CCP regime as China, PRC analysts (and some non-PRC ones too) tend to scrupulously view the cross-Pacific competition as a dreaded zero-sum game between the two great nations. In spring 2023, a PRC analyst openly concluded that "there is now no possibility for the Sino-American relationship to improve, while the chance for major, ominous and dangerous incidents further increased [so the CCP-PRC must] embrace the fully developing China-US struggle."[4]

Smokescreens and wishful thinking aside, it is easy to see that the PRC-USA rivalry is indeed existential in nature—the existence of each other's political system and worldview, if not exactly statehood and nationhood, is at stake. It may be possible, especially for the US, with its open, pluralist democracy and a legalistic society of immigrants, for the two competitors to live and let live, coexisting in a rule-based, sports-like relationship to decide, periodically and peacefully, the power and fate of the two opposing political systems and worldviews. Yet, as I have attempted to demonstrate, the system-altering CCP is innately mandated to take over the whole club and rewrite the rules in its way, thus rendering the vision of sustained fair play for the PRC-USA rivalry unreal and delusional. The outcome and peacefulness of the rivalry and the overall China Race, therefore, will be mostly a function of the cross-Pacific balance of power and how the US and its allies respond to the rising challenge from the CCP-PRC state.

The US has always symbolized the great, seemingly insurmountable, external power that the CCP does not control, acutely feels, deeply envies, and profoundly dreads. The dominant power of the US economy and military is, in fact, well appreciated by the CCP leadership, and has always aroused intense sensations in Beijing, despite its propaganda over seven decades—mostly for the purpose of intoxicating the Chinese people with crafty, make-believe stories painting the US as a "paper-tiger," an immature parvenu, a declining or already-declined nation, a self-defeating evildoer, or simply a corrupt country of spoiled and incompetent people.[5]

144 | The China Race

Talk aside, however, for as long as it has been in power, the CCP has been chasing the holy grail of surpassing and thus overwhelming the US in capability and resources, particularly as measured by economic output, financial resources, and military prowess—from the chimerical shortcut of the Great Leap Forward to surpass the US by 1965 (or 1975, or "around 2000"), which ended in great depression and massive famine, to the national mobilization of the military-industry complex, led by the "Central Focus Committee," to develop military hardware since 1962, the "modernization of national defense by 2000" since the 1980s, and the "second centennial goal of struggle" to overtake the US and make the PRC the "world's great power" by 2049 (or even by 2035).[6]

Mighty struggles, colossal squandering of lives and resources, enormous opportunity costs, and many failures and delays later, however, the CCP-PRC is still stuck in the ranks of developing countries in the 2020s, in terms of socioeconomic development and lack of technological innovation.[7] While China remains distinctively behind the US and its Western allies overall, as I have attempted to demonstrate earlier in this book and *The China Record*, the PRC state has risen to become a top contender with formidable power on the world stage, with its extraordinary extraction from the world's second-largest economy, its accumulation of the world's largest foreign currency reserve, its centralized and opaque spending of life and money with little scrutiny or constraints, and its massive access, legal and illegal, to the world's latest technology. With about two-thirds of the American GDP, the CCP-PRC state is already able to spend significantly more than the US government, and without the congressional monitoring, public scrutiny, and substantial entitlement spending that characterize the US federal budget. It is likely to be a long time before the PRC could possibly surpass the US by major indicators like technological innovation, economic efficiency, per capita GDP, and living standards.[8] However, the CCP-PRC state has already amassed world-class resources, becoming a suboptimal giant with growing weight, enabling it to have a systemic and global impact in its contest with the United States. Judging by how often sheer force and cunning ruses have combined to conquer the worthier and more powerful opponents in human history (particularly Chinese history), the CCP, with its centralized preponderance of physical force and targeted diplomacy, may not be too mistaken in betting on winning the China Race by unscrupulously employing all sorts of means, rather than counting on the desirability and popularity of its governance and the superiority of its socioeconomic performance.

The Challenger

The positive statement of the China Race and the normative analysis of the reasons and means for the US and its allies to manage and prevail in the China Race rest on the understanding and assessment of the CCP-PRC state as a system-altering, suboptimal, and undesirable, but viable and formidable challenger. The PRC is not contending with the USA for the usual relative international gains, nor in a fair-play scenario such as a sports match, which are both normal and familiar to Americans in the Westphalian world. The CCP is in a global long game of winner-takes-all, including the very existence of the loser politically and ideologically, if not physically. A quick recap and elaboration of three specific findings about the CCP-PRC state as the challenger to the United States in the China Race, based on what I have attempted in this book and its two prequels is in order here.

First, the CCP-PRC state represents a different mode of political governance, a competing model of socioeconomic development, and an alternative vision of world order. It inevitably challenges the existing Westphalian world order, the liberal international order (LIO) led by the United States and its allies. For its regime survival and security, the PRC state has been in an eternal, exacting, expensive, and perpetual struggle with the Chinese people at home, and the West-dominated world abroad. During the first three decades of the PRC's history, this mighty struggle produced a series of failures that inflicted a grand tragedy for the Chinese people and also brought the regime to the brink of demise. The post-Mao CCP conditionally and partially surrendered to its archnemesis during the Cold War, submitting to the very world order it had always fought to overthrow. Saved and protected by the LIO, the CCP retained its political system and returned to China's pre-1949 path of diplomacy and development. Over the past four decades, the Maoist party-state has managed to survive and emerge significantly enriched and considerably accepted by the world. Yet, the innate logic of the authoritarian Qin-Han polity of the CCP-PRC state preordains or condemns the regime to battle and seek to change the LIO and

146 | The China Race

the US leadership in the world, which are fundamentally incompatible with the party-state's goals and worldviews. Beijing's partial surrender to the West in exchange for survival and wealth has, over the decades of the 1980s–2010s, greatly Westernized Chinese society and at the same time petrified the partocracy "hiding" in retreat. The CCP leadership, sensing its mortal danger and new wealth, therefore has persisted in its opportunistic, incessant, and omnidirectional ventures abroad for power and regime security, with renewed vengeance and energy.

To resist, reduce, and replace the United States whenever and wherever possible and with whatever means and ruses available, so as to recenter and reorder the world, is at the core of the PRC objectives in the China Race, particularly in the PRC-USA global rivalry. A Beijing victory in the Race would mean, at minimum, a world safer for authoritarian polities at the expense of democratic rule of law and, at maximum, an alternate world leadership that would end the LIO, replace the overall Westphalian system with a China Order–like world empire, and steer humanity into a repeat of the history of the post-Qin Sinic world. In the official CCP-PRC lingo, the minimum and maximum objectives are "organically" and "dialectically" linked as the aim of "coexisting" (*gongsheng*), which ensures a harmonious "international coexistence of diverse sociopolitical systems" and the "grand mission" of constructing a new, uniform world order of "global community" (*gongtongti*). The "international ethics of the reality of coexistence," once secured, is then to be "used and elevated" to effectively "facilitate the construction of the community of common destiny for humanity."[9] In September 2021, Xi Jinping redeclared at the UN the dual objectives of "ensuring a world for different civilizations and various routes of development to coexist," and "pushing for a better world with the construction of the community of common destiny for humanity."[10]

Second, the record of governance of the CCP-PRC has been mixed and mediocre, mostly suboptimal, and often disastrous, as evidenced by its performance in political governance, socioeconomic development, and preservation of antiquities and the environment. The oxymoronic "people's democratic dictatorship" of the CCP is actually a premodern (pre-Enlightenment) sociopolitical system, a revived Qin-Han polity of authoritarianism-totalitarianism. It is qualitatively a less desirable substitute for the US and the West as world leader, and a regressive force in human civilization, representing an undesirable choice for world leader and world order. Under the so-called China Tragedy and China Suboptimality, China has experienced a giant leap backward institutionally and ideologically and a grand detour of history; the Chinese people have endured a massive loss of lives and rights, enormous destruction of wealth and ecology, and a colossal waste of time. The ruling clique of the PRC is ultra-self-centered, incredibly indulgent, eternally insecure, and inherently incompetent, but excels at safeguarding and strengthening its dictatorial power unscrupulously and ruthlessly. The CCP-PRC state is institutionally, ideologically, and historically a force for building a world-empire disguised as a nation-state. Beijing thus treats the Chinese people as useful but dispensable captives rather than citizens, despite its self-identification as the people's savior and the people's servant. The Chinese nation and the Chinese people have made extraordinary sacrifices for the CCP's extravagant foreign ventures but have been poorly served and often disserved both at home and abroad.

The CCP's chronic lack of political legitimacy has formed a symbiotic relationship of reciprocal causation with its autocratic and suboptimal way of governance, which together make the regime uniquely undesirable, extremely costly, ruthlessly formidable, and remarkably vulnerable. As an indicator of regime cost-inefficiency, a European study reports that while the Chinese per capita GDP is less than 16% of that in the US, the PRC's per capita spending on domestic security is 50% of that in the US (or twice as much in total); in "strategic locations" like Tibet and Xinjiang, the per capita cost of policing is 134% to 140% of that in the US.[11] In the 2020s, Beijing's per capita direct budgetary subsidy to Tibet alone was over 150% of the median national per capita income, or more than 270% of the median Tibetan per capita income.[12]

Third, while indisputably suboptimal and undesirable for the Chinese people, the PRC has delivered a so-called CCP Optimality of ruling and extraction, giving the regime great resilience in staying in power and controlling China. The rise of China as a rich, developed, advanced, and desirable nation is at best still a work in progress, a process that may have already entered a more difficult phase in the 2020s.[13] But the rise of CCP-PRC state power as a formidable force concentrating on its global pursuit of influencing, recentering, and reordering the world is already real and growing. While lagging the West and the US in just about every aspect of international comparison of resources and capability, the CCP-PRC state has a chance to outmaneuver the US politically and strategically and win the China Race. For that purpose, Beijing enjoys an extraordinary capability of extraction from the

148 | The China Race

world's largest (prior to 2024) population and second-largest economy, an unmonitored and largely unchecked freedom of action, and infinite unscrupulousness of means. The open and rules-based norms and institutions of the LIO in the era of globalization disproportionally enable and assist the CCP, which can selectively ignore rules of engagement and moral constraints. Perhaps paradoxically, a suboptimal polity could readily produce a formidable or even superior state power to compete optimally in world geopolitics, potentially overwhelming its richer, more advanced, and better-governed opponents with focused force, the right ruses, enough luck, and the defections and defeatism or self-sabotage of its adversaries, caused by exorbitant domestic and foreign policies—such as the so-called "global war on terror" in the early 21st century, which resembles a severe allergic overreaction that harms much more than the allergen could ever do on its own.[14] The result of the China Race therefore remains uncertain. However unlikely it may appear, the less undesirable world political order of the Westphalian system could very well be swiftly replaced by a decidedly more undesirable world political centralization. The ability to use the liberal order to destroy the liberal system constitutes a unique source of power for the CCP and presents an extraordinary challenge to the US and the West.

Aiming High and Globally

Driven by its innate logic as a revitalized Qin-Han polity in the post–World War II world, which features a US-led liberal iteration of the Westphalian world order, the CCP-PRC state is compelled to always focus on its top external and existential threat, the presence and power of the United States. It has relied on a national mobilization of resources and unscrupulous ruses, its rather effective recipe for power and control, to deal with the US, in pursuit of its manifested mandate to recenter and reorder the world. The US has thus remained the so-called "key of the key issues" (*zhongzhong zhizhong*) that has "the largest impact on China" to all CCP leaders from Mao to Xi.[15] In this book and its two prequels, I have discussed probably more than enough about the objective importance and the subjective significance of the US to the CCP's power and well-being since the 1940s, as well as the CCP's consistent strategy of the so-called four Rs (resisting, reducing, replacing, and reordering) toward the United States. Here, a brief look at the way the

CCP is modernizing and expanding its military in recent years may help to illustrate Beijing's fixation on and concrete efforts toward emulating, competing with, surpassing, and unseating the US. Whatever grand ideals the CCP has been trying to convince the Chinese people to believe, when it comes to its power and security, the party-state has always been very serious, leaving no stone unturned, aiming high and globally in its existential rivalry with the US.

In late 2021, an influential Beijing-based magazine declared in classic Maoist political lingo that "the rising Sino-American contradiction is becoming the world's main contradiction," with "a comprehensive, omnidirectional, and global impact," particularly concerning which side will be the "number one [power and leader] in the world," and the PRC must act accordingly, smartly and forcefully, in order to prevail.[16] Having already reached parity with the US to quietly usher in an "era of parallel" between two "globalization systems," according to PRC analysts, the PRC now just needs to focus on competing and winning.[17] For that, the CCP seems to hope to first divide the Pacific Basin with the US in a so-called "new type of great power relations"—Chairman Xi Jinping repeatedly proposed to Presidents Barack Obama and Donald Trump (in 2014–18) that "the Pacific is big enough to contain the two countries of China and the US."[18] Soon, however, Xi raised the level of pomposity by asserting to President Joe Biden via video conference in November 2021, and repeated in person to the visiting US secretary of state Antony Blinken in June 2023, that "the Earth is big enough for China and the US."[19]

Military power seems to feature prominently in the CCP's global effort to outmatch the US. The People's Liberation Army (PLA, the Chinese military), has always been critically important to the CCP party-state. Beyond his famously argued and practiced saying, "the truth of 'political power comes from the barrel of gun,'" first stated in the late 1920s, Mao Zedong told his comrades in 1949 that "the so-called People's Republic [of China] is in fact just the People's Liberation Army."[20] The PLA has therefore been tightly controlled by the CCP's top rulers, often personally, enjoying all sorts of perks and priorities in the PRC.[21] Due to its top priority of domestic control, and following the Maoist "People's War" doctrine of total war, which effectively mobilizes and uses civilians as human shields, the PLA has always been the world's largest army by number of personnel, and a predominantly land-based force extensively imbedded in the general population. Since the 1990s, as part of the

150 | The China Race

CCP's enhanced search for political legitimacy in nationalism, patriotism, and populism, the PLA has been rebranded as the guardian of the motherland and fighters for Han-Chinese interests, power, and respect in the world, and a "world-class" modern force, "protecting world peace" and upholding a "more just international order."[22]

In the 21st century, as the CCP speeds up the China Race, hoping for a so-called "overtaking at the curve" or leapfrogging, with both symmetric and asymmetric efforts, Beijing has been massively investing in the military, at a speed much faster than the growth of the economy.[23] The aim seems to be to make the PLA into an equal of—if not yet kinetically defeating and fully overpowering—the US military, at least in appearance. In late-2007, the PLA changed its uniforms wholesale for the nth and, so far, the final time, completely and blatantly copying those of the US military, down to every detail of the rather un-Chinese ribbons and ensigns.[24] The People's War doctrine was updated with a US-inspired "professional military capable of winning wars under any conditions with high tech and information."[25] After purging almost all of the high command he inherited, Xi Jinping raised the salary and benefits of the officers, reorganized the PLA into five forces—army, navy, air force, rocket, and strategic support force (space, cyber, and psycho warfare)—and five "theater commands" or war zones (*zhanqu*) modeled after the US joint-commands, and massively built up military hardware that seemingly aims at long distance and even global projection of capabilities.[26] Becoming more symmetric than asymmetric, the PLA is massively and rapidly building up its "global combat capability," with more nuclear weapons and advanced conventional and unconventional means, like stealth aircraft and warships, aircraft carriers, heavy destroyers and amphibious platforms, submarines, supersonic missiles, space and cyber capabilities, global positioning system technology, artificial intelligence, and allegedly also bioweapons.[27]

The PLA Navy, in particular, has graduated from a brown water (coastal) force to a blue water (ocean) navy, with a fleet that in 2021 had more warships (360, projected to be 425 by 2030) than the globally committed US Navy (298); counting auxiliary and coast guard ships, the PRC had 777 ships versus 490 for the US in the early 2020s.[28] At their current rapid speed building warships, like "making dumplings," the PLA Navy is projected to make the US Navy number two in the world in total fleet tonnage by 2040, for the first time in over a century.[29] With the inexplicable accommodation and even open assistance the US offered to the PLA for years, not to mention the massive flow, legal or illegal, of military and dual-use technology from the West, the PLA now literally sails to all corners of the globe, drilling and deploying in faraway places like the Black Sea, the Red Sea, the Atlantic, the Artic, and Antarctica. In the Western Pacific, the PLA has reportedly achieved the "full ability" to breach the so-called first island chain.[30]

Real fighting capability notwithstanding, militarily and perception-wise, quantity is a quality of its own. Unlike many other bubbles of investment created by the CCP inside and outside the PRC, as reported in this book and *The China Record*, a massive military force with expensive gears is available for use; such a force also inevitably demands and creates new purposes and actions to rationalize and justify itself. In the first PRC National Defense White Paper of 1995 and its subsequent editions in1998 and 2000, the CCP always reaffirmed its decades-old "solemn pledge" of "never basing any soldier in any foreign country." In 2002, after the PRC successfully neutralized US trade scrutiny by entering the WTO with grand promises (that it now appears it never intended to keep) and years of military buildup, however, this pledge was unceremoniously omitted in the fourth such White Paper, being replaced with a strategy of "active and proactive defense" and the new "solemn pledge" of "not deploying any nuclear weapon abroad." In the 2004 White Paper two years later (and the subsequent 2006, 2008, and 2010 editions), the CCP called on the PLA to "leapfrog and break through," in order to "win wars" against an expanded list of specific threats and enemies. In 2013 and 2015, "safeguarding international sea lanes" and extensively "pushing more pragmatic military cooperation" abroad to "actively protect the state's overseas interests" became part of the declared military strategy. In 2017, the PLA formally opened its joint base in Djibouti as part of its "international responsibility as a great power." In 2019, the PLA proclaimed in its White Paper its new mission of "providing the public good of international security" to other nations so as to "protect world peace" and "construct the community for the common human destiny."[31] At the very least, it seems that the CCP is putting huge amounts of money where its mouth is: to seriously compete with the US globally, advancing methodically in stages and overtaking opportunistically, to grow its international power in a rather traditional way by acquiring military supremacy in the world.

152 | The China Race

Further Reflections on PRC Power and Aims

To be sure, many have arrived at similar findings regarding the fundamental and systemic challenge to the US-led world order by the rising power of the PRC, reflected in a multitude of predictions in recent years about the "coming struggle," even war, between the two great powers over the world's political leadership and organization, with US national security squarely at stake.[32] Some predicted as far back as 1993 that "[m]uch of the future of humanity will hinge on" the US-China interaction.[33] These viewpoints, while perceptive, tend to focus on aspects of the rise of Chinese power through conventional Western lenses, mostly related to subsystemic ideological conflict or power struggle.[34] Many are based on overtly cultural or ethnically contingent concepts and archaic metaphors, such as "Han-centrism," "Sino-centrism," the historiography of Greek international relations, or European ideologies like communism, nationalism, and state-capitalism. The West and China are just representing two competing models of the same system, "liberal meritocratic capitalism" versus "state-led political, or authoritarian, capitalism," according to the former chief economist of the World Bank.[35] In this view, while the PRC and the US are following two different paths, Beijing's global ambitions are not fundamentally unlike those that drove the US and its predecessors to rise to positions of "global domination."[36]

In discovering what is supposedly just another common, inevitable, and thus normal international competition between China and the US, many analysts and advocates appear to be mainly defending Western- and American-centrism, or a particular episode (the LIO) of the Westphalian system, instead of safeguarding the Westphalian system itself. As awakening and acerbic as they may be, many if not most works dealing with the rise of China have tended to dull and draw out the epical China Race with misleading labels, framing it as a normal and reasonable occurrence under the Westphalian system—namely, the necessary, inevitable, legitimate, and even welcome competition and change of leadership among nations. In 2005, US senior officials expressed the laudable aspiration of incorporating China into the current world order as a like-minded, "responsible stakeholder."[37] That quite sensible wish, however, flopped quickly, as it was based on a misreading of the CCP's intent, and a premature understanding of the PRC's actions. The restraint and successful transformation of the CCP-PRC required to achieve that noble aim are directly at odds with Beijing's nonnegotiable core interests as an autocratic regime that can only be content with a position of worldwide domination. In 2020, seemingly oblivious to the fundamental incompatibility of institutions and ideas in the West and the PRC, a noted voice on world affairs still touted "a policy of engagement plus deterrence" to provide more and longer accommodation of Beijing's "legitimate pursuits."[38] In 2021, a senior scholar of international affairs opined that "Washington shouldn't assume its values are more attractive to others than Beijing's"; since "neither the United States nor China lives up to these normative declarations" under the LIO regarding human rights and the world order, "neither the United States nor China poses a genuine threat to the other's sovereignty or independence [and] neither country is likely to convert the other to its preferred political ideology."[39]

An adequate understanding of the true nature of the rising PRC power, something I attempted to develop in the two prequels to this book, still appears imperative and worthy of a quick recap. The renowned sociopolitical historian Francis Fukuyama, famed for proposing the bold thesis of "the end of history" in 1992, shared some highly insightful advice in May 2020, specifically that the PRC carries the legacy of Qin-style Legalist institutions and is now "an aspiring totalitarian country like the mid-20th century Soviet Union[. . . .] The CCP's aspiration toward total control unfortunately now reaches into liberal democracies around the world. [. . .] What Americans need to keep in mind is that their enemy and rival right now is not China, but a Chinese Communist Party that has shifted into high-totalitarian mode." All that said, he still overlooks the mega China Race, instead attributing the CCP's Maoist totalitarian politics to the personality of Xi Jinping and his anti-corruption.[40] "A former senior government official with deep expertise and experience dealing with China" anonymously published *The Longer Telegram* in early 2021, impressively arguing that Xi's leadership rather than the CCP is the source of the problem for the United States.[41] A long-time British China watcher published in mid-2021 a treatise on how a fated coup d'état in Beijing, caused by the crushing problems the CCP faces, and facilitated by "liberal democracies" led by the "newly awakened" US, will replace Xi with Li Keqiang, end China's one-party dictatorship, and launch a transition to democracy and the rule of law.[42] Insightful and inspirational as they all are, however, such views risk a profound misreading of the nature of the CCP-PRC state, which has always mandated a reordering of the world in its image, with variations only due to its sense of power calculus and opportunities.

154 | The China Race

The rising power of the CCP-PRC is not just another international competition for power and leadership, vanity, or financial and territorial gains. Beijing eyes all that and has a much larger, more fundamental ambition to convert the entire Westphalian system and replace it with an alternative world empire order. A world imperium, whether Han-Chinese dominated or not, is destined to be undesirable and disastrous, as I have attempted to show in this book and its prequels, and would thrill any aspiring autocrat. The China Race, centered around the PRC-USA rivalry, is, at minimum, about replacing the tested and tolerable US-Western leadership with the uncertain and opaque CCP-PRC leadership, which I have attempted to demonstrate is more suboptimal and undesirable. The CCP, as one of its "theorists" writes, has openly articulated that the world ought to return to the "natural and logical" history of world empire, after a 400-year "detour" under the Westphalian world order. To rebuild a singular and truer world empire, or "empire of the world," so as to "liberate" and better govern the whole of humanity, to challenge and replace the ineffectual and waning "Anglo-American World Empire," for "either perpetual peace or communism," is the inevitable "new great struggle," with a "historical mandate of heaven" for the rising Chinese power under Xi Jinping, the "leader with *charisma*."[43]

A legitimate question may still arise here: If the current CCP-PRC state is a suboptimal way of governance, would it, realistically, be able to lead and transform the world? A theme of my assessment of the PRC has been that the party-state maintains the symbiotic coexistence of the so-called CCP Optimality for control and power, and the China Suboptimality for the people. Underperforming and undesirable to the Chinese people, the partocracy has provided a rather optimal and resilient service to the ruling elites (or just a single ruler) for control and exploitation. The US has remained firmly at the center of the global value chain.[44] Measured by efficiency, innovation, and per capita GDP, the Chinses economy is unlikely to match let alone surpass that of the United States in the foreseeable future.[45] The sheer size of the Chinese economy and Beijing's massive and growing use of "second best" technology, however, is making the PRC a formidable force, with advantages in its rivalry with the US. The CCP potently extracts labor and resources from nearly one-fifth of humankind, the 1.4 billion industrious and enduring, but long manipulated, misinformed, and mistreated Chinese people. It is capable of being competitive in international relations, engaging in a full China

Race for the world order, not just a classic and costly territorial expansion and administrative domination.[46]

The China Race is as much an ideological race as it is an imperialist or colonial conquest of the nations. Beijing is not simply acting for the sake of abstract dogma, but for the control of other nations and ultimately to shape the whole world in its image, and it is doing so in concrete and consequential ways that are often overlooked. Recent, illuminating instances of how the CCP spares no effort and observes no limits in its rivalry with the US in order to win the China Race include Beijing's abundant activities in the South China Sea, in international organizations, and in places ranging from Hong Kong, Xinjiang, and Taiwan to the Korean Peninsula, Southeast and Central Asia, Latin America, Africa, and even US airspace.[47] Beijing's "partnership without limits" with Russia, declared days before Moscow invaded Ukraine in February 2022,[48] and its use of small nations in "the global South to constrain America,"[49] are some of the latest examples. The explosive growth of the PRC's military machine and the significant changes to its declared strategy and doctrine, briefly discussed earlier, clearly demonstrate that Beijing is running at full speed in its quest for ever more power over its rivals—power in all its forms: soft and hard, traditional and unusual, and globalist and national-imperialist.

The China Order, dressed in the sophisticated phraseology of globalism, humanism, and socialism and communism, has become to many an alluring Mandate of the People, a contemporary update of the Mandate of Heaven. With unrestrained access to the lives and funds of the Chinese people for the purpose of influence and control, Beijing has already gained a considerable following, a variety of willing and eager executioners, sympathizers, supporters, bribees, accomplices, and converts—often pejoratively labeled by observers as "tankies," "useful idiots," or *baizuo* (white leftists)—from many corners of the world.[50] Quite a few of these sympathizers are prominent and capable, generous and selfless, but often arrogant and even racist Western elites who tend to heedlessly project their own ideals and fantasies onto the "progressive and revolutionary" CCP-PRC, based on false and controlled information, dreaming of or pretending to enlighten and "salve" the Chinese people, direct and change China, and thus "save" and "better" the world in their preferred ways.[51] Quite a few capable and even ambitious Westerners, frustrated or marginalized at home, have chosen to help the CCP, which has indeed often rewarded them with gratifying recognition and concrete benefits in the name of one-fifth of humanity. Some are avaricious and calculating but ultimately suicidal capitalists and their tunnel-visioned apologists who would trade everything including common sense for quarterly profits and abstract "world economic efficiency." There are foreign-turned-PRC scholars living off of the construction of sophisticated apologies and promotions for not just the CCP but the whole Confucian-coated Legalist Qin-Han polity, with the enigmatic potions of "Eastern/Chinese meritocracy" and "just" sociopolitical hierarchy.[52] An influential American economist has been openly called "China's apologist" for his defense of the CCP with the illogic of "whataboutism."[53] "Scientists around the world," often "leaders in areas of advanced research that are strategic priorities, are targeted by [the CCP's] well-funded sophisticated engagement that plays on their vanity, naivete, and greed," noted a Canadian scholar in 2021.[54] There are also former and current autocrats and dictators, large and small, even in the West, who benefit from the PRC's money and moral justifications. Some observers have openly asserted that many "top Western elites" appear to be "cheerleaders for Xi's China."[55]

Beyond the less noble motivations, the rising and often genuine concerns over allegedly "global" issues in addition to war and peace, such as climate change, pandemics, human suffering, and terrorism, provide additional justification and momentum for a world government that, as I have attempted to argue, is much more likely to become a China Order–like world empire than a Kantian "Federation of Free States."[56] The CCP-PRC state therefore has a chance to capture the imaginations of the self-serving and the high-minded, the powerful and the humble—and this support, together with Beijing's possession of world-class resources, could give it a realistic chance of winning the China Race. A China Order for the whole world may eventually not even be Han-Chinese dominated; its power center may not necessarily be located in today's China; it may not even bear the name of China; but it will most certainly change the course of human civilization. The ever-improving and ever-more-"humane" Westphalian system, under the iteration of the LIO led by the US, with its expanding "universal" rights for everyone equally, in fact harbors the genes and the energy that could allow a determined power to remake it. Hot wars with unimaginable physical destruction and death may result from the China Race; but a full-scale, once-and-for-all USA-PRC war is in fact much less likely than constant, non-kinetic warfare resulting in piecemeal gains that eventually add up to a tipping point of final victory for the CCP, which can cleverly avoid repeating a Pearl Harbor–style showdown. The CCP is known to emphasize "political warfare [. . .] to win without fighting."[57] The well-justified horror of modern warfare may in fact neutralize resistance and enable the determined challenger who, by its DNA, cares much less about the cost of war or failing its people.

When a democracy faces off with an autocracy under a de jure or de facto Westphalian system, it may indeed enjoy certain distinct and decisive advantages.[58] It is theoretically convincing and empirically proven that democracies are often superior and more peaceful than autocracies under the Westphalian system. A worldwide democracy, a centralized federation populated by similar or even identical democracies, may be the ideal polity for human civilization, as envisioned by influential advocates like Clarence Streit long ago.[59] If the CCP promises or even appears to democratize China—Beijing's well-documented insincerity and duplicity aside—then a world order under the world-uniting PRC might still be quite acceptable. However, as a proposition discussed in chapter 1 of this book, a world government, even one started and led by a democracy, when unconstrained and unchallenged by peer forces, has a much greater propensity (even an inevitability) to become an authoritarian or even totalitarian regime of world empire than to adhere to democratic rule of law. This is because democracy (or a federal system), which is based on rules and compromises, is not nearly as natural a way of establishing and executing public authority for governance as autocracy. The maintenance of democratic rule of law, just like social etiquette, whether at the dinner table or on the playground, requires deliberate and constant efforts to maintain and must be adjusted through continued education, socialization, and internalization. The authoritarian tendency identified in all human organizational life requires conscious and constant efforts to mitigate.[60] This is especially the case at the national and global levels, where the stakes are high and "external" intervention to fortuitously slow or reverse that trend is both rare and costly. Constant external competition akin to the peer pressure of socialization is key to ensuring a chance for democracy in politics. Internal constraints, even under a federal/feudal system of democratized power, are not themselves enough to ensure that a sole sovereign power remains in check. Therefore, a lone and externally unconstrained world government is almost certain to degenerate into an autocratic regime of world empire or a dysfunctional

158 | The China Race

polity, in which case costly global "civil wars" would drag humanity back into raw international political anarchy, a de facto and less desirable Westphalian order, just like what happened in the Chinese world numerous times before—the cycles of "world" unity and "world" civil war that devastated and stagnated the Chinese people for many centuries.

The US-led worldwide LIO, the post–Cold War iteration of the de jure Westphalian world order is more preferred to a de facto kind but undergoes pressures and produces impulses for political globalization, and perhaps is already approaching the functional limit of a rules-based international coalition without itself morphing into a global governance or world government and toppling the Westphalian system. The dysfunction of the World Trade Organization and many other international institutions in the 2010s and 2020s, the setback of "humanitarian" interventions since the 1990s, and the prolonged and overblown "global war" on terrorism since 2001, especially after the destruction of al-Qaeda and particularly the invasion of Iraq in 2003—akin to a serious allergic overreaction—have all raised alarms.[61] As mentioned earlier in chapter 1 of this book, a key insight about human nature is that unconstrained power corrupts and drives even "good" people to quickly become evil, especially under the "right" conditions, such as a putative sense of need, uncertainty, danger, or fear.[62] The "natural" inclination and impulse for authoritarianism over democracy, and centralized power (and "solutions") over decentralized competition, in combination with the power of the enabling modern technology (produced by competition under democracy) could win the China Race against the imperative for democracy and the Westphalian world order.[63] The power of the CCP-PRC state in a systemic transformation of the world order and hence a redirection of human civilization, therefore, could in fact be much mightier and more far-reaching than the material capability Beijing seems to possess and exercise. Thus, a critical challenge for the US-led West in the China Race seems to be to outcompete the PRC without becoming a bigger PRC—to preserve democratic rule of law and the Westphalian system, without creating a China Order under a different name. This situation calls into mind the monstrous rebirth of the "dragon slayers" described by the philosopher Friedrich Nietzsche.[64] One may also look to the moral of Georgie Orwell's brilliant story *Animal Farm*, or the Burmese legend depicting the tragedy of brave young heroes who slay the evil dragon for the villagers but always end up becoming the evil dragon themselves.[65]

The State of Sinology

The epistemological challenge in discerning the nature and implications of the rising power of the CCP-PRC state, and that of the PRC-USA rivalry and the overall China Race, has often been compounded by the rather sorrowful state of Sinology (often termed *China studies*), particularly in the US. The confusion and hesitance in perceiving, reporting, and heeding the message regarding the meaning and the magnitude of the China Race have been truly remarkable given the consequences of inaction. In 2021, while some American Sinologists were openly bemoaning the "ending" of the US policy of "engagement" toward China since the late 1970s and wondering what the community of China scholars might have done differently to perhaps avoid that fate, some PRC analysts were pleased by their knowledge that many Sinologists in the West had effectively "protected and aided" the "overlooked" rise of PRC power.[66]

Countless complex and contentious volumes have been produced about China by some of the brightest people, especially in recent years, as Beijing has become undeniably more assertive and powerful.[67] In 2018, a volume including writings by some of the most established scholars in the field addressed 36 major questions about China.[68] A report by the Center for Strategic and International Studies (CSIS) proposed a "policy framework" of "seven Chinas."[69] Months later, a RAND report suggested that it is better to use accommodation and dissuasion to maintain the rising Chinese power as a "conditional supporter" with an "expanding role" in a collaborative, "shared," multilateral world order.[70] Then, possibly signaling an awakening, two former senior managers of America's China policy (both rejoined the government in a similar capacity in 2021) wrote in 2018, in *Foreign Affairs*, concluding that the United States had basically gotten it wrong about China for decades.[71] A year later, a Task Force on US China Policy comprised of some of the leading American Sinologists and former senior officials and diplomats published a report with the apt title *Course Correction*, advocating a more "effective and sustainable China policy." Together with a few other published pieces, the task force acknowledged the US failures in dealing with the PRC and the inevitable shift in the distribution of world power. It pointed out the sour mood about Beijing and "the sharp deterioration of the U.S.-China relationship," but was cautious about what to do about the rising PRC power and ambition.[72] In short, the suggestions by some of the best American minds on China seemed to remain a reasonable but hesitant blend of doing the usual and going with the flow, working rather than racing with Beijing, and keeping hopes high so that both sides might exhibit enough flexibility and pragmatism for continued coexistence with accommodation.

In 2020, amid the middle of the PRC-originated COVID-19 pandemic, which swept the world with staggering death and financial ruin, an unprecedented but perhaps justified "global backlash against China" by elites and the general public emerged.[73] The reactions of mainstream Sinologists and China hands, however, still featured ambiguity and hesitance, mixed with tenacious hope and goodwill, based on diverse conjectures. An edited volume published in 2020 (likely composed before the pandemic) offers an impressive survey of various aspects of the PRC's foreign policy, featuring a consensus among the 15 well-established China watchers that experts should simply provide "a full and detailed understanding of the complexities of China's progressive integration into the international order."[74] Among many of the keenest observers of China, wishful thinking and goodwill about the one-fifth of our fellow human beings under CCP rule seem to remain as strong and earnest as they are seemingly misplaced and inept. In early 2021, a RAND report found "a much more significant threat to vital U.S. interests from China than from Russia," yet, citing several Sinologists, called for further and more accommodation of the PRC, including "giving up" Taiwan and the South China Sea, as part of its advocacy for US restraint and retreat worldwide.[75]

In 2021, a group of leading American scholars of China studies openly admitted that the era of "engagement" with the PRC was probably over and that the discipline had perhaps suffered from extensive inaccuracies, stupor, whimsies, and tardiness. Many, if not most, however, seemed to express more sorrow and defensiveness than the delight of awakening from their misapprehensions and correcting mistakes with the passing of a "flawed" strategy—one in which they had invested enormous amount of energy and time, often believing that it was Xi personally, rather than the CCP inherently, that had doomed the engagement policy.[76] The same Task Force on US China Policy mentioned earlier issued its third report in 2021 with a sharper tone. It identified, among other things, the "surprising sense of siege on the part of the Chinese government," which is "overly centralized," and that "Beijing has done more to 'decouple' its supply chain from dependence on the U.S. than the other way around." It provided a long list of specific policies, however, that appear to be quite incoherent and fragmented, and that are lacking the underpinning of a holistic strategy. Some of the otherwise thoughtful ideas seem disjointed and mutually contradictory, with traces of wishful thinking.[77] In early 2022, a dean of American Sinology, who has been barred by Beijing since 1989 for his association with Chinese political dissidents, called the "existential threat" from the rising Chinese power politicized rhetoric "strengthening fascism in the United States," since China does not really have "an alternative vision for the world order" beyond its own national security needs.[78]

It is quite curious, and perhaps also reflective of the state of the China Race and Beijing's rising influence in the West, that the latest calls for reframed, different, and more forceful measures from the West in response to the PRC have often come from outside the "mainstream" community of Sinologists or China scholars. Moreover, these warnings and entreaties almost automatically draw fire from many of those more established in the field. In fall 2020, in the prestigious forum of *Foreign Affairs*, a group of prominent China hands derogatorily labeled a noted political scientist (who is, however, not quite a major Sinologist) a "hawk" for his call to "push back against Beijing" as "an answer to aggression." The accused was obliged to explain that he was not for "total decoupling but partial disengagement," and did not really harbor "regime-change impulses" toward Beijing.[79] It seems many established Sinologists and China specialists tread the lines vigilantly and tactfully, dismissing harsh ideas about the CCP-PRC as self-evidently wrong and inherently sinful. Months later, in April 2021, *Foreign Affairs* published on its website an article by a PRC scholar calling for a "new engagement consensus" featuring "a Chinese vision of global order" to be co-led by a PRC-USA "G2 of responsible stakeholders."[80] Hawkish or dovish, it went without much rebuttal.

The state of Sinology in the West, and particularly in the US, may be indicative of the limits of the cultureless liberalism and relativism in the West—in a paradoxically illiberal turn, to pass judgment upon an "alien" political or cultural entity seems to forfeit one's precious status as a purveyor of liberal intellectual values.[81] As Thomas Sowell has discovered, intellectuals in the West are often "grossly and disastrously wrong in their prescriptions" based on various utopian "visions of the anointed" rather than real-world considerations.[82] This phenomenon is observable in Sinology. As a Sinologist and economist concluded in 2021, there were "wrong" readings and "failed" anticipations of the political economy in the CCP-PRC by the profession, which "did not reckon with the incredibly robust and comprehensive power of the Chinese Communist Party," "did not foresee" important features of the party-state, and was "extraordinarily slow to perceive [. . .] and it has hampered our response to the China challenge."[83] Like the many Western (particularly American) intellectuals who have misread and over-applauded the post–Cold War globalization, countless Sinologists appear to have simply and consequentially misinterpreted the nature, mind, and actions of the CCP.[84]

According to a sociological study of the Sinologist/China hand community in the US, published in 2022, a "paradigmatic turnover away from engagement" among US China experts took place only after 2017, driven by "three processes: *politicization, professional status competition, and personalization*" or "three forms of struggle: political, professional, and personal."[85] The vocal critics of the standard, four-decade-old China "engagement" policy have usually been less established, nonmainstream, nontraditional, or even marginalized China watchers, including ex-military and ex-intelligence officials and journalists, as well as experts previously outside the limelight.[86] Some of the most penetrating and insightful analyses of CCP-PRC strength and strategy to undermine and destroy the West and the US by means of ploys aiming "to strangle you with your own systems"—such as freedom of speech, open markets, open information, and equal human and civil rights—have been articulated by people associated with organizations considered by many Sinologists to be fringe or tainted.[87] On the other hand, as a former US national security official has lamented, some highly regarded American sages are "decades late in recognizing China's aggressive nature."[88] In late 2021, just as the US-led West seemed to be starting to view the rising PRC power as a common "global challenge," two American scholars put out essentially identical articles in two of the most influential forums to extenuate the concern about Beijing's global ambitions and capacity with a call for a mixture of understanding and acclimatization of a jittery CCP leadership, whose power may have already "peaked," and measures to "deter" the PRC from launching a hot war out of desperation.[89]

It is remarkable that, for about four decades now, many established and noted Sinologists and China hands of both Chinese and non-Chinese ethnicity in the West have closed ranks to cautiously avoid upsetting Beijing, frequently bending over backwards to defend and "help" the PRC, and unilaterally justifying engagement and appeasement policies even where these policies have evidently failed.[90] I have personally heard many stories of well-established Sinologists quietly and earnestly advising their pupils and protégés to avoid being seen as "unfriendly" to their PRC hosts and interlocutors lest they offend the CCP and "lose the [career] valuable access to China." I have also witnessed some well-known American China experts demand the removal of their names from the published reports of relatively insignificant research sponsored by the US government because Beijing "might not like" the reports, as they touch on "sensitive issues" like Taiwan. Yet the same people have no problem openly publishing criticism of US leaders using language like "rogue government" and "insane policies," calling it folly and evil for the US to possibly have "a Cold War mentality" in dealing with the PRC. As one colleague dryly noted, attacking Washington is always safe and likely profitable; criticizing Beijing is risky and career-damaging, even outside the PRC.[91] Indeed, anecdotes recounting heavy and skillful influence by the CCP abound in the field of Sinology, illustrating the real fear of consequential retribution by the vengeful and resourceful PRC state.

For decades, many, if not most, highly recognized and widely published Sinologists and prominent China experts or China hands have not made the critical distinction in their discourses between the CCP and China, and between the CCP-PRC state and the Chinese people. Such a rudimentary mistake seems embarrassingly common among even the most established China experts, often leading to well-intended but faulty predictions and abysmal prescriptions.[92] On July 4, 2019, 100 Sinologists, scholars, and former senior officials in the US signed an open letter published in the *Washington Post*. With the apt title of "China Is Not an Enemy," it called for a restoration and continuation of the four-decade-old China policy.[93] Sensible points and goodwill notwithstanding, the letter, drafted by five well-known Sinologists and China hands, appeared to conflate the CCP-PRC regime (and its consistent mission and recent policies) with the Chinese people and the respectable and justified interests of China the country. Four days later, a rebuttal published online with the title "China Is Not an Enemy of the US and the World, but the CCP Is" was authored by three certainly lesser known Sinologists belonging to a three-year-old "China political risk consultancy" based in New York.[94] Two weeks later, another open letter was published in a small outlet urging the US government to "stay the course on China," departing from the past policy. It was drafted by a retired US Navy captain (intelligence officer), and its over 100 signatories were distinctively less

164 | The China Race

famous, with only a handful of Sinologists.[95] Some may therefore have reason to suggest that the CCP "has been able to capture a significant portion of [the Western] China policy elite class and let them do China's bidding in the corridors of Western capitals and think tanks, where the U.S. is under constant criticism for our alleged 'China bashing' and other American sins by 'fringe lunatics' who have impure and incorrect thoughts about the CCP regime."[96]

Worrying about the quality of decision-making in Western democracies, some have lamented that "ignorance, especially of anything related to public policy, is an actual virtue," and so "a cult of ignorance in the United States" has led to rejection of established expertise, with significant consequences.[97] Worse still for the discourse on US China policy, it seems, even the established expertise itself appears to be often beleaguered by ignorance and biases of several kinds.

A Study of China Studies

My cursory look at the meager state of Sinology in the West, and particularly the US, suggests that the field of China studies itself could use a good study, in order to become more apt and accurate, given the ultrahigh stakes of the response to the rising power of the CCP-PRC state.[98] Granted that the sheer size and volume of information from China, with the many existing "myths" and the countless manufactured distortions, can easily frustrate even the sincerest and most diligent observers.[99] Vast amounts of material published on China end up being "simplistic, 'surface readings' of PRC behaviour," according to a political scientist.[100] Here, I will offer only partial observations to hopefully start the discussion and highlight where improvements might be attempted, in order to reach a fuller understanding of the CCP party-state, and better assistance to the aim of competing well in the PRC-USA rivalry and the China Race—for the West, the Chinese people and, ultimately, the world. It will certainly take significant efforts by many more people to update and upgrade Sinology in the West. A legitimate and consequential question to begin with seems to be: Why is Sinology (or China studies) in the West in such a doleful state?

The existence and energy of the "useful idiots" mentioned earlier, and the powerful and increasingly documented efforts by CCP agents and surrogates, "old friends," in disguise or in the open, likely all matter.[101] The CCP's influence appears to have extensively permeated the US, from federal and local governments, universities and think tanks, to corporations and social groups, fully justifying the need for American "vigilance."[102] Additional pervading Sinophile characteristics in the West may also play considerable roles. Since the 1950s or earlier, the US (and the West at large) has had a rather paternalistic, monopolistic, and even centralized lineage of producing and promoting Sinologists, with prized positions and rewards allocated based on connections (*guanxi*), patronage, and deference to existing (or even dead) authorities that "lazily repeat false narratives for too long."[103] In the scathing words of a prominent Chinese-American scholar, influential American Sinologists, including masters like John King Fairbank, for many decades were "wrong almost every time in predicting the CCP."[104] The "professional status competition" in the field seems to have led to a quite unique erudition, featuring the long and persistent "influence and epistemic hegemony of the elite China hands" with long-standing ties to the PRC.[105] Consequently, the leaders and luminaries of the field have become increasingly inbred and form a stable hierarchy reinforcing their positions. Thin scholarship, group-thinking and wishful-thinking, echo-chambers, and self-censorship among many Sinologists in the West have helped to facilitate "the China fantasy" that "got China wrong" collectively and continuously, thereby sustaining "one of the biggest strategic miscalculations of the post–Cold War era."[106] Between the so-called "Blue Team" and "Red Team" or the caricatured "Dragon Slayers" and "Panda Huggers,"[107] established Sinologists seem to automatically lean toward the latter and shy away from the former. Moreover, as recounted by a leading American scholar on China, some US Sinologists appear to be more eager to help the PRC in keeping its access to Western science and technology than to protect fellow colleagues disliked and "punished" by the CCP.[108]

In the West, Sinology or China studies often seems to have degenerated into "asylums for dilettantes and refuges for mediocrities," as some of the finest in the field warned 60 years ago.[109] According to two separate reports, among the hundreds of most-cited political scientists in the United States (and the world), none appears to be a Sinologist.[110] Some who have written influentially about China using ancient metaphors like the so-called Thucydides's trap, on the other hand, seem to know little about the country, much less the CCP-PRC state.[111] Soviet and CCP agents in American organizations like the Institute of Pacific Relations (1925–60) seem to have left some marks

166 | The China Race

on the ideology genealogy of Sinology in the West. Perhaps people, over time, consciously and subconsciously emulate and even become their subjects of study, especially when constantly bathed in the powerful and alluring fumes of authoritarianism, the culture of emperor-envy and head-slave mentality, and the pleasure and rewards associated with the refined, "dialectic," and mesmerizing but illogical wordsmithery, games of concepts and games of numbers well-brewed over centuries under the Qin-Han polity.[112] A PRC scholar observed in 2020 that the "mostly white" American Sinologists tend to "like China more the more they study China."[113] Though often personally warm, polite, kind, and even deceptively humble, as erudite Confucian patriarchs or matriarchs are supposed to be, quite a few influential Sinologists seem to act, forcefully and above all else, in the interest of their authority and positions, much like revered Legalist patresfamilias.

Perhaps it is also the language and cultural barriers that are responsible for the embarrassing naivete and striking superficiality displayed among many China watchers. Many if not most of the non-native-speaking Sinologists in the West tend to have limited command of written Chinese; they barely converse orally and are rarely able to write comprehensibly in Chinese.[114] Precisely because of the awareness of such handicaps, perhaps, many established Sinologists in authority tend to eagerly display and emphasize their "nuanced understanding" of China and their critical and even exclusive access to the PRC. Consequentially, such an "attempt to nuance the debate over US China policy" may miss important facts and the big picture, risking continuing the "four decades of head-in-the-sand thinking on China."[115] One researcher sharply concluded in 2021 that many Sinologists and China-watchers "keep talking nonsense about Chinese words" used by CCP wordsmiths who are in fact culturally unsophisticated and ideologically impoverished; those "spurious dissections" of exotic, "cryptic and arcane" Chinese characters are often passed off as "impressive sociolinguistic insight" and mesmerizing shortcuts to interpreting precious nuances and profound meanings that are actually nonexistent.[116] "Access," or the simple permission/visa to visit the PRC to presumably conduct fieldwork or "exchanges" there, often in lieu of solid research to cover up a deficiency in knowledge, has become a coveted prize among Western Sinologists, and has been cleverly used by the CCP to influence and intimidate.[117] To oblige and even ingratiate, or at least not to irritate or risk possibly offending or antagonizing, the party-state, is an unspoken norm commonly observed in the behavior of many Sinologists.

This dynamic perhaps started with CCAS (the Committee of Concerned Asian Scholars), a group of "pacifists, anti-war liberals, new leftists, Maoists, enlightened academics and many others," which initiated visits and "access" for China specialists to the PRC in 1971.[118] This group, which has had an outsized and lasting impact on China studies to this day, has been maligned by some fellow Sinologists for projecting its populist values onto China, "polarizing the field," and uncritically "romanticizing" and promoting Maoist doctrine.[119] The "reorganization" in 2020–21 by the Hong Kong Chinese University of the fabled University Service Centre for China Studies, a "mecca to China researchers" since the 1960s, only signals the further CCP control of access and information.[120] Perhaps a simple "follow the money" cui bono would help to decipher the naivete and timidity exhibited by many otherwise intelligent academic elites in the West who, despite their seemingly impeccable record of independent and liberal thinking, often ignore or mask the obvious, such as the fact that "you can't offer a liberal education in an authoritarian state."[121]

Similar to other "regional studies," like Sovietology, Sinology in the West is often stuck in a catch-up game attempting to just explain, with meager or even nonexistent ability to predict.[122] Unlike Sovietology, where native-speaking experts, often first-generation immigrants and exiles, are highly noted and even instrumental,[123] Sinologists originally from China are often seriously hampered; they are "grossly under-placed and under-appreciated," as noted privately by an old friend of mine who is a major non-Chinese Sinologist himself.[124] Beyond the barriers of language and culture, which usually impede the publication and promotion of nonnative speakers of English in social science, humanities, and policy discourse, the émigré Sinologists in the US since World War II have certain peculiarities that are noteworthy. Many of them often exhibit the strong residue of their previous education in the CCP-PRC (and to a lesser extent in the KMT-ROC, the Republic of China, led by the Kuomintang, the Nationalist Party). Such education typically leads to an inadequate practice of scientific methodology, a more confined spirit of free and independent inquiry, and a heavy dose of Sinocentric values and concepts in the reading of history and facts, even by some of the most established émigré Sinologists.[125] Many of them habitually prize and pursue a mission of benefiting and bolstering China, holding a lin-

168 | The China Race

gering and often misplaced but genuine sense of duty and responsibility to China (frequently meaning the regime of China) and displaying a simulated "neutrality," as mostly soi-disant "bridges" or intermediaries between their ancestral land and their chosen homeland, sometimes with traces of inexplicable trepidation toward the West, where they are actually based or educated.[126] Some working in US think tanks openly declare their mission to be "fairly explaining Chinese foreign policy from Chinese perspectives [and] in the language Americans can understand."[127]

Such a sense of identity, attachment, mission, and obligation is frequently romanticized, dignified, and justified by the so-called culture of nostalgia or homesickness for hometown (*xiangchou*), the cherished value and virtue of reminiscence and belonging for the ancestral land that is commonly associated with ancestor worship and the natural religion of earth worship—both of which tend to be prevalent in more stagnant and paternalistic agrarian societies and apparently not exclusively Chinese.[128] In the era of the post–Industrial Revolution, however, such a sentiment for hometown has dwindled worldwide due to the twin forces of population mobility and urban development. In just 2010–20, at least 360,000 villages, or 13% of the total number, have vanished in the PRC.[129] As perhaps part of its nature as a premodern polity, however, the CCP has long heavily politicized, skillfully magnified, and extensively used and abused this natural but passé sensation as an effective part of its United Front scheme.[130] In May 2022, for example, the PRC ambassador to the US (who became the PRC foreign minister months later) openly told an elite Chinese-American civic group, the Committee of 100, that "yellow-skinned" Chinese-Americans are forever "naturally connected to China"; they therefore must always work to improve PRC-USA relations, since "no egg will survive when the nest is overturned."[131] Many immigrant scholars from China seem unable to transcend this increasingly imagined sentiment for ancestral land; by contrast, Chinese intellectual giants like Bai Juyi (772–846) and Su Shi (1037–1101) wisely did so long ago with their healthier attitude that "my hometown is wherever my soul is at peace."[132] Among many Sinologists with Chinese heritage, there seems to be a lack of the enlightened view that "*la patrie sans justice est la prison*" (homeland without justice is prison) by the French statesman Georges Clemenceau (1841–1929); the confidence of the German writer Thomas Mann (1875–1955) who declared in exile that "German culture is where I am"; or the stance that has been often, though perhaps inexactly, attributed to the American sage Benjamin Franklin (1706–90)

The PRC-USA Rivalry | 169

and the Chinese scholar Hu Shi (1891–1962): "My country is wherever liberty/freedom is."[133]

Such educational and cultural residues, attachments, and sentiments have often limited the freedom and independence of many ethnic Chinese Sinologists (and ethnic Chinese movers and shakers) in the West, especially among first-generation immigrants. These individuals have also been routinely and cleverly targeted, used, and manipulated by the CCP-PRC state for its United Front ploys, with perks, access and pay, and playing to their vanity, in ways similar to but decisively more abhorrent and aggressive than those of many other foreign governments, including the earlier KMT-ROC.[134] Interestingly, quite a few established non-PRC Chinese scholars and notables in the West have managed to seamlessly morph from KMT loyalists to CCP surrogates over the past three decades, as many Chinese elites did back in the 1930s–50s under the successful United Front program of the CCP.[135] Some Chinese-American scholars who formerly supported the KMT had no problem cheering for "the era of Xi Jinping" and the grand "second rise of China," which would lead to a "Pax Sinica" for the whole world.[136] A noted exception is perhaps Ying-shih Yu.[137] While masterfully advancing a critical study of the history of Chinese culture and gallantly maintaining his principles before the autocracies of both the KMT and particularly the CCP, however, Yu still devoted great efforts to "rediscover" and glorify the "inner-core" values of Confucianism—the paternalistic ideology of an agrarian society, and the traditional Chinese institution of gentleman-scholar-official (*shidaifu*) in the Confucian-coated Legalist political governance, as the approximation, complement, and even somehow equal of the post-Enlightenment liberalism, humanitarianism, and democratic rule of law in the West.[138]

All this has created peculiar, lingering, and somewhat-warranted perplexity, misperceptions, misgivings, and even distrust in the West about China-born and raised Sinologists. Some Sinophile, nonnative-speaking China experts, who are otherwise linguistically and culturally uncompetitive and unperceptive, are naturally inclined to seize an easy opportunity in a rather Chinese way: to effortlessly and somewhat justifiably marginalize or even exclude immigrant or exile Sinologists, commonly reducing them to the unvoiced secondary role of mere research assistants and data collectors, at a profound cost to the quality of research and education about China.

Finally, perhaps the problem is that many influential China watchers in the West, especially among the nonnative speakers, are frequent visitors

170 | The China Race

to the PRC but are essentially only occasional tourists and pampered guests. They tend to lack the sociocultural "feel" and hence miss many contextual and underlining nuances, and are all closely monitored and cleverly "managed" during their visits.[139] Many if not all are constantly monitored, indulged, and spoiled, with exceptional hospitality, and spoon-fed well-cooked delicacies, perks, benefits, and pleasures along with the official party lines.[140] As a corner-cutting substitute for the hard work of research, "understanding China" in this way gives the CCP excellent opportunities to easily handle and "work" the visitors "at home court"—a polished extension of its prized "thought work" or brainwashing.[141] Even a leading émigré Chinese-American historian with a mastery of Chinese culture, was capable of being deceived by the CCP into writing "a series of articles" propagating the party lines, which he years later openly regretted and wanted to "forget."[142] When a visiting US president demanded a meeting with Chinese people, which the CCP could not refuse, every detail was meticulously planned and rehearsed as a show of perfect deception—down to who showed up, where they sat, what they said, and when they said it.[143] President Barack Obama, for example, vividly recalled in his memoir how doggedly and comically the CCP tried to hack, surveil, and follow him and the American visitors during their time in China.[144] The party-state reportedly harasses and frames critics and protestors in the West as well.[145]

Countless idealistic and friendly Westerners, particularly Americans, have devoted their talent and time to helping the Chinese people and often directly the Chinese government, resulting in profound accomplishments and lasting impact, but also great disillusionment and disappointments.[146] Undying idealism and friendliness and perhaps other reasons, however, seem to have locked many of them into obliging the CCP-PRC state. It is remarkable to see how a number of wise, able, and influential US leaders, officials, and scholars seem to have been hypnotized by the luster of the realpolitik rapprochement with the failing CCP-PRC, and to take that tactic, originally intended to counter the Soviet Union in the 1970s–80s, as a lasting, historic success.[147] Perhaps operating under an egoistic delusion reinforced by the lure of being treated as "friends of the Chinese people," they appear incapable of anything but knee-jerk calls for ever more "understanding" and accommodation of the PRC, thus perpetuating the misexecuted, incomplete, often abused, and substantially obsolete "engagement" as a panacea.[148] Unsurprisingly, being treated as a dear friend or a deadly enemy "of China" is entirely up to the CCP's momentary and fickle political wishes, and thus highly tenuous and often reversable.[149] In human epistemology and action, the proposition of the causality between understanding and liking something often has neither logic nor evidence. It is sensible and increasingly fitting, after all these decades, that often the more Westerners get to know the CCP-PRC, with expansive and persistent efforts, the stronger their reasons for detesting and distancing.[150] Therefore, those "friends" of the PRC in fact just end up experiencing a form of "cognitive dissonance," making endless excuses in the name of ever more "understanding" of something that has been in plain sight for decades, effectively defending and assisting the CCP party-state in the China Race.

Reframing the Paradigms

I have attempted to outline the necessity, desirability, urgency, and achievability for the West and the world, including the Chinese people, to engage and prevail in the China Race versus the CCP-PRC state so as to preserve the liberal iteration of the Westphalian system. To manage and triumph in the global rivalry between the PRC and the USA is at the heart of the Race. For that effort to reach fruition, a reframing of the paradigm for action, or thinking outside the box, has been long overdue. Labels that have recently been applied to the PRC, from strategic partner, cooperative rival, strategic competitor, and competitive coexistence, to sworn enemy, all reflect various paradigms with consequences.[151]

The West and particularly the US should holistically and assertively reaffirm the principles and desirability of the Westphalian world order, reconsider and reorient the US-led post–World War II globalism, and reassess the application of the universal and post–Cold War equal values that have characterized much of American foreign policy for decades. To be sure, these values, as stated in the 1948 United Nations' Universal Declaration of Human Rights, are also shared by the Chinese people, whose representatives like Peng Chun Chang literally participated in the drafting of the Declaration.[152] More specifically, an open recognition of and a conscious effort to consistently distinguish the CCP and the PRC state from China and the Chinese people is a critical step for the US to efficiently devise and launch precision strikes against CCP ventures with minimum collateral damage to the Chinese people. The creation of the "US House Select Committee on Strategic Competition between the United States and the Chinese Communist Party" in early 2023 appears to be an appropriate signal. The reasonable and benevolent US/Western policy of offering blanket engagement since the 1980s, particularly after the late 1990s, has transformed China greatly, with enormous tangible and intangible benefits for many if not all. China has already been irreversibly affected by its membership in the WTO, for example, with remarkable economic growth and considerable sociocultural diversification, progress, and Westernization.[153] But the CCP regime, with its structural incompatibility with and inherent hostility toward the West, has successfully managed to maintain a selective engagement, a partial coupling or partial decoupling, with the West. Thus, it has so far survived with its new power to predictably undermine the West with a vengeance, seeking an ultimate recentering and reordering of the world in its image. Consequently, "this Party/state and its doctrine are the biggest threat the United States and the free world have ever faced," and Beijing wants "a radically transformed international system," a world radically different from that of today.[154]

The CCP, not China, therefore, should be the target of concerted efforts toward diminution and transformation, through firm containment and smarter and more selective engagement, this time at the choice of the US. Sharply targeting the CCP as "the central threat of our time," in solidarity with the Chinese people, is a new paradigm that shall profoundly adjust and reorient the US China policy.[155] A narrow distinction could also be made between the CCP-PRC's foreign ventures and internal Chinese affairs, between Beijing's actions abroad and its governance at home, in order to increase the accuracy and efficiency of managing the China Race. Such distinctions are intellectually not novel ideas but have rarely been articulated and contemplated by China watchers and policy-makers in the West in recent decades. A reframed paradigm should help to minimize or even avoid the wasteful and abhorrent racial-ethnic biases the China Race might otherwise produce against Chinese-Americans and even Asian-Americans.[156] Such a paradigm shift likely has hit the Achilles's heel of the CCP with a potent lethality, as evidenced by Beijing's extraordinarily angry and frightened responses to the message and its messengers—calling, for example, the then US secretary of state "the public enemy of humanity," as opposed to the traditionally vilest sins of "public enemy of the people" (or class, revolution, or China), and a "political virus" that is "anti-world," for his rhetoric of distinguishing the CCP from the Chinese people.[157] In July 2021, Chairman Xi Jinping conspicuously protested, in a way that mimics the acute puncturing of a very sensitive nerve and well illustrates the ancient Chinese idiom of "three hundreds taels of silver are not hidden here" (a very poor lie which actually reveals the truth), by publicly exclaiming, "Any attempt to separate the Chinese Communist Party from the Chinese people and contrast the two is bound to fail! The more than 95 million party members do not accept [such an attempt]! The more than 1.4 billion Chinese people do not accept [that attempt] either!"[158]

Understandably, any shift of paradigm is arduous, often personally unpleasant, and carries considerable cost and significant risks. Identity and esteem are at risk, and "years of scholarly labor" could be wasted, as a sociologist sharply observed regarding the China field,[159] not to mention status, influence, funding, and even culpability. But a paradigmatic shift is necessary, generally beneficial, and mostly manageable for running the PRC-USA rivalry and the overall China Race well. "Knowledge, humility, and honesty will be the things that help the outside world deal with the historic challenge of China's rise," commented a seasoned observer of China in 2020.[160] Indeed, back in 1997, I myself not only wrote an article titled "To Incorporate China: A New Policy for a New Era" for *The Washington Quarterly*, published by the Center for Strategic and International Studies (CSIS), but also actually lobbied in the halls of Washington for granting the PRC "most favored nation" trade status delinked from Beijing's record of human rights violations, in hopes of peacefully incorporating and changing the PRC through the engagement of open and preferential trade and exchanges.[161] It took me a few years and a timely personal awakening to see and say in places like the *New York Times*, starting in 2005, that, without sufficient internal sociopolitical changes and constraints, the rise of the PRC power would be a disaster for the world and for the Chinese people.[162] The engagement policy as it was being practiced was simply inadequate. In 2017, I published *The China Order*, the first prequel to this book, also launched through CSIS, to report on the deep institutional and ideological incompatibility between the CCP-PRC and the West. In 2023, I published *The Chinese Record*, the second prequel to this book, to report on the feasibility and undesirability of the CCP-PRC as an alternative world leader.

Though perhaps overdue, it is never too late to change one's mind and actions, based on evidence and reasoning. The influential *New York Times* columnist Thomas Friedman, after cheering for globalization and praising Chinese economic successes with admiration for many years, for

174 | The China Race

example, publicly admitted in 2022 that he "was wrong about Chinese censorship," and then voted for "Chexit" to decouple the PRC, with a new investment motto of "A.B.C.—Anywhere But China."[163] With the proper and timely reframing of paradigms, the US and its allies still have ample and formidable tools and leverage to address and manage the rise of PRC power, preserving and improving the current world order through highly feasible, affordable, and sustainable efforts. As a leading scholar of the liberal international order has written, the CCP-PRC is set to "tilt the world away from democratic values and the rule of law," and the US needs "the partnership of other liberal states [. . .] in reclaiming the core premise of the liberal international project: building the international institutions and norms to protect societies from themselves, from one another, and from the violent storms of modernity."[164]

Skillful management of the PRC-USA rivalry and the overall China Race will not be easy. It requires a serious and comprehensive appreciation of the nature and strength of the CCP-PRC state. The Qin-Han polity certainly has a clear record of political suboptimality and socioeconomic underperformance as well as a cost-ineffective foreign policy, as I have attempted to demonstrate in this book and its two prequels. Such suboptimalities, deficiencies, and flaws could certainly be rewardingly explored and exploited. Yet, with its historically tested and proven strengths of extraction, manipulation, and mobilization, the Qin-Han polity could have great staying power in the PRC and beyond, resisting sociopolitical changes that would alter its international objectives and worldviews. It is fully able to muster great military and diplomatic resources even without an optimal economy or good governance for its people. Unscrupulousness, a trait that is disproportionately prominent in authoritarian rulers, is always a key source of power and a means for a determined dictator to win the seemingly unwinnable. Like the Qin Empire in the 3rd century BCE (and many other victorious world empires in their respective worlds), the PRC could mobilize, concentrate, and apply world-changing force even with suboptimal socioeconomic development. It is now also greatly aided by its almost unfiltered access to the latest technology in the West and worldwide resources through its gaming of the world trade regime and its exploitation of global interconnectivity. The PRC thus does not need to be innovative and optimal to possess leading-edge technology, great economic resources, and alluring financial power.[165] Some of the best Western technology is readily and "dangerously" acquired and mismanaged by the PRC in real time by transfer (or gifting) of sensitive technology, like the P4 biolab in Wuhan, nuclear processing, and Airbus plants.[166] Massive collaboration between Western and PRC scientists over the years has directly and extensively assisted the PLA, according to a consortium of European investigators in 2022.[167] While the West is strictly banned from data collection of almost any kind in China, PRC state-owned firms have built a "dozen partnerships with hospitals and labs in the US" to store and process the biodata of "up to 80% of Americans." When the US government developed a breakthrough battery technology, it took almost no time for it to simply "give it away" to the PRC.[168]

The CCP-PRC state therefore is both destined to *and* has the capacity to fundamentally challenge not just the leadership of the US and the West, but the basic world order that has existed since the 17th century. The distribution of power in the international system and the very ordering principle of the units in the system, the two fundamental paths for systemic change in the world order described by the realist and constructivist theorists of international relations, are both affected.[169] The CCP-PRC is realistically threatening, in another vernacular, to significantly shift the balance of power in the Westphalian system and redefine the leadership and legitimacy of that system.[170]

The China Race is about the future of the world, the fortunes of human civilization, and the well-being of the Chinese people, who are not inherently less or more deserving, peaceful, or militant than any other people. China, as a nation- or multination-state, is capable of being a full, peaceful, content, and contributing member of the international system. However, as a sharp young observer from the PRC concluded, "[t]he Chinese, as any people, are capable of great cruelty, especially when violence is incited and institutionalized by the state."[171] To prevail in the China race, the West must recognize and act on the fact that the CCP-PRC rule of force and ruse has misled and misinformed the Chinese people for generations, in the same way as the great German and Japanese peoples were corrupted and intoxicated by their fascist and militaristic leaders in the 1930s–40s. As an informed interviewee based in Beijing repeated to this author many times in 2020–22: "We the Chinese people are now often as immoral, ignorant, and liable as our leaders; we need liberation and detoxification."

It is obviously a matter of principle to treat the Chinese people the same as any other human beings; but it is crucially important to have the wisdom and courage to treat PRC citizens, especially the yet-to-bedetoxified ones, with the necessary and justified vigilance. To manage the China Race, the world must treat the CCP-PRC state as a pariah state harboring a secretive gang. A civilized, rule-abiding player cannot play high-stakes competitions in a civilized and rule-abiding manner with an unscrupulous, manipulative, and gaming player that has long been determined to destroy its competitors and take over and remake, not just "win," the contest. The PRC state needs to be treated as an abnormal state with a clear record of atrocities, injustice, and deception. The CCP regime openly flouts the key values and norms of most other nations, especially those of the West, and so it should be belittled, chastened, segregated, and shunned. Many Chinese people, especially the elites, are the willing or unwilling accomplices and executioners of the CCP. They unfortunately must bear some of the culpability until they wake up and take their lives and their fates into their own hands. The victory by the West and the world in the PRC-USA rivalry and the overall China Race is in the long-term best interest of humanity, including the Chinese people; but it is a mission that is larger than China and much more important than some PRC citizens' temporary interests or feelings, many of which are contrived, distorted, and arrogated by the CCP.

In 2020, an international survey found that in countries with many recorded issues of mismanagement and suffering related to the COVID-19 pandemic, a significant percentage of people understandably assigned their governments low scores: 37% in the UK, 36% in Iran, 26% in France, and 41% in the US. Even in places where the management and results of the pandemic were widely recognized as better, people were still critical of their government's job, with approval scores of only 50% in Taiwan, 48% in Singapore, 41% in Germany, 31% in South Korea, and 16% in Japan. In China, the pandemic's origin, the government imposed draconian measures and only offered the public very opaque and openly doctored information, yet a whopping 86% of Chinese approved of their government's performance, much higher than in any other country.[172] In 2022, another survey by a major public relations firm found that "trust in government" was 82% in Saudi Arabia, 74% in Singapore, 53% in Canada and France, 42% in South Korea and the UK, 39% in the US, and 36% in Japan, but 91% in China, the "world's highest" for several years in a row.[173] Probable inaccuracy of the supposedly anonymous Chinese opinion data due to fears in a country without freedom of speech, and possible data manipulations notwithstanding, this twist illustrates the success of the CCP's information control and manipulation of "thought work" or brainwashing; it also likely reflects a lack of critical and independent thinking among many if not the majority of PRC citizens. With this in mind, the detoxification of the minds of the Chinese people in order to transform the CCP-PRC state seems both imperative and challenging.

As an ethnic Chinese who prizes my Chinese heritage and culture, I am fully aware that the PRC-USA rivalry and the China Race involve inevitable and perhaps required "collateral damage" to both PRC citizens and non-PRC people of Chinese (and even Asian) descent. It is thus obviously agonizing to see the need for a "whole-of-government," "whole-of-society," and "whole-of-the-world" approach to win the China Race for the West and the world including the Chinese people. Racial, ethnic, and other identity-based biases and bigotry always exist in all nations, not least of all in China. Therefore, to run the PRC-USA rivalry and the China Race well, it is essential to keep the public alert and take effective legal measures against racism and discrimination in the West, which has been qualitatively better than most other nations in managing the discriminative impulses and actions inevitable in any sizable human grouping. Lists of the worst episodes of modern American racial prejudice and political persecution often include the Jim Crow laws, the rise of the KKK, and McCarthyism in the 1950s, all of which are very unlikely to repeat in force, and none of which come even close to the countless and grave acts of discrimination in today's PRC against the various segments of the Han majority, not to mention non-Han peoples and foreigners, Africans in particular.[174]

Managing the China Race well for the world and the Chinese people includes, therefore, respecting, cherishing, and advancing the Chinese people and their accomplishments and aspirations. The CCP-PRC state itself deserves to be restricted, weakened, and transformed. A clear and loud message to the Chinese people might be like this: resisting, disobeying, disabling, and transforming your government and its policies, especially its foreign ventures, is imperative, or you cannot and will not receive the equal treatment as a great people that you fully merit. In the China Race, some PRC citizens, especially the ruling elites (as well as Beijing's beneficiaries and "friends" all over the world) might necessarily be viewed as CCP accomplices, pending their verified repentance and actual change. This is not an issue of human rights or civil rights, nor is it discrimination or exclusion based on who the Chinese people are or what they have. Rather, it is about the behavior of collaborators and its consequences.

178 | The China Race

It is both unwise and unnecessary for the West and the US to target every person of the massive CCP-PRC state, as there are deep fault lines and hidden (and even not-so-hidden) dissentions inside the party-state that could be nurtured and used. Ultimately, short of a full-scale, world war–like showdown, it is the job of and by the Chinese people to settle their scores with the CCP. However, it is the CCP regime, not just one singular leader, that "presents a serious problem for the whole of the democratic world."[175] A targeted effort to single out the high echelons, especially all those who are responsible for grave deeds, rather than just one specific person or the entire nation, will be more effective. After all, as I have detailed in *The China Record*, the CCP-PRC ruling elites only comprise about 3% of the 98 million CCP members, and are fewer than 0.2% of the 1.4 billion Chinese people.[176] The vast majority of the Chinese people, including many members of the CCP, could and should be allowed, encouraged, and assisted to build up their reason, will, and energy to transform their own government and take charge of their own destiny. To rid the world of what the Chinese people have long endured, the suboptimal, the undesirable, and the disasters, amply justifies new paradigms and actions for prevailing in the PRC-USA rivalry and the overall China Race.

The Reorientation of US China Policy

The recent history of US China policy seems to suggest that, while the CCP has sped up its drive in the PRC-USA rivalry and the overall China Race, the US and the West have also reoriented themselves. After the Great Recession of 2007–9, Beijing sensed an opening and came out of the self-preserving defensive stance it had taken since the late 1980s. The ascent of Xi Jinping, starting in 2012, launched "regressive" politics in the PRC, epitomized by the cultivation of a new cult of personality surrounding the leader, and his pursuit of personal rule for life as Mao II, both of which were legalized in early 2018 and cemented in 2022.[177] Warning signs, ranging from the rhetoric of the China Dream to actions like the Belt and Road Initiative and the fortification of artificial islands in the South China Sea, compelled American leaders of both major parties to fully reexamine their China policy.[178]

The glacially paced but substantial change in US China policy has taken place in stages over the past two decades, mostly as reaction to the aggressive foreign ventures of the increasingly rich and powerful CCP-PRC state. As one seasoned scholar of international relations noted, "the effort to confront a rising China began long before Trump."[179] The Bush Administration started calling the PRC a "strategic competitor" in 2001 and pledged to defend Taiwan "with whatever it took," but then quickly got distracted by the 9/11 attacks and the subsequent global "war on terror," only to return in its second term with a new India policy aimed at rethinking "the lengthening shadows cast by China's growing power."[180] Realization slowly emerged in the West that the CCP had successfully taken advantage of anti-terrorism to suppress Chinese Muslims and the Chinese people in general.[181] Considering how Beijing systematically continued "evading, bending, or breaking just about every agreed-upon rule of international commerce," a response in-kind emerged as a growing bipartisan consensus around 2009, to counter "China's gaming of the international trading system," though this effort was weakened and hampered by the Great Recession.[182] A PRC analysis in 2022 traced the "qualitative change of US China policy" to 2009–10, triggered by issues like the rising tensions in the South China Sea.[183] With its Pivot to Asia and especially its effort for the Trans-Pacific Partnership (TPP) as an upgraded international trade regime substituting for the World Trade Organization (WTO), which has been dysfunctional in addressing Beijing's duplicitous mercantilism, the Obama administration pushed the reorientation of China policy further, albeit still subtly.[184] Years later, Obama recalled his realization as president that, "[i]f any country was likely to challenge U.S. preeminence on the world stage, it was China," while believing such a challenge "was still decades away [. . . and will] most likely happen as a result of America's strategic mistakes."[185]

American rhetoric and actions departing from the decades-old China policy proliferated with the 2016 election as US president of Donald Trump, who vowed to be "tough on China." Trump probably took this stance more to capitalize on the rare bipartisanship in Washington centered around the reorientation of China policy than out of any innate anti-China or anti-CCP conviction. With the US-PRC tariff war that started in 2018, a relocation/reshoring of certain production and supply chains out of China, the so-called friendshoring or allyshoring, as part of "decoupling" on West's terms, has accelerated in 2022–23.[186] As described by a RAND researcher, a realization emerged that, "at its core, the United States and China are competing to shape the foundational global paradigm—the essential ideas, habits, and expectations

180 | The China Race

that govern international politics. It is ultimately a competition of norms, narratives, and legitimacy."[187] Whatever his motivation, Trump, according to a noted columnist, "forced a long-overdue reckoning within the United States over China's audacious foreign-influence operations, horrific human rights abuses, and creeping digital despotism. Ironically, this awakening was one of the biggest foreign-policy victories of Trump's fractious term in office."[188] In 2020, a bipartisan group of leading US foreign policy experts called candidly for a technology race and a grand strategy of "smart competition" to "blunt China's illiberal order" and to "struggle for power."[189]

The Trump administration was heavily unilateral in its approach to countering the CCP-PRC, quitting some multinational institutions such as the World Health Organization (WHO), a UN agency that allegedly misbehaved under undue influence of the PRC.[190] The heat increased with suspicions and allegations about the origin of the COVID-19 pandemic—a mismanaged jump of the virus from bat to human, or a lab leak of some supercharged "gain-of-function" virus in Wuhan that was the result of research partially financed by US government grants—which indeed put the PRC in the crosshairs for its opacity and noncooperation and even alleged bioweapon programs.[191] This increased concern was evident in other Western nations as well; clear warnings about how "time is running out for the West to stop China's global takeover," and "we Westerners shouldn't be too naïve" about the CCP's ambition for global leadership to replace the LIO with an "authoritarian century" appeared in the UK and the EU.[192]

Specific policy recommendations by influential analysts for "implementing [a new] grand strategy toward China" were published by the Council on Foreign Relations in 2020, though not exactly authored by the usual Sinologists.[193] Writing about relations with the PRC, a former US military leader openly warned that "[w]inter is coming. And we have much to do to prepare."[194] Sharp outcries became louder, urging the US to push back against "China's threat to world order" and combat the CCP's "six-front war on America's economy, military, diplomacy, technology, education, and infrastructure."[195] Exposés have detailed the CCP's extravagant cultivation of influence on Wall Street in particular and the West in general.[196] Leading China watchers who have long advocated "cooperation with criticism" with the PRC started, semi-privately, to ponder the hard choice "between desirable containment and dangerous containment" of Beijing by mid-2020.[197] In mid-2021, the RAND Corporation issued its "analysis of Chinese international and defense strategies to outcompete the United States," summarizing the reoriented American views and concerns about "China's quest for global primacy," which is inevitable, methodical, formidable, and consequential.[198]

The US Congress held an open hearing on "Beijing's promotion of alternative global norms and standards" in March 2020.[199] In May 2020, the White House issued its Strategic Approach to the PRC, officializing a significant departure from the decades-old paradigm with a China policy "guided by a return to principled realism," singling out the CCP (as distinct from China and the Chinese people) and advocating an all-government and all-society response to the rising PRC power and policies. It instructed, "first, to improve the resiliency of our institutions, alliances, and partnerships to prevail against the challenges the PRC presents; and, second, to compel Beijing to cease or reduce actions harmful to the United States' vital, national interests and those of our allies and partners."[200] Soon after that, US officials delivered a series of speeches on the PRC with quotable words like this from the US attorney general, a nontraditional spokesman on US China policy:

> The CCP rules with an iron fist over one of the great ancient civilizations of the world. It seeks to leverage the immense power, productivity, and ingenuity of the Chinese people to overthrow the rules-based international system and to make the world safe for dictatorship. How the United States responds to this challenge will have historic implications and will determine whether the United States and its liberal democratic allies will continue to shape their own destiny or whether the CCP and its autocratic tributaries will control the future.[201]

The Anticipated Zigzags

The latest reorientation of the US China policy has had an interesting formulation and execution. Donald Trump had encountered broad and open distaste and rejection from the established elites of his own party since before he was elected president. In an unprecedented move, 75 former senior diplomats released an open letter on September 21, 2016, in opposition to Trump. Just about all leading China hands of the Republican Party, not to mention those of the Democratic Party, openly or semi-openly vowed never to serve Trump if he were elected.[202] These open and strong opinions and actions by the so-called Washington establishment of both parties may explain why Beijing, seriously dismayed by the Obama administration's Pivot Strategy and TPP move, mobilized its resources inside and outside the US, without much disguise, to support and enchant Trump, who was supposedly an unworldly and pliable businessman and could sow conflict and discord in Washington.[203] The Trump administration had an unusual lack of the uninterrupted expertise of the two parties, which had taken turns employing an essentially similar China policy for four decades. That interruption contributed to the sharper reorientation, steered by a group of rather unestablished and untraditional experts and policy makers.[204] The dynamic internal US politics thus made Trump a "disrupter,"[205] allowing for new people and ideas about China to emerge inside the Beltway. Events like Beijing's strangulation of Hong Kong and the COVID-19 pandemic, highlighting the severity of the threat of the CCP-PRC state, provided the suitable backdrop.

Some conservative political warriors became persistent voices warning about the CCP-PRC as the biggest threat to the US.[206] Kenneth Weinstein, who is not strictly a Sinologist, declared a "new Cold War between the U.S. and China" in early 2019.[207] In July 2020, via the unusual messenger mentioned earlier, the FBI director, Washington outlined the following: Beijing poses "the greatest threat to American economic and national security," a threat that is not from the Chinese people but "the government of China and the Chinese Communist Party," and the CCP "is in a generational fight to surpass" the US and "in a whole-of-state effort to become the world's only superpower by any means necessary."[208] In July 2022, joined by his British counterpart, the MI5 chief, the director repeated the same warning about a global "game changing challenge" from the CCP.[209] Trump's national security adviser, a former US Army lawyer, openly wrote that the US policy toward China had been "a miscalculation that stands as the greatest failure of U.S. foreign policy since the 1930s" and the CCP had become a worldwide "threat to the idea of democracy itself, including in the United States."[210] Under the directorship of Peter Berkowitz, a political scientist who had lost his litigated tenure-bid at Harvard University, the Policy Planning Staff of the US Department of State, with a large role played by Miles Maochun Yu, a US Naval Academy history professor who had immigrated from the PRC more than three decades before, published *The Elements of the China Challenge*, which included a list of "ten tasks" to fend off the CCP's worldwide challenge to freedom.[211] In the waning days of the Trump administration, the director of national intelligence openly wrote with all the authority of his office that,

> [i]f I could communicate one thing to the American people from this unique vantage point, it is that the People's Republic of China poses the greatest threat to America today, and the greatest threat to democracy and freedom world-wide since World War II. [. . .] Beijing is preparing for an open-ended period of confrontation with the U.S. Washington should also be prepared. Leaders must work across partisan divides to understand the threat, speak about it openly, and take action to address it. This is our once-in-a-generation challenge. Americans have always risen to the moment, from defeating the scourge of fascism to bringing down the Iron Curtain. This generation will be judged by its response to China's effort to reshape the world in its own image and replace America as the dominant superpower. The intelligence is clear. Our response must be as well.[212]

According to an insider, however, the disruptive Trumpian zig of US China policy featured disconcerting politicization and careless discordance.[213] Some critics have pointed out that President Trump, despite his tough and sometimes inflammatory rhetoric, was in fact enacting a China policy of "bluster masking appeasement," with almost all key issues "decided in China's favor." It was only during its final months that the Trump administration decreed actions like delisting PRC firms on Wall Street, which were beyond symbolic moves like closing a consulate (in Houston) and imposing some visa restrictions.[214] Nevertheless, the new discourse and policy moves, dubbed by the national security adviser as a national awakening "to the threat posed by China,"[215] have continued since the tumultuous 2020 election. A form of "Trumpism" without Trump seems to have taken hold in some aspects of American politics, including the US China policy.[216] Consequently, "China looms large for Biden," who, commentators have asserted, "must not fall into China's smooth relations trap" and "should reinforce Trump's transformation of China policy."[217] Indeed, there has been a clear continuity in the reorientation

184 | The China Race

of US China policy since 2021.[218] Chinese commentators and analysts have observed this and quickly accused it of being "Trumpism with a new face," and "even more vicious."[219]

The reorientation of US China policy appears to enjoy a strong bipartisan support.[220] The US Congress has passed, with very rare unanimity, several bills opposing the CCP-PRC since 2018. The 2020 Democratic Party platform had changed from four years prior, adopting language almost identical to the Republican Party platform (which was the same for 2016 and 2020) regarding China and Taiwan. President Joe Biden, beyond his strong stances on China on the campaign trail, has put forth more-consistent criticism of the CCP on human rights grounds without President Trump's flattering of the CCP leaders.[221] Back in August 2020, candidate Biden condemned the CCP policy in Xinjiang as "genocide," a grave labeling that Trump's secretary of state Michael Pompeo officialized on January 19, 2021, the day before leaving office, and Biden's secretary of state Antony Blinken reaffirmed later on the same day.[222] In December 2020, the bipartisan US Congressional Commission on China issued its 500-page annual report detailing the "U.S.-China global competition [. . .] for power and influence," including a long list of recommended actions.[223] On January 5, 2021, the departing national security advisor declassified and released the 2018 *United States Strategic Framework for the Indo-Pacific* 21 years early, with the explicit hope of continuing the reoriented US China policy following the change of administration.[224] In 2021–22, President Biden repeatedly reaffirmed President George W. Bush's 2001 declaration that the US would defend Taiwan if the PRC attacked it. With sweeping efforts to selectively decouple, or "de-risk," from the PRC in areas such as the semiconductor industry, Biden was viewed in late 2022 as "all-in on taking out China." The latest National Security Strategy and National Defense Strategy of the United States, both released in October 2022, simply declared that "the PRC remains our most consequential competitor for the coming decade" and the US must "outcompete China" since "the PRC is the only competitor with both the intent to reshape the international order and, increasingly, the economic, diplomatic, military, and technological power to do it."[225]

Biden's senior appointees in areas related to China seem to include no Wall Street types, setting the administration apart from all others since the 1990s. The new diplomacy, defense, and intelligence chiefs all openly told the US Senate that they concurred with the previous administration on the reoriented China policy, though they might disagree on some tactics.[226] President Biden himself openly shared his predecessor's view about the critical importance of the US-PRC competition.[227] His administration quickly acted to continue and expand the Trump-era measures countering the "China technology threat," including a ban on American ties with additional PRC entities.[228] In March 2021, Biden issued his *Interim National Security Strategic Guidance* to reaffirm the 2017 National Security Strategy, with a sharpened focus on the "strategic competition" with China.[229] Senior officials in charge of China policy in the Biden administration reaffirmed that "the era of engagement with Xi's China is over" and the US "is determined to out-compete China."[230] In July 2021, the director for China in the US National Security Council, a rising Sinologist of a new generation, published a book analyzing the CCP's profound "long game" of displacing the US-led world order, and advocating a grand but "asymmetric" US strategy to counter the PRC.[231] In 2022, in a very rare public speech, the CIA director declared the PRC to be the greatest and most formidable "worldwide" challenger to the US "for as long as we can see."[232] In April 2023, the US secretary of homeland security publicly called the PRC "an especially grave threat" to the US homeland that "does touch all of our Department's missions." With a more methodical approach, a more multilateral effort, and multiple toolkits, the Biden administration appears to be pursuing the same course and may in fact be "harder and more threatening," as acknowledged by senior PRC analysts.[233]

To be sure, the reorienting US China policy has not yet reached a full rerun of the Cold War, at least not the same fight between the same two European ideologies, even though there are American calls for a "hard break" with the PRC.[234] As one seasoned observer noted in summer 2021, Biden's foreign policy team, somewhat similar to that of his predecessor's, "says China is the priority, but [. . .] lacks China expertise."[235] This truancy of the so-called establishment of Sinologists and China hands seems to suggest that the profound reorientation of China policy is still a work in progress. A rising star Sinologist, tirelessly represents quite a few in advocating that the CCP is reacting abroad aggressively or not according to its sense of insecurity, rather than running an ultrahigh-stakes "ideological competition" against the US and the West; that it is unwarranted for the US to focus on competition with the PRC, since "Westphalian principles" could coexist well with the CCP's way of governance if the West could just adjust its LIO to accommodate more of the Chinese "illiberal" authoritarianism at home

186 | The China Race

and abroad; and that the PRC-USA rivalry is somehow automatically the same as a dreaded zero-sum competition.[236] Reacting quickly, an official PRC analyst openly praised such views as "the rational voices in the US debate of its China policy," to hopefully help in "averting [a PRC-USA] crisis and creating new opportunities" for Beijing.[237] In October 2021, *Foreign Affairs* asked 65 "authorities with specialized expertise" (mostly Americans) to comment on the proposition "U.S. foreign policy has become too hostile to China." The answers, unsurprisingly, were literally all over the place, suggesting a clear lack of consensus among the specialists.[238] A year later, in November 2022, the Brookings Institution released a report advising on US China policy, with the ideal: "to manage inescapable points of competition without resorting to confrontation or conflict."[239] To compete with the PRC while openly pledging to be conflict- and confrontation-averse, an admirable intention that is as nice and thoughtful a wish as it is a deluded and unviable strategy, appears to continue ensnaring many "China hands" in the US.

In practice, while facing the historic Russian invasion of Ukraine in 2022, Washington seemed to stay focused on its competition with the PRC but still "try to limit damage to the U.S.-China relationship."[240] As always, in the absence of a total national mobilization, a pluralist, liberal democracy necessitates disagreement and contestation, experimentation and setbacks, hesitations and dissents, compromise and adjustment, even within the ranks of the same party.[241] Therefore, Washington is naturally and fully expected to undergo zigzags and ups and downs in the PRC-USA rivalry and the overall China Race ahead.[242]

The China Race in the United States

As mentioned earlier, Beijing has always focused on the United States as its main rival in the China Race. Since World War II, the CCP has understood and appreciated, directly and indirectly, the might of American power and the unbridgeable gulf between its political mandate and American norms. To surpass the US in power by possessing more raw capability or simply usurping American power and to replace Washington as the leader of the usurped international community have always been burning desires and an open dream for CCP leaders. From the fiasco of the Great Leap Forward under Mao to today's all-out and omnidirectional competition, Beijing plays all games in the China Race to catch up and outdo.[243] Based on my interviews and readings of PRC officials and analysts over the past four decades, very few if any in Beijing genuinely believe that the US is not beneficial and positive for China and the Chinese people. But, as I have attempted to analyze, the political logic of the CCP regime drives the PRC to deceive and intoxicate the Chinese elites and the Chinese people endlessly about an American plot to annihilate "us Chinese." In response, the CCP has been doing just about everything and anything possible to resist, reduce, and replace the United States, in order to recenter and reorder the world. The open and pluralist society of America itself has quite logically been a major battleground for the CCP's total war on America for resources, influence, and power. The PRC-USA rivalry and the overall China Race, therefore, have become prominent in the United States. Beijing's action is directly consequential in the US: for example, a team of American economists has found that there is a direct correlation between the PRC's state-supported growth of certain industrial sectors and the subsequent decline of the same sectors in the United States.[244]

The rather direct business and personnel connections, and the influence that Beijing has obtained through those connections, have reportedly reached the highest levels of the US government, including the families of former Presidents George Bush and Donald Trump, the two-time cabinet member Elaine Chao and her husband US Senate majority/minority leader Mitch McConnell, and others like former Secretary of Commerce Wilbur Ross.[245] Similar allegations about leaders in the Democratic Party, including Presidents Bill Clinton and Joe Biden and their families, have been around since the 1990s.[246] Both parties are reported to have ceded ground to Beijing on important issues.[247] Venerable US media organizations may have given in to extortion to suppress negative reports about CCP leaders.[248] Revelations since 2021 have shown how "cooperation" between some Western and PRC scientists has led to a deep and complex web of money and politics that, allegedly, might have turned the noble course of catching and preventing coronaviruses into a global pandemic.[249] According to exposés in 2022 and 2023, a toxic brew of greed, corruption, hypocrisy, misguided impulses, and misplaced good intentions has over three decades led many American movers and shakers, from Henry Kissinger and Madeleine Albright to the Bush family and Rob Iger, and many others in business, journalism, Hollywood, Silicon Valley, nonprofit groups, and universities, to become agents "for Chinese influence," "making China stronger," and "push Chinese talking points" at the expense of the US.[250] In the words of the US attorney general and his FBI director, the CCP has successfully used bribery, infiltration, and extortion to build deep and extensive connections and influence in corporate America, higher education, and the media-exertainment complex.[251]

The CCP-PRC state has emulated but far exceeded its political rival in China, the KMT-ROC government, which once actively lobbied Washington through politicians and think tanks. The infamous old China Lobby, however, faded in the early 1970s. It was partially revived as a Taiwan Lobby after the 1990s to quite effectively advance Taipei's new interest of defying Beijing.[252] The powerful and much better funded new China (PRC) Lobby is now viewed by some as rising strong, though not yet reaching the same level of effectiveness as the fabled Israel Lobby.[253] The PRC was reported for its active interference "on both sides of the 2020 [US] election."[254] Accompanying the CCP's extensive persuasion, propaganda, and disinformation, the unrestricted recruitment and use of ethnic Chinese in the US (often with non-PRC lineage) has played a special, important, and "expanding role" in ensuring Beijing's political influence.[255] Sinologists in the US seem especially vulnerable to temptation and coercion; Beijing openly ranks and praises, for example, about 158 American Sinologists as "scholars who comprehend China," often offering them special attention, access, and privileges.[256]

Since the 1970s, the PRC has invested massively to cultivate friends and sympathizers in powerful financial institutions, major and minor think tanks, serious and trivial journals, and prestigious and lower-tier universities in order to influence Americans and the West.[257] Some of these allies have indeed acted like enthusiastic agents and apologists for Beijing. In the late 2010s, China (including Hong Kong) was the largest source of foreign donations to US universities, reportedly contributing almost twice as much as the second-largest source, Britain.[258] Many big capitalists on Wall Street seem to have paradoxically become strong supporters of the Chinese Communists, pocketing quick profits and eying the often-illusive greater earnings.[259] The US NBA (National Basketball Association), among others, is reported to have silenced its players critical of the CCP so as to keep its lucrative market in the PRC.[260]

In 2020, at a time when cross-Pacific political tensions were rising rapidly, "five big US banks had $70.8 billion exposure in China"; Wall Street giants like Goldman Sachs, Morgan Stanley, and JP Morgan all eagerly cheered Beijing's new (but characteristically baseless) promise of "opening its $45 trillion financial market this year."[261] In July 2021, the trio "shamelessly [. . .] collected millions of dollars" for the IPO of the PRC firm Didi, a giant knockoff of Uber, on Wall Street despite the fact that 30% of the billions Americans invested in it evaporated in just four days when the CCP ordered the firm's app offline "for state security concerns."[262] Ben Meng, the deputy chief investment officer of the PRC's State Administration of Foreign Exchange (recruited through the CCP's "Thousand Talents" program) was appointed chief investment officer of the $400-billion Californian State Pension Fund right after he finished his 3-year job in Beijing.[263] Li Lu, one of the 21 most wanted student leaders of the 1989 Tiananmen Uprising, became a successful venture capitalist in exile and founded Himalaya Capital to specialize in investing in the PRC, and persuasively promoted, in the 2010s, the "different but great" growth potential of the Chinese economy.[264] In 2020–21, Ray Dalio, chairman of the mega investment firm Bridgewater, argued enthusiastically for more confidence and investment in the PRC, where "the fundamentals clearly favour" growth in comparison to the US.[265] Some of the best-known American firms seem to have bent to Beijing's will. Apple, for example, has reportedly compromised its famous privacy policy for presence and profits in China.[266] In 2021, LinkedIn made a non-Chinese member's profile not "viewable in China" for its listing of his China-related publications, before it was forced to scale back its operations in China for fear of espionage.[267] The consultancy McKinsey and Company, long bullish about promoting the Chinese economy, blindly cheered Beijing's new edict in late 2021 that "China offers a $5 trillion consumption growth opportunity over the next decade."[268] BlackRock Inc., the largest American asset manager, which also manages the entire US Federal Retirement Thrift Investment (except its G Fund), became the first foreign company to run mutual funds in China in August 2021, a move that was soon criticized by the billionaire-activist George Soros (who funded the NGO Open Society) as a "blunder" that will cost BlackRock clients billions of dollars and also "imperils the U.S. national security."[269]

The China Race in the US seems to have scored quite impressively for the CCP in other, softer but still potent, ways. For example, a Harvard University team declared in 2020 that 81% to 96% of Chinese were happy with the CCP based on its 17-year "survey" in the PRC.[270] A University of California San Diego team announced in 2020 that

190 | The China Race

its "survey" found that among the Chinese people, 89% trust the CCP and 86% "prefer living under China's political system."[271] Another study in English by a supposedly German team concluded in 2020 that only 46% of Japanese and 49% of Americans thought their respective countries were democracies, but over 73% of Chinese believed the PRC was democratic.[272] What is not disclosed, however, is that these and many other similar opinion surveys about China are mostly if not all done through PRC contractors, of whom I personally know quite a few, with the implicit or even explicit vetting and approval of the CCP. To treat the findings from such influenced studies as factual seems more than just sloppy and misinforming: it risks passing on CCP number games as scientific discoveries. They may be "better-than-nothing," but are inherently faulty in their methodological premise—that the Chinese people could freely speak their minds on sensitive political subjects to foreign-funded interviewers.

For years, the influential Brookings Institution has released reports about the democracy-approximating faction politics and "collective leadership" inside the CCP, and Beijing's "leadership role" in anchoring the world.[273] A University of Pennsylvania "global list" ranked PRC "think tanks" as peers of think tanks in the West.[274] A leak in 2020 revealed that a renowned sociology professor at Princeton University had been serving as the "chief academic adviser" of a Beijing-based "research" entity for years, advising the CCP on using AI and big data for opinion monitoring and social control through censorship and disinformation, such as that presented "internally" in the wake of the death of the whistleblower Dr. Li Wenliang during the COVID-19 pandemic.[275] That entity appeared to also work closely with the CCP to smear Didi, the Chinese knockoff of Uber, on its "American ties."[276] In 2021, the flagship journal of American economists published an article by PRC scholars showing the "positive impact" on rural basic education of the 16 million urban students "sent down" to the countryside by Mao during the Cultural Revolution. This premise was based on complex and refined-looking mining of official data, mainly from PRC-era chorography books that leading Chinese specialists of the historiography of chorography have openly deemed "often fake and useless."[277] This is akin to arguing for the positive impact of Moscow's internal exiles to the Gulag Archipelago on Siberian society or the Arctic region based on local Czarist-Stalinist official reports.[278] A tenured faculty member at the London School of Economics, the Harvard-educated child of a senior CCP official, has prolifically defended

Xi's policies, promoted "China's steroids model of growth," cheered for "China's role in the new global order," and doubted if the West "can ever understand China."[279]

Major American newspapers like the *Washington Post*, famed for reporting the Watergate scandal, published many issues of the CCP-edited *China Daily* inserts at the price of $250,000 each.[280] Known CCP agents have published repeatedly in major US journals, chanting "Xi Jinping is a 'Good Emperor.'"[281] It was curious to see the editor-in-chief of the respected medical journal the *Lancet* straying far out of his field to decry the "anti-China" racism in the West when different questions about the origin of the COVID-19 virus were raised.[282] At the same time, the chief of the leading British think tank Chatham House openly extolled the "economic opportunity," based on the PRC's official GDP figures and the need for a "stronger and richer China," regardless of what Beijing was doing at home and abroad.[283] Through funding interlocutors and intermediaries, and sending staff and visitors, the CCP seems to have successfully peddled its party lines and policy preferences as academic and policy reports, with influential names like the UN, World Bank, IMF, Asian Development Bank, and foreign universities, think tanks, and media outlets.[284] Perhaps to inundate and "take over," "academic" research and policy essays from the PRC now increasingly flood Western outlets of China studies even when those outlets are commonly banned or restricted in China. In 2021, for example, the *China Quarterly*, a leading journal of Sinology that is mostly banned in the PRC, received 37% of its over 400 paper submissions from the PRC plus 12% from Hong Kong, as compared to 12% from the US and 9% from the UK, where the magazine is based.[285] American colleges, including elite schools like Harvard and Princeton, have reportedly felt the chilling impact of the CCP-PRC on freedom of speech in their classrooms.[286] Similar effects of CCP power in the China Race have been felt in academic institutions and the media in many other Western countries, from Australia to Singapore and Switzerland.[287]

At the same time, the ultraselfish CCP elites, and even leaders, with their characteristic perfidy, often regard the US as the ideal place for their families and their fortunes. Many "sons and daughters" of CCP leaders have landed cushy jobs at major Western financial firms on the strength of their promised lucrative connections.[288] Beyond the massive cross-Pacific trade, investment and travelers, hundreds of PRC businesses (mostly state owned or controlled) have launched mega IPOs on

192 | The China Race

Wall Street. Chinese venture capitalists have snatched quite a number of American assets and talents in places like Silicon Valley, including iconic landmarks like the Waldorf Astoria New York. The CCP-PRC state itself has built a significant presence in the US. For over a decade since 2010, the PRC held over $1 trillion in US Treasury bills ($1.3 trillion in the mid-2010s and $981 billion in May 2022), accounting for about 16% of total US government debt and 26% of US government debt owed to foreigners.[289]

This situation evidently increases the complexity and difficulty for the legalistic and capitalistic US to pull itself together and race against Beijing. Some may rationally resign themselves to the fact that the PRC is already critically important and even decisive to the fortune of the Americans, hoping instead to strive for even the faintest possibility of win-win cooperation, as it is in their own financial interest. This standard stance of many American economists and businesspeople has also been frequently echoed by foreign policy experts.[290] Others justifiably fear that a full rivalry with Beijing will just lead to a senseless and futile "Pyrrhic victory."[291] A leading specialist and practitioner of US China policy warns of the coming of "a potential tragedy in U.S.-China relations and a potential tragedy for the world," and suggests "six areas in which the United States and China should seek cooperation," especially with regard to the effort to deal with the pandemic.[292] The potential impact on US allies, forcing them into the uncomfortable position of choosing sides, seems to only exacerbate the concerns about confronting the PRC.[293]

The Glacier in Motion

Slowly but steadily, as I have outlined, there has been a profound reorientation in US China policy in recent years.[294] Typical of a pluralist democracy under no unanimously recognized present emergency, the change in national attitude and policy is slow, full of hesitance, second thoughts, pauses, curves, counterforces, and even reversals. Like a glacier, however, once the flow has started, the earth-moving force is hard to stop before it has run its course. "China has already decided Cold War II has begun and [. . . is] escalating," observed the chief of the Atlantic Council; three years later, the president of the Heritage Foundation reaffirmed in 2023 that "[i]t is time to acknowledge reality: The United States is in a New Cold War with the PRC."[295] And the US urgently needs a new foreign policy including "retrenchment, restoration, and reinvention" to cope, argued the chief of the Carnegie Endowment.[296] A noted historian, who coined the eye-catching term "Team Chimerica" in 2008, illuminatingly reversed himself, describing the Chinese app TikTok as an "ugly digital fentanyl" in 2020 and warning about "the coming Chinese imperium" for the world and a Cold War II.[297] The basic strategy of US China policy of the past four decades, generally named engagement, was viewed by many in the 2020s as "dying in practice [and] already dead in spirit."[298] In 2022, a "clash of empires" is seen in a "new Cold War" between the USA and the PRC.[299] In 2021–23, a whopping 83%–89% of Americans (highest in decades) viewed the PRC unfavorably and "consider China a competitor or enemy" and nearly half "think limiting China's power and influence should be a top foreign policy priority for the U.S., up from 32% in 2018."[300] The mighty glacier seems to be in full motion.

The PRC-USA rivalry and the overall China Race in the US have picked up momentum since 2018, when the US and PRC started a trade war, which soon intensified after the SARS-CoV-2 virus moved out of Wuhan, China, to cause a global pandemic in 2020.[301] Rhetorically at least, the US and the CCP-PRC seem to have openly entered a Cold War–like confrontation by mid-2020 at the latest, as the then US national security adviser declared that America had finally awoken to the threat of the CCP and would "resist the Chinese Communist Party's efforts to manipulate our people and our governments, damage our economies, and undermine our sovereignty. The days of American passivity and naivety regarding the People's Republic of China are over."[302] Whether Americans fully agree with President Trump's characterization of the PRC-originated COVID-19 pandemic as "worse than Pearl Harbor and 9/11 attacks" and mobilize to action accordingly depends on more and better knowledge about the origin and the spread of the disease, as investigations may discover more, in the "narrative arms race" between the PRC and the US over the origin of the pandemic.[303]

Even before the pandemic, the notoriously partisan and polarized US Congress passed China-related bills unanimously or near unanimously many times, showing cooperation very rarely seen on the Hill and openly touching on some of Beijing's declared "core interests" like Taiwan, Xinjiang, and Hong Kong. This reflects the strong bipartisan consensus behind the reorientation of US China policy that I have discussed earlier, and the massive ground shift in American politics. In

194 | The China Race

May 2019, the House unanimously passed a resolution reaffirming the US commitment to Taiwan and the Taiwan Assurance Act of 2019. Then the updated Taiwan Allies International Protection and Enhancement Initiative (TAIPEI) Act of 2019 was passed by both chambers unanimously during October 2019–March 2020 and signed into law on March 28, 2020. Both chambers passed the Hong Kong Human Rights and Democracy Act of 2019 unanimously before it was signed into law days later on November 20, 2019. The Uyghur Human Rights Policy Act of (2019) 2020 was passed by the Senate twice unanimously and the House twice by votes of 407–1 and 413–1 during September 2019–May 2020, before being signed into law on June 17, 2020. On July 14, 2020, the Hong Kong Autonomy Act of 2020, having also unanimously passed both chambers of Congress, was signed into law. Since 2021, such rare bipartisanship regarding US China policy appears to have continued in Washington. In addition to the comprehensive United States Innovation and Competition Act, which explicitly uses the US-PRC competition as a pretext, Congress passed three China-specific bills with basically unanimous votes, including the Uyghur Forced Labor Prevention Act, which was promptly signed into law within days on December 23, 2021.[304]

Democrats have openly shared Republican sentiments about the fundamental "incompatibility" between American and CCP institutions and objectives since 2019.[305] The former Democratic presidential candidate Hillary Clinton, long known for her "globalist" views, wrote in late 2020 about China, using language of great power competition that was almost identical to that of the supposedly more "nationalist" Republican leaders.[306] While many in Beijing had bet on the end of the Trump era in early 2021, the new administration seems to have taken an even tougher and more comprehensive stance against the PRC, with more multilateral and nuanced efforts.[307] To "build a united front of U.S. allies and partners to confront" China and to ensure US leadership in technology and world politics, President Biden convened the first Quad summit with Australia, India, and Japan to upgrade the group.[308] In 2021, the glacial change to the US China policy seem to have moved, with bipartisan support, beyond the point of no return.[309] Secretary of State Antony Blinken declared in March 2021 and in May 2022:

> China is the only country with the economic, diplomatic, military, and technological power to seriously challenge the stable and open international system—all the rules, values,

and relationships that make the world work the way we want it to, because it ultimately serves the interests and reflects the values of the American people. Our relationship with China will be *competitive when it should be, collaborative when it can be, and adversarial when it must be.*

The Biden administration's strategy can be summed up in three words—*invest, align, compete.* And to the people of China: *we'll compete with confidence; we'll cooperate wherever we can; we'll contest where we must.* (italics added)[310]

Since 2019 at the latest, the CCP appears to have grasped this US reorientation, evidenced by the firing on all cylinders of its propaganda machine with its nine predictions, reminiscent of the Maoist propaganda of some four decades ago, that "the US will surely fail."[311] In late 2020, a PRC analyst outlined "six principles to guide China's policy toward the US," stressing the CCP's historic mission, the "dual circulation" for the further rise of the PRC's economic power, "Sun Tzu's directive" of clever ruses, and the importance of winning "friends and influence" in the US and elsewhere.[312] Perhaps in line with its "new era" calculation about the world's balance of power and the party-state's pressing political needs, the CCP under Xi has evidently decided to run the China Race against the US head-on and at full steam, and with many means recycled from the Mao era. Militant PRC diplomats have ratcheted up their "wolf warrior" rhetoric inside and outside of the US, mostly for domestic consumption and to please their boss; old "red movies" featuring anti-American stories have been released, with new ones made, to prepare the Chinese people.[313] Beijing enacted rounds of tit-for-tat sanctions, however symbolic, with the stern warning that "we will keep our words [of fighting the US] to the end" of the "downhill" run; in February 2023, for example, Beijing imposed new sanctions against American firms Lockheed Martin and Raytheon, which have little business in the PRC, including levying heavy fines (twice the amount of their weapon sales to Taiwan).[314] In August 2021, the official Xinhua News Agency published a long editorial, in a rather traditional style circa the 1960s, detailing the "seven sins of the US-led alliance system" in the world.[315] In July 2022, the PRC government officially declared 21 "blunders" in the US China policy to demonstrate that "the US is the biggest source of chaos in the world order" and "the biggest human rights violator in the world," instituting "a bottomless and all-around containment to attack

196 | The China Race

China."[316] In February 2023, the PRC Foreign Ministry issued an official report, *US Hegemony and Its Perils*, detailing American evildoings and documenting the reasons why the PRC, and the world, should rise up to oppose the US leadership.[317]

Realizing that "the politically-divided US now shockingly has a rare consensus on China," with more than three-quarters of Americans in both parties holding negative views about the PRC (a development that is "not driven by the [COVID] pandemic"),"[318] the opportunistic masters of Chinese Legalism and the "dark" art of ruses in Beijing have quietly, voluntarily and involuntarily, made tactical changes in response.[319] They closed many Confucius Institutes, curtailed some aggressive acts, such as paying to insert pages of *China Daily* into leading US newspapers, and hid some of its criticized activities, like the "Thousand Talents" program in the US. The PRC ambassador to the US (July 2021–December 2022, who then returned to Beijing to became the PRC foreign minister for a few months till July 2023) seemed less fiery than his "wolf warrior" colleagues, pompously equating his job to the secret visit to Beijing by Henry Kissinger 50 years ago, softly wanting to "push the Sino-American relationship to return to the correct tracks of development" for an "equal coexistence" and "win-win cooperation" like before, and telling some "old American friends" that "[w]e never take surpassing the US as our goal, and we never have the ambition to challenge and displace America, or to seek hegemony in the world."[320] In September 2021, in yet another impressive acrobatic move, likely aimed at a repeat of what it did to successfully swindle the West with its WTO membership application 20 years ago, the PRC applied to join the Comprehensive and Progressive Agreement for Trans-Pacific Partnership (CPTPP), the replacement of the TPP, which had been designed to replace the WTO but was later abandoned by the Trump administration.[321] Like in any good race, full sprints, tactical pauses, and even deceptive retreats and patient outflanking are all parts of the PRC-USA rivalry.

To be sure, the United States may still hesitate, citing the need for time and reason, to fully engage in the China Race inside and outside the US. Contradictory rhetoric and moves are always expected. Donald Trump used strong language such as "Chinese virus," "China Plague," and "the rape of America by China," reaping the political benefits of shifting public opinion, but he also displayed open admiration for Xi Jinping (and other authoritarian leaders like Kim Jong-Un). He was more reluctant than his national security team to criticize the CCP's sociopolitical record in China, allegedly due to his hope of making "big and good deals" with Beijing. Many from both left and right have both criticized Trump's ineffective, "soft and weak," go-it-alone, "double-standard," and counterproductive actions toward the PRC.[322] His signature, "historical," Phase One trade deal with the PRC signed in January 2020 quickly proved rather empty, as Beijing characteristically only honored about half of its treaty obligations related to imports from the US.[323] The call for mobilizing "whole-of-state," "whole-of-society," and "whole of government" action seemed lacking.[324] Some Chinese analysts believe that Trump "has further accelerated the decline of the US and the American leadership in the world [and thus] created lots of cracks and gave us many useful opportunities."[325] Others commented that, as long as he "damages the US more than" he causes "damage to China's interests," the "anti-China" Trump was actually preferable to its alternative.[326]

The Biden administration inevitably must also balance the various American interests, views, and wishes in its response to the CCP-PRC. Four signs, however, seem to suggest that the glacier or reorientation has accelerated in its motion and the US is getting its act together to pursue a serious run of the PRC-USA rivalry and the overall China Race, both inside and outside the US. First, as I have outlined so far in this chapter, there is a remarkable continuity in the reorientation of US China policy over the past decade. Despite the unprecedented political heat of the 2020 election and serious disagreements on many issues, the Biden administration seems to have quietly inherited and built on the China policy of its predecessor. Its rhetoric seems more disciplined and lowkey, while its actions seem more coherent and coordinated, especially with allies. Basically, all of Trump's actions related to countering the PRC have continued, with some considerably expanded and enhanced. In several areas, like the South China Sea, Biden appears to have gone beyond his predecessor in making a firm and transparent stand, fully endorsing the 2016 South China Sea Arbitration by the International Arbitral Tribunal.[327] So far, Washington has appeared to be remarkably consistent and firm in its professed focus of winning a comprehensive "competition with the PRC."[328] It is indicative that a democratic rule of law could readily overcome partisan divides to gather its national will and resources to move forward with its national interests, the constant and expected zigzags notwithstanding.

Second, as part of the commendable strategy of global retrenchment and reorientation, which also started years ago, the Biden administration

198 | The China Race

has taken the political risk of finally pulling out from Afghanistan after two decades, ending a war that had been too long and costly, and had drifted from its purpose and no longer served the US national interest, especially in terms of meeting more important challenges such as the PRC-USA rivalry. The "serious competition with China" is used by Biden to defend the withdrawal, as "there's nothing China or Russia would rather have, would want more in this competition than the United States to be bogged down another decade in Afghanistan."[329] The speedy fall of the Afghan government after the withdrawal of the US military seems to be a bonanza to the CCP's anti-US propaganda and its captive nationalist audience at home, as the strange surge in the PRC of praise and celebrations of the Taliban's "victory" over the US has indicated.[330] There will always be Americans concerned about humanitarian issues who criticize this sort of downsizing and retrenching moves as a selfish cut-and-run. But, as I have attempted to argue in this book, the US is in no position to safeguard, build, and perfect other nations according to American standards. It is long overdue for the US to curtail its noble or selfish idealism for global governance and responsibility for universal equality of rights. Washington must learn from the past to control and moderate its arrogated fear of and allergic reactions to the evildoers, radical lunatics of terrorism, and sheer criminals in other countries.[331] The often noble and idealistic actions based on universal human rights and ethics, such as using force to carry out the so-called "right to intervene" (RTI) or even "duty to intervene" (DTI) in another country's domestic matters based on the so-called "responsibility to protect" (RTP) for worthy-appearing objectives, including saving lives in other countries, should be minimized and restricted by the overall value of preserving the equal sovereignty of fellow nation-states.[332] As I will elaborate in the next chapter, the US should adjust its passé fixation on places like the Middle East and concentrate on critical goals abroad, such as safeguarding its leadership position and its preferred international order.

Third, substantially mitigating its predecessor's abrasive and aggravating style of diplomacy, in both rhetoric and action, the Biden administration seems to have made quick and significant progress reaffirming and reorienting the extensive American system of alliances, and promoting a multilateral approach to addressing the rising power of the CCP-PRC state. In addition to efforts to calibrate views on the PRC with allies in the region, from the Quad to South Korea and the Philippines, Washington managed to have the G7 and NATO, both for the first time, declare in mid-2021 the PRC to be a global and "systemic" challenger, criticize Beijing's human rights policy in Hong Kong and Xinjiang, and call for collective action addressing China's "nonmarket" economic practices and lack of transparency and cooperation, particularly with regard to the international investigation of the origin of the COVID-19 virus.[333] A year later, the G7 did more to call the PRC out on many issues from trade to Taiwan. Also in mid-2022, NATO for the first time ever in its decennial Strategic Concept openly targeted "the systemic challenges posed by the PRC to Euro-Atlantic security [. . . and to] our interests, security and values." NATO then redeclared this China policy with elaboration in July 2023.[334] Aside from the Quad and the Five Eyes (Australia, Canada, New Zealand, the UK, and the US), Paris seemed to have had its own "French awakening" about the China Race.[335] In December 2021 (held again in March 2023), the US convened a global "Summit for Democracy" of leaders from 111 countries, excluding the PRC but including Taiwan.[336] It is a strong testimony and enhancement of US leadership and power in the China Race.

Fourth, and finally, the Biden administration seems to have continued the wise but often distracted and delayed proposal by both parties to invest at home through actions like the Invest in America Act of 2021, to improve the American economy and social tranquility—specifically infrastructure, innovation, and education.[337] The legendary American superiority of ingenuity and efficiency is the ultimate source of power for the United States to prevail in the global PRC-USA rivalry and the overall China Race. The US apparently still attracts talent from all over the world, far better than the PRC. In the 2020s, even though China provides the largest share (29%) of the world's "top-tier AI researchers" (the US provides 20%), over 59% of these were working in the US compared to only 11% in the PRC, and the US appears to command an overwhelming lead over the PRC in AI research.[338] That competitive edge deserves more care and cultivation. The American self-strengthening, with ambitious, concerted, and massive investments, and smart policy-adjustments, holds the key to the fortune and fate of both the US and the world, including the Chinese people. The importance and urgency of the China Race, according to a former US senior official, "require us to consider in every policy we adopt, every bill we introduce, and each public-private partnership that government and U.S. industry undertake—whether each initiative increases American leverage in this competition, or surrenders leverage to a hostile dictatorship in Beijing."[339] With that, the PRC-USA rivalry, the global competition for existence and the world, now seems to be engaged in both rhetoric and action.

4

Contaformation

A Strategy for Managing the China Race

In this book, I have described the China Race, the competition between the CCP-controlled China and the US-led West for the leadership and political order of the world. It is a lengthy and global rivalry between great powers, the PRC and the USA, featuring contestation, constraint, conflict, cooperation, and co-optation. While not yet a full-scale, all-around hostility, neither contender is likely to capitulate, as they are in an existential race with an uncertain ending. The China Race is becoming a defining juncture of history, an inflection point, with the fortune and fate of all of human civilization at stake, depending on the actions and interactions of the contenders. As in any genuine competition and contestation, not everyone agrees on who should be the winner of the China Race. However, given the normative analysis and the assessment of the CCP-PRC polity I have presented in this book and its two prequels, it seems clear that it is desirable for the world, including the Chinese people, for the US-led West to prevail in the Race. Thus, the question is no longer an issue of should or could but how.

This chapter will, immodestly, outline the strategic framework of *Contaformation* (containment and engagement for transformation and incorporation) for the US-led West and the world to achieve three hierarchical objectives in the China Race, ranked in descending order of importance. *Objective 1* is the nonnegotiable top goal: the US and its allies must race to prevent the CCP-PRC state from recentering and reordering the world by taking over leadership of the world. *Objective*

2 is that the US should prepare for but deter and avoid an all-out war with the PRC, to the fullest extent possible. *Objective 3* is that the West should seek a sociopolitical and ideological transformation of the PRC so as to truly incorporate China as a contributing, constructive, and complete peer within the international community. As a seasoned American analyst argued in 2022, a clarity of strategic objectives must be established for a bipartisan, "U.S.-led [world] coalition with targeted, issue-specific efforts to contest Chinese assertiveness," in order to achieve its overall goal of ensuring "that Beijing is either unwilling or unable to overturn the regional and global order."[1]

The CCP-PRC state is a powerful and viable systemic challenger, representing a feasible but suboptimal mode of governance and an alternative but undesirable world order. It should no longer be normalized and equalized as just another contender in the international game for respect, power, glory, and wealth.[2] At the same time, we must recognize that the China Race itself is a normal occurrence of great power competition in international relations that is fully sanctioned by and fundamentally sustaining of the Westphalian world order. The constant "insecurity" and "ambition" great states feel under the Westphalian world order are ceaselessly driving national competitions for innovation.[3] The PRC-USA comparison and competition generated by a fully engaged and well-run China Race could therefore be a mighty engine for innovation and efficiency at a grand scale, benefitting the entire world, including the Chinese people.

The Parameters

With the significance, urgency, difficulty, peculiarity, and benefits of the China Race now hopefully known, it is up to the US-led West to formulate and implement a suitable strategy for managing and prevailing in the Race. It is the West's race to lose. It is expected, natural, and mostly beneficial for the West to have many divisions and disagreements. It is, after all, an open and diverse society that inevitably generates many sincere public debates, noble ideals, parochial advocacies, experimental ideas, distracting noises, sheer fallacies, self-serving schemes, and wishful thinking. It is always advisable to heed the wise proverb about "not throwing the baby out with the bathwater." In a plural society, however,

Contaformation | 203

it is often hard to agree on what is the bathwater and what is the baby before it is too late.

Echoing the normative analyses presented in chapter 1 of this book, the West should hold the strategic vision that, in the China Race, the challenger to be defeated is the CCP-PRC state and its dream of recentering and reordering the world, not the captive Chinese people or the imperfect but least undesirable Westphalian system.[4] The China Race itself, or international comparison and competition in general, is not the target. The West should treat the China Race as an unusually critical but still normal occurrence under the Westphalian world order, an event that could positively drive human civilization forward and uplift humanity, if managed well. The West should also be confident that, resilient and resourceful as it is, the PRC state has deep flaws and many weaknesses, and is fully constrainable and vincible. The Westphalian system, fragile as it is, has survived many challenges, including two world wars and the Cold War in the 20th century alone, and can prevail again this time. As a French study concluded, some "tactical successes" notwithstanding, the PRC state as "its own worst enemy" has had "a strategic failure overall" in its expansive and expensive effort for global influence.[5]

Like any serious race, critical and rewarding as it is, the China Race is neither painless nor costless, and the race course is long and perilous, with great uncertainty about the time to completion and the outcome. Unlike many other races, however, the existential rivalry of the China Race between the CCP-PRC state and the US-led Western polity is also an ultrahigh-stakes competition poised to reshape the future trajectory of all human civilization with a likely irreversibility. The rewards and risks for the racers feature a profound but clouded asymmetry. A victory by the West would likely affect the existence of the CCP regime, but not Chinese nationhood and statehood, as, under the preserved Westphalian system (especially the LIO variant), it is fully expected for the competitors to live and let live, while their internal organizations and norms either change or remain intact. A victory by the PRC, on the other hand, would impact the existence of the Western polity *and also* diminish or even erase the nationhood and statehood of the Western (and most other) countries, as under a world order of authoritarian centralization, sovereign nations and states would predictably wither and fade. In the natural selection process in the biological world, the exhaustion or demise of either or both competitors ends a rivalry and

204 | The China Race

results in a new equilibrium, often by sheer chance. The China Race, the existential selection in the political world between two competing modes of human organization, hopefully, shall decisively favor the preferred competitor, by conscious and concerted choice. A well-reasoned strategy and its determined implementation could generate a variety of imaginable and unimaginable ways and means for the West that do not leave the China Race to chance. Given the stakes of the Race and the track record of unrivaled unscrupulousness of the CCP, the West should also be prepared for considerable costs, side effects, and various risks, including some uncivilities and even iniquities that are hopefully all manageable and transient.

In light of the above, for maximizing the benefits and minimizing the risks and costs for the West and the world, including the Chinese people, I summarize the discussions presented in this book so far to propose five sets of parameters or considerations for contemplating the questions of what, whom, how, where, and when, related to succeeding in the China Race.

Parameter 1: Racing for What?

The China Race is essentially about world polity or world order, the political organization of humanity, which is a common good or bad for all. It is about which of the competing political systems, the Qin-Han polity of authoritarian-totalitarian party-state/partocracy or the Western democratic rule of law, should be the center and the leader of an international community of sovereign nations. Ultimately, it is about which of the competing world orders, the China Order of world empire and the Westphalian system of international relations, should organize humankind beyond nation-states. The first and foremost objective of a good management and victorious ending of the China Race is the prevention of the CCP-PRC from becoming the world leader. More broadly, it is about securing the Westphalian system of sovereign nations as the world order against a world political unification and centralization.

Achieving this main objective requires taking important risks. The China Race is impactful to world peace, commerce, international cooperation on issues like climate change, and many other valuable human pursuits. Defined as the lack of war (or full-scale confrontation) between major powers, peace is always of high value in world politics. *Pax optima rerum* (peace is the greatest good) and *he wei gui* (peace/

harmony is supreme) express the shared value of peace in both the West and the East since ancient times.[6] The self-evidently essential objectives of human politics, peace and order, however, should not obscure the top objective in the China Race. Peace, harmony, and order are unquestionably precious, but not priceless; the cost and manner of achieving and maintaining these desirables matter critically to the health and prosperity of human civilization. Peace and order can and have been provided by different world orders and different states: from a centralized polity of world empires like the Pax Romana (Rome Order), Pax Mongolica or Pax Tatarica (Mongol Order), and Pax Sinica (China Order) to the decentralized world polity of Pax Westphalia, featuring great powers and hegemonic leaders, of which Pax Britannica and Pax Americana and the LIO are just some varieties. I have attempted to demonstrate the critical differences in the two modes of providing world order and world peace in *The China Order* and in this book, of which the central normative viewpoint is the definitive undesirability of world political unification in relationship to other political values. The indisputably high value of avoiding a Sino-American war in the era of weapons of mass destruction (WMDs), to the fullest extent of possibility, should be a secondary objective that in fact is entirely attainable in a well-run China Race firmly focused on the main goal.

Of course, the China Race not only affects world peace but, more importantly, decides the kind of world peace, how it is provided, by whom, and at what cost to other human values and pursuits. The preservation of the Westphalian system and, so far, the least undesirable West/US leadership of it, should rightfully overweigh the fear of the real or imagined beast of war. Peace and how it is provided are intertwined values, and the latter must often take the priority so as to achieve genuine, just, and hence lasting peace. As Martin Luther King, Jr., eloquently proclaimed: "[T]here can be no justice without peace and there can be no peace without justice."[7] How to provide and maintain political order is key to maximizing both peace and justice. Both democratic rule of law and autocratic dictatorship can provide order and peace; but only under the former can a Mahatma Gandhi/Martin Luther King/Nelson Mandela way of pursuing peace and harmony based on justice at minimal cost be possible. Both world empire and the Westphalian system can provide order and peace for the whole known world, but only the latter has enabled and facilitated the qualitatively much fuller blossoming of innovation, efficiency, and progress of human civilization, and with

206 | The China Race

much less death and destruction. As I have analyzed in chapter 1 of this book, the Westphalian Peace is by no means perfect or ideal, but it provides the institutional and ideological feasibility and mechanisms to dynamically maximize the multidimensional and ever-growing human values aggregately, for all of humanity. It allows nations to experiment and innovate through constant and consequential comparison and competition; it is also the last line of defense preventing any ambitious and powerful state from centrally ordering the world through the political monopoly of a world empire. The China Race is about that last line.

In addition, the West and the world should not be in the China Race to extinguish international competition, but to win a serious, existential round of the contest in order to ensure its continuation. The Race is about how to prevent and stop the rising Chinese power used by the CCP from recentering and reordering the world; it is not about depriving the Chinese people of the rights of full and equitable membership in the international community. On the contrary, once the CCP-PRC is transformed, constrained, or both—another major, albeit secondary objective of the China Race—and Chinese power thus becomes safe to the Westphalian world order, the West and the world should welcome, fully incorporate, and benefit from the new China as another leading power of the world, with all of its reoriented competitiveness and contributions.

Parameter 2: Racing against Whom?

A key to managing and prevailing in the China Race at minimum cost is to focus on the real contender. A major source of strength for the PRC state, at home and abroad, has been the intentional or inadvertent conflation of the CCP regime with the nation of China and the Chinese people. As some observers put it, "China is not an enemy of the US and the World; but the CCP is."[8] The West, the world, and especially the Chinese people must be mindful that the CCP-PRC state is akin to a mighty and masterful captor that has captivated and even enslaved the great Chinese people with ruthless violence and unscrupulous ruses, for the interests of the party, and mainly its ruling clique. The Chinese people have suffered much more from the China Tragedy and the China Suboptimality under the CCP than any other peoples. They have been made to sacrifice endlessly for the CCP's struggle against the world for regime survival. Should the CCP win the China Race to recenter and reorder the world, the Chinese people would be worse off, reliving the calamitous lives of the Qin people in the 3rd century BCE, but this time sharing the misery with the rest of humanity.

It is wise, ethical, pragmatic, and efficient to focus on the force of the CCP-PRC state in the China Race, and particularly on its political system and ideology. A two-level game seems imperative. On one level, the US should frustrate, weaken, contain, discredit, delegitimize, defeat, and undermine the CCP regime whenever and wherever possible, with the restraint of PRC state power as the objective. The goal must not be the suppression of the Chinese nation or the exploitation of the Chinese people, beyond the unavoidable collateral damage. The purpose is to "both challenge and coexist with China," as proposed by two leaders of the Biden administration's National Security Council in 2019 when they were still civilians.[9] On another level, it is strategically critical and tactically smart to distinguish the PRC state from the Chinese people and explore the deep gap between the CCP's pursuits and Chinese people's interests, so as to strip Beijing of the cover and power of Chinese nationalism and patriotism. Minimizing the possible impact on ethnic Chinese and Asians inside and outside the PRC is vital, and will provide powerful leverage. It is morally imperative to engage the one-fifth of humankind captured by the CCP, enabling, empowering, and assisting them in their liberation and detoxification, providing nudges and even coercion if necessary, so they will take their fate into their own hands. The transformation of the CCP regime would be an ideal ending to the China Race.[10]

A "regime change" in Beijing may indeed be both imperative and possible.[11] But the Chinese people should be given the opportunity to liberate themselves and become masters of their own country. They have every right to pursue their genuinely nationalist objectives rather than the CCP's agenda disguised as Chinese national interests. Rallying and aligning with the Chinese people would be a major shortcut for the West and the world to prevail in the China Race, speedily and inexpensively.

Parameter 3: Racing with What?

Given the ultrahigh stakes and the fact that the CCP-PRC has been racing for decades against the US-led West by waging unscrupulous and unrestricted total warfare, the so-called "people's war" and *chaoxian zhan* (war without limits),[12] running the PRC-USA competition as a life-or-death fight, the China Race is not to be treated like a fair derby or ball game played with rulebooks and referees, annual beauty pageant, or business biding. It is an all-in rivalry between two political systems (and the peoples under their respective governance) to decide the way in which they and humanity are to be organized and governed, and hence the fate and future of human civilization. The West and indeed the world, including the Chinese people, should ready themselves for some rough rides, including military standoffs in the era of WMDs. As I have analyzed earlier in this book and its prequel *The China Record*, however, the CCP leadership has long been highly opportunistic, perfidious, self-preserving, and even risk-averse, with a vast vested interest in peace for their families and cronies. The likelihood of Beijing really using military force, much less WMDs, to fight a massive war with a credible opponent is, in fact, slim.[13] In 2022, the five nuclear-weapon states, including the PRC and the US, issued a joint-declaration on preventing a nuclear war, which "cannot be won and must never be fought."[14] This seems to evidence and augment the confidence about avoiding a cross-Pacific nuclear exchange, reaffirming, whatever the sincerity of the parties, a shared view about nuclear deterrence, which the US has held since the late 1950s and had persuaded Moscow to accept by the late 1970s.[15] With its joining of the Treaty on the Non-Proliferation of Nuclear Weapons (NPT) in 1992, the PRC officially accepted the US view; although its reluctance and second-thoughts regarding the nuclear arms race and the use of nuclear weapons have remained visible to this day.[16]

The Chinese military, the PLA, seems to be stuck in the role of the party's "bodyguards"—its pledged first duty is to "provide strategic support to the CCP leadership and socialist system," "under the guidance of Xi Jinping thought."[17] To observers, China's massive military force appears to have many showy "clunkers" and a very difficult geography,[18] and it is designed "for a *fait accompli*, aiming to control escalation below total war."[19] The most recent real war the PLA fought was against the Vietnamese over three decades ago, and its performance left much to be desired.[20] With the reported deaths of 31,119 troops, killing "only" 57,152 Vietnamese soldiers (and about the same number of Vietnamese civilians), the PLA's 28-day invasion with an overwhelming force of 300, 000 (versus 100,000 Vietnamese troops), was seen by its own senior officers as "an embarrassment for the country and a shame of the military."[21] Over seven decades, very few PLA general officers were lost in battles (in the single digits at most), but in the past decade alone many

Contaformation | 209

hundreds of generals, including several top commanders (and thousands more lower-ranking officers), have been purged and jailed (some for life and others sentenced to death with suspension). This suggests a force that is seriously beleaguered by widespread corruption and fierce political infighting.[22] Compared to the West, the PRC power, though formidable in appearance, may actually be a "paper dragon."[23] Still, the will and ability of the US and its allies to outrace the CCP in arms buildup and in the forward deploying and use of military force as needed must be strong and unyielding.[24] Beijing's belligerent moves must be met and its bluffs must be called.[25]

More importantly, the China Race is a multidimensional and multi-directional competition that calls for and justifies a whole-of-government, whole-of-society, and whole-of-alliance approach. Beyond military pre-paredness and an arms race, as I have attempted to show in the prequel to this book, the Chinese economy itself has many traps and bubbles that can be intelligently utilized to compromise and disable CCP power.[26] The PRC's political governance and social system are full of flaws and injustices that could also be fruitfully exploited to kill two birds with one stone: to help better the lives and rights of the Chinese people and to constrain and undermine the CCP regime. Chinese foreign policy is highly cost-ineffective even for the narrow purpose of safeguarding the CCP regime. Concerted, targeted, and precision counteractions will powerfully consolidate and improve the position and power of the West while draining and trapping the PRC's power and diminishing Beijing's stature and influence at home and abroad.

More specifically, out of the numerous means available to the West for fending off the CCP-PRC in the China Race, a highly cost-effective, fully justified, and greatly beneficial option for the Chinese people and humanity is to break China's so-called Great Firewall as quickly and as completely as possible. A well-administered cocktail of reciprocity, transparency, and issue-linkage would be very potent for that purpose. Promoting and facilitating freedom of speech and information inside the PRC will lead to a critical rereading of Chinese history and a reexam-ination of the world by the Chinese people and for the Chinese people, leading to the destruction of the PRC's state program of misinformation and disinformation, and hence the CCP's power of control.[27] This would be a detoxification of Chinese minds, turning them from slave-pawns to full citizens, and a mighty liberation of the creative power of the 1.4 billion Chinese, which will infinitely benefit human civilization.

210 | The China Race

This will also help encourage a peaceful transformation of the CCP-PRC regime. Making the long list of banned works by Chinese authors available in China would be a good start.[28] Publicizing and highlighting the gap between the democratic rule of law in the West and the PRC's authoritarian rule by law, essentially just rule of man by force and ruse, would be a smart move.[29] I elaborate on this below.

PARAMETER 4: WHERE AND WHEN TO TAKE PAUSES AND BREAKS?

The China Race is comprehensive, high-stake, arduous, and likely long. The CCP maintains that it has a mission and mandate that will last for dozens of generations, or many centuries, wishful-thinking and pretentiousness notwithstanding.[30] There are places where and moments when the West and the world could and should take some well-justified and beneficial pauses and breaks.[31] Mindful of the main goal of the China Race, the US, in its effort to stop the CCP, should guard against excesses that may damage or even ruin the Westphalian system, although, as analyzed in chapter 1 of this book, the US has been and will be by far the least likely world power to subvert the Westphalian system. The West, however, should guard against the many natural impulses of globalism for universal rights and equality beyond the nation-states that have been readily used by Beijing to disguise and assist in its recentering and reordering of the world. The noble ideals of equality of rights should be primarily a national phenomenon. To preserve the Westphalian system, which currently centers around the West-led LIO, and to prevail in the China Race, the US could seek to adjust and improve the LIO with a membership that may limit and even exclude the PRC, but not to mutilate or abandon the system in the name of more global governance for all.[32] Nation-building and state-building for better governance in various countries is ultimately the responsibility of those peoples.

A careful balance is key to benefiting from, managing, and prevailing in the China Race. As Friedrich Nietzsche warned long ago, "Whoever fights monsters should see to it that in the process he does not become a monster. And if you gaze long enough into an abyss, the abyss will gaze back into you."[33] The China Race is totally manageable without irreversibly taking away the sovereignty and diversity of decision-making of the nations. As in a democracy, where action can be indecisive and inefficient at times, the defense of the Westphalian system requires strong leadership, masterful alliance politics, and patient diplomacy, not an irrevocable dictatorship of world government. Under an improved LIO that may be somewhat smaller and less global, the US and its allies could continue their natural pursuits of relative gains, conditioned to minimizing the chance of impairing the LIO with their inadvertent assistance to the so-called "barbarians at the gate." To lift a page from the CCP's playbook, the West must work "to form a united front" of democracies and even of all that are willing, to deny Beijing's ability to "divide and rule."[34] A balanced coordination will enable the US and its allies to efficiently manage the waves of tense confrontation and relaxed cooperation for deserving causes. By pacing itself, interspersing speedy dashes with leisurely breaks, the West stands an excellent chance of prevailing in the China Race without unduly damaging the Westphalian system or overly sacrificing the (relative) interests of the nations.[35]

Competition can be tough and unpleasant, and even excessive to the contenders. But it is ultimately beneficial to most if not all, so long as the competition itself, the Westphalian system in this case, remains intact. International competition, even a contestation with a systemic challenger like the CCP-PRC, is not always system-threatening or completely zero-sum. A prudent assessment of the China Race, its progress and successes, and the resultant adjustment of policies and actions would allow for properly chosen and well-timed pauses and breaks to pace and replenish. Some positive-sum competition between the West and China could and should be facilitated, as some reciprocal, competitive cooperation with Beijing on genuinely common concerns is both beneficial and attainable. Obvious examples of such concerns include the control of global pandemics and pollution of the high seas.[36] As some have analyzed, comprehensive competition and contestation, as opposed to a "partnership," with the PRC, may actually work better to address issues like climate change.[37]

Certain actions by the CCP-PRC could be viewed as normal competition among nations, and as a key benefit under the Westphalian world order; all Chinese behaviors are not necessarily system-challenging. For instance, the PRC has engaged in a costly competition with the West in space, with projects like its 20-year-old Big Dipper global positioning system, which was fully deployed in June 2020.[38] The US-led West should naturally watch such projects for their military use and seek to outdo them, but should also consider them as competitions that could still benefit humanity by providing redundancy, choices, and stimuli. Similarly, Chinese social media apps and platforms such as WeChat,

212 | The China Race

TikTok, MICO, Yalla, and YoHo seem to have offered services with value in many places, especially the Global South.[39] The Chinese tradition of commerce in Southeast Asia could be a path to positive competition, and would also benefit and safeguard the nations involved.[40] In short, while systemic challenges by the CCP-PRC state must be viewed with utmost seriousness, the competition of the China Race itself is both natural and normal, and often beneficial. The China Race should be assessed and reassessed to adequately restrain common human greed, gullibility, and excesses, to ensure that international competition, the "game" itself, continues fruitfully.

PARAMETER 5: HOW TO ASSESS THE RACE?

A key to an accurate assessment of the China Race is the full awareness of some fundamental differences between an authoritarian-totalitarian polity and a plural democratic rule of law. The West must read and treat Beijing verifiably based on what it is and does, not by what it says or pledges or signs, nor by what the West assumes and wishes. It is an elementary but common mistake to view and treat the CCP-PRC the same as the West, which strives or is forced to be open and pluralistic, legalistic, and rule-abiding. The CCP-PRC state, by its nature and tradition, is secretive and unscrupulous, and excels in playing countless games of numbers, treating laws, rules, contracts, and promises with a consistent cynicism and expediency. Beijing's sincere-sounding promises and agreements, like its fiery warnings and threats, are mostly neither legal obligations nor moral constraints for CCP leaders. Even treaties and laws that are signed and ratified are just the bare first step, not the deal, least of all the end of the deal, and are subject to constant ad hoc bargaining and unilateral changes. A past example is the way in which Beijing ferociously fought its patron Moscow as a deadly enemy, starting in the 1960s, when the Sino-Soviet Treaty of Friendship, Alliance and Mutual Assistance was barely halfway into its 30-year term.[41] A more recent illustration was in 2017, when the Sino-British Joint Declaration, barely 20 years into its intended lifespan of a half century, was dismissed by Beijing as "just a historical document, no longer relevant today," followed by PRC actions in 2019–20 to effectively trash its treaty obligations under the Declaration.[42] But when the UK responded by offering residency to some Hong Kong people, the CCP furiously accused London of "brazen violation of its legal obligations under the Declaration."[43]

Thus, verifiable deeds and facts, not words or wishes, are the only ways to measure any change in the CCP-PRC state and hence the progress of the China Race. Even the traditionally useful field surveys by polling professionals should be viewed with well-justified skepticism. It turned out that Gallup, for example, was producing "findings" about the PRC during 2005–18 based on interviews only conducted in three cities in China (Beijing, Shanghai, and Guangzhou).[44] It may be positive and progressive to envision a possible ideal "cultural equality between China and the OECD nations, particularly the United States";[45] efforts for such equality are indeed potentially fruitful, but highly treacherous without genuine changes in the underlying institutions, ideologies, and behaviors. Whenever and wherever in doubt, of course, given the unscrupulous nature and the perfidious record of the CCP, the West must think and act agilely and prepare for the worst. As the Chinese writer Lu Xun tersely declared a century ago, "never be afraid to make the most malicious speculation about the Chinese" (read, more properly here, the Chinese rulers).[46] As the then US secretary of state suggested in 2020, when dealing with the CCP, "we must distrust and verify."[47] Or as the then US envoy for climate characterized the situation in 2021, "it would be stupid and malpractice" to simply trust Beijing's words.[48] Only in such an arguably overcautious way could the West have some cooperation with China but always firmly compete with the CCP to prevail in the China Race, allowing the world to evade the same tragic fate of the peoples in the pre-Qin Sinic world.

Contaformation: Components and Objectives

Given the above considerations, I now sketch out *Contaformation*, a portmanteau for containment and engagement for the transformation and incorporation of China, as a strategy for the West and the world, including the Chinese people, to engage, manage, and prevail in the China Race. As mentioned in chapter 1 of this book, the China Race resembles the Cold War in many ways, and contaformation also shares significant commonalities with the containment strategy, which facilitated the Western victory in the Cold War, albeit there are important differences between these two episodes of great power competition and the two strategies. The containment strategy went through profound changes as it evolved in implementation, with many improvisations, set-

214 | The China Race

backs, and adjustments before accomplishing its main goal of frustrating and disabling the Soviet Union–led systemic challenge to the West-led world order. As a living strategic vision, contaformation will also evolve and develop, with, hopefully, a better chance of minimizing the costs, detours, and pitfalls, and benefiting from the rich lessons of the past.

Contaformation has two key components: a firm containment and effective constriction of CCP-PRC state power, and a smart engagement and full communication with the Chinese people to facilitate the transformation of the CCP-PRC state and the incorporation of China as a country.[49] The endgame is to incorporate the politically and ideologically transformed China into the Westphalian system. This strategy mandates that the rising power and the peculiar ambition of the PRC state must be constrained and prevented from recentering and reordering the world. It advocates and promotes the idea that the CCP regime should be pulled and pushed through an institutional and ideological transformation and reorganization. It also presumes that the US-led West, if wholly and smartly engaged, is fully capable of managing and prevailing in the China Race, probably competing more efficiently and peacefully than it did in the Cold War.

Accordingly, this strategy has three hierarchical objectives—in descending order of importance: (1) Preventing the CCP-PRC from taking over the world's leadership; (2) the avoidance of all-out war between China and the US to the fullest extent possible; and (3) the sociopolitical and ideological transformation of the PRC in order to truly incorporate China into the Westphalian system. As a historian of the Cold War wisely suggested, the China Race should follow a "complicated, nuanced path—a patient mix of sustained confrontation and cooperation, containment and engagement, isolation and integration [. . . that] must avoid war, but also abandon the false hope of partnership."[50]

A key element of contaformation is *to always focus on the main, top-level, goal.* The US and its allies (including other nations and the Chinese people) must never lose sight of the top objective of the China Race—the preservation of the West-led Westphalian system of international relations. This goal requires fending off the revisionist power of the PRC state, and safeguarding both the organizing principle and the leadership of the current world order above all other objectives, short of a global disaster genuinely threatening the survival of the entire human species (or, perhaps, an invasion by some powerful extraterrestrials bent on annihilation).[51]

To that end, the US and its allies should lead and sustain a comprehensive rethinking and firm course change regarding globalization and world governance. A curbing of the idealistic but toxic enthusiasm for world uniformity and unification, even among the most earnest enthusiasts, seems overdue.[52] Multilateral organizations such as the United Nations, based on the universal equality of rights, together with its overgrown agencies, should not be allowed or used to compromise the nation-state system. The evolving ideals of RTI (the right to intervene) in other sovereign countries for RTP (the responsibility to protect) other country's citizens should remain an inspiring ideal rather than a legal norm, only being attempted extremely rarely. In actual practice, RTI has often been prohibitively cost-ineffective in pursuing the illusive universal equality of human rights among nations, and easily appears to be colonialist and even imperialistic to many.[53] RTI for RTP, especially when it is undertaken unilaterally, severely compromises national sovereignty and thus undermines the Westphalian system. International organizations, alliances, and global norms and rules are for the preservation and betterment of nation-states, not for their replacement. The structural and normative differences among the nations should be preserved to ensure lasting international comparison, choice, and competition, which fundamentally energizes and drives human civilization. Vicious and purposeful gaming and manipulation of multilateral organizations and agreements must be routinely and effectively monitored and controlled. Strong insistence on principles and strict discipline of international clubs are imperative. Unsavory players in the club, once caught and refusing to change, no longer belong; if the club is hijacked and rigged, then it must be rejected, restructured, and replaced.

Humans may be born equal as biological beings; they are not and should not be fantasized as equal political and economic beings globally, since they live and work in different groups and nations under varied sociopolitical systems and cultural norms. While respecting the equality of national sovereignty, ideally a popular sovereignty with national self-determination, the hallucinatory fallacy of the equality of all polities and cultures must be rejected. Ideas from all cultures are indeed potentially useful to human civilization and are thus valuable, especially when they are compared and contested in an open and fair marketplace. But to treat sociopolitical and economic norms and ideas that have gone through extensive and repeated debates, tests, efforts of falsification and validation, and constant evolution as the same as those

216 | The China Race

from a monopolistic, monolithic, and mysterious source of authoritarian dictation, is an outrageous mistake with grave consequences. It is akin to equating the nutritional value of an apple with that of a sesame seed, or the health value of a cabinet of modern medicines with a barrel of ginseng root or some other "panacea." To use a metaphor from the natural world, valuing biodiversity does not mean treating cows the same as rats or intestinal flora the same as cholera and Ebola. In the effort to preserve cultural diversity or multiculturalism in the sociopolitical world, we should not treat freedom of faith the same as indoctrination by force, variations in family structure the same as misogyny, or high heels the same as foot binding.

As I have argued in chapter 1 of this book, in balancing order, security, and equality with efficiency and innovation to ensure the health and prosperity of human civilization, national division is the last reliable institutional guarantor. The noble pursuits of globally equal human rights and identical living standards and conditions for all individual humans must be treated with utmost respect but great caution. These are wonderful and intoxicating ideals, much like grand harmony and eternal happiness, and worth all efforts (cost permitting), but should never be allowed to compromise and destroy the fundamentals that have given rise to those ideals and enabled the possibility of approaching a maximization of those ideals. It is the primacy of personal rights and freedoms allowing individuals a modicum of choice and competition, perhaps unpalatable in appearance to some believers in globalist liberalism, that ultimately drives creativity and progress in human civilization.

The contaformation strategy requires *sound leadership* for the West and the world. Given that the US has been the leading power least threatening to the Westphalian system when compared to its likely replacements, the Americans therefore should unapologetically strengthen US power through maintaining a dominant financial position, military superiority, excellence in education and innovation, and admired sociocultural and environmental conditions at home. It is in the greater interest of the world to "put America First," "make America strong," "rebuild America back better," and let America "lead again," as the US presidential contenders in 2016 and 2020 all advocated.[54] Those ideas should be delinked from the shortsightedness of isolationism and disassociated from any particular politician. It is not just to maintain and improve America the Beautiful and the Strong as the home for Americans and anyone who joins them, but also to continue the least undesirable world order under the least destructive leadership, as a highly rewarding grand experiment for the whole of humankind.[55]

Other than those nations that institutionally and ideologically share the same basic objectives and norms, especially regarding safeguarding the LIO or more generically the Westphalian system—the so-called "like-minded and capable democracies"[56]—no other country should be allowed to approach, let alone surpass, the level of power and influence that the US holds in the world. More specifically, the US should project its power and influence abroad especially in the Chinese neighborhood and on China itself. The US (and the West) should impenitently consolidate and enhance its national competitiveness and relative power versus the PRC, to ensure its ability to lead the world—representing the least tyrannical sociopolitical institutions, the least irrational economic system, and the least undesirable cultural norms that humankind has ever been able to attain aggregately through comparison and competition. Constantly working on its problems and issues at home to perpetuate "a more perfect union," as envisioned by the US Constitution, is always the key.

To prevail in the China Race, the US must do well in the international competition for power, using all means allowed by its own adaptive norms. Despite the possible distastefulness and the negativity associated with some leaders and messengers, the effort to enrich and strengthen the US first and foremost should be regarded as both critical and beneficial, and not just for the West. It is not just a selfish undertaking for the American people but also an altruistic endeavor, a "positive externality," for the world, including the Chinese people. Concrete actions, possibly seen by some as offensive, selfish, and costly, may include that the US and the West stop financing the CCP through massive trade imbalances; restrict the supply or leak of important technology to the PRC; oppose and limit Beijing's influence in the world, particularly in international organizations; cleanse the international financial system to stop the internationalization of the RMB; and crack down on Chinese malfeasance in cyberspace, following India's lead in banning digital hardware and software from the PRC. All these actions would amount to a precision hit on the CCP's Achilles's heel, according to a longtime observer of China.[57]

A coalition of the like-minded in the Western Pacific and Indian Ocean is critical to US leadership. In the Indo-Pacific, the PRC seems to be locked into a more defined yet ceaseless and near zero-sum geopolitical competition with the US and its allies. Thus it has become vital both

218 | The China Race

symbolically and substantially for them to "stand their ground" in the face of Beijing's growing, often veiled, and likely insatiable appetite for expansion in its neighborhood.[58] Significant territorial demands against India and in the South and East China seas aside, some in the PRC have argued for years, for example, for "reassessing" and "assisting the independence of Ryukyu (Okinawa)," so as to beat Tokyo and eventually "retake" the Japanese islands in the same way as "reuniting with" Taiwan. Since 1986, there have been 18 biannual "international academic conference" on "Sino-Ryukyu relations in history."[59] Expanding the Quad of the Australia-India-Japan-US alliance, a larger umbrella organization for collective security, an Asian-Pacific or Indo-Pacific treaty organization (APTO or IPTO) may form, accompanied by enhanced US-forward deployment in the region with smarter systems and strategy, at some possible trade-off of a drawdown of the US military commitment in other parts of the world.[60] A NATO-Japan/South Korea partnership has already appeared, a promising development.[61]

There should be a candid and enforced policy for the countries in and beyond the region to take sides in addressing the rising PRC power. Between the current world order and the clearly inferior and disastrous alternative represented by the CCP-PRC state, it is not only politically and socioeconomically rational but also morally imperative for nations and states to choose sides in order to protect and better themselves together. Empirically, many countries easily perceive that their top interests of national independence and security are identical to those of the US and its allies in the preservation of the Westphalian world order and have thus already taken a side in the China Race, though, for economic reasons or "free-riding" calculus, they may still not be rhetorically explicit.[62] In 2022, 57% of those people surveyed in the 10 countries of the Association of Southeast Asian Nations (ASEAN) would "align" with the US against the PRC if they "were forced to take sides," up (slightly) from 56% a year before.[63] In 2022, South Korea elected as president Yoon Suk-Yeol, who has consistently argued for closer ties with the US and Japan.[64] Since Russia's invasion of Ukraine (with the PRC's support) in 2022, the West has unified further, strengthening and expanding NATO with strong Pacific extensions.[65]

The contaformation strategy suggests *running and winning the China Race in China.* An ideal ending of the China Race that is beneficial for the world and for the Chinese people would involve institutional and ideological reconfiguration and transformation of the PRC political

Contaformation | 219

system, hopefully in a peaceful way. In this way, the mighty power and the enormous potential of the Chinese people will no longer be manipulated and wasted in an effort to replace the Westphalian system, but instead put to work toward the betterment of life for everyone, first and foremost for the Chinese people themselves. In addition to safeguarding the Westphalian system, liberating a fifth of humankind from a proven suboptimal, inferior, and repressive regime (that only provides a perceived optimal service to the very few ruling elites) and making their lives qualitatively better would be, in and of itself, an incredible accomplishment of human progress.

The United States and its allies must forcefully expose the PRC, treating it as an abnormal and powerful challenger, not just to the US and the West but to the current world order and world peace, representing a qualitatively less desirable alternative. The CCP-PRC challenge must be met and dealt with at the same level and in the same manner in which Beijing operates, with temporary races to the bottom when necessary. The US and its allies should engage in a smart contest with the CCP. The PRC's financial power, military strength, and propaganda capacity should all be curbed, reduced, undermined, and weakened. Thoughtful and concerted reciprocity, including tit-for-tat reactions, will be effective, peaceful, and inexpensive.

A key to the PRC-USA rivalry seems to be how to reduce and prevent "American money and institutions" from being used by Beijing for its ends, and to "pull Wall Street and Silicon Valley onside" to help in winning the ultrahigh-stakes "political warfare" with the CCP.[66] The US and its allies should adjust their cost-benefit calculations to actively reallocate the global chains of production and supply out of the PRC as much as possible, especially those involving key industries such as pharmaceuticals, ITC (information, transportation, and communication), and dual-use technology.[67] The operations of all PRC-based or -invested media firms and business platforms, such as Huawei, Alibaba, Tik Tok (Byte Dance), WeChat (Tencent), Temu (PDD), and Shein must be closely monitored and restricted or prohibited, unless and until the PRC genuinely opens its market to Western competitors of those firms.[68] The UK has exemplarily started to remove all Huawei products, a process set to be complete by 2027.[69] India went further, banning 177 (increased to over 300) PRC-made or -based apps on the grounds of "sovereignty and security," and openly limiting and squeezing out PRC firms.[70] PRC firms (261 listed in the US stock exchanges with a capitalization of $1.3

trillion in mid-2022), including those nominally based in offshore tax havens, especially those that evade accountability, should all be delisted in the West, unless US regulators can fully access their company audit records, a move that could help to profoundly transform state-market relations and information dissemination in China.[71] Western institutional investors should be required to regularly disclose their ties to and dealings with PRC entities. As I reported in the prequel to this book, *The China Record*, such moves will undermine the PRC's financial power, job programs, and access to Western technology, slashing deep into the CCP's political legitimacy, which is based on claims of developmentalist populism. With the consensus view by the West of the PRC as a nonmarket economy, Beijing's RMB should not be allowed to become a credible medium of exchange, a hard currency, outside of the PRC. The West should routinely and closely scrutinize and restrict PRC students and researchers, especially those maintaining double identities, those with ties to the CCP partocracy, and those ferrying back and forth to profit from both sides. The West should monitor and expose CCP sympathizers and agents, such as PRC-funded "media" and community outfits.[72]

The US and its allies ought to force the CCP-PRC to either back down or engage in a long and comprehensive arms race, including competition in the so-called "gray zone" of unconventional and nonkinetic capabilities,[73] which is almost certain to disfavor the innovation-challenged PRC under the West's comprehensive and effective control of technology export.[74] Outside of the Indo-Pacific region, as elaborated below, the US and its allies should work in a smart, concerted way to create an ever more costly drain for the CCP abroad in places like Africa and Latin America, while concurrently benefitting local nations. The West should invest wisely to raise the bar and force the CCP to spend exponentially more with sharply diminishing returns in its long game of procuring political influence in those places though bequest and bribery.

Last but clearly not least, the US and its allies must support the Chinese people, to transform and reorganize their government and redirect their resources and energy. The West must call for and act on the premise of transformation and liberalization. If US/Western policy circa 1978–2008, generally entitled "engagement," was not really or not seriously concerned with "political liberalization" in China,[75] from now on, the US and the West should be much more conscious and clear about aiming at and focusing on facilitating sociopolitical changes in its engagement or any dealings with the PRC. Belittling and depowering the CCP regime as well as fostering its demoralization, division, and disintegration are efficient ways to prevail in the China Race.

The CCP leaders and their representatives should no longer be dignified as equals or normal partners, other than in the realm of basic and common diplomatic courtesy. CCP leaders' faces, reputations, personal and family fortunes, and especially their hidden assets and their relatives secretly living overseas, should all be fair subjects for focused exposé, constant investigation, and targeted regulations. Anyone who is a part of the CCP-PRC ruling elite, particularly active and retired "leading cadres" and their immediate families (comprising a very tiny minority, fewer than 0.2% of the Chinese population), should be singled out with special scrutiny, not the favorable deference they often enjoy, in immigration, education, employment and business opportunities, and other rights, access, and privileges abroad, particularly in the West. In December 2020 and May 2021, perhaps as tentative steps in that direction, Washington started denying visa applications from certain CCP-PRC officials and their families as a punitive responses to Beijing's human rights violations and noncooperation with the repatriation of 40,000 illegal Chinese immigrants.[76] Such an adjustable policy of "precision strike" would offer ambitious Chinese a choice between chaining themselves to the ladder of the party-state and pursuing other ways of upward mobility. It would steadily reduce and deny the CCP's access to the vast talent pool in China and recruitment abroad. Having seen and tasted the wide world outside, especially in the West, the Chinese people, including many members of the PRC's ruling elite, could and should be encouraged, assisted, and even required to build up their reason, will, and energy in order to transform their own government and take charge of their own destiny.

The State of the Race

To many if not most observers, it is by now an open secret that the CCP-PRC is moving forcefully to grab the world's leadership at the expense of the US and the West, with the rather explicit aim of replacing the existing world order with a set of "alternative global norms and standards."[77] The global competition of the China Race is preordained by the innate logic of the CCP-PRC political system for the regime's survival and security, rather than motivated by the national interests of

222 | The China Race

the Chinese people, as I have attempted to demonstrate in this book and its two prequels. This competition will not go away until either the world is recentered and reordered as a world empire like the China Order, or the CCP regime withers and fades in China. The common realpolitik practice of accommodating and appeasing the nationalist demands of a rising power in order to extinguish spikes of aggression will not stop the China Race, as the CCP is not really seeking to promote Chinese national interest for the sake of the Chinese people. The CCP is destined to seek control of the entire world, far beyond the traditional disputes among the nations for territory, treasure, score-settling, or glory. The China Race is about the very existence, identity and sovereignty of all nations, and the direction and fortune of all human civilization. "Until China changes, a prolonged period of [West-PRC] rivalry is therefore all but inevitable."[78]

To recap what I have demonstrated earlier in this book, the China Race actually started from day one of the PRC in 1949, or possibly even earlier in the 1920s when the CCP was founded by Moscow as part of the Leninist-Stalinist world Communist revolution. For the West, it was largely an ignorable nuisance and a dismissible illusion, never really the focus of international relations until the 21st century. However, by the mid-2010s, the China Race had assumed a global reach and the CCP-PRC became increasingly capable of making decisive gains and even to approach the tipping point for victory. Either to project its confidence, rally for battle, or propagandize for domestic governance and extraction, Beijing declared before and after the global pandemic of COVID-19 that the PRC was "unprecedentedly approaching the center of the world stage," ready and capable of leading and improving the world as a whole, with its "China Ideas, China Wisdom, and China Solution" to "construct the community of common human destiny and a new type of international relations."[79] As mentioned earlier in this book, Xi Jinping and the CCP have publicly hailed the China Race as "the greatest transformation of the world in the last one hundred years"—since World War I (or the Russian Revolution or the creation of the CCP), or in the last 400 years—since the Peace of Westphalia (or the Industrial Revolution).[80] The CCP has also proclaimed itself, rather than its captive China, as a force that "has deeply altered the trajectory of human history" and "led the construction of a better common world," and thus fully deserves to be "a model for all political parties of the world."[81]

In the China Race, the rising power of the CCP-PRC challenges the existing institutions and norms of a world that now has nearly 200 sovereign units, all of which would see their independence and sovereignty diminish or disappear if Beijing were to win the Race. Yet, the logic of collective action and the nature of a Westphalian system, which values self-help and prioritizes relative gains, have determined that most if not all the affected nations tend to be free-riding bystanders and hedging bandwagoners.[82] Calculating the relative costs and gains and naturally counting on the "more affected" to bear the burden, nation-states prefer avoidance, even when they may see that the whole system is in danger. Many leaders of the nation-states paradoxically but unsurprisingly assist and enable their gravedigger through countless short-term behaviors for their legitimate or perceived "tangible" benefits. The current state of international relations featuring the China Race may have already become a defining juncture of human civilization with or without the full acknowledgement and appreciation of the nations affected. In many ways, the world today seems to this author akin to a reenactment of the history of the pre-Qin Warring States, which ended with the well-known undesirable power of the Qin "unexpectedly" conquering and uniting the whole known Sinic world. Many of the richer and more advanced Warring States fell one after the other to the Qin's superb application of brutal force and cunning diplomacy. The fiasco of collective inaction by those states in defending the de facto Westphalian system in east Eurasia defined, sealed, and retarded Chinese civilization for most of the subsequent two millennia.[83]

The West and the world, including the Chinese people, are all better served by the continuation of the Westphalian system—in the form of the West-led LIO or an improved version led by some similar or better power—than by any possible world governance of the China Order (or a like system under some other name) led by the CCP or its variant. Running the China Race against Beijing, the West as a group is by far richer, more advanced, and more powerful with a tested alliance in place. But some if not many of the Western countries will predictably behave like normal nation-states, not too differently from those Warring States in ancient China, inadvertently but significantly helping the systemic challenger to extinguish them. In the era of globalization, multilateralism, and multiculturalism, and with seemingly countless reasons to dislike and defy Washington, many Westerners among the US allies easily and

224 | The China Race

comfortably find a friend or at least a ride sharer in the CCP-PRC, and work with Beijing to pursue a variety of good values and worthy objectives, such as multipolarity, certain issues in the global agenda, and wealth, as well as experiencing the considerable pleasure of being well received and pampered by the ruler of nearly one-fifth of humankind.

The China Race, therefore, essentially boils down to being a contest of the PRC-USA rivalry for existence and the world. The grossly asymmetric values and calculations of costs and benefits, as well as the very unalike rules of engagement, suggest that the still much stronger and more influential US is not necessarily leading in the China Race, and is not guaranteed to prevail. In the absence of sufficient national mobilization, which is hard to muster without a compelling reason, such as unrestricted submarine warfare, the Pearl Harbor bombing or the 9/11 attack, the United States tends to be mostly reactive and is thus constantly losing ground in a piecemeal fashion to the PRC. Beijing, for all its inherent incompetence and lack of policy discourse, seems to have learned lessons from the Germans and the Japanese and picked up from the Americans the game of brinkmanship.[84] The CCP's plan for its omnidirectional offense is to maximize any possible gains and advances, with bluffs and ruses, but not give Washington an excuse strong enough to mobilize Americans before the US is outweighed and outmaneuvered. This, of course, is also lifted from the traditional Chinese art of ruling and art of war, the so-called "subduing the enemy without fighting."[85]

Beijing, with its bottomless bank account financed by nearly one-fifth of humankind toiling as tireless, bitterness-eating worker bees enduring "muted suffering and enforced silence,"[86] is betting that it can successfully train and numb American and Western elites, and even societies at large, to tolerate its increasingly egregious actions at home and abroad. This strategy, if successful, will prevent timely mobilization and concerted responses by the superior American power. With this intention, Beijing has indeed gone all-out, in an omnidirectional and meticulous manner, seemingly covering just about every country from Australia to Switzerland, with a great variety of means: "grand external propaganda"; the infiltration and deployment of agents and sympathizers (the so-called "useful idiots") through open and hidden united fronts; the cultivation of vested interests and entanglements in the West through economic activities that purposefully and deliberately transfer wealth and benefits in a targeted way; simple bribery and recruitment; and the capture and manipulation of West-created international organizations and fora.[87] It is as if the CCP is following its own version of contaformation to selectively engage and extensively influence, transform, convert, and control the West and the world, albeit with opposing values and single-minded tenacity.

By the mid-21st century, as Beijing has publicly announced for years, the CCP-PRC could be on par with or surpass the US in at least hard national power defined mostly as financial resources and military capabilities with leadership in industry and technology.[88] By then, the rational and "selfish" Americans would have to face the incredible choice between a peaceful and graceful capitulation and a cruel Armageddon of a showdown with an opponent fully armed with WMDs, capable of crushing nuclear, biological, and financial warfare. The US, with its pluralist democracy and prevalent individualism, has been widely viewed by my Chinese interviewees over the years as incapable and unwilling to risk mutually assured destruction to oppose a "clearly stronger and superior" PRC that can also skillfully soften and sweeten the initial terms of subjugation. A snowball effect then would end the China Race in Beijing's favor. Without a meaningful opponent or constraint, the CCP-PRC, or the same polity under some other name, such as "the united people of the world," would then easily have the whole globe at its willful disposal, which, as I have attempted to show in the case of the Chinese world under the China Order,[89] would result in endless cycles of the same nightmare for all of humanity in the whole known world.

Crushing the Party and Quashing the Peculiar Racism

A key development in the China Race has been the emergence of a renewed, conscious, and bipartisan effort in the United States to dis-tinguish the CCP-PRC party-state from the Chinese nation and the Chinese people.[90] As a symbol of that, in February 2023, the US House of Representatives specially formed a "Select Committee on Strategic Competition between the United States and the Chinese Communist Party."[91] As reported earlier in this book, this development has the poten-tial to create true devastation for the regime of the self-styled "people's democratic dictatorship," in effect detaching the CCP leaders from their human shields. Some precision strikes against CCP ventures and the PRC regime itself seem to have taken shape to create a new path forward and map a new landscape, a fait accompli, for future US policy toward

226 | The China Race

China. Given the analysis presented in this book, to target and crush the Party represents major progress, sharpening the focus of the China Race and opening a major shortcut to an efficient victory for the West and the world including the Chinese people. The questions then are why the US did not act this way earlier and whether this effort will sustain.

Ever since the mid-1970s, the call for "regime change" in the PRC has been a taboo proposition drawing kneejerk condemnation in the West and in the US.[92] The reasoning behind the gentle treatment of the CCP (a self-professed communist autocracy that seeks revolutionary changes in the world) as an acceptable and normal peer consistently cites the regime change that has occurred in many other states ruled by communist or other radical parties since the 1940s. Tenacious and oblivious (but also genuine and benign) wishful thinking, a persistent naivete, and misconceived fear of CCP power, perpetrated by its effective propaganda and "united front" ploys, assisted by many misguided Sinologists as described earlier, may together help to explain the self-prohibition of anti-CCP theses.

Going deeper, however, there seems to be a hidden, ugly, obstinate, and peculiar form of racism that is responsible for the Western misconception about China and the CCP-PRC in particular. This subtle but strong bias holds the Chinese people, Han and non-Han, to be somehow inherently unique and unequal, often inferior, and less worthy, human beings who are uniquely incapable or unwilling to adopt or enjoy "universal" values, rights, and norms. This nonsensical bigotry in fact strongly echoes a lasting and deeply internalized CCP party line maintaining that the so-called "low quality (*disuzhi*) of the [Chinese] people" has always deemed democracy and "Western" liberty somehow premature, inapplicable, and unfeasible in China, even in the 21st century.[93] This attitude combines all the pitfalls commonly associated with racism, such as misjudgments, self-injurious actions, costly blunders, and avoidable disasters. Over a century ago, Western intellectuals like Henry Wandesforde, the British journalist, and especially Frank Goodnow, the first president of the American Political Science Association and later the long-time president of a prestigious US university, went to China to enlighten and advise the Chinese elites and rulers. Among other things, they earnestly urged Yuan Shikai, the president of the Republic of China, to turn a just-born constitutional republic into a disastrous monarchy, a model of governance they thought to be more "suitable" to China, a special country, where the "standard of intelligence," people's "self-discipline and social cooperation," and the "suitability" of republicanism and constitutional democracy were all too low, and thus political order and stability would require a hereditary and "illiberal" regime of imperial rule.[94] The first and so far the only direct conflict between the US and the PRC, the Korean War, was also plagued by such racism-related misconceptions and misactions.[95]

The same hidden or not-so-hidden racism has contributed to the persistent wishful thinking about a natural or even automatic political change in the PRC through open trade, ignoring how such sociopolitical changes have historically taken place in the world: through conscious and concerted political organization and action, often with a role for force. In the 21st century, racist biases seem to possess many foreign "friends" who, with their misreading of history, distortion of Chinese ideas, and fascination with the CCP, promote a "China Model"—a "new society" filled with Chinese peculiarities—as an alternative governance of so-called "political meritocracy"; these are essentially repackaged pre-Enlightenment political ideals that never existed let alone prospered anywhere in reality, yet somehow "suit" and best serve the Chinese people today and also tomorrow.[96] In this view, the West is better advised to tolerate, accept, appreciate, and reward the CCP for its rather effective "control" of the massive numbers of inscrutable, menacing but lesser Chinese people of "low quality."

Sadly, given the long history of suboptimality and tragedies of governance and brainwashing under the imperial version and the CCP version of the Qin-Han polity, as I have attempted to outline in the two prequels to this book, the prejudice that views the Chinese people as somehow enigmatic aliens and lesser beings may not be totally incomprehensible. This increasingly unwitting and often unconscious racism is just like all other forms of racism in terms of its significance and fallaciousness, but with two profound twists. As the infamous China Exclusion Act (1882–1943) illustrated, it unfairly treats the Chinese people, rather than Chinese sociopolitical organization and political culture, as inferior and threatening. Moreover, it often materializes as overzealous fascination, simulated and misplaced admiration, or unreasoned and categorical dismissal about anything Chinese, so as to tolerate and normalize or overlook the seemingly inscrutable Chinese governance and way of life. In practice, this peculiar racism often, ignorantly or dishonestly, contrives to display an outsized and unjustified empathy for the CCP-PRC state to disguise a deep sense of superiority toward the Chinese people. On the one hand, to curb the

228 | The China Race

so-called Yellow Peril and promote the so-called Yellow Promise, many American and Western elites seem to have caught the so-called Yellow Fever,[97] eagerly and easily pointing to the unscrupulously manufactured words and gestures of the CCP to declare the compatibility, equality, promise, and even superiority of the PRC. On the other hand, there seems to be a hidden belief, a "double standard," among many Western elites that, for the lower and lesser Chinese people, the CCP has already done an acceptable and even remarkable job worthy of support and praise, despite all those undeniable atrocities, blunders, and disasters. Thus, while the Serbian leaders were prosecuted for the deaths of tens of thousands of Yugoslavians and the Russian leader censured for poisoning political dissidents, the CCP leaders continue to wine and dine with Western leaders as respected peers despite their role in the mistreating and even killing of many more (tens of millions of) Chinese.[98]

Seeing the great utility of this peculiar racism in the service of its power and ambition, the CCP has shrewdly used accusations of racism and propaganda to harvest political capital from Chinese nationalists and to deceive and fend off Westerners. It has also sought to capitalize on such Western bigotry to fend off criticisms of the party-state with, for example, Xi Jinping's blunt declaration that "those spoiled foreigners" who dared to criticize the CCP should just shut up, since "we first don't export revolution, second don't export famine and poverty, and third don't go to torment you," yet.[99] A double-standard in the West about the CCP-PRC state, often echoing Beijing's party line on those peculiar and impregnable "Chinese characteristics" or "national conditions,"[100] has thus persisted, helping to sustain and empower the CCP. The CCP is often misconceived as an overly sensitive pupil with a teenage temper (or the guardian with endless wisdom of the very unique and "only undisrupted" human civilization, as Xi Jinping put it[101]), inscrutable and unbendable, trying its best but needing special patience and tolerance. It is abominably common for this author to observe Western movers and shakers implying that, in comparison to the Soviet regimes in Russia and Eastern Europe that presided over Christians and Caucasians, an even more autocratic version of Leninist-Stalinist communism is somehow not *that* bad, perhaps even apposite, needed, and justified, for the "peculiar" and less deserving people in China. As a former PRC political prisoner in exile wrote in 2021 regarding "regime change" in Beijing, "the majority of western observers and politicians, for nearly two past decades, have lost the academic and political imagination to envision a free China"[102] The ongoing debate in the West over the accuracy and appropriateness of Washington's accusations of "genocide" in Xinjiang and other human rights abuses in the PRC, for example, seems to reaffirm such an observation.[103]

The US is poised to have a comprehensive "rules-based competition that cooperates and confronts [. . .] China's combined effects strategy."[104] The accompanying "whole-of-state" and "whole-of-society" rhetoric, however, may sound like a "red scare," which is traditionally and normatively un-American and haphazardly implemented, reminding many of the infamous (though not entirely incorrect in hindsight) activities of McCarthyism in the 1950s.[105] However, so long as Washington and the Americans are fully aware of the difference and distinction between the CCP-PRC state and the Chinese nation/people, and even more critically between the CCP and Chinese/Asian-Americans, then the sociopolitical and moral costs of running the China Race in the US should remain at a manageable minimum.[106]

It is necessary and possible to crush both the Party and racism against Chinese. Many of those automatically crying "red scare"[107] tend to be witting or unwitting scaremongers with specific agendas. They often exaggerate and misappropriate the real but limited political harassment and social chagrin very few American liberals briefly suffered during the McCarthy era as somehow morally equivalent to the decades-long deadly purges of millions in places like the Soviet Union or the PRC. Their ostentatious alarm is not only perilously illogical and deceitful but also morally deficient, harboring serious racism that grossly discounts and dismisses "other" peoples like the Chinese. Zero collateral damage in the China Race is unrealistic but, fortunately, it is now over a half-century since the civil rights movement. The US policy and action toward Muslims during the two-decade-long global war on terrorism after the 9/11 attack should provide considerable confidence and comfort. The US in the 21st century, after all, is very different from what it was in the 1940s–50s. For example, reasoned worries and balanced scrutiny regarding the possible overuse of the US Department of Justice's investigations under its "China Initiative" appeared loudly just months after the program was announced in 2018; the "Initiative" was replaced in February 2022 with a less "myopic" effort "to address threats from a broader array of hostile nations."[108]

The actions of engaging the China Race in recent years offer hope that the US can target the CCP Party while avoiding anti-Chinese discrimination, that is, walking and chewing gum at the same time.[109] Washington has launched a series of legal and administrative actions related to Taiwan and Xinjiang and escalated sanctions against dozens of PRC entities including Huawei and Hikvision.[110] In response to Beijing's effective destruction of Hong Kong's treaty-promised autonomy, as reported earlier in this book, the US has started to end its special treatment of the former British colony and may shut a major backdoor for the CCP's significant access to Western technology and capital.[111] But there has not been anything close to a blanket embargo. At home, the US has started to restrict the presence and actions of CCP-controlled PRC media, suspend visas for PLA-related visitors, gradually tighten regulations on Chinese firms (mostly state owned and all CCP-controlled) listed on Wall Street,[112] and apply the Global Magnitsky Act to financially punish CCP cadres and entities for their violations of human rights in places like Xinjiang and in cases like religious persecution.[113] The US national security advisor openly pointed out in October 2020 that "nearly every Chinese-language news outlet in the United States is owned by the CCP or follows its editorial line."[114] But, at the same time, the US has kept its doors open to the same massive number of incoming Chinese students since the global pandemic subsided in 2021.[115] The US trade war of tariffs with the PRC and its enhanced border controls attempting to stamp out the massive inflow of deadly fentanyl from the PRC via Mexico, an effort that was probably long overdue, has not significantly affected the massive imports from China.[116]

The US law enforcement community in general, as the FBI director told Congress and the public in July 2020, seems mobilized to counter "the greatest threat" from the CCP, with an "all-tools and all-sectors approach." "The FBI is now opening a new China-related counterintelligence case every 10 hours" and "of the nearly 5,000 active counterintelligence cases currently under way across the country, almost half are related to China."[117] Despite this, there has been very limited evidence of systemic racial discrimination against Chinese-Americans. In August 2020, in announcing its new efforts for the "expansion of clean network," the US government started to ban PRC apps and restrict and expel PRC IT firms, and called on its allies to do the same.[118] Most of these firms and apps, however, are still operating in the US over three years later with no chance of being totally banned administratively, as they have been in India. The US has publicly stated that "it's time for a new grouping of like-minded nations, a new alliance of democracies" to effectively meet the comprehensive challenge of the CCP.[119] Military leaders have openly envisioned a disciplined, fully combined, and multidimensional approach to restraining and countering Beijing, as the US and its "broader networks of capable, like-minded partners [. . .] are ready to defend every front" against the PLA.[120] Still, Washington sent cabinet-level envoy John Kerry to China "separately" to discuss climate change, and included Xi at the virtual global summit on climate, reaching at least some symbolic agreements on common concerns.[121]

Ideas on Racing Well

There are many scholars, analysts, and politicians who are smarter, better-informed, more experienced, more capable, and more articulate than this author in crafting a sound China policy for the American effort to prevail in the China Race.[122] A task force organized by the Asia Society that included leading Sinologists and former senior China hands from the US government, for example, produced eight "memos" in fall 2021 with specific and often sharp policies to extensively address the various aspects of US-China relations.[123] A former US defense planner bluntly argued that the US must make the total defeat of the rising power of the PRC, militarily if necessary, the center of the American national security strategy in the new era of great power competition, so as to stop Beijing's international ambitions.[124] In general, it seems imperative to make America strong, to "focus on the strength of Detroit, Disney, and the dollar," in order to race well with the CCP.[125] The Biden administration's proposal for massive investment in US infrastructure is a move in the right direction.[126] It is both wise and challenging "to renew America's advantages in its competition with China" (read the CCP) but "not to turn a rising [Chinese] power into an enemy."[127] In spring 2023, a long report by the Heritage Foundation presented a detailed action plan for "countering China" and "winning the new Cold War."[128] It is increasingly apparent, as this book has attempted to argue, that the CCP-led PRC state power is now seen inside and outside the Beltway as a long-term adversary with its fixation on replacing the US as world leader.

The contaformation strategy outlined in this book presupposes an unyielding effort to keep the US strong for the sake of effective containment and smart engagement. The central value is the delicate but worthy goal of crushing the CCP party, not the nation of China. One

232 | The China Race

young analyst has succinctly outlined "five interrelated and overlapping strategies required to defeat the CCP: 1) Defend, 2) Ally, 3) Contain, 4) Divide, and 5) Democratize."[129] An anonymous report via a major US thinktank outlined in 2021 a thoughtful US China strategy that resonates well with this book, especially on competing with superior ideas and ideals, making the US a strong leader, consolidating the US dollar and the current world order, and working with allies.[130] The engagement part of contaformation parallels sensible ideas like "cooperative rivalry," "balance between global competition and cooperation," and "constructive competition."[131] With "no time left to waste," the US must do "whatever" it takes to "peak" or maximize its capacity and will to deter the PRC in the critical 2020s, according to two American analysts.[132] With more urgency, more calls are already out for leveraging American power at home and abroad to manage the China Race. Given our understanding of the CCP and its strengths and weaknesses, and in the context of the normative principles and policy parameters discussed earlier, I immodestly present the following ideas with the hope of helping to create a sustained China policy, in the context of contaformation, to win the PRC-USA rivalry with effectiveness and efficiency.

First, with "all-tools and all-sectors," the US should focus on weakening and dismantling the CCP's Great Firewall, which is designed to control information and advance propaganda, foremostly in the United States itself. Propaganda with adroit misinformation, boundless disinformation, and targeted manipulation has been one of Beijing's key weapons at home and abroad. In 2009, the CCP reportedly put down ¥45 billion ($7 billion) to launch and then several billions more every year to operate the "grand external propaganda" (*dawaixuan*) program to upgrade and expand the promotion of the CCP-PRC state's image abroad so as to "grab the power of narratives of the world."[133] That program is getting ever stronger under the prettified new name of "grand promotion" (*dachuanbo*) in the 2020s.[134] The omnipresent "defensive" censorship at home costs even more. Financially and technologically, the CCP is stuck fighting an endless and uphill battle, which presents the US a shortcut to run the China Race efficiently. The widespread use of mobile devices like smart phones inside the PRC, for example, has already shown its usefulness for political contention that resists the CCP's information control.[135] Washington should leverage that and seek to make both the Great Firewall and the "grand external propaganda" ever more cost-ineffective and technologically challenged, with measures to subsidize, sponsor, and provide for any efforts and toolkits, such as VPN, space-based direct Wi-Fi access, Bluetooth transmission, and smart apps like Podcasts, Telegram, WhatsApp, and Clubhouse, to penetrate and break Beijing's censorship and control of information flow on the Internet.[136] Translating the CCP's domestic propaganda and making it available to foreigners could help to counter the party's double talk; politically inconvenient Internet hacking and leaking apparently can also happen in the PRC.[137] To reduce or even eliminate the "radical secrecy" of the CCP would make China more predictable and the world safer.[138]

Federal statutes and criminal investigations should be invoked to reduce and prevent American technology from being used for social surveillance and information control and gathering in the PRC and increasingly abroad.[139] All media and educational institutions and social groups in the US should disclose and declare their administrative and financial ties to the CCP-PRC, if any, beyond just their tax filings, so as to warn their consumers and members. This would be no different than the warning labels on canned food or cigarette packs. For example, up until 2019, CCP propaganda and United Front cadres, perhaps in their zeal to please their bosses, published a list of Beijing-subsidized, influenced, and controlled organizations and individuals in the US (and abroad in general) working for the "grand external propaganda"—they met biannually in the PRC.[140] "U.S. institutions must get smarter about Chinese Communist Party money," two American analysts argued in 2021; the simple identification and exposure of those names would go a long way toward disrupting and diminishing the CCP's propaganda and united front machines abroad.[141] Regarding the presence of the CCP on American campuses via Confucius Institutes (CIs) or other channels,[142] the US should demand equal treatment for the federally sponsored American educators of social sciences and humanities on Chinese campuses and require the CIs to register as PRC state entities and move off campus.[143] A fair policy of reciprocity would enable the US government and corporate operators to limit or even stop the CCP's crafty propaganda and disinformation on American social media and broadcast media that are banned in China. What Twitter did in June 2020—deleting 170,000 PRC accounts—should be supported and emulated by the whole industry, including Facebook, Instagram, and YouTube,[144] unless and until Beijing allows uncensored American postings on WeChat, TikTok, and Weibo inside the PRC.

Second, the US should better leverage the massive number of Chinese students in the country. Starting from 1978, generations of students

234 | The China Race

from the Chinese Mainland have studied in the US, a development viewed by many in the PRC as "the 40-year American assistance to China."[145] In 2018–19, for the 10th consecutive year, China remained the largest source of international students in the US, with 369,548 students in undergraduate, graduate, nondegree, and optional practical training programs (and this does not even include the increasing number of Chinese students attending American high schools, middle schools, and even elementary schools). This number grew every year from 2005 to 2020. In 2021, despite the negative impact of the COVID pandemic, Chinese students accounted for a whopping 34% of all international students in America, far higher than the Chinese proportionate population in the world (roughly 19%), almost double the number of students from India, the number two country of origin, and 10 times the number from South Korea, the third largest country of origin.[146] Even when the pandemic literally halted cross-Pacific travel, the US remained the top study-abroad destination for 97% of Chinese students and their families surveyed.[147] In the 2010s, around 5,000 Chinese students earned PhD degrees each year from US colleges (6,182 in 2018 and 6,305 in 2019, for example), comprising about 11% of the total PhD degrees granted; over 90% majored in STEM (science, technology, engineering, and mathematics) and 79.3% (in 2019) remained in the US after graduation.[148] As of February 2017, 90% of the 55,000 Chinese recipients of PhD degrees in STEM in the 15-year period 2000–15 were still living and working the US.[149] Overall, more than 85% of all Chinese students earning degrees in STEM have stayed indefinitely, becoming productive and contributing new Americans by choice.[150] Some will ultimately return to China and others will frequently shuttle across the Pacific. All of them are key assets to a good running of the China Race in both the US and the PRC.

The CCP has worked hard to exploit these students—an effort that has been effective in acquiring technology.[151] A simple, extra effort that is truly win-win-win for the PRC students, the United States, and the Chinese people in general would be to require all students from the PRC, especially those above the high school level and majoring in STEM, to take or retake a sufficient number of history courses (particularly Chinese history), civics and logic, philosophy and ethics, social sciences especially political science, and other humanities from accredited American educators. These could be existing courses or specially tailored cluster or module courses. Such a requirement could be extended to students from other countries that have high school and college social science and humanities curricula incompatible with what a good American education should entail. Other Western allies should and could do the same. An American/Western degree of higher learning without an American/Western education in the social science and humanities is incomplete and substandard, and certainly shortchanges the recipient, with grave consequences. With the incomplete curriculum, for example, Western-educated engineers from the Muslim world have "disproportionately" become radical jihadists against the West.[152]

For nearly two decades, tens of thousands of PRC mothers have traveled to the US each year to deliberately give birth here; affluent PRC parents have also used surrogacy to have their children born in the US, even during the COVID-19 pandemic.[153] By 2023, such a backdoor emigration through birth—lawful and innovative but often abusive of the American legal and health-care systems—has resulted in an estimated half-million and increasing future US citizens, who are "mostly educated in the PRC and will probably all come to the US as adults with full rights to immediately participate in American politics," yet without the learning and adaptation associated with the gradual naturalization process. It will therefore be a novel and consequential challenge, with many unknowns and uncertainties, for the US to accommodate so many CCP-educated American citizens in its society, politics, and military.[154] Reeducating these special citizens, similarly to reeducating the Chinese students as discussed above, seems advisable and even imperative but could be difficult and even controversial.

Third, the US should minimize its dependence on critical supplies from the PRC. While it seems that this shift is already taking place,[155] more and sustained government action related to industrial policy, infrastructure development, trade, and investment are sorely needed to compensate for the CCP's well-funded industrial policy and investment schemes.[156] Prevailing in the China Race and having a healthy and strong US economy are symbiotic and mutually reinforcing. Significant but selective and smart delinking and disconnection of the American and Chinese economies must take place, understandably at a certain but transient cost. National security requires a secure supply of key products and ingredients, such as health-care products.[157] For common labor-intensive consumer products and services, the US should establish and use issue-linkages in combination with reciprocity to promote green standards for labor rights and environmental protection in the PRC, and

236 | The China Race

to open the Chinese market for competitive American firms in areas that are also beneficial for running the China Race, such as financial services, telecommunications, education, media, and entertainment. The distancing of the two economies will not really hurt the bottom-lines of American firms, as Beijing's talking points would have people believe. Lessons from the Nippon-American economic negotiations a few decades ago can still be useful.[158]

The so-called "decoupling" between China and the US in fact has been an often-obscured reality ever since the PRC was founded in 1949. The CCP violently imposed a nearly full decoupling with the US-led West during the Mao era. The post-Mao rulers have modified that to a more selective decoupling (selective engagement and disengagement or a conditional "surrender" in another perspective) since the so-called "reform and open" era began in the late 1970s. As I have attempted to show in this book and its two prequels, the CCP has spent astronomically to maintain a parallel and walled-off universe in the PRC, especially regarding human rights and social values, political institutions and norms, worldviews, and the flow of information. It is only logical for the US to fully join the game and refashion that partial decoupling more on Western terms, moving to a full decoupling when necessary, so as to slow or even stop the CCP from draining and poisoning the well of Western technology and wealth; it would be helpful in inducing the CCP-PRC to change its behavior (and hopefully its composition and mindset as well, for a more sustainable alteration in its behavior) in order to have a real and full coupling that is clearly beneficial to the American people and critically valuable to the Chinese people. Selective and manipulative coupling by one side never sustains a fair, lasting, and healthy relationship. Either a verified full coupling, a selective decoupling on Western terms as well, or a full decoupling would be a responsible and cost-effective way for the US to act in its effort to prevent the CCP from recentering and reordering the world. Beijing's attempt to import the West's technology without its sociopolitical norms was deemed, starting in the late-19th century, as ineffective or even impossible;[159] Today, however, such a selective coupling or decoupling appears to be cleverly doable and ever more dangerous, and should be stopped. One must follow the "universal" rules to drive and fly, or return to walking and crawling. While, as Robert Atkinson argued in 2020, the US-led West may choose to counter Beijing's "power trade" game "bravely, strategically, and expeditiously,"[160] the moral burden associated with the sociopolitical cost of that hefty choice should be rightfully on the CCP. Encouragingly, many PRC analysts seem to see the choice and its fatefulness for the Chinese nation and the Chinese people, especially in the aftermath of the united Western sanctions against Russia since 2022.[161]

Driven by its innate political musts in tandem with its questionable power calculus, the CCP has accelerated its efforts to control, squeeze, and expel foreign firms, usually as soon as a craved technology is transferred, as most recently illustrated by the cases of Tesla, Bain, and others in 2021–23.[162] As one commentator observed, American investors have begun to "acknowledge that funneling Americans' money into Chinese companies that have zero transparency, zero accountability and zero independence from the CCP is both bad for investors and bad for America."[163] In fact, after all, as Chinese analysts have acknowledged, foreign-invested firms in the PRC earn the majority of the hard currencies used by Beijing to power its military and diplomatic ventures.[164] A smart, proactive and selective policy of distancing and even decoupling in the PRC-West economic and technological exchanges is therefore justified and imperative; it also creates new opportunities for American businesses.[165] The price increases and inconvenience for American consumers are in all likelihood manageable and temporary, as the global chains of production can relocate quickly, and Chinese exports to the West are mostly very substitutable.[166] A so-called "Altasia" (alternative Asian supply chain), for example, appears to have already quietly and effectively replaced many PRC suppliers.[167] This is in fact a highly economical investment, because, as one observer put it, "we wouldn't have to spend so much on military etcetera if we didn't chase the much smaller money saved on cheap Chinese imports."[168] Far beyond superficial moral concerns of fairness or theoretical calculations of "global" economic efficiency, the question of where to buy and at what true cost is critically important to the long-term prosperity and security of the US and to world peace.

If properly mobilized and well led, the US could prevail in the PRC-USA rivalry and the overall China Race swiftly and efficiently, with its still apparent, albeit eroding, superiority in its power relationship with the PRC, especially with regard to so-called soft power.[169] As mentioned earlier, the US and its major allies (Germany, UK, and Japan) all enjoy a higher rank of soft power than the PRC, whose global soft power is viewed as less than countries like Poland and Brazil. In terms of business brand recognition, in 2023, seven American firms were in the top 10 and 50 in the top 100 lists of the most valued brands in the world,

238 | The China Race

while only 1 and 13 Chinese brands (decreased from 2 and 24 in the previous year) made the two lists, respectively.[170] During the COVID-19 pandemic, the PRC actively launched a so-called "vaccine diplomacy" for soft power but with only mixed, limited, and even counterproductive results to show for it, even in the developing countries.[171]

Western democracies, particularly the US, seem capable of perceiving and sounding alarms about the rising power of the CCP-PRC and its "Sino-formation of the world" to "assimilate" the nations.[172] America's scientific community seems to have started to see the "tipping point" at which the US would lose its preeminence in science and technology to China.[173] Even if fully appreciating and benefiting from these wake-up calls, though, there may still be a considerable margin of error for trials, distractions, and indulgences, such as idealist assumptions, wishful thinking, lassitude, procrastination, and other self-injurious policies and activities. But time is clearly of the essence for a preferable management and ending of the China Race, especially in terms of cost-effectiveness. The vastly different costs of World War II and the Cold War illustrate the price differential for the different ways of fending off a systemic threat to the West-led Westphalian world order. A sound and timely US China policy will determine how much humanity pays this time for managing and prevailing in the China Race. The odds for exceeding the Cold War in efficiency, however, remain excellent.

The Worldwide Race

The China Race concerns the world and is thus global in nature. The CCP-PRC has made considerable headway all over the world, literally from Africa to Antarctica and the Arctic. The United States and its allies must react accordingly, and run the Race as a global game rather than just a bilateral, cross-Pacific dispute. To continue my immodest and illustrative effort, here are a few more considerations for efficiently managing and prevailing in the worldwide China Race, with a holistic approach that combines both "hard balancing" and "soft balancing" to deal with the CCP-PRC state.[174]

First, the US/West must safeguard its world leadership position, especially where it matters. The codified Westphalian world order, specifically the LIO version since World War II, has been under American leadership with four major pillars: (1) the superior national power of the

US, as measured in economic and military prowess; (2) the international organizations the US has initiated and led; (3) the American-Western dominated international financial system, centered around the quasi world currency of the US Dollar; and (4) the set of liberal norms and values, centered around freedoms and human rights for all citizens, which are shared and practiced by Western polities of democratic rule of law. The US and its allies should audaciously and unapologetically defend their leadership of the international community and the four pillars that support it. As a principle of the Westphalian system, of course, any nation is allowed and welcome to compete for the leadership position, provided that the challenger credibly respects and preserves the fundamental rules of the Westphalian system. The contender for leadership must be internally organized and ideologically oriented to share political power with its people and with peers abroad, or constrained and balanced to do so. For a new national power to become an equal or better leader to continue the Westphalian system, it must be institutionally and ideologically sanctioned, both internally and externally, to allow for political comparison and competition. As this book and its prequels have argued at length, the CCP-PRC state, with its internal political organization, ideology, and track record, shares political power neither internally nor externally and thus proffers no real possibility of upholding the Westphalian system let alone the LIO, no matter what it claims. Therefore, without a fundamental sociopolitical and ideological transformation, the CCP-PRC must be contained and constrained worldwide through external competition and, ideally, internal remodeling. This "greatest game" for the world is up to the US and other democracies to win or lose.[175]

More specifically, the US and its allies must be *realist* enough to pursue a rather old-fashioned game for relative gains vis-à-vis the PRC. Beijing should not be viewed as a normal partner, let alone deserving of any preferential privilege, in its access to and share of the world's economic and technological resources. The PRC's trade imbalance must be scrutinized and curtailed, its investors and merchants monitored and restricted. Any vestige of the massive foreign aid to the PRC and the numerous preferences and open accesses granted by the West over the past four decades should cease. Beijing's forceful and crafty push to internationalize its currency, the RMB, should be strictly conditioned on the requisite reforms of its internal structures and policies, particularly its state-society and state-market relationships and its fiscal and monetary policies. The financial and money laundering centers of Greater China,

240 | The China Race

Hong Kong and Macau, which are now ever more tightly controlled by the CCP, should be distanced from the international financial apparatus like the rest of the PRC.[176] Beijing's critical access to the West-led cross-border financial transaction network, the Society for Worldwide Interbank Financial Telecommunication (SWIFT)—in which the PRC and Hong Kong together have 2 votes out of 22—could be limited or even discontinued. This would deal a major blow to the CCP's power and ambitions at home and abroad, despite its backup plan, the Cross-Border Interbank Payment System (CIPS), launched in 2015.[177] The use of such a so-called "financial nuclear option" could be fine-tuned by a good study of the cutting-off of major Russian banks from SWIFT since 2022 in response to Moscow's invasion of Ukraine.[178] Similarly, Beijing's role in international organizations, especially functional agencies that make impactful policies, should be carefully monitored and countered. The PRC should not take more than its share of leadership positions. The US and the West ought to continuously put Beijing on the defense for its poor record of governance at home. When an international organization or forum is hijacked and corroded by CCP ruses and money, the West should simply cut the loss and pull the plug to start anew.

The US should also be *constructivist* enough to enact and lead organizations like the Comprehensive and Progressive Agreement for Trans-Pacific Partnership (CPTPP), the Indo-Pacific Economic Framework (IPEF), the Transatlantic Trade and Investment Partnership (TTIP), and the 18-nation Supply Chain Forum as the upgrade and replacement of the dysfunctional World Trade Organization (WTO).[179] The West should affirm and enforce the qualifications for the PRC's membership in any international organization it leads, controlling its noble but self-defeating urge to offer equal rights to all nations in the era of globalization. Selective and meaningful divergence, if not a total decoupling, is always a smart strategy.[180] The West should especially scrutinize the PRC's 2021 application for membership in CPTPP, for example—to fully verify first the prerequisite actions required of Beijing to qualify; to resist the temptation of wishful or greedy thinking; and to avoid falling once again for CCP's "united front" gimmicks and vain pledges.[181]

Second, the US must strengthen and defend the Western alliance. The CCP-PRC, as analyzed earlier, is structurally and ideologically unwilling and unable to work the magic of alliance among equal nations. Its approach of unilateral efforts combined with united front tricks is inherently costly if not always cost-ineffective, thus offering its opponent a chance to race against it efficiently. Accordingly, the US should strengthen and expand its vast and tested alliance networks, to better leverage the far superior power of the defenders of the LIO and the Westphalian system, based on and beyond the Democracy Quartet of the US, Australia, India, and Japan in the region.[182] A network could connect the alliances and partnerships of the Quad, the Five Eyes, AUKUS, and NATO with bilateral and even multilateral ties with South Korea, the Philippines, Singapore, and Thailand. With the momentum of Western unity in the aftermath of Russia's invasion of Ukraine, a larger aim could be working with Indonesia, Vietnam, Central Asian countries, and even Taiwan to form a "NATO in Asia" or North-Atlantic-Indo-Pacific Treaty Organization (NAIPTO).[183] In February 2023, Japanese prime minister Fumio Kishida and NATO's secretary general Jens Stoltenberg indeed publicly outlined that prospect.[184] The US could also explore possibilities with Mongolia and even with Russia, whose fear of the PRC over the vast, empty land of Eastern Siberia and ambition for a Moscow-dominated Eurasian unity are real and not that hidden.[185] While attempting to reforge a shared ideological identity under Vladimir Putin and Xi Jinping, Moscow and Beijing are in reality far from a position where "they have reconciled all their divergent interests or that they will co-ordinate all their policies, including a joint challenge to the West."[186] Despite their pledges of "limitless and restriction-less cooperation," Beijing and Moscow offer each other decidedly limited and unreliable support as in the case of Russia's invasion of Ukraine since 2022.[187] A post-Ukraine and post-Putin Russia is likely to reconsider its ties with the CCP in the interest of bettering its relationship with the West.[188] As Richard Nixon envisioned more than 50 years ago, it is "in their own interest that the nations in the path of China's ambitions move quickly to establish an indigenous Asian framework for their own future security" with American assistance.[189] The US should be unabashed but skillful in requesting, convincing, and even coercing the nations to substantively, if not symbolically, take sides whenever needed.[190]

At the same time, the US should be forceful about confronting the PRC and wining a comprehensive arms race, including nuclear weapons, missile-defense systems, cyber capabilities, and a space force.[191] If "China has already won Asia's arms race" against its neighboring countries in East and Southeast Asia, it is imperative for the US to counter with its own strengthened presence there, together with more investment in security by its regional allies.[192] Naturally, sensible negotiations and verifiable arms control agreements with the PRC are desirable on issues such as the permissible methods of anti-satellites, launch-on-warning systems, and nuclear-nonnuclear entanglement.[193] The US should maintain the strategic pivot started by the Obama administration to consolidate and strengthen its forward military deployment in the Indo-Pacific, with efficient new weapon systems like land-based ballistic, cruise, and hypersonic missiles, and unmanned vehicles on the so-called first and second island chains.[194] The US military could sufficiently negate the PLA in Asia-Pacific without a major budget hike, and could be freed from the overburden of peacekeeping and nation-building in other places where the needs of anti-terrorism in the future could be effectively met with good intelligence and surgical strikes. The pullout of the US military from Afghanistan in 2021 to end the US's longest war was the right move, albeit not costless. Two more potent (though provocative) geostrategic moves that the US could make to prevail in the China Race in the Western Pacific are more military and diplomatic leveraging of Taiwan, and controlled relaxation of the standing policy of nuclear nonproliferation for Japan and even South Korea, thus addressing the military and particularly the nuclear buildup by the PRC and North Korea.[195]

Third, the US should prioritize some areas over others in the global China Race. Aside from focusing on consolidating the West/US power and leadership position relative to the PRC, the US and its allies should pick and choose how and where to run the China Race effectively and efficiently. The geographical focus should always be the Indo-Pacific, as mentioned above.[196] In other areas like Africa and South America, particularly areas outside the key international shipping lanes and far from the US homeland, Washington should play smart to leverage its still formidable power there to mostly trap and drain the PRC, rather than attempting to match Beijing in every case and every step. The PRC's efforts have typically been cost-ineffective, beyond fickle favors from a few local elites and politicians, in winning the hearts and minds of the peoples, due to its incompetence and corruption, as reported in this book and by others.[197] The US should run the China Race there differently than in the Indo-Pacific. The West should encourage more PRC ventures in Africa and South America, such as the snowballing BRI (Belt and Road Initiative), while investing strategically and working smartly with locals to constantly raise the bar of ethics in business, labor rights, and environmental protection, pressuring Beijing to behave and improve. Well-targeted US efforts, such as the new Development

Finance Corporation and Transaction Advisory Fund in the US, armed with "robust anti-corruption campaigns," could asymmetrically counter and cancel Beijing's influence.[198] The global infrastructure initiative of the Blue Dot Network of project certification on transparency and sustainability, adopted by the G7 and G20 in 2018–19 and revived in 2021, as well as the 2022 G7 Infrastructure Partnership to "invest, align, compete," are steps in the right direction.[199] In this way, peoples in Africa, Asia, and Latin America would get more and better infrastructure and other tangible economic development as benefits from the PRC and the West, while the West maintains its relevance and influence there in an efficient way, and the inevitable "debt-traps" would only entrap Beijing there, draining its resources. The PRC is attempting a unique "power-building mechanism" and "extending its political influence" in Africa,[200] but, short of an unwise, highly costly, and improbable repeat of colonialist takeover by force, the PRC would have to constantly write off significant investments in those places, gaining little more than some bragging rights at home and laundered wealth for a few in the partocracy. The now rising needs and practice of Chinese security contractors in Africa, already costing billions of dollars annually, are indicative signs.[201] Beijing's ventures in places like Montenegro and Hungary may enable the West to easily trip, trap, and drain the CCP there by leveraging existing EU rules and influence.[202] Similarly, Canberra and Wellington could effectively lead efforts to counter the PRC's aggressive ventures in the South Pacific.[203]

The vast land from Central, West, and Southwest Asia to Eastern Europe, including much of the Middle East reaching the Maghreb Countries, is an important but complicated track of the China Race. For at least two decades now, the CCP-PRC has seemed to have a "go west" strategy, mimicking the geostrategic theory of "world-island and heartland," which was articulated by the British Halford Mackinder about 120 years ago.[204] Efforts like the Shanghai Cooperation Organization and especially the BRI have advanced Beijing's position in this region through trade, investment, and aid sprees.[205] As the world's largest importer of crude oil, the PRC has obtained significant power over the OPEC nations, including some traditional US allies.[206] Like in Africa and Latin America, however, the characteristic cost-ineffectiveness of Chinese foreign policy is also rampant here. The ambitious and omnidirectional pursuit of the CCP's overall goal in the China Race is intertwined with and even hampered by some genuine Chinese national interest. To simultaneously attempt to

244 | The China Race

please countries there that are sharply divided and in eternal opposition has become an inherently disadvantageous position for Beijing. The PRC supports countries it views as anti-American comrades—Iran, Syria, Hussein's Iraq, and Qadhafi's Libya—or leaders with authoritarian aspirations, like Vladimir Putin in Russia and Viktor Orbán in Hungary. It also craves advanced technology from Israel and Ukraine, seeks oil supplies (and chases the dream of a petrol-RMB) in Saudi Arabia and the Gulf states, while it struggles to maintain its solidarity with "class-comrades" like the Palestine Authority and quasi-allies like Iran.[207] Beijing's latest overtures to the Taliban in Afghanistan likely will cost it in its relationship with countries like Iran, Tajikistan, Turkmenistan, and even Russia. Investing heavily to cultivate friendship with leaders of Islamic states with schemes like the BRI, Beijing seems to have created new complications for its pursuits abroad and its subjugation of Muslims at home in Xinjiang.[208]

It seems unlikely, if at all possible, for the PRC to dominate this vast region through financial means. The region's internal dynamics are enough to frustrate the genuine expansion of PRC power there, with "anti-Chinese sentiment" already seen rising in Central Asia.[209] What the US should do, other than maintaining its traditional position in the region, is engage in some specific and targeted actions to block the petrol-RMB, stop the leak of sensitive technology, and reveal Beijing's business deals, which are often tainted by bribes, abusive labor practices, and Muslim policy at home, to keep raising the cost of Beijing's ventures in the region.[210] Efforts such as the Better Utilization of Investments Leading to Development Act of 2018, the Blue Dot Network of certification of infrastructure projects since 2019, and the G7's Build Back Better World Partnership announced in 2021 and enhanced in 2022 are significant countermeasures in that direction.[211] American allies and partners like India could do a lot to help with the China Race here.[212] The ultra-expensive BRI, already appearing unsustainable and even less well-managed than the massive funding poured into Africa, could easily become a cost-effective way for opponents to drain and distress the PRC.[213]

For other regions from the Arctic to Antarctica, while a close watch is always warranted, the US requires little additional spending. A key goal should be to slow the transmission of sensitive Western technology to the PRC and to deny, as much as possible, propaganda gains for the CCP. For that, the US just needs to work with allies to better implement those regulations of technology export to Greater China and of Chinese investment in the West, including countermeasures to Beijing's efforts in recruitment and thievery.[214] In 2022, it was reported that "80 per cent of all economic espionage prosecutions brought by the US Department of Justice allege conduct that would benefit the Chinese state [. . . and estimated] the cost to the US of stolen trade secrets, pirated software and counterfeiting by China at between $225bn and $600bn a year."[215] PRC technology firms of a certain size, especially those industry monopolies, should all be rightfully regarded as owned or controlled by the CCP-PRC state and carefully targeted accordingly.[216] Perhaps engaging in "cold-eyed economic warfare" by slipping in flawed technology, a strategy reportedly used against the Soviet Union, could make Beijing's extensive technology thievery backfire.[217]

Washington should develop a hierarchy of issues and encourage a division of labor among the Western countries to avoid directly racing with China everywhere and at every moment with the same intensity. Some Western nations like Australia and Canada have started to take the China Race increasingly seriously and have made strong responses.[218] With some reluctance, the European Union seems to have decided to side fully with the US. Revitalizing and creating "multilateral forums and linkages between European and Indo-Pacific allies" would pool the resources of the entire West.[219] The US should be more conspicuous and consistent about its hierarchy of relations with the nations—yielding on some of its trade and regulatory disputes with the EU and South Korea, for example, and viewing its relative losses to allies rightfully as investments toward the much bigger goal of prevailing in the China Race, shouldering the cost of its leadership of the West to safeguard the LIO. The suspension of the Boeing–Air Bus trade dispute in June 2021, for instance, was a sensible move. The US could certainly handle intelligently the "selfish" and unhelpful but normal and understandable pursuits for relative gains by some allies, such as the French president "Emmanuel Macron's cozy visit to Xi Jinping" in April 2023 for his vision of "strategic autonomy" and "third superpower."[220] The lasting dividend of leadership comes with a management cost. This price for the consolidation of the US-led Westphalian system may indeed be viewed as a smart investment generating ever more dividends for the US, shared by its allies and partners worldwide.[221]

The China Race in the PRC

To reach the three objectives of the contaformation strategy, the main and ultimate track or battleground for the China Race is inside the PRC

246 | The China Race

itself. The reason for this lies in the very strengths, flaws, and weaknesses of the CCP party-state, as I wrote in 2006 in the *New York Times*:

> The only reliable assurance [for peace and security of the current world order and the best interest of the Chinese people] is that the rising Chinese power become structurally constrained, first of all internally [. . .] by developing effective internal constraints on its own political power based on well protected individual rights and property rights, freedom of speech, democratic governance, diversified civil society, and genuine rule of law. [. . .] For a start, the Chinese people must not be misled about their own history any longer; there must be a marketplace for competing ideas, open discourse, and judicious reasoning. Only by facing its own record truthfully can a government become accountable."[222]

Some key observations about the nature of the China Race are worthy of reiteration and further reflection. To begin with, the CCP-PRC is not the same as the nation of China, much less the Chinese people. The CCP's political interests at home and abroad differ profoundly from the national interests of the Chinese people. There is a deep divide between the regime's political interests and the nation's interests, which provides a key shortcut for running and winning the China Race in China for the world and the Chinese people. A China institutionally and ideologically reorganized and renewed, and without the CCP Qin-Han polity, will fundamentally change its worldviews and foreign policy, becoming much more peaceful and constructive. As such, China should rise as a great power, competing and contributing to human civilization under the Westphalian world order. A secure, prosperous, and respected China, free from the paranoia and scourge of the CCP, which has cursed nearly one-fifth of humankind to challenge the world, destroy the West and reorder the Westphalian system, would be a great ending to the China Race, as I wrote back in 2005 in the *New York Times*:

> China should and can be powerful and rich. More important, the Chinese people deserve to be free: free from poverty and backwardness, free from the hurtful feelings of past humiliations, free from deeply trenched ethnocentrism and chauvinism, and free from political tyranny. Such a rise of China would

enrich the world and truly glorify Chinese history. Chinese people and the world must work together to devise and further social, political and institutional changes, in addition to promoting economic development, to ensure the peaceful rise of China.[223]

The safeguarding of the Westphalian world order and the transformation of the CCP-PRC should be pursued as peacefully as possible in an era of WMDs. Whether humanity will repeat the world wars or the Cold War, or worst of all, the history of the post-Qin Chinese world, depends on how the China Race is run in China. An avoidance of a full-scale war between the US and the PRC is highly probable and, with conscious and concerted efforts, the China Race could end peacefully and in a speedy manner. The latest military technology would certainly help to minimize the cost of an open war should it ever be needed, and means that there would be little to no reason for Americans to ever invade Mainland China. Similar to the Stalinist regime in Moscow in the 1940s, as classically analyzed by George Kennan, the CCP-PRC today is also ferociously feeble and fragilely forceful, and mostly risk- and confrontation-averse internationally because of its deep dread of actual war with real opponents.[224] As a RAND study concluded in 2021, a top aim of Beijing's in fact is "to avoid war with the United States" prior to reaching its hoped-for goal of outcompeting the US and achieving "global primacy" by the mid-21st century.[225]

As this book and its prequels have attempted to show, the CCP leaders are self-aggrandizing, arrogant, brutal, and unscrupulous, but also essentially opportunistic, insecure, ultraselfish, overly indulgent, and cynically pragmatic. They see "the world as, first and foremost, a jungle," where survival and raw power matter.[226] The CCP elites today have significant personal and family stakes in peace, with many not-so-hidden nests and eggs in the West. They have deeply indulged themselves in the West-created (and still often only West-provided) modern comforts and luxury, and are spoiled to the bone by that, making them qualitatively different from the earlier CCP leaders, most of whom were destitute and desperate rebels. Other than believing in self-preservation, selfish indulgence, raw power, cunning ruses and, ideally, a world empire at their disposal, they are not ideologues of any serious faith that provides inner sanctum, moral restraint, or principled impulses. Their extraordinary security needs, endless perfidy, split personalities, and "special provisions"

248 | The China Race

of nearly all kinds for the sake of their ultra-luxurious lifestyles are good evidence of this. They are fully aware of the great places around the world suitable for a comfortable life in exile. They are also malignant, selfish, and cynical enough to be content with their power and perks even if their country is reduced, impoverished, and isolated, like the Maoist PRC, Cuba, North Korea, or post-1979 Iran. In fact, Xi Jinping has repeatedly alerted the CCP since 2013, with much enhanced emphasis in 2020, to "be prepared for the bottom-line [or worst case] thinking" and ever more "hard struggles."[227] This has been wittily and penetratingly interpreted by some as a North Korean reenactment or "turning the PRC into a West Korea"—namely, to preserve the regime at all costs to the nation, like the Kim regime in Pyongyang has done, sprouting belligerent rhetoric but avoiding action when facing a very uncertain and likely suicidal war with the United States and its allies.[228]

The massive buildup and "modernizing" reorganization of the PLA with the aim of generating a "world-class military," such as the setup of joint commands and the expensive procurement of air, naval, and space hardware discussed earlier in this book, may give the CCP the confidence to try more calculated (or miscalculated) brinkmanship, risking kinetic clashes with the US military. But, as illustrated by the PLA's overseas base in Djibouti, the CCP appears to aim mostly for more centralized control of the guns, domestic bragging rights, foreign posturing, and opportunistic encroachment, rather than fighting an all-out global war.[229] Of course, the US and the West should never overlook the crude logic of what the vested interest of a massive arms-buildup could lead to and the unreliable mindset and sanity of an autocrat. The Pentagon has identified at least three areas in which "China is already ahead of the United States": shipbuilding, land-based ballistic and cruise missiles, and integrated air defense systems.[230] The PLA Navy, in particular, which has become the world's largest by quantity of vessels, and soon by fleet-tonnage too, naturally justifies effective counteractions for worst-case contingencies.[231] The deployment of more surface-to-ship missiles and unmanned platforms in the Western Pacific in order to race qualitatively with new tools, not just quantitatively with the same gear, and joint sailing by warships from allies in the region, are advisable ideas.[232]

To always prepare for the worst behavior from the CCP is prudent and justified. At the same time, it is wise to be cognizant of the smokescreens of the CCP ruses and propaganda so as not to miss the party-state's weaknesses. Avoiding "excessive overconfidence," the US should observe and leverage the CCP's problems of "insecurity, political uncertainty, and even [. . .] Xi's longevity and succession."[233] As long as the US maintains its superior military power and calls Beijing's bluff, pushing back and stopping in a timely way any CCP ventures similar to the *Rheinlandbesetzung* (remilitarization of the Rhineland by Nazi Germany in 1936), the only likely way for massive war to break out during the possibly long China Race is probably just by accident. For the ultrahigh stakes of the China Race, that is a fully acceptable risk. Facing the increased decoupling with the US and the West, for example, CCP leaders have so far called for a "protracted war" (read no real fighting) and steered toward an isolationist economy of "mostly relying on internal circulation," rather than reforming the Chinese political economy further or launching a full outburst of aggression.[234] Some senior PRC analysts have already argued that the CCP must avert a potentially annihilating hot war or an equally devastating economic decoupling with the US.[235] A leading hawkish voice in Beijing opined in 2021 that "a club-based international system [of China vs. US] bipolar configuration [. . .] will be far less dangerous than all-out, Cold War–style competition," let alone a hot war.[236] If the CCP leaders indeed followed their own isolationist prescription for self-preservation, the top objective of the China Race would be within reach. If "regime change is not an option in China," as some have argued,[237] then verified and sustained alteration and restraint of Beijing's ability and behavior would work just as well for the US-led West to prevail in the China Race. If the PRC indeed turns out to be "a declining power" that self-isolates and faces a "looming demographic and economic collapse,"[238] the China Race would have been successful for the world including the Chinese people, although an autocracy facing the loss of power and control could still go belligerent to gamble with the use of force for aggressions abroad.

Should the top objective of the China Race be secured, namely, the West-led Westphalian world order remains intact due to the isolation, stagnation, depowering, and dissipation of CCP-PRC power, there would be no need to require a total surrender from Beijing. Continued competition generated by the China Race, assuming a secure constraint on the PRC's power to challenge, is mostly beneficial. A declining Chinese economy at home and a battered image abroad would likely propel the China Race in China to the accomplishment of the secondary but highly desirable objective of political and ideological transformation of the PRC. Although democracy would be something wonderful to have

250 | The China Race

in China, first and foremost for the best interests of the Chinese people, there is no need to push for a hasty and likely half-baked Western-style democratization in China, especially not imposed by force from outside. Essentially, what happens in China after the CCP is thwarted abroad is a matter that should be left for the Chinese people to decide, and "America would be better off letting China drag itself down."[239] The common bipolar belief—that the West must either pacify the CCP's simulated "anger" through acquiescing to its endless demands, or risk fighting World War III with nuclear weapons against one-fifth of humankind—persists because of natural or artificial fearmongering, ignorance, irrationality, paranoia, or deception, or all of the above.[240]

In July 2020, after endless bluffs and battle cries from the CCP's "wolf warriors" against the US and another barrage of US actions opposing Beijing on multiple fronts, including trade, Hong Kong, and human rights, the PRC foreign minister suddenly started to talk about the need to "follow and defend the historical and natural trend of Sino-American cooperation," on the basis that "we both should not attempt to change [the institutions and actions of] the other." His deputy, who had previously threatened to "cut the black hand [from the US and West]" and defeat the US in a grand struggle, also suddenly changed tack, declaring that "the mega trend of cooperation between China and the US is irresistible."[241] While these are typical diplomatic ploys that probably signal little real action, such statements nonetheless reveal that the CCP leadership, probably feeling the impact of US actions, habitually rolls and pleads "do not disconnect us," "refuse decoupling," and "say no to decoupling," willingly slapping its own face as it "tastes bitterness for later revenge."[242] The high-level talks in Anchorage in March 2021, other than revealing the "widening gulf of distrust and disagreements" across the Pacific,[243] were little more than a bravado-filled talk show by the top CCP diplomats Yang Jiechi and Wang Yi, glossing over the CCP's failure abroad for domestic consumption. Then again, in March 2023, Li Qiang, the new PRC premier (number two in the CCP leadership) told reporters that Beijing does not see or want any decoupling with the US after all. And "to reconstruct a stable structure for Sino-American relations" became a new theme in Beijing by mid-2023.[244]

Logically, the global China Race will eventually be decided back in China where it all started in 1949, with the decisive and final participation of the Chinese people. It is likely to be surprisingly peaceful in the end. Concurrently with the China Race in the US and around the world, to run the Race well in China, the US should focus on crushing the CCP party with figurative precision strikes, while befriending, enabling, and empowering the Chinese people through smart engagement and exchange, which will help advance the genuine national interests of both China and the United States.

Empowering the Chinese People

The CCP is structurally and genetically preordained to challenge the US for world leadership, while seeking to recenter and reorder the world. This is a seemingly eternal mission that is essential to the Party's claim to rule and extract from the Chinese people autocratically and indefinitely. As analyzed earlier, the CCP-PRC's power comes from its captivation of the Chinese people with the tested Maoist "secret weapons" of force, propaganda, and United Front. Beyond the sustained will and sufficient ability to use military and diplomatic force to deter and defeat the CCP, the US and the world should also attempt to debilitate and constrain the CCP through a comprehensive engagement to empower the Chinese people. A key aspect of this involves targeting the CCP's other two pillars of governance: information control and manipulative ruses. Here, a smart play of reciprocity with precision strikes, a "long game" of "political warfare" to arrest, affect, and alter the CCP,[245] is critical to prevailing in the China Race in China.

The US and its allies should firmly, constantly, and consistently demand equal and reciprocal treatment for their people and information in China vis-à-vis the treatment that the PRC receives in their countries. This is crucial to frustrating and canceling Beijing's propaganda and united front activities abroad without damaging the principles of freedom at home; it is also critical to the detoxification and empowerment of the Chinese people inside the PRC.[246] This policy of "reciprocity and candor," as advised by a senior US official in 2020,[247] will compel the CCP to choose between either decoupling from the West, and thus face self-isolation and decline, or risking the enlightenment and empowerment of its own people, who will inevitably take their destiny into their own hands and change the PRC. With a great variety of means at its disposal and the policy of issue-linkage, the US should focus on working to undermine and dismantle Beijing's Great Firewall so as to enable a freer flow of information and speech in the PRC. This shortcut to prevailing in the

252 | The China Race

China Race is financially and technologically feasible and efficient; it also defends and advances the key values of freedom and equality, which are socioeconomically rewarding, politically desirable, and ideologically and ethically appealing to peoples (if not rulers) around the world.

As this book and its two prequels have analyzed, before it can control and reorder the world, the CCP-PRC state, for the sake of its power and survival, must keep its people away from the world and away from debatable and verifiable history and reality. At great cost to Chinese taxpayers, the PRC blocks over 600,000 "undesirable" websites, including almost all of the world's most visited sites, such as Google, YouTube, Wikipedia, Twitter/X, Instagram, Dropbox, Reddit, Blogpost, Facebook, Tumblr, and most non-PRC media outlets and social media apps.[248] If making a clear distinction between the CCP and the Chinese people is hitting the Achilles's heel of the rising PRC power, as I have discussed earlier, freedom of information and speech will evidently have a similar effect. With the penetration and tearing-down of the Great Firewall, the CCP will rapidly wither and crumble at home. Moreover, it is itself great liberation and progress for humanity and a wonderful public good for all (except the CCP rulers) to ensure that the Chinese people, nearly one-fifth of humankind who are endowed with great potential for creativity, have options for free access and full contribution to the knowledge store of human civilization. Systemic deprivation of people's right to information and open communication without due legal process is itself a flagrant violation of human rights. Locking so many human beings out of the bulk of human civilization for so long through thought work and information control is simply cruel, immoral, and criminal.

Countless fieldwork projects have revealed that the Firewall is unmistakably one of the most unpopular CCP policies among the Chinese people, even the so-called "pinkies" or "fifty-cents party" netizens who are often programmed to blindly support the CCP.[249] If the Chinese people have free access to information and are free from persecution when rereading their own history, exploring facts, comparing ideas, and speaking their minds, a powerful enlightenment, detoxification, and empowerment will certainly take place to peacefully sweep away the CCP power and agenda, if not the CCP regime itself. It is exemplarily encouraging to see that, after just a few years of *glasnost* (openness and transparency), the Soviet Communist Party, the creator, longtime tutor, and benefactor of the CCP, peacefully lost its dictatorial power without suffering systemic purges, massive retribution, and violent revenge.[250] Of course, the Russians had the power of organized national religion, the revived Orthodox Christian Church, which may have critically facilitated their peaceful political transition with considerable social tolerance and the ability to forgive, a lesson some Chinese in the PRC seem to have also noticed recently.[251] Indeed, neighboring Japan has been a relevant and inspiring illustration of the successful and profound detoxification and transformation of an ancient autocratic polity possessed with a world-empire ideology acting under the force of outside pressures, facilitated by its violent defeat in a world war.[252]

In 1987, almost four decades ago, President Ronald Reagan historically proclaimed at the Brandenburg Gate by the Berlin Wall, "Mr. Gorbachev, open this gate! Mr. Gorbachev, tear down this wall!"[253] Four years later, the symbolic wall of the Cold War fell. American and world leaders should similarly stand up and declare, as often as needed, "Mr. Xi Jinping, tear down this Firewall!" The US should facilitate and invest in private and government efforts to create and provide the technology to increase free access to the Internet in the PRC and deprive Beijing of the technology for information control, as discussed earlier in this chapter. Just blacklisting and embargoing certain entities like Hikvision, Huawei, and Tencent is not effective, since the CCP has a near-totalitarian ability to easily expropriate things sold to any entity under its jurisdiction or within its reach. Any officials and technical professionals who have facilitated the building and management of the Great Firewall could be sanctioned, in the same fashion as targets of the Global Magnitsky law. Americans and other foreigners could be allowed to sue the PRC government, entities, and individuals in American or international courts for damages caused by the information and communication control, similar to legal actions against other human rights violations or even commercial frauds.[254]

An efficient way to target the party through empowering the people is to expose and inconvenience CCP leaders, senior cadres, and their allies in order to decrease the lure and power of the party. For example, in addition to those on the sanction list, all visiting PRC citizens should declare their CCP affiliation, if any. Such information may involve special scrutiny for visa applications, school admissions, job applications, and immigration.[255] Certain visas, schools, jobs, events, and fora could be specifically listed as off-limits to active CCP members. The overseas assets owned by or linked to CCP leaders and cadres should be carefully traced and constantly reported, perhaps simply via leaks and tips to the

254 | The China Race

media. The CCP's many atrocities, irrationalities and incompetence, failures and scandals, and unethical and duplicitous activities should all be fair game for Western governments and media to expose.[256] CCP leaders are highly sensitive about their face as they have shaky legitimacy and many vulnerabilities in the court of public opinion. The West just needs to share with the Chinese people what it knows about the CCP leaders' fortunes hidden overseas, houses purchased abroad, emigrated families and illegitimate children, ultra-luxurious indulgences, and endless blunders and waste. This is, legally and morally, a fully justified defense of information freedom and offers a great service to the Chinese people, while also powerfully useful in the China Race.

If in the aftermath of the COVID-19 pandemic, as some analysts have concluded, the CCP "is using an arsenal of spin, obfuscation, hyperbole, and outright disinformation to win back its reputation" and "succeeding at shaping global narratives" about the pandemic,[257] the West should simply counteract. A highly potent way to prevail in the China Race is to show and highlight the striking gap and often complete divorce between the CCP's interests and the interests of the Chinese nation and the Chinese people, fracturing the party-state's fabricated image and false reputation as Chinese nationalists. The worldwide "narrative arms race" with the CCP must not be left unattended, particularly inside the PRC.[258] To further neutralize the CCP's prized weapon of United Front, the full display of the abnormality and illegitimacy of the CCP-PRC is useful, as it will hamper Beijing's efforts in recruiting, captivating, and manipulating people at home and abroad. The Chinese people, especially the young, curious, ambitious, talented, and self-respecting, should see the CCP being defamed, shamed, isolated and disrespected, at least in the West. Working for the CCP for sociopolitical and economic benefits should not be cost-free abroad, especially in the West. Active and unrepentant executioners of the CCP agenda deserve the taint of complicity, and should even be held legally accountable when applicable.

As the sage Confucius was recorded to have said, "If names are not correct, language will not flow well; if language does not flow well, things will not be accomplished."[259] Proper language is critical to effective communication and truthful ways of thinking; it also powerfully shapes mindsets, worldviews, and policies.[260] Thus, to prevail in the China Race, the West should indeed use the proper language and the right names. Whenever possible, the PRC should be called what it is, the CCP-PRC or the PRC, rather than China. Xi Jinping, for example should be rightfully addressed as general secretary of the CCP, his most important title, or chairman of the PRC, rather than the misleading "President of China."[261] The PLA should be rightfully named "the CCP military" rather than "the Chinese military" or the people's military. In fact, because they have to swear allegiance only to the CCP as party-guards rather than serving proudly as China's national military, many if not most professional soldiers in the PLA rightfully harbor deep indignation.[262] To awaken and reinforce that emotion, the PLA Navy and PLA officers, for instance, should be correctly referred to as "CCP Navy" and "CCP officers," instead of "Chinese Navy" and "Chinese officers."

The widespread "second-class foreigner" status suffered by PRC citizens abroad, a potent source of discontent targeted at the CCP and its foreign policy, should be constantly highlighted. Western governments should rightfully broadcast that the CCP and its policies are the real reason for the unfairness and humiliation, real or imagined, that PRC citizens may encounter abroad.[263] Differential treatment of PRC citizens, especially those with strong CCP ties, may be misconstrued and spun as anti-China or unfair and even racist discrimination, but the West should transparently state that any such inconvenience is the price individuals pay for their tolerance and support of the CCP policies. A clear message should be that, as long as the CCP is unchallenged and unconstrained in its actions at home and abroad, the Chinese people will not get their otherwise fully deserved normal and proper stature and respect in the world.

Finally, the US could patiently encourage the development of intraparty diversity and decentralization as a peaceful way to transform the CCP-PRC. Internal democracy in the CCP, as this author tried but failed to convince the CCP leadership two decades ago, is an efficient and peaceful way for China to rise up rich, strong, and dignified, with a smooth transition toward long lasting domestic tranquility.[264] In addition to applying the Global Magnitsky law to punish CCP officials and entities who are human rights violators, the West could also seek to list and punish some CCP "discipline inspectors," whom the CCP leadership uses to purge, abuse, and eliminate political dissidents, often grossly violating the human and civil rights of nonconformists or losers of power struggles. There is little meaningful policy debate in the CCP-PRC, but the diversifying Chinese society seems to still harbor varied and nuanced ideas on foreign policy.[265] Grassroots and elitist proponents of liberty and democratization inside the PRC are clearly repressed and tormented, but they courageously survive and persist in uncertain but likely significant numbers, and they consistently gain more sympathizers.[266] In 2020, a

256 | The China Race

Peking University professor openly ridiculed the CCP's illogic of staying in power forever.[267] In 2022, amid the draconian lockdown of entire cities in the name of containing the COVID-19 pandemic, "tens of thousands" Chinese netizens continued to voice their resistance, "overwhelming the censors."[268] A Beijing-based economist argued that the party-state, like an insatiable and savage dragon, is creating *lanwei* (unfinished projects) everywhere: from real estate, poverty-reduction, and economic reform at home to the BRI abroad, "devouring itself by the tail" and "turning the China Dream into a nightmare for all of us."[269] One just-retired CCP cadre wrote on the popular PRC social media platform WeChat in 2022 that "[t]he criteria for judging a good or bad government should be whether this government is good to its people. [. . .] Our government should respect the change of status of our people, applying universal rules in the treatment of our people; it absolutely should not take the lead in harming the people. It must be known that times have changed; we are no longer the coolies of the past."[270]

It is not impossible for a new and different CCP leader like Mikhail Gorbachev to emerge, wise enough to steer the PRC away from its confrontation with the West. Such a leader might even autocratically start a sociopolitical liberalization and democratization in China. Likely "mistakes" and misfortune of autocrats could start Chinese democratization, as it seems to be the case in many other nations.[271] The development of a peaceful reform or a forceful revolution would be desirable for an efficient pause in or even an end to the China Race.[272] Some have indeed envisioned a decisive regime change in Beijing through a "China coup," analogous to the coup d'état after the death of Mao, to be launched by self-preserving CCP leaders opposing Xi, with better assistance from "liberal democracies." Others hope that the sheer force of nature may do the trick with an expected succession crisis.[273] Intriguing uncertainties and dramatic possibilities like these have certainly made so-called Pekingology or Zhongnanhai studies interesting. However, given our overall understanding of the CCP, the role of one single person, rather than a whole clique within the structured system, may be limited.

More Tracks and Shortcuts

To generate both hard and soft power to counter and restrain the CCP-PRC state, the US and the West in fact have a deep well of resources and a vast arsenal. As some American leaders have reasoned, the critical need does not necessarily require new means, but rather new ways of thinking and action to maximize the immense effects of the available means in an altered strategic landscape.[274] Other than the considerations already presented, there are many more possibilities regarding additional tracks and shortcuts in the China Race. I will discuss three below as illustrations.

The tragedy of Hong Kong and Macau, the two special administrative regions (SARs) of the PRC, has provided the justification and opportunity for the US and the West to plug a leak in the dam constraining the PRC's power. The two former colonies are now strangled by the tightening control of the CCP for its political interests.[275] Their special treatment granted in 1997 and 1999 should therefore be conveniently reduced or even revoked. The two SARs' full access to the West has been of critical assistance to the PRC in obtaining Western technology and capital, and has enabled the CCP's money laundering and "united front" ploys.[276] As a Beijing-friendly offshore venture capital firm focusing on TMT (technology, media, and telecom) investment in China outlined in 2022, somewhat self-servingly, Hong Kong as a financial center and a technology conveyer belt has been of critical value to the CCP-PRC state and its grand plan of "defeating the US."[277] In the China Race, the special privileges of Hong Kong and Macau have become a strategic liability rather than an asset. Hong Kong alone has always provided or facilitated the overwhelming majority of foreign investment: 51.1% of total FDI to China in the four decades since the mid-1980s is from Hong Kong, and the SAR provided over 65% of annual FDI to China in the late-2010s.[278] The considerable financial interests a few Western capitalists built there over the decades are important, but, given the high fluidity of international capital these days, they could easily relocate for a strategic adjustment of the West's Hong Kong policy.[279] Costly efforts by the CCP in recent years, such as the expansion of Macau to Hengqin, the integration of the "Guangdong–Hong Kong–Macau Greater Bay Area," and the Qianhai development bordering Hong Kong, all strongly indicate Beijing's critical need to control and exploit the two major loopholes in the China Race.[280]

Another idea is to invest in better and fuller leverage of Taiwan, which is increasingly pursuing the control of its own destiny as a fully contributing member of the international community and collective security.[281] This track of the China Race is similar to improving ties

258 | The China Race

with Han-Chinese political exiles, Tibetans and Uyghurs, protecting and working with them as catalysts and conduits for the strategic constriction and sociopolitical transformation of the PRC.[282] The US could continue and crystallize its security protection to support the status quo of the de facto independence of the ROC (Republic of China) in Taiwan.[283] After 20 years of distraction by the war on terrorism, President Joe Biden openly repeated in 2021 and 2022 that the US would militarily defend Taiwan against the PRC like an ally, the same US commitment first publicly clarified by President George W. Bush in April 2001.[284] Moreover, this time, unlike two decades ago, the president's "vow" has been echoed and elaborated by his national security advisor and top officials for East Asia at the State Department and the Pentagon, with clear bipartisan support in the US Congress, as well as thinktanks like CFR.[285] The so-called "one-China" policy regarding the two sides of the Taiwan Strait is seen as increasingly obsolescent.[286] Washington could continue its "one China policy" (for the PRC) as opposed to Beijing's "one China principle" (for both the PRC and the ROC/Taiwan), and even upgrade its relationship with Taipei to support a full, de jure, independence of Taiwan as a new nation-state in a paradigm shift, if so warranted.[287] After a half century of evolution, the "one China framework" regarding Taiwan, comprising the "one China policy" and the "one China principle" is now seen facing "unprecedented challenges."[288] Indeed, even the CCP itself has not been consistent about the legal status of Taiwan, which was first conquered by the Manchu-Qing empire, "legally" occupied by the Han-Chinese national government of the ROC only once for four years from 1945 to 1949 (the ROC has continued its rule of the island since 1949, but basically as a "refugee" and "local" government), and has never been under PRC rule.[289]

A peaceful resolution of the Beijing-Taipei dispute has now become perhaps a "waning dream."[290] However, the US and the world could still try to facilitate a conditional unification of the two sides of the Taiwan Strait to magnify the power of Taiwan as a potent catalyst for sociopolitical changes on the Chinese Mainland. This would neutralize the power of rising Chinese nationalism, which has been conveniently expropriated by the CCP, and turn it to undermine the CCP's nationalist credibility by clearly posing the question of what the party is really for: either its own eternal monopoly of power or China's national interests. An open, constrained, democratic China, with a political system resembling that in Taiwan, could be the common and better home as a federation or confederation for both the Taiwanese and the Chinese, bolstering both world order and world peace.[291]

On the other hand, if the CCP uses force to invade and conquer Taiwan, the US and its allies ought to react more forcefully than the UK and its allies did in March 1939, when Germany invaded Czechoslovakia, even though the US Navy may not prevail immediately in the theater.[292] Left alone, Taiwan would have a hard time fending off the PRC. But the brutal Winter War between Finland and the Soviet Union in 1939–40, among many other examples, illustrates well how a small and unaided but determined country can protect itself fighting against a much larger aggressor.[293] There is both a solid rationale and strong feasibility for Taiwan to be a "force for good" on the frontline of the democratic alliance, as its President Tsai Ing-wen opined in 2021.[294] The Taiwanese chip-maker TSMC, for example, plays a much-noted role in the PRC-USA "technology competition."[295] To be sure, Taiwan has been instrumental to the economy of the PRC for decades: its investment produced 40% of China's critical export and constituted seven of the top 10 Chinese exporters in the early 2020s. Perhaps realizing that economic ties are enriching the CCP rather than compelling it to change and rethink its priorities, Taiwan's investments in the PRC declined by 15% in 2020–21, "a major change unseen in decades," while its overall overseas investments increased more than 30% (investments in the US jumped over 600%).[296]

Yet one more idea involves taking control, and even setting the pace and timing of the China Race per its inexorable logic. We know that, by its nature or structural DNA, the CCP-PRC is fundamentally incompatible with the current world order and antagonistic toward the current world leader. The regime, not just a single leader, is highly resistant to internal transformation and has a survival instinct to recenter and reorder the world at all costs. This global and systemic challenge, existential and intensifying in nature, is beyond appeasement by the challenged, short of a total surrender. Sooner or later, there will inevitably be a deciding moment for the future of human civilization, when the US-led West must choose between submission and showdown. In fact, that moment may be so disguised, gradual, lopsided, and piecemeal that the West, though powerful and advantaged, could simply be too blinded and paralyzed to react in time. We know that there are only two ways the West and the world could avoid that moment of dreaded choice: an effective restraint and sufficient weakening of Chinese power under the CCP or an apposite transformation of the PRC regime along with an acceptable change to its foreign policy. In running the China Race, passive engagement alone is insufficient, and hence unwise and perilous:

260 | The China Race

it helps the destined adversary to grow stronger and readier on its chosen path and to set the pace. It is more rational, responsible, and ethical to proactively manage the China Race, draining, trapping, diverting, and preempting a known foe. There is a fringe conspiracy theory that the US "allowed" the Pearl Harbor attack when it knew in advance that it would occur, in order to create the momentum needed to mobilize and join World War II.[297] But, counterfactually, the Allies would have indeed been in a more disadvantageous and costly position had the US delayed its entry into the war by another year or two.

It is both benevolent and economical for the US and its allies to pick a time and place they feel is most suitable to battle for the maximum impact with minimal collateral damage. Possible choices for the "spark" that ignites a duel for the West might include a new Taiwan policy, a naval clash in the South China Sea over the PRC's artificial islands or in the East China Sea over the Senkaku (Diaoyu) islets, a blockage of sea lanes like the Malacca Strait,[298] a breakthrough in the arms race, evidence of China's biological warfare capabilities,[299] litigation leading to a freeze of the CCP leaders' assets overseas, an engineered or exacerbated financial crash or a major cyber-attack, or an out-of-control riot or disaster in the PRC. In the overall scheme, having a smart run and a speedy triumph in the China Race, at the timing and place of the West's choice, would be a great and virtuous service for the world, including the Chinese people.

Winning the Race versus Transforming the PRC

Like countless others who have observed and written attentively and passionately about China, this author has an unshakable empathy for the Chinese people. The Chinese people fully deserve ever more prosperity, peace, dignity, liberty, and freedom. Beyond China, all people are securer and happier under a world polity that maximizes order and innovation for everyone. The China Race merely continues the millennia-old human struggle between different polities and world orders and their contending ways of organizing people within and beyond nations.[300] Unlike in the past, I argue, we now have enough reason and evidence to be confident about the preferable option in this round. For national polity, the least-bad system is the widely tested democratic rule of law; for world order, the proven less undesirable system is the decentralized world polity of international relations under the Westphalian system.[301] The great variety and the constant variation of the two systems, the natural and mostly desirable results of the competitive and experimental dynamics inherent and inevitable in the two systems, give individual nations colorful life-styles, lasting vitality, ceaseless innovation, varied but optimizing balances between efficiency and equality, endless possibilities and choices, and an ever more promising future for human civilization.[302] More specifically, in the current PRC-USA rivalry, the preservation and improvement of the United States (the grand "American Experiment") together with its allies, as the world leader is critically important to both the sociopolitical systems of democratic rule of law and the Westphalian system overall.

In defense of those values, the contaformation strategy defines the path to victory in the China Race, for the West and the world, including the Chinese people, through three main objectives, hierarchically ranked in importance: (1) safeguarding the West-led Westphalian world order; (2) avoidance of a Sino-American hot war to the fullest extent possible; and (3) sociopolitical and ideological transformation of the CCP-PRC. These goals, as I have attempted to demonstrate, are organically related and mutually reinforcing, and are all attainable through a well-run China Race. Only the accomplishment of the top objective (related to world leadership and world order) is necessary for a pause and even a con-clusion of the China Race. However, the inability to achieve the other two objectives certainly means a less ideal, and likely also less efficient path of managing and prevailing in the Race.

To further ponder the hierarchy of these values and objectives, it is necessary to discuss the relationship between the China Race and the democratization of the PRC. Contaformation aims at the aggregate opti-mization of key values for the most human beings, rather than an ideal result for everyone. To be sure, world politics and politics in general are all about balances and possibilities—hardly a precision science yielding perfect results, since multiple values and objectives always present in the endless blending and interaction of seemingly infinite competing actors and variables, with always scarce resources and finite time, for the construction and exercise of public authority.

The democratization of China and the sociopolitical transformation of the PRC, while high-value objectives, remain mostly domestic agenda issues in China, tasks of, for, and by the Chinese people. These would tremendously assist in a successful conclusion to the China Race, but the Westphalian system, even in its LIO version, stipulates that nations are

262 | The China Race

entitled to choose and experiment with whatever political system they see fit, especially for a large country like China. To promote democracy is to share the most tested and least evil form of government known to humankind; but to impose it identically at the expense of the Westphalian system would be a true Pyrrhic victory or worse. A Chinese democracy is not sufficient or necessary for the West's victory in the China Race, but a Chinese democratization will enable and energize a grand choice for the Chinese people: whether to continue the CCP autocracy and its inevitable challenge to the West, with its endless sacrifices by the Chinese nation and the Chinese people, or to transform the organization and governance of China, enabling it to fully join the international community and maximize the great potential of the rights and interests of the Chinese nation and the Chinese people. As a Chinese-American scholar put it, "Ultimately, the CCP, Chinese government and the Chinese people must make the historic choice: how to define state-society relationship, how to define party-state relationship, and how to define the relationship between the so-called core values with Chinese characteristics and the universal values of freedom, democracy and peace."[303]

To achieve the top objective of the China Race efficiently, it is wise and justified for the US and its allies to explore a global united front, a grand alliance, to defend and promote core Western values and norms so as to safeguard its leadership of the Westphalian world order. However, the West should be fully aware of the risk of a centralized world government in the name of any singular political ideology. The American "exceptionality," which, so far, has resisted the trend of building a world empire in its image, like the entire American experiment itself, is not irreversible, uncompromisable, or always invincible. It is still human-made and thus vulnerable to human blunders or *force majeure*. It would be greatly counterproductive to win the China Race with a global government of a singular governance of the world, as that would be, in fact, a great failure of the world in the China Race. A world empire is a world empire no matter what it is entitled and colored. To stop the Chinese version of world empire with a different world empire to replace the Westphalian system would still be a tragedy for all.

In this regard, victory in the China Race is not about the USA subjugating and remodeling China in its image; nor is it about extinguishing cross-Pacific competition. It is about ensuring that the contenders are competing productively and as peacefully as possible in a decentralized world polity, the Westphalian system of sovereign nations, without transforming the system itself. The China Race may lead to and will certainly benefit from the transformation of the PRC. But the West in the China Race should not pursue the worthy transformation of the PRC at the expense of the Westphalian system. Great powers and leaders of the system may rise and fall, peacefully or violently, in great power competitions featuring hegemonic struggles and power transitions.[304] With variations in peacefulness and prosperity among nations, the world order can be a globalizing LIO or a less liberal collection of rival blocks and groups of diverse nations, some in disconnection and isolation. But the basics of the Westphalian system should remain intact: nations have equal sovereign status, full independence of their existence, and complete freedom of action within their own abilities, choices, consequences of their policies, and others' reactions to their actions. Nations compete ceaselessly through self-help, internal changes, balance of power politics, and utilization of international institutions to ensure that no state, especially not a suboptimal and undesirable one, singularly denominates the whole world and rules all other nations.

The relationship between the PRC-USA rivalry and Chinese democratization is often and easily misconstrued. Some suggest that a democratized China without the CCP would be more peaceful and content with the current world order, so the US should focus on overthrowing the CCP regime and promoting democratization in China as the avenue to victory in the PRC-USA rivalry.[305] Others treat the CCP and China as inseparable, warning that a liberalized and democratized China could be more aggressive, militant, and even imperialistic, so the US should work equitably with the survival-focused CCP autocracy to reign in the beast of Chinese nationalism.[306] Both arguments are informative but reductionist. It is the CCP autocracy (or a more generic Qin-Han polity of authoritarianism) for the sake of regime survival, not Chinese democracy, that has been fanning irrational and aggressive nationalism and militarism in China; it will not cease without replacing the US and recentering and reordering the world in its own image.[307] In November 2022, a newly elevated top CCP leader openly reiterated the party's now standard packaging of its real goal with the contrived accusation that "hostile [foreign] forces are always trying everything to block the process of the great rejuvenation of the Chinese nation," so the Party and Xi Jinping must continuously lead the "unprecedented and unparalleled" great struggles at home and abroad for the nation.[308] Considerable uncertainties notwithstanding, a democratization will likely deliver a better governance

264 | The China Race

in China, making it truly strong and attractive. A reformed China with democratic rule of law, sharing the core values and norms of the West, would be qualitatively less threatening to the Westphalian world order, but could be more capable in international competition. Sociopolitical transformation of China seems beneficial for the safeguarding and improvement of the Westphalian system and human civilization—the top objective in the China Race. Yet it will likely produce a possibly more formidable competitor, driving the US to do more and better if it desires to stay on as the world leader, with all the benefits, burdens, and privileges that position entails. Therefore, regarding world leadership and the contenders' relative gains and power, the PRC-USA rivalry is independent from the question of whether China is a democracy or not; but a democratized China will make that rivalry decidedly more peaceful, much less threatening to the Westphalian system, less vicious, and more rewarding to both sides and the whole world.

The CCP-PRC autocracy, with its raw power and confidence, is the less preferred contender in the China Race, as it will inevitably challenge the US and reorder the world with all it has. A weakened, contained, and undermined CCP-PRC autocracy could be just as low impact on the current world order as a strong and transformed Chinese democracy, and largely peaceful to the world. A democratic but nationalist Chinese superpower could still be a system-impacting competitor in its pursuit of national power and interests, possibly sharing and even replacing the US leadership in the world. But the *new* China will have much less unscrupulousness, qualitatively more effective internal and normative constraints, reoriented worldviews about preserving the Westphalian system, and little drive "to compel ideological conformity" worldwide,[309] as it will itself be internally diverse and constrained. The sociopolitical transformation of China, just like the depowering of the PRC, means victory in the China Race for the world and the Chinese people; but the former is clearly a more preferable game-changer, for all except the few who just dread international competition from a better governed and hence likely more competitive China. With an effective sociopolitical transformation of the PRC, it would be a very different kind of *new* China Race, one that is transformed from an existential struggle for an alternative world order to a much more virtuous and peaceful international competition, with the benefits of ever more efficiency and innovation, to enrich and uplift human civilization. A downside of that, of course, is the possibly more and tougher international competition, discomforting the few competition-averse monopolies or monopoly-wannabes, which is neither American nor good for human civilization: Americans and humankind have always thrived in competition and will surely continue to excel in the *new* China Race. The critical transformation is for the main contenders of the China Race to all be governed internally by the known least-bad polity—a stable democratic rule of law (with variations), hence driven by little or no innate mandate to politically replace the known less-undesirable world order of the Westphalian system with a centralized polity of world empire.

In short, victory in the China Race, for the West and the world, including the Chinese people, requires comprehensively frustrating, weakening, and undermining the CCP-PRC state whenever and wherever possible. An effective constraint and containment of PRC state power abroad is the minimum requirement, and a successful delegitimization and transformation of the CCP regime in China is perhaps the maximum. Sociopolitical transformation of China *and* hence the transformation of the PRC-USA rivalry would be the truly ideal win-win outcome of the China Race. Ultimately, however, how to organize China politically, after PRC state power is contained and Beijing's worldview altered, is the decision of and by the Chinese people when they are free to exercise their right to choose as a sovereign member of the Westphalian world. The visible resentment toward and open defiance of the CCP, exhibited in the so-called "white-paper movement" in 2022 and 2023, only reaffirmed that the Chinese people are capable of fighting for their own lives an rights.[310] Over 150 years ago, Anson Burlingame, the legendary American diplomat then heading the Chinese Mission to the US, said with passion in New York City that the Chinese people are "a great, a noble people, [. . .] a polite people; it is a patient people; it is a sober people; it is an industrious people" that has been under tyranny and excluded from "the council hall of the nations." He then wisely advised that, so long as China was open and engaged in genuinely fair play with other nations, "let her alone" to manage herself.[311]

The Race and Peace: Matrices of Cost

Analysis of costs and benefits and cost-effectiveness is always key to determining the desirability and shaping of preferences in political decisions, especially those with definitive and irreversible consequences. The

266 | The China Race

cost of winning the global race with the PRC, often touted by many with exaggeration and scaremongering, is very tolerable to the US, especially considering the ultrahigh stakes and the alternative payoffs. The US has had a global leadership and worldwide presence for eight decades with extensive networks of operational bases and tested allies, unrivaled infrastructure for resource mobilization and power projection, and unmatched soft power and credibility. Most of the massive imports from China are easily substitutable, while much if not the majority of US exports to the PRC is decidedly less substitutable; the loss of value and profits due to resourcing away from China will in fact be more than compensated by savings in the ever-increasing US spending needed to counter the rising PRC power, which has been fueled by American orders, investment, and technology. The kneejerk condemnation of a dreaded Sino-American decoupling, for the alleged economic inefficiency and noncooperation, simply overlooks the fact that the PRC-USA relationship (including business ties) has always been only partially coupled and selectively decoupled, mostly at Beijing's choosing. To win the China Race, the US (and the West) need merely to continue that selective decoupling, now more on the American/Western terms, for hopefully a genuine full coupling eventually.

The risk of a cross-Pacific military conflict, possibly resulting from the PRC-USA rivalry, constitutes a hefty cost that rightfully worries many. To keep peace between the world's two largest economies, both armed with all sorts of weapons of mass destruction, is obviously in itself a worthy objective. A major goal of winning the China Race, therefore, is that the United States should prepare for but deter and avoid an all-out war with the PRC, to the fullest extent possible. However, conflicts among nations are a normal byproduct or cost of business for the critical international comparison and competition under the Westphalian system. War between great powers, dreadful but actually very rare, is the ultimate price for the upkeep of world order and world peace.

Gainful human endeavors all necessarily entail matching price tags for success or failure, including the human migrations out of Africa; the fierce interstate competitions that laid the foundation of human civilization on the Eurasian continent—in the Hellenic-Roman world on the West side and the pre-Qin Sinic world on the East side; the establishment of world empires like the Rome Order and the China Order; the codification and globalization of the Westphalian world order; and the wars against the world Fascist and Communist movements. The China

Race is no exception. There will be costs for the racers in the China Race, win *or* lose: they naturally hold directly opposing cost-benefit matrices to justify their competing preferences, while their calculus of cost-effectiveness may conceivably be quite similar. Below, I speculate on the two sets of desirabilities, costs, and preference hierarchies in the China Race (see table 4.1).

Table 4.1. Matrices on Desirability, Cost, and Preference

For the US, the West, and the World, including the Chinese People:
Outcome A > B > C > D

A. High Desirability, Low Cost CCP-PRC constrained and, maybe, transformed peacefully Contaformation Precedent: Cold War	**B. High Desirability, High Cost** CCP-PRC constrained and transformed violently Military showdown Precedent: World War II
C. Low Desirability, Low Cost CCP-PRC leads and reorders the world peacefully Appropriated political globalization Precedent: None yet	**D. Low Desirability, High Cost** CCP-PRC recenters and reorders the world violently Military showdown Precedent: Qin unification of Chinese world

For the CCP-PRC State and Its Comrades and Fellow Travelers:
Outcome I > II > III > IV

I. High Desirability, Low Cost CCP-PRC leads and reorders the world peacefully Appropriated political globalization Precedent: None yet	**II. High Desirability, High Cost** CCP-PRC recenters and reorders the world violently Military showdown Precedent: Qin unification of Chinese world
III. Low Desirability, Low Cost CCP-PRC constrained and, maybe, transformed peacefully Contaformation Precedent: Cold War	**IV. Low Desirability, High Cost** CCP-PRC constrained and transformed violently Military showdown Precedent: World War II

268 | The China Race

For the United States and its allies, the contaformation of containment and engagement for the transformation and incorporation of China seems the most desirable and least costly option. The hierarchy of preference is Outcomes A > B > C > D. It is wise and preferable to have a "responsible competition" with "all measures short of war."[312] But the West must also be prepared to deter or decisively win a hot war against the PRC state when and where necessary. Considering the ultimate cost in terms of the fortune and future of human civilization, even the high cost of a hot war, Outcome B, appears fully justified and is preferable to Outcome C.[313] The riskiest and most undesirable outcome is clearly Outcome D, a CCP conquest of the world by force. A key variable of determination is probably a function of time and seriousness: the later the China Race is fully engaged, the more likely for Outcome B, C, or even D to take place.

For the CCP-PRC state and its comrades and fellow-travelers, the hierarchy of preference is Outcomes I > II > III > IV. The effect of time here is different: the later the US and the West seriously engage in the China Race to oppose the PRC, the more likely for Outcome I or II to happen. While increasingly pursuing its goals omnidirectionally with all its resources, the CCP has been hiding behind its captivated Chinese people with the rather believable pretention that the party-state is synonymous with China and the Chinese people.[314] Another method the CCP uses is the standard, kneejerk accusation of "Cold War mentality" or "hegemonism" in the West. In 2020, while officially calling a senior US official who tried to distinguish the CCP from the Chinese people a "public enemy of humanity," Beijing funded a group of CCP agents, "useful idiots," and fringe "anti–Cold War" activists to promote the slogan "A new Cold War against China is against the interests of humanity." A variant of this is the so-called "China solution of 'new multilateralism' to counter anti-globalization" and "to crush the talk for Cold War." In early 2023, as I have mentioned earlier in this book, the then PRC foreign minister simply proclaimed that "the world will have no security if we [PRC] are not secure."[315] Irony, pretentiousness, and obliviousness aside, such utterings probably indicate precisely what the CCP really prefers and what it fears the most.

It is a profound realization that the two sides in the China Race seem to potentially share a common preference for the avoidance of a hot world war. Indeed, among all the direct costs and opportunity costs associated with running the China Race, the ultimate sacrifice is the large loss of human life in a possible Sino-American war. This is perhaps even the case for rulers who customarily discount and dismiss their people as mere assets and tools, since modern warfare, particularly its capability for precision strikes and decapitation, has made it unsafe to hide behind the frontlines. It is natural to question the resolve and capacity of the West to risk human lives, possibly in substantial numbers, even for a clearly seen choice involving the well-being of human civilization. Yet, this author is confident that the US and its allies still have what it takes to make consequential decisions that may put some lives at risk. A democratic, well-informed, and thoroughly reasoned process is fully expected to be more rational, effective, and life-saving than a process relying on any single person, however smart and powerful, on such life-and-death choices. The visible and stable bipartisanship in Washington on the reorientation of US China policy over the past decade and the coming together of "like-minded" nations led by the US in the 2020s seem to suggest that the die has been cast.

While it is indisputably imperative to minimize the loss of life, especially in today's West, where popular votes direct the rulers, human life has been and will continue to be sacrificed for worthy causes and purposes, ranging from neighborhood policing, to construction projects, to earth and space exploration, to fighting just wars. How many human lives would and should be risked for the China Race? As early as 431 BCE, Pericles of Athens argued in his timeless "Funeral Oration" that a democracy must constantly weigh the risk and value the sacrifice of life for worthy causes.[316] This book makes the immodest argument that virtually no cost of life and treasure is too high to preserve the least evil form of governance and the least undesirable type of world order, currently represented by the LIO of the Westphalian world order led by democratic rule of law in the West. Such a world order has been indisputably proven much more life- and peace-preserving and prosperity- and wealth-creating than its alternative, the world empire, of which the China Order has been among the most prominent. Of course, the physical existence of the entire human species is obviously more important than how human beings are politically organized. The powerful and often debilitating fear of species extinction caused by international competition, confrontation, and war certainly appears humane, rational, and even credible. However, a total annihilation of humanity, or the fear of "the end of the world" as a consequence of human behavior, which features in many Hollywood products, is essentially a fantasy, a nightmarish fabrication passing as a

270 | The China Race

persuasive argument that has been construed and propagated for various sociopolitical purposes. As such, it appeals to raw, primitive emotions and is supported by neither factual evidence nor logical foundation. In practice, it may paralyze critical decision-making and forestall correct and sober choices, allowing for timidity, laziness, and vested interests to dominate, and enabling and empowering the ruthless and the brutal to mislead and disserve humanity through force and bluff.[317]

Two simple facts may help to dispel this urban legend of Armageddon, which is often propagated as a dreadful result of the PRC-USA rivalry in the era of WMDs. First, civil wars and bad governance have always been much more murderous and destructive than any international conflicts and wars; this is especially true in a united world state (namely, a world empire).[318] One American Civil War, for example, killed more Americans than all the international wars the US has ever fought, from the War for Independence beginning in 1776 to the invasion of Iraq in 2003. Second, many more human beings, measured both in proportion and absolute numbers, have died unnaturally as a consequence of human behavior completely unrelated to the use of WMDs, which only appeared around the mid-20th century. In fact, the most unnatural losses of human life have been associated with bad policies and low-tech weapons: the meat-grinding of the religious wars in medieval Europe, the genocides committed by Asian nomads like the Mongol cavalry, the disappearance of half or more of the total population at the downfall of a Chinese or Inca world empire, the world-record death tolls of the Taipei Rebellion in the 19th century and the Maoist Great Famine in 1958–62, the Stalinist purges and famine in the 1920s–30s, and the massacres (mostly with pistols and machetes) in places like the Khmer Rouge's Cambodia and Rwanda in the late-20th century. Factually and logically, though perhaps a bit counterintuitively, international competition and WMDs (and the collective dread of the awesome power of those weapons) together have massively reduced human-caused death and destruction. The ever mightier the latest technology becomes, the more imperative is it to keep that technology in the "right" hands with its power reliably constrained—a fundamental reason why the world must triumph in the China Race for the maximum preservation of human life.

Though the CCP leaders may indeed discount and disregard people's lives, they too have a good reason to avoid war with the US, as much as possible. They are ultraselfish and totally self-indulgent autocrats, as I have attempted to demonstrate in The China Record, and hence not

Contaformation | 271

interested in insane or ideological suicide, especially when facing opponents armed with WMDs and the improving capability of regime (and targeted individual) decapitation. The risk of a hot war thus remains low in a well-run race with the PRC.[319] As the top US military leader, General Mark Milley, testified in Congress in March 2023, war with China and Russia is not inevitable, as long as the US remains "the most powerful nation on Earth" and fully prepared.[320]

The grand choice between alternative world orders, therefore, should not be enervated by the unnecessary and often false fear of confrontation, whether cold or hot. Important choices all have costs; maintaining or deconstructing a world order is unlikely to be bloodless, though its lethality can certainly be minimized. People have fought for worthy principles for eons and have died in countless numbers—sometimes heroically for the preservation of desirable values, sometimes tragically for the wrong causes. Here, it may be illustrative to examine the costs in lives of the last two major wars between large nations, World War II and the Korean War, which has so far been the only hot war between the PRC and the USA (see table 4.2 below). World War II was very costly in terms of life, a grave price, however, that seems well compensated by the war's outcome. The winning of World War II preserved the Westphalian world order and consolidated the leadership of the international community by the democratic rule of law. The unparalleled world peace, economic prosperity, sociopolitical justice, human rights, civil rights, and technological revolution ever since have benefited the overwhelming majority, if not all, of humanity to unprecedentedly advance human civilization, both quantitatively and qualitatively. Tellingly, the human species itself has grown explosively in size since the conclusion of that war, accompanied by the highest-ever living standard and ever-longer life expectancy. In fact, the death toll of World War II itself could probably have been significantly lower had the international community acted earlier and more forcefully to stop militarist Japan, Fascist Italy, and Nazi Germany at critical junctures, such as the Japanese invasion of Manchuria in 1931, the Second Italo-Abyssinian War in 1935, and the *Rheinlandbesetzung* (remilitarization of the Rhineland) in 1936; or responded in a smarter and more determined way, such as by starting a cold war to constrain the Fascist powers in the late 1920s and early 1930s and pushing back more forcefully from day one of the conflict, rather than being paralyzed by the hesitancy and wishful inaction that finally ended with the demand for unconditional surrender of the Axis powers in 1943. It may be somewhat

272 | The China Race

Table 4.2. Costs of Two Wars

World War II Deaths (1939–45)	Percentage*	Korean War Deaths (1950–53)
Battle: 15 million	15%	Battle: 1 million
Civilian: 45 million	2.0%	Civilian: 2 million
Total: 60 million	2.8%	Total: 3 million
Loss of Life: Selected Countries**	**World War II**	**Korean War**
United States	418,500	36,066
China	21 million (1937–1945)	197,653–900,000***
Korea	473,000	2 million
Soviet Union	24 million	—
Germany	6.6–8.8 million	—
Japan	2.6–3.1 million	—
France	567,600	262
Italy	457,000	—
UK	450,000	1,078

*   Of the world's military force (100 million in 1945) and total population (2.3 billion in 1939).

**   Total of battle and civilian deaths.

*** By various estimates. Other than vague, one-line mentions like "salute the 197,653 martyrs" by the CCTV in 2019 or "197,653 Chinese soldiers were killed in the [Korean] war" by the *China Daily* in 2020—this number has been questioned by many; the PRC government has never formally released or confirmed this data, providing no verifiable names or details.

Sources: Bian Xiuyue (2004); Cumings (2010, 35); F. Wang (2017, 240); "6/25 War Casualties," Monument in the ROK Ministry of Defense, Seoul, 2013; CCTV (2019; Zhang Zhouxiang (2020); Rhem (2020); Monument in National World War II Museum, New Orleans, Louisiana, 2022.

understandable to now question the US/West "economic decoupling" with Japan in 1940–41 for "leading" to the horrific Pacific War.[321] Yet it is the belated timing, not the sanctions, that may be most regrettable.

The Korean War, technically still under an armistice, stopped the advance of the Soviet Bloc and preserved the post–World War II international order in Northeast Asia. It rescued South Korea, which ultimately blossomed to become in 1996 one of the only two Asian members of the OECD, and in 2021 a new "developed nation"—the only such upgrade made by the UN Conference on Trade and Development since 1964. It also saved Taiwan, enabling it to evolve into the first ever Chinese democracy.[322] But the war was brutal and deadly. More than half of it, from November 27, 1951 (when other key issues were resolved at the ceasefire negotiation in Panmunjom), to July 27, 1953 (when the armistice was finally signed), was in fact fought for neither battleground gains nor the conditions of surrender, but for the previously "trivial" issue of how to repatriate the POWs (prisoners of war). The CCP vehemently demanded a mandatory and full repatriation of its people, dictated by its political rationale. But the US insisted on voluntary or unforced repatriation to give the Chinese POWs a choice between the PRC on the Chinese Mainland and the ROC on Taiwan. Fierce fighting continued for 15 months alongside 575 rounds of additional truce talks, mainly due to this disagreement. Beijing eventually relented (by the wish of new leaders in Moscow) to accept the US principle. Two-thirds (66.8% or 14,342) of the Chinese POWs went to Taiwan and one-third (33.1% or 7,109) returned to the PRC. Out of about 3,770 American POWs, 21 "voluntarily" chose to go to China (one died within months of arrival there). These American POWs, however, soon left the PRC with only one staying there, till his death in 2004.[323] Shockingly, for every one of the Chinese POWs who exercised his freedom of choice, almost one American soldier, at least six Chinese soldiers, 10 Korean civilians, and an unknown number of soldiers from other countries died on the battlefield.[324] For politicians and historians, this was indeed a costly victory for American "moral and humanitarian principles" against forced repatriation to "slaughter or slavery."[325] The somewhat unexpectedly huge death toll resulting from the disagreement over this principle may have tarnished the glory of the win, especially in a society that values human life highly. Nevertheless, it was a much-needed triumph of public relations for the ROC in Taipei, a bitter defeat and big loss of face for the CCP in Beijing after it had sacrificed so much and so long for nothing—a fact that has been well concealed inside the PRC—and a major humiliation for the international communists in general.

In hindsight, it may be easy, though a bit unfair, to view this incredible cost of precious human life as an overly brutal sacrifice on both sides over a trivial dispute, with the "Chinese anti-Communist" POWs morally judged as having "hijacked the Korean War" for their own interest.[326] To the Chinese POWs who escaped the hellish, more than three-decade-long period of mistreatment suffered by their former comrades who returned to the PRC, however, it was definitely a price-

274 | The China Race

less choice that bettered life for them and their offspring.[327] The family stories of I. M. Pei, the world-class architect, Lin Ching-hsia, one of the most renowned actresses in Greater China, and countless others illustrate quite vividly the "heaven and hell" life chance that the choice to abscond from the PRC to Taiwan could make.[328] Decades later, the CCP's treatment of the Chinese POWs returning from its invasion of Vietnam evidently remained the same hellish ordeal.[329]

Liberal democracies may value human life distinctively more than illiberal autocracies and thus tend to be more reluctant to act when loss of life is possible. This cost-benefit calculus may be justifiably viewed by many, especially democracy's detractors, as a major weakness of the West in international competition and confrontation. However, the unconditional surrender demanded and won by the Allies to end World War II, and the voluntary repatriation insisted upon and secured by the US to reach the Korean War armistice powerfully and unmistakably demonstrate the resolve and capacity of the West to fight for core values, fundamental principles, and well-reasoned objectives, even when substantial lives are at risk. Hopefully, such a firm and deliberate resolve remains to guide, in an ever smarter and better way, the management of and the ultimate victory in the China Race. The world should be mindful that "America and China are one military accident away from disaster";[330] winning the China Race, however, is much more important than avoiding confrontation and war.

Over 12 centuries ago, around 752 CE, Du Fu, later venerated as perhaps the greatest poet of China, or the "Sage/Saint of Poetry," wrote a poem so timeless that it could have been just composed for the China Race today:

> When drawing a bow, draw a strong one
> When using an arrow, use a long one
> To shoot the raider, shoot the horse first
> To seize the foe, capture the chief first
>
> Killing too has its limits
> States all keep their own boundaries
> So long as aggression is restrained
> No point shedding any more blood[331]

Epilogue

The Future of China and the World

With the completion of my trilogy on China, after nearly two decades of work, I feel a sense of relief mixed with delight, humility, and hope. It is of course probably an old cliché to say that people all naturally assert that their individual time is the most crucial and consequential piece of history. But, as I have labored to show in this book and its two prequels, the intensifying China Race, with its rare combination of choice and tempo, constitutes a critical juncture of history that will determine how humanity will be organized. In September 2021, speaking before the United Nations, US president Joe Biden declared that a "clear and urgent choice" must be made as the world stands "at an inflection point of history," and "we face here at the dawning of what must be a decisive decade for our world—a decade that will quite literally determine our futures." To the same audience, PRC Chairman Xi Jinping seemed to echo this sentiment by declaring that "the world is once again at the crossroad of history."[1]

The stakes and alternatives in this global competition centered around the PRC-USA rivalry are as certain and evident as they are weighty and urgent. There are clear paths and also shortcuts to reach a more desirable outcome of the China Race both efficiently and securely, and very likely also speedily and peacefully. The actual ending of the Race, however, is neither certain nor guaranteed, as human fallibility and misfortune are never in short supply when so many different players with vested interests, countless ideas, diverse ideals, and disposed beliefs are involved. The ultrahigh-stakes global competition between the US-led West and the CCP-led PRC tests and will continue to demand

276 | The China Race

ever more wisdom, vision, will, ability, resources, and luck to shape the future of human civilization. Naturally, the reader is more than welcome to critique, dispute, and falsify these and all other findings, deductions, and inferences I have attempted to present in this trilogy. It is now the time, however, for me to pause for a brief speculation about the future of the China Race, and the future of China and the world. It is always exciting and rewarding to witness and strive to explain human behavior; it is more intimidating and humbling to analyze and attempt to predict trends and the future.

The economist Robert Fogel, winner of the 1993 Nobel Prize in Economics, wrote at the turn of the 21st century his predictions for the world of the future:

> We should not be afraid of the future, [. . .] my predictions for the next six decades include longer and healthier lives, more abundant food supplies, improved housing and environments, higher levels of education for larger numbers of people, the narrowing of both material and spiritual inequality (not only within the country but internationally), better-paying and more flexible jobs, more time for parenting, stronger families that spend more leisure time together, lower rates of crime and corruption, and greater ethnic and racial harmony. [After envisioning that there will be a rise in Chinese values (authority, filial obedience, and discipline), he wondered if Americans should] prepare for a cataclysmic war or learn to endure a protracted cultural and political stalemate."[2]

Years later, I considered, with decidedly much less fame and authority, in my 2017 book, the first volume of my trio on China, the following four likely scenarios about the PRC:

> First, the PRC could evolve further politically and ideologically to be a more open and less illiberal Qin-Han polity [. . .], if not a functional liberal democracy with rule of law, so to live long with security and prosperity under the Westphalian world order. Beijing would reread its history, refocus its worldviews and reorient its strategy, to suppress and even abandon the tianxia (all under heaven) world empire ideal with sufficient institutional, international, and ideological assurances.

Second, the PRC could return to a Maoist revolutionary state and beyond, a hardcore authoritarianism, even totalitarianism and militarism, in order to survive through reshaping and reordering the world. [. . .] Mao failed miserably in that approach. But the new wealth and technology that have been strengthening the PRC could offer Beijing confidence and resources to retry it with more force and smarter ruses. [. . .] A PRC China Order may be surprisingly victorious in due time to unite the world, however improbable as it may seem today, like what the Qin Empire did to the Chinese World twenty-four centuries earlier and the CCP did to the Centralia seven decades ago.

Third, the PRC could be torn apart by itself between [. . .] the Qin-Han rulers' inherent desire and attempts for the China Order and [. . .] the changed and ever changing Chinese demography, economy, culture, and ideology that are increasingly Westernized and internationally connected [. . .], leading to political chaos and possibly civil war. The Centralia could eventually lose some of its peripheries. A collapse of the CCP-PRC, either peacefully or violently, could result in a phoenix rebirth of a Chinese nation-state like post–World War II Germany and Japan or a failed state armed with weapons of mass destruction.

[F]ourth, though likely only a transitional scenario: the PRC could continue [. . .] to hide its mandate for the China Order. Instead of trying to resist, reduce, and replace the United States to reorder the world, the PRC could pragmatically and selectively follow the Westphalian system and the Western leadership to resist sociopolitical and ideological changes at home while suppressing its urges of leading and reordering the world. Growing, enriching, and carefully opportunistic, the CCP may get by and muddle through with its Qin-Han polity without the China Order for some time to come, with whatever discontent, difficulty, and precariousness accompany that option.[3]

In 2020, a group of Sinologists concluded that "the future of China is highly contingent" and will be shaped by how "Chinese actors manage hundreds of complex interconnected challenges" and the accumulating

278 | The China Race

"critical problems" at home and abroad. However, the team had "little consensus" and great disagreements within itself regarding the academic assessment of and the policy advice about the challenges and problems Beijing faces. The "good leadership, good policies, and good fortune" that have been critical to the rise of the PRC in recent decades are no longer certain but may still be regained and retainable.[4] The future of China, and substantially the whole world, seems unknowable with any certainty. The Chinese and humanity are not just at some crossroad or juncture, they seem to be wandering in the middle of nowhere.

In mid-2020, a team of experts at the RAND Corporation envisioned four scenarios for China in 2050, which largely correspond to the four scenarios I outlined above:

> 1. triumphant China, in which Beijing is remarkably successful in realizing its grand strategy; 2. ascendant China, in which Beijing is successful in achieving many, but not all, of the goals of its grand strategy; 3. stagnant China, in which Beijing has failed to achieve its long-term goals; 4. imploding China, in which Beijing is besieged by a multitude of problems that threaten the existence of the communist regime.
>
> A triumphant China is least likely because such an outcome presumes little margin for error and the absence of any major crisis or serious setback between now and 2050—an implausible assumption.
>
> An imploding China is conceivable, it is not likely because, to date, Chinese leaders—for the most part—have proved skilled at organizing and planning, adept at surmounting crises, and deft at adapting and adjusting to changing conditions.
>
> By 2050, [. . .] the most plausible scenarios would be an ascendant China or a stagnant China.[5]

In October 2020, Joseph Nye, famous for coining the phrase "soft power," described five possible scenarios, by 2030, in the post–COVID pandemic world, with a 10% probability for each of the first four scenarios and 60% probability for the fifth scenario, representing continuity:

> The end of the globalized liberal order with its system manager the US weakened.

Epilogue | 279

A 1930s-like authoritarian challenge with more hospitable conditions for authoritarian politics worldwide.

A China-dominated world order. China's government and major companies are able to reshape institutions and set standards to their liking.

A green international agenda with an international agenda defined by countries' focus on green issues, while the US may recapture the leadership of the world.

More of the same. The US, still the largest power but with declining influence, and China manage to cooperate on pandemics and climate change, even as they compete on other issues.[6]

In spring 2021, two teams of scholars of international relations speculated on the future of the current world order, the LIO (or a newer version, LIO II) of the Westphalian system:

We envision three possible scenarios. First, contestations dwindle and leave LIO II more robust. In this scenario, liberal international institutions would meet reformist demands to address grievances against exclusion and inequality by changing the way liberal authority is exercised. [. . .] Second, the current tide of contestations sees the reconstitution of national and international politics as a conflict between those who seek greater international openness and cooperation versus those who advocate the return to the nation-state. [. . .] Third, the pushbackers succeed in cutting back the liberal intrusiveness of LIO II. [. . .] The ensuing reconstitution of politics would result in a fundamentally different international order, be it in the form of a reversion to the power politics of the Westphalian order in the nineteenth century or a new Chinese hegemony based on a one-world ideology. [. . . And,] we need to grasp nonliberal and non-Western normative principles and belief systems, [as . . .] it takes a truly global IR approach that transcends the divide between the "liberal" West and the "nonliberal" rest.[7]

Will the LIO gradually disappear, giving rise to the renaissance of an old-fashioned "Westphalian" order based on sovereignty as its key principle, as neorealism would argue? Or

280 | The China Race

will we see the transformation of the LIO into a new international order that preserves some of its principles (economic liberalism, principled multilateralism), while transforming others (rule of law, human rights, democracy)?[8]

A year later in 2022, a leading US think tank released a report entitled "Perspectives on the Future of the Global Order," which pointed to the arrival of "a new Cold War" between the PRC and the USA and called for nations to "project to the world an inclusive, eclectic, practical, respectful, and responsible strategic vision of convergence toward a new era in the global order that [. . .] must be managed to reestablish a single international community for all." More specifically, by late-2023, the much-talked rise of PRC power, mostly the so-called "China's economic miracle," is seen ending by experts of international economics.[9]

The list of speculations on the future of China and the world can in fact grow much longer, with more diverse and detailed predictions on a wide spectrum. Learning from the insights of all these viewpoints, and based on the data-driven positive statements and the normative analyses I have attempted to present in this book and its two prequels, I suggest, with all due respect and humility, the following three possible futures of the China Race, China, and the world:

First, and preferably, there will be a continuation of, or "a return to"—as seen from the liberal institutionalist and globalist perspectives—the Westphalian order of decentralized world polity, based on the equality of sovereignty of nation-states. This is the outcome this book strongly favors as a distinctively more desirable political future for the world, including the Chinese people. The continued leadership by the democratic rule of law in the West, particularly the US as the least systemic-subverting hegemonic power, will persist in the world. Disunity, differences, disparities, discrimination, and, yes, inequalities and exclusions, will exist among the nations to facilitate constant international comparison and competition through national experimentations with sociopolitical reform, economic efficiency, and technological innovation, as well as by way of international alliances, realignments, cooperation, institutions, and conflicts. The systemic challenge of both the rising power of the CCP-PRC state and the various forces for political globalization will be constrained and curtailed if not completely neutralized.

The likelihood of this future is excellent, with odds way above 50%, as long as the US and its allies fully and forcefully engage and prevail

Epilogue | 281

in the China Race. The peacefulness and the overall cost for achieving and securing this future are directly linked to the seriousness, speed, style, and skills of the running of the China Race by the US-led West. The fear of firmly countering a formidable systemic challenger in the era of weapons of mass destruction is genuine but grossly overstated and exorbitantly manipulated. The trendy emphasis on a globalist agenda of equality for all and on a uniform world political governance, purportedly ever more liberal and fair, may be ideal and even commendable, but is dangerously mis-prioritized and extensively abused. A thorough rejection of the various wishful or indoctrinated fantasies and the indolent or intentional ignorance about the rising power of the CCP-led PRC is already seriously overdue.

Second, an even more ideal and desirable future for China and the world, as I have outlined in chapter 4 of this book, is for China to become a fully integrated member of the continuing Westphalian international community, with a sufficiently transformed sociopolitical system and worldview. This may happen concurrently or sequentially with the PRC state being contained and constrained in the China Race, though not a necessity or a prerequisite.

Such a future is clearly preferable to all, and chiefly to the Chinese people (excluding the tiny ruling group of the CCP-PRC autocracy). A successful sociopolitical and ideological transformation of the PRC state and its worldview will result in the rising Chinese power and the great energy of the Chinese people being securely redirected away from recentering and reordering the world to focus instead on bettering the livelihood of the Chinese people and indeed all humanity. Profound reorganization and optimization of the Chinese state, economy, social life, and nationhood will take place. The likelihood of this future is also high, but heavily depends on the China Race proceeding in the favor of the West. A decisive frustration and loss of the China Race by the CCP party-state will be critical to the coming of this future, though it is neither necessary nor sufficient. The West, for its main objective of prevailing in the China Race, should fully engage the Chinese people, to assist and empower them for the transformation of the PRC. But it is essentially a cause of, for, and by the Chinese people, who must take their fate into their own hands.

Third, as I have demonstrated repeatedly in this trilogy, the CCP-PRC state has long openly declared its full-scale, all-around, and nonstop struggle for the future of the world, featuring a singular authoritarian or

282 | The China Race

even totalitarian polity, in its image, to order the nations and peoples. At the minimum, the CCP will make steady progress in the China Race, ensuring a safer world for its autocratic, illiberal, governance featuring state/party-capitalism or crony capitalism, at the expense of democratic rule of law, the market economy, civil society, and human rights. At the maximum, this future means that the US loses its leadership in the world to the CCP-PRC, the West is displaced and diminished, and the world recentered and reordered into a world empire like the China Order, which ruled and stagnated the whole known Sinic world for many centuries.[10]

Such a "China Dream" or, more precisely, a CCP Dream, is clearly an undesirable outcome of the China Race for the world including the Chinese people. It will steer human civilization onto a slippery slope that will be hard to reverse, if not be irreversible, on its way to long stagnation, repeated tragedies, and endless suboptimality. With perhaps a biased confidence, I see the likelihood of this future as less than the two futures outlined above, but still a frighteningly grave outcome with a serious feasibility. The odds of its realization, however partially and incrementally, is in fact not that small at all, since the "good" tends to have built-in disadvantages in an existential rivalry with the "evil." As Franz Kafka noted in November 1917 (when the world was being bled by the Great War and the Russian Revolution), "Evil knows of the Good, but Good does not know of Evil."[11] Unlike in Hollywood, human history is littered with examples showing that the preferred and the desirable do not always, let alone automatically, win against the unpreferred and the undesirable. Tragedy, like comedy, has featured prominently and eternally in the human psyche, aesthetics, and dramas for good reasons.

And with that, I leave my take on the rise of China and what to do about it to the reader, hoping the darkish omens and upbeat hopes contained among my murmurs and musings are heard and heeded or refuted in time. I hope this trio of books will never have the honor of a counterfactual vindication with a "what if" sigh of "but it is too late now." No joy would be greater than seeing my concerns and worries proven wrong and unnecessary. Immodestly following many others, I have come, I have seen, I have spoken, and I shall now trust in the collective wisdom of my fellow human beings.

Notes

Introduction

1. F. Wang (2017; 2023).

2. Kahn (1966, 23–47); Hardin (1968, 1243–48); Capoccia and Kelemen (2007, 341–69).

3. Lebow (2010). For an attempt by historians to present such fruits, see Cowley (1999). For a counterfactual theory of knowledge of epistemology, see Nozick (1981). For study of counterfactual causality in the social sciences, see Morgan and Winship (2007).

4. In the pre-Qin Chinese world, for example, to unite all the states into one was a prominent ideal promoted by diverse schools of thought including Confucianism, Legalism, Mohism, and Taoism. For a Judaic-Christian rumination and a wholistic historical survey of "world empire" over "the global ecumene," the global society with police powers in "a unity of mankind," see Voegelin (1962). For the Japanese ambition of the Nippon-Manchu-China "East" defeating the US-led "West" (and the world) in a 30-year protracted war with a battle of Armageddon in the end to unify the whole world for the "ultimate peace for all," see Ishiwara ([1940] 1953).

5. F. Wang (2017, 3); Buzan and Little (2000, 176). For an effort to contrast and "bridge" the "classic" or Western and the ancient Indian and Chinese ideas of political order, see Acharya et al. (2023).

6. Bernstein (1998).

7. Earlier, I described the China Race as "the China Struggle between Tianxia and Westphalia" (F. Wang 2017, ch. 7). Conceptually, it is in many ways analogous to (but often broader than) the following notions: "century-long marathon," "the superpower marathon," "the long game," "an open-ended period of confrontation," and "a long war" between the US and the PRC (Pillsbury 2015; Doshi 2021; M. Brown 2020; Ratcliffe 2020; Brands 2022). Relatedly and more internally, the China Race also portends the long struggle between the forces generated by the Chinese socioeconomic modernization generally in the

283

284 | Notes to Chapter 1

direction of Westernization and the CCP-PRC partocracy's ability to control China to continue its Qin-Han style authoritarian polity.

8. For a mathematical approach to the study of historical dynamics or "cliodynamics," see Turchin 2003.

9. Spruyt 1994.

10. Blackwill and Wright (2020); CFR (2019); Stares et al. (2020).

11. Lake, Martin, and Risse (2021, quote on pp. 235–36).

12. Shu Jianzhong, Da Wei, and Ren Ling (2021); Wu Hailong (2022).

13. Atanassow (2022).

14. US NIC (2021, 9, 90–105).

15. Xi Jinping (April 20, 2021).

16. Xi Jinping (September 21, 2021; March 15, 2023).

17. In a way, the China Race has its roots in "the race in Asia" seen a half century ago (Nixon 1967). For a sketch of Beijing's vision, ambition, and action to remake the international system, see Economy (2022 and 2022a).

18. For a general discussion on this linkage, see Chayes (2016).

19. Biden (September 21, 2021).

20. Collins and Erickson (2021).

21. Qin Yaqing (2022); Zhang Weipeng (2023).

22. Russell (1922).

23. It may be soothing and agreeable to assert that "competition cannot become an end in itself" in international politics or between the USA and the PRC; but it is naive and fanciful to pursue "human progress, peace, and prosperity" without competition (Weiss 2022). Much more on this later in this book.

24. Neumann and Morgenstern ([1944] 2004); Myerson (1991).

25. Heath (2023).

Chapter 1

1. In this book, "West" refers to the member countries of the OECD (Organization for Economic Cooperation and Development), 38 in 2023, plus a few other "developed countries" (as categorized by the United Nations) with similar sociopolitical systems, not necessarily geographically or ethnoculturally Western European or North American. Many differences certainly exist in the West, such as cultural diversity, varied state-society relationships, economic disparity, and diplomatic priorities. "Western powers" refers to the US, Canada, the EU, the UK, Japan, South Korea, Australia, and New Zealand. "Western values" refers to the sociopolitical norms centered around democratic rule of law and popular sovereignty, including meta-rules such as individual freedom or liberty and equality; people's right to life, consent (*quod omnestangit, ab omnibus approbetur* or "approval of a law by the effected"), property, procedural justice (due process),

Notes to Chapter 1 | 285

and self-defense; and the dispensability of any particular political leader. As some in the PRC have also understood it, the jaded phraseology of the East-West (or PRC-USA) dichotomy should be better seen as describing the contrasting and alternative modes of human organization and world order, "the barbarian and backward versus the civilized and advancing," which can exist in both the East and the West (Ren Jiantao 2016). For an economic history of the modern West, see North and Thomas (1973). For the anthology of Western ideas, see Heer (1968), Stromberg (1993), and Frame 2015. For art and aesthetics in the West, see Sennett (1994). For a *longue durée* history of the Western culture since the 16th century, see Barzun (2000) and Figes (2019). For a Chinese scholar's focus on the "spirits of rationality and freedom" that critically separate the "the superior" Western culture/civilization form the Chinese one, see Deng Xiaomang (2022).

2. The state is defined by Max Weber as "a compulsory political organization with continuous operation [. . .] insofar as its administrative staff successfully upholds the claim to the *monopoly* of the *legitimate* use of physical force in the enforcement of its order" (Weber [1922] 1978, 54). Sovereignty refers to the supreme authority of the state over a land and society, independent from peers and without superiors (Spruyt 1994, 3–7). For a description of the "modern" state (or nation-state) in recent centuries, see Lachmann (2010). For a "postmodern" anthropological conceptualization of sovereignty deconstructing the centrality of the state, see Hansen and Stepputat (2006, 295–315).

3. Lake, Martin, and Risse (2021).

4. T. Bai (2019); Niu Tiansheng (2020, 61–68).

5. Morgenthau (1948); Organski (1968); Waltz (1979); Gilpin (1981); P. Kennedy (1987); Wendt (1992, 391–425); Mearsheimer ([2001] 2014).

6. Du Shangze (2016, 1); He Cheng (2020, 1); Yuan Peng (2016, 2020); Dong Zhengrui (2020); Yuan Peng (2022).

7. For an institutionalist take on "critical junctures" in political history, see Capoccia and Kelemen (2007, 341–69).

8. The CCP still periodically reveals what it really is and does, such as in 1989 when, some now think, the "long game" of the PRC-USA rivalry started (Doshi 2021).

9. Wang Jisi (2021).

10. As defined by a few key landmarks: the PRC-USA diplomatic relationship in December 1978; the Tiananmen crackdown in June 1989; Bill Clinton's presidential visit to the PRC in 1998 and the PRC's subsequent membership in the WTO (World Trade Organization) in 2001; the Great Recession of 2007; and the rise of Xi Jinping in 2012.

11. Wang Zihui (2021); Mo Lin (2021).

12. *Zhongguo jingji zhoukan* (January 2010).

13. PRC officials/scholars, however, often simplistically attribute the China Race to "the change of the US China policy" (Qin Yaqing 2021).

286 | Notes to Chapter 1

14. Obama (2020, 475); Rappeport (2019, B6); Group of Seven (2021, 2022); North Atlantic Council (2021). NATO (2022: 10, 5) for the first time targeted "the systemic challenges posed by the PRC to Euro-Atlantic security [. . . and to] our interests, security and values," and elaborated that a year later (2023: items 6, 23–5).

15. Mitter (2021).

16. For the concepts, modern history, mindset, and "logic" of authoritarianism and totalitarianism, and the broader concept of "autocracy," see Arendt ([1951] 1976), Gleason (1995), Drucker ([1939] 2017), F. Wang (2017, 40–2), Desmet (2022) and Gerschewski (2023).

17. In fact, with indispensable thanks to the US-led LIO, the Chinese people have attained security and prosperity with their highest living standard ever (F. Wang 2017, 2023).

18. A. Goldman (2021). For a critique of a "Schmitt fever" among many in the PRC since the late 1990s, see Liu Yu (2010).

19. For embellishment of the CCP-PRC by authors educated in the West, see Zhang Weiwei (2016) and Zheng Yongnian (2021).

20. For the sociopolitical impact of the Enlightenment, see Acton (1949), Fitzpatrick et al. (2004), Israel (2011), and Jacob (2021).

21. The Legalist regime of the CCP-PRC is also frequently identified as a communist dictatorship of Leninism-Stalinism (Albert and Xu 2019).

22. With its "cumulative organizational complexity" under the "law of diminishing returns," and without "peer" state(s) to engineer regime change and innovation to sufficiently reenergize and resupply, a world polity inevitably disintegrates, leading to calamitous collapse and even disappearance of the society and civilization (Tainter 1988).

23. For an account of Beijing's ambitions wrapped up in liberal and globalist phraseology, see Da Wei (2021, 99–109).

24. Kornai (1992) published early on the flaws and follies of the Soviet-style socialism. For a history of world communism since 1917, see Pons et al. (2017).

25. 天下一统 and 共托邦. Zhao Tingyang (2006, 2018, 2020). For more about the revival of the *tianxia* idea in the PRC since the 1990s and critiques of it, see F. Wang (2017, 210–14).

26. Pan Yue (2020). For a Chinese rebuttal of the East-West dichotomy, see Shi Bo (2022).

27. B. Wang (2017); Uhl (2021).

28. D. Goldman (2020, 2020a).

29. 人类命运共同体. The official PRC English translation of this phrase appears somewhat nebulous: "community with a shared future for humanity" (CCP Central Party School 2018; Yuan Zongze 2020; Xi Jinping, April 20, 2021).

30. Xuan Yan (June 7, 2021, 1; June 8, 2021, 1).

31. *Cankao xiaoxi* (2021).

Notes to Chapter 1 | 287

32. Xuan Yan (2022, 1).

33. Taleb (2010); Kissinger (1994).

34. Cline (2015); Münkler ([2005] 2007); Darwin (2009).

35. Dalio (2021).

36. Shepherd (2020); Office of the Secretary of State (2020).

37. Ren Jiantao (2022, 23–38).

38. For a short historical portrait of hegemons and hegemony, see P. Anderson ([2017] 2022).

39. Wucker (2016).

40. Cheong (2021); Maizland and Albert (2021).

41. 楷模, 合作, 红利 and视野. Wang Wen (2021).

42. For a PRC promotion of the "Chinese Dream" in English that omits the CCP's global aspiration for the "China Dream," see Lu (2021). For a dialogue about "China Dream" versus "Chinese Dream," see M. Wan (2013).

43. Ikenberry and Yan Xuetong (2021).

44. Piketty (February 15, 2022).

45. Chu and Zheng (2021); S. Chan et al. (2021).

46. F. Wang (2023, chs. 2 and 3).

47. Ferguson (2008); Schularick (2009); Schell (2020).

48. In 2017, Schwarzman served as chairman of Trump's Strategic and Policy Forum; he was an early partner of the BlackRock Inc., which now manages the entire US Federal Retirement Thrift Investment (except G Fund) (Wu Su 2020; Schmidt 2022).

49. 潘石屹, 张欣. L. Wei (December 2, 2020); G. Lee (2021).

50. F. Wang (2017, 114–34).

51. 超国家主義. Maruyama ([1946] 2015).

52. Theoretically and historically, there are only three types of international political structures: an "anarchical system of states," a "world imperial system," and a "feudal system" (Nye 2008).

53. Scheidel (2019); "Europe shaped the modern world" from MacLennan (2018); Strange (1999, 345–54).

54. Aristotle ([350 BCE] 1912); Aquinas ([1485] 1911); Locke ([1690] 1980); Rousseau ([1762] 1923); Habermas (2019); UNESCO (2015).

55. John Maynard Keynes, for example, saw in Confucian ideas many common theorems and moral issues of modern economics (Keynes 1912, 584–88).

56. Bhargava (2021).

57. F. Wang (1998a, 1–5, 16–20). For a take on modernity as "a state of mind," in addition to an institutional or structural state of organization, see S. Smith (2016).

58. Wilson ([1975] 2000, 1979, 2019); Galor (2011, 2022).

59. Phillips and Reus-Smit (2020, 45); Turchin et al. (2022).

60. Acemoglu and Robinson (2006); Atanassow (2022, 155–74).

288 | Notes to Chapter 1

61. F. Wang (2017, 30–38); Fried (2009; 2015, 305, 512–25). For a limited take by a Chinese scholar on the impact of the decentralized world polity in Europe, which created the marvels of the modern world for all, see Zhang Xiaoyu (2021).

62. Williamson (1975, 1996). Like most writers, I treat innovation broadly to include technological, institutional, managerial, ideological, policy, and behavioral innovations.

63. For a sketch of the LIO, see Ikenberry (2011). For a sociological interpretation of the evolution of the Westphalian system, see S. Tang (2013). For legal efforts to outlaw war, see Hathaway and Shapiro (2017). For a critique of the operationality of the LIO concept, see A. Johnston (2019, 9–60).

64. Mearsheimer (2019, 7–50).

65. B. Scott et al. (2021).

66. Börzel and Zürn (2021, 282–305).

67. Kissinger (1994, 2014). For "great statesman" needed in international relations today, see Byman and Pollack (2001, 107–46). For the European "anomaly," see Scheidel 2019: 30–48.

68. For the disruptive development of a "constitutionalism" with "far-reaching consequences" on US politics and policy, for instance, see Loughlin (2022).

69. Bryan (1899); J. Burns (1981–89); Merk and Merk (1995); David and Grondin (2006).

70. Michels ([1911] 1962); Lipset, Trow, and Coleman ([1956] 1977); Voss and Sherman (2000, 303–49); Leach (2005, 312–37).

71. B. Johnson (2022).

72. Darwin (2009a, 2013).

73. Schake (2017); O'Rourke (2019); Moore (2019).

74. Franklin Roosevelt and Winston Churchill, the Atlantic Charter, August 14, 1941; Joe Biden and Boris Johnson, the New Atlantic Charter, June 10, 2021.

75. K. Lee (2020).

76. Ron Paul (and later Paul Broun, followed by Mike Rogers), the American Sovereignty Restoration Act, congressional bill was introduced but failed with a large margin, 1997–2023 (congress.gov/bill/117th-congress/house-bill/7806/text).

77. Haass (October 15, 2001); Münkler ([2005] 2007, 146–54); Groh and Lockhart (2015); Hopkins (2018). For Chinese use of the term, see Ding Ling (2014); Xia Yafeng (2017); Liu Ming (2019); Jiang Shigong (2020).

78. For an example of such effort, see Khong (2013, 1–47).

79. Russell, Rennison, and Karaian (2022).

80. Kissinger (2014, 1).

81. J. F. Kennedy (1963).

82. Burns (1981–89); Kirk (2003).

83. Nixon (1967).

Notes to Chapter 1 | 289

84. Campbell ([1992] 1998).

85. There were also border skirmishes between China and India (1962 and later), and between China and Soviet Union (1969). In the 1960s–1970s, PRC "volunteers" secretively manned many positions such as antiaircraft turrets in North Vietnam against the US, with thousands of casualties (Shen Zhihua and Yang Kuisong 2000).

86. Kissinger (1957).

87. Those wars include 1821–32 (Britain, Russia vs. Ottoman), 1839–41 (Britain, Russia, Ottoman vs. France, Spain), 1839–40 (Britain vs. Qing), 1853–56 (Britain, France, Ottoman vs. Russia), 1856–60 (Britain, France vs. Qing), 1870–71 (France vs. Prussia), 1874 and 1894–95 (Japan vs. Qing), 1877–78 (Russia vs. Ottoman), 1883–86 (France vs. Qing), 1895–98 (US vs. Spain), 1899–1901 (Eight-Nation Alliance vs. Qing), 1904–5 (Japan vs. Russia), 1907–15 (Britain vs. Ottoman), 1914 (Ottoman vs. Russia), 1914 (US vs. Mexico), and the Great War of 1914–18.

88. Ikenberry (2020, 2020a).

89. For the push for a USE by many movers and shakers in Europe, some three decades before Jean Monnet et al. set the European Union in motion in 1950, see M. Bond (2021).

90. An influential example of such prophecies is P. Kennedy (1987). A recent warning is Levitsky and Ziblatt (2018).

91. Huntington (1988, 76–96); Prowse (1992); Hall (2011); Chomsky (2011); Zakaria (2021); Kagan (2021); Calhoun, Gaonkar, and Taylor (2022); Wolf (2023).

92. Packer (2021). One could easily list many imperfections and flaws of the US system, from dated election mechanisms and gun politics to mismanagement of health care.

93. Cooley and Nexon (2020).

94. Beckley (2018, 2020).

95. Power (2021).

96. Y. Lee (2021); *Economist* (April 13, 2023; April 15, 2023).

97. Hannah and Gray (2021).

98. F. Wang (2017, 2023).

99. Russell (1922). Russell hoped that somehow the ancient, good wisdom of China could combine with Western science to build a better society.

100. J. F. Kennedy (1949); MacArthur (1964).

101. Doshi (2021).

102. Allan, Vucetic, and Hopf (2018, 839–69).

103. India's population might have overtaken China's as early as 2023 (Hegarty 2022).

104. John Adams, "From John Adams to Massachusetts Militia," letter, October 11, 1798 (founders.archives.gov/documents/Adams/99-02-02-3102).

290 | Notes to Chapter 1

105. Huntington ([1996] 2011, 51).

106. Moscovici ([1981] 1985).

107. Chu and Zheng (2021).

108. Schwab and Vanham (2021, 86, 180–85).

109. Andersen (2020).

110. Goddard (2018, 1).

111. For one report on the role of such ideas in China, see E. Wong (2018, SR4).

112. For a possible "death" of American democracy, see Levitsky and Ziblatt (2018). For regression of democracy as the failure of American liberal universalism, see Holmes and Krastev (2020).

113. Applebaum (2021).

114. Li and Westad (2021); G. Chang (2021a).

115. Kotkin (2022); Gleason (1995).

116. As reported by CCTV (中央电视台) on November 15, 2022, and Li Xuemei (2022).

117. C. Parton (2020). For religion and values as the "soul" during the Cold War, see Inboden (2008).

118. Foa et al. (2022).

119. The 39 countries are Germany, Albania, Australia, Austria, Belgium, Bosnia and Herzegovina, Bulgaria, Canada, Croatia, Denmark, Estonia, Finland, France, Haiti, Honduras, Iceland, Ireland, Italy, Japan, Latvia, Liechtenstein, Lithuania, Luxembourg, the Republic of the Marshall Islands, Monaco, Nauru, the Kingdom of the Netherlands, New Zealand, North Macedonia, Norway, Palau, Poland, Slovakia, Slovenia, Spain, Sweden, Switzerland, the United Kingdom, and the United States. The 26 countries are China, Angola, Antigua and Barbuda, Belarus, Burundi, Cambodia, Cameroon, Cuba, the DPRK, Equatorial Guinea, Eritrea, Iran, Laos, Myanmar, Namibia, Nicaragua, Pakistan, Palestine, Russia, Saint Vincent and the Grenadines, South Sudan, Sudan, Suriname, Syria, Venezuela, and Zimbabwe (German Mission to UN 2020; Xinhua, October 6, 2020).

120. Japanese Foreign Ministry, December 8, 2020 (https://www.mofa.go.jp/press/release/press1e_000162.html).

121. The Group of Friends in Defense of the Charter of the United Nations includes Algeria, Angola, Belarus, Bolivia, Cambodia, China, Cuba, Eritrea, Iran, Laos, Nicaragua, North Korea, Palestine, Russia, Saint Vincent and the Grenadines, Syria, and Venezuela (O'Connor 2021).

122. Muhammad (2021).

123. Fassihi and Myers (2021, A12).

124. Wang Dan (April 14, 2021).

125. Polzsar (2022).

126. Shi Yinhong (September 2021); She Gangzheng (2022); Small (2022); Yan Xuetong (2023). For a US-led "Coalition of Democracies" versus a PRC-led "Axis of Authoritarians," see Friedberg (2023).

Notes to Chapter 1 | 291

127. Charon and Vilmer (2021).

128. French (2022).

129. Sibley (2004); Klehr and Radosh (1996); Steil (2013); Unger (2021, 7, 36).

130. Bērziņa-Čerenkova (2022); Medeiros (2022). In March 2023, Xi's first foreign visit after securing his third term as the PRC Chairman was to see Putin in Moscow (PRC-Russian Federation joint communiqué, Moscow, March 22, 2023).

131. Lippmann (1947); Kort (2001, 3); Glass (2020).

132. McFaul (2021, 1–39); Brands (March 31, 2021).

133. X (1947); Kennan (1948); Gaddis (2011). For an imitation of Kennan on "the sources of Chinese conduct," see Mandelbaum (2023).

134. Office of the Secretary of State (2020, 45).

135. Kennan ([1946] 1969, 696–709).

136. Blinken (March 4, 2021).

137. Stephens (2021).

138. While the US persisted with the policy of containment, there were attempts to roll back in places like East Germany during the Cold War (Ostermann 2021).

139. Kennan (1992, A21).

140. Kennan (1972, 54–58).

141. John Lewis Gaddis, comment at "100 Years of Foreign Affairs," CFR, July 26, 2022.

142. For concise historical surveys of the containment and the demise of the USSR, see Gaddis ([1982] 2005) and Kotkin (2001).

143. For Kennan's thinking about China, see Heer (2018).

144. 中华民族 and 各民族平等. For the artificialness of "Chinese" nation, see Hayton (2020, 75–100). For the CCP's self-contradictory and somewhat debilitating nationality policy, see Xi Jinping (August 28, 2021).

145. Kennedy (Sept 9, 2020); Maizland (2021); IMPC (2021); Wong and Buckley (2021, A9); Al Jazeera (2022).

146. United States-China Economic and Security Review Commission (2020, 31).

147. Brands and Cooper (2020).

148. Hirsh (2022); Greenberg (2022).

149. Wolf (2021).

150. Christensen (2021).

151. Khalilzad (1999, 6–8).

152. Garside (2021a).

153. Weiss (2022).

154. Y. Tan (2021).

155. Nixon (1967).

156. Millward (2019).

292 | Notes to Chapter 1

157. Mann (2022).

158. In mid-2022, PRC analysts seemed to have already started to caution, however timidly, about the need to "keep sufficient connection to the West" Da Wei (June 14, 2022).

159. Crabtree (2020); Pei (December 16, 2020); Pao (2022); Jin and Zhou (2022).

160. McFaul (2020, 26, 28).

161. For an optimistic "manifesto" declaring that more "social progress" and a "better society" are within reach, see Fleurbaey et al. (2018).

162. Friedberg (2021, 115).

163. The nomenclature of the virus has been itself a symbolic contest in international politics. While the PRC official media first used the term Wuhan Virus or Wuhan Pneumonia for the initial months of the pandemic (December 2019–February 2020), the WHO (with strong influence from China) named it COVID-19 in mid-February 2020 for the explicit reason of political correctness. The ongoing search for the origin of the virus has already produced piles of literature sustaining suspicions about the outbreak, the cover-ups ordered by the CCP leadership, the management of the crisis in China, and the misinformation and distortion. For two concurrent early reports on the CCP's relevant acts at home and abroad, see Wong, Barnes, and Rosenberg (2020) and Li Yuan (April 23, 2020). For a typical effort to self-glorify the CCP and traditional Chinese herb medicine, see *China Daily* (2020) and the PRC government (State Council 2020a). For an investigation asserting the Wuhan origin and the CCP's responsibility for the pandemic, see Philipp (2020). For an analysis of the origin of the virus, see Leitenberg (2020) and Metzl (2020, 2021). For US government action, see Biden (May 26, 2021). The CCP, however, has promoted the idea of the US origin of the virus (Zhao Lijian 2021). The origin of the virus remains a hot issue in 2023–24.

164. F. Wang (2017, 114–34); Rosenthal and Wong (2011, 228–32).

165. Heer (July 27, 2020).

166. Desch (2022).

167. Anonymous (2021, 7).

168. Gao Ertai (2021).

169. For efforts "to colonize" extraterrestrial worlds, see Davenport (2018) and SpaceX (2022).

170. Wendt and Duvall (2008, 607–33).

171. Kennan ([1946] 1969, 696–709).

172. Chen Shenshen (2020).

173. Ci (2019).

174. Dante Alighieri ([1313] 1904).

175. The least known of these is perhaps the utopian ideal of "world city" or "cosmic city" of Stoicism, which envisions a sociopolitical uniformity

Notes to Chapter 1 | 293

transcending boundaries and divisions (Sedley 1998; Strange and Zupko 2004, 156–61; Sellars 2006, 130–31).

176. Kant ([1795] 2003; [1781–90] 2008).

177. Nagel and Newman (2008); Popper ([1945] 2013); Pinker (2021).

178. Hobbes ([1651] 2011).

179. Wendt (2003, 491–542; 2005, 589–98; n.d.).

180. Rousseau ([1755] 1992; [1762] 1923).

181. Michels ([1911] 1962); Rohrschneider (1994, 207–38).

182. Culturally and psychologically, such an urge may also persist for simple and "benign" aesthetic joy and comfort, such as in making and owning pets (Tuan 1984). For how humans, when vested with unconstrained power, tend to quickly become pure evil, see Zimbardo (2007).

183. Zhang Hongjie (2013, 300); Desmet (2022, 2).

184. Satel (2021); *Economist* (September 4, 2021); Matovski (2021). For a take on the crisis of "democratic capitalism" of our time, see Wolf (2023).

185. Hayek ([1944] 2007, 15, 43, 144–46); Feser (2007, 100).

186. For the dreaded involution, see Geertz (1969). For "political involution" in China, see Duara (1988). For involution in Chinese socio-economy, see P. Huang (1990). For it in today's PRC, see Y. Liu (2021) and Huang Jing-Yang (2021).

187. Börzel and Zürn (2021, 282–305).

188. Adler and Drieschova (2021).

189. Visentin (2021).

190. For the "positive," even "critical," role of war-preparation in sociopolitical, economic, and technological innovation, see Gat (2006), Ruttan (2006), and Morris (2014).

191. Elleman, Kotkin, and Schofield (2013).

192. L. Wei (2023).

193. Raby (ex-Australian ambassador to China) (2020).

194. For the construction of "Chinese nationalism" and the CCP's use of it, see Hayton (2020) and S. Zhao (2021, 141–61).

195. Author's interviews with senior PRC officials and analysts, 2015–22.

196. Pempel (2021). For the developmental state in East Asia, see Slater and Wong (2022).

197. A long-time observer of China concluded that a major transformation of the CCP polity held the key to the PRC's avoidance of stagnation and more tragedy (Overholt 2018).

198. Robespierre ([1790] 1950, 643); Constitution de la République d'Haïti, article 4, 1987.

199. Rawls (1971, 2001). For critics of Rawls from different angles, see R. Smith (2016) and Britton-Purdy (2019).

200. Forrester (2019).

294 | Notes to Chapter 1

201. Berkowitz (2000, 5, 32, 77).

202. Beitz (1999, 2009).

203. Waldron (2002).

204. Fogel (2000, 37).

205. Hanson (2018).

206. Nozick ([1974] 2013). For an ostentatious effort to use Confucian ideals of *ren* (仁 benevolence), *yi* (义 righteousness), and *li* (礼 propriety) to "supplement" equality, democracy, and freedom—key values of "Western liberalism in decline"—so to form "the modernized universal values of fairness, justice and civility" as the moral foundation of a new world order, see Yan Xuetong (2021a).

207. Kohler and Smith (2018).

208. Harden (2021).

209. Berlin (1969, 47, 68, 171–2, 215).

210. Berkowitz (2000, 110–11).

211. Hume ([1740] 2003); Burke ([1790] 1993); Lively (1971).

212. Fogel (2000, 238).

213. For my earlier and lengthier discussion on human needs, desires, and institutions, and the central role of the state (political system) in shaping and altering the overall domestic organization of a given nation, see F. Wang (1998a, 5–32).

214. F. Wang (1998a, 13).

215. Thomas (1979, 538–53); Carter (2011, 538–71).

216. Mark (2019); Sandel (2020).

217. Follesdal and Pogge (2005, 88).

218. 不患寡而患不均. Confucius ([5th—3rd centuries BCE] 2016). It is followed with "worry not about poverty, worry about disorder" (不患贫而患不安). English translation is mine.

219. Rawls (1971, 152, 302).

220. Von Mises ([1922/1951] 2010); Hayek ([1944] 2007).

221. Schumpeter ([1941] 1991).

222. Piketty ([2013] 2014; [2019] 2020; [2021] 2022).

223. Blitzer (2021).

224. Rappeport (2021); Alderman, Tankersley, and Nelson (2021).

225. Stiglitz, Tucker, and Zucman (2021).

226. Piketty ([2019] 2020, 47, 1027 [table 17.2], 1036–37; [2021] 2022, 226–44).

227. B. Sanders (2021); Bardhan (2022).

228. For a normative ranking of the four identifiable basic types of institutional exclusion, see F. Wang (2005, 1–22).

229. Einstein (1933).

230. Stuurman (2017).

Notes to Chapter 1 | 295

231. The literature on the determinants and importance of efficiency and innovation is so vast, rich, and well-known that there is little reason to cite it here. However, for two succinct takes by economists on the central role of "competition policy" on efficiency and innovation at the communal, industrial, national, and international levels, see Neumann (2001) and Gilbert (2020).

232. Terms like liberal have become a semantic swamp that may contain too much to be meaningful. Here, liberal political values refer primarily to individual rights, freedom of choice, and the liberty to be different and innovative. For a definition of liberalism, see Gaus, Courtland, and Schmidtz (2018). For more on liberty and freedom of choice, see Friedman and Friedman (1990) and Hayek (2011).

233. With small, flexible, and targeted efforts, rather than big and uniform schemes, abject or absolute poverty could also be eradicated even globally (Banerjee and Duflo 2011).

234. For a history of capitalism, see Braudel (1992). For the political impact of relative poverty, see Karadja, Mollerstrom, and Seim (2017, 201–12).

235. Social Darwinism has been easily dismissed on many grounds. However, an agnostic contemplation on the impact of evolution and selection probably serves humanity, still a biological species, better than a total denial (Hofstadter [1944] 1992; Bowler 2009).

236. James (2006).

237. Dawkins ([1976] 2016); Wilson ([1975] 2000, 547–76; 2019, 79–126). Human biological evolution today continues its selective removal of harmful genes (Mostafavi et al. 2017).

238. Loewe et al. (2008, 59).

239. Deborah Gordon (2010, 2016); Werber (2013). And "policy can change culture" (Bau 2021).

240. Shafik (2021).

241. Even in domestic settings, diverse thinkers like John Rawls (2001) and Friedrich Hayek ([1944] 2007) both have allowed for the existence of "just inequality," as an elaboration of the wisdom of the second half of article 1 of the French Declaration of the Rights of Man (1789): "Men are born and remain free and equal in rights. Social distinctions may be founded only upon the general good."

242. For a spirited defense of nationalism and the nation-state system, see Hazony (2018).

243. Kuttner (2020).

244. Milanovic (2019).

245. Paine ([1776] 2016, 1).

246. For two enthusiastic takes on globalization, see T. Friedman (2005) and Sheth and Sisodia (2006).

296 | Notes to Chapter 1

247. Wolf (2004).

248. Myrdal (1968); Migdal (1988).

249. For a report about how the PRC has effectively lured and used Western financiers to strengthen itself, see Hamilton and Ohlberg (2020; 2020a). For a stronger accusation of "globalist billionaires" of Wall Street acting as the CCP's agents to influence US policy, see Navarro (2018). Of course, the impact of the great lure of the massive number of Chinese consumers to greedy but naive international capitalists is nothing new (Crow 1937).

250. Klein (2020). For a Chinese analysis on how the PRC in economic globalization has contributed to the crisis of welfare states in the West, see Qin Hui (July 3, 2015).

251. Strange (1999).

252. Daudin, Morys, and O'Rourkeet al. (2010).

253. Lenin ([1916] 2021).

254. Hathaway and Shapiro (2017); Walt (2017).

255. Pogge and Mehta (2016); Parijs and Vanderborght (2017).

256. EU Commission (2019, 2020); K. Chan (October 21, 2020).

257. *New York Magazine* (2018).

258. Fick and Miscik (2022).

259. Allen-Ebrahimian (2021).

260. Zeihan (2022).

261. For a discussion about "just war" and limited versus unlimited wars, see Gentry and Eckert (2014), Lango and Simmons (2014), and Weisiger (2013).

262. Parker (1996); A. Goldstein (2006, 445–673); Morris (2014, 3–26).

263. Walt (2017).

264. Waltz (1979); Kant ([1795] 2003).

265. F. Wang (2017, 32–38, 132).

266. For democracy peace, see Mansfield and Snyder (2002) and Gat (2005). For free trade peace (sometimes called "capitalist peace"), see McDonald (2004) and Gartzke (2007). The belief that open exchanges of ideas and visits facilitate peace is the guiding principle of countless groups and individuals promoting international interactions; for example, see the mission statement by Bachner (2022).

267. There seem to be two kinds of democracy peace theory: "democratic peace," a lasting ideal that a global democratic political system will ensure sustained peace for all, and "democracy peace," an empirically observed pattern that democratic nations tend to be significantly less war-prone with each other (Reiter 2012).

268. Griffiths (2019); Strittmatter (2020); Dimitrov (2022).

269. For the stable but evolving human "nature," see Wright (1994). For the potential of fusion, see "Fusion Energy" on www.iter.org (last accessed, July 2023). The much talked-about AI, according to Sam Altman, the CEO of

OpenAI that created ChatGPT, at a CFR meeting on June 21, 2023, remains just a "new tool," unaltering human nature or sociopolitical structures.

270. K. Chang (2022).

271. He Jiankui (贺建奎). J. Cohen (2019); Wee (2019). After three years, He was released and seemed to have resumed his research on gene therapy (Wang Cong 2023).

272. Münkler ([2005] 2007, 154–61).

273. For a meditative albeit early reflection on the performances of liberal democracy and centralized authoritarianism during the COVID Pandemic, see Qin Hui (July 24, 2020).

274. For the variety of the "same" prototype human institution and the varied forms of interconnection and interaction among human institutions, such as liberal versus elite democracies, and the American state/society-market relationship versus that in Japan, see F. Wang (1998a, 18–40). For the rise and possible decline of democracy, see Hobson (2015), Levitsky and Ziblatt (2018), and Bardhan (2022). For democracy in different nations and at different times, see Stasavage (2020). For how illiberalism or authoritarianism could emerge to ruin a democracy, from the left just as easily as from the right, see Lilla (2016, SR1; 2020) and T. Friedman (2020, A14).

275. Sullivan (2020).

276. For a critique of the American style of capitalism in health care, which sorely needs improvement, for instance, see Case and Deaton (2020).

277. Yao Yao (2014).

278. For two recent exposés of this, see Hernández (2020), Hernández and Zhong (2020).

279. F. Wang (2017, 105–10, 172–75; 2023, 4–2); Wallace (2023, 1–17).

280. 特供. F. Wang (2023, 64–69). Mao Zedong was "diagnosed by experts" to have a "confirmed" lifespan of 150 years. *Great News* (最好消息), Red Guards, Beijing, December 1966, reposted online by many including @zhanglifan on Twitter, December 25, 2019.

281. Hayek ([1944] 2007, 147–70, 193–222). The Soviet-style communist polity has long been called an "atheist theocracy" (Heimann 1953, 311–31). To widely varying degrees, perhaps all governments (and public figures and authorities) tend to maximize their power and revenue in this way (Higgs 1987, 2021).

282. For those grand worldviews and plans, see CCP Central History and Archives Bureau (2020). For interpretation of CCP slogans in Chinese foreign policy, see J. Zeng (2020).

283. F. Wang (2017, 21–29). PRC scholars today still cannot face, for example, the archeological evidence of early Caucasian people living in the heartland of ancient China (Tang Jigen 2020). A new but still insufficient effort by Chinese historians to rectify the official narrative distorting the Qin Empire is Liu Sanjie (2020).

298 | Notes to Chapter 2

284. F. Schwarz (1960).

285. CCP Constitution, 2017, 1. "Party constitution revisions" (党章历次修订概览, 1921–2017), *Gongchan dangyuan* (共产党员), Beijing, accessed August 6, 2022.

286. Author's interviews with Chinese official and scholars, 2000–2022.

287. 天可汗. First invoked in 630 CE. Sima Guang ([11th century] 2009). Yan Xuetong (阎学通), speech at East-West Scholar forum of Princeton University Press, March 4, 2021.

288. Brands and Beckley (2021); Beckley and Brands (2021); Will (2022).

289. For a classic discussion of party-state dictatorship, see Friedrich and Brzezinski ([1956] 1965). For a take on the dynamics of personality cults, see Postoutenko and Stephanov (2021).

290. Zhou Xinmin (2020); He Yiting (2020, 1).

291. The powerful human emotions of fear and hatred are both exploitable and controllable (Dozier 1998, 2002); Furedi (2006, 2018).

292. Xi Jinping (July 1, 2021; October 16, 2022; March 16, 2023).

293. Wu Jicheng and Yang Yuning (2006).

Chapter 2

1. F. Wang (2017, 135–58,195–214). For a recent take on the relations between China and the outside world prior to the PRC, see Brook (2020). For a Chinese take, see Zhang Guogang (2019). For a meticulous story of it set in the 19th century, see Hanser (2019).

2. F. Wang (1998, 76–77, 93–115; 2017, 198).

3. For an early but penetrating discussion on this, see Schwartz (1968, 228–44).

4. F. Wang (2005, 199; 2012; 2017, 157–78).

5. The revolutionary Sun Yat-sen, "father of the ROC," revered by both the KMT and the CCP, however, opposed China's joining of the Allied Powers in World War I (Yang Tianshi 2019).

6. Unsurprisingly, PRC analysts always define China's national interests and "external threats" first and foremost in terms of the CCP's political interests (CICIR 2021a; CISS 2022).

7. S. Zhao (2023).

8. For a vivid summary of how the suboptimal diplomacy of the Qin-Han polity (of the Qing Empire) is readily seen in the PRC today, see Guo Songtao ([1883] 1983, 469).

9. Hannas and Tatlow (2021).

10. Tse, Ming, and Ong (2019).

Notes to Chapter 2 | 299

11. 亡我之心不死. This assertion, allegedly coined by Mao Zedong, is used in a great variety of circumstances, depending on what is the declared and targeted evil enemy at a particular time or occasion. For its recent reiterations, see Lao Wantong (2018) and Qian Xiang (2020).

12. Y. He (2018, 741–66).

13. Hu Haiou (2018).

14. Stalin ([1931] 1954). 落后/贫穷/弱小就要挨打/受人欺负/任人宰割 and 弱国无外交, Mao Zedong (1999, 500); Chen Kaizhi (2015); Wang and Li (2022); Jiedu Shishi (2023). For reflections on this by PRC scholars, see Fang Ning (2000) and Huang Chuanchang (2020).

15. 落后就要挨打, 贫穷就要挨饿, 失语就要挨骂. Xi Jinping (Dec. 11, 2015).

16. *Constitutional Oath* (宪法宣誓制度). NPC, Beijing, Febraury 24, 2018.

17. Christensen (2015, 288–89).

18. 枢纽. Shi Zhan (2018, ch. 8).

19. For world affairs as viewed by senior CCP official-scholars, see Xie Fuzhan (2021).

20. Li Shaowei (2021).

21. Gohale (2020).

22. Brands and Sullivan (2020).

23. Niu Jun (2012).

24. Fravel (2020, 97).

25. *Wenhua Zongheng* (2021).

26. Hillman and Sacks (2021).

27. Green, Nelson, and Washington (2020).

28. Fung and Lam (2020).

29. UNBigData (unstats.un.org/bigdata/index.cshtml; last accessed August 2023).

30. Frachon (2021).

31. Large (2021).

32. Ahmed et al. (2020).

33. Cao Yuanzheng (2022).

34. Mobley (2019, 52–7); Chatzky and McBride (2020).

35. Zhang Chenjing (2021).

36. Xi Jinping (September 17, 2021; September 16, 2022). By 2023, the SCO had expanded to include 9 members (the PRC, India, Iran, Kazakhstan, Kyrgyzstan, Pakistan, Russia, Tajikistan, Uzbekistan), 3 observers (Afghanistan, Belarus, Mongolia), and 14 dialogue partners (Azerbaijan, Armenia, Bahrain, Cambodia, Egypt, Kuwait, Maldives, Myanmar, Nepal, Qatar, Saudi Arabia, Sri Lanka, Turkey, UAE) (SCO official website: chn.sectsco.org, 2023).

37. Xinhua (July 12, 2022). More on wicwuzhen.cn (last accessed August 2023).

300 | Notes to Chapter 2

38. 国际调解院. The nine are: Algeria, Belarus, Cambodia, Djibouti, Indonesia, Laos, Pakistan, Serbia, and Sudan (PRC Foreign Ministry Press Release, fmprc.gov.cn/web/wjbzhd/202302/t20230216_11025952.shtml; posted February 16, 2023).

39. Chan et al. (2021).

40. For official elaborations of the China Solution, see Chen Shuguang (2018, 11), Huang Ping (2019), and Cheng Zhiqiang (2020). For PRC foreign policy in 2023 and beyond, announced by the CCP's new top diplomat, see Wang Yi (December 25, 2022).

41. F. Wang (2017, 198–203).

42. Mao's decision to enter the Korean War itself was greatly motivated by his domestic political needs (Chen Jian 2021, 13–15). He was also ordered so by Stalin (Xu Zerong 2023).

43. Song Yongyi (2007, 212–20).

44. Wang Yiwei (June 30, 2020).

45. Meyskens (2020).

46. F. Wang (2017, 170–218). For the US prevention of Moscow's nuclear attack on China, see Xu Ni (2008).

47. F. Wang (2023, 15–83).

48. Hayton (2020, 9–10, 5).

49. 国家安全 and 总体国家安全观. National People's Congress (2015); CICIR (2021).

50. Blanchette (2021); Naughton and Boland (2023).

51. Qin Gang (February 21, 2023).

52. Buckley (June 20, 2020). By the end of 2022, at least 230 US citizens were reportedly jailed or detained in the PRC opaquely on "arbitrary grounds" (Areddy and Spegele 2022).

53. PRC Foreign Ministry press conferences/releases, June 7, 2012, April 26, 2013, and December 13, 2019. Ren Qinqin and Wang Jianhua (2015); *Renmin Ribao* (May 9, 2019, 1).

54. Li Jing (July 29, 2009).

55. "China is firm in upholding its core interests, which include the following: state sovereignty, national security, territorial integrity and national reunification, China's political system established by the Constitution and overall social stability, and the basic safeguards for ensuring sustainable economic and social development" (State Council Press Office 2011, III).

56. Wang Jisi (2015, 2021).

57. Sheng Dingli (2020).

58. "总体国家安全观[是 . . .]捍卫中国共产党的领导和[. . .] 维护国家政权安全和制度安全" (Yang Jiechi, 2020, 6). "核心利益就是核心的利益," (Liu Shangnan 刘尚南, correspondence, May 2023).

59. Li Zhiwei (2021).

Notes to Chapter 2 | 301

60. Xinhua (July 26, 2021); Wang Yi (2022, 2022c).

61. 总体国家安全. Fu Xiaoqiang (2021).

62. S. Zhao (2023, 23–114).

63. Richardson (2010).

64. Allison (2016).

65. Garver (2017); Shambaugh (2013, 56).

66. For an official elaboration of Xi's foreign policy, see Su Ge (2020).

67. Hitler (1943, 49, 373–75); Cecil (1972, 56).

68. *Tianxia datong* (天下大同), in Confucius ([5th–3rd centuries BCE] 2016).

69. 人类命运共同体. Li Yun Shi (李陨石), *Datong Declaration* (大同宣言) for Big Harmony Party (大同党), Georgetown, Guyana, 2006. Information about this declaration is banned in the PRC. Li's party was suspended in 2009 and dissolved in 2014 for lack of funding (Zhuang Weizheng 2019).

70. *Renmin Ribao* (September 7, 2007); Xinhua (May 21, 2011); State Council (2011).

71. Qian Tong (2012).

72. 世界大同, 天下一家. Xi Jinping (January 1, 2017; January 1, 2021).

73. Zhu Xili (2017).

74. Wang Yi (2013, 2016, 2022).

75. Jin Canrong, "Seminar on Sino-US Strategy" (金灿荣:中美战略讲座), Guangzhou, July 2016 (www.jcrfans.com/html/2016-08-29-1024.html [page blocked since January 2023]).

76. "为中国人民谋幸福, 为中华民族谋复兴, 为世界谋大同 . . . 积极推动构建新型国际关系" (Xi Jinping, April 20, 2021).

77. 全人类共同价值 v 普世价值. Xi Jinping, speeches at the 70th & 75th UN Assembly meetings, Sept 28, 2015 and Sept 22, 2020 (Wang Tingyou 2016; Han Aiyong 2022).

78. Wu Pengfei (2022).

79. Fang Kecheng (2014, 305–9). For personal accounts on how "foreign friends" could be jailed as "enemies" and maybe later become "friends" again, see Rittenberg and Bennett (2001) and Savitt (2016).

80. Orwell (1949, 113).

81. 外事/外交无小事. Chen Lifeng (2007); Chen Yuanyuan (2013). This author was told by insiders that, in the 1960s–70s, Zhou ordered harsh measures including executions to punish cadres for trivial things like "improper" dish arrangement at a diplomatic banquet. This rule is legally reaffirmed in *The PRC Law on Foreign Relations*, article 5, July 1, 2023.

82. Even in the 21st century, Mao apologists still cite his overture to the West for regime survival, "opening China to the world," as evidence of his wisdom and accomplishment (Deng Liqun 2004; Yan Shenlang 2015).

83. Price and Dayan (2008).

84. Nossel (2021); Kaplan (2023).

302 | Notes to Chapter 2

85. 举国体制. Beech (2021). An interesting twist on that is the CCP's successful employment of an American skier (Athey 2022; Shepherd 2022).

86. *Caijing toutiao* (2016).

87. For more about Mao's frantic efforts to promote global revolution, see F. Wang (2017, 200–203).

88. Lovell (2019, 195).

89. One report asserts that "at least" thousands of "Red Guards" died in Burma in the 1960s–1970s (Sun Wenyi 2009).

90. Mao's secret speech to CCP leaders on May 17, 1958, cited in Li Rui (1999, 390).

91. Nhem (2013); Starn (1995); Rochlin (2003); Galway (2022).

92. Rogin (2018); P. Martin (2021).

93. Unger (2021, 44).

94. K. Fang (2022).

95. Worden (2020).

96. The CCP's blunter comrade, Nikita Khrushchev, infamously declared in 1956 that the Soviet Bloc would bury the West (*Time* 1956). For an example of the vow to "bury the American Imperialism" during the Mao era, see *Renmin Ribao* (April 6, 1966, 2; January 30, 1969, 5). Officially, the CCP has stopped using such language since the 1980s, though various PRC analysts still use it in the 2020s, such as Zhang Yanping (2021).

97. Zhang Hongzhi (1994); Zhu Binyuan (2019); Xi Jinping (August 2019).

98. Clayton et al. (2023).

99. Hughes (1988); Siegel (1996); Wong (2023, 213–46).

100. Zhu Huayan (2018); CCTV (2017); Le Zi (2018); Zhong Shan (PRC Minister of Commerce) (2019); Ren Zeping (2020). An appreciative report of FDI in China is Enright (2017).

101. McAuliffe and Khadri (2020).

102. Zheng Cunzhu (2019).

103. Author's interviews in Beijing and Shanghai, 2001–4 and 2010.

104. For an Australian protestor framed as a "terrorist," see Wondracz (2022). More Western "critics of the CCP" appear to have experienced similar smears and entrapment by fake emails and social media postings (Kevin Carrico, posted on listserv, July 23, 2022).

105. Zheng Rui (2020); Aroor (2020).

106. Wang Tianyi (2021, 1).

107. K. McGregor (2009); Britton (2018).

108. Borao (1998).

109. "Wang Yi Met with Afghanistan's Taliban Leaders" (王毅会见阿富汗塔利班政治委员会负责人), July 28, 2021 (mfa.gov.cn/wjbzhd/202107/t20210728_9137717.shtml).

Notes to Chapter 2 | 303

110. Then PRC Chairman Hu Jintao inexplicably visited the remote Namibia in 2007 and showered a huge amount of aid to stop the business bribery investigation against his son there (Fairclough, Childress, and Champion 2009; author's interviews in Windhoek, Namibia, 2013).

111. State Council Press Office (2018); Zhou Hong (2007). For the "extravagant and unbearable" foreign aid and ventures, see the articles and data collection by Tencent Reviews, *The Gains and Losses of 60-Years of China's Foreign Aid* (中国对外援助六十年的得与失) (view.news.qq.com; last accessed August 2022).

112. By 2022, the PRC had 13,427 "development" projects (mainly aid programs) in 165 countries, totaling $843 billion (*AidData*, College of William & Mary; accessed Mar 20, 2022).

113. Wheatley, Cotterill, and Yu (2022). For the impact of PRC international lending, see Dreher et al. (2022).

114. Chatzky and McBride (2020). For vague second thoughts regarding the BRI by a Peking University–based PRC analyst, see Zhu Keren (2020). For the reception of BRI projects in Southeast Asia, see Lampton, Ho, and Kuik (2020). For the CCP's "Cooperative Alliance of BRI Think Tanks" to coordinate over 140 "high level" institutions for the BRI, see (一带一路智库合作联盟) *Belt Road Portal* (yidaiyilu.gov.cn).

115. Fassihi and Myers (2020, A18).

116. BBC (August 6, 2021).

117. Wang Mingyuan (2018).

118. Hu Xingdou (胡星斗), quoted in Qiao Long (2015).

119. Ministry of Commerce (2018).

120. Guo Yuhua (2018); UNESCO (2020).

121. Took a hit from Western critics and went into retreat, the CIs, however, made a comeback with new guises in the 2020s (Peterson, Oxnevad, and Yan 2022).

122. Sahlins (2014).

123. The funds, via Hanban (Chinese language office), appear mostly from the CCP Central Department of Propaganda (National Association of Scholars 2020; Han Ban 2020; US Congressional Research Service, 2019).

124. Costs are calculated based on author's data from CIs in Georgia, Michigan, Maryland, and New York (2012–18), Xiong Binqi (2018), and Ministries of Education and Finance (2019).

125. Allen-Ebrahimian (2017); *AidData*, College of William & Mary, March 16, 2022.

126. Wang Yi (January 2, 2022); Xinhua (February 4, 2022). During Putin's nine-hour visit to Beijing, the two sides signed 15 deals (Ministry of Foreign Affairs, February 4, 2022; Chen Aizhu 2022). Xi reaffirmed the partnership with Putin during his state visit to Moscow in March 2023.

304 | Notes to Chapter 2

127. Buckley (2022, A1).

128. Cankao Xiaoxi (2022); E. Cheng (2022).

129. 策应. Li Zhanshu (栗战书), Vladivostok, Russia, State Duma video, September 13, 2022.

130. M. O'Neill (2022); P. Zhang (2022); Pei (2022); Ni (2022); Holland (2022); Erickson (2022); R. Martin (2022).

131. E. Wong (2022, A11); W. Mauldin (2022); Colby (2022); Schultheis (2022); Boot (2022). PRC analysts saw "long-term strategic damage to China" as "the nature of this war" (Bai Sen Xin 2022; Magnus 2022; Singleton 2022; Mitchell et al 2022; Blanchette 2022).

132. 大外宣. Dudley and Kao (2020).

133. Tang Shiping (2020).

134. For tales of white gloves, see Shum (2021).

135. Cao Yuan (2019).

136. Duan Xiujian (2010).

137. Zhong et al. (June 10, 2020).

138. For one "white glove" who swindled ¥40 billion from Chinese bank depositors and continued as a prominent agent of the CCP's "grand external propaganda" campaign in the US, see Henan Xinwen (2022).

139. Collins (2020); Hasson (2020); Feldwisch-Drentrup (2020).

140. Jiang Tianfeng (2021); Yunzhong Shiji (2021); Zhihu Zhuanlun (2023).

141. Ministry of Foreign Affairs (2020a).

142. Jie Shu (2020).

143. Kiplagat (2020); Alden and Otele (2022).

144. Wheatley, Cotterill, and Yu (2022).

145. Wang Yi Hao (Jan. 17, 2023). Qin, in a very dramatic way, was removed as foreign minister after only seven months on the job and one month of absence (Xinhua, July 25, 2023, news.cn/politics/2023-07/25/c_1129767587.htm).

146. Lynch, Andersen, and Zhu (2020).

147. Fernandez (2019); Turkish Radio and Television Corporation (2019); Parkinson, Areddy, and Bariyo (2020); Fabricius (2020).

148. Brautigam (2009, 273–312); Y. Huang (2019); Brautigam and Rithmire (2021).

149. Author's observation in East Africa and Oceania, 2013–14; CBS News, 60 Minutes, February 2, 2020; Wingo (2020); State Council (November 26, 2021).

150. Dube and Steinhauser (2023).

151. Driessen (2019).

152. For the Realist definition of national interest, see Morgenthau (1949). For the take by idealists, see Bull (2012). For an early effort to bridge and synthesize the two, see Cook and Moos (1952).

Notes to Chapter 2 | 305

153. For how the lack of trust decidedly raises the risk for a nation to face conflicts and war, see Copeland (2014).

154. The practice of extracting from and sacrificing its own people to please and placate foreigners seems to have its roots in the late-Qing court, which allegedly would "rather gift to friend countries than give to [our] slaves at home" (宁赠友邦不与家奴) (Liang Qichao [1899] 2010, ch. 4; Chen Tianhua [1903] 2002).

155. The CCP eventually abandoned all its demands, large or small, including the US leaving Taiwan and Korea, Beijing taking Taipei's seat in the United Nations, and the repatriation of all POWs, in order to reach the 1953 Armistice (F. Wang 2017, 164, 199).

156. Elleman (1997); Jersild (2019); Liu Hui (2020); Bie De (2022).

157. Torigian (2022).

158. Repnikova (2022).

159. McClory et al. (2019, 38); Cook (2020).

160. Ronen et al. (2014). Xiong Yan (熊焰), public speech, Beijing, May 22, 2023.

161. Silver, Devlin, and Huang (April 21, July 30, October 6, 2020); Smeltz and Kafura (2020); Silver, Huang, and Clancy (2023).

162. Mapping Militant Organizations (2018); Espina and Rinoza (2020).

163. NBC Universal data, New York, February 2022.

164. Sheng Zhihua (2013); Davies (2021); Pompeo (2023).

165. Xin Ziling (2010).

166. J. Yuan (2019).

167. Wei Zhi (2014); Su Qun (2004).

168. Sun Jing (2014, A11); Xinhua (January 10, 2013); *Zhongguo jianzhu bao* (2013, 4).

169. Fang Fenghui (房峰辉, PLA chief of staff), vowed to the press on May 14, 2014, during his official visit to Washington, that "not an inch of our ancestor's land can be lost." The PRC Ministry of Defense has repeated the decades-old line to the press almost every year (for example, chinanews.com.cn/gn/2021/03-01/9421513.shtml), even though Gen. Fang himself was purged in 2018 and sentenced to life in prison for corruption.

170. Heinzig (2004, 363).

171. Fravel (2005). For a Chinese list of the "great amount of territories lost since 1949," see Wang Peiyao (2021).

172. Qin Hui (2012).

173. Garver (2001). Chinese nationalists today often bitterly call it a loss to the Chinese national interest for Mao's psychological satisfaction (Jin Hui 1995). For a recent bloody border clash, see Aroor (2020).

174. Yang Kuisong (2009, 259).

306 | Notes to Chapter 2

175. Sheng Zhihua (June 2014; August 2014).

176. Palmer (2014); *Economist* (2014); Ramzy and Ives (2020).

177. *Economist* (2019). For "Hong Kong nationalism," see Carrico (2022).

178. S. Lewis (2016); Kaiman (2017); Cheung and Hughes (2020).

179. National People's Congress (2020).

180. Ewing (2020); Desiderio (2020).

181. Kwan (2020); M. Davis (2020); Ye and Cheng (2022).

182. Lee and Blanchard (2020).

183. Xi Lisheng (2020); Gao Yang (2021); Qin and Chien (2022, 2022a).

184. Lu and Xie (2020); 1992–2023 surveys by the National Cheng-chi University, Taipei, (esc.nccu.edu.tw/PageDoc/Detail?fid=7804&id=6960; last accessed August 2, 2023).

185. Author's interviews with Taiwanese, 1995–2022.

186. Wang Yi (August 5, 2022); Ministry of Foreign Affairs (August 5, 2022).

187. Adragna (2023).

188. For the PRC's conquest and colonization in the greater Tibet region, see Li Jianglin (2011) and X. Liu (2020). For just one horrific massacre of Mongolians in the 1960s, the case of "Neiren Party" (内人党), see Hao Weimin (2019). For just one massacre of Yunnan Muslims in 1975, the "Shadian Incident" (沙甸事件), see Gladney (1996, 137–38). For the Xinjiang camps, see Watson and Westcott (2020) and Alecci (2022).

189. For a French study of Tibetan nationalism, see Donnet (1993). For a revelation by a Tibetan-Chinese of Tibetan life under the PRC's colonial-style rule, see Wei Se (2003).

190. *Jingji ribao* (2014). The natural gas produced in Xinjiang has been pipelined all the way to Shanghai (author's field notes in Xinjiang and Shanghai, 2001 and 2004).

191. Zenz (2018).

192. In addition to the Qinghai-Lhasa Railway ($47 billion), which was completed in 2006, the Sichuan-Lhasa Railway ($32 billion) is to be completed in 2025 (Daqiong and Luo Wangshu 2016; Hao Yu and Gu Yu 2022).

193. Pinchuk (2013); *Bloomberg* (Dec 22, 2014); Roblin (2020); Pubby (2020).

194. Zhang Bin (2014).

195. Stevenson (June 1 and July 1, 2020); Wise and Talley (2020).

196. A new addition to the massive and creative migrants is the thousands of asylum seekers from the PRC, literally walking all the way from Ecuador to Texas (Fan and Lu 2023).

197. Author's interviews in Tanzania and Zimbabwe, 2013.

198. Lawler (2020).

Notes to Chapter 2 | 307

199. Evans-Pritchard (2020).

200. Qian Tong et al (2008); Xinhua (February 7, 2022).

201. Wang Huiyao et al. (2014, 57).

202. *The Henley Passport Index 2020 Q2* (henleyglobal.com/passport-index/ranking; posted June 2021); Ministry of Foreign Affairs (2020); *Summary of China and Foreign Countries' Agreements on Mutual Visa Waiver* (中国与外国互免签证协定一览表) (cs.mfa.gov.cn; last accessed August 2, 2023).

203. 内外有别. Brady (2000); Lien Xiaotong (2016).

204. F. Wang (2017, 105–10).

205. Meng Weizhan (2019, 121–35); *WeChat* posts, April 2020. For similar schemes to "win over the American left," see MZIRI (2020).

206. Mugabe's speech at the 2010 and 2015 Sino-African Forum summits in Johannesburg and Beijing (focac.org, accessed June 8, 2022).

207. Wang and Elliot (2014).

208. Mendes (2015).

209. Zhihu (2016). The original thread was deleted by the censors in 2020.

210. Roosa (2006); Purdey (2006).

211. Ministry of Foreign Affairs (1978); Y. Chan (2011); author's field notes in Siberia, Russia, 2011; Sun Yue, "Russia's 'De-Chinese' Phenomena" (孙越: 俄罗斯的去中国化现象), Sina Blog, January 15, 2014 (censored by 2021); Wang Qiang (2009); Ma Singshen (2010).

212. G. Wang (2000).

213. Chen Chuanren (2006); Suryadinata (1978, 1995); J. To (2014); Ruiz et al (2023).

214. Kynge, Hornby, and Anderline (2020). For the united front "for covert influence and technology transfer," see Joske (2020).

215. Busch (2019).

216. Wang Yaqiu (2020); H. Zhang (August 19, 2019).

217. Bowe (2018); Parker (2020); Fan Jiayang (2020).

218. Tatlow (2020, 2023). For CCP's "media offensive," see Kurlantzick (2022).

219. Federal Bureau of Investigation (2022).

220. Charon and Vilmer (2021).

221. Dorfman (2018); Qin Weiping (2020, 73).

222. Wen Shan (2019).

223. Saul (2017); Allen-Ebrahimian (2018, 2018a); Izambard (2019); K. Smith (2020); Espiner (2021); Human Rights Watch (2021); J. O'Connor (2021); Parliament of Australia (2022).

224. Yang Yijun (2021); Xinhua (July 7, 2021).

225. Shen and Li (2000).

226. Pehe (1998); Leira (2019).

308 | Notes to Chapter 2

227. For details, see F. Wang (2017, 21–32, 154–58; 2023, 47–54).

228. Li Rui (1999, 152–95, quote on 168). Similar views are in Xin Ziling (2009, 1–22, 454–82).

229. Potter (2021).

230. For a Chinese summary of such efforts in recent years, see Kong Dapeng (2021), Zhou Ziheng (2022), and IMI (2012–22).

231. Author's field notes and interviews in Africa, Latin American and Southeast Asia, 1999–2013 and 2016–20.

232. Nhem (2013); Killing Fields Museum of Cambodia (killingfields museum.com).

233. Author's interviews in Kenya and Tanzania, 2013; Klomegah (2022).

234. Dyer (2019); Wang and Harsono (2020); Mirovalev (2020); Serhan (2022).

235. Some call this a "financial Cold War" between the PRC and the US (Fok 2022).

236. PRC State Administration of Taxation data, 1993–2011. Comments by Gao Peiyong, deputy director of China Institute for Fiscal and Trade Studies, in *Zhongguo caijing bao* (中国财经报), August 21, 2007. He reaffirmed his views in Gao Peiyong (2013, B06).

237. Zhou Tianyong (professor of CCP Central Party School, 2010); US Congressional Budget Office (2002); US Office of Management and Budget (2014).

238. 人民币. Rolnick and Weber (1986).

239. Xinhua (April 7, 2020); IMF (2022).

240. Subramanian (2010); Frieden (2016); F. Wang (2023, 98–129).

241. Autor, Dorn, and Hanson (2013, 2121–68; 2016, 205–40).

242. Feygin and Leusder (2020); Schwartz (2020).

243. Evans (1979).

244. Piketty ([2013] 2014; [2019] 2020).

245. Klein and Pettis (2020).

246. F. Wang (2023, 110–29).

247. Databases of US Federal Reserve, US Department of Commerce, People's Bank of China, accessed August 2022.

248. Subacchi (2017, 3–4, 9–28).

249. For the "Nixon shock," see Gowa (1983).

250. Di Dongshen (2013: 115–26; June 2020; April 4 and May 3, 2020); Ju Jiandong (2023).

251. Turrin (2020).

252. Wang Yongli (ex-deputy governor of Bank of China) (2021).

253. Sun Jiayi (2020); Tran and Matthews (2020); Fan Yifei (deputy governor of the PRC central bank) (2020); Kshetri (2022). For digital currency in general, see Hockett (2019).

Notes to Chapter 2 | 309

254. For an insider's take, see Zhou Xiaochuan (ex-governor of People's Bank) (2020).

255. Subacchi (2017); *Economist* (May 7, 2020).

256. *Bloomberg* (July 13, 2020).

257. Lian Ping (2020).

258. Chey and Li (2020).

259. Zhang Sheng (2018).

260. 天下货币 and 世界人民元. Ma Xia (2021).

261. Kumar and Rosenbach (2020).

262. Macleod (2020).

263. Qian Xue (2019); Yan Yan (2021). For an American warning on this, see Chorzempa (2022).

264. In 2021, the basket was adjusted (once every five years) to RMB 12.28%, yen 7.59%, pound 7.44%, USD 43.38%, and euro 29.31% (imf.org/en/Topics/special-drawing-right; last accessed August 2, 2023).

265. Economy (2019, 94).

266. Guan Tao (2020).

267. IMF (2022).

268. Excluding Eurozone, RMB ranked lower with a share of only 1.47%, further behind Canadian dollar (2.29%) and Swiss franc (1.67%) (SWIFT 2023, 3–7).

269. Wen Kejian (2022).

270. Zhu Jun et al (2021); Liu Jun (2021).

271. A basket-based reserve currency comprised of reals, roubles, rupees, RMB, and rand as an alternative to the IMF's SDR (Turner 2022); BIS (2022); Jin Tou Wang (2022).

272. Dahir (2018); Lewis and Trevisani (2014); Griffith-Jones (2014); Liu Weidong et al. (2019); Jin Liqun (president of AIIB) (2021).

273. Liu Jun (2021).

274. Tai Meiti (2022).

275. For PRC investment abroad, see *China Global Investment Tracker* by the American Enterprise Institute, (aei.org/china-global-investment-tracker), *Mapping China's Global Investments and Inequality* by AidData (aiddata.org/china-project-locations), and *Belt and Road Tracker* by CFR (cfr.org/article/belt-and-road-tracker), all last accessed August 2023.

276. Kamel and Wang (2019); Hong Shen (2019); D. Ren (2020).

277. State Council (2020); National People's Congress (2021).

278. Leng and Zheng (2020).

279. People's Bank of China et al. (2019).

280. Tham and Leng (2019).

281. F. Wang (2023, chs. 1 and 4).

310 | Notes to Chapter 2

282. Vedrenne (2019).

283. Francis (2014).

284. International Consortium of Inverstigative Journalists, *The Panama Papers* (panamapapers.icij.org; last accessed August 2023).

285. Or $3.79 trillion in 2005–12 (Gascoigne 2014). Or $200 billion annually in 2015–20 (Zhang Ming 2020).

286. Global Financial Integrity (2020, 51, 47–51, 59, 64).

287. 与世界接轨, 中国特色 and 中国方案引领世界 have been three slogans central to Beijing's internal and external propaganda in the post-Mao era (State Council Press Office, September 27, 2019).

288. K. Tsai (2006); Y. Huang (2008).

289. L. Pang (2012); F. Wang (2023, 175–213, 219–25).

290. Chambers (2012). For the conviction of Patrick Ho for bribery in the UN, see M. Goldstein (2018, B7). For a case involving a PRC company, see C. Sanders (2020).

291. Jing Yang (2020).

292. Mu Xi (2020); Yao Yun (2020); Indo-Asian News Service (2022).

293. Beyoud and Chen (2022).

294. P. Adams (2019); Godfrey (2020); Mantesso (2020).

295. McGahan (2020); Allen-Ebrahimian and Dorfman (2020).

296. M. Campbell (2015).

297. Hillman (2019); Doig (2019).

298. Author's interviews in Chile, EU, India, Israel, Japan, Jordan, New Zealand, Peru, Singapore, Siri Lanka, South Africa, South Korea, Turkey, UAE, UK, and US, 2003–22.

299. Yglesias (2021).

300. ShareAmerica (2020).

301. McMahon (2020).

302. Author's interviews in Africa in 2013. The PRC sponsored a UN "Comparative Study on Special Economic Zones in Africa and China" (UNDP 2015). For reports, see Olander, van Staden, and Wan (2015); Pairault (2019); Okere (2019); Mierzejewski (2022).

303. Author's field studies, 2013; Jayaram, Kassiri, and Sun (2017); Africa Research Initiative database, Johns Hopkins University, accessed August 2022.

304. A leader's personality and emotions are viewed as meaningful to foreign policy making (Lebow 2008, 2010a).

305. Pantsov and Levine (2015, 377–94).

306. Deng issued the strategy in September of 1989: "To keep a low profile, be good at pretending and hiding, never take the lead, act out selectively, preserve ourselves, and gradually and quietly expand and develop" (韬光养晦, 善于守拙, 绝不当头, 有所作为, 保存自己, 徐图发展) (Leng Rong et al. 2004, 1346); Jiang Zemin (2006, 202).

Notes to Chapter 3 | 311

307. Ci (2019).

308. *Economist* (April 3, 2021).

309. C. Lee (2022).

310. Mattingly et al. (2023).

311. Mann (2007); Freeland (2011).

312. F. Wang (1998); Robert Zoellick (deputy secretary of state) (2005); Patrick (2010).

313. Liu Zhongjing, "The Remolding of the World Order after World War I" (刘仲敬: 一战后世界秩序的重塑). Public lecture, Guangzhou, March 14, 2015.

314. Biden (August 31, 2021).

315. With the loss of his business empire in China after 1949, Sassoon asked his niece and heir "promise me you will never go to China" (Kaufman 2020, 211, 250, 328).

316. M. Cooper (2021).

317. Patey (2021).

318. Pearson, Rithmire, and Tsai (2022).

319. Galston (2019); I. Bond (2020); Forgey and Kine (2022).

Chapter 3

1. Tian Feilong (2022).

2. Sun Liping (2021, 2022).

3. *Zhongzhi zhiku*, a Beijing think tank (2022).

4. An Gang (2023).

5. This staple of CCP propaganda started in the later 1940s, when Mao coined the phrase "paper tiger" to describe the US (Mao Zedong [1946] 1991; [1958] 1999). For a 2021 "research" effort by three PRC "think tanks," published by the top CCP media, which called the US the worst in the world in eight ways, see Yang Xun and Wang Fang (2021).

6. Mao Zedong ([1958] 1999, 368); Qi Weiping and Wang Jun (2002); F. Wang (2017, 201–2); Xinhua (March 5, 2021); Xie Chuntao (2021).

7. F. Wang (2023, chs. 2 and 4).

8. As I discussed before (F. Wang 2023, ch. 2), the various assertions that the PRC possesses some special or even magical ability, a "steroids model," for superior and sustained growth tend to be erroneous, invalidated, or fanciful (J. Lin 1999, 2012; L. Zhou [2008] 2017; T. Zhu 2021; Xing Yuqing 2022; K. Jin 2019, 2023).

9. 共生 and 共同体. Hu Shoujun (2012); Jin Yingzhong (2011); SIIS (2014); Cai Liang (2014); Wang Yi (2016); Wang Gonglong (2019); Ren Xiao (2019); Xie Xinshui (2020); Xia Liping (2021); Pan Zhongqi (2021).

10. Xi Jinping (September 21, 2021).

312 | Notes to Chapter 3

11. Zenz (2018); World Bank Data website (accessed August 3, 2022).

12. PRC State Statistical Bureau database (accessed August 10, 2022).

13. Fingar and Oi (2020(b), 67–84); Beckley and Brands (2021).

14. Applebaum (2021).

15. 重中之重. Bao Shenggang (2015); Mission statement of the American Studies Center (美国研究中心), Peking University (website accessed September 14, 2022).

16. *Wenhua Zongheng* (2021).

17. Di Dongsheng (2021, 2023).

18. Xi repeated those words to the US leaders and senior officials many times, as reported as frontpage news by CCP's flagship newspaper *People's Daily* on, for example, May 18, 2015, September 26, 2015, November 10, 2017, and December 3, 2018.

19. CCTV (2021, 2023).

20. Shao Jianbin (2017); He Yiting (2019).

21. F. Wang (2017, 184–85; 2023, 58–9). Other than securer jobs and higher pay, the families of PLA personnel all get free health care starting in 2022 (Liu and Sun 2021).

22. The Han-Chinese chauvinism fantasizing world domination by force, copycatting European colonialism of the 19th century, indeed has long roots, as shown by Jin Zuoli ([1908] 2008).

23. Fei Chai (2020); Wang Wentao (2021).

24. Xinhua (2007). The US military, however, noticeably changed its uniform by the 2020s; it remains to be seen if the PLA will emulate again.

25. Zhang Xinyi (2017).

26. 战区. BBC (July 9, 2021).

27. Office of the Secretary of Defense (2020); Wuthnow (2021). Others, however, think that is a "threat inflation" in assessing the PLA capabilities (Swaine 2022).

28. Ziezulewicz (2021); Roblin (2021).

29. Wang Li (2021); Fanell (2020).

30. Lang Yage (2016) and Ma Haoliang (2023).

31. State Council or Ministry of Defense (1995–2019).

32. Pillsbury (2015); Callahan (2016); Allison (2017); Mosher (2017); Friend and Thayer (2018); Mauldin (2019); Rolland (2020); T. Brook (2020); Ratcliffe (2020).

33. Overholt (1993, 416).

34. Manning (2020).

35. Milanovic (2019, 5, 12–128).

36. Brands and Sullivan (2020).

37. Zoellick (2005).

Notes to Chapter 3 | 313

38. Zakaria (2020).

39. Walt (2021).

40. Fukuyama (1992, 2020).

41. Anonymous (2021, 4–7).

42. Garside (2021, 173–87).

43. Jiang Shigong (2018, 2019, 2020).

44. Asian Development Bank (2021).

45. *Economist* (August 30, 2021; May 11, 2023). For a take on some unique factors that have helped but will doom the rising PRC power, see Y. Huang (2023).

46. Unlike in the nostalgic Moscow under Putin, the "traditional" territorial expansion appears cost-ineffective for the PRC, at least for now (Fravel 2010).

47. Stories circulating in PRC cyberspace for a decade have alleged "at least 10 overseas military bases by the end of 2021," including the Coco Islands (Myanmar), Gwadar (Pakistan), and Lourdes (Cuba) (Chen Junji 2021). For boasting of PLA's influence in Africa, see Yuanfang Qingmu (2022). For the strange case of the PRC surveillance airship shot downed the US, see Cooper, Wong, and Buckley (2023).

48. Wang Yi (January 2, 2022); Xinhua (Feb 4, 2022).

49. Rolland (2022).

50. For the notion of "willing executioners," see Goldhagen (1997). For "tankie," see Rickett (2017). For "useful idiots," see Hollander ([1981] 1997), Safire (1987), Mirsky (2010), and F. Wang (2017, 206, 242). "White leftists" refers to "the naïve and ignorant Western idealists paradoxically embracing the CCP" (Perry Link, conference speech, December 10, 2020).

51. Palmer (2015). For early generations of such Westerners, see Spence ([1969] 2002) and Inboden (2008, 157–89).

52. D. Bell (2015); Bell and Wang Pei (2020).

53. Teng Biao (April 14, 2021); Quinn (2021).

54. Unruh (2022).

55. Moynihan (2020); G. Chang (December 30, 2021).

56. Kant ([1795] 2003).

57. Gershaneck (2020).

58. Kroenig (2020).

59. Streit (1939).

60. Michels ([1911] 1962); Voss and Sherman (2000, 303–49).

61. Graff (2021).

62. Zimbardo (2007, 8–10, 230–232).

63. Scharfstein (1995). In the 2010s–20s, the fascination and support for unscrupulous authoritarianism was clear also in the US, with advocacy for more centralized state power, regulations, and enforcement from both the right and

314 | Notes to Chapter 3

the left proliferating. The "end of history" euphoria (Fukuyama 1992) seemed to have misread the human proclivity for authoritarian rule especially in times of challenge, danger, uncertainty, and ever more new "needs" (Desmet 2022).

64. Nietzsche ([1872] 2005, 11).

65. Orwell ([1946] 1990); Larkin (2004, 108).

66. Mertha (2021, 89–119); Ning Nanshan (2021). Furedi (2006, 2018).

67. A Google Scholar search for "rise of China" in October 2021 yielded 45,800 and 37,000 English publications for 2019 and 2020, respectively.

68. Rudolph and Szonyi (2018).

69. D. Kelly (2018).

70. Mazarr, Heath, and Cevallos (2018).

71. Campbell and Ratner (2018, 60–70).

72. Schell and Shirk et al. (February 2019, 46).

73. Erlanger (2020).

74. Shambaugh (2020, xi).

75. Priebe et al. (2021, 52).

76. Thurston (2021).

77. Schell, Shirk, et al. (2021).

78. Barboza (2022).

79. Swaine et al. (2020). For the "hawkish" ideas, see Boustany and Friedberg (2019) and Friedberg (2020).

80. Wang Dong (2021).

81. Katherine Thompson is acknowledged for this point, March 2021.

82. Sowell (1995, 2009).

83. Naughton (2021, 174–96).

84. For a critique of both, see M. Yu (2022).

85. McCourt (2022, 47–81; 2022a, 583–633, quotes on 594 and 608; italics original).

86. Recent examples include Michael Pompeo, Matthew Pottinger, and Navarro (2011, 2015). Also, Corr (2018, 2021) and Bosco (2021, 2021a). Reflecting the pluralistic America, some ex-intelligence and military officials have continued arguing for a "cooperative and constructive and peaceful U.S.-China relationship" through more "mutual understanding" with the PRC (Heer May 13, 2020; Oct 20, 2020; Packard and Jensen 2020).

87. Such as Joshua Philipp (2020, 2020a), senior investigative reporter for *Epoch Times* and host of *Crossroads* online.

88. Bosco (2020).

89. Brands and Beckley (2021); Beckley and Brands (2021).

90. McCourt (2022, 2022a).

91. Greitens and Truex (2020); Morgan (2022); Fish (2022a); Alpermann (2022).

92. Mitter (2020); Kirby (2022); Weiss (2022).

Notes to Chapter 3 | 315

93. Fravel et al. (2019). Some of the signatories soon published their important disagreements with the letter (Jerome Cohen 2019; Millward 2019).

94. Don Tse, Chu-cheng Ming, and Larry Ong (2019).

95. Fanell et al. (July 18, 2019).

96. Miles Maochun Yu, a historian at the US Naval Academy working at the US Department of State's Planning Staff in 2018–20, quoted in Gertz (2020).

97. Nichols (2017, x, 1).

98. The study of China, or China studies, as an academic discipline, has had various names: 国学/國學 (national studies) and 中国研究 (China study) in Chinese; 漢学 (Han studies) in Japanese; Sinology, chinoiserie, China watch, and Chinese studies in English. There have been continued disagreements on the nomenclature, content, and approaches of the field, one of the most famous of which was the call for "multidisciplinary" China studies replacing the "dead" Sinology focusing on linguistic-culture and history (Skinner 1964). I use the terms of Sinology and China Studies interchangeably, with a full appreciation of the difference between linguistic and anthropological works and the attempt to study China as a comparative and holistic inquiry in social sciences especially political science. For an authoritative description of studies of comparative politics, see Munck and Snyder (2007).

99. For a personal recollection of the arduous understanding of Chinese history, see P. Cohen (2019).

100. T. Hall (2020, 184).

101. For vivid boasting about having those powerful "friends" and the invincible power of money in the US, see Di Dongsheng (November 28, 2020).

102. Diamond and Schell (2018). A noted example is the aptly named Bush China Foundation, created in 2017 (bushchinafoundation.org).

103. Millward (2020).

104. Yu Ying-shi ([1991] 2006).

105. McCourt (2022a, 621).

106. Mann (2007, 2018); Brands (2019); Carrico (2018); Page (2020); Friedberg (2022).

107. Kaiser and Mufson (2000, A01); Gifford (2010); Epstein (2010); Lowsen (2017).

108. Perry Link (2023).

109. Schafer (1958, 119–20).

110. Kim and Grofman (2019); Bouchrika (2023).

111. Allison (2017). For critiques, see Waldron (2017) and Kirshner (2019). For a Chinese critique, see Chen Cunfu (2020, 356–63). A noted liberal Chinese thinker openly called Allison's points "very dumb" (Qin Hui July 6, 2020).

112. Thomas (1974). For such mentality and its intoxicating lure, see F. Wang (2017, 101–20).

113. Di Dongsheng (August 5, 2020).

316 | Notes to Chapter 3

114. Wong Young-tsu (2010, 139–49; 2020).

115. McCourt (2022a, 624–25).

116. Eberts (2021). Tellingly, Qin Gang (then PRC ambassador to the US), for one, asserted that a US official or analyst must know the Chinese language first, before knowing anything about China (us.china-embassy.gov.cn/dshd/202206/t20220601_10697523.htm; posted June 1, 2022).

117. Greitens and Truex (2020).

118. Committee of Concerned Asian Scholars (founded in 1968), "China Through the Lens of Friendship Delegations in the 1970s," exhibition at UC San Diego since December 2017. Characterization is by E. Friedman (2018). For the group, see Lanza (2017). For CCAS publications, see the open-access *Bulletin of Concerned Asian Scholars* (renamed the quarterly journal *Critical Asian Studies* after 2001), 1969–2023.

119. Madsen (1993); Baum (2010: 236–39); E. Friedman (2018).

120. Si Ying (2020).

121. H. Lewis (2020). For an effort to beautify the CCP polity, see D. Bell (2015). An example of how accomplished American scholars could be risibly bought by the CCP's money may be the case of Charles Lieber (US Attorney's Office 2021; Barry 2021, A22; Fischer 2021).

122. For how some of the most influential American scholars got the Soviet Union very wrong for many years, see Levy and Peart (2011).

123. For how Sovietologists, native and émigré, influentially disagreed and debated on assessing the Soviet Union, see Malia (1994) and Trachtenberg (2018).

124. For a report that "China is now a major source of talent for North American humanities and social sciences" but émigré Sinologists "with Chinese origin" face challenging career prospects and tend to have a "higher self-censorship," see Luce/ACLS China Studies Advisory Group (2021).

125. For impressive examples of confusing "rule of law" with "rule by law," misreading Chinese political history, and misapplying Western jargon, see Y. Wang (2015, 2022).

126. For examples, see some of the contributions to Feng and He (2020). For an illustration of the feeling of homesickness and self-assumed duties to China, see P. Huang (2020, preface). For reflections by 31 US-trained historians from the PRC, see Yao, Wang et al. (2022).

127. Zhang Song (2022).

128. 乡愁 or *natsukashii* (懐(なつ)かしい) in Japanese (Farese and Asano-Cavanagh 2019, 213–41). For the environmental/locational effect of place on people, see Tuan (1974).

129. Ministry of Housing and Urban-Rural Development (2020, 138–39). Like many others, I personally felt an overwhelming sense of disappointment and detachment when, after just two decades, I visited my childhood hometown

Notes to Chapter 3 | 317

in Anhui; the place had become a complete stranger to me, worse than it was in my memory, with nobody there I could relate to anymore. For home towns and home villages in China being socially dispersed and displaced and also physically mutilated and demolished, see Meyer (2008), Bai Yun (2012), Smith (2021), and Zhang Feng (2021).

130. For a firm rebuttal by a leading American Sinologist of the use of *xiangchou*, see Y. Yu (2006) and Yu Jie (2021).

131. Yu Donghui (2022); Xu Wenxin (2023). Such a racist wish seems hopeless for the CCP, as more Chinese-Americans (62% vs. 41%) like Taiwan over the PRC (Ruiz et al., 2023).

132. "I really have no hometown, which is wherever my soul is at peace" (我生本无乡,心安是归处) (Bai Juyi [9th century] 1999); "Hometown is wherever this heart settles down" (此心安处是吾乡) (Su Shi [11th century] 2021).

133. Koopmann (1982); "Citations de Georges Clemenceau" (citation-ce-lebre.leparisien.fr); Library of Congress (2010, 65); Ren Jiantao (2013). A noted exception is the leading Malaysian-Australian Sinologist of Chinese descent, Wang Gungwu, whose memoir is titled *Where Is My Home? My Home Is Where My Heart Is at Peace* (2020).

134. Bachrack (1976); Jim Mann (1996); Hrebenar and Thomas (2011).

135. Yu Jie (2017).

136. J. Hsiung (2012) and J. Hsiung et al. (2015).

137. Yu Jie (2021).

138. 士大夫. Y. Yu (1987, 2003, 2015, 2016).

139. Baum (2010). For accounts by more Sinologists, see K. Liu (2012).

140. Hu Ping (2013, 2020). For rare studies about the CCP's "magic weapon" of united front at home and abroad against foreigners and overseas Chinese, see Brady (2003, 2017) and Glaser (2017). For the multifaceted ethical issues faced by foreign researchers in the PRC, see Alpermann (2022).

141. For early and recent reports on CCP's thought work, see Hunter (1951), F. Wang (2023, 47–54), and Song and Xia (2023). For a deep lament by PRC analysts over the lack of such opportunities "for two very long years" due to bilateral tensions and the COVID-19 pandemic, see Wang and Miao (2022, 7).

142. Ho Ping-ti (2004, 393).

143. This started with Richard Nixon's visit in 1972 (Pei Yiran 2012). Ronald Reagan and Bill Clinton were exemplarily "handled" this way on university campuses in 1984 and 1998 (author's interviews in China, 1998 and 2000; Lishi Yanjiu 2017).

144. Obama (2020, 472–73).

145. Roy (2019); Wondracz (2022).

146. Kroncke (2016); Lautz (2022).

147. MacMillan (2008).

318 | Notes to Chapter 3

148. Bosco (2020b); Maté (2020). Speeches by Kissinger, Freeman, and others at the "Commemoration of Kissinger's Secrete Visit to China in 1971," Beijing and online, July 9, 2021. Wu Liming (2022); Kennedy and Wang (2023).

149. Genuine friends of China like Pearl Buck and John Leighton Stuart are condemned while Moscow/CCP agents like Edgar Snow and Anna Louise Strong are praised. For how an American in China was treated as friend, then enemy, then friend again by the same CCP, see the obituary of Sidney Rittenberg by Robert McFadden in the *New York Times*, August 25, 2019.

150. Chinoy (2023).

151. Traub (2020); Rummler (2020); Nye (June 11, 2020); S. Kennedy (2019); National Intelligence Council (2021).

152. 张彭春. H. Roth (2018).

153. Y. Tan (2021, 2021a).

154. Prestowitz (2021, 293); Economy (2022, 208).

155. Millward (2019); Pompeo (2019; July 23, 2020); Santora (2020, A4).

156. For earlier cases of such prejudice, see Heale (2009, 19–47).

157. Waller (2020); CCTV (2020).

158. 此地无银三百两. Xi Jinping (July 1, 2021).

159. McCourt (2022, 629).

160. K. Brown (2020).

161. F. Wang (1998, 67–81).

162. F. Wang (July 21, 2005; April 10, 2006).

163. T. Friedman (July 21, 2022; November 1, 2022).

164. Ikenberry (2020).

165. Breznitz and Murphree (2011).

166. Lasserre (2020).

167. Follow the Money et al. (2022).

168. CBS, *60 Minutes*, January 31, 2021; National Public Radio (2022).

169. Morgenthau (1948); Waltz (1979); Gilpin (1981); Wendt (1992; 1999).

170. Kissinger (2014, 365).

171. Y. Cheng (2020).

172. Gilchrist (2020).

173. *Edelman Trust Barometer 2022*, January 2022.

174. F. Wang (2005). For racism in the PRC, see Distelhorst and Hou (2014) and Y. Cheng (2019). For Chinese racism against Africans, see Francavilla (2022). Many in the PRC openly call for the expulsion of Africans in China to address racist concerns (Pan Qinglin [2017] 2021).

175. Anonymous (2021, 6, 18).

176. CCP Organization Department (2023).

177. F. Wang (2023, 27–34).

178. Marlow (2020).

179. Walt (2018, 227).

Notes to Chapter 3 | 319

180. Lippman (1999, A9); Sanger (2001, A1); Twining (2006).

181. Roberts (2020).

182. Obama (2020, 475).

183. Gao Jianbo et al. (2022).

184. Anderson and Cha (2017).

185. Obama (2020, 338). An insiders' look at the Bush–Obama era is in Hadley et al. (2023, 416–44).

186. K. Kim (2022). For early assessment, see Saha and Feng (2020), J. Lee (2020), and Kynge (2020). For anecdotes, see Wu Wei (2021). For overall evidence, see IMF (2023).

187. Mazarr (2019, 131–38).

188. Rogin (2021a). For the paradigmatic shift in Washington enabled by Trump, see McCourt (2022, 2022a).

189. Aspen Strategy Group (2020).

190. That move was stopped and reversed a few months later in 2021.

191. Page and Khan (2020); Carrico (2020); Mallapaty et al. (2021); Sprunt (2021); Pompeo and Yu (2021); Bloom et al. (2021, 694); Biden (May 26, 2021); Jacobsen (June 2, 2021); Quay and Muller (2021); Liptak and Sullivan (2021); Wade (2021); Pekar et al. (2022); Gordon and Strobel (2023).

192. Lucas (2020); Vervaeke en Vlaskamp (2020); Eban (2022); Bond and Godement (2022); Ogden (2023).

193. Blackwill (2020).

194. Winnefeld (2020).

195. Spalding (2019); Thayer and Han (2020).

196. Hamilton and Ohlberg (2020, 2020a); Thorley (2020); L. Wei, Davis, and Lim (2020).

197. Jeromy A. Cohen is acknowledged for this quote, May 22, 2020.

198. Heath, Grossman, and Clark (2021).

199. US Congress (March 13, 2020).

200. White House (May 20, 2020).

201. Barr (2020).

202. Saldin and Teles (2020). Eighty-eight retired general and admirals, however, issued an "open letter from military leaders" on September 6, 2016, to endorse Trump (Johnson and Brown 2017).

203. Author's interviews in East Asia and the US, 2016–17.

204. Schweller (2018, 133–43).

205. Gavrilis (2021, 165).

206. B. Huang (2019); Barboza (May 24, 2020).

207. Weinstein (CEO of the Hudson Institute) (March 22, 2019).

208. Wray (2020).

209. Thorburn (2022).

210. O'Brien (October 21, 2020).

320 | Notes to Chapter 3

211. Office of the Secretary of State (Policy Planning Staff) (2020).

212. Ratcliffe (2020).

213. Bolton (2020).

214. Millward (2019); Scissors (2023); Rogin (2021).

215. Associated Press (2020).

216. Sullivan (2020a); Pompeo (December 9, 2020).

217. Rogin (November 19, 2020); Bosco (2020a); Pomfret (November 10, 2020).

218. Glaser and Price (2021, 29–42).

219. *China Daily* (2021); Zhu Feng (2021); Wang Jianwei (2021); Cui Liru (2021); Wu Lingming (2021).

220. For a review on China from the left that is almost identical to that from the right, see Senator Markey (2022).

221. Strobel and Siddiqui (2020); Ganesh (May 20, 2020); Schlesinger (2020).

222. Basu (2020); Pompeo (January 19, 2021); Weiss (January 23, 2021).

223. United States-China Economic and Security Review Commission (2020, 31).

224. O'Brien (2021).

225. Sanger (2001); Stephanopoulos (2021); Liptak (2021); CBS, *60 Minutes*, September 18, 2022; Bateman (2022); US DOD (October 2022); White House (October 2022); Sullivan (2023).

226. Brunnstrom and Pamuk (2021); Shelbourne (2021); Singman (2021).

227. Biden (February 4, 2021).

228. McKinnon (2021); Magnus (2021); Biden (June 3, 2021). The US Department of Commerce later added many more PRC entities to the blacklist (DOC website, last accessed August 2023).

229. Biden (March 2021, 20–21; October 12, 2022, 3, 23).

230. Campbell and Rosenberger (2021).

231. Doshi (2021).

232. William Burns (CIA Director), speech at the Georgia Institute of Technology, Atlanta, Georgia, April 14, 2022. He also declared the principle of distinguishing the Chinse people from the PRC state and the creation of the only country mission center on China inside the CIA.

233. Mayorkas (2023); Stavridis (2020); Shi Yinhong (2020; March 7, 2021); Yan Xuetong (2020).

234. Yan Xuetong (2018); Christensen (2021); Case and Rodrigues (2023).

235. Overholt (July 7, 2021; October 14, 2021).

236. Weiss (2019, 2020, 2022, 2023); Weiss and Wallace (2021,635–64); Weiss and Pepinsky (2021).

237. Dong Chunling (2022).

Notes to Chapter 3 | 321

238. "Is U.S. Foreign Policy Too Hostile to China?," *ForeignAffairs.com*, October 19, 2021 (foreignaffairs.com/ask-the-experts/2021-10-19/us-foreign-policy-too-hostile-china).

239. Hass, Kim, and Bader (2022, 4).

240. White House (February 11, 2022); Colby (2022); Eckstein (2022); Losey (2022); A. O'Neal (2022); Biden (March 1, 2022; October 12, 2022); Martina (2023).

241. Mordecai and Fagan (2021).

242. Walt (2020); Bosco (2021); B. Sanders (2021).

243. Mina and Chipchase (2018).

244. Chen, Fos, and Wei Jiang (2022).

245. Markay and Allen-Ebrahimian (2021); McIntire (2020, A1); Forsythe et al. (2019, A1); Pathikonda (2020); Barboza (April 25, 2021); Wang and Berens (2022).

246. Timperlake and Triplett (1998); *Wall Street Journal* (October 20, 2020).

247. B. Powell (2020).

248. Demick (2015).

249. Eban (2021); C. Ford (former US assistant secretary of state, 2021).

250. Fish (2022); Hvistendahl et al (2023).

251. Barr (2020); Wray (2020). For a scholarly report on these, see Kurlantzick (2022).

252. *New York Times* (1970, 14); Koen (1974); Bachrack (1976); Mann (1988, 1996).

253. Hrebenar and Thomas (2011).

254. Rogin (October 30, 2020).

255. Koehn and Yin (2002); Allen-Ebrahimian (2018, 2018a). For Singaporeans recruited by the CCP to spy in the US, see Yong (2020). For an alarmist report on the efforts and successes by the PRC Ministry of State Security to disinform, recruit, and influence Western elites, see Joske (2022).

256. 知华派. The "top 20 American scholars who comprehend China" are David Lampton, David Shambaugh, Avery Goldstein, Robert Ross, Susan Shirk, Robert Sutter, Cheng Li, M. Taylor Fravel, Bates Gill, Kenneth Lieberthal, Aaron Friedberg, Michael Chase, Richard Bush, Dali Yang, Thomas Christensen, Andrew Mertha, Anne-Marie Slaughter, James Mulvenon, Thomas Rawski, and Carla Freeman (China Foreign Affairs University 2015).

257. For a hectic such "track-two" effort made by a CCP outfit, see Center for China and Globalization (2022).

258. Out of the $1.2 billion Chinese donation (23% of the total foreign donations reported during 2014–19), over 8% came from the PRC government directly via Confucius Institutes (Reale 2020). By that ratio, another $1.4

322 | Notes to Chapter 3

billion in Chinese gifts to US colleges in the 2010s could be unreported (US Department of Education 2020).

259. Perkowski (2012); Gold (2019); W. Tan (2020); Hamilton and Ohlberg (2020); Stevenson (July 1, 2020, A1); Wei and Hutzler (2022).

260. S. Wong (2022); Thiessen (2022).

261. *Bloomberg* (May 28, 2020); J. Zhu (September 5, 2020); Fish (2021).

262. Rogin (July 8, 2021). Didi's market capitalization was $60 billion, ranked 7th among the 244 PRC firms listed on Wall Street (Stockmarketmba. com, accessed July 15, 2021).

263. Gittelsohn, Natarajan, and Leonard (2020).

264. Li Lu (2019). Li has been the only political exile linked to 1989 ever allowed by Beijing to visit the PRC (since 2010) (BBC in Chinese 2019).

265. Dalio (2020). For the US billionaire's cheerleading for China and his worldview of "big cycles," see Dalio (2021, chs. 6–7). For his defense and retraction, see Sorkin et al (2021). For his call for more cooperation with Beijing so to avert a "war," see Dalio (2023).

266. Fruen (2021); Niewenhuis (2021); McGee (2023).

267. Reported by J. Michael Cole, at an online forum, June 2, 2021. Y. Lee (2019); Subin (2021).

268. Zipser, Seong, and Woetzel (2021).

269. Lim and Xie (2021); Soros (September 6, 2021).

270. Cunningham, Saich, and Turiel (2020).

271. Guang Lei et al. 2020.

272. Deveaux (2020).

273. C. Li (2016); Petri and Plummer (2020).

274. McGann (2019).

275. Qi and Xie Yu (2020). For how the CCP-PRC smeared Li, see Zhong et al. (2020).

276. Zhu Linagcai (July 6, 2021).

277. Y. Chen et al. (2020, 3393–430); Zou Yilin (2015). Similarly, the flagship journal of the American Political Science Association published in 2022 an article (Y. Wang 2022) that attempted to explain the "the rise and fall of Imperial China," illustrating the common spectacle of GIGO (garbage in, garbage out) according to noted Sinologist Zhao Dingxin (2023).

278. Much has been published about the brutal internal exile (see, for examples, Y. Pan 2003; Xu Xiaoni 2012; Rene 2013; Bonnin 2013).

279. Keyu Jin (2019, 2023); Jin Keyu (2020).

280. Diresta et al. (2020, 9).

281. E. Li (May 14, 2020).

282. R. Horton (2020).

283. J. O'Neill (2020).

284. Author's interviews of PRC scholars and officials, 2018–23. One example is *Global Economic Prospects*, a "Flagship Report" periodically released by the World Bank and "co-launched" with the CCG (Center for China and Globalization), an official PRC think tank aiming at a "global vision for China, Chinese wisdom for the world," in 2019–22 (Kurlantzick 2022).

285. Chang Siying (2022).

286. Craymer (2020).

287. Radio New Zealand (2021); Rhyn (2021); Mahtani and Chandradas (2023).

288. Barboza (2013); Levin (2015); Egan (2016).

289. US Department of the Treasury/Federal Reserve Board (2014, 2022).

290. Posen and Ha (2017); Chin (2020); Greenberg (2022).

291. Weiss (2020).

292. Christensen (2020).

293. Tharoor (2020).

294. For a representative argument, see Haley (2019).

295. Kempe (2020a); Carafano et al. (2023, 1, 3).

296. W. Burns (2020).

297. Ferguson (2008, 2020).

298. Schell (2020a); Barboza (November 7, 2021). For an opposing view, see Johnston (2019a).

299. H. Hung (2022).

300. Silver, Devlin, and Huang (2021); Silver, Huang, and Clancy (2023).

301. Pence (2018); Davis and Wei (2020); Krueger (2020).

302. O'Brien (June 21, 2020).

303. Phillips (2020); Nsoesie et al. (2020); Bandeira et al (2021).

304. For those bills, see www.congress.gov/bill/117th-congress/senate-bill/1260 and www.congress.gov/bill/117th-congress/house-bill/1155 (last accessed August 2023).

305. Medeiros (2019).

306. Clinton (2020).

307. Strobel and Siddiqui (2020); Ganesh (May 20, 2020; July 15, 2020).

308. White House (March 12, 2021).

309. Wong and Myers (2020); Pomfret (August 21, 2020).

310. Blinken (March 3, 2021; May 26, 2022).

311. Zhong Sheng (2019).

312. Jie Dalei (2020).

313. P. Martin (2021); Dai and Luqiu (2021).

314. Zhong Sheng (2021); Y. Huang (2021); Sebastian (2023).

315. Xinhua (August 3, 2021).

316. Ministry of Foreign Affairs (June 19, 2022).

324 | Notes to Chapter 4

317. Ministry of Foreign Affairs (February 20, 2023).

318. Wu Xiaogang (2021); Wang and Miao (July 18, 2022, 7).

319. R. Hass (2022).

320. Sun Xingjie (2021); Qin Gang (2021).

321. Bloomberg (May 17, 2021); *Global Times* (September 17, 2021).

322. Kristof (2020, SR9); Hass and Denmark (2020); Bolton (2020); Bannon (2020); Swanson (2020, A1). In 2023, the former president Trump openly praised Xi Jinping "smart, brilliant, everything perfect" (*Wall Street Journal* 2023).

323. Bown (2020).

324. Retired General David Petraeus, webinar at NDU, Washington, DC, October 15, 2020.

325. Zhu Zhihong (2020).

326. Yan Xuetong, quoted in Sudworth (2020). Reportedly, the PRC gave monetary support to Trump's reelection bid (N. Anderson 2022).

327. US DOS (January 2022).

328. White House (November 14, 2022).

329. Biden (August 16, 2021; August 31, 2021).

330. BBC (August 6, 2021); *Economist* (August 21, 2021).

331. Furedi (2006, 2018); Graff (2021).

332. For the evolving conceptualization and practice of RTI (DTI) and RTP, see Cutler (1985), Orford (2003), Nardin (2013), and UN OGPRP (2023).

333. Group of Seven (2021); North Atlantic Council (2021).

334. Group of Seven (2022); NATO (2022, 10, 5; 2023, items 6, 23–25).

335. Charon and Vilmer (2021, 640–43).

336. White House (December 23, 2021; March 29, 2023).

337. White House (August 2, 2021).

338. The US attracted 88% of Chinese AI PhD students and 85% of other foreign AI PhD students after their graduation (*Global AI Talent Tracker*, Macro Polo Institute, searched August 2022); Deep Tech Research 2022.

339. Pottinger (March 10, 2021).

Chapter 4

1. Fontaine (2022).

2. A standard equalization or normalization tends to resemble this: "Washington has legitimate concerns about Beijing's excessive domestic political control and aggressive foreign policy stances, just as Chinese leaders believe the United States still has futile designs on blocking their country's inevitable rise to great-power status" (C. Li 2021).

3. Aum and Wang (2022).

4. Well summarized by Antony Blinken (2022).

Notes to Chapter 4 | 325

5. Charon and Vilmer (2021, 638–45).

6. Silius Italicus ([1st century CE] 1934, 11595); 和为贵, Confucius ([5th century BCE] 2016).

7. Dawn (2010).

8. Tse, Ming, and Ong (2019).

9. Campbell and Sullivan (2019).

10. Corr (2019); Li Fan (2020).

11. Garside (2021a).

12. Qiao Liang and Wang Xiangsui ([1999] 2010).

13. Zhao Tong (2020).

14. White House (January 3, 2022).

15. Treaty Between the United States of America and the Union of Soviet Socialist Republics on the Limitation of Strategic Offensive Arms (SALT II), June 18, 1979.

16. Zhou Baogen (2003); Li and Xiao (2010). PRC analysts and military officers have continued, often openly, suggesting active and assertive "first use" of "more" and "better" nuclear weapons, "just like other legit (conventional) weapons" for international conflicts, and even for attacking another nuclear power like the US, should Beijing's "core interests" be touched. Fenghuang Wang (2005); author's interview with PLA Major Gen. Zhu Chenghu (朱成虎), 2013; senior Chinese analysts, speaking at the "U.S.-China Seminar on Chinese Nuclear Perspectives," Washington, May 12, 2015; Hu Xijin (2020); Sheng Dingli (2020); McLeary (2021).

17. State Council Press Office (July 24, 2019).

18. Carey (July 11, 2020).

19. Winnefeld (July 2020).

20. X. Zhang (2016). For accounts by PLA's officers and soldiers on its woeful experience, heavy losses, poor performance, indiscriminate killing of POWs and civilians, and its *sanguang* (三光 three-clear) policy of taking, burning, and destroying everything in Vietnam, see Song Zipei ([1990] 2014) and Liu Minglu (2021). For an insider's account of corruption, fragility, and failures of the PLA in the 1940s–2010s, see Liu Jiaju (2020).

21. 辱国辱军. Liu Minglu (2021). The death-ratio may be 26,000 versus 30,000 (K. Chen 1987, 114; Tonnesson 2010, 2).

22. P. Wang (2016).

23. Frum (2021).

24. US Congressional Research Service (2020).

25. The US "could have nipped the problem in the bud" in places like the South China Sea (Anders Corr, correspondence July 15, 2020).

26. Acemoglu (October 28, 2022).

27. For collections of some Chinese "liberal" ideas dreaded and punished by the CCP, see Beijing Municipal Committee of CCP (1989) and Hui Da (2020).

326 | Notes to Chapter 4

Noted attempts of rereading history in the PRC include Qin Hui (2016), Zhang Ming (2021), and Zhang Qianfan (2021).

28. A journalistic example is Xiao Jiansheng (2007). It is critical to have serious discourse and debates like the ones PRC authors have had overseas (Xi Shuguang 2021).

29. Bosco (2020c).

30. Xi Jinping's speech to the new CCP Central Committee members, Beijing, January 5, 2013, in Party Literature Research Center (2014).

31. For a PRC analysis viewing the PRC-USA rivalry as a longer repeat of the "Anti-Japanese War," with phases, pauses, and buffers, see Huang Renwei (2022).

32. Ikenberry (2020a).

33. Nietzsche ([1885] 2018, 31).

34. Tsang (2020).

35. Brunnermeier, Doshi, and James (2018).

36. Chinese analysts list only four "areas" of feasible US-PRC cooperation in the 2020s: denuclearization of Korea, reconstruction of Afghanistan, control of narcotics (fentanyl), and balanced economic relations (Qiao Qiao 2020).

37. Erickson and Collins (2021).

38. Li Guoli et al. (2020). The PRC cost of space flight, however, appears to be many times higher than the US, and still at or above the level of Soyuz and even Saturn V a half-century ago (Venditti 2022).

39. Dai Er (2021).

40. Tagliacozzo and Chang (2011); Lampton, Ho, and Kuik (2020); Kuik (2021); He and Tritto (2022). For China's "asymmetrical" connectivity in the region, see Womack (2023).

41. The treaty took effect in 1950 and auto-expired in 1979.

42. Bai Yunyi (2017); National People's Congress (June 30, 2020); Joyu Wang (2020).

43. State Council Office of Hong Kong and Macau Affairs (2021).

44. "Gallup Worldwide Research Methodology-Country Data Set Details," Gallup Worldwide Research Data 2005/2006–2018 (accessed February 10, 2022).

45. Fogel (2000, 231).

46. 不憚以最壞的惡意來推測中國人. Lu Xun (1926).

47. As contrasted with "trust and verify," Ronald Reagan's motto in dealing with the Soviet Union (Pompeo, July 23, 2020).

48. Kerry (2021).

49. For some early ideas on this, perhaps ahead of its time, see Sullivan (1992, 3–23).

50. McFaul (2020, 30–31).

51. For possible advanced extraterrestrials on Earth, see CBS, "UAP," 60 Minutes, May 16, 2021. For a fictional take on a dire survival need for global

Notes to Chapter 4 | 327

"coalition government," see Liu Cixin (2008). The movie, based on the novel about Chinese "saviors" of humanity, became a blockbuster in the PRC (Guo Fan 2019).

52. An impressive such rethinking by Western scholars is in the special issue of *International Organization*, edited by Lake et al. (2021).

53. Hippel (1995); Orford (2003); Xypolia (2022).

54. National Security Council (2020); Clinton (2020); Biden (August 2020). Other than infrastructure and education, many efforts certainly could and should be made, for example, to better manage firearms, money in politics, and the cost of health care in the US.

55. Ikenberry (2020a); Sullivan (2023).

56. Jain (2013); Kempe (2020); EAI (2020); Scott and Reynolds (2020).

57. S. Li (2022, 249–77). For US actions in this area, see Schneider and Zhang (2022).

58. For Chinese Indo-Pacific strategy, see Zhang Wenmu (2016).

59. *Huanqiu shibao wang* (2017); Yang Chen (2021); Zhang Haipeng (2023).

60. Roche (2020); White House (March 12, 2021.

61. Mesmer (2022).

62. Patey (2021); Jones and Yeo (2022). For the taking-sides strategies of China's smaller neighbors, see S. Kim (2023); Grano and Huang (2023).

63. Beijing had more support only in three smaller countries of the 10: Cambodia, Laos, and Brunei (ISAS 2022, 32).

64. Yeung, Seo, and Hancocks (2022); Cha (2023).

65. In 2022, NATO invited Finland and Sweden to join it as new members, and Australia, Japan, South Korea, and New Zealand to attend its summit as partners (nato.int/cps/en/natohq/news_196144.htm; last accessed August 2023).

66. Pottinger (2021).

67. Jones and Chandler (2021); Dreyer (2022); US DOS (July 20, 2022). For PRC analyses reflecting deep concern about this, see Zhao Jian (2022) and Qin Shu (2022).

68. WeChat is alleged to serve the CCP, including surveillance outside of the PRC. So is Zoom (*Washington Post*, December 20, 2020). For more, see Kenyon (2020), Mozur (2020), and Kaplan (2023).

69. Kelion (2020). For the PRC 5G industry, see Ceci and Rubin (2022).

70. ET Bureau (2020); Yasir and Kumar (2020, A21); Zhang Yadong (2022).

71. Reuters (December 10, 2020); Chowdhury (2021); United States-China Economic and Security Review Commission (2022); Beyoud and Yilun (2022).

72. For how a "voluntary" agent of such in the US named Qiao Mu (乔木) who was exposed as cleverly using three identities to praise the CCP as a "scholar in political exile" and making a living from online "immigration consulting," see Jiu Dian (2021).

73. B. Lin et al. (2022).

328 | Notes to Chapter 4

74. For a PRC assessment about its technology gap, see IISS (2022). For the US efforts to keep innovating military technology by trial and error, see Martin, McBride, and Tiron (2023) and M. Gordon (2023).

75. F. Wang (1998, 67–81); Overholt (July 7, 2021; October 14, 2021).

76. Mozur and Zhong (2020, A13); Xue Xiaoshan (2021); A. Wang (2021).

77. US Congress (March 13, 2020).

78. Friedberg (2020).

79. Liu Hong (2017); *Renmin Ribao* (August 13, 2019); State Council Press Office (2019); Xu Xiangli (2020); Chen Wenling (May 18, 2020); Shang Qian (2020); Yang Jiechi (May 10, 2021).

80. Du Shangze (2016); He Cheng (2020); Dong Zhengrui (2020); Yuan Peng (2016, 2020, 2022).

81. CCP Foreign Liaison Department (2020). For a summary of "Xi Jinping Thought on diplomacy" by the CCP official media, see Hao Weiwei (2022).

82. For articulation of this logic, see Olson (1965).

83. F. Wang (2017, 31–55).

84. Ambrose (2010, 109).

85. 不战而屈人之兵. Sun Tzu (6th century BCE) 2007; author's interviews with Chinese officials and analysts, 1995–2022.

86. Dimon Liu is acknowledged for this, July 2020.

87. Mattis and Brazil (2020); Joske (2020). CCP's overt and covert influence campaigns in Taiwan seem strong and sophisticated (Tseng and Shen 2020; Hsu and Cole 2020; R. Weber 2020).

88. Ward (2019).

89. F. Wang (2017, 99–134).

90. Pompeo (October 30, 2019); Santora (2020, A4); Blinken (May 26, 2022); US DOS (July 2022).

91. Select Committee on the Strategic Competition Between the United States and the Chinese Communist Party (clerk.house.gov/committees/ZS00; accessed April 6, 2023).

92. Such as Heer (July 27, 2020).

93. 低素质. Xu Boyuan (2005); Lai Hairong (2014); Zi Xun (2022).

94. Woodhead (1925); Goodnow (1926); Jenne (2015); Kroncke (2016, 132–57).

95. Chen Jian (2020); Wells et al. (2020).

96. Naisbitt and Naisbitt (2010); Bell (2015).

97. Doromal (2007); Dower (2008); Tchen and Yeats (2014).

98. Link (2012).

99. Xi Jinping (2009).

100. 中国特色or 国情. Li Honsen (2017); Qiu Shi (2018).

101. Xi Jinping (November 30, 2020).

102. Teng Biao (滕彪), on an online forum, May 3, 3021.

Notes to Chapter 4 | 329

103. Roberts (2020); Mattis (2021).

104. Drohan (2020).

105. Haynes and Klehr (1999); Marshall (2001); Goldberg (2003).

106. Even during the McCarthy era of the 1950s, due process and decent protection of the accused were largely in place. See, for example, Simpson (2000).

107. Swanson (2019).

108. M. Lewis (2020); Guo et al (2021); Lynch (2022). The program reported that "about 80 percent of all economic espionage [cases] would benefit the Chinese state [and] at least some nexus to China in around 60 percent of all trade secret theft cases" (DOJ 2021).

109. Pillsbury (2020).

110. Alper and Ali (2020).

111. Trump (July 14, 2020); US DOS (March 31, 2022).

112. Lardy and Huang (2020); Michaels (2020); Magnus (2020); Associated Press (February 7, 2022).

113. Ortagus (2020); White House (May 29, 2020); US DOS (June 26, 2020; May 2021); US DOT (July 9, 2020).

114. O'Brien (October 21, 2020).

115. Zeng and Jia (2021); Wang Xiaofeng (2021); May (August 25, 2021).

116. Case and Deaton (2020, 112, 120); Brunnstrom (2020). For the major role of the PRC in sustaining the US opioids overdose crisis, see McLaughlin (2017), Drug Enforcement Administration (2020), Felbab-Brown (2020), and census.gov/foreign-trade/index.html (last accessed August 2023).

117. Wray (July 7, 2020); BBC (July 8, 2020); Federal Bureau of Investigation (2020).

118. Pompeo (August 5, 2020); Trump (August 6, 2020).

119. Pompeo (July 23, 2020); Blinken (May 26, 2022).

120. Winnefeld (2020); Esper (August 24, 2020); Garamone (March 15, 2021).

121. H. Kim (2021); DOS (April 23, 2021).

122. For some prudent ideas on "smart competition" with the PRC, see Nye (WQ 2020), Friedberg and Boustany (2020), and Wyne (2020).

123. Schell, Shirk, et al. (2021).

124. Colby (2021a, 9–25).

125. Magnus (2021).

126. Biden (April 28, 2021).

127. Hass (2021).

128. Carafano et al. (2023).

129. Corr (2020).

130. Anonymous (2021).

131. Nye (June 11, 2020); Astorino-Courtois et al. (November 2020; May 2021).

132. Collins and Erickson (2021).

330 | Notes to Chapter 4

133. 大外宣, 夺取世界话语权. Chen Yan (2009); "Grand External Propaganda Archives" (大外宣), *China Digital Times*, Berkeley, CA (last accessed August 2023).

134. 大传播. Xi Jinping (May 31, 2021). For the unscrupulousness, resourcefulness, and meticulousness of how-to from a top propaganda cadre, see Shen Haixiong (June 7, 2021).

135. J. Liu (2020).

136. M. Chan (2021); S. Lu (2020). Internet hacking and leaking, apparently, could also be used effectively against the CCP (Hao and Liang 2022).

137. Chang Xi (2022); Hao and Liang (2022).

138. McGregor (2022).

139. Cadell (2021); Kakutani (2022).

140. Han Hui (2019); Jin Yun (2022).

141. Eisenman (2021).

142. Perhaps reacting to backlashes, in mid-2020, the HQ of the CIs changed its name from *Hanban* (汉办Chinese Language Office) to the less official-looking Center for Sino-Foreign Language Exchange and Cooperation of the "nongovernmental" China Foundation for International Chinese Education (press release, July 5, 2020, Hanban.gov).

143. By 2022, the CIs had had a significant downsizing and creative repackaging in the US (Peterson, Oxnevad, and Yan 2022).

144. Conger (2020). Meta (Facebook and Instagram) deleted 9,000 such accounts in 2023.

145. Huanggong Wangjiang (2021).

146. "Leading Places of Origin" (OpenDoorsData.org; accessed April 2023).

147. IIE (2019); Wang and Miao (2021); Stacey (2021).

148. NCSES (2020).

149. The same rate for the 178,000 international PhD recipients is 77% (Corrigan, Dunham, and Zwetsloot 2022).

150. Zweig and Kang (2020).

151. Lloyd-Damnjanovic and Bowe (2020).

152. Gambetta and Hertog (2016).

153. E. Feng (Oct 22, 2022); F. Wang (2023, 167).

154. Author's interviews with US diplomats and officials, 2022–23.

155. Grimshaw (2020); Hippold (2020); Zumbrun (2021).

156. For some thoughtful ideas along this line, see CSIS (2021).

157. Lind (2020).

158. Prestowitz (1990).

159. *New York Times* (July 23, 1881, 4).

160. Atkinson (2020).

161. Chen Wenling (December 7, 2020); Zhang Zhikun (2022); Mei Zhu (2022).

162. Lopez 2021; Bloomberg (2023).

Notes to Chapter 4 | 331

163. Rogin (July 8, 2021); Nikakhtar and Duffy (2021); Mok and Kwok (2021).

164. Zhi Hu (2021).

165. Davis and Wei (2020); Saleen (2020); Beene (2022).

166. Senior Director for international economics and competitiveness Peter Harrell, White House briefing, Washington, DC, February 24, 2021.

167. *Economist* (March 3, 2023). For the profound shift of FDI away from China, see IMF (2023).

168. Gordon Chang is acknowledged for this quote, 2019.

169. Gewirtz (2020).

170. The one Chinese brand was ICBC (bank). ICBC was the first PRC brand that made it into the top 10 in 2015 (Brand Finance 2022; 2016–23).

171. J. Palmer (2021); Mole (2021); S. Wee (2021); Connors (2021); María de Ávila (2022); Watanabe and Takeda (2022); Kobierecka (2022).

172. D. Goldman (2020a).

173. AAAS (2020); Van Noorden (2022). For a more, perhaps overly, alarmist report on PRC's technology prowess, see Gaida et al (2023).

174. Paul (2018, 119–45).

175. Shepherd (2020, 70).

176. Hong Kong is also envisioned by Beijing as a shortcut for the all-important RMB internationalization (*Lianhe zaobao* 2021).

177. C. Leng (2020); Scott and Zachariadis (2014).

178. Kowsmann, Norman, and Talley (2022).

179. White House (May 23, 2022); US DOS (July 20, 2022).

180. Parton (2020).

181. Reuters (September 17, 2021); Gao and Zhou (2021).

182. Makichuk (2020).

183. The Japanese politician Shigeru Ishiba (石破茂) openly called for an Asian-Pacific NATO in 2014 (Ishiba 2014). For a PRC analysis, see Zheng Rongjian (2021). After Japan (in 2010 and 2018), Seoul in 2022 joined NATO intelligence network and set up a formal liaison office to NATO (Jo He-rim 2022; Shin Ji-hye 2022). Japanese and South Korean leaders attended the NATO summit for the first time in 2022 (Mesmer 2022; M. Yu 2022a, 2022b).

184. Stoltenberg and Kishida (2023).

185. Larin (1995: 280–301); Dugin (2014); Shi Chang (2021); Pieper (2022). For the complex and uncertain relationship between China and Russia, see Snow (2023).

186. C. Chen (2016); Kaczmarski (2015, 172); *Economist* (April 9, 2022).

187. Blackall (2022); Wintour (2022); McDonell (2022); L. He (2022).

188. According to a PRC analysis, "anti-China" is Moscow's "only bargaining chip" to regain the trust and friendship of the West (Wei Ci 2022).

332 | Notes to Chapter 4

189. Nixon (1967).

190. Lee Hsien Loong (2020).

191. Cheng et al. (2018); T. Zhao (2020, 2020a). Author's interviews with US defense industry analysts, 2022.

192. Bratton (2021); Sharp (2022).

193. Acton (2019); Grego (2012); Hippel (2020).

194. US DOD (2019).

195. F. Wang (2017a, 157–78; 2023a, 149–72).

196. Cliff (2020); Esper (US secretary of defense, July 21, 2020); Garamone (March 13, 2021; March 15, 2021); Hynes and Vittachi (2021).

197. Field observations in South America have convinced this author that Beijing's power gains there are even less cost-effective and more superficial than those in Africa (author's field notes in Chile, Ecuador, Panama, and Peru, 2014–20). For Beijing's debacle of public relations, the so-called "wolf warrior diplomacy," in places like Brazil, see Stuenkel (2020) and Kennon (2020).

198. US Congress (2018); Bellows (2020); Hillman and Sacks (2021).

199. Group of Seven (2018); Group of 20 (2019); A. Fang (2021); Wahba (2022).

200. Benabdallah (2020); Eisenman and Shinn (2023).

201. Nantulya (2020).

202. Areddy (2012); Strupczewski (2021); Szabolcs (2021); Spike (2021); Higgins (2021).

203. Tewari (2022).

204. Mackinder (1904, 421–37); Liu Yazhou (2010); Hu Weixing (2022).

205. Rippa (2020).

206. Gordon, Tong, and Anderson (2020); Carrai, Defraigne, and Wouters (2020).

207. Tatlow (2022); Samuels and Megiddo (2023).

208. Ma Lirong (2015); Qina Benli (2019).

209. Khanna (2020); Kyzy (2020).

210. Halegua (2020, 225–57); Emily Feng (2019); Halegua and Ban (2020).

211. Washburne (2018); White House (June 26, 2022); US DOS, *Blue Dot Network* (state.gov/blue-dot-network/; accessed March 2023).

212. Ganguly et al. (2023). According to Indian scholars (July 2022), during the Sino-Indian border skirmish in June 2020, the US provided "very helpful live intelligence" to India. The "closest" partnership between India and the US, affirmed by President Biden and Prime Minister Narendra Modi in mid-2023, was a major step (White House, June 22, 2023).

213. Maçães (2019); M. Ye (2020). Some PRC analysts seemed to have also vaguely seen this (Lu Gang 2019; Kynge and Wheatley 2020).

214. Zweig and Kang (2020). For cases of PRC "economic espionage" in the US, see Mattis and Brazil (2020, 145–94). For 14 policy measures recommended by a US Senate report, see US Senate (2019, 11–13).

Notes to Chapter 4 | 333

215. *Financial Times* (April 18, 2022).

216. Cave et al. (2019).

217. Reed (2004, 266–70).

218. Cao and Poy (2011); Hamilton and Ohlberg (2020a); S. Tan (2020).

219. Charles Michel (president of the European Council, 2020); Ford and Goldgeier (2021); Binnendijk et al. (2021); ETNC (2015–22).

220. Amaro and Josephs (2021); R. Cohen (2023); Anderlini and Caulcutt (2023).

221. Stiftun (2020); Pompeo (June 19, 2020; June 25, 2020); Kemp (2022).

222. F. Wang (April 10, 2006).

223. F. Wang (July 21, 2005).

224. X (1947); Kennan (1948); Mastro (2018).

225. Heath, Grossman, and Clark (2021, 10, 34–5, 97–9).

226. Pei (July 8, 2020).

227. CCP Central Party School (2020, 7); Xi Jinping (May 10, 2022).

228. Wei Pu (2016); Pei (May/June 2020); Fan Haixing (2020); Xu Zhangrun (2020).

229. Saunders et al. (2019). The PLA may appear more menacing at a more regional and local level (Gill, Ni, and Blasko 2020; Cabestan 2020, 731–47).

230. US DOD (2020, i–ii).

231. Lendon (2021).

232. The author acknowledges US defense policy experts for these inspiring ideas, 2020s.

233. Scobell (2021); Magnus (2021); Pomfret and Pottinger (2023).

234. 以国内循环为主. Duan Siyu and Huang Siyu (2020); Wang Jingwen (2020).

235. Wang Jisi (王缉思), Wu Xinbo (吴心伯) et al., conversations, fall 2020; IISS (2022).

236. Yan Xuetong (July/August 2021). Yan was, however, later criticized in the PRC for his "pro-US" concerns about the Russian invasion of Ukraine (De Na 2022).

237. Medeiros and Tellis (2021).

238. Brands and Beckley (2021); G. Chang (2022); Cochrane, Ferguson, and McMaster (2022).

239. Matt Pottinger (deputy national security advisor, 2020); Tsang (2023, 49).

240. Johnson and Gramer (2020); Furedi (2006, 2018). For the perennial *nucleomituphobia* (irrational fear of nuclear weapons) in the West, see Orland (2022).

241. Wang Yi (July 9, 2020); Le Yucheng (July 8, 2020).

242. Wang Yi (August 5, 2020). For arguments that "we must above all prevent the US-PRC decoupling," see Wei Jianing (2019). For "enduring the

334 | Notes to Chapter 4

bitterness and hardship to get revenge later" (卧薪尝胆), see Sun Lipeng (2020) and Zhong Sheng (2020, 3).

243. Jakes and Myers (2021).

244. Li Qiang (李强), pres conference, Beijing, March 13, 2023. Beida (2023).

245. Friedberg (September/October 2020); Gershaneck (2020).

246. Joske (2020).

247. Matt Pottinger, deputy national security advisor, "Remarks to London-based Policy Exchange," White House, October 23, 2020.

248. Great Fire Wall Check (gfwcheck.com and zh.greatfire.org; accessed July 2022).

249. 小粉红. One interesting twist is that quite a few of those misinformed human robots complain that Beijing's Firewall has prevented them from "doing more abroad" for the CCP (author's interviews, 2015–22). For a discussion of little pinkies, see Fang and Repnikova (2017).

250. Melville and Lapidus (1990); Gibbs (1999); Medvedev (2002); Beissinger and Kotkin (2013); Dutkiewicz, Kulikov, and Sakwa (2016).

251. Johnson, Stepaniants, and Forest (2005); Bai Yue (2017).

252. Maruyama (1963, 1998). For evidence on policy reshaping minds, see Bau (2021).

253. Reagan (1987).

254. Simons (2020).

255. For how investment immigration is abused by many PRC citizens, see Crane (2020).

256. For examples of actions proposed in this regard, see Carafano et al. (2023, 77–91).

257. Gilsinan (2020); China Power Team (2021).

258. Bandeira et al. (2021). A US effort in this regard is the "To Refute Lies" (揭谎频道), by the Washington-based Voice of America in Chinese (美国之音) (voachinese.com/p/7645.html). New Congressional action is also seen (Harris 2022).

259. 名不正, 则言不顺; 言不顺, 则事不成. Confucius, *Analects-Zilu* (孔子: 论语·子路).

260. Chase (1959). For how Nazi Germany imposed its own language with profound implications, see Klemperer ([1957] 2013) and Grunberger (1971).

261. Wilhelm (2022).

262. Author's interviews, 1996–2022.

263. Some PRC bloggers have already openly asserted that, instead of the so-called "shame" caused by foreigners, the "real national humiliation" of China is the result of CCP governance, including the coverup of massive war dead, the Great Famine, the Cultural Revolution, and fake history (Gao Ren 2017).

264. F. Wang ([2000] 2003).

Notes to Chapter 4 | 335

265. Breslin and Ren (2020). For a recent insider-turned-dissenter openly critical of Xi, Cai Xia, see Buckley (August 10, 2020). For a detectable "divergence in foreign policy" in Beijing, see G. Wu (2022). For disagreement in the PRC over Beijing's pro-Putin policy, see Buckley (2023).

266. Zha (2007); Teng Biao (May 2, 2021); author's interviews and observations, 1989–2023; Cai Xia (February 6, 2022). For a long list of open and anonymous PRC critics of Xi, see Jessie (2021). For an "insider" account of an alleged coup-like showdown at the highest level of the CCP, see Xiang (2022). For a scholarly analysis of the deep political and economic problems in the PRC, see Tao Ran (2023).

267. Zheng Yefu (2020).

268. Hancock and Li (2022). For examples of biting denunciation of Xi in PRC cyberspace, see Fang Zhou (2022, 2022a). For the melodramatic cat-and-mouse games between the critics and the censors in PRC cyberspace, see J. Pan (2022) and Brouwer (2022).

269. 烂尾. Tao Ran (陶然), "How Did China Dream Turn Out to Be a Nightmare for All of Us?," unpublished essay, Shenzhen, July 2022.

270. Shi Ming (2022).

271. Treisman (2020).

272. For "the current race between reform and revolution" in the PRC, see Zhou and Yang (2014).

273. Blanchette (2020); Winnefeld and Morell (2020); Garside (2021).

274. Winnefeld, Morell, and Allison (2020).

275. S. Cheng (2021).

276. Carrol (2022).

277. PAC (2022).

278. The 2nd through 14th largest sources of FDI to China only provided 37.2%, while "all others" only 11.7% in the four decades (Ministry of Commerce 2019, 6, 35).

279. The great flow of capital from Hong Kong to Singapore illustrates this well (Ng 2022; *Economist*, July 2, 2022).

280. State Council Press Office (2021); Guangdong–Hong Kong–Macau Greater Bay Area (粤港澳大湾区) (cnbayarea.org.cn; last accessed August 8, 2023).

281. David Stilwell (assistant secretary of state for East Asian and Pacific affairs, 2020); Gregson et al. (2021); Qin and Chien (2022).

282. To many in Beijing, "retaking" Taiwan is simply the key to the rise of China as global power (Jiang Shigong 2022).

283. Such as the publication and legislation of the "six assurances," penned by President Ronald Reagan (Chen and Lim 2020). For similar advice based on different reasoning, see Haass and Sacks (2020). Also, Colby (January 26, 2021); Blackwill and Zelikow (2021); R. Wang (2021). For a call by 14 noted

336 | Notes to Chapter 4

Sinologists and formal "China hands" for firmer and smarter US policy to "avoid war over Taiwan," see Task Force on U.S.-China Policy (2022).

284. Sanger (2001); Stephanopoulos (2021); Liptak (2021); CBS, 60 Minutes, September 18, 2022.

285. "Press Briefing by Press Secretary Jen Psaki and National Security Advisor Jake Sullivan," White House, December 7, 2021; "The Future of U.S. Policy on Taiwan," Hearing by Committee on Foreign Relations, US Senate, December 8, 2021; CFR (2023).

286. Kanapathy (2022).

287. Miles Yu (2022a); Gregory and Ho (2022); Pedrozo (2022); Carrico (2022). The new chairman of the ruling DPP Lai Ching-te (賴清德) asserted that Taiwan has a de jure independence (Lai 2023). Taipei is poised to accept the PRC as a diplomatic peer (ROC foreign minister's press conference, March 26, 2023).

288. Liff, Lin, et al. (2022).

289. Li Xiaofeng (2015); van der Wees (2022).

290. Dittmer (2017, 283); "Taiwan Update" (carlford.substack.com; August 1, 2022).

291. F. Wang (Sep 19, 2006). Indeed, many in the PRC seem to feel that "thankfully China has a Taiwan [to contrast with the PRC]" (Gu Yuchuan 2012).

292. "The Pentagon has reportedly enacted 18 war games against China over Taiwan, and China has prevailed in every one" (Zakaria 2020; Glaser and Funaiole 2020).

293. Chew (1971). Still ongoing, the Ukrainian resistance to Russia in 2022–23, with more external aid, has more strongly proven this point.

294. Tsai Ing-wen (2021).

295. Kuzub (2023); Madhok (2023). For the consequential PRC-USA "chip war," see Miller (2022).

296. Zhi Gu (2021); Murphree (2022).

297. Prange (1986).

298. Anders Corr is acknowledged for these ideas, June 18, 2020. Sutton (2020). For the PRC's island-building, see Di Li Ren (2022).

299. G. Chang (2020).

300. Kroenig (2020).

301. As discussed earlier in this book, this normative assertion will naturally adjust if some of the key parameters change due to, for example, interaction between Earth and extra-terrestrial civilizations, the common threat of genuine species annihilation, bio/genetic alteration of the human nature or capacity, or new technology that can eliminate the energy- or resource-scarcity.

302. A polity of democratic rule of law can be parliamentary or presidential, republic or constitutional monarchy, proportional-representation or simple-major-

ity, federation or unitary state; the Westphalian world order can be de jure or de facto, multipolar or bipolar or even transiently unipolar (hegemonic), peaceful or warring, with hierarchies and exclusions (as in colonies, alliances, blocks, and the UN Security Council), or with an equal arrangement of all units (as in the UN General Assembly and the International Olympics).

303. Xia Ming (2020).

304. Tammen et al. (2000); Mearsheimer (2001); T. Lynch (2021).

305. Corr (2019).

306. Fravel et al. (2019).

307. The CCP has crafted potent "destructive nostalgia" and xenophobia of Han-nationalism that thrives on claims like antisemitism (Carrico 2017; Hayton 2020).

308. Ding Xuexiang (2022).

309. White House (May 20, 2020).

310. Associated Press (November 29, 2022); "Call for 'White Paper Movement'" ("白纸运动"发起倡议书) (www.baizhi.org; posted January 31, 2023).

311. Burlingame (1868). For Burlingame's diplomatic career in the Qing empire, see von Gumpach (1872). For assessments of his role, see Williams (1912) and Babones (2017).

312. T. Wright (2017, 187–222).

313. Some US politicians appear to disagree with this hierarchy of preference and consider a Cold War–like confrontation in and of itself the worst disaster (Sanders 2021).

314. Xi Jinping (July 1, 2021).

315. Ross, Wang, et al. (2020); Wang Huiyao (2021); Qin Gang (February 2023).

316. Pericles, "Funeral Oration," in Thucydides ([5th century BCE] 1972, ch. 6).

317. Furedi (2006, 2018). The fear-mongering about a dire and obliterating war whenever the West/US is seen somewhat serious about the PRC-USA rivalry has been unceasing and inventive. A latest example is the invocation of a new phantom of "AI war" or "AI risks" (C. Li 2022; Wong and Chen 2023).

318. F. Wang (2017, 35–8, 119–23).

319. P. Johnston (2012); Cone (2019).

320. Mark Milley, chairman of the Joint Chiefs, testimony at Congress, March 29, 2023.

321. Johnson and Gramer (2020).

322. F. Wang (2017, 199); Lorenzo (2013); Yonhap (2021).

323. Gui Yu (2006).

324. D. Chang (2020).

325. Truman (1952).

338 | Notes to Epilogue

326. D. Chang (2020).

327. For how the Chinese POWs were brutally purged after their return—almost 100% blacklisted for life (relaxed only after 1980), see He Ming (1998), Yang Dongxiao (2013), Zhao Feipeng (2013), and Yu Jin ([1988] 2020); also, the best-selling fictional memoir, Ha Jin (2015).

328. Li Shu (2017); Jiao Ni (2020). For more examples of similar family stories, see Mu Guangfeng (2022), Z. Li (2022), and Zhou Zhixing (2022).

329. Fu Chun (2021). Perhaps, the US was mindful of "the great betrayal," the forced repatriation of Soviet POWs, and Russian diaspora after World War II (Epstein 1973; Naumenko 2015).

330. *Economist* (January 15, 2022).

331. 诗圣. "挽弓当挽强,用箭当用長。射人先射馬, 擒賊先擒王。殺人亦有限, 列國自有疆。苟能制侵陵, 豈在多殺傷" (Du Fu (杜甫; [8th century] 2021), translation is mine. For Du's works in English, see Owen (2016). For the poet, see BBC (April 2020).

Epilogue

1. Biden (September 21, 2021); Xi Jinping (September 21, 2021). In March 2023, when meeting the visiting Belarusian president, Xi reemphasized the need "to cope with global challenges" during "the once-in-a-century great change of the world" (CCTV, March 2, 2023). For an extensive and official elaboration of the CCP's grand design and action plan for that "great change" of world order, see *Build Together the Community of Common Human Destiny: China's Proposals and Actions* (携手构建人类命运共同体: 中国的倡议与行动), White Paper, Beijing: PRC State Council Press Office, September 26, 2023.

2. Fogel (2000, 13, 241–2, 302–3).

3. F. Wang (2017, 216–17).

4. Fingar and Oi (2020a, x, 3–4, 8).

5. Scobell et al. (2020, x).

6. Nye (October 6, 2020). Three years later, he imagined a "smart competition" of "soft power" would allow a PRC-USA "cooperative rivalry" to avoid a new Cold War (Nye 2023).

7. Börzel and Zürn (2021, 303–4).

8. Lake et al. (special issue, 2021, 252).

9. Bradford (2022); Posen (2023).

10. For a report illustrating and forewarning such a scenario, see B. Allen (2023).

11. Kafka ([1917] 2004).

Works and Sources Cited

AAAS. *The Perils of Complacency: America at a Tipping Point in Science and Engineering.* Cambridge, MA: American Academy of Arts and Sciences, 2020.

Acemoglu, Daron. "China's Economy Is Rotting from the Head." Project Syndicate, October 28, 2022.

Acemoglu, Daron, and James A. Robinson. *Economic Origins of Dictatorship and Democracy.* New York: Cambridge University Press, 2006.

Acharya, Amitav, Daniel Bell, Rajeev Bhargava, and Yan Xuetong. *Bridging Two Worlds: Comparing Classical Political Thought and Statecraft in India and China.* Oakland: University of California Press, 2023.

Acton, James. "Why Is Nuclear Entanglement So Dangerous?" Carnegie Endowment for International Peace, January 23, 2019.

Acton, John Emerich Edward Dalberg-Acton, Baron. *Essays on Freedom and Power.* Boston: Beacon, 1949.

Adams, Paul. "Is China's Fishing Fleet Taking All of West Africa's Fish?" BBC, March 25, 2019.

Adler, Emanuel, and Alena Drieschova. "The Epistemological Challenge of Truth Subversion to the Liberal International Order." *International Organization* 75, no. 2 (2021): 359–86.

Adragna, Anthony. "McCarthy, Taiwan's Leader Meet in California Despite Threats from China." *Politico*, April 5, 2023.

Ahmed, Shazeda, Natasha E. Bajema, Samuel Bendett, Benjamin Angel Chang, Rogier Creemers, Chris C. Demchak, Sarah W. Denton, et al. *AI, China, Russia, and the Global Order.* Washington, DC: Department of Defense Strategic Multilayer Assessment (SMA) Program, 2018.

Albert, Eleanor, and Xu Beina. "The Chinese Communist Party." Council on Foreign Relations, September 27, 2019.

Alden, Chris, and Oscar M. Otele. "Fitting China In: Local Elite Collusion and Contestation along Kenya's Standard Gauge Railway." *African Affairs* 121, no. 484 (2022): 443–66.

340 | Works and Sources Cited

Alderman, Liz, Jim Tankersley, and Eshe Nelson. "U.S. Proposal for 15% Global Minimum Tax Wins Support from 130 Countries." *New York Times*, July 1, 2021.

Alecci, Scilla. "The Faces of China's Detention Camps in Xinjiang." International Consortium of Investigative Journalists, March 24, 2022.

Al Jazeera. "What Will It Take to Stop China's Uighur Genocide?" June 2, 2022.

Allan, Bentley, Srdjan Vucetic, and Ted Hopf. "The Distribution of Identity and the Future of International Order: China's Hegemonic Prospects." *International Organization* 72, no. 4 (2018): 839–69.

Allen, Bethany. *Beijing Rules: How China Weaponized Its Economy to Confront the World*. New York: Harper, 2023.

Allen-Ebrahimian, Bethany. "Russia Is the Biggest Recipient of Chinese Foreign Aid." *Foreign Policy*, October 11, 2017.

———. "China's Long Arm Reaches into American Campuses." *Foreign Policy*, March 7, 2018.

———. "The Chinese Communist Party Is Setting Up Cells at Universities across America." *Foreign Policy*, April 18, 2018a.

———. "Former Google CEO and Others Call for U.S.-China Tech 'Bifurcation.'" *Axios*, January 26, 2021.

Allen-Ebrahimian, Bethany, and Zach Dorfman. "Suspected Chinese Spy Targeted California Politicians." *Axios*, December 8, 2020.

Allison, Graham. "Of Course China, like All Great Powers, Will Ignore an International Legal Verdict." *Diplomat*, July 11, 2016.

———. *Destined for War: Can America and China Escape Thucydides's Trap?* New York: Houghton Mifflin Harcourt, 2017.

Alper, Alexandra, and Idrees Ali. "Trump Administration Says Huawei, Hikvision Backed by Chinese Military." Reuters, June 24, 2020.

Alpermann, Björn. "Ethics in Social Science Research on China." *Made in China Journal* 7, no. 1 (2022): 36–43.

Amaro, Silvia, and Leslie Josephs. "US and EU Resolve 17-Year Boeing-Airbus Trade Dispute." CNBC, June 15, 2021.

Ambrose, Stephen. *Rise to Globalism: American Foreign Policy Since 1938*. New York: Penguin, 2010.

An Gang. "Embrace the Fully Developing China-US Struggle." *Zhongmei jujiao* (中美聚焦), Febraury 28, 2023.

Anderlini, Jamil, and Clea Caulcutt. "Europe Must Resist Pressure to Become 'America's Followers,' Says Macron." *Politico*, April 9, 2023.

Andersen, Ross. "Chinese AI Is Creating an Axis of Autocracy." *Atlantic*, September 2020.

Anderson, Natasha. "Two Chinese-Born New Yorkers Are Charged with Funneling Foreign Money to Trump's 2020 Campaign." Reuters, July 19, 2022.

Works and Sources Cited | 341

Anderson, Nicholas, and Victor Cha. "The Case of the Pivot to Asia: System Effects and the Origins of Strategy." *Political Science Quarterly* 132, no. 4 (2017): 595–617.

Anderson, Perry. *The H-Word: The Peripeteia of Hegemony*. New York: Verso, (2017) 2022.

Anonymous. *The Longer Telegram: Toward A New American China Strategy*. Atlantic Council, January 2021.

Applebaum, Anne. "The Autocrats Are Winning." *Atlantic*, December 2021.

Aquinas, Thomas. *The Summa Theologiae*. New York: Benziger, (1485) 1911.

Areddy, James. "European Project Trips China Builder." *Wall Street Journal*, June 4, 2012.

Areddy, James, and Brian Spegele. "Dozens of Americans Are Barred from Leaving China." *Wall Street Journal*, November 13, 2022.

Arendt, Hannah. *The Origins of Totalitarianism*. New York: Harvest, (1951) 1976.

Aristotle. *Politics*. Translated by Williams Ellis. New York: Dutton, (350 BCE) 1912.

Aroor, Shiv. "3 Separate Brawls, 'Outsider' Chinese Troops and More." *India Today*, June 21, 2020.

Asian Development Bank. *Global Value Chain Development Report 2021: Beyond Production*. Manila, November 2021.

Aspen Strategy Group. *The Struggle for Power: U.S.-China Relations in the 21st Century*. Washington: Aspen Institute, 2020.

Associated Press (AP). "Trump's National-Security Adviser Says U.S. 'Has Finally Awoken to the Threat' Posed by China." June 24, 2020.

———. "China Lockdown Protests Pause as Police Flood City Streets." November 29, 2022.

———. "Commerce Dept. Adds 33 Chinese Companies to Red Flag List." February 7, 2022.

Astorino-Courtois, Allison, et al. *Present and Future Challenges to Maintaining Balance between Global Cooperation and Competition*. SMA Perspectives, DOD, November 2020.

———. *US versus China: Promoting "Constructive Competition" to Avoid "Destructive Competition*. SMA Perspectives, DOD, May 2021.

Atanassow, Ewa. *Tocqueville's Dilemmas, and Ours: Sovereignty, Nationalism, Globalization*. Princeton, NJ: Princeton University Press, 2022.

Athey, Amber. "The Twisted Love Affair with Eileen Gu." *Spectator World*, February 10, 2022.

Atkinson, Robert. "A Remarkable Resemblance: Germany from 1900 to 1945 and China Today—Time for a NATO for trade?" *International Economy*, Fall 2020.

Aum, Daniel, and Fei-Ling Wang. "Insecurity and Ambition: Dual Drivers of Chinese Innovation?" *Defense and Peace Economics*, December 2022.

342 | Works and Sources Cited

Autor, David, David Dorn, and Gordon H. Hanson. "The China Syndrome: Local Labor Market Effects of Import Competition in the United States." *American Economic Review* 103, no. 6 (2013): 2121–68.

———. "The China Shock: Learning from Labor-Market Adjustment to Large Changes in Trade." *Annual Review of Economics* 8 (2016): 205–40.

Babones, Salvatore. "The Burlingame Mission: How an 1867 Embassy Prefigured Chinese and American Power." *Foreign Affairs*, November 23, 2017.

Bachner, David. "A Very Practical Approach to Peace: The Case for International Exchange." 2022. https://static1.squarespace.com/static/56167d1de4b0141a0f9a9378/t/5697c32b40667adbe8f8dce6/1452786476282/PracticalApproachToPeace.pdf.

Bachrack, Stanley. *The Committee of One Million: China Lobby Politics, 1953–1971.* New York: Columbia University Press, 1976.

Bai Juyi. *First Farewell to the City* (白居易: 初出城留别). In *Collected Works by Bai Juyi* (白居易集). Beijing, China: Zhonghua Shuju, (9th century) 1999.

Bai Sen Xin Consultancy. "Nature of the Russo-Ukrainian Crisis I" (百森新咨询: 俄乌危机的本质1). Beijing, February 28, 2022.

Bai, Tongdong. *Against Political Equality: The Confucian Case.* Princeton, NJ: Princeton University Press, 2019.

Bai Yue. "Observation on the Change of Faith by the Russian Communist Party" (白约: 俄罗斯共产党信仰转型观察). *Boke zhongguo* (博客中国), Beijing, January 8, 2017.

Bai Yun. "Disappeared Hometown" (白云: 消失的故乡). *Financial Times in Chinese*, September 23, 2012.

Bai Yunyi. "Foreign Ministry: Sino-British Joint Declaration Is Irrelevant Historical Document" (白云怡: 外交部: 中英联合声明是历史文件已不具现实意义). *Huanqiu Shibao* (环球时报), June 30, 2017.

Bandeira, Luiza, Nika Aleksejeva, Tessa Knight, Jean le Roux, Graham Brookie, Iain Robertson, Andy Carvin, and Zarine Kharazian. *Weaponized: How Rumors about COVID-19's Origins Led to a Narrative Arms Race.* Atlantic Council, 2021.

Banerjee, Abhijit, and Esther Duflo. *Poor Economics: A Radical Rethinking of the Way to Fight Global Poverty.* New York: Public Affairs, 2011.

Bannon, Steve. "Tired of Winning." *War Room*, October 9, 2020.

Bao Shenggang. "US Still Remains the Key of Key Issues to Chinese Diplomacy" (鲍盛刚: 美国依然是中国外交重中之重). *Aisixiang* (爱思想), Beijing, March 13, 2015.

Barboza, David. "Andrew Nathan on the Politicization of the 'China Threat.'" *Wire China*, January 23, 2022.

———. "Many Wall St. Banks Woo Children of Chinese Leaders." *New York Times*, August 20, 2013.

———. "Steve Bannon on Hong Kong, COVID-19, and the War with China Already Underway." *Wire China*, May 24, 2020.

Works and Sources Cited | 343

———. "David Shambaugh on Why U.S. Engagement with China Is Already Dead in Spirit." *Wire China*, November 7, 2021.

———. "Peddling the President: Elliott Broidy's Efforts to Lobby the President Came Close to Succeeding." *Wire China*, April 25, 2021.

Bardhan, Pranab. *A World of Insecurity: Democratic Disenchantment in Rich and Poor Countries*. Cambridge, MA: Harvard University Press, 2022.

Barr, William. "Remarks on China Policy at the Gerald R. Ford Presidential Museum." Public speech in Grand Rapids, Michigan, July 16, 2020.

Barry, Ellen. "In a Boston Court, a Superstar of Science Falls to Earth." *New York Times*, December 22, 2021.

Barzun, Jacques. *From Dawn to Decadence, 1500 to the Present: 500 Years of Western Cultural Life*. New York: HarperCollins, 2000.

Basu, Zachary. "Biden Campaign Says China's Treatment of Uighur Muslims Is 'Genocide.'" *Axios*, August 25, 2020.

Bateman, Jon. "Biden Is Now All-In on Taking Out China." *Foreign Policy*, October 12, 2022.

Bau, Natalie. "Can Policy Change Culture?" *American Economic Review* 111, no. 6 (2021): 1880–1917.

Baum, Richard. *China Watcher: Confessions of a Peking Tom*. Seattle: University of Washington Press, 2010.

BBC. *Du Fu: China's Greatest Poet*. Documentary, April 2020.

———. "FBI Director: China Is 'Greatest Threat' to US." July 8, 2020.

———. "China Becomes Taliban's New Friend." August 6, 2021.

———. "China Is Reported to Construct a Global Military Supply Network." July 9, 2021.

BBC in Chinese. "Thirty-Year Anniversary of June 4th" (六四30週年). June 4, 2019.

Beckley, Michael. *Unrivaled: Why America Will Remain the World's Sole Superpower*. Ithaca, NY: Cornell University Press, 2018.

———. "Rogue Superpower: Why This Could Be an Illiberal American Century." *Foreign Affairs*, November/December 2020.

Beckley, Michael, and Hal Brands. "The End of China's Rise: Beijing Is Running Out of Time to Remake the World." *Foreign Affairs*, October 1, 2021.

Beech, Hannah. "The Chinese Sports Machine's Single Goal: The Most Golds, at Any Cost." *New York Times*, July 30, 2021.

Beene, Ryan. "American Factories Are Making Stuff Again as CEOs Take Production out of China." *Bloomberg*, July 5, 2022.

Beida (Peking University). International Conference on Reconstructing a Stable Structure for Sino-American Relations. World Peace Forum, Beijing, July 3, 2023.

Beijing Municipal Committee of CCP, ed. *Collection of Ideas of Bourgeoisie Liberalization* (北京市委: 资产阶级自由化言论辑录). Beijing: Zhongguo Qingnian, December 1989.

344 | Works and Sources Cited

Beissinger, Mark, and Stephen Kotkin. *Historical Legacies of Communism in Russia and Eastern Europe*. New York: Cambridge University Press, 2013.

Beitz, Charles. *Political Theory and International Relations*. Princeton, NJ: Princeton University Press, 1999.

———. *The Idea of Human Rights*. New York: Oxford University Press, 2009.

Bell, Daniel. *The China Model: Political Meritocracy and the Limits of Democracy*. Princeton, NJ: Princeton University Press, 2015.

Bell, Daniel, and Wang Pei. *Just Hierarchy: Why Social Hierarchies Matter in China and the Rest of the World*. Princeton, NJ: Princeton University Press, 2020.

Bellows, Abigail. *Regaining U.S. Leadership on Anti-Corruption*. Carnegie Endowment for International Peace, July 1, 2020.

Benabdallah, Lina. *Shaping the Future of Power: Knowledge Production and Network-Building in China-Africa Relations*. Ann Arbor: University of Michigan Press, 2020.

Berkowitz, Peter. *Virtue and the Making of Modern Liberalism*. Princeton, NJ: Princeton University Press, 2000.

Berlin, Isaiah. *Liberty*. Oxford: Oxford University Press, 1969.

Bernstein, Peter. *Against the Gods: The Remarkable Story of Risk*. New York: Wiley, 1998.

Bērziņa-Čerenkova, Una Aleksandra. *Perfect Imbalance: China and Russia*. Singapore: World Scientific, 2022.

Beyoud, Lydia, and Lulu Yilun Chen. "US, China Reach Preliminary Deal in Push to Avoid Delistings." *Bloomberg*, August 26, 2022.

Bhargava, Rajeev. "Without War and Conquest: The Idea of a Global Political Order in Asoka's Dhamma." Conference paper, 2021.

Bian Xiuyue. "Study on the Chinese Loss of Life during Anti-Japanese War" (卞修跃:抗日战争时期中国人口损失问题研究). PhD thesis, Chinese Academy of Social Sciences, 2004.

Biden, Joe. "Explained: How to Build Back." Posted August 8, 2020. youtube.com/watch?v=6MNY6EQmQxo.

———. "Why America Must Lead Again: Rescuing U.S. Foreign Policy after Trump." *Foreign Affairs*, March/April 2020.

———. "Address to a Joint Session of Congress." April 28, 2021.

———. "Executive Order on Addressing the Threat from Securities Investments That Finance Certain Companies of the People's Republic of China." White House, June 3, 2021.

———. "Remarks by President Biden Before the 76th Session of the United Nations General Assembly." New York, September 21, 2021.

———. "Remarks by President Biden on Afghanistan." White House, August 16, 2021.

———. "Remarks by President Biden on America's Place in the World." White House, February 4, 2021.

Works and Sources Cited | 345

———. "Remarks by President Biden on the End of the War in Afghanistan." White House, August 31, 2021.

———. *Renewing America's Advantages: Interim National Security Strategic Guidance.* White House, March 2021.

———. "Statement by President Joe Biden on the Investigation into the Origins of COVID-19." White House, May 26, 2021.

———. *2022 State of the Union Address.* White House, March 1, 2022.

———. *National Security Strategy.* White House, October 12, 2022.

Bie De. "The 'Expelled' Chinese in Russia" (别的: 被"驱逐"的俄罗斯华人). *Wangyi* (网易), July 12, 2022.

Binnendijk, Hans, Sarah Kirchberger, James Danoy, Franklin D. Kramer, Connor McPartland, Christopher Skaluba, Clementine G. Starling, and Didi Kirsten Tatlow. *The China Plan: A Transatlantic Blueprint for Strategic Competition.* Atlantic Council, March 2021.

BIS. "Announces Renminbi Liquidity Arrangement." Press release, Zurich, June 25, 2022.

Blackall, Molly. "UN Security Council: Why Did China Abstain in Ukraine Vote." *Inews*, February 26, 2022.

Blackwill, Robert. "Implementing Grand Strategy toward China: Twenty-Two U.S. Policy Prescriptions." Council on Foreign Relations Special Report no. 85, January 2020.

Blackwill, Robert, and Thomas Wright. *The End of World Order and American Foreign Policy.* Council on Foreign Relations Special Report no. 86, May 2020.

Blackwill, Robert, and Philip Zelikow. *The United States, China, and Taiwan: A Strategy to Prevent War.* Policy Report, Council on Foreign Relations, February 2021.

Blanchette, Jude. "What Happens If Xi Jinping Dies in Office?" CSIS podcast, September 24, 2020.

———. *From "China Inc." to "CCP Inc.": A New Paradigm for Chinese State Capitalism.* Hinrich Foundation, February 2021.

———. "Xi Jinping's Faltering Foreign Policy: The War in Ukraine and the Perils of Strongman Rule." *Foreign Affairs*, March 16, 2022.

Blinken, Antony. "Confidence, Humility, and the United States' New Direction in the World: A Transcript of Remarks on U.S. Foreign Policy." *Foreign Policy*, March 4. 2021.

———. "A Foreign Policy for the American People." US Department of State, March 3, 2021.

———. "The Administration's Approach to the People's Republic of China." George Washington University, May 26, 2022.

Blitzer, Ronn. "Majority of Democratic Voters Now Prefer Socialism to Capitalism, Poll Finds." Fox, August 12, 2021.

346 | Works and Sources Cited

Bloom, Jesse D., Yujia Alina Chan, Ralph S. Baric, Pamela J. Bjorkman, Sarah Cobey, Benjamin E. Deverman, David N. Fisman, et al. "Investigate the Origins of COVID-19." *Science*, May 14, 2021.

Bloomberg. "China Buys Record Russia Crude as Putin Seeks to Avoid Recession." December 22, 2014.

———. "China Renews Push for Increased Global Role for the Yuan." July 13, 2020.

———. "Wall Street Has Billions to Lose in China from Rising Strain." May 28, 2020.

———. "China Steps Up Efforts to Join Trade Pact Created to Exclude It." May 17, 2021.

———. "Foreign executives in China ask 'who's next?'" April 28, 2023.

Bolton, John. *The Room Where It Happened: A White House Memoir*. New York: Simon and Schuster, 2020.

Bond, Ian. "Europe Must Stand Up to China before It's Too Late." *Foreign Policy*, June 16, 2020.

Bond, Ian, François Godement, Hanns W. Maull, and Volker Stanzel. *Rebooting Europe's China Strategy*. German Institute for International and Security Affairs, May 2022.

Bond, Martyn. *Hitler's Cosmopolitan Bastard: Count Richard Coudenhove-Kalergi and His Vision of Europe*. Montreal: McGill-Queen's University Press, 2021.

Bonnin, Michel. *The Lost Generation: The Rustication of China's Educated Youth (1968–1980)*. Hong Kong: Chinese University of Hong Kong Press, 2013.

Boot, Max. "The Case for American Empire." *Weekly Standard*, October 15, 2001.

———. "Putin's War of Aggression Has Mobilized the Strongest International Outrage since 9/11." *Washington Post*, February 27, 2022.

Borao, José Eugenic. "The Massacre of 1603: Chinese Perception of the Spanish in the Philippines." *Itinerario* 22, no. 1 (1998): 22–40.

Börzel, Tanja, and Michael Zürn. "Contestations of the Liberal International Order." *International Organization* 75, no. 2 (2021): 282–305.

Bosco, Joseph. "Henry Kissinger Is Decades Late in Recognizing China's Aggressive Nature." *Hill*, Oct. 20, 2020.

———. "Biden Should Reinforce Trump's Transformation of China Policy." *Hill*, November 17, 2020a.

———. "Kissinger Tells Biden to Go Easy on China." *Hill*, November 24, 2020b.

———. "America's Rule of Law v. China's 'Rule by Law.'" *Hill*, December 29, 2020c.

———. "Biden Just Weakened His China Policy and Did Xi Jinping a Big Favor." *Hill*, May 18, 2021.

———. "Biden Must Be Clear with Beijing: It's One China, One Taiwan." *Hill*, December 21, 2021a.

Bouchrika, Imed. *World Ranking of Top Law & Political Scientists*. Research.com, 2023.

Works and Sources Cited | 347

Boustany, Charles, and Aaron Friedberg. *Partial Disengagement: A New U.S. Strategy for Economic Competition with China*. Seattle: National Bureau of Asian Research, 2019.

Bowe, Alexander. *China's Overseas United Front Work: Background and Implications for the United States*. U.S.-China Economic and Security Review Commission, August 24, 2018.

Bowler, Peter. *Evolution: The History of An Idea*. Berkeley: University of California Press, 2009.

Bown, Chad. "US-China Phase One Tracker: China's Purchases of US Goods." Peterson Institute for International Economics, October 26, 2020.

Bradford, Colin. "Perspectives on the Future of the Global Order." Brookings, May 4, 2022.

Brady, Anne-Marie. "Treat Insiders and Outsiders Differently." *China Quarterly* 164, 2000.

———. *Making the Foreign Serve China: Managing Foreigners in the People's Republic*. Lanham, MD: Rowman and Littlefield, 2003.

———. *Magic Weapons: China's Political Influence Activities under Xi Jinping*. The Hague: Clingendael Institute, 2017.

Brand Finance. *Global 500 Brands* (2015–23). London, 2016–23.

———. *Global Soft Power Index, 2022*. London, 2022.

Brands, Hal. "The 'China Hands' Got China Wrong, but Listen to Them Now." Opinion, *Bloomberg*, September 15, 2019.

———. "The Cold War's Lessons for US-China Diplomacy." *Bloomberg*, March 31, 2021.

———. *Getting Ready for a Long War with China*. American Enterprise Institute, July 25, 2022.

Brands, Hal, and Michael Beckley. "China Is a Declining Power—and That's the Problem." *Foreign Policy*, September 24, 2021.

Brands, Hal, and Zack Cooper. "The Great Game with China Is 3D Chess." *Foreign Policy*, December 30, 2020.

Brands, Hal, and Jake Sullivan. "China Has Two Paths to Global Domination." *Foreign Affairs*, May 22, 2020.

Bratton, William. "China Has Already Won Asia's Arms Race: Regional Powers Must Act to Curtail Beijing's Military Supremacy." *Nikkei Asia*, February 14, 2021.

Braudel, Fernand. *Civilization and Capitalism, 15th–18th Century*. 3 vols. Translated by Siân Reynold. Berkeley: University of California Press, 1992.

Brautigam, Deborah. *The Dragon's Gift: The Real Story of China in Africa*. New York: Oxford University Press, 2009.

Brautigam, Deborah, and Meg Rithmire. "The Chinese 'Debt Trap' Is a Myth." *Atlantic*, February 6, 2021.

Breslin, Shaun, and Ren Xiao, eds. "China Debates Its Global Role." Special issue, *Pacific Review* 33, no. 3/4 (2020).

348 | Works and Sources Cited

Breznitz, Dan, and Michael Murphree. *Run of the Red Queen: Government, Innovation, Globalization, and Economic Growth in China*. New Haven, CT: Yale University Press, 2011.

Britton, Jack. "20 Years Later, Victims of Indonesia's May 1998 Riots Are Still Waiting for Justice." *Diplomat*, May 18, 2018.

Britton-Purdy, Jedediah. "What John Rawls Missed." *New Republic*, October 29, 2019.

Brook, Timothy. *Great State: China and the World*. New York: HarperCollins, 2020.

Brouwer, Joseph. "List of Derogatory Nicknames for Xi Leaked amid Crackdown on 'Typos.'" *China Digital Times*, July 20, 2022.

Brown, Kerry. "Why the West Needs to Stop Its Moralising against China." *E-International Relations*, August 10, 2020.

Brown, Michael. "Preparing the United States for the Superpower Marathon with China." Brookings, April 2020.

Brunnermeier, Markus, Rush Doshi, and Harold James. "Beijing's Bismarckian Ghosts: How Great Powers Compete Economically." *Washington Quarterly* 41, no. 3 (2018): 161–76.

Brunnstrom, David. "U.S. Sanctions Four China-Based Individuals, Firm over Fentanyl." Reuters, July 17, 2020.

Brunnstrom, David, and Humeyra Pamuk. "U.S. Secretary of State Nominee Blinken Sees Strong Foundation for Bipartisan China Policy." Reuters, January 19, 2021.

Bryan, William Jennings. *Republic or Empire?* Chicago: Independence, 1899.

Buckley, Chris. "China Readies Strict Security Law for Hong Kong." *New York Times*, June 20, 2020.

———. "She Was a Communist Party Insider in China—Then She Denounced Xi." *New York Times*, August 10, 2020.

———. "'Abrupt Changes': China Caught in a Bind over Russia's Invasion of Ukraine." *New York Times*, February 26, 2022.

———. "Defying China's Censors to Urge Beijing to Denounce Russia's War." *New York Times*, March 21, 2023.

Bull, Hedley. *The Anarchical Society: A Study of Order in World Politics*. New York: Columbia University Press, 2012.

Burke, Edmund. *Reflections on the Revolution in France*. Oxford: Oxford University Press, (1790) 1993.

Burlingame, Anson. "Speech in New York." June 23, 1868. china.usc.edu/anson-burlingame-speech-new-york-june-23-1868.

Burns, James Macgregor. *The American Experiment*. 3 vols. New York: Knopf, 1981–89.

Burns, William. "The United States Needs a New Foreign Policy." *Atlantic*, July 14, 2020.

Busch, Gary. "Organised Crime and International Politics in Asia: Part 2, Greater China." *Ocnus.Net*, February 24, 2019.

Buzan, Barry, and Richard Little. *International Systems in World History*. New York: Oxford University Press, 2000.

Byman, Daniel, and Kenneth Pollack. "Let Us Now Praise Great Men." *International Security* 25, no. 4 (2001): 107–46.

Cabestan, Jean-Pierre. "China's Military Base in Djibouti: A Microcosm of China's Growing Competition with the United States and New Bipolarity." *Journal of Contemporary China* 29, no. 125 (2020): 731–47.

Cadell, Cate. "China Harvests Masses of Data on Western Targets." *Washington Post*, December 31, 2021.

Cai Liang. "Optimizing the International System of Coexistence: From Peaceful-Coexistence to Community of Common Destiny" (蔡亮: 共生国际体系的优化-从和平共处到命运共同体). *Shehui Kexue* (社会科学), no. 5, 2014.

Cai Xia. "The Infighting of the CCP If Full of Possibilities before the 20th Party Congress" (蔡霞: 二十大前中共内斗充满变数). *Yibao* (議報), Washington, DC, February 6, 2022.

Caijing toutiao (财经头条). "The cost of an Olympic gold medal for China is 600 million" (中国一枚奥运金牌的成本是6亿). Beijing, August 17, 2016.

Calhoun, Craig, Dilip Parameshwar Gaonkar, and Charles Taylor. *Degenerations of Democracy*. Cambridge, MA: Harvard University Press, 2022.

Callahan, William. "China 2035: From the China Dream to the World Dream." *Global Affairs* 2, no. 3 (2016): 247–58.

Campbell, David. *Writing Security: United States Foreign Policy and the Politics of Identity*. Minneapolis: University of Minnesota Press, (1992) 1998.

Campbell, Kurt, and Ely Ratner. "The China Reckoning: How Beijing Defied American Expectations." *Foreign Affairs*, March/April 2018.

Campbell, Kurt, and Laura Rosenberger. "Speeches on U.S.-China Relations." Stanford University, May 27 2021.

Campbell, Kurt, and Jake Sullivan. "Competition without Catastrophe." *Foreign Affairs*, September/October 2019.

Campbell, Matthew. "A Chinese Casino Has Conquered a Piece of America." *Bloomberg Businessweek*, February 18, 2015.

Cankao Xiaoxi. "World Decodes the Centennial Great Party" (世界解码百年大党). *Cankao Xiaoxi* (参考消息), Beijing, May 1, 2021.

———. "Russia Becomes China's Largest Oil Provider" (俄罗斯成为中国最大石油供应国). *Cankao Xiaoxi* (参考消息), Beijing, June 21, 2022.

Cao, Huhua, and Vivienne Poy. *The China Challenge: Sino-Canadian Relations in the 21st Century*. Ottawa: University of Ottawa Press, 2011.

Cao Yuan. "Blame the Beggars" (草原: 穷逼国背锅). Weibo (微博), January 26, 2019.

350 | Works and Sources Cited

Cao Yuanzheng. "The Dollar Zone, Euro Zone, and RMB Zone May Form a Tripolarity of International Currency" (曹远征: 美元区、欧元区、人民币区: 国际货币格局或将"三足鼎立"). *China Daily*, Febraury 11, 2022.

Capoccia, Giovanni, and Daniel Kelemen. "The Study of Critical Junctures: Theory, Narrative, and Counterfactuals in Historical Institutionalism." *World Politics* 59, no. 3 (2007): 341–69.

Carafano, James, Michael Pillsbury, Jeff M. Smith, and Andrew Harding. *Winning the New Cold War: A Plan for Countering China*. Heritage Foundation, March 28, 2023.

Carey, Merrick. "Has China's Rise Peaked?" *National Interest*, July 11, 2020.

Carrai, Maria, Jean-Christophe Defraigne, and Jan Wouters. *The Belt and Road Initiative and Global Governance*. Cheltenham, UK: Edward Elgar, 2020.

Carrico, Kevin. *The Great Han: Race, Nationalism, and Tradition in China Today*. Oakland: University of California Press, 2017.

———. "China Studies: Between Censorship and Self-Censorship." *Made in China Journal* 3, no. 2 (2018): 12–15.

———. "Pizza Originated in China, and COVID-19 Originated in Italy?" *Apple Daily*, December 4, 2020.

———. *Two Systems, Two Countries: A Nationalist Guide to Hong Kong*. Oakland: University of California Press, 2022.

Carrol, John. *The Hong Kong-China Nexus: A Brief History*. New York: Cambridge University Press, 2022.

Carter, Ian. "Respect and the Basis of Equality." *Ethics* 121, no. 3 (2011): 538–71.

Case, Anne, and Angus Deaton. *Deaths of Despair and the Future of Capitalism*. Princeton, NJ: Princeton University Press, 2020.

Cass, Oren, and Gabriela Rodriguez. "The Case for a Hard Break with China: Why Economic De-risking Is Not Enough." *Foreign Affairs*, July 25, 2023.

Cave, Danielle, Samantha Hoffman, Alex Joske, Fergus Ryan, and Elise Thomas. *Mapping China's Technology Giants*. Issue Paper no. 15, Australian Strategic Policy Institute, International Cyber Policy Center, 2019.

CCP Central History and Archives Bureau. *Digest of Xi Jinping's Treaties on Great Power Diplomacy with Chinese Characteristics* (中共中央党史和文献研究院.习近平关于中国特色大国外交论述摘编). Beijing: Zhongyang wenxian, 2020.

CCP Central Party School. "Fully Understand Sticking to the Bottom Line Thinking" (深刻认识坚持底线思维). *Renmin ribao* (人民日报), Beijing, June 25, 2020.

CCP Foreign Liaison Department. "The CCP Deeply Altered the Trajectory of Human History" (中国共产党深刻改变了人类历史的发展轨迹). *Renmin Ribao* (人民日报), July 1, 2020.

CCP Organization Department of the Chinese Community Party. *Internal Statistical Report of the CCP* (中国共产党党内统计公报). Beijing, June 2 023.

Works and Sources Cited | 351

CCTV. "FDI Leaving Affects 45 Million Rice Bowls" (外资出走动4500万人饭碗). February 26, 2017.

———. "Salute! Please Repost Today for 197,653 Martyrs" (致敬! 今天请为197653名烈士转发). October 25, 2019.

———. *International Commentaries of News Simulcast* (新闻联播国际锐评). April 30, 2020.

———. "Xi Jinping meets Biden virtually" (习近平与拜登举行视频会晤). November 16, 2021.

———. "Xi Jinping meets Blinken (习近平会见布林肯). June 19, 2023.

Ceci, Michael, and Lawrence Rubin. "China's 5G Networks: A Tool for Advancing Digital Authoritarianism Abroad?" *Orbis* 66, no. 2 (2022): 270–88.

Cecil, Robert. *The Myth of the Master Race: Alfred Rosenberg and Nazi Ideology.* London: Batsford, 1972.

Center for China and Globalization. "30 Events in 10 days: CCG Visits the US" (十天三十场活动 CCG访美). CCG, July 12, 2022.

Central Committee of the Chinese Communist Party. "What Is Community of Common Destiny for Humanity?" (什么是人类命运共同体). Beijing, January 2018.

CFR. "Insights from 8th Council of Councils Conference." Council on Foreign Relations, May 7–May 9, 2019.

———. *U.S.-Taiwan Relations in a New Era*, Task Force Report No. 81, June 2023.

Cha, Sangmi. "South Korea Pivots to 'Hard-Line Stance' With China." *Bloomberg*, June 13, 2023.

Chambers, David. "The Past and Present State of Chinese Intelligence Historiography." *Studies in Intelligence* 56, no. 3 (2012): 31–46.

Chan, Kelvin. "After Years Grappling with Google, Europe Has Tips for US." Associated Press, October 21, 2020.

Chan, Melissa. "China Ends the Clubhouse Spring." *Foreign Policy*, February 8, 2021.

Chan, Steve, Huiyun Feng, Kai He, and Weixing Hu. *Contesting Revisionism: China, the United States, and the Transformation of International Order.* New York: Oxford University Press, 2021.

Chan, Yuk Wah, ed. *The Chinese/Vietnamese Diaspora: Revisiting the Boat People.* New York: Routledge, 2011.

Chang, David Cheng. *The Hijacked War: The Story of Chinese POWs in the Korean War.* Stanford, CA: Stanford University Press, 2020.

Chang, Gordon. "China Seeds: A Biological Attack on America?" *Online Report*, Gatestone Institute, July 30, 2020.

———. "American Traitors: Academics Working for China." *Gatestone*, December 30, 2021.

———. "China Is Becoming the Soviet Union." *19FortyFive*, December 26, 2021a.

352 | Works and Sources Cited

————. "Disaster for Everyone: China Cuts Itself off From the World." *Newsweek*, August 25, 2022.

Chang, Kenneth. "Scientists Achieve Nuclear Fusion Breakthrough with Blast of 192 Lasers." *New York Times*, December 13, 2022.

Chang Siying. "Interview of Chief Editor of the China Quarterly" (常思颖: 专访当代中国研究知名学刊《中国季刊》主编). BBC in Chinese, September 2, 2022.

Chang Xi. "Can 'Great Translation Campaign' Counter Great External Propaganda" (昌西: "大翻譯運動"能否對抗大外宣). *Initium Media* (端傳媒), Hong Kong, March 24, 2022.

Charon, Paul, and Jena-Baptiste Jeangène Vilmer. *Chinese Influence Operations: A Machiavellian Moment*. 2nd ed. Institute for Strategic Research (IRSEM) report. Paris: Ministry of Armed Forces, 2021.

Chase, Stuart. *The Tyranny of Words*. New York: Harper, 1959.

Chatzky, Andrew, and James McBride. "China's Massive Belt and Road Initiative." Council on Foreign Relations, 2020.

Chayes, Sarah. *Thieves of State: Why Corruption Threatens Global Security*. New York: Norton, 2016.

Chen Aizhu. "Russia, China Agree 30-Year Gas Deal via New Pipeline, to Settle in Euros." Reuters, February 4, 2022.

Chen, Cheng. *The Return of Ideology: The Search for Regime Identities in Postcommunist Russia and China*. Ann Arbor: University of Michigan Press, 2016.

Chen Chuanren. "Overseas Chinese Form Special Political Force" (陈传仁: 海外华人形成特殊政治力量). *Huanqiu Shibao* (环球时报), Beijing, June 9, 2006.

Chen Cunfu. "Was There Ever a Thucydides' Trap in Ancient Greece?" (陈村富: 古希腊有过"修昔底德陷阱"吗). *Nanguo Xueshu* (南國學術) 10, no. 3 (2020): 356–63.

Chen Jian. "Chinese and American Misjudgment and the Making and Prolonging of the Korean War." Wilson Center, June 23, 2020.

————. *Cannot Let History All Become Ashes: Critical Notes on the Political History of the Cultural Revolution* (陳兼: 怎忍青史盡成灰: 文革政治史批判筆記). Hong Kong: Oxford University Press, 2021.

Chen Junji. "Dispute over China's Overseas Military Bases" (陈俊杰: 中国海外军事基地之争). *Fuxing Wang* (复兴网), December 1, 2021.

Chen Kaizhi. "Remembering the Southern Trip by Deng Xiaoping in 1992" (陈开枝: 回忆邓小平1992年南方之行). *Renmin wang* (人民网) Beijing, August 17, 2015.

Chen, King C. *China's War with Vietnam, 1979*. Stanford, CA: Hoover Institution, 1987.

Chen Lifeng. "Zhou Enlai Planned Ahead to Forge the Backbone of the New China's Diplomacy." *Zhongguo Gongchandang Xinwen Wang* (中国共产党新闻网), Beijing, February 2007.

Works and Sources Cited | 353

Chen Shenshen. "The Political Logic of the Zhongnanhai Empire" (陈申申: 中南海帝国的政治逻辑). Blog essay, Shanghai, November 16, 2020.

Chen Shuguang. "Contribute the China Solution for the World" (陈曙光: 向世界贡献中国方案). *Guangming Ribao* (光明日报), October 10, 2018.

Chen Tianhua. *Alarm to Awaken the Age* (陳天華: 警世鐘). Beijing: Huaxia, (1903) 2002.

Chen Wenling. "Several Dimensions of Cooperation Exist between China and the US in the Next 4 years" (陈文玲: 中美未来4年存在多种合作面向). *China News*, December 7, 2020.

———. "The World after the Pandemic, De-Chinese or De-American" (陈文玲: 疫情之后, 世界去中国化还是去美国化). China Center for International Economic Exchanges, May 18, 2020.

Chen, Xiao, Vyacheslav Fos, and Wei Jiang. "Race to Lead: How China's Government Interventions Shape U.S.-China Industrial Competition." SCCEI Brief, Center on China's Economy and Institutions, Stanford University, August 1, 2022.

Chen Yan. "China Spends 45 Billion to Start State PR Strategy to Remake New Image" (陳焱:中國耗資450億啟動國家公關戰略重塑形象). *Xin shiji zhoukan* (新世紀周刊), March 11, 2009.

Chen, Yi, Ziying Fan, Xiaomin Gu, and Li-An Zhou. "Arrival of Young Talent: The Send-Down Movement and Rural Education in China." *American Economic Review* 110, no. 11 (2020): 3393–430.

Chen Yuanyuan. "Nothing Is Small in Diplomacy" (陈媛媛: 外交无小事). Ministry of Foreign Affairs, November 1, 2013. fmprc.gov.cn.

Chen, Yun-yu, and Emerson Lim. "Declassified Cables Reveal U.S. Assurances on Taiwan's Defense." *Focus Taiwan*, August 31, 2020.

Cheng, Dean, Peter Garretson, Namrata Goswami, James Lewis, Bruce W. MacDonald, Kazuto Suzuki, Brian C. Weeden, and Nicholas Wright. *Outer Space; Earthly Escalation? Chinese Perspectives on Space Operations and Escalation*. Strategic Multilayer Assessment Periodic Publication, August 2018.

Cheng, Evelyn. "China's Xi Says Trade with Russia Expected to Hit New Records in the Coming Months." CNBC, June 17, 2022.

Cheng, Selina. "Now Macau's Pro-Democracy Politicians Face a Hong Kong–Style Crackdown." *Hong Kong Free Press*, July 13, 2021.

Cheng, Yangyang. "The Battlefield of Memory." *Los Angles Review of Books*, December 15, 2020.

Cheng, Yinghong. *Discourses of Race and Rising China*. London: Palgrave, 2019.

Cheng Zhiqiang. "China Solution to Promote World Peace and Development" (程志强: 促进世界和平与发展的中国方案). *Renmin Ribao* (人民日报), April 2, 2020.

354 | Works and Sources Cited

Cheong, Ching. "The Fall of Hong Kong: China's Strategic Plan to Conquer Hong Kong and Purge It of Its People." Middle East Media Research Institute, February 24, 2021.

Cheung, Helier, and Roland Hughes. "Why Are There Protests in Hong Kong? All the Context You Need." BBC News, May 21, 2020.

Chew, Allen. *The White Death: The Epic of the Soviet-Finnish Winter War.* East Lansing: Michigan State University Press, 1971.

Chey, Hyoung-Kyu, and Yu Wai Vic Li. "Chinese Domestic Politics and the Internationalization of the Renminbi." *Political Science Quarterly* 135, no. 1 (2020): 37–65.

Chin, Josh. "U.S. Foreign-Policy Experts Call for Cooperation with China on Coronavirus." *Wall Street Journal,* July 8, 2020.

China Daily. China's Fight Against COVID-19. Beijing, April 21, 2020.

———. "Biden's China Policy Smacks of Trumpism." Editorial, Beijing, February 25, 2021.

China Foreign Affairs University. *Report assessing American scholars who comprehend China* (外交学院： 美国知华派评估报告), January 15, 2015.

China Power Team. "Is China Succeeding at Shaping Global Narratives about COVID-19?" Washington: CSIS, October 22, 2021.

China Watch Institute et al., eds. *China's Fight against COVID-19.* April 22, 2020.

Chinoy, Mike. *Assignment China: An Oral History of American Journalists in the People's Republic.* New York: Columbia University Press, 2023.

Chomsky, Noam. "American Decline: Causes and Consequences." *Al-Akhbar,* August 24, 2011.

Chorzempa, Martin. *The Cashless Revolution: China's Reinvention of Money and the End of America's Domination in Finance and Technology.* New York: Public Affairs, 2022.

Chowdhury, Naoreen. "Why the U.S. Is Threatening to Delist China Stars like Alibaba." *Bloomberg,* March 30, 2021.

Christensen, Thomas. *The China Challenge: Shaping the Choices of a Rising Power.* New York: Norton, 2015.

———. *A Modern Tragedy? COVID-19 and US-China Relations.* Brookings, May 2020.

———. "There Will Not Be a New Cold War: The Limits of U.S.-Chinese Competition." *Foreign Affairs,* March 24, 2021.

Chu, Yun-han, and Zheng Yongnian, eds. *The Decline of the Western-Centric World and the Emerging New Global Order.* Abingdon, UK: Routledge, 2021.

Ci, Jiwei. *Democracy in China: The Coming Crisis.* Cambridge, MA: Harvard University Press, 2019.

CICIR (China Institutes of Contemporary International Relations). *Series on State Security in Totality* (中国现代国际关系研究院: 总体国家安全观系列丛书). 6 vols. Beijing: Shishi, April 2021.

Works and Sources Cited | 355

———. *Strategic and Security Review 2020–2021* (中国现代国际关系研究院: 国际战略与安全形势评估2020/2021). Beijing, 2021a.

CISS (Center for International Security and Strategy). *Report on China's External Security Risk 2022* (清华大学战略与安全研究中心: 2022年中国外部安全风险展望报告). Beijing: CISS, 2022.

Clayton, Christopher, Antonio Coppola, Amanda Dos Santos, Matteo Maggiori, and Jesse Schreger. *China in Tax Havens*. NBER Working Paper no. 30865, January 2023.

Cliff, Roger. *A New U.S. Strategy for the Indo-Pacific*. NBR Special Report no. 86, National Bureau of Asian Research, June 2020.

Cline, Eric H. *1177 B.C.: The Year Civilization Collapsed*. Princeton, NJ: Princeton University Press, 2015.

Clinton, Hillary R. "A National Security Reckoning: How Washington Should Think about Power." *Foreign Affairs*, November/December 2020.

Cochrane, John, Niall Ferguson, and H. R. McMaster. "Ameri-Can or Can't? China's Looming Demographic and Economic Collapse." Seminar at the Hoover Institution, August 25, 2022.

Cohen, Jerome. "More Thoughts on the Open Letter 'China Is Not an Enemy.'" Jerome A. Cohen blog, July 11, 2019.

Cohen, Jon. "Inside the Circle of Trust." *Science*, August 2, 2019, 430–37.

Cohen, Paul. *A Path Twice Traveled: My Journey as a Historian of China*. Cambridge, MA: Harvard Asia Center, 2019.

Cohen, Roger. "French Diplomacy Undercuts U.S. Efforts to Rein China In." *New York Times*, April 8, 2023.

Colby, Elbridge. "America Can Defend Taiwan." *Wall Street Journal*, January 26, 2021.

———. *The Strategy of Denial: American Defense in an Age of Great Power Conflict*. New Haven, CT: Yale University Press, 2021a.

———. "The U.S. Must Support Ukraine, but China Must Be Our Priority." *Time*, February 27, 2022.

Collins, Gabriel, and Andrew Erickson. *U.S.-China Competition Enters the Decade of Maximum Danger*. Houston: Rice University Baker Institute for Public Policy, 2021.

Collins, Michael. "The WHO and China: Dereliction of Duty." Council on Foreign Relations (blog), February 27, 2020.

Cone, Paige, ed. *Assessing the Influence of Hypersonic Weapons on Deterrence*. Future Warfare Series no.59, US Air Force, June 2019.

Confucius et al. *Book of Rituals—Destiny of Rituals* (孔子: 论语·礼记–礼运); *Jishi 16* (季氏第十六); *Xueer* (学而). Beijing: Zhonghua Shuju, (5th–3rd centuries BCE) 2016.

Conger, Kate. "Twitter Removes Chinese Disinformation Campaign." *New York Times*, June 17, 2020.

356 | Works and Sources Cited

Connors, Emma. "Thailand, Indonesia Consider Booster Jab amid Sinovac Doubts." *Australian Financial Review*, July 6, 2021.

Cook, Sarah. "China's Media Influence Has Gone Global—So Has the Pushback." *Diplomat*, June 18, 2020.

Cook, Thomas, and Malcolm Moos. "Foreign Policy: The Realism of Idealism." *American Political Science* 46, no. 2 (1952): 343–56.

Cooley, Alexander, and Daniel Nexon. *Exit from Hegemony: The Unraveling of the American Global Order*. New York: Oxford University Press, 2020.

Cooper, Helene, Edward Wong, and Chris Buckley. "China Condemns U.S. Decision to Shoot Down Spy Balloon." *New York Times*, February 5, 2023.

Cooper, Marshall. "Your New China Problem: The Calculus for Doing Business in China Just Changed." Corporate Board Member, unpublished paper, April 2021.

Copeland, Dale C. *Economic Interdependence and War*. Princeton, NJ: Princeton University Press, 2014.

Corr, Anders. *Great Powers, Grand Strategies: The New Game in the South China Sea*. Annapolis, MD: Naval Institute Press, 2018.

———. "Democratizing China Should Be the U.S. Priority." *Journal of Political Risk* 7, no. 7 (2019).

———. "Defeating China: Five Strategies." *Journal of Political Risk* 8, no. 4 (2020).

———. *The Concentration of Power: Institutionalization, Hierarchy and Hegemony*. Montreal: Optimum, 2021.

Corrigan, Jack, James Dunham, and Remco Zwetsloot. *The Long-Term Stay Rates of International STEM PhD Graduates*. CSET Issue Brief, Georgetown University, April 2022.

Cowley, Robert, ed. *What If? The World's Foremost Historians Imagine What Might Have Been*. New York: Berkley Books, 1999.

Crabtree, James. "China's Radical New Vision of Globalization." *Noema Magazine*, December 2020.

Crane, Brent. "The Price of Admission: How Chinese Money and American Greed Turned the EB-5 Visa Program into a Cesspool of Illegality." *The Wire*, August 23, 2020.

Craymer, Lucy. "China's National-Security Law Reaches into Harvard, Princeton Classrooms." *Wall Street Journal*, August 19, 2020.

Crow, Carl. *400 Million Customers*. Hong Kong: Earnshaw, 1937.

CSIS. Confronting Chinese State Capitalism. Conference, February 16, 2021. csis.org/events/confronting-chinese-state-capitalism.

Cui Liru. "Some Assessment of the Biden Administration's Policy" (崔立如: 对拜登政府政策的几点判断). Chinese Society of America Studies, April 25, 2021.

Cumings, Bruce. *The Korean War: A History*. New York: Modern Library, 2010.

Cunningham, Edward, Tony Saich, and Jesse Turiel. *Understanding CCP Resilience: Surveying Chinese Public Opinion through Time*. Ash Center, Harvard University, July 2020.

Works and Sources Cited | 357

Cutler, Lloyd N. "The Right to Intervene." *Foreign Affairs*, Fall 1985.

Da Wei. "Direction of the Evolution of Current International Order and China's Choices" (达巍: 现行国际秩序演变的方向与中国的选择). *Guoji Wenti Yanjiu* (国际问题研究), no. 1, 2021.

———. "China Should Emphasis the Big Picture and Keep Sufficient Connection to the World" (达巍: 中国要着眼于大势, 保持同全球充分连接). Tsinghua University, June 14, 2022.

Dahir, Abdi Latif. "The Growing Membership of a China-Led Development Bank Challenges the IMF-World Bank Orthodoxy." *Quartz*, May 9, 2018.

Dai Er. "100 Million Middle Eastern Fans Addicted to Chinese App" (戴尔:1 亿中东老铁迷上中国APP). *Global Insights—36kr* (霞光社—36氪), Beijing, May 12, 2021.

Dai Yaoyao and Rose Luwei Luqiu. "China's 'Wolf Warrior' Diplomats Like to Talk Tough." *Washington Post*, May 12, 2021.

Dalio, Ray. "Don't Be Blind to China's Rise in a Changing World." *Financial Times*, October 23, 2020.

———. *The Changing World Order*. New York: Avid Reader, 2021.

———. "What I Think Is Going On." Essay, LinkedIn, April 26, 2023.

Dante Alighieri. *De monarchia*. Translated by Aurelia Henry. New York: Houghton, (1313) 1904.

Daqiong and Luo Wangshu. "Sichuan-Tibet Railway to Be Completed in 2025." *China Daily*, November 8, 2016.

Darwin, John. *After Tamerlane: The Rise and Fall of Global Empires, 1400–2000*. New York: Bloomsbury, 2009.

———. *The Empire Project: The Rise and Fall of the British World-System, 1830–1970*. Cambridge: Cambridge University Press, 2009a.

———. *Unfinished Empire: The Global Expansion of Britain*. New York: Bloomsbury, 2013.

Daudin, Guillaume, Matthias Morys, and Kevin H. O'Rourke. "Globalization, 1870–1914." In *The Cambridge Economic History of Modern Europe*, vol. 2, edited by Stephen Broadberry and Kevin O'Rourke, 5–29. Cambridge: Cambridge University Press, 2010.

Davenport, Christian. *The Space Barons: Elon Musk, Jeff Bezos, and the Quest to Colonize the Cosmos*. New York: Public Affairs, 2018.

David, Charles, and David Grondin. *Hegemony or Empire?* Farnham, UK: Ashgate, 2006.

Davies, Christian. "North Korea Looks across the Border for Its Biggest Threat." *Financial Times*, December 11, 2021.

Davis, Bob, and Wei Lingling. *Superpower Showdown*. New York: Harper, 2020.

Davis, Bob, and Lingling Wei. "The Soured Romance between China and Corporate America: For Years, Big U.S. Firms Were Beijing's Most Reliable Allies in Washington—Now They're Taking a Harder Stand." *Wall Street Journal*, June 5, 2020.

358 | Works and Sources Cited

Davis, Michael. "Hong Kong Is Part of the Mainland Now." *Foreign Affairs*, July/August 2020.

Dawkins, Richard. *The Selfish Gene*. Oxford: Oxford University Press, (1976) 2016.

Dawn, Aurora. "Forget Glenn: Remembering Dr. Martin Luther King, Jr., in His Own Words." *Daily Kos*, August 31, 2010.

De Na. "Comments on Yan Xutong's Latest Views" (德纳: 对阎学通近期言论的评论). *Kunlunce* (昆仑策), Beijing, July 1, 2022.

de Ávila, María, Bosco Marti, Riyad Insanally, and Claudia Trevisan. *US-China Vaccine Diplomacy: Lessons from Latin America and the Caribbean*. Atlantic Council, February 23, 2022.

Deep Tech Research. *AI Research Rankings 2022: Sputnik Moment for China?* Thundermark Capital, May 2022.

Demick, Barbara. "The Times, Bloomberg News, and the Richest Man in China." *New Yorker*, May 5, 2015.

Deng Liqun, ed. *Diplomatic Strategist Mao Zedong* (邓力群: 外交战略家毛泽东). Beijing: Zhongyang Minzu Daxue, 2004.

Deng Xiaomang. "Why the Western Culture Became the Superior Culture Today?" (邓晓芒: 西方文化凭什么成为当今的强势文化？). *Aisixiang* (爱思想), Beijing, May 24, 2022.

Desch, Michael. "War Is a Choice, Not a Trap." *Defense Priorities*, July 19, 2022.

Desiderio, Andrew. "Senate Passes China Sanctions Bill after White House Relents." *Politico*, June 25, 2020.

Desmet, Mattias. *The Psychology of Totalitarianism* (De physchologie van totalitarisme). Translated by Els Vanbrabant. London: Chelsea Green, 2022.

Deveaux, Fred. *Democracy Perception Index 2020*. Berlin: Dalia, 2020.

Di Dongsheng. "The Renminbi's Rise and Chinese Politics." In *The Power of Currencies and Currencies of Power*, edited by Alan Wheatley, 115–26. Abingdon, UK: Routledge, 2013.

———. "The Economics and Politics of China's Currency Internationalization." *Global Asia* 12, no. 2 (2020): 58–64.

———. "Should Push for RMB Internationalization This Time" (翟东升: 这次该推进人民币国际化了). *Sina Caijing* (新浪财经). Beijing, April 4 and May 3, 2020.

———. "We Have Old Friends inside the Core Circles of American Power and Influence—Nothing in the World Cannot Be Settled with US$" (美国的权势核心圈有我们的老朋友-天下没有美元搞不定的事情). *Guan Media* (观视频), November 28, 2020.

———. "Why Sino-American Relations Got to This Point" (中美关系为什么走到了这一步). Yiwan Academy (亿万学院), Beijing, August 5, 2020.

———. *Parallel and Competition: Governance of China in the Era of Two Circulations* (平行与竞争—双循环时代的中国治理). Beijing: Dongfang, 2021.

———. "Thoughts on 'New Cold War'" (关于"新冷战"的几点思考). Essay, April 29, 2023.

Di Li Ren. "How's the Construction of First Artificial Island in the South China Sea" (地历人: 南海第一人工岛建设如何). *Baidu baike* (百度百科), June 28, 2022.

Diamond, Larry, and Orville Schell, eds. *Chinese Influence and American Interests*. Stanford, CA: Hoover Institution, 2018.

Dimitrov, Martin K. *Dictatorship and Information: Authoritarian Regime Resilience in Communist Europe and China*. New York: Oxford University Press, 2022.

Ding Ling. "Is the US an Empire?" (丁霖: 美国是不是一个帝国). *Ershiyi Shiji Jingji Baodao* (21世纪经济报道), June 6, 2014.

Ding Xuexiang. "To Unite and Struggle to Fully Promote the Great Rejuvenation of the Chinese Nation" (丁薛祥: 为全面推进中华民族伟大复兴而团结奋斗). *Renmin Ribao* (人民日报), November 2, 2022.

Diresta, Renée, Carly Miller, Vanessa Molter, John Pomfret, and Glenn Tiffert. *Telling China's Story: The Chinese Communist Party's Campaign to Shape Global Narratives*. Internet Observatory, Stanford Cyber Policy Center, 2020.

Distelhorst, Greg, and Yue Hou. "Ingroup Bias in Official Behavior: A National Field Experiment in China." *Quarterly Journal of Political Science* 9, no. 2 (2014): 203–30.

Dittmer, Lowell. *Taiwan and China: Fitful Embrace*. Oakland: University of California Press, 2017.

Doig, Will. "The Belt and Road Initiative Is a Corruption Bonanza." *Foreign Policy*, January 15, 2019.

Dong Chunling. "Reflection on China Policy in US Strategy Circles and Its Revelations" (董春岭: 美国战略界的对华政策反思及启示). China Institutes of Contemporary International Relations (中国现代国际关系研究院), *Zhongmei Jujiao* (中美聚焦), Beijing, October 5, 2022.

Dong Zhengrui. "Synopsis on Recent Studies on 'Once in a Century Change' among Domestic Scholars" (董振瑞: 近年来国内学术界关于"百年未有之大变局"研究述评). *Dangde Wenxian* (党的文献), Beijing, August 5, 2020.

Donnet, Pierre-Antoine. *Tibet mort ou vif* (Life and Death in Tibet). Paris: Folio, 1993.

Dorfman, Zach. "The Disappeared: China's Global Kidnapping Campaign Has Gone on for Years. It May Now Be Reaching inside U.S. Borders." *Foreign Policy*, March 29, 2018.

Doromal, Krystle. "From Yellow Peril to Yellow Fever." *Offscreen* 11, no. 5 (2007).

Doshi, Rush. *The Long Game: China's Grand Strategy to Displace American Order*. Oxford: Oxford University Press, 2021.

Dower, John W. "Yellow Promise/Yellow Peril." *Visualizing Cultures*, MIT, 2008.

Dozier, Rush, Jr. *Fear Itself*. New York: St. Martin's, 1998.

360 | Works and Sources Cited

———. *Why We Hate*. Chicago: Contemporary Books, 2002.

Dreher, Axel, Andreas Fuchs, Bradley Parks, Austin Strange, and Michael J. Tierney. *Banking on Beijing: The Aims and Impacts of China's Overseas Development Program*. New York: Cambridge University Press, 2022.

Dreyer, June Teufel. "Rare Earths, Scarce Metals, and the Struggle for Supply Chain Security." Foreign Policy Research Institute, March 30, 2022.

Driessen, Miriam. *Tales of Hope, Tastes of Bitterness: Chinese Road Builders in Ethiopia*. Hong Kong: Hong Kong University Press, 2019.

Drohan, Thomas. "A Basic Strategy toward China: Rules-Based Competition That Cooperates and Confronts." International Center for Security and Leadership, June 26, 2020.

Drucker, Peter. *The End of Economic Man: The Origins of Totalitarianism*. New York: Routledge, (1939) 2017.

Drug Enforcement Administration (DEA). *Fentanyl Flow to the United States*. Intelligence report, January 2020.

Du Fu. *Out Frontier-First Series-VI* (杜甫: 前出塞其六). In *Collection of Poems by Du Fu* (杜甫诗集). Shanghai: Guji, (8th century) 2021.

Du Shangze. "Big Strides on the Historical March towards the Great Rejuvenation of the Chinese Nation" (杜尚泽: 阔步走在中华民族伟大复兴的历史征程上). *Renmin Ribao* (人民日报), January 5, 2016.

Duan Siyu and Huang Siyu. "Liu He: A New Sate of Two-Circular Economy Is Forming in China" (段思宇&黄思瑜: 刘鹤-中国双循环发展新格局正在形成). *Yicai* (第一财经), June 18, 2020.

Duan Xiujian. "Sky High Price Bid for CI Website" (段修健: 孔子学院网站天价中标). *Xinjing Bao* (新京报), January 22, 2010.

Duara, Prasenjit. *Culture, Power, and the State: Rural North China, 1900–1942*. Stanford, CA: Stanford University Press, 1988.

Dube, Ryan, and Gabriele Steinhauser. "China's Global Mega-Projects Are Falling Apart." *Wall Street Journal*, January 20, 2023.

Dudley, Renee, and Jeff Kao. "The Disinfomercial: How Larry King Got Duped into Starring in Chinese Propaganda." *ProPublica*, July 30, 2020.

Dugin, Alexander. *Eurasian Mission: An Introduction to Neo-Eurasianism*. Budapest: Arktos, 2014.

Dutkiewicz, Piotr, V. V. Kulikov, and Richard Sakwa, eds. *The Social History of Post-Communist Russia*. Abingdon, UK: Routledge, 2016.

Dyer, Gwynne. "Xinjiang: The Silence of the Muslims." *Japan Times*, March 22, 2019.

EAI (East Asia Institute). *Like-Minded Democracies under Shared Vision*. Seoul, September 24, 2020.

Eban, Katherine. "The Lab-Leak Theory: Inside the Fight to Uncover COVID-19's Origins." *Vanity Fair*, June 3, 2021.

Works and Sources Cited | 361

———. "'This Shouldn't Happen': Inside the Virus-Hunting Nonprofit at the Center of the Lab-Leak Controversy." *Vanity Fair*, March 31, 2022.

Eberts, Jake. "Why Do Analysts Keep Talking Nonsense about Chinese Words?" *Foreign Policy*, July 6, 2021.

Eckstein, Megan. "Navy Says China Fight Is Most Likely in 2020s." *Defense News*, March 3, 2022.

Economist. "Hong Kong's Protests: A Tough Test for China's Leaders." September 29, 2014.

———. "China Wants to Make the Yuan a Central-Bank Favourite." May 7, 2020.

———. "China Is Betting That the West Is in Irreversible Decline." April 3, 2021.

———. "China Is Happy to See America Humbled in Afghanistan." August 21, 2021.

———. "The Threat from the Illiberal Left" and "Left-Wing Activists Are Using Old Tactics in a New Assault on Liberalism." September 4, 2021.

———. "Why China Will Not Surpass the United States." August 30, 2021.

———. "America and China Are One Military Accident Away from Disaster." January 15, 2022.

———. "The Battle between Asia's Financial Centres Is Heating Up." July 2, 2022.

———. "Don't Underestimate Xi Jinping's Bond with Vladimir Putin." April 9, 2022.

———. "America's Economic Outperformance Is a Marvel to Behold." April 13, 2023.

———. "Peak China?" May 11, 2023.

———. "Riding High: The Lessons of America's Astonishing Economy." April 15, 2023.

———. "These Countries Could Lure Manufacturing away from China: Call Them 'Altasia.'" March 3, 2023.

Economy, Elizabeth. *The Third Revolution: Xi Jinping and the New Chinese State*. New York: Oxford University Press, 2019.

———. *The World According to China*. Cambridge, UK: Polity, 2022.

———. "Xi Jinping's New World Order." *Foreign Affairs*, January/February 2022a.

Egan, Matt. "JP Morgan Fined for Hiring Kids of China's Elite to Win Business." CNN, November 17, 2016.

Einstein, Albert. "Einstein's Final Speech Given in Europe, at the Royal Albert Hall." London, October 3, 1933.

Eisenman, Joshua. "U.S. Institutions Must Get Smarter about Chinese Communist Party Money." *Foreign Policy*, August 31, 2021.

Eisenman, Joshua, and David Shinn. *China's Relations with Africa: A New Era of Strategic Engagement*. New York: Columbia, 2023.

Elleman, Bruce. *Diplomacy and Deception: Secret History of Sino-Soviet Diplomatic Relations, 1917–27*. London: Routledge, 1997.

362 | Works and Sources Cited

Elleman, Bruce, Stephen Kotkin, and Clive Schofield, eds. *Beijing's Power and China's Borders: Twenty Neighbors in Asia.* Armonk, NY: Sharpe, 2013.

Enright, Michael. *Developing China: The Remarkable Impact of Foreign Direct Investment.* Abingdon, UK: Routledge, 2017.

Epstein, Gady. "Panda Hugger vs. Dragon Slayer." *Forbes,* January 29, 2010.

Epstein, Julius. *Operation Keelhaul: The Story of Forced Repatriation from 1944 to the Present.* New York: Devin-Adair, 1973.

Erickson, Andrew. "2013 PRC-Ukraine Treaty of Friendship and Cooperation/ Joint Communiqué." March 13, 2022. AndrewErickson.com.

Erickson, Andrew, and Gabriel Collins. "Competition with China Can Save the Planet." *Foreign Affairs,* May/June 2021.

Erlanger, Steven. "Backlash Builds against China over Coronavirus." *New York Times,* May 3, 2020.

Esper, Mark. "The Pentagon Is Prepared for China." *Wall Street Journal,* August 24, 2020.

———. "U.S. Vision for Security in the Indo-Pacific Region." IISS webinar, July 21, 2020.

Espina, Nonoy, and Jojo Rinoza. "Philippine Communist Leadership Orders Guerrillas to Go after Chinese Firms." *BenarNews,* October 14, 2020.

Espiner, Guyon. "Chinese Communist Party Spies in NZ Universities." *New Zealand Herald,* June 27, 2021.

ET Bureau. "India Bans 59 Chinese Apps Including TikTok, Helo, WeChat." *India Times,* July 13, 2020.

ETNC. *Annual Report on European-Chinese Relations.* Brussels: European Think-Tank Network on China, 2015–22.

EU Commission. *Antitrust: Commission Fines Google €1.49 Billion.* March 20, 2019.

———. *Antitrust: Commission Sends Statement of Objections to Amazon.* November 10, 2020.

Evans, Peter. *Dependent Development: The Alliance of Multinational, State, and Local Capital in Brazil.* Princeton, NJ: Princeton University Press, 1979.

Evans-Pritchard, Ambrose. "Lone Wolf: The West Should Bide Its Time, Friendless China Is in Trouble." *Sydney Morning Herald,* July 10, 2020.

Ewing, Philip. "Trump, Retaliating against Beijing, Revokes Privileges for Hong Kong." NPR, May 29, 2020.

Fabricius, Peter. *Is COVID-19 Enabling Debt-Trap Diplomacy, Will Mombasa and Port Sudan Be Ceded to Foreign Powers to Repay Debt?* Institute for Security Studies, Pretoria, April 30, 2020.

Fairclough, Gordon, Sarah Childress, and Marc Champion. "Probes Involve Firm Linked to China Leader's Son." *Wall Street Journal,* July 22, 2009.

Fan Haixing. "Red China's Endgame Is North Korean-ization" (范海辛: 红色中国最后的归宿就是北韩化). IPK Media (光传媒), May 26, 2020.

Works and Sources Cited | 363

Fan Jiayang. "How My Mother and I Became Chinese Propaganda." *New Yorker*, September 14, 2020.

Fan, Wenxin, and Shen Lu. "Determined to Flee China, Thousands Take a Long, Dangerous Route to the Southern U.S. Border." *Wall Street Journal*, April 16, 2023.

Fan Yifei. "Analysis of the Policy Implication of M0 Position of Digital RMB" (范一飞: 关于数字人民币M0定位的政策含义分析). *Renmin Wang* (人民网), Beijing, September 15, 2020.

Fanell, James. "China's Global Navy." *Naval War College Review* 73, no. 4 (2020).

Fanell, James, et al. "Stay the Course on China: An Open Letter to President Trump." *Journal of Political Risk*, July 18, 2019.

Fang, Alex. "Biden Pushes Belt and Road Rival 'Blue Dot' with Japan and Australia." *Nikkei Asia*, June 9, 2021.

Fang Kecheng. *Old Friends of the Chinese People* (方可成: 中国人民的老朋友). Beijing: Renmin Ribao, 2014.

———. "Praise from the International Community: How China Uses Foreign Experts to Legitimize Authoritarian Rule." *China Journal* 87, no. 1 (2022): 72–91.

Fang, Kecheng, and Maria Repnikova. "Demystifying 'Little Pink.'" *New Media and Society* 20, no. 6 (2017): 2162–85.

Fang Ning. "On 'Behind Will Be Beaten'" (房宁":落后挨打"辨). *Zhongguo baodao* (中国报道), April 4, 2000.

Fang Zhou. "His Crises" (他的危机). WeChat (微信公众号), April 27, 2022a.

———. "Xi Jinping and New China" (方舟: 习近平与新中国). Matters.news, January 19, 2022.

Farese, Gian Marco, and Yuko Asano-Cavanagh. "Analysing Nostalgia in Cross-Linguistic Perspective." *Philology* 4 (2019): 213–41.

Fassihi, Farnaz, and Steven Lee Myers. "Defying U.S., China and Iran Near Trade and Military Partnership." *New York Times*, July 12, 2020.

———. "China, with $400 Billion Iran Deal, Could Deepen Influence in Mideast," *New York Times*, March 28, 2021.

Federal Bureau of Investigation (FBI). *China: The Risk to Academia*. Washington, 2020.

———. "Five Individuals Charged Variously with Stalking, Harassing, and Spying on U.S. Residents on Behalf of the PRC Secret Police." USDJ, March 16, 2022.

Fei Chai. "World's Number One! Our Country Realizes Overtaking at the Curve" (废柴: 世界第一! 我国实现弯道超车). *Sohu* (搜狐), March 27, 2020.

Felbab-Brown, Vanda. *Fentanyl and Geopolitics: Controlling Opioid Supply from China*. Brookings, July 22, 2020.

364 | Works and Sources Cited

Feldwisch-Drentrup, Hinnerk. "How WHO Became China's Coronavirus Accomplice." *Foreign Policy*, April 2, 2020.

Feng, Emily. "China's Global Construction Boom Puts Spotlight on Questionable Labor Practices." NPR News, March 30, 2019.

———. "Chinese Families Navigate a Maze of Laws and COVID Rules to Have Babies in the U.S." NPR News, October 22, 2022.

Feng, Huiyun, and Kai He, eds. *China's Challenges and International Order Transition: Beyond "Thucydides's Trap."* Ann Arbor: University of Michigan Press, 2020.

Fenghuang Wang. "True Story of 'PLA Major General Calls for Attacking the U.S. with Nuclear Weapons'" (凤凰网: "解放军少将核武袭美论"真相). September 5, 2005. aisixiang.com/data/8554.html.

Ferguson, Niall. "Team 'Chimerica.'" *Washington Post*, November 17, 2008.

———. "TikTok Is Inane—China's Imperial Ambition Is Not." *Bloomberg*, August 9, 2020.

Fernandez, Minelle. "Is China's Investment in Sri Lankan Project a Debt Trap?" *Al Jazeera*, January 16, 2019.

Feser, Edward. *The Cambridge Companion to Hayek*. Cambridge: Cambridge University Press, 2007.

Feygin, Yakov, and Dominik Leusder. "The Class Politics of the Dollar System." *Phenomenal World*, May 1, 2020.

Fick, Nathaniel. and Jami Miscik. *Confronting Reality in Cyberspace: Foreign Policy for a Fragmented Internet*. New York: Council on Foreign Relations, 2022.

Figes, Orlando. *The Europeans: Three Lives and the Making of a Cosmopolitan Culture*. New York: Metropolitan, 2019.

Financial Times. "America Is Struggling to Counter China's Intellectual Property Theft." Editorial, April 18, 2022.

Fingar, Thomas, and Jean Oi. "China's Challenges: Now It Gets Much Harder." *Washington Quarterly* 43, no. 1 (2020): 67–84.

———, eds. *Fateful Decisions: Choices That Will Shape China's Future*. Stanford, CA: Stanford University Press, 2020a.

Fischer, Karin. "What the Lieber Verdict Says, and Doesn't Say, about Future Probes of Scholars' Ties to China." *Chronicle of Higher Education*, December 27, 2021.

Fish, Isaac Stone. "Beijing Wants U.S. Business Leaders to Plead Its Case—Here's Why They Shouldn't." *Washington Post*, January 18, 2021.

———. *America Second: How America's Elites Are Making China Stronger*. New York: Knopf, 2022.

———. "The Censorship Circus: How Can the U.S. Hope to Understand China If Its Scholars Are Struggling to Figure Out How to Speak about It?" *Wire China*, February 27, 2022a.

Fitzpatrick, Martin, Peter Jones, Christa Knellwolf, and Ian McCalman, eds. *The Enlightenment World*. London: Routledge, 2004.

Works and Sources Cited | 365

Fleurbaey, Marc, Olivier Bouin, Marie-Laure Salles-Djelic, Ravi Kanbur, Helga Nowotny, and Elisa Reis. *A Manifesto for Social Progress*. Cambridge: Cambridge University Press, 2018.

Foa, Roberto S., Margot Mollat, Han Isha, Xavier Romero-Vidal, David Evans, and Andrew J. Klassen. *A World Divided: Russia, China and the West*. Cambridge, UK: Centre for the Future of Democracy, 2022.

Fogel, Robert. *The Fourth Great Awakening and the Future of Egalitarianism*. Chicago: University of Chicago Press, 2000.

Fok, James A. *Financial Cold War*. Chichester, UK: Wiley, 2022.

Follesdal, Andreas, and Thomas Pogge, eds. *Real World Justice: Grounds, Principles, Human Rights, and Social Institutions*. Dordrecht: Springer, 2005.

Follow the Money et al. *China Science Investigation*. May 19, 2022. ftm.eu/ chinascienceinvestigation.

Fontaine, Richard. "Washington's Missing China Strategy." *Foreign Affairs*, January 14, 2022.

Ford, Christopher. "The 'Lab-Leak' Inquiry at the State Department: An Open Letter." June 10, 2021.

Ford, Lindsey, and James Goldgeier. *Retooling America's Alliances to Manage the China Challenge*. Brookings, January 25, 2021.

Forgey, Quint, and Phelim Kine. "Blinken Calls China 'Most Serious Long-Term' Threat to World Order." *Politico*, May 26, 2022.

Forrester, Katrina. *In the Shadow of Justice: Postwar Liberalism and the Remaking of Political Philosophy*. Princeton, NJ: Princeton University Press, 2019.

Forsythe, Michael, Eric Lipton, Keith Bradsher, and Sui-Lee Wee. "A 'Bridge' to China, and Her Family's Business, in the Trump Cabinet." *New York Times*, June 3, 2019.

Frachon, Alain. "Beijing Intends to Translate the Gradual Shift in Power from West to East at the United Nations" (Pékin entend traduire aux Nations Unies le glissement progressif du pouvoir d'ouest en est). *Le Monde*, September 30, 2021.

Frame, John M. *A History of Western Philosophy and Theology*. Phillipsburg, NJ: P&R, 2015.

Francavilla, Chiara. "Africa Eye: Racism for Sale." BBC, June 13, 2022.

Francis, Diane. "Why $10B of China's Money Is Laundered Every Month." *New York Post*, July 26, 2014.

Fravel, M. Taylor. "Regime Insecurity and International Cooperation: Explaining China's Compromises in Territorial Disputes." *International Security* 30, no. 2 (2005): 46–83.

———. "International Relations Theory and China's Rise: Assessing China's Potential for Territorial Expansion." *International Studies Review* 12, no. 1 (2010): 505–32.

———. "China's 'World-Class Military' Ambitions: Origins and Implications." *Washington Quarterly* 43, no. 1 (2020, 97).

366 | Works and Sources Cited

Fravel, M. Taylor, J. Stapleton Roy, Michael Swaine, Susan Thornton, and Ezra Vogel. "China Is Not an Enemy." *Washington Post*, July 3, 2019.

Freeland, Chrystia. "The U.S. Capitalist Love Affair with Communist China." Reuters (opinion), April 29, 2011.

French, Howard. "China's Engagement with Africa Has a Cold War Parallel." *World Politics Review*, January 19, 2022.

Fried, Johannes. *Medieval History and Culture* (Das Mittelalter: Geschichte und Kultur). Munich: Beck, 2009.

———. *The Middle Ages*. Translated by Peter Lewis. Cambridge, MA: Belknap Press, 2015.

Friedberg, Aaron. "An Answer to Aggression: How to Push Back against Beijing." *Foreign Affairs*, September/October 2020.

———. "The Growing Rivalry between America and China and the Future of Globalization." *Texas National Security Review* 5, no. 1 (2021): 95–119.

———. *Getting China Wrong*. Cambridge, UK: Polity, 2022.

———. *A World of Blocs*. Marshall Papers, CSIS, April 6, 2023.

Friedberg, Aaron, and Charles Boustany. "Partial Disengagement." *Washington Quarterly* 43, no. 1 (2020): 23–40.

Frieden, Jeffry. "Macroeconomic Rebalancing in China and the G20." *China and World Economy* 24, no. 4 (2016): 15–33.

Friedman, Edward. "Myths of Maoism." *Dissent*, November 16, 2018.

Friedman, Milton, and Rose Friedman. *Free to Choose*. New York: Harcourt, 1990.

Friedman, Thomas. *The World Is Flat: A Brief History of the Twenty-First Century*. New York: Farrar, 2005.

———. "Even before a Winner, America Was the Loser." *New York Times*, November 5, 2020.

———. "How China Lost America." *New York Times*, November 1, 2022.

———. "I Was Wrong about Chinese Censorship." *New York Times*, July 21, 2022.

Friedrich, Carl, and Zbigniew Brzezinski. *Totalitarian Dictatorship and Autocracy*. Cambridge, MA: Harvard University Press, (1956) 1965.

Friend, John, and Bradley Thayer. *How China Sees the World: Han-Centrism and the Balance of Power in International Politics*. Lincoln, NE: Potomac, 2018.

Fruen, Lauren. "Apple Allows State Officials Process Personal Data of Chinese Users." *Daily Mail*, May 18, 2021.

Frum, David. "China Is a Paper Dragon." *Atlantic*, May 3, 2021.

Fu Chun. "May History Eventually Treat Them Well" (福春: 历史终将善待他们). WeChat blog (微信公众号), November 23, 2021.

Fu Xiaoqiang (vice-president of the China Institutes of Contemporary International Relations 中国现代国际关系研究院). "Accurately Understanding the Perspectives and Methodologies of Total State Security" (傅小强: 准确把握总体国家安全观方法论). Beijing, September 2, 2021.

Works and Sources Cited | 367

Fukuyama, Francis. *The End of History and the Last Man*. New York: Free Press, 1992.

———. "The China Challenge: What Kind of Regime Does China Have?" *American Interest*, May 18, 2020.

Fung, Courtney, and Shing-Hon Lam. "China Already Leads 4 of the 15 U.N. Specialized Agencies—and Is Aiming for a 5th." *Washington Post*, March 3, 2020.

Furedi, Frank. *Culture of Fear Revisited*. London: Continuum, (1997) 2006.

———. *How Fear Works*. New York: Bloomsbury Continuum, 2018.

Gaddis, John Lewis. *Strategies of Containment*. New York: Oxford University Press, (1982) 2005.

———. *George F. Kennan: An American Life*. New York: Penguin, 2011.

Gaida, Jamie, Jennifer Wong-Leung, Stephan Robin, and Danielle Cave. *ASPI's Critical Technology Tracker*. Australian Strategic Policy Institute, March 2, 2023.

Galor, Oded. *Unified Growth Theory*. Princeton, NJ: Princeton University Press, 2011.

———. *The Journey of Humanity: The Origins of Wealth and Inequality*. New York: Dutton, 2022.

Galston, William. "Is It Too Late to Counter China's Rise?" *Wall Street Journal*, April 2, 2019.

Galway, Matthew. *The Emergence of Global Maoism*. Ithaca, NY: Cornell University Press, 2022.

Gambetta, Diego, and Steffen Hertog. *Engineers of Jihad: The Curious Connection between Violent Extremism and Education*. Princeton, NJ: Princeton University Press, 2016.

Ganesh, Janan. "America's Eerie Lack of Debate about China: The US Is Entering an Open-Ended Conflict without Much Dissent." *Financial Times*, July 15, 2020.

———. "China Has Much to Lose from a Joe Biden Presidency." *Financial Times*, May 20, 2020.

Ganguly, Sumit, et al. *The Sino-Indian Rivalry: Implications for Global Order*. New York: Cambridge University Press, 2023.

Gao Ertai. "I Worry about the Emergence of a Kind of World Government" (高尔泰：我担心出现一种全球政府). *Dunjiao Wang* (钝角网), July 12, 2021.

Gao, Henry, and Weihuan Zhou. "China's Entry to CPTPP Trade Pact Is Closer Than You Think." *Nikkei Asia*, Tokyo, September 20, 2021.

Gao Jianbo et al. "Has the Sino-American Relationship Changed Qualitatively" (高剑波等：中美关系发生质变了吗). *Wenhua Zongheng* (文化纵横), Beijing, January 16, 2022.

Gao Peiyong. "'Tax Civilization' Needs Progress" (高培勇："税收文明"待进步). *Xinjing Bao* (新京报), August 15, 2013.

368 | Works and Sources Cited

Gao Ren. "Major National Shames since 1945" (高人: 1945年以来的重大国耻). *Dongfang toutiao* (东方头条), January 17, 2017.

Gao Yang. "Mainland Will Unite by Force" (高杨：大陆必武统). *Renmin zhenxie bao* (人民政协报), Beijing, March 22, 2021.

Garamone, Jim. "Austin, Blinken Trip All about Partnerships with Asian Allies." *DOD News*, March 13, 2021.

———. "DOD Officials Describe Conditions in Indo-Pacific." *DOD News*, March 15, 2021.

Garside, Roger. *China Coup: The Great Leap to Freedom.* Oakland: University of California Press, 2021.

———. "Regime Change in China Is Not Only Possible, It Is Imperative." *Globe and Mail*, April 30, 2021a.

Gartzke, Erik. "The Capitalist Peace." *American Journal of Political Science* 51, no. 1 (2007): 166–91.

Garver, John. *Protracted Contest: Sino-Indian Rivalry in the Twentieth Century.* Seattle: University of Washington Press, 2001.

———. *China's Quest: Foreign Relations of the People's Republic of China.* New York: Oxford University Press, 2017.

Gascoigne, Clark. "China's Illicit Outflows Were US$1.08 Trillion from 2002–2011." Global Financial Integrity, September 23, 2014.

Gat, Azar. "The Democratic Peace Theory Reframed: The Impact of Modernity." *World Politics* 58, no. 1 (2005): 73–100.

———. *War in Human Civilization.* New York: Oxford University Press, 2006.

Gaus, Gerald, Shane D. Courtland, and David Schmidtz. "Liberalism." In *Stanford Encyclopedia of Philosophy*, substantive revision January 22, 2018, edited by Edward Zalta. Stanford, CA: Stanford University Department of Philosophy, 2018.

Gavrilis, George. *The Council on Foreign Relations: A Short History.* New York: Council on Foreign Relations, 2021.

Geertz, Clifford. *Agricultural Involution.* Berkeley: University of California Press, 1969.

Gentry, Caron, and Amy Eckert. *The Future of Just War.* Athens: University of Georgia Press, 2014.

German Mission to UN. *Joint Statement on the Human Rights Situation in Xinjiang and the Recent Developments in Hong Kong.* New York, October 6, 2020.

Gerschewski, Johannes. *The Two Logics of Autocratic Rule.* Cambridge, UK: Cambridge University Press, 2023.

Gershaneck, Kerry. *Political Warfare: Strategies for Combating China's Plan to "Win without Fighting."* Quantico, VA: Marine Corps University Press, 2020.

Gertz, Bill. "From Mao's China to Foggy Bottom." *Washington Times*, June 15, 2020.

Gewirtz, Julian. "China Thinks America Is Losing: Washington Must Show Beijing It's Wrong." *Foreign Affairs*, November/December 2020.

Works and Sources Cited | 369

Gibbs, Joseph. *Gorbachev's Glasnost: The Soviet Media in the First Phase of Perestroika*. College Station: Texas A&M University Press, 1999.

Gifford, Rob. "Panda-Huggers and Dragon-Slayers: How to View Modern China Today." *Social Education*, January/February 2010.

Gilbert, Richard. *Innovation Matters: Competition Policy for the High-Technology Economy*. Cambridge, MA: MIT Press, 2020.

Gilchrist, Karen. "China Gets Top Score as Citizens Rank Their Governments' Response to the Coronavirus Outbreak." CNBC, May 6, 2020.

Gill, Bates, Adam Ni, and Dennis Blasko. "The Ambitious Reform Plans of the People's Liberation Army." *Australian Journal of Defence and Strategic Studies* 2, no. 1 (2020): 5–26.

Gilpin, Robert. *War and Change in World Politics*. New York: Cambridge University Press, 1981.

Gilsinan, Kathy. "How China Is Planning to Win Back the World." *Atlantic*, May 28, 2020.

Gittelsohn, John, Sridhar Natarajan, and Jenny Leonard. "CalPERS' Top Money Man Is Targeted in Fears of Chinese Espionage." *Los Angeles Times*, February 25, 2020.

Gladney, Dru. *Muslim Chinese: Ethnic Nationalism in the People's Republic*. Cambridge, MA: Council on East Asian Studies, Harvard University, 1996.

Glaser, Bonnie. "China's Political Influence Activities: A Conversation with Anne-Marie Brady." *ChinaPower* (podcast), CSIS, December 4, 2017.

Glaser, Bonnie, and Mathew Funaiole. "Poll Shows Increase in American Support for Defending Taiwan." *Diplomat*, October 23, 2020.

Glaser, Bonnie, and Hannah Price. "(US-China) Continuity Prevails in Biden's First 100 Days." *Comparative Connections* 23, no. 1 (2021, 29–42).

Glass, Andrew. "Bernard Baruch Coins Term 'Cold War.'" *Politico*, April 16, 2020.

Gleason, Abbott. *Totalitarianism: The Inner History of the Cold War*. New York: Oxford University Press, 1995.

Global Financial Integrity (GFI). *Trade-Related Illicit Financial Flows in 135 Developing Countries: 2008–2017*. Washington, DC, March 2020.

Global Times. "China Officially Applies to Join CPTPP, as the US Increasingly Isolated in Trade." Beijing, September 17, 2021.

Goddard, Stacie. *When Right Makes Might: Rising Powers and World Order*. Ithaca, NY: Cornell University Press, 2018.

Godfrey, Mark. "Chinese Overfishing Threatens Development of West African Fishing Sector." *Seafood Source*, June 26, 2020.

Gohale, Vijay. "China Doesn't Want a New World Order—It Wants This One." *New York Times*, June 4, 2020.

Gold, Howard. "Wall Street Doubles Down on China while Corporate America Now Moves the Other Way." *MarketWatch*, October 25, 2019.

370 | Works and Sources Cited

Goldberg, Jonah. "Two Cheers for 'McCarthyism'?" *National Review*, February 26, 2003.

Goldhagen, Daniel Jonah. *Hitler's Willing Executioners: Ordinary Germans and the Holocaust*. New York: Vintage, 1997.

Goldman, Addis. "Why Carl Schmitt Matters to China: Uncovering the Pathology of Schmitt Fever." *Hedgehog Review*, October 21, 2021.

Goldman, David. "The Chinese Challenge: America Has Never Faced Such an Adversary." *Claremont Review of Books*, Spring 2020.

———. *You Will Be Assimilated: China's Plan to Sino-form the World*, New York: Bombardier, 2020a.

Goldstein, Azar. *War in Human Civilization*. New York: Oxford University Press, 2006.

Goldstein, Matthew. "Ex-Hong Kong Official Convicted in Bribe Case Involving Chinese Oil Company." *New York Times*, December 6, 2018.

Goodnow, Frank. *China: An Analysis*. Baltimore: Johns Hopkins Press, 1926.

Gordon, David F., Haoyu Tong, and Tabatha Anderson. *Beyond the Myths— towards a Realistic Assessment of China's Belt and Road Initiative: The Security Dimension*. International Institute for Strategic Studies, September 2020.

Gordon, Deborah. *Ant Encounters: Interaction Networks and Colony Behavior*. Princeton, NJ: Princeton University Press, 2010.

———. "The Queen Does Not Rule." *Aeon*, December 19, 2016.

Gordon, Michael R. "The U.S. Is Not Yet Ready for the Era of 'Great Power' Conflict." *Wall Street Journal*, March 6, 2023.

Gordon, Michael, and Warren Strobel. "U.S.-Funded Scientist among Three Chinese Researchers Who Fell Ill amid Early Covid-19 Outbreak." *Wall Street Journal*, June 21, 2023.

Gowa, Joanne. *Closing the Gold Window: Domestic Politics and the End of Bretton Woods*. Ithaca, NY: Cornell University Press, 1983.

Graff, Garrett. "After 9/11, the U.S. Got Almost Everything Wrong: A Mission to Rid the World of 'Terror' and 'Evil' Led America in Tragic Directions." *Atlantic*, September 8, 2021.

Grano, Simona A., and David Wei Feng Huang, eds. *China-US Competition Impact on Small and Middle Powers' Strategic Choices*. Singapore: Palgrave, 2023.

Green, Will, Leyton Nelson, and Brittney Washington. *China's Engagement with Africa: Foundations for an Alternative Governance Regime*. U.S.-China Economic and Security Review Commission, May 1, 2020.

Greenberg, Maurice. "We Want to Rebuild U.S. Relations With China." *Wall Street Journal*, July 6, 2022.

Grego, Laura. "A History of Anti-satellite Programs." Union of Concerned Scientists, January 2012.

Gregory, E. John, and Lillian Ho. "Getting 'International Recognition' of Taiwan Right Before It's Too Late." *National Interest*, March 28, 2022.

Works and Sources Cited | 371

Gregson, Chip. "How the Biden Administration Can Support Taiwan." *Diplomat*, April 30, 2021.

Greitens, Sheena, and Rory Truex. "Repressive Experiences among China Scholars: New Evidence from Survey Data." *China Quarterly* 242 (2020): 349–75.

Griffith-Jones, Stephany. *A BRICS Development Bank*. Geneva: United Nations Conference on Trade and Development, 2014.

Griffiths, James. *The Great Firewall of China: How to Build and Control an Alternative Version of the Internet*. London: Zed, 2019.

Grimshaw, Jack. "U.S. Companies Set to Move Supply Chains out of China." *Supply Chain*, May 18, 2020.

Groh, Tyrone, and James Lockhart. "Is America an Empire?" *War on the Rocks*, August 27, 2015.

Group of Seven (G7). *Charlevoix Commitment on Innovative Financing for Development*. 2018.

———. *Carbis Bay G7 Summit Communiqué*. Cornwell, UK, June 13, 2021.

———. *G7 Leaders' Communiqué*. Elmau, Germany, June 28, 2022.

Group of 20 (G20). *G20 Principles for Quality Infrastructure Investment*. 2019.

Grunberger, Richard. *The 12-Year Reich: A Social History of Nazi Germany*. New York: Da Capo, 1971.

Gu Yuchuan. "'Thankfully China Has a Taiwan' Microblog Went Viral" (古玉川: "幸亏中国有个台湾" 微博走红). *QQ*, April 24, 2012.

Guan Tao. "14th Five-Year Plan on Cautiously Promoting RMB Internationalization" (管涛: 十四五规划部署稳慎推进人民币国际化). *Diyi Caijing* (第一财经), November 16, 2020.

Guang Lei et al. "Pandemic Sees Increase in Chinese Support for Regime." China Data Lab, University of California San Diego, June 30, 2020.

Gui Yu. "They Chose China" (贵余: 他们选择了中国). *Qinnian cankao* (青年参考), Beijing, March 1, 2006.

Gumpach, Johannes von, ed. *The Burlingame Mission: A Political Disclosure*. London: Trübner,1872.

Guo, Eileen, et al. "The US Crackdown on Chinese Economic Espionage Is a Mess." *MIT Technology Review*, December 2, 2021.

Guo Fan. *The Wandering Earth* (郭帆: 流浪地球). Beijing: China Film Corporation, 2019.

Guo Songtao. *Diary* (郭嵩焘日记). Beijing: Renmin, (1883) 1983.

Guo Yuhua. "Are We Rich or Not?" (郭于华: 我们究竟是有钱还是没钱). *Wanxiang Digest* (万象文摘), Beijing Oct 6, 2018.

Ha Jin. *War Trash*. New York: Vintage, 2015.

Haass, Richard. "Imperial America." Brookings, November 11, 2000.

Haass, Richard, and David Sacks. "American Support for Taiwan Must Be Unambiguous." *Foreign Affairs*, September 2, 2020.

372 | Works and Sources Cited

Habermas, Jürgen. *This Too a History of Philosophy* (Auch eine Geschichte der Philosophie). Berlin: Suhrkamp, 2019.

Hadley, Stephen, et al. *Hand-Off: The Foreign Policy George W. Bush Passed to Barack Obama.* Brookings, 2023.

Halegua, Aaron. "Where Is the Belt and Road Initiative Taking International Labour Rights?" In *The Belt and Road Initiative and Global Governance,* edited by Maria Carrai, Jean-Christophe Defraigne, and Jan Wouters, 225–57. Cheltenham, UK: Edward Elgar, 2020.

Halegua, Aaron, and Xiaohui Ban. "Labour Protections for Overseas Chinese Workers." *Chinese Journal of Comparative Law* 8, no. 2 (2020): 304–30.

Haley, Nikki. "How to Confront an Advancing Threat from China." *Foreign Affairs,* July 18, 2019.

Hall, Robert. *The Coming Collapse of the American Republic.* Des Plains, IL: Old Jarhead, 2011.

Hall, Todd. " 'I'll Tell You Something about China': Thoughts on the Specialist Study of the International Relations of the People's Republic of China." *St. Antony's International Review* 16, no. 1 (2020).

Hamilton, Clive, and Mareike Ohlberg. "Bulls in a China Shop: How Beijing Cultivated Wall Street's Giants." *Sydney Morning Herald,* June 13, 2020.

———. *Hidden Hand: Exposing How the Chinese Communist Party Is Reshaping the World.* London: Oneworld, 2020a.

Han Aiyong. "What Are the Fundamental Differences between Common Values for All Humanity and So-Called 'Universal Values' " (韩爱勇: 全人类共同价值与所谓"普世价值"有何根本区别). *Xuexi Shibao* (学习时报), Beijing, July 18, 2022.

Han Ban. *2019 Annual Report.* Confucius Institute US Center, 2020.

Han Hui. "The Overseas VIPs of the Tenth World Chinese Media Forum" (韩晖: 第十届世界华文传媒论坛境外嘉宾人员名单). *Zhongxinshe* (中新社), Beijing, October 10, 2019.

Hancock, Tom, and Jing Li. "Outpouring of Resentment on Chinese Social Media Is Overwhelming Censors." *Bloomberg Businessweek,* April 27, 2022.

Hannah, Mark, and Caroline Gray. *Democracy in Disarray: How the World Sees the U.S. and Its Example.* New York: Eurasia Group, 2021.

Hannas, William, and Didi Tatlow, eds. *China's Quest for Foreign Technology: Beyond Espionage.* Abingdon, UK: Routledge, 2021.

Hansen, Thomas, and Finn Stepputat. "Sovereignty Revisited." *Annual Review of Anthropology* 35, no. 1 (2006): 295–315.

Hanser, Jessica. *Mr. Smith Goes to China.* New Haven, CT: Yale University Press, 2019.

Hanson, Victor Davis. "Ten Paradoxes of Our Age." *Defining Ideas,* June 6, 2018.

Hao, Karen, and Rachel Liang. "Vast Cache of Chinese Police Files Offered for Sale in Alleged Hack." *Wall Street Journal,* July 4, 2022.

Hao Weimin. "Inner Mongolia during the 10-Year Holocaust" (郝维民: 十年浩劫中的内蒙古). Xinhua (新华), December 5, 2019.

Hao Weiwei. "Route of Destiny and Common March" (郝薇薇: 命运与共行大道). Xinhua (新华), September 29, 2022.

Hao Yu and Gu Yu. "China Built World's First Desert-Encircling Railway" (郝玉、顾煜: 中国建成世界首条环沙漠铁路线). Xinhua (新华), June 16, 2022.

Harden, Kathryn Paige. *The Genetic Lottery: Why DNA Matters for Social Equality*. Princeton, NJ: Princeton University Press, 2021.

Hardin, Garrett. "The Tragedy of the Commons." *Science* 162, no. 3859 (1968): 1243–48.

Harris, Lee. "Congress Proposes $500 Million for Negative News Coverage of China." *American Prospect*, February 9, 2022.

Hass, Ryan. *Stronger: Adapting America's China Strategy in an Age of Competitive Interdependence*. New Haven, CT: Yale University Press, 2021.

———. "Beijing's Response to the Biden Administration's China Policy." *China Leadership Monitor*, no. 71, March 2022.

Hass, Ryan, and Abraham Denmark. "More Pain than Gain: How the US-China Trade War Hurt America." Brookings, August 7, 2020.

Ryan Hass, Patricia M. Kim, and Jeffrey A. Bader. *A Course Correction in America's China Policy*. Washington, DC: Brookings, 2022.

Hasson, Peter. "China Helped Put This Man in Charge of the World Health Organization—Is It Paying Off?" *National Interest*, March 22, 2020.

Hathaway, Oona, and Scott Shapiro. *The Internationalists: How a Radical Plan to Outlaw War Remade the World*. New York: Simon and Schuster, 2017.

Hayek, Friedrich A. *The Road to Serfdom*. Chicago: University of Chicago Press, (1944) 2007.

———. *The Constitution of Liberty*. Chicago: University of Chicago Press, 2011.

Haynes, John, and Harvey Klehr. *Venona: Decoding Soviet Espionage in America*. New Heaven, CT: Yale University Press, 1999.

Hayton, Bill. *The Invention of China*. New Haven, CT: Yale University Press, 2020.

Hazony, Yoram. *The Virtue of Nationalism*. New York: Basic Books, 2018.

He Cheng. "To Completely Understand the 'Great Change Once in 100 Years'" (何成: 全面认识和理解"百年未有之大变局"). *Guangming ribao* (光明日报), January 3, 2020.

He, Laura. "China Can't Do Much to Help Russia's Sanction-Hit Economy." CNN, March 4, 2022.

He Ming. *Loyalty: the Bumpy Life of the Returned Volunteer Army POWs* (贺明: 忠诚-志愿军战俘归来人员的坎坷经历). Beijing: Zhongguo wenshi, 1998.

He Yinan. "Domestic Troubles, National Identity Discourse, and China's Attitude towards the West, 2003–2012." *Nations and Nationalism* 24, no. 3 (2018, 741–66).

374 | Works and Sources Cited

He Yiting. "Adhere and Perfect the Fundamental System of Socialism with Chinese Characteristics" (何毅亭: 坚持和完善中国特色社会主义根本制度). *Xuexi Shibao* (学习时报), November 29, 2019.

———. "Xi Jinping Thought Is Marxism in the 21st Century" (何毅亭: 习近平新时代中国特色社会主义思想是21世纪马克思主义). *Xuexi Shibao* (学习时报), June 15, 2020.

He Yujia and Angela Tritto. "Urban Utopia or Pipe Dream? Examining Chinese-Invested Smart City Development in Southeast Asia." *Third World Quarterly* 43, no. 9 (2022): 2244–68.

Heale, M. J. "Anatomy of a Scare: Yellow Peril Politics in America, 1980–1993." *Journal of American Studies* 43, no. 1 (2009): 19–47.

Heath, Timothy. *The Return of Great Power War: Scenarios of Systemic Conflict Between the United States and China.* RAND Corporation, 2023.

Heath, Timothy, Derek Grossman, and Asha Clark. *China's Quest for Global Primacy: An Analysis of Chinese International and Defense Strategies to Outcompete the United States.* RAND Corporation, June 2021.

Heer, Friedrich. *The Intellectual History of Europe.* 2 vols. New York: Doubleday, 1968.

Heer, Paul. *Mr. X and the Pacific: George F. Kennan and American Policy in East Asia.* Ithaca, NY: Cornell University Press, 2018.

———. "America's Coronavirus Blame Game Must End." *National Interest,* May 13, 2020.

———. "Mike Pompeo Challenges China's Governing Regime." *National Interest,* July 27, 2020.

———. "Understanding U.S.-China Strategic Competition." *National Interest,* October 20, 2020.

Hegarty, Stephanie. "World Population Day: India Will Overtake China in 2023." BBC, July 11, 2022.

Heimann, Eduard. "Atheist Theocracy." *Social Research* 20, no. 3 (1953): 311–31.

Heinzig, Dieter. *The Soviet Union and Communist China, 1945–1950: The Arduous Road to the Alliance.* Armonk, NY: Sharpe, 2004.

Henan Xinwen. "Resume of the Real Boss of Henan Xincaifu Lü Yi Exposed" (河南新闻: 河南新财富实控人吕奕简历曝光). *Wangyi* (网易), June 19, 2022.

Hernández, Javier C. "China Peddles Falsehoods to Obscure Origin of COVID Pandemic." *New York Times,* December 14, 2020.

Hernández, Javier C., and Raymond Zhong, et al. "No 'Negative' News: How China Censored the Coronavirus." *New York Times,* December 19, 2020.

Higgins, Andrew. "A Pricey Drive Down Montenegro's Highway 'from Nowhere to Nowhere.'" *New York Times,* August 15, 2021.

Higgs, Robert. *Crisis and Leviathan: Critical Episodes in the Growth of American Government.* New York: Oxford University Press, 1987.

Works and Sources Cited | 375

———. "The Political Economy of Fear." *Mises Daily Articles*, April 16, 2021.

Hillman, Jennifer, and David Sacks. *China's Belt and Road: Implications for the United States.* New York: Council on Foreign Relations, 2021.

Hillman, Jonathan. "Corruption Flows along China's Belt and Road." CSIS, January 18, 2019.

Hippel, Karin von. "The Non-interventionary Norm Prevails: An Analysis of the Western Sahara." *Journal of Modern African Studies* 33, no. 1 (1995): 67–81.

Hippold, Sarah. "33% of Supply Chain Leaders Moved Business Out of China or Plan to by 2023." News release, Gartner, June 24, 2020.

Hirsh, Michael. "The U.S. and China Haven't Divorced Just Yet." *Foreign Policy*, June 22, 2022.

Hitler, Adolf. *Mein Kampf.* Munich: Nachf, 1943.

Ho Ping-ti. *Six Decades of Reading History and Viewing the World* (何炳棣: 讀史閱世六十年). Hong Kong: Shangwu, 2004.

Hobbes, Thomas. *Leviathan.* Seattle: Pacific, (1651) 2011.

Hobson, Christopher. *The Rise of Democracy: Revolution, War and Transformations in International Politics since 1776.* Edinburgh: Edinburgh University Press, 2015.

Hockett, Robert. "The Capital Commons: Digital Money and Citizens' Finance in a Productive Commercial Republic." *Review of Banking and Financial Law* 39 (2019): 345–498.

Hofstadter, Richard. *Social Darwinism in American Thought.* Boston: Beacon, (1944) 1992.

Holland, Steve. "China Asked Russia to Delay Ukraine Invasion until after Olympics." Reuters, March 2, 2022.

Hollander, Paul. *Political Pilgrims: Western Intellectuals in Search of the Good Society.* Piscataway, NJ: Transaction, (1981) 1997.

Holmes, Stephen, and Ivan Krastev. *The Light That Failed: Why the West Is Losing the Fight for Democracy.* New York: Pegasus, 2020.

Hong Shen. "China's Oil Futures Give New York and London a Run for Their Money." *Wall Street Journal*, March 27, 2019.

Hopkins, A. G. *American Empire: A Global History.* Princeton, NJ: Princeton University Press, 2018.

Horton, Richard. "This Wave of Anti-China Feeling Masks the West's Own Covid-19 Failures." *Guardian*, August 3, 2020.

Hrebenar, Ronald, and Clive Thomas. "The Rise of the New Asian Lobbies in Washington, D.C.: China, India and South Korea." APSA annual meeting, Seattle, 2011.

Hsiung, James C. *China into Its Second Rise: Myths, Puzzles, Paradoxes, and Challenge to Theory.* Singapore: World Scientific, 2012.

Hsiung, James C., et al. *The Xi Jinping Era.* Beijing: Shidai, 2015.

376 | Works and Sources Cited

Hsu, Szu-Chien, and J. Michael Cole, eds. *Insidious Power: How China Undermines Global Democracy*. Manchester, UK: Eastbridge Books, 2020.

Hu Haiou. "Rid the Nightmare of 'Always Want to Annihilate Us'" (胡海鷗: 擺脫「亡我之心不死」的夢魘). *China Times* (中國時報), June 22, 2018.

Hu Ping. "Commenting on *Deng Xiaoping Time* by Ezra Vogel" (胡平: 点评傅高义的邓小平时代). *Zhongguo Renquan Shuanzhoukan* (中国人权双周刊), New York, February 7, 2013.

———. "Ezra Vogel's Limitation" (傅高义的局限). TenCent (腾讯), December 21, 2020.

Hu Shoujun. *On Social Coexistence* (胡守钧: 社会共生论). Shanghai: Fudan, 2012.

Hu Weixing. "Great Power Geopolitical Competition Returns to 'Heartland' of Eurasia Continent" (胡伟星: 大国地缘政治竞争重回欧亚大陆 "心脏地带"). *Yatai anquan yu haiyang yanjiu* (亚太安全与海洋研究), Nanjing, no. 4, July, 2022.

Hu Xijin. "China Needs More Nuclear Weapons" (胡锡进: 中国需要更多核武). *Weibo* (微博), Beijing, May 8, 2020.

Huang, Billy. "Steve Bannon Is Right about Overseas Chinese." *South China Morning Post*, Hong Kong, April 26, 2019.

Huang Chuanchang. "Rethinking 'the Weak Can't Have Diplomacy'" (黄传昶: "弱国无外交"再思考). *Lishi jiaoxue* (历史教学), Beijing, no. 10, 2020.

Huang Jing-Yang. "Age of Involution: Uncontrolled Investment, Redundant Competition, and the End of the Chinese Model of Growth" (黃靖洋: 內卷時代: 無節制的投入、同質化的競爭，與中國增長模式的極限). *Initium* (端傳媒), Hong Kong, January 7, 2021.

Huang, Philip. *The Peasant Family and Rural Development in the Yangzi Delta, 1350–1988*. Stanford, CA: Stanford University Press, 1990.

———, ed. *Guide to Practical Social Science Research* (黄宗智: 实践社会科学研究指南). Nanning: Guangxi Shida, 2020.

Huang Ping. "Community of Common Destiny for Humanity Provides the 'China Solution' for Global Governance" (黄平: 人类命运共同体为全球治理提供" 中国方案"). *Hongqi Wengao* (红旗文稿), October 24, 2019.

Huang Renwei. "The Phase of Sino-US Strategic Holding and Battle Buffering" (黄仁伟: 中美战略相持阶段与战役缓冲). *Guoji Guanxi Yanjiu* (国际关系研究), Shanghai, July 2022.

Huang, Yanzhong. "After the Lab-Leak Theory, US-Chinese Relations Head Downhill." *Bulletin of the Atomic Scientists*, July 16, 2021.

Huang, Yasheng. *Capitalism with Chinese Characteristics: Entrepreneurship and the State*. New York: Cambridge University Press, 2008.

———. "Can the Belt and Road Become a Trap for China?" Project Syndicate, May 22, 2019.

———. *The Rise and the Fall of the EAST: How Exams, Autocracy, Stability, and Technology Brought China Success, and Why It Might Lead to Its Decline?* New Haven, CT: Yale University Press, 2023.

Works and Sources Cited | 377

Huanggong Wangjiang. "The 40 Years History of Studying in the US, Is the History of the US Assisting the New China" (黄公望江: 四十年的留美史, 就是美国帮助新中国的历史). WeChat blog (微信公号), August 22, 2021.

Huanqiu shibao wang. "China Can Support Ryukyu Independence" (环球网: 中国可支持琉球独立). Beijing, January 16, 2017.

Hughes, Thomas. "How America Helped Build the Soviet Machine." *American Heritage*, December, 1988.

Hui Da. "What Inappropriate Opinions Prof. Yu Lingqi Voiced?" (回答: 于琳琦老师发什么不当言论). *Jinri Toutiao* (今日头条), May 10, 2020.

Human Rights Watch. *They Don't Understand the Fear We Have: How China's Long Reach of Repression Undermines Academic Freedom at Australia's Universities.* New York, 2021.

Hume, David. *A Treatise of Human Nature.* Mineola, NY: Dover, (1740) 2003.

Hung, Ho-fung. *Clash of Empires: From "Chimerica" to the "New Cold War."* Cambridge: Cambridge University Press, 2022.

Hunter, Edward. *Brain-Washing in Red China: The calculated destruction of men's minds.* New York: Vanguard, 1951.

Huntington, Samuel. "The U.S.: Decline or Renewal?" *Foreign Affairs*, Winter 1988.

———. *The Clash of Civilizations and the Remaking of World Order.* New York: Simon and Schuster, (1996) 2011.

Hvistendahl, Mara, et al. "A Global Web of Chinese Propaganda Leads to a U.S. Tech Mogul." *New York Times*, August 5, 2023.

Hynes, Phill, and Nury Vittachi. "Strategists Admit West Is Goading China into War." *FridayEveryday*, November 23, 2021.

Ibrahim, Azeem. "China Has No Room for Dissenting Friends." *Foreign Policy*, October 4, 2019.

IIE. "Number of International Students in the United States Hits All-Time High." November 18, 2019.

IISS. *Sino-American Strategic Competition in Technology* (北京大学国际战略研究院: 技术领域的中美战略竞争). Beijing: Institute of International and Strategic Studies, 2022.

Ikenberry, G. John. *Liberal Leviathan: The Origins, Crisis, and Transformation of the American World Order.* Princeton, NJ: Princeton University Press, 2011.

———. "The Next Liberal Order: The Age of Contagion Demands More Internationalism, Not Less." *Foreign Affairs*, July/August 2020.

———. *A World Safe for Democracy: Liberal Internationalism and the Crises of Global Order.* New Haven, CT: Yale University Press, 2020a.

Ikenberry, G. John, and Yan Xuetong. "Princeton East-West Scholar Talk." Princeton University Press (YouTube channel), March 4, 2021. youtube.com/watch?v=s_ASEYTeK7c&ab_channel=PrincetonUniversityPress.

378 | Works and Sources Cited

IMF (International Monetary Fund). "Currency Composition of Official Foreign Exchange Reserves (COFER)." IMF Data, updated March 2022.

———. *World Economic Outlook*. April 2023.

IMI. *Report on RMB Internationalization* (人民币国际化报告). Beijing: Renmin University, International Monetary Institute, annually, 2012–22.

Inboden, William. *Religion and American Foreign Policy: The Soul of Containment*. New York: Cambridge University Press, 2008.

Indo-Asian News Service (IANS). "US Lists More Chinese Firms to Delist Them from American Exchanges." *Business Standard*, May 5, 2022.

Inner Mongolia People's Congress. "Rules on Improving National Solidarity in Inner Mongolia Autonomous Region" (内蒙古自治区促进民族团结进步条例). Hohhot, January 30, 2021.

Institute of Party History and Literature of the CCP Central Committee. *Digest of Xi Jinping's Treaties on Great Power Diplomacy with Chinese Characteristics* (中共中央党史和文献研究院: 习近平关于中国特色大国外交论述摘编). Beijing: Zhongyang Wenxian, 2020.

ISAS (Institute of Southeast Asia Studies). *The State of Southeast Asia*, February 2022.

Ishiba, Shigeru. "Ishiba's Lecture Mentions Asian Version of NATO" (アジア版NATO, 言及 石破氏講演). *Chugoku Shimbun* (中国新聞), Hiroshima, Japan, March 7, 2014.

Ishiwara, Kanji. *On the World's Final War* (石原莞爾: 世界最終戰論). Tokyo: Rutuimei (立命館), (1940) 1953.

Israel, Jonathan. *Democratic Enlightenment: Philosophy, Revolution, and Human Rights*. New York: Oxford University Press, 2011.

Italicus, Silius. *Punica*. Cambridge, MA: Harvard University Press, (1st century CE) 1934.

Izambard, Antoine. *France China: Dangerous Liaisons* (France Chine: Les liaisons dangereuses). Paris: Stock, 2019.

Jacob, Margaret. *The Enlightenment: A Brief History with Documents*. Boston: Bedford, 2021.

Jacobsen, Rowan. "How Amateur Sleuths Broke the Wuhan Lab Story and Embarrassed the Media." *Newsweek*, June 2, 2021.

Jain, Ash. *Like-Minded and Capable Democracies*. Council on Foreign Relations, January 2013.

Jakes, Lara, and Steven Lee Myers. "Tense Talks with China Left U.S. 'Cleareyed' about Beijing's Intentions." *New York Times*, March 25, 2021.

James, Paul. *Globalism, Nationalism, Tribalism: Bringing Theory Back In*. London: Sage, 2006.

Jayaram, Kartik, Omid Kassiri, and Irene Yuan Sun. *The Closest Look Yet at Chinese Economic Engagement in Africa*. McKinsey and Company, June 28, 2017.

Jenne, Jeremiah. "The Perils of Advising the Empire: Yuan Shikai and Frank Goodnow." *ChinaFile*, December 30, 2015.

Works and Sources Cited | 379

Jersild, Austin. "Chinese in Peril in Russia: The 'Millionka' in Vladivostok, 1930–1936." Wilson Center, October 29, 2019.

Jessie. "Last Straw to Crush the CCP" (压死中共的最后一根稻草). March 9, 2021. ipkmedia.com/30861.

Jiang Shigong. "Philosophy and History: Interpretation of 'Xi Jinping Era' from 19th CCP National Congress Report" (强世功: 哲学与历史 - 从党的十九大报告解读"习近平时代"). *Kaifang Shidai* (开放时代), Guangzhou, no. 1, 2018.

———. "The Internal Logic of Super-Sized Political Entities: 'Empire' and World Order" (强世功: 超大型政治实体的内在逻辑: "帝国"与世界秩序). *Wenhua Zhongheng* (文化纵横), April 2019.

———. "'New Roman Empire' and 'New Great Struggle'" (强世功: "新罗马帝国"与"新的伟大斗争"). *Guanchazhe* (观察者), Shanghai, September 5, 2020.

———. "Ruse of Great Power and Civilizational Rejuvenation: The Taiwan Issue under 'the Protracted War between Civilizations'" (强世功: 大国崛起与文明复兴—"文明持久战"下的台湾问题). *Wenhua zhongheng* (文化纵横), August 2022.

Jiang Tianfeng. "The Lesson of Tedros' 'Turn' for China" (江天风: 谭德塞的"反转"给中国的警示). *Zhihu Zhuanlun* (知乎专论), Beijing, April 21, 2021.

Jiang Zemin. *Selected Works of Jiang Zemin* (江泽民文选). Beijing: Renmin, 2006.

Jiao Ni. "Lin Ching-hsia and Her Sister in Henan" (教你: 林青霞与河南亲姐). *Caijing* (财经), Beijing, August 1, 2020.

Jie Dalei. "Six Principles to Guide China's Policy toward the United States." Carnegie–Tsinghua Center for Global Policy, Beijing, December 3, 2020.

Jie Shu. "Nigeria Demands Compensation from China, Why the Rise of 'Anti-China' Waves in Many African Nations" (杰叔: 尼日利亚要求中国索赔, 为什么非洲很多国家"反华"声浪突起). *Caixin* (财新), Beijing, May 5, 2020.

Jiedu Shishi. "Falling Behind Will Be Beaten, the Weak Can't Have Diplomacy" (杰读史实: 落后就要挨打, 弱国无外交). *Jinri toutiao* (今日头条), Beijing, January 7, 2023.

Jin Hui. *Seduction of Tibet's Motuo* (金辉: 西藏墨脱的诱惑). Shanghai: Dongfang, 1995.

Jin Keyu. "China's Role in the New Global Order" (金刻羽: 中国在全球新秩序中的角色). *Sina caijing* (新浪财经), March 26, 2020.

Jin, Keyu. "The West Is Wrong about Xi Jinping." Project Syndicate, April 6, 2018.

———. "China's Steroids Model of Growth." In *Meeting Globalization's Challenges: Policies to Make Trade Work for All*, Luís Catão and Maurice Obstfeld, 77–93. Princeton, NJ: Princeton University Press, 2019.

———. *The New China Playbook: Beyond Socialism and Capitalism*. New York: Viking, 2023.

Jin Liqun. "Reform of International Financial System and China's Power of Influence" (金立群: 国际金融体系改革和中国影响力). International Financial Forum, May 16, 2021.

380 | Works and Sources Cited

Jin Tou Wang. "Accelerating De-dollarization" (金投网: 去美元化提速). *Sohu*, June 28, 2022.

Jin Yilong and Zhou Manqin. "'International Schools' No More" (金贻龙, 周缦卿: "国际学校"渐成往事). *Caijing* (财经), July 17, 2022.

Jin Yingzhong. "Theory on Coexistence of International Society" (金应忠: 国际社会的共生论). *Shehui Kexue* (社会科学), no. 10, 2011.

Jin Yun. "How the World Chinese Media Forum Is 'Forged'" (津云: 世界华文传媒论坛是怎样"炼"成的). *Sina* (新浪), July 7, 2022.

Jin Zuoli. *New Era* (碧荷馆主人/金作砺: 新纪元). Nanning: Guangxi Shida, (1908) 2008.

Jing Yang. "Behind the Fall of China's Luckin Coffee: A Network of Fake Buyers and a Fictitious Employee." *Wall Street Journal*, May 28, 2020.

Jingji ribao (经济日报). "Xinjiang Energy" (新疆能源). Beijing, January 20, 2014.

Jiu Dian. "Eating a Fish Three Ways" (玖点: 一鱼三吃). *Wanwei* (万维), August 6, 2021.

Jo He-rim. "South Korea's Intelligence Agency Joins NATO's Cyber Defense Center as First in Asia." *Korea Herald*, May 5, 2022.

Johnson, Boris. "Resignation Speech." AP News, July 7, 2022.

Johnson, Dennis, and Lara Brown. *Campaigning for President 2016*. New York: Routledge, 2017.

Johnson, Juliet, Marietta Stepaniants, and Benjamin Forest, eds. *Religion and Identity in Modern Russia: The Revival of Orthodoxy and Islam*. London: Routledge, 2005.

Johnson, Keith, and Robbie Gramer. "The Great China-U.S. Economic Decoupling." *Foreign Policy*, May 14, 2020.

Johnston, Alastair Iain. "China in a World of Orders: Rethinking Compliance and Challenge in Beijing's International Relations." *International Security* 44, no. 2 (2019): 9–60.

———. "The Failures of the 'Failure of Engagement' with China." *Washington Quarterly* 42, no. 2 (2019a): 99–114.

Johnston, Patrick. "Does Decapitation Work?" *International Security* 36, no. 4 (2012): 47–79.

Jones, Bruce, and Andrew Yeo. *China and the Challenge to Global Order*. Brookings, 2022.

Jones, Trevor, and Treston Chandler. "Sweeping U.S. Lists Seek to Restrict Trade and Investment That Support the Chinese Military." Wisconsin Project on Arms Control, 2021.

Joske, Alex. "The Party Speaks for You: Foreign Interference and the Chinese Communist Party's United Front System." Brief no. 32, Australian Strategic Policy Institute, 2020.

———. *Spies and Lies: How China's Greatest Covert Operations Fooled the World*. San Francisco: Hardie Grant, 2022.

Works and Sources Cited | 381

Ju Jiandon. "RMB Becoming International Currency Is the Necessary Condition of World Peace" (鞠建东:人民币成为国际货币是世界和平的必要条件). Beijing: Tsinghua-CIFER, February 26, 2023.

Kaczmarski, Marcin. *Russia-China Relations in the Post-Crisis International Order.* Abingdon, UK: Routledge, 2015.

Kafka, Franz. "The Second Octavo Notebook—Nov. 21." In *Blue Octavo Notebooks.* Cambridge, MA: Exact Change, (1917) 2004.

Kagan, Robert. "Our Constitutional Crisis Is Already Here." *Washington Post,* September 23, 2021.

Kahn, Alfred E. "The Tyranny of Small Decisions: Market Failures, Imperfections, and the Limits of Economics." *Kyklos* 19, no. 1 (1966): 23–47.

Kaiman, Jonathan. "Mystery Deepens over Apparent Abduction of Chinese Billionaire in Hong Kong." *Los Angeles Times,* February 13, 2017.

Kaiser, Robert, and Steven Mufson. "'Blue Team' Draws a Hard Line on Beijing." *Washington Post,* February 22, 2000.

Kakutani, Yuichiro. "Star American Professor Masterminded a Surveillance Machine for Chinese Big Tech." *Daily Beast,* August 22, 2022.

Kamel, Maha, and Wang Hongying. "Petro-RMB? The Oil Trade and the Internationalization of the Renminbi." *International Affairs* 95, no. 5 (2019): 1131–48.

Kanapathy, Ivan. *The Collapse of One China.* CSIS Brief, June 17, 2022.

Kant, Immanuel. *To Perpetual Peace: A Philosophical Sketch* (Zum ewigen Frieden: Ein philosophischer Entwurf). Translated by Ted Humphrey. Indianapolis: Hackett, (1795) 2003.

———. *Three Critiques: Critique of Pure Reason, Critique of Practical Reason, Critique of Judgment* (Kritik der reinen Vernunft, Kritik der praktischen Vernunft, Kritik der Urteilskraft). New York: Penguin, (1781–90) 2008.

Kaplan, Seth. "China's Censorship Reaches Globally Through WeChat: The All-in-One App Is Also a Propaganda Tool for the Chinese Communist Party." *Foreign Policy,* February 28, 2023.

Karadja, Mounir, Johanna Mollerstrom, and David Seim. "Richer (and Holier) than Thou? The Effect of Relative Income Improvements on Demand for Redistribution." *Review of Economics and Statistics* 99, no. 2 (2017): 201–12.

Kaufman, Jonathan. *The Last Kings of Shanghai: The Rival Jewish Dynasties That Helped Create Modern China.* New York: Viking, 2020.

Kelion, Leo. "Huawei 5G Kit Must Be Removed from UK by 2027." BBC News, July 14, 2020.

Kelly, David. "Seven Chinas: A Policy Framework." Working paper, CSIS, February 2018.

Kemp, Ted. "U.S. Announces Major Asia Economic Deal in Effort to Boost Profile, Counter China." CNBC, May 23, 2022.

382 | Works and Sources Cited

Kempe, Frederick. "Biden Has a Plan to Rally the World's Democracies." CNBC, September 13, 2020.

———. "China Has Already Decided Cold War II Has Begun—Now It's Escalating." Atlantic Council, July 19, 2020a.

Kennan, George. *Policy Planning Study.* PPS 23. Washington: DOS, 1948.

———. "Long Telegram." In *Foreign Relations of the United States, 1946.* Vol. 6, *Eastern Europe, The Soviet Union,* 696–709. Washington, DC: Department of State, 1969.

———. *Memoirs, 1950–1963.* Boston: Little Brown, 1972.

———. "Report by the Policy Planning Staff." PPS 23. In *Foreign Relations of the United States, 1948.* Vol. 2, pt. 2, edited by the Department of State, document 4. Government Printing Office, 1976.

———. "The G.O.P. Won the Cold War? Ridiculous." *New York Times,* October 28, 1992.

Kennedy, Ellen. "China, Tibet, and the Uighurs: A Pattern of Genocide." *MinnPost,* September 9, 2020.

Kennedy, John F. "Remarks of Representative John F. Kennedy at the Philip J. Durkin Testimonial Dinner." January 30, 1949.

———. "Commencement Address at American University." Washington, DC, June 10, 1963.

Kennedy, Paul. *The Rise and Fall of the Great Powers: Economic Change and Military Conflict from 1500 to 2000.* New York: Random House, 1987.

Kennedy, Scott. "Is China a Strategic Partner or Rival Power?" *Washington Post,* July 2, 2019.

Kennedy, Scott, and Wang Jisi. "America and China Need to Talk." *Foreign Affairs.* April 6, 2023.

Kennon, Isabel. "China-Brazil Relations under COVID-19." Atlantic Council, May 20, 2020.

Kenyon, Miles. "WeChat Surveillance Explained." Citizen Lab, University of Toronto, May 7, 2020.

Kerry, John. "Kerry Says Trusting China on Climate Would Be 'Stupid and Malpractice.'" *Politico,* May 12, 2021.

Keynes, John Maynard. "Review of The Economic Principles of Confucius and His School by Chen Huan Chang." *Economic Journal* 22, no. 88 (1912): 584–88.

Khalilzad, Zalmay. *Congage China.* Issue paper, RAND Corporation, 1999.

Khanna, Parag. "All Roads Need Not Lead to China." *Noēma,* Berggruen Institute, July 2020.

Khong, Yuen Foong. "The American Tributary System." *Chinese Journal of International Politics* 6, no. 1 (2013): 1–47.

Kim, Hannah, and Bernard Grofman. "The Political Science 400." *PS: Political Science and Politics* 52, no. 2 (2019): 296–311.

Works and Sources Cited | 383

Kim, Hyung-Jin. "US, China Agree to Cooperate on Climate Crisis with Urgency." AP, April 18, 2021.

Kim, Kisoo. "The Accelerated Decoupling with China: The Background and Progress of the U.S. Decoupling Strategy." Current Issues and Policies, no. 42, Sejong Institute, September 1, 2022.

Kim, Sung Chull. *China and Its Small Neighbors: The Political Economy of Asymmetry, Vulnerability, and Hedging*. Albany: State University of New York Press, 2023.

Kiplagat, Sam. "Appellate Court Rules SGR Construction Flouted Laws." *Daily Nation*, Nairobi, June 19, 2020.

Kirby, William. *Empires of Ideas: Creating the Modern University from Germany to America to China*. Cambridge, MA: Harvard University Press, 2022.

Kirk, Russell. *Roots of American Order*. Wilmington, DE: ISI Books, 2003.

Kirshner, Jonathan. "Handle Him with Care: The Importance of Getting Thucydides Right." *Security Studies* 28, no. 1 (2019): 1–24.

Kissinger, Henry. *Diplomacy*. New York: Simon and Schuster, 1994.

———. *A World Restored*. New York: Grosset and Dunlap, 1957.

———. *World Order*. New York: Penguin, 2014.

Klehr, Harvey, and Ronald Radosh. *The Amerasia Spy Case*. Chapel Hill: University of North Carolina Press, 1996.

Klein, Ezra. *Why We're Polarized*. New York: Avid, 2020.

Klein, Matthew, and Michael Pettis. *Trade Wars Are Class Wars: How Rising Inequality Distorts the Global Economy and Threatens International Peace*. New Haven, CT: Yale University Press, 2020.

Klemperer, Victor. *Language of the Third Reich: LTI—Lingua Tertii Imperii*. London: Bloombury, (1957) 2013.

Klomegah, Kester. "China Opens Its First Political Party School in Africa." *Eurasia Review*, July 5, 2022.

Kobierecka, Anna. "Post-COVID China: 'Vaccine Diplomacy' and the New Developments of Chinese Foreign Policy." *Place Branding and Public Diplomacy*, May 14, 2022.

Koehn, Peter, and Yin Xiao-huang. *The Expanding Roles of Chinese Americans in U.S.-China Relations: Transnational Networks and Trans-Pacific Interactions*. New York: Sharpe, 2002.

Koen, Ross. *The China Lobby in American Politics*. London: Octagon, 1974.

Kohler, Timothy, and Michael Smith, eds. *Ten Thousand Years of Inequality: The Archaeology of Wealth Differences*. Tucson: University of Arizona Press, 2018.

Kong Dapeng. "RMB Exchange Rate and Internationalization in the New Situation of Financial Openness" (孔大鹏: 金融开放新格局下的人民币汇率及国际化问题). *Lingdao Wencui* (领导文萃), Fuzhou, September 2021.

Koopmann, Helmut. "'German Culture Is Where I Am': Thomas Mann in Exile." *Studies in 20th Century Literature* 7, no. 1 (1982).

384 | Works and Sources Cited

Kornai, János. *Economics of Shortage*. Amsterdam: North-Holland, 1980.

———. *Socialist System: The Political Economy of Communism*. Princeton, NJ: Princeton University Press, 1992.

Kort, Michael. *The Columbia Guide to the Cold War*. New York: Columbia University Press, 2001.

Kotkin, Stephen. *Armageddon Averted: The Soviet Collapse, 1970–2000*. New York: Oxford University Press, 2001.

———. "The Cold War Never Ended: Ukraine, the China Challenge, and the Revival of the West." *Foreign Affairs*, May/June 2022.

Kowsmann, Patricia, Laurence Norman, and Ian Talley. "West Orders Seven Russian Banks Off Swift." *Wall Street Journal*, March 1, 2022.

Kristof, Nicholas. "China's Man in Washington, Named Trump." *New York Times*, June 21, 2020.

Kroenig, Matthew. *The Return of Great Power Rivalry: Democracy versus Autocracy from the Ancient World to the U.S. and China*. New York: Oxford University Press, 2020.

Kroncke, Jedidiah. *The Futility of Law and Development: China and the Dangers of Exporting American Law*. New York: Oxford University Press, 2016.

Krueger, Anne. "Trump's Spectacular Trade Failure." Project Syndicate, September 22, 2020.

Kshetri, Nir. "China's Digital Yuan: Motivations of the Chinese Government and Potential Global Effects." *Journal of Contemporary China* 32, no. 139 (2022): 87–105.

Kuik, Cheng-Chwee. "Irresistible Inducement? Assessing China's Belt and Road Initiative in Southeast Asia." *Foreign Affairs*, June 15, 2021.

Kumar, Aditi, and Eric Rosenbach. "Could China's Digital Currency Unseat the Dollar? American Economic and Geopolitical Power Is at Stake." *Foreign Affairs*, May 20, 2020.

Kurlantzick, Joshua. *Beijing's Global Media Offensive: China's Uneven Campaign to Influence Asia and the World*. New York: Oxford University Press, 2022.

Kuttner, Robert. "Can We Fix Capitalism?" *New York Review of Books*, September 24, 2020.

Kuzub, Alena. "US Leverages Its Relationship with Taiwan to Help Rebuild the Domestic Semiconductor Industry." *Northeastern Global News*, January 13, 2023.

Kwan, Macro Yuk-sing. "China's Great Wall of Finance Shows First Signs of a Crack—in Hong Kong." *Diplomat*, June 25, 2020.

Kynge, James. "US-China Economic Decoupling Accelerates in First Quarter of 2020." *Financial Times*, May 11, 2020.

Kynge, James, Lucy Hornby, and Jamil Anderline. "Inside China's Secret 'Magic Weapon' for Worldwide Influence." *Financial Times*, October 26, 2020.

Kynge, James, and Jonathan Wheatley. "China Pulls Back from the World: Rethinking Xi's 'Project of the Century.'" *Financial Times*, December 11, 2020.

Kyzy, Aruuke. *Rising Anti-Chinese Sentiment in Central Asia: A Harbinger of Regional Unrest.* Istanbul: TRT Research Centre, 2020.

Lachmann, Richard. *States and Power.* New York: Polity, 2010.

Lai Ching-te. "Taiwan Has Already Been an Independent Sovereign Country" (賴清德: 台灣已是主權獨立國家). Inaugural ceremony as chairman of the DPP, Taipei, January 18, 2023.

Lai Hairong. *Prospects of Reform: China and the World* (赖海榕: 改革的前景: 中国与世界). Beijing: Zhongyang Bianyi, 2014.

Lake, David A., et al., eds. "Challenges to the Liberal International Order: International Organization at 75." Special issue, *International Organization* 75, no. 2 (2021).

Lake, David, Lisa L. Martin, and Thomas Risse. "Challenges to the Liberal Order: Reflections on International Organization." *International Organization*, 75 no. 2 (2021): 225–57.

Lampton, David, Selina Ho, and Cheng-Chwee Kuik. *Rivers of Iron: Railroads and Chinese Power in Southeast Asia.* Oakland: University of California Press, 2020.

Lang Yage. "Chinese Carrier Group Broke Through the First Island Chain" (蓝雅歌: 中国航母编队突破第一岛链). *Huangqiu shibao* (环球时报), December 26, 2016.

Lango, John, and Richard Simmons. *The Ethics of Armed Conflict: A Cosmopolitan Just War Theory.* Edinburgh: Edinburgh University Press, 2014.

Lanza, Fabio. *The End of Concern: Maoist China, Activism, and Asian Studies.* Durham, NC: Duke University Press, 2017.

Lao Wantong. "American Imperialists Never Cease to Annihilate Us" (美帝亡我之心不死). SinoVision, July 10, 2018.

Lardy, Nicholas, and Huang Tianlei. "Despite the Rhetoric, US-China Financial Decoupling Is Not Happening." Peterson Institute for International Economics, July 2, 2020.

Large, Daniel. *China and Africa: The New Era.* Oxford, UK: Polity, 2021.

Larin, Viktor. "'Yellow Peril' Again? The Chinese and the Russian Far East." In *Rediscovering Russia in Asia: Siberia and the Russian Far East*, edited by Stephen Kotkin. New York: Sharpe, 1995.

Larkin, Emma. *Finding George Orwell in Burma.* New York: Penguin, 2004.

Lasserre, Isabelle. "The Worrisome Transfer of Technology from France to China" (Les inquiétants transferts de technologies de la France vers la Chine). *Le Figaro*, May 3, 2020.

Lautz, Terry. *Americans in China: Encounters with the People's Republic.* New York: Oxford University Press, 2022.

386 | Works and Sources Cited

Lawler, Dave. "The 53 Countries Supporting China's Crackdown on Hong Kong." *Axios*, July 3, 2020.

Le Yucheng. "The Mega Trend of Cooperation between China and the US Is Irresistible" (乐玉成: 中美走向合作的大势是挡不住的). Public speech, Beijing, July 8, 2020.

Le Zi. "FDI Affects One Hundred Million Jobs" (乐之: 外企影响数以亿计人的就业). Tencent, August 8, 2018.

Leach, Darcy K. "The Iron Law of What Again? Conceptualizing Oligarchy across Organizational Forms." *Sociological Theory* 23, no. 3 (2005): 312–37.

Lebow, Richard Ned. *A Cultural Theory of International Relations*. New York: Cambridge University Press, 2008.

———. *Forbidden Fruit: Counterfactuals and International Relations*. Princeton, NJ: Princeton, 2010.

———. *Why Nations Fight: Past and Future Motives for War*. New York: Cambridge University Press, 2010a.

Lee, Ching Kwan. "Global China at 20: Why, How and So What?" *China Quarterly* 250 (2022): 313–31.

Lee, Georgina. "Blackstone Drops US$3.05 Billion Offer for Soho China amid Regulatory Review of Takeover of the Largest Developer in Beijing." *South China Morning Post*, Hong Kong, September 10, 2021.

Lee Hsien Loong. "The Endangered Asian Century: America, China, and the Perils of Confrontation." *Foreign Affairs*, July/August 2020.

Lee, John. "Can Japan Successfully Decouple from China?" *Diplomat*, April 16, 2020.

Lee, Kristine. "The United States Can't Quit on the UN." *Foreign Affairs*, September 24, 2020.

Lee, Yen Nee. "China Is Reportedly Using LinkedIn to Recruit Spies Overseas." CNBC, August 28, 2019.

———. "The U.S. Will Remain Richer than China for the Next 50 Years or More, Says Economist." CNBC, March 26, 2021.

Lee, Yimou, and Ben Blanchard. "Taiwan President Rejects Beijing Rule." Reuters, May 19, 2020.

Leira, Halvard. "The Emergence of Foreign Policy." *International Studies Quarterly* 63, no. 1 (2019): 187–98.

Leitenberg, Milton. "Did the SARS-CoV-2 Virus Arise from a Bat Coronavirus Research Program in a Chinese Laboratory? Very Possibly." *Bulletin of the Atomic Scientists*, June 4, 2020.

Lendon, Brad. "China Has Built the World's Largest Navy—Now What's Beijing Going to Do With It?" CNN, March 5, 2021.

Leng, Cheng. "Chinese Banks Urged to Switch away from SWIFT as U.S. Sanctions Loom." Reuters, July 29, 2020.

Leng Rong et al., eds. *Chronicles of Deng Xiaoping* (冷容等: 邓小平年谱). Vol. 2. Beijing: Zhongyang Wenxian, 2004.

Leng, Sidney, and William Zheng. "China Unveils Plan to Make Hainan a Free Trade Hub like Hong Kong." *South China Morning Post*, Hong Kong, June 4, 2020.

Lenin, Vladimir. *Imperialism, the Highest Stage of Capitalism.* Eastford, CT: Martino, (1916) 2021.

Levin, Ned. "J. P. Morgan Hired Friends, Family of Leaders at 75% of Major Chinese Firms It Took Public in Hong Kong: Program Known Internally as 'Sons and Daughters.'" *Wall Street Journal*, November 30, 2015.

Levitsky, Steven, and Daniel Ziblatt. *How Democracies Die.* New York: Viking, 2018.

Levy, David, and Sandra Peart. "Soviet Growth and American Textbooks: An Endogenous Past." *Journal of Economic Behavior and Organization* 78, no. 1/2 (2011): 110–25.

Lewis, Harry. "Harvard, Hong Kong, and China." *Bits and Pieces*, July 29, 2020.

Lewis, Jeffrey, and Paulo Trevisani. "BRICS Agree to Base Development Bank in Shanghai." *Wall Street Journal*, July 15, 2014.

Lewis, Margaret. "Criminalizing China." *Journal of Criminal Law and Criminology* 111, no. 1 (2020).

Lewis, Simon. "China Has Finally Told Hong Kong It Is Holding the 3 Missing Booksellers." *Time*, February 16, 2016.

Li Bin and Xiao Tiefeng. "Rethink the Role of Nuclear Weapons" (李彬, 肖铁锋: 重审核武器的作用). *Waijiao Pinglun* (外交评论), no. 3, 2010, 3–9.

Li Chen and Odd Arne Westad. "Can Cold War History Prevent U.S.-Chinese Calamity?" *Foreign Affairs*, November 29, 2021.

Li, Cheng. *Chinese Politics in the Xi Jinping Era.* Brookings, 2016.

———. *Middle Class Shanghai.* Brookings, 2021.

———. "Pelosi's Visit to Taiwan: Provoking the First. AI War in History?" *China and US Focus*, August 26, 2022.

Li, Eric. "Xi Jinping Is a 'Good Emperor.'" *Foreign Policy*, May 14, 2020.

Li Fan. "Don't Give Up on Chinese Democracy: Times Are Dark, but Civil Society Is Quietly Growing." *Foreign Policy*, July 8, 2020.

Li Guoli et al. "Chinese Big Dipper, Serves the World" (李国利等: 中国北斗 服务全球). *Xinhua* (新华), June 23, 2020.

Li Honsen. "Analyze the 'Characteristics' of Socialism with Chinese Characteristics" (刘洪森: 中国特色社会主义之"特色"探析). *Gaoxiao Makesi Zhuyi Lilun Yanjiu* (高校马克思主义理论研究) 3, no. 1 (2017): 137–44.

Li Jianglin. *1959 Lhasa* (李江琳: 1959 拉萨). Hong Kong: Xinshiji, 2011.

Li Jing. "First Round of Sino-American Economic Dialogue" (李静: 首轮中美经济对话). *Zhongxin* (中新), July 29, 2009.

388 | Works and Sources Cited

Li Lu. "The Future of the Chinese Economy from a Foreign Investor's Perspective" (李录: 从外国投资人角度看中国经济的未来). International Investors' Conference, Beijing, 2019.

Li Rui. *Witness Account of the Great Leap Forward* (李锐: 大跃进亲历记). Vols. 1–2. Haikou: Nanfang, 1999.

Li, Shaomin. *The Rise of China, Inc.* New York: Cambridge University Press, 2022.

Li Shaowei. "The US Is Not Coming Back" (李少威: 美国回不来了). *Nanfengchuan* (南风窗), Guangzhou, March 24, 2021.

Li Shu. "I. M. Pei at 100 and His Pei Clan" (李舒: 100岁的贝聿铭和他的贝氏家族). *Lianhe zobao* (联合早报), Singapore, May 1, 2017.

Li Xiaofeng. "The CCP Was for Taiwanese Independence Before" (李筱峰: 中共以前是贊成台獨的). *Apple Daily* (蘋果日報), Hong Kong, May 6, 2015.

Li Xuemei, et al. "Chairman Xi Jinping's Speech at the First Phase of the 17th G-20 Summit Meeting Leads the Direction of Global Development" (李学梅等: 习近平主席在二十国集团领导人第十七次峰会第一阶段会议上的重要讲话引领全球发展方向). Xinhua (新华), November 16, 2022.

Li Yuan. "With Selective Coronavirus Coverage, China Builds a Culture of Hate." *New York Times*, April 23, 2020.

Li Zhiwei. "Yang Jiechi and Wang Yi Hold High-Level Sino-American Strategic Dialogue with Blinken and Sullivan" (李志伟: 杨洁篪、王毅同布林肯、沙利文举行中美高层战略对话). *Renmin Ribao* (人民日报), March 21, 2021.

Li, Zhuqing. *Daughters of the Flower Fragrant Garden: Two Sisters Separated by China's Civil War.* New York: Norton, 2022.

Lian Ping. "Seven Major Moves to Accelerate the Steps of RMB Internationalization" (连平: 七大举措加快人民币国际化发展步伐). *Shouxi Jingji Xuejia* (首席经济学家), November 27, 2020.

Lianhe zaobao (联合早报). "Hong Kong Financial Bureau Works with Mainland to Expand the Use of RMB in Security Market" (港金管局与内地研究扩大人民币股市交易使用). Singapore, September 29, 2021.

Liang Qichao. *Record of the Wuxu Coup* (梁啟超: 戊戌政變記). Nanning: Guangxi Shida, (1899) 2010.

Library of Congress. *Respectfully Quoted: A Dictionary of Quotations.* Mineola, NY: Dover, 2010.

Lien Xiaotong. "The Tradition, Dilemma and Future of 'Neiwai Youbie' Principle" (连小童: "内外有别"原则的传统、困境与未来). *Today's Media* (今传媒), Beijing, December 21, 2016.

Liff, Adam P., Dalton Lin, et al. "'One China' Framework and International Politics after Fifty Years (1972–2022)." Special section, *China Quarterly* 252 (2022).

Lilla, Mark. "The End of Identity Liberalism." *New York Times*, November 20, 2016.

———. "When Will My Fellow Liberals Learn?" *UnHerd*, November 4, 2020.

Works and Sources Cited | 389

Lim, Dawn, and Stella Yifan Xie. "BlackRock Gets Go-Ahead for a Mutual-Fund Business in China." *Wall Street Journal*, August 29, 2021.

Lin, Bonny, Cristina L. Garafola, Bruce Mcclintock, Jonah Blank, Jeffrey W. Hornung, Karen Schwindt, Jennifer D. P. Moroney, Paul Orner, Dennis Borrman, Sarah W. Denton, and Jason Chambers. *Competition in the Gray Zone: Countering China's Coercion against U.S. Allies and Partners in the Indo-Pacific.* RAND Corporation, 2022.

Lin, Justin Yifu. *China's Miraculous Development Strategy and Economic Reform* (林毅夫: 中国的奇迹发展战略与经济改革). Shanghai: Shanghai Renmin, 1999.

———. *New Structural Economics* (新结构经济学). Beijing: Beida, 2012.

Lind, Michael. "The China Question." *Tablet Magazine*, May 19, 2020.

Link, Perry. "Why We Should Criticize Mo Yan." *New York Review*, December 24, 2012.

———. "Recounting My 60 Years of Studying China" (林培瑞:回顾中国研究六十年). VOA Chinese, January 12, 2023.

Lippman, Thomas. "Bush Makes Clinton's China Policy an Issue." *Washington Post*, August 20, 1999.

Lippmann, Walter. *Cold War.* New York: Harper, 1947.

Lipset, Seymour Martin, Martin A. Trow, and James S. Coleman. *Union Democracy.* New York: Free Press, (1956) 1977.

Liptak, Kevin. "Biden Vows to Protect Taiwan in Event of Chinese Attack." CNN, October 22, 2021.

Liptak, Kevin, and Kate Sullivan. "G7 Calls for New Study into Origins of Covid and Voices Concern on China." CNN, June 14, 2021.

Lishi Yanjiu. "1984, President Reagan Walked into Fudan Classroom" (历史研究: 1984, 里根总统走进复旦课堂). *Sohu* (搜狐), Shanghai, November 9, 2017.

Liu Cixin. *The Wandering Earth* (刘慈欣: 流浪地球). Wuhan: Changjiang, 2008.

Liu Hong et al. "China Approaches the Center of the World Stage" (刘洪等: 走近世界舞台中央的中国). Xinhua (新华), July 31, 2017.

Liu Hui. "The Chinese Citizens Caught in Russia's Covid-19 Crackdown." *Sixth Tone*, Shanghai, March 13, 2020.

Liu Jiaju. *Behind the Glory: My Observation inside the PLA* (刘家驹: 光荣的背后: 我的军旅见闻). Austin, TX: Huayi, 2020.

Liu Jun. "New Drivers and New Mission of Internationalizing RMB" (刘珺: 人民币国际化的新动力新使命). *Zhongguo Jinrong* (中国金融), no. 17, September 2021.

Liu, Jun. *Shifting Dynamics of Contention in the Digital Age: Mobile Communication and Politics in China.* New York: Oxford University Press, 2020.

Liu, Kin-Ming, ed. *My First Trip to China: Scholars, Diplomats and Journalists Reflect on their First Encounters with China.* Hong Kong: Hong Kong University Press, 2012.

Liu Ming. "How to Interpret the American 'Worldview'" (刘明: 如何解读美国的"世界观"). *Huanqiu* (环球), Beijing, no. 15, July 24, 2019.

Liu Minglu. "My 26 Days of Life and Death in the Counterattack War on Vietnam" (刘明录: 我在对越还击战中的生死26天). WeChat blog (微信公众号), November 22, 2021.

Liu Sanjie (Liu Song). *Qin Bricks: Revelation of the Rise and Fall of the Great Qin Empire* (刘三解 <刘嵩>: 秦砖: 大秦帝国兴亡启示录). Beijing: Lianhe, 2020.

Liu Weidong et al. *Third-Party Assessment on BRI Construction 2013–2018* (刘卫东等: 一带一路建设进展第三方评估报告2013~2018). Beijing: Shangwu, 2019.

Liu, Xiaoyuan. *To the End of Revolution: The Chinese Communist Party and Tibet, 1949–1959*. New York: Columbia University Press, 2020.

Liu Yang and Sun Xingwei. "New Healthcare Policy for Military Families" (刘阳、孙兴维: 军人家庭医疗待遇保障新政策). *Jiefangjun bao* (解放军报), Beijing, October 27, 2021.

Liu Yazhou. *Treatise on the West Region* (刘亚洲: 西部论) (2004). Excepted in *Fenghuang zhoukan* (凤凰周刊), Hong Kong, August 5, 2010.

Liu, Yi-Ling. "China's 'Involuted' Generation." *New Yorker*, May 14, 2021.

Liu Yu. "Have You Had Schmitt Today?" (刘瑜: 今天您施密特了吗). *Caijing* (财经), Beijing, no. 18, 2010.

Lively, Jack, ed. *The Works of Joseph de Maistre*. New York: Schocken, 1971.

Lloyd-Damnjanovic, Anastasya, and Alexander Bowe. *Overseas Chinese Students and Scholars in China's Drive for Innovation*. U.S.-China Economic and Security Review Commission, 2020.

Locke, John. *The Second Treatise of Government*. Indianapolis: Hackett, (1690) 1980.

Loewe, Laurence, et al. "Negative Selection." In *Evolutionary Genetics*, edited by Bob Sheehy and Norman Johnson, 59. London: Nature Education, 2008.

Lopez, Linette. "Beijing's Campaign to Rein in Tesla Has Begun." *Business Insider*, April 30, 2021.

Lorenzo, David. *Conceptions of Chinese Democracy: Reading Sun Yat-sen, Chiang Kai-shek, and Chiang Ching-kuo*. Baltimore: Johns Hopkins University Press, 2013.

Losey, Stephen. "Kendall: Despite Russian Invasion, China Remains Military's Top Challenge." *Defense News*, March 3, 2022.

Loughlin, Martin. *Against Constitutionalism*. Cambridge, MA: Harvard University Press, 2022.

Lovell, Julia. *Maoism: A Global History*. New York: Knopf, 2019.

Lowsen, Ben. "The Four Types of China Engager: Which Are You? Dragon Slayer, Diplomat, Sinologist, or Panda Hugger, Where Do You Fit In?" *Diplomat*, January 28, 2017.

Lu Gang. "Strategic Restrictions of BRI and Ways to Avoid Them" (陆钢: "一带一路"建设的战略制约因素及其规避策略). *Shehui Kexue* (社会科学), Shanghai, no. 3, 2019.

Lu, Mai, ed. *The Chinese Dream and Ordinary Chinese People*. Singapore: Springer, 2021.

Lu, Shen. "New Wave of Podcasts Is Shaking Up Chinese-Language Media." *Politico*, July 23, 2020.

Lu Xun. "In Memory of Ms. Liu Hezheng" (鲁迅: 記念劉和珍君). *Yusi* (語絲), 74, April 1926.

Lu, Yi-hsuan, and Dennis Xie. "New High of 83.2% See Themselves as Taiwanese." *Taiwan Times*, February 25, 2020.

Lucas, Edward. "Time Is Running Out for the West to Stop China's Global Takeover." *Times*, April 25, 2020.

Luce/ACLS China Studies Advisory Group. *China Studies in North America: A Report on Survey Research*. American Council of Learned Societies, 2021.

Lynch, Leah, Sharon Andersen, and Tianyu Zhu. *China's Foreign Aid: A Primer for Recipient Countries, Donors, and Aid Providers*. CGD Note, Center for Global Development, July 9, 2020.

Lynch, Sarah. "U.S. Justice Department to End Trump-Era Program Targeting Threats Posed by China." Reuters, February 23, 2022.

Lynch, Thomas, III, ed. *Strategic Assessment 2020: Into a New Era of Great Power Competition*. Washington, DC: Institute for National Strategic Studies, National Defense University, 2021.

Ma Haoliang. "Carrier Shangdong Broke Island Chains, Deter Western Pacific" (马浩亮: 山东舰破岛链 慑西太). Takunpao (大公报), April 10, 2023.

Ma Lirong. "Assessing the Impact on 'Xinjiang Independence' in the Security Context of BRI" (马丽蓉: 中国"一带一路"战略安全环境中"疆独"问题影响评估). *Guoji guancha* (国际观察), Shanghai, no. 3, 2015, 109–20.

Ma Singshen. "[North] Korea Gunned Down Chinese, PLA Looks the Other Way (朝鲜枪杀中国边民, 解放军网开一面). *Sina* (新浪), June 12, 2010.

Ma Xia. *Tianxia Currency—to Break and End the USD Hegemony* (马霞: 天下货币-美元霸权的突破与终结). Beijing: Zhongguo Caifu, 2021.

Mações, Bruno. *Belt and Road: A Chinese World Order*. London: Hurst, 2019.

MacArthur, Douglas. *Reminiscences*. New York: McGraw Hill, 1964.

Mackinder, H. J. "The Geographical Pivot of History." *Geographical Journal* 23, no. 4 (1904).

MacLennan, Julio. *Europa: How Europe Shaped the Modern World*. New York: Pegasus, 2018.

Macleod, Alasdair. "China Is Killing the Dollar." *Goldmoney*, September 17, 2020.

MacMillan, Margaret. *Nixon and Mao: The Week that Changed the World*. New York: Random House, 2008.

Madhok, Diksha. "World's Top Chip Maker Mulls Global Expansion with Plants in Europe, Japan." CNN, January 13, 2023.

Madsen, Richard. "The Academic China Specialists." In *American Studies of Contemporary China*, edited by David Shambaugh, 163–74. New York: Sharpe, 1993.

392 | Works and Sources Cited

Magnus, George. "A Messy Financial Divorce for the US and China." Project Syndicate, December 30, 2020.

———. "Economics, National Security, and the Competition with China." *War on Rocks*, March 3, 2021.

———. "China Has Little to Gain but Much to Lose as Russia's Ally." *Guardian*, March 4, 2022.

Mahtani, Shibani, and Amrita Chandradas. "In Singapore, Loud Echoes of Beijing's Positions Generate Anxiety." *Washington Post*, July 24, 2023.

Maizland, Lindsay. *China's Repression of Uighurs in Xinjiang*. New York: Council on Foreign Relations, 2021.

Maizland, Lindsay, and Eleanor Albert. *Hong Kong's Freedoms: What China Promised and How It's Cracking Down*. Backgrounder, Council on Foreign Relations, February 17, 2021.

Makichuk, Dave. "Malabar 2020: A Show of Force on China's Doorstep." *Asia Times*, November 4, 2020.

Malia, Martin. *The Soviet Tragedy: A History of Socialism in Russia, 1917–1991*. New York: Free Press, 1994.

Mallapaty, Smriti, Amy Maxmen, and Ewen Callaway. "'Major Stones Unturned': COVID Origin Search Must Continue after WHO Report, Say Scientists." *Nature*, February 10, 2021.

Mandelbaum, Michael. "The Sources of Chinese Conduct." *American Purpose*, January 24, 2023.

Mann, James. "Donations Add to Influence in U.S.: Taiwan a Big Contributor to Think Tanks." *Los Angeles Times*, September 5, 1988.

———. "Taiwan Lobbying in U.S. Gets Results." *Los Angeles Times*, November 4, 1996.

———. *The China Fantasy: Why Capitalism Will Not Bring Democracy to China*. New York: Penguin, 2007.

———. "How the West Got China Wrong." *Economist*, May 1, 2018.

———. "How Nixon's Fabled Trip to China, 50 Years Ago This Week, Led to Today's Taiwan Crisis." *Los Angeles Times*, Febraury 21, 2022.

Manning, Robert. "The United States Can Negotiate with a China Driven More by Power than Ideology." *Foreign Policy*, December 4, 2020.

Mansfield, Edward, and Jack Snyder. "Democratic Transitions, Institutional Strength, and War." *International Organization* 56, no. 2 (2002): 297–337.

Mantesso, Sean. "China's 'Dark' Fishing Fleets Are Plundering the World's Oceans." Australian Broadcasting Corporation (ABC), December 18, 2020.

Mao Zedong. "Conversation with US Reporter Anna Louise Strong" (和美国记者安娜·刘易斯·斯特朗的谈话). In *Selected Works of Mao Zedong* (毛泽东选集), vol. 4. Beijing: Renmin, (1946) 1991.

———. "Opinion on Industry Papers of the Beidaihe Conference" (毛泽东: 对北戴河会议工业类文件的意见). In *Mao Zedong's Manuscripts since the Founding of the State* (建国以来毛泽东文稿), vol. 7. Beijing: Zhongyang Wenxian, (September 2, 1958) 1992, 368.

———. *Collected works* (毛泽东文集). Vols. 1–7, Beijing: Renmin, 1999.

———. "On the Question If Imperialism and All Reactionaries Are Real Tigers" (关于帝国主义和一切反动派是不是真老虎的问题). In *Selected Works of Mao Zedong* (毛泽东文集), vol. 7. Beijing, China: Renmin, (1958) 1999.

Mapping Militant Organizations. "Communist Party of the Philippines—New People's Army." Mapping Militant Organizations, Stanford University, August 2018.

Mark, Clifton. "A Belief in Meritocracy Is Not Only False: It's Bad for You." *Aeon*, March 8, 2019.

Markay, Lachlan, and Bethany Allen-Ebrahimian. "Bush Family Nonprofit's $5 Million Deal with China Influence Group." *Axios*, June 5, 2021.

Markey, Edward. *Speech on China*. CSIS, November 17, 2022.

Marlow, Iain. "Bill Clinton Says China's Direction under Xi Upended U.S. Ties." *Bloomberg*, November 16, 2020.

Marshall, Joshua. "Exhuming McCarthy." *American Prospect*, December 19, 2001.

Martin, Peter. *China's Civilian Army: The Making of Wolf Warrior Diplomacy.* New York: Oxford University Press, 2021.

Martin, Peter, Courtney McBride, and Roxana Tiron. "Russia's War on Ukraine, China's Rise Expose US Military Failings." *Bloomberg*, February 21, 2023.

Martin, Rachel. "If China Aligns Itself with Russia, That Could Impact Its Reputation and Economy." *Morning Edition*, NPR, March 16, 2022.

Martina, Michael. "Why the US Delayed China Sanctions after Shooting Down a Spy Balloon." Reuters, May 11, 2023.

Maruyama, Masao. *Thought and Behaviour in Modern Japanese Politics*. Oxford: Oxford University Press, 1963.

———. *Loyalty and Rebellion: State of Japan's Spiritual History during the Period of Transition* (丸山眞男: 忠誠と反逆 - 転形期日本の精神史的位相). Tokyo: Chikuma, 1998.

———. *The Logic and Psychology of Ultra-Statism* (丸山眞男:超国家主義の論理と心理の論理と心理). Tokyo: Iwanami, (1946) 2015.

Mastro, Oriana. "The Theory and Practice of War Termination: Assessing Patterns in China's Historical Behavior." *International Studies Review* 20, no. 4 (2018): 661–84.

Maté, Aaron. "Veteran Diplomat Chas Freeman on U.S. vs. China." *Grey Zone*, December 25, 2020.

Matovski, Aleksandar. *Popular Dictatorships: Crises, Mass Opinion, and the Rise of Electoral Authoritarianism*. New York: Cambridge University Press, 2021.

Mattingly, Daniel, Trevor Incerti, Changwook Ju, Colin Moreshead, Seiki Tanaka, and Hikaru Yamagishi. "Chinese State Media Persuades a Global Audi-

394 | Works and Sources Cited

ence That the 'China Model' is Superior: Evidence from A 19-Country Experiment." OSF Preprints, Center for Open Science, January 18, 2023.

Mattis, Peter. "Yes, the Atrocities in Xinjiang Constitute a Genocide." *Foreign Policy*, April 15, 2021.

Mattis, Peter, and Matthew Brazil. *Chinese Communist Espionage: An Intelligence Primer*. Annapolis, MD: Naval Institute Press, 2020.

Mauldin, John. "China's Grand Plan to Take over the World." *Forbes*, November 12, 2019.

Mauldin, William. "U.S. Looks to Make China Pay for Close Ties to Russia in Ukraine Crisis." *Wall Street Journal*, February 27, 2022.

May, Tiffany. "International Students Return to Pre-pandemic Levels with Chinese Students Accounting for Nearly Half of Them" (赴美留学人数回升至疫前水平, 中国学生占比近半). *New York Times in Chinese*, August 25, 2021.

Mayorkas, Alejandro. "Tackling an Evolving Threat Landscape." Speech at CFR, April 21, 2023.

Mazarr, Michael, Timothy R. Heath, and Astrid Stuth Cevallos. *China and the International Order*. RAND Corporation, June 2018.

———. "US/China Competition." In *Chinese Strategic Intentions*, edited by Nicole Peterson, 131–38. Strategic Multilayer Assessment (SMA) white paper, US DOD, December 2019.

McAuliffe, Marie, and Binod Khadri, eds. *World Migration Report 2020*. UN, IOM, 2020.

McClory, Jonathan, et al. *The Soft Power 30*. Los Angeles: USC, 2019.

McCourt, David. "The Changing U.S. China Watching Community and the Demise of Engagement with the PRC." *Journal of American-East Asian Relations* 29, no. 1, 2022.

———. "Knowledge Communities in US Foreign Policy Making: The American China Field and the End of Engagement with the PRC." *Security Studies* 31, no. 4, 2022a.

McDonald, Patrick. "Peace through Trade or Free Trade?" *Journal of Conflict Resolution* 48, no. 4 (2004): 547–72.

McDonell, Stephen. "The Ukraine Crisis Is a Major Challenge for China." BBC, February 28, 2022.

McFaul, Michael. "Cold War Lessons and Fallacies for US-China Relations Today." *Washington Quarterly* 43, no. 4 (December 2020): 7–39.

McGahan, Jason. "How José Huizar Became Embroiled in the Worst Corruption Scandal in Almost a Century." *Los Angeles Magazine*, June 23, 2020.

McGann, James. *2018 Global Go to Think Tank Index Report*. Philadelphia: University of Pennsylvania, 2019.

McGee, Patrick. "How Apple Tied Its Fortunes to China." *Financial Times*, January 18, 2023.

Works and Sources Cited | 395

McGregor, Katharine E. "The Indonesian Killings of 1965–1966." In *Mass Violence and Resistance* (Violence de masse et résistance), August 4, 2009.

McGregor, Richard. "Xi Jinping's Radical Secrecy." *Atlantic*, August 21, 2022.

McIntire, Mike. "Trump Records Shed New Light on Chinese Business Pursuits." *New York Times*, October 21, 2020.

McKinnon, John. "U.S. to Impose Sweeping Rule Aimed at China Technology Threats." *Wall Street Journal*, February 26, 2021.

McLaughlin, Kathleen. "Underground Labs in China Are Devising Potent New Opiates Faster Than Authorities Can Respond." *Science*, March 29, 2017.

McLeary, Paul. "Pentagon Predicts 5 Times Increase in China's Nuclear Weapons over Next 10 Years." *Politico*, Novmeber 3, 2021.

McMahon, Dinny. "The Wanda Warning: Behind Wang Jianlin's Global Aspirations Was a Comedy of Errors." *Wire China*, June 28, 2020.

Mearsheimer, John. *The Tragedy of Great Power Politics*. Updated ed. New York: Norton, (2001) 2014.

———. "Bound to Fail: The Rise and Fall of the Liberal International Order." *International Security* 43, no. 4 (2019): 7–50.

Medeiros, Evan. "The Changing Fundamentals of US-China Relations." *Washington Quarterly* 42, no. 3 (2019): 93–119.

———. "China's Strategic Straddle: Analyzing Beijing's Diplomatic Response to the Russian Invasion of Ukraine." *China Leadership Monitor*, no. 72, June 1, 2022.

Medeiros, Evan, and Ashley Tellis. "Regime Change Is Not an Option in China: Focus on Beijing's Behavior, Not Its Leadership." *Foreign Affairs*, July 8, 2021.

Medvedev, Roy. *Post-Soviet Russia*. Translated by George Shriver. New York: Columbia University Press, 2002.

Mei Zhu. "The Future of China: Cooperation over Confrontation" (梅竹: 中国的未来: 合作>>对抗). WeChat blog (微信公众号), March 13, 2022.

Melville, Andrei, and Gail Lapidus, eds. *The Glasnost Papers: Voices on Reform from Moscow*. Boulder, CO: Westview Press, 1990.

Mendes, Candido. "Chinese Officials Complain about Angolan Kidnapping Scourge." *Bloomberg*, November 9, 2015.

Meng Weizhan (孟维瞻). "Unity, Democracy, and Anti-Americanism in China." *Washington Quarterly* 42, no. 3 (2019): 121–35.

Merk, Frederick, and Lois Merk. *Manifest Destiny and Mission in American History*. Cambridge, MA: Harvard University Press, 1995.

Mertha, Andrew. "A Half Century of Engagement: The Study of China and the Role of the China Scholar Community." In *Engaging China: Fifty Years of Sino-American Relations*, edited by Anne Thurston, 89–119. New York: Columbia University Press, 2021.

396 | Works and Sources Cited

Mesmer, Philippe. "Japan and South Korea Want NATO to Look toward Asia." *Le Monde*, June 29, 2022.

Metzl, Jamie. "How to Hold Beijing Accountable for the Coronavirus: Why Did China Cover Up the Epidemic?" *Wall Street Journal*, July 28, 2020.

———. "10 Questions for Zhao Lijian." Jamie Metzl blog, April 13, 2021.

Meyer, Michael. *The Last Days of Old Beijing: Life in the Vanishing Backstreets of a City Transformed*. New York: Walker, 2008.

Meyskens, Covell. *Mao's Third Front: The Militarization of Cold War China*. New York: Cambridge University Press, 2020.

Michaels, Dave. "White House Seeks Crackdown on U.S.-Listed Chinese Firms." *Wall Street Journal*, August 6, 2020.

Michel, Charles. "A Stronger and More Autonomous European Union Powering a Fairer World." Speech to the UN General Assembly, September 25, 2020.

Michels, Robert. *Political Parties: A Sociological Study of the Oligarchical Tendencies of Modern Democracy*. New York: Free Press, (1911) 1962.

Mierzejewski, Dominik, Bartosz Kowalski, and Jarosław Jura. "The Domestic Mechanisms of China's Vertical Multilateralism." *Journal of Contemporary China*, August 2022.

Migdal, Joel. *Strong Societies and Weak States*. Princeton, NJ: Princeton University Press, 1988.

Milanovic, Branko. *Capitalism, Alone: The Future of the System That Rules the World*. Cambridge, MA: Harvard University Press, 2019.

Miller, Chris. *Chip War: The Fight for the World's Most Critical Technology*. New York: Scribner, 2022.

Millward, James. "We Need a Better Middle Road on China." *Washington Post*, August 6, 2019.

———. "China as Polylith: It's Time for a New Paradigm in Chinese History." Personal blog, October 11, 2020.

Mina, An Xiao, and Jan Chipchase. "Inside Shenzhen's Race to Outdo Silicon Valley." *MIT Technology Review*, December 18, 2018.

Ministries of Education and Ministry of Finance. *Statistical Communique on National Education Spending in 2018* (2018年全国教育经费执行情况统计公告). Beijing, Oct. 10, 2019.

Ministry of Commerce. "China Declares $60 Billion in Aid to Africa" (中国宣布将拨款600亿美元援助非洲). Beijing, September 10, 2018.

———. *Statistical Report of FDI in China 2019*, Beijing, 2019.

Ministry of Foreign Affairs. *On Viet Nam's Expulsion of Chinese Residents*. Beijing: Waiwen, 1978.

———. *Ordinary Chinese Passport Holder Entrance Privilege* (持普通护照中国公民前往有关国家和地区入境便利待遇). January 1, 2020.

———. "Suspend Debt Payment from 77 Developing Countries and Regions" (外交部: 向77个发展中国家和地区暂停债务偿还). Beijing, June 7, 2020a.

———. "China and Russia Signed a Series of Cooperation Documents" [中俄签署一系列合作文件]. Beijing, February 4, 2022.

———. "Countermeasures in Response to Nancy Pelosi's Visit to Taiwan." Xinhua (新华), Beijing, August 5, 2022.

———. *Mistakes in US Views of China and the Facts and Truth* (外交部: 美国对华认知中的谬误和事实真相). Beijing, June 19, 2022.

———. *US Hegemony and Its Perils* (美国的霸权霸道霸凌及其危害). Beijing, February 20, 2023.

Ministry of Housing and Urban-Rural Development. *2020 Yearbook of China's Urban-Rural Development* (中国城乡建设统计年鉴). Beijing, 2020.

Minzhi International Research Institute (民智国际研究院). "Why It Is Necessary to Win over the American Leftists" (为何必须争取美国左派). Beijing, April 24, 2020.

Mirovalev, Mansur. "Why Are Central Asian Countries So Quiet on Uighur Persecution?" *Al Jazeera*, February 24, 2020.

Mirsky, Jonathan. "Many Poisoned Rivers." *Literary Review*, July 2010.

Mitchell, Tom, Demetri Sevastopulo, Sun Yu, and James Kynge. "The Rising Costs of China's Friendship with Russia." *Financial Times*, March 10, 2022.

Mitter, Rana. *China's Good War: How World War II Is Shaping a New Nationalism*. Cambridge, MA: Belknap Press of Harvard University Press, 2020.

———. "The World China Wants." *Foreign Affairs*, January/February 2021.

Mo Lin. "Debating Prof. Wang Jisi on How to Deal with the US" (牟林: 就中国和美国相处之道与王缉思教授商榷). *Qinan Zhanlue* (秦安战略), Beijing, September 13, 2021.

Mobley, Terry. "The Belt and Road Initiative: Insights from China's Backyard." *Strategic Studies Quarterly* 13, no. 3 (2019): 52–72.

Mok, Charles, and Dennis Kwok. "China's Neo-nationalism Poses Risks for International Businesses." *Diplomat*, November 2, 2021.

Mole, Beth. "Early Adopters of Chinese Vaccines See Case Surges; China Plows Ahead Anyway." *Ars Technica*, June 4, 2021.

Moore, Charles. "Margaret Thatcher's Battle over Europe." *Wall Street Journal*, December 6, 2019.

Mordecai, Mara, and Moira Fagan. "Americans' Views of Key Foreign Policy Goals Depend on Their Attitudes toward International Cooperation." Pew Research Center, April 23, 2021.

Morgan, John. "When Do Professors Self-Censor? British Professors Are More Likely to Do So When They Are Teaching a Class That Includes Chinese Students, Study Finds." *Times Higher Education*, February 25, 2022.

Morgan, Stephen, and Christopher Winship. *Counterfactuals and Causal Inference*. New York: Cambridge University Press, 2007.

Morgenthau, Hans. *Politics among Nations: The Struggle for Power and Peace*. New York: Knopf, 1948.

398 | Works and Sources Cited

———. "The Primacy of the National Interest." *American Scholar* 18, no. 2 (1949): 207–12.

Morris, Ian. *War! What Is It Good For? Conflict and the Progress of Civilization from Primates to Robots.* New York: Farrar, Straus and Giroux, 2014.

Moscovici, Serge. *The Age of the Crowd: A Historical Treatise on Mass Psychology* (L'age des foules: Un traité historique de psychologie des masses). Translated by J. C. Whitehouse. Cambridge: Cambridge University Press, (1981) 1985.

Mosher, Steven. *Bully of Asia: Why China's Dream Is the New Threat to World Order.* Washington, DC: Regnery, 2017.

Mostafavi, Hakhamanesh, Tomaz Berisa, Felix R. Day, John R. B. Perry, Molly Przeworski, and Joseph K. Pickrell. "Identifying Genetic Variants that Affect Viability in Large Cohorts." *PLOS Biology* 15, no. 9 (2017): 1–29.

Moynihan, Maura. "Top Western Elites Are Now Cheerleaders for Xi's China." *Asian Age*, May 8, 2020.

Mozur, Paul. "Forget TikTok—China's Powerhouse App Is WeChat, and Its Power Is Sweeping." *New York Times*, September 6, 2020.

Mozur, Paul, and Raymond Zhong. "U.S. Tightens Visa Rules for Chinese Communist Party Members." *New York Times*, December 4, 2020.

Mu Guangfeng. "Story of Duan Family Reunion" (牟广丰: 段家寻亲记). WeChat blog (微信公众号), January 15, 2022.

Mu Xi. "154 Stocks in US Face Delisting" (木樨: 154只美股股票濒临退市). ChinaIPO.com (资本邦), Beijing, May 12, 2020.

Muhammad, Jeannette. "U.S. Joins EU in Sanctions against China over Treatment of Uyghur Muslims." NPR, March 22, 2021.

Munck, Gerardo, and Richard Snyder, eds. *Passion, Craft, and Method in Comparative Politics.* Baltimore: Johns Hopkins University Press, 2007.

Münkler, Herfried. *Empires: The Logic of World Domination from Ancient Rome to the United States.* Translated by Patrick Camiller. New York: Polity, (2005) 2007.

Murphree, Michael. "Whither Global Value Chains: The Shifting Role of Taiwanese FDI in Mainland China." In *China's New Development Strategies*, edited by Gary Gereffi, Penny Bamber, and Karina Fernandez-Stark, 141–66. Singapore: Palgrave, 2022.

Myerson, Roger. *Game Theory: Analysis of Conflict.* Cambridge, MA: Harvard University Press, 1991.

Myrdal, Gunnar. *Asian Drama.* New York: Pantheon, 1968.

MZIRI (Minzhi International Research Institute 民智国际研究院). "Why Is It Necessary to Win Over the American Leftists" (为何必须争取美国左派). Beijing, Apr 24, 2020.

Nagel, Ernest, and James Newman. *Gödel's Proof.* Rev. ed. New York: New York University Press, 2008.

Naisbitt, John, and Doris Naisbitt. *China's Megatrends: The 8 Pillars of a New Society*. New York: Harper, 2010.

Nantulya, Paul. "Chinese Security Contractors in Africa." Carnegie-Tsinghua Center for Global Policy, Beijing, October 8, 2020.

Nardin, Terry. "From Right to Intervene to Duty to Protect: Michael Walzer on Humanitarian Intervention." *European Journal of International Law* 24, no. 1 (2013): 67–82.

National Association of Scholars. "How Many Confucius Institutes Are in the United States?" National Association of Scholars, May 15, 2020.

National Intelligence Council. *Global Trends 2040: A More Contested World*. NIC, 2021.

National People's Congress. National Security Law of the People's Republic of China. Beijing, July 1, 2015.

———. Law of the People's Republic of China on Safeguarding National Security in the Hong Kong Special Administrative Region. Beijing, June 30, 2020.

———. Law of the People's Republic of China on the Hainan Free Trade Port (中华人民共和国海南自由贸易港法). Beijing, June 10, 2021.

National Public Radio. "The U.S. Made a Breakthrough Battery Discovery—Then Gave the Technology to China." *All Things Considered*, NPR, August 3, 2022.

National Security Council. "President Trump on China: Putting America First." November 2, 2020.

NATO. *2022 Strategic Concept*. Madrid: North Atlantic Organization, 2022.

———. *Vilnius Summit Communiqué*. North Atlantic Organization, July 11, 2023.

Naughton, Barry. "A Perspective on Chinese Economics." In *Engaging China: Fifty Years of Sino-American Relations*, edited by Anne Thurston, 74–198. New York: Columbia University Press, 2021.

Naughton, Barry, and Briana Boland. *CCP Inc.: The Reshaping of China's State Capitalist System*. Washington, DC: CSIS, 2023.

Naumenko, Vyacheslav. *Great Betrayal: Repatriation of Cossacks at Lienz and Other Places*. Tanslated by William Dritschilo. New York: All Slavic, (1962) 2015.

Navarro, Peter. *Death by China: Confronting the Dragon—a Global Call to Action*. New York: Pearson, 2011.

———. *Crouching Tiger: What China's Militarism Means for the World*. Buffalo: Prometheus, 2015.

———. "Economic Security as National Security." CSIS, November 9, 2018.

NCSES. *Survey of Earned Doctorates 2019*. Washington, DC: National Science Foundation, 2020.

Neumann, Manfred. *Competition Policy: History, Theory and Practice*. Cheltenham, UK: Edward Elgar, 2001.

Neumann, Manfred, and Oskar Morgenstern. *Theory of Games and Economic Behavior*. Princeton, NJ: Princeton University Press, (1944) 2004.

400 | Works and Sources Cited

New York Magazine. "In 20 Years, the Internet Will Split in Two—Then Go to War with Itself." Editorial, October 25, 2018.

New York Times. "China in the United States." Editorial, July 23, 1881.

———. "'China Lobby,' Once Powerful Factor in U. S. Politics, Appears Victim of Lack of Interest." April 26, 1970.

Ng, Abigail. "Hong Kong Residents Are Flocking to Singapore." CNBC, April 27, 2022.

Nhem, Boraden. *Khmer Rouge: Ideology, Militarism, and the Revolution That Consumed a Generation.* Westport, CT: Praeger, 2013.

Ni, Vincent. "They Were Fooled by Putin." *Guardian,* February 27, 2022.

Nichols, Tom. *The Death of Expertise: The Campaign against Established Knowledge and Why It Matters.* New York: Oxford University Press, 2017.

Nietzsche, Friedrich. *The Birth of Tragedy.* New York: Penguin, (1872) 2005.

———. *Beyond Good and Evil.* Suwanee, GA: Twelfth Media, (1885) 2018.

Niewenhuis, Lucas. "What Did Apple Get Out of Its Secret, $275 Billion China Deal in 2016?" *SupChina,* December 7, 2021.

Nikakhtar, Nazak, and Mark Duffy. "Biden Import Ban Could Slow Infrastructure Advancement, but It Doesn't Have To." *Washington Examiner,* July 12, 2021.

Ning Nanshan. "Who Has Protected the Rise of China?" (宁南山: 是谁掩护了中国崛起). *Zhihu Zhuanlun* (知乎专论), Beijing, May 23, 2021.

Niu Jun. *Cold War and the Origin of New China's Diplomacy* (牛军: 冷战与新中国外交的缘起). Beijing: Sheke Wenxian, 2012.

Niu Tiansheng. "Late Imperialism: Historical End of Capitalist World Order." *World Socialism Studies,* Beijing, no. 6 (2020): 61–68.

Nixon, Richard. "Asia after Vietnam." *Foreign Affairs,* October 1967.

North, Douglass, and Robert Thomas. *The Rise of the Western World: A New Economic History.* New York: Cambridge University Press, 1973.

North Atlantic Council (NAC). *Brussels Summit Communiqué.* June 14, 2021.

Nossel, Suzanne. "Chinese Censorship Is Going Global." *Foreign Policy,* October 26, 2021.

Nozick, Robert. *Philosophical Explanations.* Cambridge, MA: Belknap Press of Harvard University Press, 1981.

———. *Anarchy, State, and Utopia.* New York: Basic Books, (1974) 2013.

Nsoesie, Elaine, Benjamin Rader, Yiyao L. Barnoon, Lauren Goodwin, and John S. Brownstein. "Analysis of Hospital Traffic and Search Engine Data in Wuhan China Indicates Early Disease Activity in the Fall of 2019." Harvard Library, Office for Scholarly Communication, 2020. dash.harvard.edu.

Nye, Joseph. *Understanding International Conflicts: An Introduction to Theory and History.* New York: Longman, 2008.

———. "Perspectives for a China Strategy." *Prism* 8, no. 4 (June 11, 2020): 121–31.

———. "Post-Pandemic Geopolitics." Project Syndicate, October 6, 2020.

Works and Sources Cited | 401

———. "Power and Interdependence with China." *Washington Quarterly* 43, no. 1, 2020.

———. *Soft Power and Great-Power Competition: Shifting Sands in the Balance of Power between the United States and China.* Berlin, Springer, 2023. Open access book.

Obama, Barack. *A Promised Land.* New York: Random House, 2020.

O'Brien, Robert C. "How China Threatens American Democracy: Beijing's Ideological Agenda Has Gone Global." *Foreign Affairs,* October 21, 2020.

———. "The Chinese Communist Party's Ideology and Global Ambitions." Public speech in Phoenix, Arizona, June 24, 2020.

———. "A Free and Open Indo-Pacific." White House, January 5, 2021.

O'Connor, Justin. "A Fearful University in Adelaide Abandons Academic Freedom in Attempts to Better Understand China." *Pearls and Irritations,* October 4, 2021.

O'Connor, Tom. "China, Russia, Iran, North Korea and More Join Forces 'in Defense' of U.N." *Newsweek,* March 12, 2021.

Office of Management and Budget. *Receipts by Source as Percentages of GDP: 1934–2018.* Washington, DC, January 2, 2014.

Office of the Secretary of Defense. *Annual Report to Congress: Military and Security Developments Involving the People's Republic of China.* Washington, DC, 2020.

Office of the Secretary of State (Policy Planning Staff). *The Elements of the China Challenge.* Washington, DC, November 20, 2020.

Ogden, Chris. *The Authoritarian Century: China's Rise and the Demise of the Liberal International Order.* Bristol: Bristol University Press, 2023.

Okere, Austine. "Specialized Economic Zones (SEZs) in Africa: Exporting Production, Performance, and Perils." *Impakter,* August 16, 2019.

Olander, Eric, Cobus van Staden, and James Wan. "China's Special Economic Zones in Africa: Lots of Hype, Little Hope." *ChinaFile,* August 25, 2015.

Olson, Mancur. *The Logic of Collective Action.* Cambridge, MA: Harvard University Press, 1965.

O'Neal, Adam. "China and the New Cold War." *Wall Street Journal,* March 18, 2022.

O'Neill, Jim. "The Logic of Sino-Western Détente." Project Syndicate, October 12, 2020.

O'Neill, Mark. "China Will Be Big Loser in Russian Invasion of Ukraine." *EJ Insight* (Hong Kong Economic Journal), February 28, 2022.

Orford, Anne. *Reading Humanitarian Intervention: Human Rights and the Use of Force in International Law.* Cambridge: Cambridge University Press, 2003.

Organski, A. F. K. *World Politics.* New York: Knopf, 1968.

Orlando, Alex. "Nuclear Anxiety Is Nothing New." *Discover,* March 17, 2022.

O'Rourke, Kevin. *A Short History of Brexit: From Brentry to Backstop.* London: Pelican, 2019.

402 | Works and Sources Cited

O'Rourke, Ronald. *China Naval Modernization: Implications for U.S. Navy Capabilities—Background and Issues for Congress*. RL33153. Washington, DC: Congressional Research Service, 2020.

Ortagus, Morgan. "Designation of Additional Chinese Media Entities as Foreign Mission." Press statement, Department of State, June 22, 2020.

Orwell, George. *Nineteen Eighty-Four*. London: Secker and Warburg, 1949.

———. *Animal Farm*. New York: Harcourt, (1946) 1990.

Ostermann, Christian. *Between Containment and Rollback*. Stanford, CA: Stanford University Press, 2021.

Overholt, William. *China's Crisis of Success*. New York: Cambridge University Press, 2018.

———. *The Rise of China: How Economic Reform is Creating a New Superpower*. New York: Norton, 1993.

———. "Biden Cannot Counter China with a Team that Lacks Expertise." *Hill*, July 7, 2021.

———. "Was US-China Engagement Premised on Chinese Political Liberalization?" *Hill*, October 14, 2021.

Owen, Stephen. *The Poetry of Du Fu*. Berlin: De Gruyter, 2016.

PAC. "Hong Kong, Hong Kong" (香港, 香港). Hong Kong, January 7, 2022.

Packard, Nathan, and Benjamin Jensen. "Washington Needs a Bold Rethink of Its China Strategy." *War on the Rocks*, June 9, 2020.

Packer, George. *Last Best Hope: America in Crisis and Renewal*. New York: Farrar, 2021.

Page, Jeremy. "How the U.S. Misread China's Xi: Hoping for a Globalist, It Got an Autocrat." *Wall Street Journal*, December 23, 2020.

Page, Jeremy, and Natasha Khan. "On the Ground in Wuhan, Signs of China Stalling Probe of Coronavirus Origins." *Wall Street Journal*, May 12, 2020.

Paine, Thomas. *Common Sense*. Dublin, OH: Coventry House, (1776) 2016.

Pairault, Thierry. "China in Africa: Phoenix Nests versus Special Economic Zones." *Hyper articles en ligne* (HAL), January 3, 2019.

Palmer, James. "What Really Scares Beijing about the Hong Kong Protests." *Spectator*, October 4, 2014.

———. "For American Pundits, China Isn't a Country—It's a Fantasyland." *Washington Post*, May 29, 2015.

———. "China's Vaccine Diplomacy Has Mixed Results." *Foreign Policy*, April 7, 2021.

Pan, Jennifer. "Controlling China's Digital Ecosystem: Observations on Chinese Social Media." *China Leadership Monitor*, no. 72, 2022.

Pan Qinglin. "To Solve the African Black People Problem Once and for All" (潘庆林: 一次性解决非洲黑人问题). *Zhihu* (知乎), (2017) 2021.

Pan, Yihong. *Tempered in the Revolutionary Furnace: China's Youth in the Rustication Movement*. Lanham, MD: Lexington Books, 2003.

Works and Sources Cited | 403

Pan Yue. "Warring States and Greece: The Roots of East-West Civilizations Compared" (潘岳: 战国与希腊: 中西方文明根性之比较). *Wenhua Zongheng* (文化纵横), Beijing, June 2020.

Pan Zhongqi, ed. *Classic Chinese Ideas of International Relations* (潘忠岐: 中华经典国际关系概念). Shanghai: Shanghai Renmin, 2021.

Pang, Laikwan. *Creativity and Its Discontents: China's Creative Industries and Intellectual Property Rights Offenses.* Durham, NC: Duke University Press, 2012.

Pantsov, Alexander, and Steven Levine. *Deng Xiaoping: A Revolutionary Life.* New York: Oxford University Press, 2015.

Pao, Jeff. "New Urgency for China's 'Dual Circulation' Drive." *Asia Times,* April 12, 2022.

Parijs, Philippe, and Yannick Vanderborght. *Basic Income: A Radical Proposal for a Free Society and a Sane Economy.* Cambridge, MA: Harvard University Press, 2017.

Parker, Charlie. "Chinese Students in Britain Told to Serve Motherland." *Times,* July 4, 2020.

Parker, Geoffrey. *The Military Revolution: Military Innovation and the Rise of the West, 1500–1800.* New York: Cambridge University Press, 1996.

Parkinson, Joe, James T. Areddy, and Nicholas Bariyo. "As Africa Groans under Debt, It Casts Wary Eye at China." *Wall Street Journal,* April 17, 2020.

Parliament of Australia. *Inquiry into National Security Risks Affecting the Australian Higher Education and Research Sector.* Canberra, March 2022.

Parton, Charles. *Not Cold War, but a Values War; Not Decoupling, but Some Divergence.* China Research Group report, UK, November 2, 2020.

Party Literature Research Center of the CCP Central Committee, ed. *Important Documents since the 18th Party Congress* (中央文献研究室: 十八大以来重要文献选编). Beijing: Zhongyang Wenxian, 2014.

Patey, Luke. *How China Loses: The Pushback against Chinese Global Ambitions.* New York: Oxford University Press, 2021.

Pathikonda, Vilas. *Follow the Money: Did Administration Officials' Financial Entanglements with China Delay Trump's Promised Tough-on-China Trade Policy?* Public Citizen, June 28, 2020.

Patrick, Stewart. "Irresponsible Stakeholders? The Difficulty of Integrating Rising Powers." *Foreign Affairs,* November/December 2010.

Paul, T. V. *Restraining Great Powers: Soft Balancing from Empires to the Global Era.* New Heaven, CT: Yale University Press, 2018.

Pearson, Margaret M., Meg Rithmire, and Kellee S. Tsai. "China's Party-State Capitalism and International Backlash: From Interdependence to Insecurity." *International Security* 47, no. 2 (2022): 135–76.

Pedrozo, Pete. "Unpacking the Distinction: One China Principle v. One China Policy." *Lawfire,* August 19, 2022.

Pehe, Jiří. "Connections between Domestic and Foreign Policy." *Perspectives,* no. 10 (Summer 1998): 61–64.

404 | Works and Sources Cited

Pei, Minxin. "China's Coming Upheaval: Competition, the Coronavirus, and the Weakness of Xi Jinping." *Foreign Affairs*, May/June 2020.

———. "China's Fateful Inward Turn." *China Leadership Monitor*, December 16, 2020.

———. "The Political Logic of China's Strategic Mistakes." Project Syndicate, July 8, 2020.

———. "Whether It Sides with Russia or Not, China Will Pay a Price." *Los Angeles Times*, February 27, 2022.

Pei Yiran. "Truth about the Deception during Nixon's Visit to China" (裴毅然: 尼克松訪華說謊紀實). *Kaifang* (開放), Hong Kong, September 5, 2012.

Pekar, Jonathan, Andrew Magee, Edyth Parker, Niema Moshiri, Katherine Izhikevich, Jennifer L. Havens, Karthik Gangavarapu, et al. "The Molecular Epidemiology of Multiple Zoonotic Origins of SARS-CoV-2." *Science*, July 26, 2022.

Pempel, T. J. *A Region of Regimes: Prosperity and Plunder in the Asia-Pacific*. Ithaca, NY: Cornell University Press, 2021.

Pence, Mike. "Remarks by Vice President Pence on the Administration's Policy Toward China." Hudson Institute, October 4, 2018.

People's Bank of China et al. *Action Plan for the Construction of Shanghai International Financial Center 2018–2020* (上海国际金融中心建设行动计划2018-2020年). Shanghai Municipal People's Government, January 2019.

Perkowski, Jack. "Wall Street, Goldman Sachs and China." *Forbes*, March 19, 2012.

Peterson, Rachelle, Ian Oxnevad, and Flora Yan. *After Confucius Institutes: China's Enduring Influence on American Higher Education*. New York: National Association of Scholars, 2022.

Petri, Peter, and Michael Plummer. "China Could Help Stop the Freefall in Global Economic Cooperation." Brookings, July 16, 2020.

Philipp, Joshua. "Tracking Down the Origin of the Wuhan Coronavirus." Documentary, *Epoch Times*, April 7, 2020.

———. "Virus Origins." *American Thought Leaders*, May 23, 2020a.

Phillips, Andrew, and Christian Reus-Smit, eds. *Culture and Order in World Politics*. Cambridge: Cambridge University Press, 2020.

Phillips, Morgan. "Trump Says Coronavirus Crisis Is 'Worse' than Pearl Harbor, 9/11 Attacks." Fox, May 6, 2020.

Pieper, Moritz. *The Making of Eurasia: Competition and Cooperation between China's Belt and Road Initiative and Russia*. London: Tauris, 2022.

Piketty, Thomas. *Capital in the Twenty-First Century* (Le capital au XXI siècle). Translated by Arthur Goldhammer. Cambridge, MA: Harvard University Press, (2013) 2014.

———. *Capital and Ideology* (Capital et idéologie). Translated by Arthur Goldhammer. Cambridge, MA: Harvard University Press, (2019) 2020.

Works and Sources Cited | 405

———. *A Brief History of Equality* (Une bréve histoire de l'égalité). Translated by Steven Rendall. Cambridge, MA: Harvard University Press, (2021) 2022.

———. "Responding to China: The Case for Global Justice and Democratic Socialism." Strategic Multilayer Assessment (SMA), February 15, 2022.

Pillsbury, Michael*The Hundred-Year Marathon: China's Secret Strategy to Replace America as the Global Superpower*. New York: St. Martin's, 2015.

———, ed. *Guide to the Trump Administration's China Policy Statements*. Hudson Institute, August 2020.

Pinchuk, Denis. "Rosneft to Double Oil Flows to China in $270 Billion Deal." Reuters, June 21, 2013.

Pinker, Steven. *Rationality*. New York: Viking, 2021.

Pogge, Thomas, and Krishen Mehta, eds. *Global Tax Fairness*. New York: Oxford University Press, 2016.

Polzsar, Zoltan. *War and Industrial Policy*. Credit Suisse analysis, August 27, 2022.

Pomfret, John. "Biden Could Execute a Strong and Effective China Policy . . . Thanks to Trump." *Washington Post*, August 21, 2020.

———. "Keep the Tough Approach or Seek Cooperation? China Looms Large for Biden." *Washington Post*, November 10, 2020.

Pomfret, John, and Matt Pottinger. "Xi Jinping Says He Is Preparing China for War, the World Should Take Him Seriously." *Foreign Affairs*, March 29, 2023.

Pompeo, Mike. "The China Challenge." Speech at the Hudson Institute, October 30, 2019.

———. "A New Transatlantic Dialogue." German Marshall Fund's Brussels Forum, June 25, 2020.

———. "Announcing the Expansion of the Clean Network to Safeguard America's Assets." Press statement, Department of State, August 5, 2020.

———. "Communist China and the Free World's Future." Richard Nixon Presidential Library and Museum, July 23, 2020.

———. "Europe and the China Challenge." Copenhagen Democracy Summit, June 19, 2020.

———. "The Chinese Communist Party on the American Campus." Speech at the Georgia Institute of Technology, Atlanta, December 9, 2020.

———. "Determination of the Secretary of State on Atrocities in Xinjiang." Press release, Department of State, January 19, 2021.

———. *Never Give an Inch*. New York: Broadside, 2023.

Pompeo, Mike, and Miles Yu. "China's Reckless Labs Put the World at Risk." *Wall Street Journal*, February 23, 2021.

Pons, Silvio, Norman Naimark, Sophie Quinn-Judge, Juliane Fürst, and Mark Selden, eds. *The Cambridge History of Communism*. 3 vols. Cambridge: Cambridge University Press, 2017.

406 | Works and Sources Cited

Popper, Karl. *The Open Society and Its Enemies*. Princeton, NJ: Princeton University Press, (1945) 2013.

Posen, Adam. "The End of China's Economic Miracle." *Foreign Affairs*, August 2, 2023.

Posen, Adam, and Ha Jiming. "US-China Cooperation in a Changing Global Economy." Peterson Institute for International Economics, June 2017.

Postoutenko, Kirill, and Darin Stephanov. *Ruler Personality Cults from Empires to Nation-States and Beyond*. Abingdon, UK: Routledge, 2021.

Potter, Pitman. *Exporting Virtue? China's International Human Rights Activism in the Age of Xi Jinping*. Vancouver: University of British Columbia Press, 2021.

Pottinger, Matt. "Reflections on China's May Fourth Movement: An American Perspective." Speech at the Miller Center, University of Virginia, May 4, 2020.

———. "Beijing's American Hustle: How Chinese Grand Strategy Exploits U.S. Power." *Foreign Affairs*, September/October 2021.

———. "Reflections on U.S.-China Relations." Hoover Institution, March 10, 2021a.

Powell, Bill. "How Bush and Obama Ceded the World Health Organization to China." *Newsweek*, April 14, 2020.

Power, Samantha. "The Can-Do Power: America's Advantage and Biden's Chance." *Foreign Affairs*, January/February 2021.

Prange, Gordon. *Pearl Harbor: The Verdict of History*. New York: McGraw-Hill, 1986.

Prestowitz, Clyde. *Trading Places: How We Are Giving Our Future to Japan and How to Reclaim It*. New York: Basic Books, 1990.

———. *The World Turned Upside Down: America, China, and the Struggle for Global Leadership*. New Haven, CT: Yale University Press, 2021.

Price, Monroe, and Daniel Dayan, eds. *Owning the Olympics: Narratives of the New China*. Ann Arbor: University of Michigan Press, 2008.

Priebe, Miranda, Bryan Rooney, Nathan Beauchamp-Mustafaga, Jeffrey Martini, and Stephanie Pezard. *Implementing Restraint*. RAND Corporation, 2021.

Prowse, Michael. "Is America in Decline?" *Harvard Business Review*, July–August 1992.

Pubby, Manu. "India Requests Quick Delivery of Missiles, Ammo from Russia." *Economic Times*, New Delhi, June 25, 2020.

Purdey, Jemma. *Anti-Chinese Violence in Indonesia, 1996–1999*. Honolulu: University of Hawaii Press, 2006.

Qi Weiping and Wang Jun. "The History of the Evolution of Mao Zedong's Thought of 'Catching Up with the UK and Surpassing the US'" (齐卫平, 王军: 关于毛泽东"超英赶美"思想演变阶段的历史考察). *Shixue Yuekan* (史学月刊), Kaifeng, no. 2, 2002.

Qi Zhongxiang and Xie Yu. "Special Report on a Critical Development of the Internet" (齐中祥, 谢宇: 重大网情专报). No. 2. Beijing: Womin Corporation (沃民公司), February 7, 2020.

Qian Tong. "CCP First Proposes 'Community of Common Destiny for Humanity'" (钱彤: 中共首提"人类命运共同体"). Xinhua (新华), Beijing, November 10, 2012.

Qian Tong et al. "World Meets under the Banner of Five Rings" (钱彤等: 世界相聚五环旗下). Xinhua (新华), August 10, 2008.

Qian Xiang. "American Imperialism Never Ceases to Annihilate Us" (黔线:美帝亡我之心不死). *Xinghuozhiku* (星火智库), March 23, 2020.

Qian Xue. "To Challenge the USD Is to Exterminate the US" (千雪: 挑战美元就是灭美国). *Zhihu Zhuanlun* (知乎专论), Beijing, September 9, 2019.

Qiao Liang and Wang Xiangsui. *Unrestricted Warfare* (乔良, 王湘穗: 超限战). Beijing: Chongwen, (1999) 2010.

Qiao Long. "Who Have You Asked before Showering Money Everywhere?" (乔龙: 四处撒钱你问过谁). RFA, December 9, 2015.

Qiao Qiao. "Compare the Lists of Cooperation" (乔桥: 比较中美合作"清单"). *US-China Perception Monitor*, no. 71, September 2020.

Qin, Amy, and Amy Chang Chien. "As China Rattles Sabers, Taiwan Asks: Are We Ready for War?" *New York Times*, June 14, 2022a.

———. "'We Are Taiwanese': China's Growing Menace Hardens Island's Identity." *New York Times*, January 19, 2022.

Qin Gang. "Keynote Speech by Ambassador Qin Gang at the Welcome Event by the National Committee on US-China Relations Board of Directors." Washington, August 31, 2021.

———. "Global Security Initiative" (秦刚:全球安全倡议). Beijing, February 21, 2023.

Qin Hui. "China Entered the Korean War to Quench Stalin's Anger" (秦晖: 中国卷入朝鲜战争是为消斯大林的恼火). Nanfang Wang (南方网), November 10, 2012.

———. "Crisis of Globalization in the 21st Century" (秦晖: 21世纪的全球化危机). *Aisixiang* (爱思想), July 3, 2015.

———. *39 Lectures on the History of Chinese Thought* (秦晖: 中国思想史39讲). *Qinghua Daxue Gongkaike* (清华大学公开课), Beijing, 2016.

———. "Globalization after the Pandemic" (秦晖: 瘟疫后的全球化). *NeoThought* (新思考), July 24, 2020. Podcast, MP3 audio, 2:07:52. https://podcasts.apple.com/us/podcast/秦晖-瘟疫后的全球化-历史与现实/id1524974550?i=1000485979780.

———. "The New Cold War May Be More like a Cold War" (秦晖: 新冷战可能更像冷战). *Caixin* (财新), July 6, 2020.

Qin Shu. "Our Total Situation May Be Reversed If Still Not to Protect China's Supply Chains" (秦朔: 再不保卫中国供应链, 我们的整个形势恐被逆转). *Jinri Toutiao* (今日头条), May 21, 2022.

408 | Works and Sources Cited

Qin Weiping. *Big Winner of China's Crisis* (秦伟平: 中国危机大赢家). New York: Shenzhou, 2020.

Qin Yaqing. "Change of US-China Strategy and the Trend of Sino-American Relations" (秦亚青: 美国对华战略转变与中美关系走向). *Renmin Luntan* (人民论坛), no. 15, 2021.

———. "100-Year Change and Global Governance" (秦亚青: 百年变局与全球治理). Shandong University, Jinan, September 17, 2022.

Qina Benli. "Domestic Impact of China's 'BRI'" (錢本立:中國「一帶一路倡議」的國內影響). *Globalization Monitor*, Hong Kong, February 18, 2019.

Qiu Shi. "Completely Apprehend and Master Our Basic National Conditions" (秋石: 全面认识和把握我国基本国情). *Renmin Ribao* (人民日报), May 3, 2018.

Quay, Steven, and Richard Muller. "The Science Suggests a Wuhan Lab Leak." *Wall Street Journal*, June 6, 2021.

Quinn, Jimmy. "Jeffrey Sachs, China's Apologist in Chief." *National Review*, April 24, 2021.

Raby, Geoff. *China's Grand Strategy and Australia's Future in the New Global Order*. Melbourne: Melbourne University Press, 2020.

Radio New Zealand. "Chinese Censorship, Surveillance Found at Australian Universities." June 30, 2021.

Ramzy, Austin, and Mike Ives. "Hong Kong Protests, One Year Later." *New York Times*, June 9, 2020.

Rappeport, Alan. "Trump Calls China a 'Threat to the World' as Trade Talks Approach." *New York Times*, September 21, 2019. Ratcliffe, John. "China Is National Security Threat No. 1." *Wall Street Journal*, December 3, 2020.

———. "Finance Leaders Reach Global Tax Deal Aimed at Ending Profit Shifting." *New York Times*, June 11, 2021.

Rawls, John. *A Theory of Justice*. Cambridge, MA: Belknap of Harvard University Press, 1971.

———. *Justice as Fairness: A Restatement*. Cambridge, MA: Belknap Press of Harvard University Press, 2001.

Reagan, Ronald. "Brandenburg Gate Speech." June 12, 1987. americanrhetoric.com/top100speechesall.html.

Reale, Hannah. "China's Donations to U.S. Universities." *Wire*, September 13, 2020.

Reed, Thomas. *At the Abyss: An Insider's History of the Cold War*. New York: Presidio, 2004.

Reiter, Dan. "Democratic Peace Theory." In *Oxford Bibliographies*, last modified 2012. 10.1093/obo/9780199756223-0014.

Ren, Daniel. "Petroyuan's Stature Grows on Shanghai Exchange." *South China Morning Post*, Hong Kong, June 12, 2020.

Ren Jiantao. "Hu Shi and State Identification" (任剑涛: 胡适与国家认同). *Kaifang Shidai* (开放时代), Guangzhou, no. 6, 2013.

Works and Sources Cited | 409

———. "It Is 100 Times More Important to Distinguish the Civilized from the Barbarian Than the East from the West" (任剑涛: 划分文明与野蛮, 比划分东西重要一百倍). *Aisixiang* (爱思想), September 7, 2016.

———. "Resentful Rise of Nations and Global Disorder" (任剑涛: 国家的怨恨性崛起与全球失序). *Sichun Daxue Xuebao* (四川大学学报), Chengdu, January 2022, 23–38.

Ren Qinqin and Wang Jianhua. "China's Core Interests Shall Not Be Challenged" (任沁沁 & 王建华: 中国核心利益不容挑战). Xinhua (新华), May 25, 2015.

Ren Xiao. *Towards World Gongshen* (任晓: 走向世界共生). Beijing: Shangwu, 2019.

Ren Zeping. *China Employment Report 2020* (任泽平:中国就业报告 2020). Beijing: Hengda (恒大), April 24, 2020.

Rene, Helena. *China's Sent-Down Generation: Public Administration and the Legacies of Mao's Rustication Program*. Washington, DC: Georgetown University Press, 2013.

Renmin Ribao (人民日报). "We Raise the 400th Serious Warning to the US" (我对美国提出第四百次严重警告). Editorial, April 6, 1966.

———. "The Day to Bury American Imperialism Is Coming Soon" (美帝被埋葬的日子不会太长了). Editorial, January 30, 1969.

———. "The Concept of 'Big Family' in the Asia-Pacific" (亚太区域的"大家庭"观念). Editorial, September 7, 2007.

———. "China Firmly Safeguards Core Interests" (中国捍卫核心利益的决心坚定不移). Editorial, May 9, 2019.

———. "To Plan Great Harmony for the World: How China Has Approached the Center of the World Stage" (为世界谋大同: 中国是怎样走近世界舞台中央的). Editorial, August 13, 2019.

Repnikova, Maria. *Chinese Soft Power*. Cambridge: Cambridge University Press, 2022.

Reuters. "S&P DJI to Remove 21 Chinese Firms from Equities and Bond Indices." CNBC, December 10, 2020.

———. "China Applies to Join Pacific Trade Pact to Boost Economic Clout." September 17, 2021.

Rhem, Kathleen. "Korean War Death Stats Highlight Modern DoD Safety Record." June 8, 2000. defense.gov/news.

Rhyn, Larissa. "A Tweet Cost Him His Doctorate: The Extent of China's Influence on Swiss Universities." *Neue Zürcher Zeitung in English*, August 4, 2021.

Richardson, Sophie. *China, Cambodia, and the Five Principles of Peaceful Coexistence*. New York: Columbia University Press, 2010.

Rickett, Oscar. "From Latte Socialist to Gauche Caviar." *Guardian*, October 23, 2017.

Rippa, Alessandro. "Mapping the Margins of China's Global Ambitions: Economic Corridors, Silk Roads, and the End of Proximity in the Borderlands." *Eurasian Geography and Economics* 61, no. 1 (2020): 55–76.

410 | Works and Sources Cited

Rittenberg, Sidney, and Amanda Bennett. *The Man Who Stayed Behind.* Durham, NC: Duke University Press, 2001.

Roberts, Sean. *The War on the Uyghurs: China's Internal Campaign against a Muslim Minority.* Princeton, NJ: Princeton University Press, 2020.

Robespierre, Maximilien. *Works by Maximilien Robespierre* (Oeuvres de Maximilien Robespierre). Vol. 4. Paris: Presses Universitaires de France, (1790) 1950.

Roblin, Sebastien. "Is China's Navy 'Larger' than America's?" *National Interest,* April 9, 2021.

———. "Tanks, Ships, and Assault Rifles: India Still Buys Most of Its Weapons from Russia." *National Interest,* January 25, 2020.

Roche, Elizabeth. "Free and Open Indo-Pacific: US, Australia, India, Japan to Discuss China's Growing Power." *Mint,* October 6, 2020.

Rochlin, James. *Vanguard Revolutionaries in Latin America: Peru, Colombia, Mexico.* Boulder, CO: Lynn Rienner, 2003.

Rogin, Josh. "Inside China's 'Tantrum Diplomacy' at APEC." *Washington Post,* November 12, 2018.

———. "Biden Must Not Fall into China's Smooth Relations Trap." *Washington Post,* November 19, 2020.

———. "There's Chinese Interference on Both Sides of the 2020 Election." *Washington Post,* October 30, 2020.

———. *Chaos under Heaven: Trump, Xi, and the Battle for the Twenty-First Century.* New York: Houghton Mifflin Harcourt, 2021a.

———. "Wall Street Is Finally Waking Up to the Reality of China." *Wall Street Journal,* July 8, 2021b.

———. "The Trump Administration Had a China Strategy after All but Trump Didn't Follow It." *Washington Post,* January 14. 2021.

Rohrschneider, Robert. "How Iron Is the Iron Law of Oligarchy?" *European Journal of Political Research* 25, no. 2 (1994): 207–38.

Rolland, Nadège. *China's Vision for a New World Order.* NBR Research, January 27, 2020.

———. "China's Southern Strategy: Beijing Is Using the Global South to Constrain America." *Foreign Affairs,* June 9, 2022.

Rolnick, Arthur, and Warren Weber. "Gresham's Law or Gresham's Fallacy." *Journal of Political Economy* 94, no. 1 (1986): 185–99.

Ronen, Shahar, Bruno Gonçalves, Kevin Z. Hua, Alessandro Vespignanib, Steven Pinkere, and César A. Hidalgo. "Links That Speak: The Global Language Network and Its Association with Global Fame." *Proceedings of the National Academy of Sciences* 111, no. 52 (2014, E5616–E5622.

Roosa, John. *Pretext for Mass Murder: The September 30th Movement and Suharto's Coup d'État in Indonesia.* Madison: University of Wisconsin Press, 2006.

Rosenthal, Jean-Laurent, and R. Bin Wong. *Before and Beyond Divergence: The Politics of Economic Change in China and Europe.* Cambridge, MA: Harvard University Press, 2011.

Works and Sources Cited | 411

Ross, John, Wang Wen, et al., "International Meeting: No to the New Cold War." July 25, 2020. www.nocoldwar.org.

Roth, Hans Ingvar. *P. C. Chang and the Universal Declaration of Human Rights.* Philadelphia: University of Pennsylvania Press, 2018.

Rousseau, Jean-Jacques. *The Social Contract.* London: Dent, (1762) 1923.

———. *Discourse on the Origin of Inequality.* Indianapolis: Hackett, (1755) 1992.

Roy, Eleanor Ainge. "'I'm Being Watched': Anne-Marie Brady, the China Critic Living in Fear of Beijing in New Zealand." *Guardian*, January 12, 2019.

Rudolph, Jennifer, and Michael Szonyi, eds. *The China Questions: Critical Insights into a Rising Power.* Cambridge, MA: Harvard University Press, 2018.

Ruiz, Neil, et al. "Most Asian Americans View Their Ancestral Homelands Favorably, Except Chinese Americans." Pew Research Center, July 19, 2023.

Rummler, Orion. "Biden Calls Russia an 'Opponent,' Sees China as a 'Serious Competitor.'" *Axios*, September 18, 2020.

Russell, Bertrand. *The Problem of China.* London: Allen and Unwin, 1922.

Russell, Karl, Joe Rennison, and Jason Karaian. "The Dollar Is Extremely Strong, Pushing Down the World." *New York Times*, July 16, 2022.

Ruttan, Vernon W. *Is War Necessary for Economic Growth? Military Procurement and Technology Development.* New York: Oxford University Press, 2006.

Safire, William. "Useful Idiots of the West." *New York Times*, April 12, 1987.

Saha, Sagatom, and Ashley Feng. "Global Supply Chains, Economic Decoupling, and U.S.-China Relations." China Brief 20, no. 6, Jamestown Foundation, April 1, 2020.

Sahlins, Marshall. *Confucius Institutes: Academic Malware.* Chicago: Prickly Paradigm, 2014.

Saldin, Robert, and Steven Teles. *Never Trump: The Revolt of the Conservative Elites.* New York: Oxford, 2020.

Saleen, Steve. "How Chinese Officials Hijacked My Company." *Wall Street Journal*, July 31, 2020.

Samuels, Ben, and Gur Megiddo. "Revealed: The Israeli-American Academic Gal Luft's Efforts to Help China Establish a Foothold in Israel." *Haaretz*, July 20, 2023.

Sandel, Michael. *The Tyranny of Merit: What's Become of the Common Good?* New York: Farrar, Straus and Giroux, 2020.

Sanders, Bernie. "Washington's Dangerous New Consensus on China: Don't Start Another Cold War." *Foreign Affairs*, June 17, 2021.

Sanders, Chris. "China's ZTE Subject to New U.S. Bribery Investigation." *Reuters*, March 13, 2020.

Sanger, David. "U.S. Would Defend Taiwan, Bush Says." *New York Times*, April 26, 2001.

Santora, Marc. "Pompeo Calls China's Ruling Party 'Central Threat of Our Times.'" *New York Times*, January 31, 2020.

412 | Works and Sources Cited

Satel, Sally. "The Experts Somehow Overlooked Authoritarians on the Left." *Atlantic*, September 25, 2021.

Saul, Stephanie. "On Campuses Far from China, Still under Beijing's Watchful Eye." *New York Times*, May 5, 2017.

Saunders, Phillip, Arthur S. Ding, Andrew Scobell, Andrew N.D. Yang, and Joel Wuthnow, eds. *Chairman Xi Remakes the PLA: Assessing Chinese Military Reforms*. Washington, DC: National Defense University Press, 2019.

Savitt, Scott. *Crashing the Party: An American Reporter in China*. Berkeley, CA: Soft Skull, 2016.

Schafer, Edward. "Open Letter to the Editor." *Journal of Asian Studies* 78, no. 2 (1958): 119–20.

Schake, Kori. *Safe Passage: The Transition from British to American Hegemony*. Cambridge, MA: Harvard University Press, 2017.

Scharfstein, Ben-Ami. *Amoral Politics: The Persistent Truth of Machiavellism*. Albany: State University of New York Press, 1995.

Scheidel, Walter. *Escape from Rome: The Failure of Empire and the Road to Prosperity*. Princeton, NJ: Princeton University Press, 2019.

Schell, Orville. "The Death of Engagement." *Wire China*, June 7, 2020a.

———. "The Ugly End of Chimerica." *Foreign Policy*, April 3, 2020.

Schell, Orville, Susan Shirk, et al. *Course Correction: Toward an Effective and Sustainable China Policy*. Asia Society and 21st Century China Center, February 2019.

———. *China's New Direction: Challenges and Opportunities for U.S. Policy*. Asia Society and 21st Century China Center, September. 2021.

Schlesinger, Jacob. "What's Biden's New China Policy? It Looks a Lot like Trump's." *Wall Street Journal*, September 10, 2020.

Schmidt, Blake. "Schwarzman College's Culture Wars Reflect a New Reality in China." *Bloomberg*, June 10, 2022.

Schneider, Jordan, and Irene Zhang. "New Chip Export Controls and the Sullivan Tech Doctrine with Kevin Wolf: How the US Intends to Outpace China in Force-Multiplying Technologies." *ChinaTalk*, October 11, 2022.

Schularick, Moritz. "How China Helped Create the Macroeconomic Backdrop for Financial Crisis." *Financial Times*, March 24, 2009.

Schultheis, Emily. "Germany's Move to Help Arm Ukraine Signals Historic Shift." AP, February 27, 2022.

Schumpeter, Joseph. *The Economics and Sociology of Capitalism*. Edited by Richard Swedberg. Princeton, NJ: Princeton University Press, (1941) 1991.

Scissors, Derek. "Trump: When in Doubt, Help China Out." AEI posting, June 13, 2023.

Schwab, Klaus, and Peter Vanham. *Stakeholder Capitalism: A Global Economy That Works for Progress, People and Planet*. Hoboken, NJ: Wiley, 2021.

Schwartz, Benjamin I. *Communism in China: Ideology in Flux*. Cambridge, MA: Harvard University Press, 1968.

Works and Sources Cited | 413

Schwartz, Herman Mark. "The Dollar and Empire." *Phenomenal World*, July 16, 2020.

Schwarz, Fred. *You Can Trust the Communists (to Be Communists)*. Upper Saddle River, NJ: Prentice Hall, 1960.

Schwarzman Scholars. "About—Schwarzman Scholars." Accessed May 16, 2023. schwarzmanscholars.org/about/.

Schweller, Randall. "Three Cheers for Trump's Foreign Policy: What the Establishment Misses." *Foreign Affairs*, September/October 2018.

Scobell, Andrew. "China's Post-Pandemic Future: Wuhan Wobbly?" *War on Rocks*, February 3, 2021.

Scobell, Andrew, Edmund J. Burke, Cortez A. Cooper III, Sale Lilly, Chad J. R. Ohlandt, Eric Warner, and J. D. Williams. *China's Grand Strategy: Trends, Trajectories, and Long-Term Competition*. RAND Corporation, 2020.

Scott, Ben, et al. *The United States and the Rules-Based Order*. Sydney, Australia: Lowy Institute, 2021.

Scott, Jason, and Isabel Reynolds. "Australia Seeks to Build Defense Ties to Counter China Squeeze." *Bloomberg*, November 18, 2020.

Scott, Susan, and Markos Zachariadis. *The Society for Worldwide Interbank Financial Telecommunication (SWIFT)*. Abingdon, UK: Routledge, 2014.

Sebastian, Dave. "China Sanctions Lockheed Martin and Raytheon as Tensions over Balloon Increase." *Wall Street Journal*, February 16, 2023.

Sedley, David. "Stoicism." In *Routledge Encyclopedia of Philosophy*, edited by Edward Craig. London: Routledge, 1998.

Sellars, John. *Stoicism*. Abingdon, UK: Routledge, 2006.

Sennett, Richard. *Flesh and Stone: The Body and the City in Western Civilization*. New York: Norton, 1994.

Serhan, Yasmeen. "The Muslim World Isn't Coming to Save the Uyghurs." *Atlantic*, February 3, 2022.

Shafik, Minouche. *What We Owe Each Other: A New Social Contract for a Better Society*. Princeton, NJ: Princeton University Press, 2021.

Shambaugh, David. *China Goes Global: The Partial Power*. New York: Oxford University Press, 2013.

———. *China and the World*. New York: Oxford University Press, 2020.

Shang Qian. "2020, World Anticipates 'China Solution' from the Two Conferences" (商婧: 2020, 世界期待来自两会的"中国答案"). Xinhua (新华), May 19, 2020.

Shao Jianbin. "The Origin and Evolution of Mao Zedong's 'Political Power Comes from the Barrel of Guns'" (邵建斌: 毛泽东"枪杆子里面出政权"的来历与演变). *Renmin Wang* (人民网), June 13, 2017.

ShareAmerica. "China's Development Projects Export Environmental Devastation." October 22, 2020. share.america.gov/chinas-projects-export-environmental-devastation.

Sharp, Andrew. "Asia's Arms Race: China Spurs Military Spending Spree." *Nikkei Asia*, February 23, 2022.

414 | Works and Sources Cited

She Gangzheng. *The Rise of Complex "Intermediate Zones."* Atlantic Council, July 12, 2022.

Shelbourne, Mallory. "SECDEF Nominee Austin Affirms Threat from China." USNI News, January 19, 2021.

Shen Haixiong. "To Deepen the Push for 'Good Feeling Promotion'" (慎海雄: 深入推进"好感传播"). CCTV, June 7, 2021.

Shen Zhihua and Li Danhui. "Sino-American Rapprochement and China's Diplomacy to Vietnam" (沈志华&李丹慧: 中美和解与中国对越外交). *Meiguo Yanjiu* (美国研究), Beijing, no. 1, 2000.

Shen Zhihua and Yang Kuisong. *China and the War in Indochina* (沈志華/楊奎松: 中国与印度支那战争). Hong Kong: Tiandi, 2000.

Sheng Dingli. "'Don't Fire the First Shot' Is Never Absolute" (沈丁立: "不开第一枪"从来就不是绝对的). *Huanqiu Shibao* (环球时报), Beijing, September 25, 2020.

Sheng Zhihua. "The Shocking Inside Story of Sino-Korean Relations" (沈志华: 中朝关系惊天内幕). *Sina lishi* (新浪历史), Beijing, Sept 3, 2013.

———. "China's Principles of Dealing with Land Border Disputes during the Cold War Years" (沈志華: 冷戰年代中國處理陸地邊界糾紛的方針). *21st Century* (二十一世紀), 143 (June 2014): 22–32.

———. "Counterproductive: Results of China's Dealing with Land Border Disputes during the Cold War Years" (事與願違: 冷戰年代中國處理陸地邊界糾紛的結果). *21st Century* (二十一世紀), 144 (August 2014): 52–61.

Shepherd, Christian. "Eileen Gu Is Beijing's Olympic Face." *Washington Post*, February 18, 2022.

Shepherd, Robin. *China vs. Democracy: The Greatest Game, a Handbook for Democracies.* Washington, DC: Halifax International Security Forum, 2020.

Sheth, Jagdish, and Rajendra Sisodia. *Tectonic Shift: The Geoeconomic Realignment of Globalizing Markets.* New Delhi: Response, 2006.

Shi Bo. "Paradox: Is the West Really the Enemy?" (施博: 悖论: 西方真是敌对势力吗). Tencent blog (腾讯博客), Beijing, February 28, 2022.

Shi Chang. "Why Russia Remains Uninterested in Sino-Russian Free Trade Zone" (势场:俄罗斯为何对中俄自由贸易区始终不感兴趣). Careerengine.us, May 26, 2021.

Shi Ming. "Coolies and World Factory" (石铭: 苦力与世界工厂). WeChat blog (微信公众号), March 12, 2022.

Shi Yinhong. "Biden Comes to Power: Good or Bad for China-US Relations?" (时殷弘: 拜登上台, 对中美关系有何利弊). *Phoenix* (凤凰), Hong Kong, November 9, 2020.

———. "Biden Administration's China Policy Expressed" (时殷弘: 拜登政府对华当今方针宣示). *Renda Meiguo Yanjiu Jianbao* (人大美国研究简报), no. 1, March 7, 2021.

———. "World's Pattern" (时殷弘:世界格局). *Eluosi Yanjiu* (俄罗斯研究), Shanghai, no. 5, September 2021.

Shi Zhan. *Pivot: China of 3,000 Years* (施展: 枢纽—3000年的中国). Nanning: Guangxi Shida, 2018.

Shin Ji-hye. "Yoon's NATO Trip 'Achieved Goals beyond Expectations.' " *Korea Herald*, June 30, 2022.

Shu Jianzhong, Da Wei, and Ren Ling. "On China and World Order" (舒建中, 达巍, 任琳: 中国与国际秩序专题). *International Studies* (国际问题研究), Beijing, no. 1 (2021): 86–122.

Shum, Desmond. *Red Roulette: An Insider's Story of Wealth, Power, Corruption, and Vengeance in Today's China*. New York: Simon and Schuster, 2021.

Si Ying. "USC at HKCU Faces 'Reorganization' " (斯影: 港中大中国研究服务中心面临"重组"). BBC in Chinese, December 25, 2020.

Sibley, Katherine. *Red Spies in America: Stolen Secrets and the Dawn of the Cold War*. Lawrence: University Press of Kansas, 2004.

Siegel, Katherine. *Loans and Legitimacy: The Evolution of Soviet-American Relations, 1919–1933*. Lexington: University Press of Kentucky, 1996.

SIIS (Shanghai Institutes for International Studies). "The 'Shanghai School' for Inclusion and Coexisting" (上海国际问题研究院: 海纳百川、包容共生的"上海学派"). *Guoji Zhanwang* (国际展望), no. 6, 2014.

Silver, Laura, Kat Devlin, and Christine Huang. *Americans Fault China for Its Role in the Spread of COVID-19*. Pew Research Center, July 30, 2020.

———. "Attitudes toward China." Pew Research Center, April 21, 2020.

———. *Unfavorable Views of China Reach Historic Highs in Many Countries*. Pew Research Center, October 6, 2020.

———. *Most Americans Support Tough Stance toward China on Human Rights, Economic Issues*. Pew Research Center, March 4, 2021.

Silver, Laura, Christine Huang, and Laura Clancy. *China's Approach to Foreign Policy Gets Largely Negative Reviews in 24-Country Survey*. Pew Research Center, July 27, 2023.

Sima Guang. *Chronicles for the Rulers* (司马光: 资治通鉴). Vol. 193. Beijing: Zhonghua Shuju, (11th century) 2009.

Simons, Marlise. "Uighur Exiles Push for Court Case Accusing China of Genocide." *New York Times*, July 6, 2020.

Simpson, Joanne Cavanaugh. "Seeing Red." *Johns Hopkins Magazine*, September 2000.

Singleton, Craig. "Putin's War Is Xi's Worst Nightmare." *Foreign Policy*, March 4, 2022.

Singman, Brooke. "Biden DNI Nominee Haines Says Aim Should Be to 'Out-Compete China.' " Fox, January 29, 2021.

Skinner, William. "What the Study of China Can Do for Social Science." *Journal of Asian Studies* 23, no. 4 (1964): 517–22.

416 | Works and Sources Cited

Slater, Don, and Joseph Wong. *From Development to Democracy: The Transformations of Modern Asia*. Princeton, NJ: Princeton University Press, 2022.

Small, Andrew. *No Limits: The Inside Story of China's War with the West*. London: Hurst, 2022.

Smeltz, Dina, and Craig Kafura. *Do Republicans and Democrats Want a Cold War with China?* Chicago Council on Global Affairs, October 13, 2020.

Smith, Kyle. "The Other Chinese Infection." *National Review*, April 5, 2020.

Smith, Nick. *The End of the Village: Planning the Urbanization of Rural China*. Minneapolis: University of Minnesota Press, 2021.

Smith, Randall. "Defeated by Default: The Abiding Influence of John Rawls." *Public Discourse*, June 13, 2016.

Smith, Steven. *Modernity and Its Discontents*. New Haven, CT: Yale University Press, 2016.

Snow, Philip. *China and Russia: Four Centuries of Conflict and Concord*. New Haven, CT: Yale University Press, 2023.

Song Yongyi, ed. *Cultural Revolution: Historical Facts and Collective Memory* (宋永毅: 文化大革命: 历史的真相和集体记忆). Hong Kong: Tianyuan, 2007.

Song Yongyi and Xia Ming, eds. *Brainwashing in Mao's China and Beyond* (宋永毅、夏明: 洗脑: 毛泽东和后毛时代的中国与世界). New York: Huayi, 2023.

Song Zipei. *Life and Death of Twenty-Eight Days: The Record of the 41st Army in Gaoping during the War against Vietnam* (宋子佩: 生死二十八天, 四十一军对越作战高平战役纪实). Guangzhou, (1990) 2014.

Sorkin, Andrew, et al. "Another Corporate Leader Clarifies His Remarks on China." *New York Times*, December 6, 2021.

Soros, George. "BlackRock's China Blunder: Pouring Billions into the Country Now Is a Bad Investment and Imperils U.S. National Security." *Wall Street Journal*, September 6, 2021.

Sowell, Thomas. *The Vision of the Anointed*. New York: Basic Books, 1995.

———. *Intellectuals and Society*. New York: Basic Books, 2009.

SpaceX. "Mars and Beyond: The Road to Making Humanity Multiplanetary." August 2022. spacex.com/human-spaceflight/mars.

Spalding, Robert. *Stealth War: How China Took Over While America's Elite Slept*. New York: Portfolio/Penguin, 2019.

Spence, Jonathan. *To Change China: Western Advisers in China*. New York: Penguin, (1969) 2002.

Spike, Justin. "Chinese University Plan Causes Security Concerns in Hungary." *AP News*, May 2, 2021.

Sprunt, Barbara. "White House: China and WHO Need to 'Step Up' on Investigation into Origin of Pandemic." *NPR*, February 21, 2021.

Spruyt, Hendrik. *The Sovereign State and Its Competitors: An Analysis of Systems Change*. Princeton, NJ: Princeton University Press, 1994.

Stacey, Viggo. "Chinese Families Continue to 'Embrace US Education as Top Choice.'" *PTE News*, March 24, 2021.

Works and Sources Cited | 417

Stalin, Joseph. "The Tasks of Business Executives." In *Works of Stalin*, vol. 18. Moscow: Foreign Language Publication, (1931) 1954.

Stares, Paul, Qingguo Jia, Nathalie Tocci, Dhruva Jaishankar, and Andrey Kortunov. *Perspectives on a Changing World Order*. New York: Council on Foreign Relations, 2020.

Starn, Orin. "Maoism in the Andes: The Communist Party of Peru-Shining Path and the Refusal of History." *Journal of Latin American Studies* 27, no. 2 (1995): 399–421.

Stasavage, David. *The Decline and Rise of Democracy: A Global History from Antiquity to Today*. Princeton, NJ: Princeton University Press, 2020.

State Council or Ministry of Defense. *China's National Defense White Paper* (中国国防白皮书) [or similar biannual and triannual reports]. Beijing, 1995–2022.

State Council (国务院). *China's Peaceful Development* (中国的和平发展). Beijing, 2011.

———. *Master Plan for the Construction of Hainan Free Port* (海南自由贸易港建设总体方案). June 1, 2020.

———. *White Paper on Chinese Action in Countering COVID-19 Pneumonia* (抗击新冠肺炎疫情的中国行动). June 7, 2020a.

———. *Sino-African Cooperation in the New Era* (新时代的中非合作). November 26, 2021.

State Council Office of Hong Kong and Macau Affairs. "Strongly Condemn the British Violation of Treaty" (国务院港澳办: 强烈谴责英国的毁约行径). January 31, 2021.

State Council Press Office (国务院新闻办公室). *China's Foreign Aid* (中国的对外援助白皮书). August 6, 2018.

———. *China and the World in the New Era* (新时代的中国与世界白皮书). September 27, 2019.

———. *China's National Defense in the New Era* (新时代的中国国防白皮书). July 24, 2019.

———. "Press Conference on Developing Hengqin and Qianhai" (横琴、前海开发建设情况新闻发布会). September 9, 2021.

Stavridis, James. "A Preview of Biden's Foreign Policy." *Bloomberg*, November 8, 2020.

Steil, Benn. "Red White: Why a Founding Father of Postwar Capitalism Spied for the Soviets." *Foreign Affairs*, March/April 2013.

Stephanopoulos, George. "Interview with President Joe Biden." ABC News, August 19, 2021.

Stephens, Bret. "China Won't Bury Us, Either." *New York Times*, July 5, 2021.

Stevenson, Alexandra. "Business Embraces Hong Kong's Security Law—the Money Helps." *New York Times*, July 1, 2020.

———. "Will the U.S. Soon Treat Hong Kong like China? Much Is at Stake." *New York Times*, June 1, 2020.

418 | Works and Sources Cited

Stiftun, Bertelsmann. *Dealing with the Dragon: China as a Transatlantic Challenge.* New York: Asia Society, 2020.

Stiglitz, Joseph, Todd Tucker, and Gabriel Zucman. "Ending the Race to the Bottom: The Global Minimum Tax Deal Is about More than Fairness." *Foreign Affairs*, September 17, 2021.

Stilwell, David. "The United States, Taiwan, and the World: Partners for Peace and Prosperity." Speech at the Heritage Foundation, August 31, 2020.

Stoltenberg, Jens, and Kishida, Fumio. *Joint Statement.* Tokyo, February 1, 2023.

Strange, Steven, and Jack Zupko, eds. *Stoicism: Traditions and Transformations.* New York: Cambridge University Press, 2004.

Strange, Susan. "The Westfailure System." *Review of International Studies* 25, no. 3 (1999): 345–54.

Streit, Clarence K. *Union Now: A Proposal for a Federal Union of the Democracies of the North Atlantic.* New York: Third Impression, 1939.

Strittmatter, Kai. *We Have Been Harmonized: Life in China's Surveillance State.* New York: Custom House, 2020.

Strobel, Warren, and Sabrina Siddiqui. "Biden Aims to Out-Tough Trump on China while Invoking His Obama Experience." *Wall Street Journal*, May 2, 2020.

Stromberg, Roland. *European Intellectual History since 1789.* New York: Pearson, 1993.

Strupczewski, Jan. "EU Says It Can't Help Montenegro on China Loan but Can on Financing." Reuters, April 12, 2021.

Stuenkel, Oliver. "China's Diplomats Are Going on the Offensive in Brazil." *Financial Times*, May 15, 2020.

Stuurman, Siep. *The Invention of Humanity: Equality and Cultural Difference in World History.* Cambridge, MA: Harvard University Press, 2017.

Su Ge, ed. *Great Transformation of the World and Great Power Diplomacy with Chinese Characteristics in the New Era* (苏格: 世界大变局与新时代中国特色大国外交). Beijing: Shijie Zhishi, 2020.

Su Qun. "When Prince Sihanouk Was in China" (苏群: 西哈努克亲王在中国的日子). *Renmin Wenzhai* (人民文摘), Beijing, no. 7, 2004.

Su Shi. *Ding Feng Bo* (苏轼: 定风波). In *Poems by Su Shi* (苏轼诗集). Beijing: Zhonghua Shuju, (11th century) 2021.

Subacchi, Paola. *The People's Money: How China Is Building a Global Currency.* New York: Columbia University Press, 2017.

Subin, Samantha. "Microsoft to Shut Down LinkedIn Website in China as Internet Censorship Increases in the Country." CNBC, October 14, 2021.

Subramanian, Arvind. "China Is the Key to Unwinding Global Imbalances." *Financial Times*, April 20, 2010.

Sudworth, John. "US 2020 Election: Who Does China Really Want to Win?" BBC News, October 20, 2020.

Works and Sources Cited | 419

Sullivan, Andrew. "Trump Is Gone. Trumpism Just Arrived." *Weekly Dish*, November 6, 2020a.

———. "Why Is Wokeness Winning? The Astonishing and Continuing Success of Left Illiberalism." *Weekly Dish*, October 15, 2020.

Sullivan, Jake (National Security Advisor). "Renewing American Economic Leadership." Remarks at the Brookings Institution, April 27, 2023.

Sullivan, Roger. "Discarding the China Card." *Foreign Policy*, Spring 1992.

Sun Jiayi. "China to Expand Digital Currency Pilot Programs, Questions Remain." *Panda Daily*, August 19, 2020.

Sun Jing. "Chinese Architects Pirating World's Famous Buildings" (孙静:中国建筑盗版全球"名筑"). *Beijing Qingnian Bao* (北京青年报), May 26, 2014.

Sun Lipeng. "US Accelerates Economic Decoupling from China" (孙立鹏: 美国加紧对华经贸脱钩). *World affairs* (世界知识), Beijing, June 11, 2020.

Sun Liping. "Between China and the US, All Conflicts Are Strategic and All Détentes Are Tactical" (孙立平: 中美之间, 任何对抗都是战略性的, 任何缓和都是策略性的). WeChat blog (微信公众号), November 17, 2021.

———. "No Matter What, Putin Has Changed the World in a Backfired Way" (无论战事结果如何, 普京都在事与愿违的意义上改变了世界). WeChat blog (微信公众号), March 10, 2022.

Sun Tzu. *The Art of War*. Open source, (6th century BCE) 2007.

Sun Wenyi. "Old Zhiqings in the Burmese Jungle" (孙文晔: 老知青的缅甸丛林记). *Zhongguo Xinwen Zhoukan* (中国新闻周刊), no. 403, Beijing, January 2009.

Sun Xingjie. "Qin Gang Starts as New Ambassador to the US" (孙兴杰: 秦刚履新驻美大使). *Xinjing Bao* (新京报), Beijing, July 30, 2021.

Suryadinata, Leo. *Overseas Chinese in Southeast Asia and China's Foreign Policy*. Singapore: Institute of South Asian Studies, 1978.

———. *Southeast Asian Chinese and China*. Singapore: Times Academic, 1995.

Sutton, H. I. "Could the Indian Navy Strangle China's Lifeline in the Malacca Strait?" *Forbes*, June 8, 2020.

Swaine, Michael. *Threat Inflation and the Chinese Military*. Quincy Paper, no. 7, Quincy Institute for Responsible Statecraft, June 2022.

Swaine, Michael, Ezra F. Vogel, Paul Heer, J. Stapleton Roy, Rachel Esplin Odell, Mike Mochizuki, Avery Goldstein, and Alice Miller, with reply by Aaron L. Friedberg. "The Overreach of the China Hawks: Aggression Is the Wrong Response to Beijing." *Foreign Affairs*, October 23, 2020.

Swanson, Ana. "A New Red Scare Is Reshaping Washington." *New York Times*, July 20, 2019.

———. "U.S. Diplomats and Spies Battle Trump Administration over Suspected Attacks." *New York Times*, October 21, 2020.

SWIFT. *RMB Tracker: Monthly Reporting and Statistics on Renminbi (RMB) Progress towards Becoming an International Currency*. La Hulpe, Belgium, January 2023.

420 | Works and Sources Cited

Szabolcs, Panyi. "Huge Chinese Loan to Cover the Construction of Fudan University in Budapest." Direct36, Hungary, April 6, 2021.

Tagliacozzo, Eric, and Wen-chin Chang. *Chinese Circulations: Capital, Commodities, and Networks in Southeast Asia*. Durham, NC: Duke University Press, 2011.

Tai Meiti. "SWIFT Sanction! Many Russian Banks Connected to CIPS" (钛媒体: SWIFT制裁! 俄罗斯多家银行接入CIPS). *Fenghuang* (凤凰), March 1, 2022.

Tainter, Joseph. *The Collapse of Complex Societies*. New York: Cambridge University Press, 1988.

Taleb, Nassim Nicholas. *The Black Swan: The Impact of the Highly Improbable*. 2nd ed. New York: Random House, 2010.

Tammen, Ronald, Jacek Kugler, Douglas Lemke, Allan C. Stam III, Mark Abdollohian, Carole Alsharabati, Brian Efird, Ronald L. Tammen, and A. F. K. Organski. *Power Transitions: Strategies for the 21st Century*. Washington, DC: CQ Press, 2000.

Tan, Su-Lin. "Why Has the China-Australia Relationship Deteriorated into What Some Are Calling 'Trade War 2.0'?" *South China Morning Post*, July 1, 2020.

Tan, Weizhen. "Trump Wants to Delist Chinese Companies from U.S. Exchanges—That Could Hurt Wall Street." CNBC, June 9, 2020.

Tan, Yeling. "How the WTO Changed China: The Mixed Legacy of Economic Engagement." *Foreign Affairs*, March/April 2021.

———. *Disaggregating China, Inc.: State Strategies in the Liberal Economic Order*. Ithaca, NY: Cornell University Press, 2021a.

Tang Jigen. "On the Bone-Marrow DNA and Race of Yinxu People" (唐际根: 关于殷墟人骨DNA和殷墟人种问题). *Kaogu* (考古), June 23, 2020.

Tang Shiping. "Cultivate National Image" (唐世平: 塑造国家形象). *The Paper* (澎湃), Shanghai, December 24, 2020.

Tang, Shiping. *The Social Evolution of International Politics*. Oxford: Oxford University Press, 2013.

Tao Ran. *Between People and Land* (陶然: 人地之间). Shenyang: Liaoning Renmin, 2023.

Task Force on U.S.-China Policy. *Policy Brief: Avoiding War Over Taiwan*. UCSD, October 12, 2022.

Tatlow, Didi. "Exclusive: 600 U.S. Groups Linked to Chinese Communist Party Influence Effort with Ambition beyond Election." *Newsweek*, October 26, 2020.

———. "China Targets Israeli Technology in Quest for Global Dominance as U.S. Frets." *Newsweek*, August 10, 2022.

———. "Kilts and Qipaos in Britain: Nearly 400 China 'United Front' Groups Thrive." *Newsweek*, June 29, 2023.

Tchen, John Kuo Wei, and Dylan Yeats. *Yellow Peril! An Archive of Anti-Asian Fear*. New York: Verso, 2014.

Works and Sources Cited | 421

Teng Biao, "Interview on *News Night*." BBC Channel Two, April 14, 2021.

————. "Is China Ready for Democracy?" Personal blog, May 2, 2021.

Tewari, Suranjana. "Pacific Islands Urge Unity in Face of China Ambition." BBC News, July 16, 2022.

Tham, Engen, and Cheng Leng. "Bankers' Exits and Zombie Accounts: China's Shanghai Free Trade Zone Sputters." Reuters, September 1, 2019.

Tharoor, Ishaan. "The World Doesn't Want to Pick between the U.S. and China." *Washington Post*, April 28, 2020.

Thayer, Bradley, and Han Lianchao. "Kissinger's Folly: The Threat to World Order Is China." *Hill*, April 19, 2020.

Thiessen, Marc. "Enes Freedom Was Cut for Exposing How U.S. Corporations Became Foreign Agents of Communist China." *Washington Post*, February 15, 2022.

Thomas, Lloyd. "Equality Within the Limits of Reason Alone." *Mind* 88, no. 352 (1979): 538–53.

Thorburn, Jacob. "Heads of MI5 and FBI Warn of Threat Posed by China in First Ever Joint Speech." *Daily Mail*, July 6, 2022.

Thorley, Martin. *Fool's Gold? Sino-British Elites and the "Golden Era" of Relations.* PhD thesis, Nottingham University, 2020.

Thucydides. *History of the Peloponnesian War.* New York: Penguin, (5th century BCE) 1972.

Thurston, Anne, ed. *Engaging China: Fifty Years of Sino-American Relations.* New York: Columbia University Press, 2021.

Tian Feilong. "New Cycle of Sino-American Relationship" (田飞龙: 中美关系的新周期). *Zhongguo Pinglun* (中国评论), Hong Kong, January 2022.

Time. "Foreign News: We Will Bury You!" November 26, 1956.

Timperlake, Edward, and William Triplett. *Year of the Rat: How Bill Clinton and Al Gore Compromised U.S. Security for Chinese Cash.* Washington, DC: Regnery, 1998.

To, James Jiann Hua. *Qiaowu: Extra-territorial Policies for the Overseas Chinese.* Leiden: Brill, 2014.

Tonnesson, Bởi Stein. *Vietnam 1946: How the War Began.* Berkeley: University of California Press, 2010.

Torigian, Joseph. *Prestige, Manipulation, and Coercion: Elite Power Struggles in the Soviet Union and China after Stalin and Mao.* New Haven, CT: Yale University Press, 2022.

Trachtenberg, Marc. "Assessing Soviet Economic Performance during the Cold War: A Failure of Intelligence?" *Texas National Security Review* 1, no. 2 (2018): 76–101.

Tran, Hung, and Barbara Matthews. "China's Digital Currency Electronic Payment Project Reveals the Good and the Bad of Central Bank Digital Currencies." Atlantic Council, August 2020.

422 | Works and Sources Cited

Traub, James. "Biden Is Now a China Hawk—with Limits." *Foreign Policy*, September 3, 2020.

Treisman, Daniel. "Democracy by Mistake: How the Errors of Autocrats Trigger Transitions to Freer Government." *American Political Science Review* 114, no. 3 (2020): 792–810.

Truman, Harry. "Statement by the President on General Ridgway's Korean Armistice Proposal." White House, May 7, 1952.

Trump, Donald. "Executive Order on Addressing the Threat Posed by WeChat." White House, August 6, 2020.

———. "The President's Executive Order on Hong Kong Normalization." White House, July 14, 2020.

Tsai Ing-wen. "Taiwan and the Fight for Democracy: A Force for Good in the Changing International Order." *Foreign Affairs*, November/December 2021.

Tsai, Kellee. *Capitalism without Democracy: The Private Sector in Contemporary China*. Ithaca, NY: Cornell University Press, 2006.

Tsang, Steve. "China Will Punish Britain for Defying Its Will—We Need Allies to Hold the Line." *Guardian*, July 12, 2020.

———. "Getting China Right." *Survival* 65, no. 4 (2023): 43–54.

Tse, Don, Chu-cheng Ming, and Larry Ong. "China Is Not an Enemy of the US and the World—But the CCP Is." *Sino Insider*, July 8, 2019.

Tseng, Poyu, and Puma Shen. *The Chinese Infodemic in Taiwan*. Doublethink Lab, July 26, 2020.

Tuan, Yi-Fu. *Dominance and Affection: The Making of Pets*. New Haven, CT: Yale University Press, 1984.

Tuan, Yi-Fu. *Topophilia: A Study of Environmental Perception, Attitudes, and Values*. New York: Columbia University Press, 1974.

Turchin, Peter. *Historical Dynamics: Why States Rise and Fall*. Princeton, NJ: Princeton University Press, 2003.

Turchin, Peter, Harvey Whitehouse, Sergey Gavrilets, Daniel Hoyer, Pieter François, James S. Bennett, Kevin C. Feeney, et al. "Disentangling the Evolutionary Drivers of Social Complexity: A Comprehensive Test of Hypotheses." *Science Advances* 8, no. 25 (2022). https://doi.org/10.1126/sciadv.abn3517.

Turkish Radio and Television Corporation (TRT). "How China's Debt Trap Diplomacy Works and What It Means." *TRT World*, December 13, 2019.

Turner, Chris. "BRICS: The New Name in Reserve Currencies." *ING Economic and Financial Analysis*, June 22, 2022.

Turrin, Rich. "China's New Digital Currency Will Foster Hi-Tech Internationalisation of the Renminbi." *China Banking News*, Shanghai, May 27, 2020.

Twining, Daniel. "The New Great Game: Why the Bush Administration Has Embraced India." *Weekly Standard*, December 20, 2006.

Uhl, Christian. "Veiling Ideology or Enabling Utopia? On the Potentials and Limitations of the Debate about *Tianxia* as a Model for a New World Order." Conference paper, 2021.

UNDP. "Comparative Study on Special Economic Zones in Africa and China." UNDP White Paper no. 6, 2015.

UNESCO (United Nations Educational, Scientific and Cultural Organization). *Rethinking Education: Towards a Global Common Good.* Paris, 2015.

———. *Global Education Monitoring Report 2020.* Paris, June 23, 2020.

Unger, Craig. *American Kompromat.* New York: Penguin, 2021.

United States-China Economic and Security Review Commission. *2020 Report to Congress.* December 1, 2020.

———. *Chinese Companies Listed on Major U.S. Stock Exchanges.* March 31, 2022.

UN OGPRP (Office on Genocide Prevention and Responsibility to Protect). "Responsibility to Protect." Accessed August 2023. un.org/en/genocideprevention.

Unruh, Bob. " 'Essentially Traitors': China Has 'Thousands' of U.S. Professors on Payroll." *Citizens Journal,* January 3, 2022.

US Attorney's Office, District of Massachusetts. "Harvard University Professor Convicted of Making False Statements and Tax Offenses." Press release, December 21, 2021.

US Congress. Better Utilization of Investments Leading to Development Act. October 2018.

———. "A 'China Model?' Beijing's Promotion of Alternative Global Norms and Standards." Hearing, Washington, DC, March 13, 2020.

US Congressional Budget Office. *A 125-Year Picture of the Federal Government's Share of the Economy, 1950 to 2075.* Washington, DC, July 3, 2002.

US Congressional Research Service. *Confucius Institutes in the United States.* April 15, 2019.

———. *China Naval Modernization: Implications for U.S. Navy Capabilities.* Washington, May 21, 2020.

US Department of Education. "U.S. Department of Education Launches Investigation into Foreign Gifts Reporting at Ivy League Universities." Febraury 12, 2020.

US Department of the Treasury/Federal Reserve Board. *Major Foreign Holders of Treasury Securities.* Department of the Treasury, May 2014.

———. *Major Foreign Holders of Treasury Securities.* Department of the Treasury, July 2022.

US DOD. *Indo-Pacific Strategy Report: Preparedness, Partnerships, and Promoting a Networked Region.* June 1, 2019.

———. *Military and Security Developments Involving the People's Republic of China—Annual Report to Congress.* August 21, 2020.

———. *National Defense Strategy of the United States.* October 2022.

US DOJ. *Information about the Department of Justice's China Initiative and a Compilation of China-Related Prosecutions since 2018.* Updated November 19, 2021.

US DOS. "Visa Restrictions on Chinese Communist Party Officials for Undermining Hong Kong's High Degree of Autonomy and Restricting Human Rights." June 26, 2020.

———. *2020 Report on International Religious Freedom.* Department of State, May 2021.

———. *Leaders Summit on Climate.* April 23, 2021.

———. *The Chinese Communist Party: Threatening Global Peace and Security.* Department of State, July 2022.

———. *Joint Statement on Cooperation on Global Supply Chains.* July 20, 2022.

———. *Limits in the Sea No. 155—People's Republic of China: Maritime Claims in the South China Sea.* Department of State, January 2022.

———. *2022 Hong Kong Policy Act Report.* Department of State, March 31, 2022.

US DOT. "Treasury Sanctions Chinese Entity and Officials Pursuant to Global Magnitsky Human Rights Accountability Act." Department of the Treasury, July 9, 2020.

US NIC (National Intelligence Council). *International: More Contested, Uncertain, and Conflict Prone.* March 2021.

US Office of Management and Budget, *Receipts by Source as percentages of GDP: 1934–2018.* January 2, 2014.

US Senate. "Threats to the U.S. Research Enterprise: China's Talent Recruitment Plans." Committee on Homeland Security and Governmental Affairs, November 19, 2019.

van der Wees, Gerrit. "When the CCP Thought Taiwan Should Be Independent." *Diplomat*, May 3, 2022.

Van Noorden, Richard. "The Number of Researchers with Dual US–China Affiliations Is Falling." *Nature*, May 30, 2022.

Vedrenne, Gabriel. "Chinese Money Launderers a 'Growing Threat' in Europe." MoneyLaundering.com, November 26, 2019.

Venditti, Bruno. "The Cost of Space Flight before and after SpaceX." *Visual Capitalist*, January 27, 2022.

Vervaeke, Leen, and Marije Vlaskamp. "China Is Already Shaping Us More Than We Think" (China vormt ons al meer dan we denken). *De Volkskrant*, May 8, 2020.

Visentin, Lisa. "University Students Will Be Trained to Spot Foreign Interference." *Sydney Morning Herald*, August 31, 2021.

Voegelin, Eric. "World-Empire and the Unity of Mankind." *International Affairs* 38, no. 2 (1962): 170–88.

von Hippel, Frank. "Eliminate the Launch-on-Warning Option for U.S. Ballistic Missiles." Physicists Coalition for Nuclear Threat Reduction, November 15, 2020.

Von Mises, Ludwig. *Socialism: An Economic and Sociological Analysis*. Whitefish, MT: Kessinger, (1922/1951) 2010.

Voss, Kim, and Rachel Sherman. "Breaking the Iron Law of Oligarchy." *American Journal of Sociology* 106, no. 2 (2000): 303–49.

Wade, Nicholas. "The Origin of COVID: Did People or Nature Open Pandora's Box at Wuhan?" *Bulletin of the Atomic Scientists*, May 5, 2021.

Wahba, Sadek. "The G7 Infrastructure Partnership Is a Step in the Right Direction." *Hill*, June 28, 2022.

Waldron, Arthur. "There Is No Thucydides Trap." *SupChina*, June 12, 2017.

Waldron, Jeremy. *God, Locke, and Equality*. New York: Cambridge University Press, 2002.

Wallace, Jeremy. *Seeking Truth and Hiding facts: Information, Ideology, and Authoritarianism in China*. New York: Oxford University Press, 2023.

Waller, Michael. "Chinese Communist Party Wants Pompeo Out." Center for Security Policy, April 4, 2020.

Wall Street Journal. "The Bidens and China Business." Editorial, October 20, 2020.

———. "'Nobody in Hollywood' Like Xi Jinping." Editorial, July 20, 2023.

Walt, Stephen. "There's Still No Reason to Think the Kellogg-Briand Pact Accomplished Anything." *Foreign Policy*, September 29, 2017.

———. *The Hell of Good Intentions: America's Foreign Policy Elite and the Decline of U.S. Primacy*. New York: Farrar, 2018.

———. "Biden Sees the A-Team—I See the Blob." *Foreign Policy*, December 11, 2020.

———. "The World Might Want China's Rules: Washington Shouldn't Assume Its Values Are More Attractive to Others than Beijing's." *Foreign Policy*, May 4, 2021.

Waltz, Kenneth. *Theory of International Politics*. New York: McGraw Hill, 1979.

Wan, Ming. "The China Dream—2." *Asan Forum*, September 6, 2013.

Wang, Amber. "US Denies Chinese Student a Visa because Father Is a Police Officer." *South China Morning Post*, May 14, 2021.

Wang, Ban. *Chinese Visions of World Order: Tianxia, Culture, and World Politics*. Durham, NC: Duke University Press, 2017.

Wang Cong. "He Jiankui Plans to Cure 3–5 Rare Diseases" (网从: 贺建奎计划在2-3年内攻克3-5种罕见病). *Shengwu Shijie* (生物世界), Shanghai, January 19, 2023.

Wang Dan. "A New Axis Is Taking Shape" (王丹: 新的軸心國正在成形). *Apple Daily* (蘋果日報), Hong Kong, April 14, 2021.

Wang Dong. "The Case for a New Engagement Consensus: A Chinese Vision of Global Order." *Foreign Affairs*, April 15, 2021.

Wang, Echo, and Michael Berens. "How a Trump Deal Got a Boost from a China-Based Financier." Reuters, February 10, 2022.

426 | Works and Sources Cited

Wang Fei-Ling. "The Best Way to Long and Peaceful Governance and Democratization in China: Inner-Party Democracy and Legitimization of Factions Inside the Party" (王飞凌: 中国政治长治久安与民主化的最佳途径—党内民主和党内派别的合法化). *China Elections and Governance*, Beijing, [2000] June 13, 2003.

Wang, Fei-Ling. "To Incorporate China—a New China Policy for a New Era." *Washington Quarterly* 21, no. 1 (1998): 67–81.

———. *Institutions and Institutional Change in China: Premodernity and Modernization*. London: Macmillan, 1998a.

———. *Organization through Division and Exclusion: China's Hukou System*. Stanford, CA: Stanford University Press, 2005.

———. "Lots of Wealth, Lots of People, Lots of Flaws: China Rising." *New York Times*, July 21, 2005a.

———. "Beijing's Incentive Structure: The Pursuit of Preservation, Prosperity, and Power." In *China Rising: Power and Motivation in Chinese Foreign Policy*, edited by Yong Deng and Fei-Ling Wang, 19–49. Lanham, MD: Rowman and Littlefield, 2005b.

———. "Heading Off Fears of a Resurgent China." *New York Times*, April 10, 2006.

———. "Taiwan: Catalyst for Change in China." *Christian Science Monitor*, September 19, 2006a.

———. "Resisting, Reducing, and Replacing: China's Strategy and Policy towards the United States." In *China's Domestic Politics and Foreign Policies and Major Countries' Strategies toward China*, edited by Jung-Ho Bae, 155–86. Seoul: KINU, 2012.

———. "Between the Bomb and the United States: China Faces the Nuclear North Korea." In *North Korea and Nuclear Weapons: Entering the New Era of Deterrence*, edited by Sung Chull Kim and Michael Cohen. Washington, DC: Georgetown University Press, 2017a.

———. *The China Order: Centralia, World Empire, and the Nature of Chinese Power*. Albany: State University of New York Press, 2017.

———. *The China Record: An Assessment of the People's Republic*. Albany: State University of New York Press, 2023.

———. "Talking the Talk and Walking the Walk: China and the Effort to Denuclearize North Korea." In Terence Roehrig and Su-Mi Lee eds. In *Negotiation Dynamics to Denuclearize North Korea: Cohesion and Disarray*. Albany: State University of New York, 2023a.

Wang, Fei-Ling, and Es`i Elliot. "China in Africa: Presence, Perceptions, and Prospects." *Journal of Contemporary China* 23, no. 90 (2014): 1012–32.

Wang Gonglong. "Transitional Community: The Historical Position of the Community of Common Destiny for Humanity" (王公龙: 过渡性共同体-人类命运共同体的历史方位). *Lilun Sheye* (理论视野), Central Party School, no. 3, 2019.

Works and Sources Cited | 427

Wang, Gungwu. *The Chinese Overseas: From Earthbound China to the Quest for Autonomy.* Cambridge, MA: Harvard University Press, 2000.

———. *Where Is My Home? My Home Is Where Heart Is at Peace* (王賡武: 家園何處是, 心安是我家). Hong Kong: Chinese University of Hong Kong Press, 2020.

Wang Huiyao. *Globalization at the New Crossroad* (王辉耀: 全球化站在新的十字路口). Beijing: Sanlian, 2021.

Wang Huiyao et al., eds. *Report on China's international migration 2014* (王辉耀等: 中国国际移民报告 *2014*). Beijing: Shke wenxian, 2014.

Wang Huiyao and Miao Lv. *Report on Development of Chinese Students Studying Abroad 2021* (王辉耀,苗绿:中国留学发展报告2021). Beijing: Shehui kexue, 2021.

———. "Close Look at US Attitudes towards China through 'Track-Two Diplomacy'" (王辉耀, 苗绿: 透过"二轨外交," 近观美国各界对中国态度). *Huanqiu Shibao* (环球时报), July 18, 2022.

Wang Jianwei. "Biden's China Policy Is Trumpism without Trump?" (王建偉: 拜登對華政策是沒有特朗普的"特朗普主義"吗). *Ershiyi Shiji* (二十一世紀), Hong Kong, April 2021.

Wang Jin Tou. "Accelerating De-dollarization" (金投网: 去美元化提速). *Sohu* (搜狐), June 28, 2022.

Wang Jingwen. "Fight a Protracted War, Promote Two Circulars" (王静文: 打持久战 促双循环). Beijing: Xinhua, August 4, 2020.

Wang Jisi. "The 'Two Orders' and the Future of China-U.S. Relations." *ChinaFile*, July 9, 2015.

———. "The Plot against China? How Beijing Sees the New Washington Consensus." *Foreign Affairs*, July/August 2021.

Wang, Joyu. "Hong Kong Security Law: How Beijing Is Cracking Down." *Wall Street Journal*, November 11, 2020.

Wang Li. "Breakthrough! From 'One Warship' a Decade to 'Making Dumplings'" (王力: 突破! 从十年磨一"舰" 到 "下饺子"). *Jiefang Ribao* (解放日报), Shanghai, April 19, 2021.

Wang Lisheng and Li Xinyu. "To Scientifically Ascertain the Historical Place of Mao Zedong and Mao Zedong Thought" (王立胜 李新宇: 科学把握毛泽东和毛泽东思想的历史地位). *Zhongguo pudong ganbu xueyuan xuebao* (中国浦东干部学院学报), Shanghai, no. 2, 2022.

Wang, Maya, and Andreas Harsono. "Indonesia's Silence over Xinjiang." Human Rights Watch, January 31, 2020.

Wang Mingyuan. "The Colossal Loss and Lessons from the Soviet Union's Diplomacy of Economic Aid in the Third World" (王明远: 苏联在第三世界经济援助外交的巨额损失和教训). *Meiri Toutiao* (每日头条), Beijing, September 7, 2018.

Wang Peiyao. "How Much Land Has China Lost since 1949?" (王培尧: 1949年以后, 中国丢失多少国土?). *Kexue Wang* (科学网), Beijing, April 12, 2021.

Works and Sources Cited

Wang, Peng. "Military Corruption in China: The Role of Guanxi in the Buying and Selling of Military Positions." *China Quarterly* 228 (2016): 970–91.

Wang Qiang. "Chinese Merchants Self-Expose How Coned by [North] Koreans" (中国商人自曝如何被朝鲜人忽悠). *New York Times in Chinese*, September 5, 2009.

Wang, Robert. "Countering China's Intimidation of Taiwan." *Foreign Service Journal*, June 2021.

Wang Tianyi. "Heroes Standing Tall on Karakoram" (王天益: 英雄屹立喀喇昆仑). *Jiafangjun Bao* (解放军报), Beijing, February 19, 2021.

Wang Tingyou. "'Common Values' Are Not the West's So-Called 'Universal Values'" (汪亭友: "共同价值"不是西方所谓"普世价值"). *Hongqi Wengao* (红旗文稿), Beijing, Febraury 2016.

Wang Wen. "Sino-American Competition" (王文: 中美竞争). *Shiping-Zhongtou Shuoqi* (视频-重头说起). Beijing: Chongyang Institute for Financial Studies, July 19, 2021.

Wang Wentao. "Building a Great Cyber Power Helps China to Develop an 'Overtaking at the Curve'" (汪闻涛: 网络强国建设助力中国发展"弯道超车"). *Renmin Luntan* (人民论坛), February 18, 2021.

Wang Xiaofeng. "85 Thousand Chinese Students Go to the US" (王晓枫: 8.5万中国学生赴美留学). *Caijing* (财经), Beijing, August 27, 2021.

Wang Yaqiu. "WeChat Is a Trap for China's Diaspora." *Foreign Policy*, August 14, 2020.

Wang Yi. "Analyzing the Building and Institutional Construction of a New Type of Global Governance System" (王毅: 试析新型全球治理体系的构建及制度建设). *Guowai Lilun Dongtai* (国外理论动态), Beijing, no. 8, 2013.

———. "Join Hands to Forge the Community of Common Destiny for Humanity" (王毅: 携手打造人类命运共同体). *Renmin Ribao* (人民日报), May 31, 2016.

———. "Special Interview with Xinhua on Sino-American Relations" (王毅就当前中美关系接受新华社专访). Beijing, August 5, 2020.

———. "Protect the Correct Direction of Sino-American Relations" (维护中美关系的正确方向). Public speech, Beijing, July 9, 2020.

———. "Raise High the Banner of Community of Common Destiny of Humanity, Forward with Big Strides" (王毅: 高举人类命运共同体旗帜阔步前行). *Qiushi* (求是), January 2022.

———. "Sino-Russia Strategic Cooperation Has No Limit, No Restriction, No Ceiling" (王毅: 中俄战略合作没有止境, 没有禁区, 没有上限). Beijing, January 2, 2022a.

———. "The So-Called Taiwan Statement by the G7 Is a Piece of Wastepaper" (王毅: G7所谓涉台声明是废纸一张). China Central Television (CCTV), August 5, 2022b.

Works and Sources Cited | 429

———. "Writing a New Chapter of Great Power Diplomacy with Chinese Characteristics" (王毅: 谱写中国特色大国外交新华章). Public speech, Beijing, December 25, 2022c.

Wang Yi Hao. "Wrote Off Debt and Debt All the Way Traveled" (网易号: 走一路免一路债务). *Wangyi* (网易), January 17, 2023.

Wang Yiwei. "Helping Africa Is Helping China Itself, Great Rejuvenation Needs Construction of a China Overseas" (王义桅: 帮助非洲就是帮助中国自己, 伟大复兴要打造海外中国). *Jinri Toutiao* (今日头条), Beijing, June 30, 2020.

Wang Yongli. "China Completely Blocks Cryptocurrencies" (王永利: 中国全面封堵虚拟货币). *Sina* (新浪), June 23, 2021.

Wang, Yuhua. *Tying the Autocrat's Hands: The Rise of The Rule of Law in China.* New York: Cambridge University Press, 2015.

———. "Blood Is Thicker than Water: Elite Kinship Networks and State Building in Imperial China." *American Political Science Review* 116, no. 3 (2022): 1–15.

———. *The Rise and Fall of Imperial China: The Social Origins of State Development.* Princeton, NJ: Princeton University Press, 2022.

Wang Zihui. "'Struggle'! This Speech by Xi Jinping Is Rich with Profound Meaning" (王子晖: "斗争"!习近平这篇讲话大有深意). Beijing, China: Xinhua (新华), September 4, 2021.

Ward, Jonathan. *China's Vision of Victory.* Fayetteville, NC: Atlas, 2019.

Washburne, Ray. "Statement as President Signs BUILD Act into Law." US International Development Finance Corporation, October 5, 2018.

Washington Post. "Zoom Is Complicit in Chinese Repression." Editorial, December 20, 2020.

Watanabe, Shin, and Kentaro Takeda. "China's Vaccine Diplomacy Spoiled by Omicron variant." *Nikkei Asia*, May 8, 2022.

Watson, Ivan, and Ben Westcott. "Watched, Judged, Detained: Leaked Chinese Government Records Reveal Detailed Surveillance Reports on Uyghur Families." CNN, February 17, 2020.

Weber, Max. *Economy and Society.* Berkeley: University of California Press, (1922) 1978.

Weber, Ralph. "Unified Message, Rhizomatic Delivery: A Preliminary Analysis of PRC/CCP Influence and the United Front in Switzerland." *Sinopsis*, December 18, 2020.

Wee, Sui-Lee. "Chinese Scientist Who Genetically Edited Babies Gets 3 Years in Prison." *New York Times*, December 30, 2019.

———. "They Relied on Chinese Vaccines—Now They're Battling Outbreaks." *New York Times*, June 22, 2021.

Wei Ci. "Vigilant for Russia Turning against China" (慰慈: 警惕俄罗斯转向反华). WeChat blog (微信公众号), June 24, 2022.

430 | Works and Sources Cited

Wei Jianing. (魏加宁:中国经济走势与政策取向). Public speech, Beijing, October 26, 2019.

Wei, Lingling. "Chinese Pressure Tactics against Other Countries Largely Ineffective, Study Finds." *Wall Street Journal*, March 21, 2023.

Wei, Lingling, Bob Davis, and Dawn Lim. "China Has One Powerful Friend Left in the U.S.: Wall Street." *Wall Street Journal*, December 2, 2020.

Wei, Lingling, and Charles Hutzler. "China Turns to Back-Channel Diplomacy to Shore Up U.S. Ties." *Wall Street Journal*, November 21, 2022.

Wei Pu. "East Korea and West Korea" (未普:東朝鮮和西朝鮮). *Boxun* (博讯), April 28, 2016.

Wei Se. *Tibetan Notes* (唯色: 西藏笔记). Guangzhou: Huacheng, 2003.

Wei Zhi. "Sihanouk, Khmer Rouge, and China" (未知: 西哈努克, 红色高棉与中国). *Gongshi Wang* (共识网), July 29, 2014.

Weinstein, Kenneth (CEO of the Hudson Institute). "A New Cold War between the U.S. and China." *Aspen Review*, March 22, 2019.

Weisiger, Alex. *Logics of War: Explanations for Limited and Unlimited Conflicts.* Ithaca, NY: Cornell University Press, 2013.

Weiss, Jessica Chen. "A World Safe for Autocracy? China's Rise and the Future of Global Politics." *Foreign Affairs*, July/August 2019.

———. "No 'Beijing Consensus': Why the U.S. Risks a Pyrrhic Victory in Confronting China." *SupChina*, June 29, 2020.

———. "Mike Pompeo Accused China of Committing 'Genocide,' an International Crime—Biden's Team Agrees." *Washington Post*, January 23, 2021.

———. "The China Trap: U.S. Foreign Policy and the Perilous Logic of Zero-Sum Competition." *Foreign Affairs*, September/October 2022.

———. "Even China Isn't Convinced It Can Replace the U.S." *New York Times*, May 4, 2023.

Weiss, Jessica Chen, and Thomas Pepinsky. "The Clash of Systems? Washington Should Avoid Ideological Competition with Beijing." *Foreign Affairs*, June 11, 2021.

Weiss, Jessica Chen, and Jeremy Wallace. "Domestic Politics, China's Rise, and the Future of the Liberal International Order." *International Organization* 75, no. 2 (2021, 635–64).

Wells, Samuel, Robert S. Litwak, Donggil Kim, and Youngjun Kim. "Korean War: Myths and Misconceptions." *Wilson Quarterly* 44, no. 3 (2020).

Wen Kejian (He Yongqin). "Pathological Analysis of RMB Internationalization" (温克坚/何永勤: 人民币国际化病理剖析报告). WeChat blog (微信公众号), September 2022.

Wen Shan. "Posting Anti-China Abroad, Arrested When Back Home" (文山: 境外发帖反华, 回国即遭逮捕). *Deutsche Welle in Chinese*, Berlin, July 29, 2019.

Wendt, Alexander. "Anarchy Is What States Make of It: The Social Construction of Power Politics." *International Organization* 46, no. 2 (1992): 391–425.

Works and Sources Cited | 431

———. *Social Theory of International Politics.* Cambridge: Cambridge University Press, 1999.

———. "Why a World State Is Inevitable." *European Journal of International Relations* 9, no. 4 (2003): 491–542.

———. "Agency, Teleology, and the World State: A Reply to Shannon." *European Journal of International Relations* 11, no. 4 (2005): 589–98.

———. "The World State Project." n.d. Accessed July 3, 2022. alexanderwendt.org.

Wendt, Alexander, and Raymond Duvall. "Sovereignty and the UFO." *Political Theory* 36, no. 4 (2008): 607–33.

Wenhua Zongheng (文化纵横). "The Era of the Rising Sino-American Contradiction as the World's Main Contradiction Is Arriving" (中美矛盾上升为世界主要矛盾的时代正在到来). Editorial, Beijing, no. 4, August 2021.

Werber, Niels. *Ant Societies* (Ameisengesellschaften). Frankfurt: Fischer, 2013.

Wheatley, Jonathan, Joseph Cotterill, and Sun Yu. "China's Pivotal Role under Scrutiny as Zambia Seeks Debt Relief." *Financial Times*, June 28, 2022.

White House. "Proclamation on the Suspension of Entry as Nonimmigrants of Certain Students and Researchers from the People's Republic of China." May 29, 2020.

———. *United States Strategic Approach to the People's Republic of China.* Report to Congress, May 20, 2020.

———. Quad Leaders' Joint Statement: "The Spirit of the Quad." Briefing, March 12, 2021.

———. *Summit for Democracy Summary of Proceedings.* December 23, 2021.

———. "Updated Fact Sheet: Bipartisan Infrastructure Investment and Jobs Act." August 2, 2021.

———. *Indo-Pacific Strategy of the United States.* February 11, 2022.

———. *Joint Statement of the Leaders of the Five Nuclear-Weapon States on Preventing Nuclear War and Avoiding Arms Races.* January 3, 2022.

———. *National Defense Strategy of the United States.* October 2022.

———. "President Biden and G7 Leaders Formally Launch the Partnership for Global Infrastructure and Investment." June 26, 2022.

———. "Readout of President Joe Biden's Meeting with President Xi Jinping of the People's Republic of China." November 14, 2022.

———. "Statement on Indo-Pacific Economic Framework for Prosperity." May 23, 2022.

———. *Joint Statement from the United States and India.* June 22, 2023.

———. "Remarks by President Biden at the Summit for Democracy." March 29, 2023.

Wilhelm, Katherine. "It's Time to Stop Calling Xi Jinping the 'President' of China." *Washington Post*, October 19, 2022.

Will, George. "Why China Will Become Ever More Dangerous as Its Baby Bust Worsens." *Washington Post*, August 24, 2022.

432 | Works and Sources Cited

Williams, Frederick. *Anson Burlingame and the First Chinese Mission to Foreign Powers*. New York: Scribner's, 1912.

Williamson, Oliver. *Markets and Hierarchies*. New York: Macmillan, 1975.

———. *The Mechanisms of Governance*. New York: Oxford University Press, 1996.

Wilson, E. O. *On Human Nature*. Cambridge, MA: Harvard University Press, 1979.

———. *Sociobiology: The New Synthesis*. Cambridge, MA: Harvard University Press, (1975) 2000.

———. *Genesis: The Deep Origin of Societies*. New York: Liveright, 2019.

Wingo, Scott. "China, COVID-19, and Developing Country Debt." Center for Advanced China Research, August 27, 2020.

Winnefeld, James. "Winter Is Coming." *Proceedings*, July 2020.

Winnefeld, James, and Michael Morell. "The War That Never Was?" *Naval Proceedings*, August 2020.

Winnefeld, James, Michael Morell, and Graham Allison. "Why American Strategy Fails: Ending the Chronic Imbalance between Ends and Means." *Foreign Affairs*, October 28, 2020.

Wintour, Patrick. "Ukraine: What Will China Do? There Are Signs It Is Uneasy about Putin's Methods." *Guardian*, February 27, 2022.

Wise, Lindsay, and Ian Talley. "Senate Passes Sanctions Bill on China over Hong Kong Law." *Wall Street Journal*, June 25, 2020.

Wolf, Martin. *Why Globalization Works*. New Haven, CT: Yale University Press, 2004.

———. "Containing China Is Not a Feasible Option." *Financial Times*, February 3, 2021.

———. *The Crisis of Democratic Capitalism*. New York: Penguin, 2023.

Womack, Brantly. *Recentering Pacific Asia: Regional China and World Order*. New York: Cambridge University Press, 2023.

Wondracz, Aidan. "Australian Anti-China Activist Pleads for Help." *Daily Mail*, July 23, 2022.

Wong, Brian, and George Chen. "AI Risks Require China and U.S. to Work Together." *Nikkei—Opinion*, July 18, 2023.

Wong, Chun Han. *Party of One: The Rise of Xi Jinping and China's Superpower Future*. New York: Avid Reader, 2023.

Wong, Edward. "A Chinese Empire Reborn: The Communist Party's Emerging Empire Is More the Result of Force than a Gravitational Pull of Chinese Ideas." *New York Times*, January 7, 2018.

———. "U.S. Officials Repeatedly Urged China to Help Avert War in Ukraine." *New York Times*, February 26, 2022.

Wong, Edward, Julian E. Barnes, and Matthew Rosenberg. "Chinese Agents Spread Messages That Sowed Virus Panic in U.S., Officials Say." *New York Times*, April 23, 2020.

Wong, Edward, and Chris Buckley. "U.S. Says China's Repression of Uighurs Is 'Genocide.'" *New York Times*, January 20, 2021.

Wong, Edward, and Steven Lee Myers. "Officials Push U.S.-China Relations toward Point of No Return." *New York Times*, July 25, 2020.

Wong, Sue-Lin. "Seeds of a Pomegranate." *The Prince*, September 26, 2022. Podcast, MP3 audio, 38:37. podcasts.apple.com/us/podcast/the-prince/id1642926713.

Wong Young-tsu. "Balderdash in Memory of Dream" (汪榮祖: 夢憶裡的夢囈). In *Modern History Series* (中央研究院近代史研究所集刊), no. 65, 139–49. Taipei: Academia Sinica, 2010.

———. "Six Worrisome Problems of Overseas Study of Chinese History" (汪荣祖: 海外中国史研究值得警惕的六大问题). *Guoji Hanxue* (国际汉学), Beijing, no. 2, 2020.

Woodhead, H. G. W. *The Truth about the Chinese Republic*. London: Hurst, 1925.

Worden, Andréa. *China at the UN Human Rights Council: Conjuring a "Community of Shared Future for Humankind"?* Seattle: National Bureau of Asian Research, 2020.

Wray, Christopher. "The Threat Posed by the Chinese Government and the Chinese Communist Party to the Economic and National Security of the United States." Speech at Hudson Institute, July 7, 2020.

Wright, Robert. *The Moral Animal: Why We Are the Way We Are*. New York: Pantheon, 1994.

Wright, Thomas. *All Measures Short of War*. New Haven, CT: Yale University Press, 2017.

Wu, Guoguang. "The Ukrainian Challenge to China's Leadership Politics: An Emerging Divergence in Foreign Policy and Its Impact on the 20th Party Congress." *China Leadership Monitor*, no. 72, 2022.

Wu, Hailong. "Resolved in Desperation to Compete with the US and the West in all Areas [and] China Must Win" (吴海龙: 横下一条心与美西方竞争, 中国必须赢). Hainan, October 29, 2022. new.qq.com/rain/a/20221101A09MC000.

Wu Jicheng and Yang Yuning. "Mao Zedong Joked about 'Venting Cannon'" (邬吉成, 杨宇宁: 毛泽东笑谈"放空炮"). *Junshi Wenzhai* (军事文摘), Beijing, no. 10, 2006.

Wu Liming. "Start with 'Celebrating Birthday' for Kissinger" (吴黎明: 从给基辛格"过生日"说起). Xinhua (新华), June 2, 2022.

Wu Lingming. "'Trumpism' with a New Face Is Even More Vicious" (吴黎明: 改头换面的"特朗普主义"更阴险). Editorial, Xinhua (新华), July 16, 2021.

Wu Pengfei. "Eight Grand Breakthroughs of Chinese Diplomacy" (吴鹏飞: 中国外交的八大突破). WeChat blog (微信公众号), January 3, 2022.

Wu Su. "Wall Street Tycoon Schwarzman Took Advantage of China Big Time" (吴苏: 华尔街大佬苏世民曾坑惨中国). *Chinese Business Strategy* (华商韬略), Beijing, April 27, 2020.

434 | Works and Sources Cited

Wu Wei. "I Manage Factories in Vietnam" (吴威: 我在越南管理工厂). *Sina Caijing* (新浪财经), May 26, 2021.

Wu Xiaogang. "Latest Survey: How Has the COVID Pandemic Affected American People's Opinion about China" (吴晓刚: 最新调查: 冠疫情如何影响美国民众对中国态度). *Zhishi Fenzi* (知识分子), Beijing, August 24, 2021.

Wucker, Michele. *The Gray Rhino: How to Recognize and Act on the Obvious Dangers We Ignore.* New York: St. Martin's, 2016.

Wuthnow, Joel, Phillip C. Saunders, and Ian Burns McCaslin. *PLA Overseas Operations in 2035: Inching Toward a Global Combat Capability.* Strategic Forum, National Defense University, May 17, 2021.

Wyne, Ali. "How to Think about Potentially Decoupling from China." *Washington Quarterly* 43, no. 1 (2020): 7–64.

X (George Kennan). "The Sources of Soviet Conduct." *Foreign Affairs* 25, no. 4 (1947): 566–82.

Xi Jinping. "Speech at the PRC Embassy to Mexico." Mexico City, February 11, 2009.

———. "Speech at the Meeting on the Work of Party Schools" (习近平: 在全国党校工作会议上的讲话). Beijing, December 11, 2015.

———. "New Year's Message" (习近平: 新年贺词). Xinhua (新华), January 1, 2017.

———. *Excerpts on "Forget Not the Original Intent, Remember Well the Mandated Mission"* (习近平: 关于"不忘初心、牢记使命"论述摘编). Beijing: Zhongyang Wenxian, August 2019.

———. "To Construct Archeology with Chinese Characters, Styles and Manners" (习近平: 建设中国特色中国风格中国气派的考古学). *Qiushi* (求是), Beijing, November 30, 2020.

———. "Enhance and Improve International Promotion Work" (习近平: 加强和改进国际传播工作). Speech at the CCP Politburo, May 31, 2021.

———. "New Year's Message" (习近平: 新年贺词). Xinhua (新华), January 1, 2021.

———. "Speech at the Central Work Conference on Nationalities" (习近平: 在中央民族工作会议上的讲话). Beijing, China Central Television (CCTV), August 28, 2021.

———. "Speech at the Meeting Celebrating the Centenary of the Chinese Communist Party" (习近平: 在庆祝中国共产党成立一百周年大会上的讲话). Beijing, July 1, 2021.

———. "Speech at the 21st SCO Heads of State Council Meeting" (习近平: 在上海合作组织成员国元首理事会第二十一次会议上的讲话). Beijing, September 17, 2021.

———. "Speech at the 76th UN General Assembly Meeting" (习近平: 在第七十六届联合国大会一般性辩论上的讲话). Speech via video link, Beijing, September 21, 2021.

———. "Video Keynote Address to 2021 Boao Asian Forum" (习近平: 在博鳌亚洲论坛2021年年会开幕式上的视频主旨演讲). Beijing, April 20, 2021.

———. *Report to the 20th CCP National Congress* (习近平: 中国共产党第二十次全国代表大会报告). Beijing, October 16, 2022.

———. "Speech at the 22nd SCO Heads of State Council Meeting" (习近平: 在上海合作组织成员国元首理事会第二十二次会议上的讲话). Samarkand, September 16, 2022.

———. "Speech at the Celebration of 100 Years of the Chinese Communist Youth League" (习近平: 在庆祝中国共产主义青年团成立100周年大会上的讲话). Beijing, May 10, 2022.

———. "Keynote Address to CCP-World Political Parties High-level Meeting" (习近平: 在中国共产党与世界政党高层对话会上的主旨讲话). Beijing, March 16, 2023.

Xi Lisheng. "Unification Enters 'Countdown'" (犀利声: 两岸统一进入"倒计时"). *Zhihu Zhuanlun* (知乎专论), Beijing, October 27, 2020.

Xi Shuguang. "The Competition of the Century between China and the US: Evolution and the Fate of China" (息曙光: 中美世纪性战略竞争: 来龙去脉与中国之命运). *Chinese Future* (中国: 历史与未来), Brussels, December 13, 2021.

Xia Liping. "Peace, Harmony, Coexistence, and Unity Direct the Development of Humanity" (夏立平: "和衷共济, 和合共生"是人类发展的前进方向). *Zhongguo Shehui Kexue* (中国社会科学), September 18, 2021.

Xia Ming. "The Ratcheting Effect in the Tough US China Policy" (夏明: 美国对华强硬政策的棘轮效应). *US-China Perception Monitor*, August 2, 2020.

Xia Yafeng. "Is the US an 'Empire'?" (夏亚峰: 美国是"帝国"吗?). *Shijie Lishi* (世界历史), Beijing, no. 2, 2017.

Xiang, Yang. *China Duel: A True Story of the Failed Coup in 2012.* Pittsburgh: Dorrance, 2022.

Xiao Jiansheng. *Rethinking the Chinese Civilization* (肖建生: 中国文明的反思). Beijing: Shehui Kexue, 2007.

Xie Chuntao. "The Plan of Action for Marching towards the Second Centennial Goal of Struggle" (谢春涛: 向第二个百年奋斗目标迈进的行动纲领). *Liaowang* (瞭望), July 19, 2021.

Xie Fuzhan, ed. *Chinese Academy of Sciences Report on International Situations 2021* (谢伏瞻: 中国社会科学院国际形势报告2021). Beijing: Chinese Academy of Sciences, February 2021.

Xie Xinshui. "Use the International Ethics of Coexistence to Facilitate the Construction of Community of Common Destiny for Humanity" (谢新水: 以共生共在的国际伦理促进人类命运共同体构建). *Xueshu Jie* (学术界), Hefei, no. 7, 2020.

Xin Ziling. *The Crash of the Red Sun: The Eternal Achievements and Crimes of Mao Zedong* (辛子陵: 紅太陽的隕落: 千秋功罪毛澤東). Hong Kong: Shuzuofang, 2009.

———. "China Has Done Everything for the Kim Father and Son (辛子陵: 中国对金氏父子已经仁至义尽). *Sina* (新浪), September 25, 2010.

436 | Works and Sources Cited

Xing Yuqing. *The Mystery of China's Exports: Decoding "Global Value Chain"* (邢予青: 中国出口之谜: 解码"全球价值链"). Shanghai: Sanlian, 2022.

Xinhua. "PLA Launches Its Largest Scale of Uniform Change in History" (解放军启动历史上最大规模三军换装). July 3, 2007.

———. "Wen Jiabao Visits Japanese Disaster Area" (温家宝访问日本灾区). May 21, 2011.

———. "Controversy over China Pirating Foreign Architecture" (中国山寨国外建筑引争议). January 10, 2013.

———. "China, on Behalf of 26 Countries, Criticizes U.S., Other Western Countries for Violating Human Rights." October 6, 2020.

———. "China's Forex Reserves Stand at 3.0606 Trln USD." April 7, 2020.

———. "14th Five-Year Plan and the Long-Term Objectives of Development by 2035" ("十四五"规划和2035远景目标). March 5, 2021.

———. "'Seven Sins' of the American Alliance System" (新华社: 美国同盟体系"七宗罪"). August 3, 2021.

———. "The World Implication of the Care for People" (人民情怀的世界意义). Editorial, July 7, 2021.

———. "Wang Yi Meets US Deputy Secretary of State Sherman" (王毅会见美国常务副国务卿舍曼). Tianjin, July 26, 2021.

———. *Joint Communiqué by the People's Republic of China and the Russian Federation on International Relations in the New Era and Global Sustainable Development* (中华人民共和国和俄罗斯联邦关于新时代国际关系和全球可持续发展的联合声明). February 4, 2022.

———. "World Internet Conference created" (世界互联网大会成立大会). July 12, 2022.

———. "Xi Jinping Meets Foreign Leaders Attending the Beijing Winter Olympics" (习近平会见出席北京冬奥会的外国政要). February 7, 2022.

Xiong Binqi. "The State Only Spends ¥4 Per Pupil?" (熊丙奇: 国家为每个小学生只花4块钱). *The Paper* (澎湃), May 25, 2018.

Xu Boyuan. "Low Quality of the Chinese Is Also a National Condition" (许博渊: 中国人素质低也是国情). Xinhua (新华), October 28, 2005.

Xu Ni. "1969, the Whole Story of the Sino-Soviet Nuclear Crisis" (许倪: 1969年,中苏核危机始末). *Zhongguo Gongchandang Xinwen* (中国共产党新闻), May 25, 2008.

Xu Wenxin. "Tenth Meeting of the World's Chinese Groups Ended Victoriously" (徐文欣: 第十届世界华侨华人社团联谊大会闭幕). Zhongxinshe (中新社), Beijing, May 11, 2023.

Xu Xiangli et al. "China Looks at the World and the World Looks at China" (徐祥丽等: 从中国看世界到世界看中国). *Renmin Ribao* (人民日报), January 23, 2020.

Xu Xiaoni. *Time Upside Down* (徐小棣: 颠倒岁月). Beijing: Sanlian, 2012.

Works and Sources Cited | 437

Xu Zerong (Tsui Ch). *China's Military Intervention in Korea: Its Origins and Objectives* (徐泽荣:重重雾释鸭绿江-抗美援朝决策探秘). New York: Blurb, 2023.

Xu Zhangrun. "The Lone Boat of China in the Great Ocean of World Civilization" (许章润: 世界文明大洋上的中国孤舟). In *China's Ongoing Crisis: Six Chapters of Year Wuxu* (戊戌六章). New York: Blurb, 2020.

Xuan Yan. "China Has Not Let Socialism Down" (宣言: 中国没有辜负社会主义). *Renmin Ribao* (人民日报), June 8, 2021.

———. "Socialism Has Not Let China Down" (宣言: 社会主义没有辜负中国). *Renmin Ribao* (人民日报), June 7, 2021.

———. "What Is the CCP? What Does the CCP Do?" (宣言: 什么是中国共产党, 中国共产党干什么). *Renmin Ribao* (人民日报), June 30, 2022.

Xue Xiaoshan. "US to Stop Issuing Visas to Multiple Chinese Officials and Their Families" (薛小山: 美国向中国政府多部门官员及家属停发签证). RFA, May 13, 2021.

Xypolia, Ilia. "From the White Man's Burden to the Responsible Saviour: Justifying Humanitarian Intervention in Libya." *Middle East Critique* 31, no. 1 (2022): 1–19.

Yan Shenlang. "China's Opening in 1972" (延伸浪: 1972年的中国对外开放). *Sina* (新浪), January 17, 2015.

Yan Xuetong. "Trump Can't Start a Cold War with China, Even If He Wants To." *Washington Post*, February 6, 2018.

———. "It Will Be More Complex to Deal with Biden than Trump" (阎学通: 应对拜登将比应对特朗普更复杂). *Caixin* (财新), Beijing, December 16, 2020.

———. "Becoming Strong—the New Chinese Foreign Policy." *Foreign Affairs*, July/August 2021.

———. "China's *Ren Yi Li* Can Save the Declined Liberalism" (阎学通: 中国的仁义礼可挽救衰落的自由主义). *Guanchazhe* (观察者), Shanghai, October 5, 2021a.

———. "Where Is the China-US Strategic Competition Headed" (阎学通: 中美战略竞争将走向何方). Speech at Qianhai Entrepreneur Summit, April 21, 2023.

Yan Yan. "Decisive Battle: Hunt and Kill the USD" (阎岩: 决战-猎杀美元). WeChat blog (微信公众号), August 12, 2021.

Yang Chen. "To Assist the Independence of Ryukyu" (杨晨: 帮助琉球独立). *Toutiao* (头条), Beijing, July 14, 2021.

Yang Dongxiao. "A Three-Decade Quest by a Volunteer Army POW" (杨东晓: 一名志愿军战俘的三十年追问). *Kanlishi* (看历史), Chengdu, August 21, 2013.

Yang Jiechi. "Actively Construct Favorable External Environments" (杨洁篪: 积极营造良好外部环境). *Renmin Ribao* (人民日报), November 30, 2020.

438 | Works and Sources Cited

———. "The Glorious Century-Long History and the Bright Future of CCP's Work of Foreign Affairs" (杨洁篪:中国共产党建党百年来外事工作的光辉历程和远大前景). *Qiushi* (求是), no. 10, May 10, 2021.

Yang, Jing. "Behind the Fall of China's Luckin Coffee: A Network of Fake Buyers and a Fictitious Employee." *Wall Street Journal*, May 28, 2020.

Yang Kuisong. *Study of the History of the Construction of the PRC* (杨奎松: 中华人民共和国建国史研究). Vol. 2. Nanchang: Jiangxi Renmin, 2009.

Yang Tianshi. "Sun Yat-sen and World War I" (杨天石: 孙中山与第一次世界大战). *Aisixiang* (爱思想), November 14, 2019.

Yang Xun and Wang Fang. "Eight 'Global Number Ones'? Truth about the US Anti-Pandemic" (杨迅, 王芳: 八个"全球第一"?! 美国抗疫真相来了). *Renmin Ribao* (人民日报), August 10, 2021.

Yang Yijun. "Wind from East Brings New Spring" (杨依军: 东方风来春色新). *Xinhua* (新华), January 16, 2021.

Yao Ping, Wang Xi, et al. *Teaching History in America* (姚平, 王希等: 在美国教历史). Beijing: Beida, 2022.

Yao Yao. *History of New China's External Propaganda: To Build Contemporary China's Right to International Narrative* (姚遥: 新中国对外宣传史: 建构现代中国的国际话语权). Beijing: Tsinghua, 2014.

Yao Yun. "Chinese Stocks Run Away from Wall Street Again" (姚赟:中概股再次逃离华尔街). *Sina Caijing* (新浪财经), Beijing, June 2, 2020.

Yasir, Sameer, and Hari Kumar. "India Bans 118 Chinese Apps as Indian Soldier Is Killed on Disputed Border." *New York Times*, September 3, 2020.

Ye, Min. *The Belt Road and Beyond: State-Mobilized Globalization in China, 1998–2018*. New York: Cambridge University Press, 2020.

Ye, Wendy, and Evelyn Cheng. "China's Rich Are Moving Their Money to Singapore—Beijing's Crackdown Is One of the Reasons." CNBC, March 29, 2022.

Yeung, Jessie, Yoonjung Seo, and Paula Hancocks. "How South Korea's New President Could Shake Up the Region." CNN, March 11, 2022.

Yglesias, Matthew. "Free Markets Are Creating a Major Free Speech Problem." *Slow Boring* (Substack), May 28, 2021.

Yong, Charissa. "Singaporean Pleads Guilty to Spying for China in the US." *Straits Times*, Singapore, July 24, 2020.

Yonhap. "UN Agency Upgrades Korea to Developed Economy." *Korea Times*, July 14, 2021.

Yu Donghui. "Qin Gang to Chinese-Americans: No Egg Can Survive When the Nest Is Overturned" (余东晖: 秦刚语美国华裔: 覆巢之下焉有完卵). *Zhongpingshe* (中评社), May 7, 2022.

Yu Jie. *Despicable Chinese* (余杰: 卑賤的中國人). Taipei: Zhuliu, 2017.

———. "Remembering Mr. Yu Ying-shih" (余杰: 懷念余英時先生). *Shangbao* (上報), Taipei, August 10, 2021.

Yu Jin. *Doomed* (于劲:厄運). Hong Kong: Tiandi, (1988) 2020.

Works and Sources Cited | 439

Yu, Miles. "Escape from Civilization's Predicaments." *Telos* 201, 2022 (Winter 2022): 51–61.

———. "The Meaning of Taiwan." *Taipei Times*, January 10, 2022a.

———. "On Taiwan: NAIPTO—Toward a Eurasian, Transoceanic Multilateral Collective Defense Alliance." *Taipei Times*, July 11, 2022b.

Yu Ying-shi. "John King Fairbank and China" (余英时: 费正清与中国). In *Modern Scholars and Scholarship* (现代学人与学术). Nanning: Guangxi Shida, (1991) 2006.

Yu, Ying-shih. *History and Thought* (余英時:歷史與思想). Taipei: Lianjing, 1976.

———. *Shi and Chinese Culture* (士与中国文化). Shanghai: Shanghai Renmin, 1987.

———. *Zhu Xi's Historical World* (朱熹的歷史世界). Taipei: Yunchen, 2003.

———. "Address of Yu Ying-shih on the Occasion of Receiving the John W. Kluge Prize at the Library of Congress." Library of Congress, Washington, DC, December 5, 2006.

———. *China and Democracy* (中國與民主). Hong Kong: Tianchuang, 2015.

———. *Chinese History and Culture*. Vol. 2. New York: Columbia University Press, 2016.

Yuan, Jingdong. "China's Core Interests and Critical Role in North Korea's Denuclearisation." *East Asian Policy* 11, no. 3 (2019): 25–38.

Yuan Peng. *Change Once in Four Hundred Years—China, US and New World Order* (袁鹏:四百年未有之变局 - 中国美国与世界新秩序). Beijing: Zhongxin, 2016.

———. "The Covid Pandemic and the Change of the Century" (新冠疫情与百年变局). *Xiandai guoji guanxi* (现代国际关系), Beijing, CICIR, May 2020.

———. "Use High Standard Security to Assure High Quality Development" (袁鹏: 以高水平安全保障高质量发展). *Renmin Ribao* (人民日报), Beijing, January 5, 2022.

Yuan Zongze. "Xi Jinping Diplomatic Thought, Community of Common Destiny for Humanity, and Great Power Diplomacy with Chinese Characteristics" (阮宗泽: 习近平外交思想, 人类命运共同体,中国特色大国外交). *International Studies* (国际问题研究), Beijing, no. 1, 2020.

Yuanfang Qingmu. "African Liberation Army, Ever Growing in Numbers" (远方青木: 非洲的解放军, 数量越来越多). *Wangyi* (网易), June 29, 2022.

Yunzhong Shiji. "Tedros Flipping: Aiding the Evil to Attack China" (云中史记: 谭德塞翻脸, 助纣为虐对华下手). *Wangyi* (网易), Beijing, August 4, 2021.

Zakaria, Fareed. "The New China Scare." *Foreign Affairs*, January/February 2020.

———. "The Decay of American Democracy Is Real." *Washington Post*, June 17, 2021.

Zeihan, Peter. *The End of the World Is Just the Beginning: Mapping the Collapse of Globalization*. New York: Harper, 2022.

Zeng Jia, and Denise Jia. "U.S. Embassy in China to Resume Student Visa Processing May 4." *Caixin* (财新), Beijing, May 1, 2021.

Zeng, Jinghan. *Slogan Politics: Understanding Chinese Foreign Policy Concepts*. London: Palgrave Macmillan, 2020.

440 | Works and Sources Cited

Zenz, Adrian. "China's Domestic Security Spending: An Analysis of Available Data." China Brief 18, no. 4, Jamestown Foundation, 2018.

Zha, Jianying. "Enemy of the State: The Complicated Life of an Idealist." *New Yorker*, April 23, 2007.

Zhang Bin et al. "Why Do People Emigrate More as They Become Richer?" (张斌等: 国人为什么越富越移民?). *Jingji Cankao Bao* (经济参考报), February 21, 2014.

Zhang Chenjing. "Iran, 'Political Obstacle' to Joining SCO Is Cleared" (张晨静: 伊朗加入上合组织的"政治阻碍"已扫除). *Guanchazhe* (观察者), Shanghai, August 12, 2021.

Zhang Feng. "You've Become a Stranger in Your Hometown" (张丰: 你已变成故乡的陌生人). *Zhongguo Qingnian Bao* (中国青年报), Beijing, February 23, 2021.

Zhang Guogang. *General History of Sino-West Cultural Relations* (张国刚: 中西文化关系通史). 2 vols. Beijing: Beida, 2019.

Zhang Haipeng. "Should Raise the Issue of Reassessing Ryuky's Status Now" (张海鹏: 应当提出琉球地位再议问题了). *Hongse wehua* (红色文化), May 14, 2023.

Zhang Han. "The 'Post-Truth' Publication Where Chinese Students in America Get Their News." *New Yorker*, August 19, 2019.

Zhang Hongjie. *The Evolutionary History of Chinese National Character* (张宏杰: 中国国民性演变历程). Changsha: Hunan Renmin, 2013.

Zhang Hongzhi. "Grasp the Main Contradiction of the World" (张宏志: 把握世界主要矛盾). *International Politics Study* (国际政治研究), Beijing, no. 1, 1994.

Zhang Ming. "2021 China's International Account" (张明: 2021年中国国际收支). *Hongguan Jinrong Yanjiu* (宏观金融研究), December 19, 2020.

———. *14 Lectures on Modern History* (张鸣: 近代史讲座14讲). *Gongshi Shalong* (共识沙龙), 2021.

Zhang, Phoebe. "Backlash in China over Vulgar Social Media Mocking of Ukraine Conflict." *South China Morning Post*, February 28, 2022.

Zhang Qianfan. *Constitutional China* (张千帆: 宪政中国). New York: Bodeng, 2021.

Zhang Sheng. "Look Out for the Landscape of New World Financial Order" (张胜: 展望世界金融秩序新图景). Xinhua (新华), Beijing, August 2, 2018.

Zhang Song. "What Are the 'China Centers' in US Think Tanks Busy for Now" (张松: 美智库的"中国中心"都在忙什么). *Huanqiu Wang* (环球网), July 25, 2022.

Zhang Weipeng. "Using Chinese Wisdom to Guide the Direction for the World in the Once-a-Century Transformation" (张伟鹏: 以中国智慧为百年变局中的世界指引前进方向). Center for the Study of Xi Jinping Thought on Diplomacy. accessed July 2023. cn.chinadiplomacy.org.cn/2023-01/10/content_85051405.shtml.

Zhang Weiwei. *The China Shock Trilogy* (张维为: 中国震撼三部曲). Shanghai Renmin, 2016.

Zhang Wenmu. "Geopolitics of the Three Continents in the Northern Hemisphere and Its Impact on China" (张文木: 北半球三大洲地缘政治特点及其对中国的影响). *Taipingyang Xuebao* (太平洋学报) 26, no. 1 (2016): 20–40.

Works and Sources Cited | 441

Zhang, Xiaoming. *Deng Xiaoping's Long War: The Military Conflict between China and Vietnam, 1979–1991*. Chapel Hill: University of North Carolina Press, 2016.

Zhang Xiaoyu. *Business-Trade and Civilization: The Birth of the Modern World* (张笑宇: 商贸与文明 - 现代世界的诞生). Vol. 2 of the Civilization trilogy (文明三部曲). Nanning: Guangxi Shida, 2021.

Zhang Xinyi. "Military High Tech and Modern Warfare" (张新一: 军事高科技与现代战争). *Junshi Wenzhai* (军事文摘), Beijing, September 9, 2017.

Zhang Yadong. "Chinese Firms Collectively in Trouble" (张亚东: 中企在印陷入集体困局). *Nanya Yanjiu Tongxun* (南亚研究通讯), July 15, 2022.

Zhang Yanping. "US Lost in Its Middle East Policy Seen from Its 'Strategic Shrink'" (张艳萍: 从"战略收缩"看美国中东政策的进退失据). *Guangming Ribao* (光明日报), August 6, 2021.

Zhang Zhikun. "The Revelation of the Russo-Ukrainian War: Get Ready for the Full Rupture of the Sino-American Relations" (张志坤: 俄乌战争启示-做好中美关系全面破裂的准备). *Kunlunce* (昆仑策), Beijing, March 12, 2022.

Zhang Zhouxiang, "Seventy Years Later, a Nation Still Remembers." *China Daily*, Beijing, September 29, 2020.

Zhao Dingxin. "The Bugs in *The Rise and Fall of Imperial China*" (赵鼎新:《中华帝国的兴衰》之病). *Dushu* (读书), July 2023.

Zhao Feipeng. "Times Erases the Scars of POW" (赵飞鹏:在岁月中慢慢消磨被俘伤痕). *Zhongguo qingnianbao* (中国青年报), June 24, 2013.

Zhao Jian. "Global Crisis and War to Protect Supply Chains" (赵建: 全球危局与供应链保卫战). *Sina* (新浪), March 14, 2022.

Zhao Lijian. "Press Conference of the Foreign Ministry" (赵立坚: 外交部记者招待会). Beijing, July 30, 2021.

Zhao, Suisheng. "From Affirmative to Assertive Patriots: Nationalism in Xi Jinping's China." *Washington Quarterly* 44, no. 4 (2021): 141–61.

———. *The Dragon Roars Back: Transformational Leaders and Dynamics of Chinese Foreign Policy*. Stanford, CA: Stanford University Press, 2023.

Zhao Tingyang. "Rethinking Empire from a Chinese Concept 'All-under-Heaven' (Tian-Xia)." *Social Identities* 12, no. 1 (2006): 29–41.

———. "Opinion: Can This Ancient Chinese Philosophy Save Us from Global Chaos?" *Washington Post*, February 7, 2018.

———. "A Constitutional Tianxia" (赵汀阳: 一个宪法性的天下). *Shijie Zhexue* (世界哲学), Beijing, no. 3, 2020.

Zhao Tong. "Size of Nuclear Arsenal and Chinese National Interest" (赵通: 核武库规模与中国国家利益). *China US Focus*, Hong Kong, May 20, 2020.

Zhao, Tong. *Narrowing the U.S.-China Gap on Missile Defense: How to Help Forestall a Nuclear Arms Race*. Washington, DC: Carnegie Endowment, 2020a.

Zheng Cunzhu. *The History of Organizing Chinese Democracy Party* (郑存柱: 中国民主党组织史). Los Angeles: Xidian, 2019.

442 | Works and Sources Cited

Zheng Rongjian. "Analysis of the Possibility of 'Asian NATO'" (郑榕健: "亚洲版北约"形成的可能性分析). *Daily Report on US Politics* (美国政治追踪), Guangzhou, January 2021.

Zheng Rui. "Why Doesn't China Release Death Toll Figures?" (郑瑞: 为何中方仍不透露死亡人数). *Duowei News*, Beijing, June 18, 2020.

Zheng Yefu. "For Whom to Stay in Power" (郑也夫: 为谁保江山). *Guang chuanmei* (光传媒), July 28, 2020.

Zheng Yongnian. *Explaining China Trilogy* (郑永年: 解释中国三部曲). Zhejiang Renmin, 2021.

Zhi Gu. "Taiwanese Investment to Mainland Declined Rapidly" (智谷: 来大陆的台资极速减少). *Fenghuang wang* (凤凰网), Hong Kong, December 31, 2021.

Zhi Hu (知乎). "Why Are the Comments on Chinese Diplomatic Services Overseas So Bad?" (为什么中国驻海外使馆的服务评价如此之差). 2016. zhihu.com/question/28535919.

———. "Who Are the Biggest Earners and Spenders of Foreign Currencies" (赚外汇和花外汇最多的企业是哪几家). 2021. zhihu.com/zvideo/1438054775586074624.

Zhihu Zhuanlun. "American Puppet Revealed True Colors" (知乎专论: 美国的傀儡终于露出真相). *Zhihu Zhuanlun* (知乎专论), January 3, 2023.

Zhong Shan. "Chinese Foreign Trade Employs over 180 Million" (钟山: 中国外贸带动就业超1.8亿人). Press conference, Beijing, September 29, 2019.

Zhong Sheng. "Nine Treatises on the US 'Will Surely Fail'" (钟声: 九论美国"必将失败"). *Renmin Ribao* (人民日报), May 23–31, 2019.

———. "'Decoupling' Is Reactionary Move by Mis-judgement" (钟声: "脱钩"是误判大势的逆动). *Renmin Ribao* (人民日报), August 17, 2020.

———. "American Side Wake Up, Don't Say You Were Not Warned!" (钟声: 美方醒醒, 勿谓言之不预!). *Renmin Ribao* (人民日报), July 24, 2021.

Zhong, Raymond, et al. "No 'Negative' News: How China Censored the Coronavirus." *New York Times*, December 19, 2020.

Zhong, Raymond, Aaron Krolik, Paul Mozur, Ronen Bergman, and Edward Wong. "Behind China's Twitter Campaign, a Murky Supporting Chorus." *New York Times*, June 10, 2020.

Zhongguo Jianzhu Bao (中华建筑报). "'Waves of Imitation' in Chinese Architecture" (中国建筑刮起"仿建风"). Beijing, July 26, 2013.

Zhongguo Jingji Zhoukan (中国经济周刊). "Redesign New Global Order" (Redesign 全球新秩序). January 2010. *Zhongzhi zhiku* (中制智库). *Be Highly Vigilant: The West Likely to Soon Win the Race against COVID* (高度警惕西方即将在与新冠的赛跑中胜出). Beijing, January 14, 2022.

Zhou Baogen. "China and the Global Nuclear Nonproliferation Regime: A Constructivist Analysis" (周宝根: 中国与国际核不扩散机制的一种建构主义分析). *Shijie Zhengzhi Yu Jingji* (世界经济与政治), no. 2, 2003, 23–27.

Works and Sources Cited | 443

Zhou Hong. "Foreign Aid and Contemporary International Relations" (周弘: 对外援助与当代国际关系). *Chinese Academy of Social Sciences Journal* (中国社会科学院院报), February 2007.

Zhou Lian and Yang Kuisong. "The Prelude of Revolution" (周濂对话杨奎松: 革命的前奏). *Dongfang lishi pinlun* (东方历史评论), Nanning, no. 4, 2014.

Zhou, Li-An. *Local Governments in Transformation* (周黎安: 转型中的地方政府). Shanghai: Shanghai Renmin, (2008) 2017.

Zhou Tianyong. *Chinese Opinions: Interviews with Economists* (周天勇: 意见中国: 经济学家访谈录). Beijing, no. 13, July 2010.

Zhou Xiaochuan. "The Prospects of RMB Internationalization from Multiple Perspectives" (周小川: 多角度关注人民币国际化前景). *Jinrong Shibao* (金融时报), Beijing, October 22, 2020.

Zhou Xinmin. "The Era of Great Change Calls for World Political Leader" (周新民: 大变局时代呼唤世界政治领袖). *Jinri Toutiao* (今天头条), June 9, 2020.

Zhou Zhixing. "Great Differences Made by a Different Choice of a Split Second" (周志兴: 一念之差的千差万别). WeChat blog (微信公众号), October 10, 2022.

Zhou Ziheng. "Petrocurrency, Petrodollar, and Petroyuan" (周子衡: 石油货币, 石油美元及石油人民币). WeChat blog (微信公众号), March 22, 2022.

Zhu Binyuan. "Two 'Inevitabilities' Is Still the General Trend of the World" (朱炳元: "两个必然"仍然是当今世界发展的大趋势). *Hongqi Wengao* (红旗文稿), March 22, 2019.

Zhu Feng. "Biden's China Diplomacy Not Out of the 'Trump Mire.'" (朱锋: 拜登对华外交未走出"特朗普泥潭"). *Huanqiu Shibao* (环球时报), March 23, 2021.

Zhu Huayan. "FDI Job Creation Five Times the National Average" (朱华燕: 外资就业吸纳能力高出全国平均水平5倍). Ministry of Commerce study, Beijing, April 24, 2018.

Zhu, Julie. "Goldman Sachs Joins Syndicate for Ant IPO of Up To $30 Billion, Say Sources." Reuters, September 5, 2020.

Zhu Jun et al. *Internationalization of RMB and Reform of International Monetary System in the New Era* (朱隽等: 新形势下的人民币国际化与国际货币体系改革). Zhongguo Jinrong, 2021.

Zhu Keren. "A Suggestion for BRI" (朱可人: 给"一带一路"出一招). *The Paper* (澎湃), July 15, 2020.

Zhu Liangcai. "Six Questions about the Didi Incident" (朱良才: "滴滴事件"背后的六问). *Wode Yuqing* (沃德舆情), Beijing, Womin Corporation (沃民公司), July 6, 2021.

Zhu, Tian. *Catching Up to America: Culture, Institutions, and the Rise of China.* New York: Cambridge University Press, 2021.

Zhu Xili. "'Building Community of Common Destiny for Humanity' Written into UN Security Resolution" (朱曦莉: 构建人类命运共同体"理念写入联大安全领域决议). CCTV, November 2, 2017.

444 | Works and Sources Cited

Zhu Zhihong. "Trump Is Basically Over" (朱志宏: 特朗普大势已去). *Zhanlue Guanchajia* (战略观察家), Beijing, November 6, 2020.

Zhuang Weizheng. "The Origin of the Name of the Chinese Datong Party" (庄维振: 中国大同党称谓的由来). *Duowei News* (多維新聞), Hong Kong, January 7, 2019.

Zi Xun. "What to Do about the Low Quality of the Chinese" (资讯: 中国人的素质太低了怎么办). *Yinzidian* (热门资讯), July 16, 2022.

Ziezulewicz, Geoff. "China's Navy Has More Ships than the US. Does That Matter?" *Navy Times*, April 12, 2021.

Zimbardo, Philip. *The Lucifer Effect: Understanding How Good People Turn Evil.* New York: Random House, 2007.

Zipser, Daniel, Jeongmin Seong, and Jonathan Woetzel. "Seven Segments Shaping China's Consumption Landscape." Report, McKinsey and Company, July 22, 2021.

Zoellick, Robert (deputy secretary of state). "Whither China? From Membership to Responsibility." National Committee on U.S.-China Relations, New York, September 21, 2005.

Zou Yilin. "Interviews on Thoughts on Chorography" (邹逸麟: 方志思想采访录). *Shizhi Yanjiu* (史志研究), Ningbo, no. 1, 2015.

Zumbrun, Josh. "U.S. Tariffs Drive Drop in Chinese Imports, as U.S. Companies Shift Purchases Elsewhere." *Wall Street Journal*, May 12, 2021.

Zweig, David, and Siqin Kang. "America Challenges China's National Talent Programs." Occasional Paper no.4, CSIS, May 2020.

Index

9/11 attacks, 138, 179, 193, 224, 229

Adams, John, 30

Afghanistan, 25, 34, 99, 100, 109, 198, 242, 244, 299n36, 326n36

Africa, 34, 72, 83–85, 91–92, 103–104, 118, 135, 155, 220, 238, 242–44, 266, 442n197

AI (artificial intelligence), 31, 69, 84, 107, 296n269

AIIB (Asian Infrastructure Investment Bank), 84, 139

Albania, 100, 123, 124, 290n119

Algeria, 123, 290n121, 300n80

Alibaba (阿里巴巴), 219

aliens/extraterrestrials, 42, 214, 227

Altasia (alternative Asian supply chain), 237

American exceptionality, 24–29, 262

American experiment, 27, 261–62

America First, 216

Anglo-American political genealogy, 25, 154

Angola, 118, 123, 290n119 & n121

anti-Americanism, 81, 99, 142

APEC, 91

Aristotle, 21, 52

arms race, 36, 48, 208, 209, 220, 241, 260

ASEAN, 218

Asian-Pacific or Indo-Pacific treaty organization (APTO or IPTO), 218

Atlantic Charter, 25

Australia, 24, 48, 107, 120, 191, 194, 199, 218, 224, 241, 245, 284n1, 290n119

authoritarianism, 10, 13–15, 18, 29, 35, 37, 40, 46–74, 50–51, 82, 124, 146, 158, 166, 185, 263, 277, 286n16, 313n64
logic/tendency of, 72, 75, 77, 80–81, 105, 136, 145–46, 148, 157, 174, 187, 221, 244, 286n16, 313n63

autocracy, 7, 14, 21, 23, 32, 46, 54, 58, 71, 101, 106, 114, 136, 142, 157, 169, 181, 205, 249, 256, 274, 282, 286n16
of CCP-PRC, 14–15, 30, 36, 43–44, 50–51, 62, 80–81, 86, 90, 128, 136, 142, 147, 153, 226, 228, 253, 262–64, 270, 281

Bank for International Settlements (BIS), 130

Belt and Road Initiative (BRI 一带一路), 83, 84, 99, 104, 130, 242–44, 256, 303n114

Bentham, Jeremy, 44

445

446 | Index

Biden, Joe, 4, 149, 183–85, 187, 194–95, 197–99, 207, 231, 258, 275, 332n211
Big Dipper system, 211
biodiversity, 22, 216
Black Swan and Gray Rhino, 17, 18
Blinken, Antony, 35, 149, 184, 194
Brazil, 29, 107, 116, 133, 237, 332n197
Bretton Woods system, 34
BRICS Development Bank, 130
Burlingame, Anson, 265, 337n311
Burma (Myanmar), 34, 106, 109, 116, 123, 290n119, 299n36, 302n89, 313n47
Bush, George W., 179, 187, 258, 315n102
Byzantine Empire, 36

Cambodia, 92, 108, 123, 124, 270, 290n119, 299n36, 300n38, 327n63
Canada, 34, 107, 116, 120, 176, 199, 245, 284n1, 290n119
capital flight, 95, 132–33
capitalism, 36, 56, 59, 65, 92, 123, 295n234
  autocratic/authoritarian/state/ partocratic, 10, 15, 62, 133, 139, 152, 282
  crony, 66, 282
  democratic, 31, 62
Catholicism, 45
CCAS (Committee of Concerned Asian Scholars), 167, 316n118
CCP (Chinese Communist Party 中国共产党), 1, 6, 9, 13–14, 15–17, 30, 34–37, 43–44, 71–76, 86–87, 91–92, 94–97, 105, 125, 132–34, 142, 171–73, 176, 178, 181–82, 184, 193, 204, 206–207, 210, 213, 222, 231–33, 236, 246, 252–53, 259, 263, 277

agents and helpers of, 14, 34, 94, 102, 106, 114, 117, 119–20, 135, 148, 155–57, 160–71, 177–78, 187–92, 219–20, 224, 226–30, 233, 235, 268, 296n249, 304n138, 313n50, 316n121, 318n149, 321n255, 327n72
  internal dissent, 255–56, 334n263, 335n265
  ruling elites of, 4, 49–51, 71–75, 90, 94, 99, 121–22, 127, 132, 141, 146, 181, 208, 221, 247–48, 250, 253–55, 270–71
  worldview and intention of, 78–85, 87–90, 92, 99–100, 136–38, 141–44, 146, 148–51, 153–54, 195, 212, 224–25, 237–28, 249, 251, 257–58, 267–68, 281–82, 298n5
CCP Inc v. China Inc., 86
CCP Optimality, 1, 15, 30, 80, 93, 147, 154
CCP-PRC, party-state or partocracy (People's Republic of China under the Chinese Communist Party 中华人民共和国), 1, 4, 6, 7, 9–10, 15, 77, 84, 86, 93, 130, 135, 142, 145–48, 154, 204, 220, 243, 283n7
  corruption in, 4, 7, 50, 102–104, 114, 117, 132, 134, 209, 242, 325n20
  extraction by, 10, 36, 72, 80, 81, 92, 125, 128, 144, 147, 174, 222
  fear of US/West, 80, 114, 142, 189, 247, 268
  influence in US/West, 48, 161, 188–92, 195, 217
  kleptocracy of, 4, 66
  normalization of, 12, 93–94, 202, 227, 324n2
  passport popularity, 113, 115–18

Index | 447

political legitimacy, 15, 23, 77,
82, 86, 91, 93–94, 99, 102, 105,
136, 138, 147, 150, 220, 254
record of, 1, 20, 40, 67, 93, 122,
137, 146, 173–74, 176, 204, 213,
240
sense of insecurity, 15, 35, 36,
79–80, 81, 113, 136, 185, 249
transformation of, 5, 7–8, 10–11,
37–38, 40, 42, 44, 48, 122, 138,
142, 152, 172, 201–202, 207,
210, 213–14, 218, 220, 239, 247,
249, 258, 259, 261–65, 268, 281
Celestial Emperor, 74
Central Asia, 87, 124, 155, 241, 244
Chanyuan (澶渊) System, 23, 70
ChatGPT, OpenAI, 107, 296n269
China Bank of Development, 99
China Card, 138
China Dream, 17, 19, 178, 256, 282
China Exclusion Act, 227
China Fantasy, 138, 165
China Hands, *also see* Sinologists,
160–63, 165, 181, 185–86, 231,
335n283
China Initiative, 229
China International Development
Cooperation Agency, 104
China Lobby, 188
China Order, see also *tianxia*, 2–3,
6–7, 10, 13–17, 18–21, 29, 31,
36, 40–41, 43–44, 47, 66, 68,
70, 77–78, 81–82, 85, 93, 96,
105, 117, 137–38, 146, 155, 156,
158, 204–205, 222–23, 225, 266,
269, 277, 282
China Race, 2–8, 9–10, 11–14,
18–21, 59, 66, 73–74, 78, 82,
138, 141–43, 145, 152–55, 159,
175, 201, 275, 283n7, 284n17
cost of, 48–51, 177, 214, 265–74
future of, 276–82

goals of, 40–48, 146, 171, 201–
202, 203–206, 214–16, 267–68
how to, 122, 158, 172–78, 197–99,
206–13, 216–21, 226–45, 251–60
in the PRC, 245–50
in the US, 186–92, 193, 195–96
new kind of, 5, 206, 264–65
odds for, 48–51, 80, 238, 280–82
state of, 136–39, 147–48, 150–51,
154, 156, 164, 221–25
versus the Cold War, 32–39
versus transforming the PRC,
260–65
China Studies, *see also* Sinology,
159–60, 164–71, 191, 315n98,
316n124
China Suboptimality, 15, 20, 40, 62,
80, 92, 93, 105, 117, 122, 137,
146, 154, 174, 206, 227, 282
China Tragedy, 15, 92, 93, 122, 145,
146, 206
China-Africa Forum, 84, 91
Chinese-Americans, 119, 120, 165,
167–69, 172, 230, 262, 317n131
Chinese Civil War, 31, 68, 97, 110,
270
Chinese Communist Party, *see*
CCP
Chinese diaspora, 96, 98, 102,
119–20
Chinese foreign policy, 7, 39,
77–140, 160, 174, 209, 243, 255,
259
core interest of, 79, 82, 85–90,
93–97, 136–37, 154–57, 300n40
cost of, 97–104
effect of, 105–35, 137–39, 150–51
toward the US, 141–45, 148–51
Chinese national interests, 7, 50, 93,
99, 101, 105–106, 110–11, 137,
142, 207, 221–22, 243, 246, 251,
258, 298n6, 305n173

448 | Index

Chinese political tradition, 1, 36, 57, 78–79, 81, 102, 117, 130, 134, 151, 169, 195, 212, 224

Chinese Soviet Republic (中华苏维埃共和国), 106

Chinese territory/territorial interests, 49, 87, 105, 108–109, 111, 154, 218, 222, 305n171, 313n46

Chinese world, *also see* Sinic world, 7, 15, 19, 36, 42, 61, 68, 70, 74, 109, 158, 225, 249, 267, 277, 283n4

Chinoiserie, 108, 315n98

CIPS (Cross-Border Interbank Payment System), 131, 240

circulation, dual and internal, 39, 195, 249

citizenship, 61, 96, 98, 113–14

civil war, 31, 50, 65, 68, 158, 270, 277

climate change, 83, 156, 204, 211, 231, 279

Clinton, Bill, 187, 285n10, 317n143

Clinton, Hillary, 87, 194

Cold War, 10, 22, 23, 25, 33–39, 83, 86, 88, 137, 138, 145, 163, 185, 192–93, 203, 213–14, 238, 247, 249, 253, 267, 271, 290n117, 291n138

new, 182, 192–93, 231, 268, 280, 308n235, 337n313, 338n6

collateral damage, 8, 171, 177, 207, 229, 260

common good, public goods, 6, 10, 21–22, 26, 31, 57, 151, 204, 252

communism, 6, 15–17, 29, 35–36, 40, 41, 43, 45, 47, 50, 65, 74, 77–78, 82, 90, 94, 105, 122, 152, 154–55, 228, 286n24

Community of Common Human Destiny (CCHD), 4, 17, 75, 84–85, 89–90, 143, 146, 222

competition, among nations, 22, 32, 42–43, 46, 48, 52, 55, 57, 60–64, 66–67, 70, 123, 202–203, 206, 215–17, 239, 266, 280

Confucianism (儒家), 10, 14, 15, 16, 22, 45, 55, 77, 100, 117, 156, 166, 169, 196, 233, 254, 283n7, 287n55, 294n206 & n218

Confucius Institute (CI), 100–101, 102, 196, 233, 321n258

Congagement, 37

Congress of Vienna, 23, 28

Constitution of the United States, 54, 217

Contaformation, 5, 7, 10, 37–39, 201–202, 216, 218, 225, 232, 261, 267

components of, 213–21, 238–45

objectives of, 201–202, 214, 261

parameters for, 202–13

shortcuts of, 225–38, 245–60

Containment, 35, 37–38, 180, 213, 291n138, 291n142

Constructivism, 45, 175, 240

counterfactual analysis, 1, 124, 260, 282, 283n3

COVID-19, 40, 103, 107, 134, 138, 143, 160, 176, 180, 182, 190, 191, 193, 196, 199, 222, 234, 235, 238, 254, 256, 292n163, 297n273

CPTPP (Comprehensive and Progressive Agreement for Trans-Pacific Partnership), 196, 240

Cultural Revolution of 1966–77, 97, 190

Czech, 107, 259

Darwinism, Darwinian System, 25, 81, 295n235

debt trap, 104, 243

Declaration of Independence, 54

Declaration of the Rights of Man 54, 295n241

decoupling, 37–39, 66, 111, 160, 174, 236–27, 240, 266, 249–50, 251, 266, 272, 333n242
  partial/selective, 38–39, 172, 179, 184, 236–37, 266

democratic rule of law, 4, 6, 9, 10, 27–28, 32, 43, 46–47, 50, 55, 58, 59, 68, 70–71, 85, 142, 146, 157–58, 169, 174, 197, 204, 205, 210, 212, 239, 260–61, 264, 265, 280, 282, 284n1
  variety of, 336n302

democratic/democracy peace, 266, 296n267

Deng Xiaoping (邓小平), 79, 136, 310n306

derisking, *see* decoupling

detoxification of the mind, 175, 177, 207, 209, 251, 252, 253

developmental state, 50, 80, 220

distinguishing between the internal and the external (内外有别 *neiwai youbie*), 117

diplomacy, 24, 62, 70, 80–81, 88, 90, 93, 98–99, 121, 144–45, 180, 198, 210, 223, 298n8

distributed processes/algorithms, 60

diversity, 22–23, 24, 27, 43, 52, 57–58, 202, 210, 246, 255, 275, 284n1
  regime of, 22–23
  of polities and socio-cultures, 22, 52, 110, 146, 172, 210, 263, 264

Democratic Progress Party (DPP 民進黨), 110

East-West Divergence, 41

Eastern Europe, 25, 228, 243

Ecuador, 104, 123, 306n196, 332n197

Egypt, 29, 124, 299n36

Einstein, Albert, 44, 57

emigration, 60, 63, 95, 100, 114, 132, 235

engagement policy, 36, 38, 153, 159, 160, 162, 170, 172, 173, 185, 193, 220

Enlightenment, 14, 27, 59, 146, 169, 227, 286n20

entropy, 63, 71

equality-liberty equilibrium, 63, 204

Ethiopia, 84, 112, 123, 124

European Union (EU), 25, 33, 34, 66, 118, 180, 243, 245, 284n1, 289n89

evolution based on fitness, 59

Export-Import Bank of China, 99

Fairbank, John King, 165

Fascism, 45, 47, 183

FDI/investment from China, 95–96, 101, 103, 118, 124, 125–35, 192, 242–43, 309n275, 331n167

FDI/investment to China, 95, 134–35, 188–89, 192, 257, 302n100, 322n262, 335n178

fear mongering, 47, 72, 75, 114, 158, 198, 205, 226, 250, 269–71, 281, 298n291, 333n240, 337n317

federalism, 25, 27, 57

feudalism, 25

Finland, 259, 290n119, 327n65

Five Eyes, 199, 241

Five Principles of Peaceful Coexistence, 88

foreign aid, 91, 99, 102, 239, 303n111

foreign currency reserve, 125, 127–29, 144

foreign trade, 94–95, 128, 133, 135

France, 54, 116, 176, 199, 245, 272, 289n87, 290n119

450 | Index

French Revolution, 51, 295n241
Friends of China/PRC, 33, 84, 90,
    100, 108, 112, 114, 118–19, 122,
    135, 164, 170–71, 177, 196, 227,
    244, 290n121, 302n79, 315n101,
    318n149

G-20, 33, 91, 243
G7, 56, 106, 111, 198–99, 243, 244
Galapagos Islands, 134
game theory, 5, 12, 18, 30, 71, 143,
    166, 202, 207, 224, 239
Germany, 18, 29, 33, 57, 65, 72, 73,
    74, 89, 107, 116, 176, 237, 249,
    259, 271, 272, 277, 290n119,
    334n260
Ghana, 98, 123
glasnost, 252
global guerrilla warfare, 85
global minimum corporate tax, 56
global minimum wage, 57
Global South, 34, 84, 155, 212
globalism, globalist, 6, 10, 14, 16, 29,
    31, 36, 56, 59, 65, 82, 94, 155,
    171, 194, 210, 216, 280, 281,
    286n23, 296n249
global war on terrorism, 148, 158,
    179, 229, 258
globalization, 4, 16, 41, 52, 62,
    64–67, 88, 90, 97, 143, 148–49,
    162, 173, 215, 223, 240, 268
    economic, 31, 39, 64–66, 129,
        296n250
    political, 25, 42, 56, 65–66, 69,
        158, 266, 267, 280
Gödel, Kurt, 45
going global, 92, 137
Gorbachev, Mikhail, 253, 256
Grand External Propaganda (大外
    宣 da waixuan), 50, 71–72, 83,
    93, 100, 102, 119, 120, 188,

    224, 226, 232–33, 251, 304n138,
    330n133 & 134
gray zone, 220
Great Famine of 1959–63, 92, 97,
    144, 270
Great Firewall, 91, 209, 232, 251–53
Great Leap Forward, 77, 92, 122,
    144, 186
Great Recession, 13, 81, 178, 179,
    285n10
Greater China, 109, 240–41, 244, 274
Greco-Roman civilization, 27
Greece, 17, 107
Gresham's Law, 124, 125, 127, 131
group selection, 60

hakkō ichiu (八紘一宇 all the world
    under a single roof), 21
Hayek, Fredrich, 47
Hobbes, Thomas, 45, 52
Hollywood, 32, 187, 269, 282
Holocaust, 74
Hong Kong (香港), 18, 88, 105,
    109–10, 113, 115, 116, 117,
    120, 132, 155, 182, 188, 191,
    193–94, 199, 212, 240, 250, 257,
    331n176
Hu Jingtao (胡锦涛), 79, 303n110
Huawei (华为), 219, 230, 253
hukou (household registration 户口),
    97
human civilization, 3, 11, 17, 19, 22,
    38, 41, 48, 55, 59–61, 63–64,
    68–69, 201, 252, 264–65, 266,
    269
    direction of, 1, 3, 5–6, 9, 12, 18,
        33, 42, 46, 51, 158, 203, 222,
        259, 268
    juncture/choice of, 43–45, 69, 146,
        156, 203, 208, 215–16, 223, 276,
        282

Index | 451

optimality of, 1, 3, 57–58, 61, 67, 78, 157, 175, 205, 209, 215–16, 246, 261, 271
Hume, David, 53
Hungary, 107, 243, 244

identity politics, 59, 64
IMF, 128, 129–30, 191, 309n271
India, 29, 34, 88, 98, 108, 113, 116, 133, 194, 218, 219, 230, 234, 241, 244, 289n85, 299n36, 310n298, 332n212
Indo-Pacific, 217, 218, 220, 240, 241–42, 245
Indonesia, 33, 98, 119, 124, 133, 241, 300
inequality, 52, 55–59, 60, 64, 276, 279
  international, 31, 46, 56, 61–64, 65
  "just," 61, 295n241
  relative, 12, 49, 59, 63, 65, 145, 211, 217, 223, 239, 245, 264, 295n234
Inner Mongolia, 36, 111
innovation, 3, 23, 29, 38, 43, 49, 55, 57–59, 61–63, 66, 68, 144, 202, 216, 260–61, 264, 280, 288n62, 295n231
International Organization for Mediation, 84
international policing, 26
international political anarchy (IPA), 11, 24, 42, 69–70, 158
international terrorism, 13, 31, 65, 96, 156, 158, 179, 198, 229, 242, 258
Internet, 66, 69, 84, 117, 217, 233, 252–53, 260, 330n136, 335n268
Iran, 33, 34, 99, 112, 124, 176, 244, 248, 290n119 & 121, 299n36
Iraq, 25, 116, 124, 158, 244, 270
iron law of oligarchy, 25, 46

Ishiba, Shigeru (石破茂), 331n183
Ishiwara, Kanji (石原莞爾), 283n4
Islam, Muslim, 45, 111, 124, 179, 229, 235, 244, 306n188
island chains, 49, 152, 242
Israel, 116, 188, 244
Italy, 107, 271, 272, 290n119

Japan, 18, 21, 29, 33, 34, 50, 65, 89, 96, 106, 107, 116, 118, 175, 176, 190, 194, 218, 224, 237, 241, 242, 253, 271, 272, 277, 283n4, 284n1, 289n87, 290n119, 297n274, 327n65, 331n183
Jiang Zemin (江泽民), 79
Johnson, Boris, 25
Jordan, 124, 310n298
Judeo-Christian tradition, 27
justice, 3, 6, 19, 40, 52–58, 60–61, 63, 64, 65, 67, 168, 205, 271, 284n1, 294n206

Kafka, Franz, 282
Kant, Immanuel, 44–45, 52–53, 156
Kennan, George F., 35–36, 43, 247, 291n143
Kennedy, John F., 27, 30
Kenya, 103, 123
Khmer Rouge, 92, 124, 270
Kim Jong-Un, 108, 198
King, Martin Luther, 205
Kishida, Fumio (岸田文雄), 241
Kissinger, Henry, 27, 187, 196
Korea, 28, 36, 82, 155, 272, 305
  North (DPRK), 33, 34, 66, 99, 100, 101, 108, 109, 112, 116, 119, 242, 248, 290n121, 326n36
  South (ROK), 25, 34, 98, 106, 107, 115, 116, 117, 176, 198, 218, 234, 241, 242, 245, 272, 284n1, 327n65

452 | Index

Korean War, 85, 97, 106, 123, 227, 271–74

Kuomintang (Nationalist Party 國民黨), KMT-ROC), 79, 114, 167, 169, 188, 298n5

lanwei (烂尾 unfinished projects), 256

Lai Ching-te (賴清德), 336n287

Latin America, 92, 117, 118, 126, 153, 155, 156, 220, 242, 243, 332n197

League of Nations, 23, 26, 65

Legalism (法家), Legalist, 14, 15, 77, 141, 166, 169, 196, 281n21, 283n4

Leninism, Leninist, 13, 16, 29, 50, 65, 77–78, 94, 105–106, 222, 228, 286n21

Li Keqiang (李克强), 153

Li Qiang (李强), 250

liberty, freedom, 45, 51–56, 58–59, 61, 62–63, 169, 226, 255, 260, 284n1, 295n232

Libya, 100, 123, 124, 244

LIO (Liberal International Order), 1, 2, 3, 6, 9, 23–24, 26–29, 31, 42, 48, 64, 77, 80, 82, 83, 136, 145–46, 148, 152, 153, 156, 158, 180, 185, 203, 205, 210–11, 217, 223, 238–39, 241, 245, 261, 263, 269, 286n17, 288n63

LIO-II, 279–80

Lippmann, Walter, 34

Liu Shaoqi (刘少奇), 82

Locke, John, 21, 52

Long Peace, 28

Lu Xun (鲁迅), 213

MacArthur, Douglas, 30

Macau, Macao (澳門), 109, 113, 116, 117, 120, 132, 240, 257

Macron, Emmanuel, 245

Magnitsky Act, 230, 253, 255

Malaysia, 84, 133, 135

Manchuria (Northeast), 106, 271

Mandate of Heaven, People or History, 49, 137, 154, 155

Manifest Destiny, 24

Mao Zedong (毛泽东), 13, 44, 77, 79, 82, 85–86, 88, 91–93, 109, 114, 121–22, 148, 149, 186, 190, 236, 256, 277, 297n280, 311n5

Mao Zedong Thought, Maoism, 75–76, 86, 137, 178, 195, 299n11, 301n82

market economy/system, 31, 43, 47, 48, 49, 64, 69–71, 112, 125, 128–31, 162, 199, 215, 220, 246, 282, 297n274

Marshall Plan, 99

Marxism, 13, 14, 16, 29, 53, 75, 77

McCarthyism, 177, 229

Melaka Strait, 49

Meta (Facebook, Instagram), 330n144

Mexico, 29, 107, 133, 230

Middle East, 198, 243

migration, 46, 60, 62, 70, 95, 114, 266

Mill, John Stuart, 52

Modi, Narendra, 332n211

money laundering, 102, 132, 239, 257

Mongolia, 25, 84, 108, 109, 241, 299n36

monopoly, 20, 31, 45–47, 48, 62, 66, 70, 71, 128, 206, 258, 265, 285n2

Mozambique, 123

multiculturalism, 53, 57, 216, 223

Munich Conference, 41

Muslim, *see* Islam

Nairobi-Mombasa Railway, 103

Index | 453

Namibia, 123, 290n119, 303n110
nation-state, 11, 16, 20, 23, 32, 64, 68, 78, 86, 93, 147, 175, 198, 204, 210, 215, 223, 258, 277, 279, 280, 285n2
national mobilization (*juguo tizhi* 举国体制), 92, 144, 148, 174, 186, 224, 266
nationalism, 22, 26, 35, 59, 122, 150, 152, 207, 258, 263, 337n307
NATO, 198–99, 218, 241, 327n65, 331n183
natural selection, 59, 203
Nazi, 14, 21, 57, 65, 72, 73, 74, 89, 249, 271, 334n260
necessary evil, 63, 70
Nepal, 109, 299n36
NGO (non-governmental organization), 96, 189
Nietzsche, Friedrich, 158, 210
Nigeria, 29, 103
Nixon, Richard, 38, 127, 241, 308249
Norway, 290n119
nuclear weapon/power, 31, 49, 86, 87, 108, 115, 150, 151, 208, 241, 250, 300n46
doctrine of, 33, 87, 92, 208, 225, 242, 325n16
nuclear nonproliferation, 208, 242
nucleomituphobia, 333n240

Obama, Barack, 149, 170, 179, 182, 242
OECD (Organization for Economic Cooperation and Development), 108, 213, 272, 284n1
Olympic Games, 13, 91, 92, 107, 115
One China Policy, 258
One China Principle, 110, 258
One Country Two Systems, 110
Orwell, George, 34, 9, 158

overseas Chinese, *see* Chinese diaspora

Pakistan, 34, 84, 99, 101, 108, 109, 112, 123, 124, 290n119, 299n36, 330n38, 313n47
paper dragon, 209
paper tiger, 143, 311n5
Pax Americana, 205
Pax Britannica, 205
Pax Mongolica/Tatarica, 205
Pax Romana, 205
Pax Sinica, 169, 205
Pax Westphalia, 205
perpetual peace, 44, 68, 154
Pearl Harbor, 37, 41, 157, 193, 224, 260
Pekingology or Zhongnanhai studies, 256
People's War doctrine, 149
Permanent Court of Arbitration, 84, 197
Peru, 92, 310n298
Philippines, 25, 98, 116, 198, 241
Piketty, Thomas, 56
pinkies, 252, 334n249
Pivot to Asia, 179, 182, 242
PLA (People's Liberation Army), 83, 98, 120, 149–51, 175, 208–209, 230, 231, 242, 248, 255, 312n21, 325n20
Poland, 29, 107, 116, 133, 237, 290n119
Pompeo, Michael, 172, 184, 213
Popper, Karl, 45
Portugal, 109
power/leadership transition, 3, 6, 10, 11, 18, 23, 65, 84, 263
PRC, *see* CCP-PRC
PRC-USA rivalry, 2, 5, 9, 38, 127, 141–45, 146, 154, 159, 161, 164, 173–78, 186–99

454 | Index

Putin, Vladimir, 101, 113, 241, 244, 291n130, 303n126, 313n46
Pyrrhic victory, 192, 262

Qin Empire (秦), 153, 174, 207, 213, 223, 277, 297n283
Qin unification, 7, 70, 146, 247, 267, 283n4
Qin-Han Polity, 10, 13–15, 29, 36, 40–41, 43–44, 50, 51, 70, 71, 73, 77–79, 82, 84, 86, 90, 96, 110, 136–37, 142, 145–46, 148, 156, 166, 174, 204, 227, 246, 263, 276–77, 283n7
Qin Gang (秦刚), 103, 168, 196, 304n145, 316n116
Qing Empire (清), 74, 96, 111, 136, 258, 305n154
Quad, 33–34, 194, 198, 199, 218, 241
race to the bottom, 19, 48, 56, 66
racism, 177, 191, 226–29, 318n174
Rawls, John, 52, 55, 295n241
Reagan, Ronald, 253, 317n143, 326n47, 335n283
realism, realist 81, 105, 175, 181, 239, 304n152
redistribution
reshoring/friendshoring/allyshoring, 66, 179
rejuvenation of the Chinese nation/civilization, 14–15, 74, 75, 89–90, 137, 142, 263
Rheinlandbesetzung, 249, 271
rise of China/PRC, 3, 18, 20, 95–96, 106, 115, 147, 152, 159, 169, 173–74, 195, 246–47, 278, 282, 314n67, 335n282
scenarios of, 276–80
RMB (Renminbi 人民币), 125, 129–31

internationalization of, 84, 123, 127–32, 217, 220, 239, 309n264 & n268 & n271, 331n176
petrol-RMB, 131, 244
ROC (Republic of China, 中華民國), see also Taiwan, 79, 91, 96, 106, 110–11, 114, 119, 167, 169, 188, 258, 273, 298n5
Roman Empire, 21, 23, 27, 205, 266
Rousseau, Jean-Jacques, 21, 44, 46
RTI (right to intervene), 198, 215, 324n332
RTP (responsibility to protect), 198, 215, 324n332
Russell, Bertrand, 5, 29–30, 289n99
Russia, see also Soviet Union, 17, 33, 34, 36, 96, 99, 100, 101, 106, 107, 109, 112–13, 116, 118, 119, 131, 133, 155, 160, 186, 198, 218, 222, 228, 237, 240, 241, 244, 253, 271, 282, 290n119 & 121, 291n130, 299n36, 331n185, 338n329

Sassoon, Victor, 138, 311n315
Saudi Arabia, 124, 176, 244, 299n36
Schwarzman, Stephen, 20, 287n48
second-class foreigner, 255
selfish gene, 60
Senkaku (Diaoyu) islets, 87, 260
Serbia, 123, 124, 228, 300n38
SEZs (special economic zones), 135
Shanghai Cooperation Organization (SCO), 84, 243, 299n36
Silicon Valley, 187, 192, 219
Sinic world, also see Chinese world, 2, 11, 14, 20, 23, 40, 70, 73, 74, 146, 213, 223, 266, 282
Singapore, 176, 191, 241, 321n255, 335n279
Sino-British Joint Declaration, 212

Sinologists, 159–71, 180, 182, 185, 188, 226, 231, 277, 317n139, 335n283
  of Chinese heritage, 84, 162, 166–69, 316n124
Sinology, *also see* China Studies, 6, 159–71, 191, 315n98
  state of, 12, 141, 159–71
social contract, 46, 55, 60
Social Darwinism, 81, 295n235
socialism, socialist, 10, 15, 16–17, 19, 29, 35, 37, 47, 56, 57, 65, 87, 90, 124, 126, 132, 155, 208, 286n24
soft power, 49, 84, 100, 107, 115, 142, 155, 237–38, 256, 266, 278, 338n6
South America, *see* Latin America
South China Sea, 83, 87, 105, 155, 160, 178, 179, 197, 260, 325n25
Southeast Asia, 83, 92, 107, 119, 120, 155, 212, 218, 241, 303n114
sovereignty, 59, 70, 87, 96, 153, 193, 198, 210, 215–16, 219, 222, 223, 279, 280, 284n1, 285n2
Soviet Bloc, 25, 72, 272, 302n96
Soviet Union (USSR), *see also* Russia, 12, 18, 25, 29, 33, 34–37, 39, 85, 36, 92, 95, 97, 99, 100, 106, 108, 109, 119, 122–23, 153, 170, 214, 229, 245, 259, 272, 289n85, 291n142, 316n122 & n133, 316n47
Spain, 98, 289n87, 290n119
Spanish-American War, 24
Sri Lanka, 84, 123, 299n36
stability maintenance, 103, 112, 147
Stalinism, Stalinist, 14, 16, 29, 36, 50, 65, 72, 94, 190, 222, 228, 247, 270, 286n21

state, the, 46, 53–57, 63, 67, 285n2, 294n213
  effectiveness and fairness of, 53–57
Stoicism, 45, 292n175
strong/great power diplomacy (大国外交), 88, 98, 99, 137
Sudan, 123, 124, 290n119, 300n38
Sullivan, Jake, 82
Summit for Democracy, 199
Sumerian city-states, 2
Sun Tzu (孙子), 195
SWIFT (Society for Worldwide Interbank Financial Telecommunication), 130–31, 240

Taiwan (台灣), *see also* ROC, 25, 87, 88, 106, 108, 110–11, 115–16, 120, 155, 160, 163, 176, 179, 184, 193–94, 195, 199, 218, 230, 241, 257–60, 273–74, 305n155, 317n131, 328n87, 335n282, 336n287 & n282
Taiwan Lobby, 188
Tanzania, 98, 123, 124
Tazara (the Tanzania-Zambia Railway), 98
technology, role of, 68–69, 73, 127–28, 174–75, 244–45, 247, 270, 336n301
Tedros Adhanom, 103
Third Front program, 85
Thousand Talents program, 189, 196
Tiananmen Uprising, 34, 189, 285n10
tianxia (天下 all under heaven), *see also* China Order, 10, 15, 16, 36, 74, 78, 85, 89, 129, 138, 276, 283n7, 286n25
Tibet (西藏), 36, 87, 111, 112, 147, 258, 306n188 & n189

456 | Index

totalitarianism, 13, 14, 15–16, 18, 29, 31, 33, 38, 40, 46–47, 72, 75, 77, 79–80, 89, 146, 153, 157, 204, 212, 253, 277, 282, 286n16
TPP (Trans-Pacific Partnership), 179, 182, 196
trade misinvoicing, 132–33
tribalism, 23, 29, 47, 59
Truman, Harry, 27
Trump, Donald, 149, 179, 180–85, 187, 193, 196–97, 319n188, 324n322 & n326
Tsai Ing-wen (蔡英文), 110, 111, 259
TSMC (台積電), 259
Turkey, 34, 107, 124, 299n36
Twitter/X, 102, 233, 252
tyranny of small decisions, 1

UK, Britain, 25, 34, 98, 116, 118, 120, 176, 180, 182, 188, 191, 199, 212, 219, 237, 259, 272, 284n1
Ukraine, 34, 101, 131, 155, 186, 218, 240, 241, 244
UN (United Nations), 26, 28, 33, 44, 83, 89, 91, 94, 112, 115, 146, 180, 191, 272, 310n290, 336n302
united front, 6, 71, 75, 90, 119–20, 168–69, 224, 226, 233, 240, 251, 254, 257, 307n214, 317n140
universal basic income, 57, 66
Universal Declaration of Human Rights, 171
US (USA, United States of America), as PRC's main target, 37, 141–51, 186–92
babies born by visiting PRC parents, 235
China Policy, 81, 159–60, 163–64, 193, 195, 197, 199, 231–32, 238

reorientation and zigzags of, 141, 172, 178–86, 192–94, 269
Chinese students in, 120, 220, 230, 233–35, 334n338
special education of, 234–35
dollar, 26, 84, 127, 129–30, 131, 231–32, 239, 309n264
domestic issues relevant to the China Race, 28–29, 56–57, 107, 120, 161, 175–76, 188–92, 195–96, 218–20, 226, 229–31, 235, 289n92, 313n63, 315n101, 327n54
foreign policy, 27, 129, 171, 180, 182, 185–86, 193
leadership of, 2, 13, 20, 24–29, 42, 78, 127, 146, 175, 194, 196–97, 199, 205, 217, 238–39, 264, 279
power of, 24, 27, 142–43, 186, 216–17, 224, 231–32, 242
useful idiots, 34, 93, 117, 155, 164, 224, 268, 313n50

vaccine diplomacy, 238
Venezuela, 33, 34, 84, 99, 100, 112, 118, 209n119 & n121
Vietnam, 25, 36, 38, 82, 97, 109, 116, 119, 121, 208, 241, 274, 289n85, 325n20

Wall Street, 130, 134, 138, 180, 183, 184, 188–89, 192, 219, 230, 296n249, 322n262
Wang Yi (王毅), 88, 89, 250, 330n40
war, just, 48, 269
Warring States, 23, 223
WeChat (微信), 212, 219, 233, 256, 327n68
welfare state, 59, 126, 296n250
Wen Jiabao (温家宝), 89
West, the concept of, 284–85n1
Westernization, 172, 283n7

Westfailure, 21, 64
Westphalian system/order, 1, 3–6, 9, 11, 14–15, 18–19, 21–24, 41–42, 157, 223, 238–39, 336n302
current variant of, *see* LIO
demise/detraction/destruction of, 1, 3–4, 11–12, 19, 23, 24–32, 40, 46, 48–50, 78–79, 81, 136, 145–47, 154, 158, 175, 210, 215–16, 219, 223, 262
desirability/role of, 6, 10, 17–18, 20–23, 38, 51, 62–71, 77, 122, 131, 145, 157–58, 171, 202–203, 260–61, 266, 276
expansion/improvement of, 1, 23–24, 156, 203, 214, 246, 264–65, 271, 288n63
future of, 276–82
preservation of, 1, 3–5, 12, 24–29, 38, 40, 42–44, 48–50, 171, 203–206, 210–11, 214, 217–19, 238, 245, 247, 261–65, 269–70
white glove (白手套), 102, 304n138
White Paper Movement, 265
WHO (the World Health Organization), 26, 83, 103, 180, 292n163
Wilson, Woodrow, 44
WMD (weapon of mass destruction), 19, 31, 205, 208, 225, 247, 270–71
wolf warrior diplomacy, 93, 195–96, 250, 332n197
World Bank, 99, 130, 152, 191, 323n184
World Communism/Communist, 6, 17, 40, 41, 78, 82, 88, 94, 106, 108, 123, 222
world empire, 2, 6, 7, 10, 13–14, 15–16, 18, 20, 21, 23–25, 32, 40, 44, 50, 68, 77, 81, 93, 105, 138, 146–47, 156–57, 204, 205,

222, 253, 262, 269, 270, 276, 282, 283n4
result/tendency of globalization, 31–32, 42–43, 47–48, 63, 66, 68, 70, 74, 154, 206, 265
US as one, 24–29, 154, 157–58, 262
world governance/government, 11, 14, 22, 26, 31, 45–46, 57, 62, 66, 68, 79, 156–58, 211, 215, 223, 262
world order, alternatives of, 1–3, 6, 7, 9–10, 16, 19, 21, 23, 29, 33, 40, 51, 67, 78, 83, 138, 142, 145, 154, 161, 173, 202, 204, 205, 218–19, 221, 260, 264, 269, 271, 284n1
world peace, 37, 44, 47, 51, 65–66, 74–75, 204, 205, 219, 237, 258, 266–67, 271
world state, 16, 32, 42, 45–47, 270
world-federation, 47, 63, 68
World War I, 12, 65, 79, 203, 222, 247, 298n5
World War II, 15, 18, 22, 24, 25, 27, 65, 79, 80, 106, 114, 146, 167, 171, 183, 186, 203, 238, 247, 260, 267, 271–72, 274, 277, 338n329
Worlds, of Mesopotamian-Persian, Indian, Chinese (Sinic), Mongolian, Mesoamerican, Mediterranean-European, 2, 17, 19, 22, 61, 174, 292n169
WTO (World Trade Organization), 105, 129, 130, 151, 158, 172, 179, 196, 240, 285n10
Wuhan (武汉), 175, 180, 193, 292n163

Xi Jinping (习近平), 13, 33, 75, 79, 84, 88, 93, 100, 101, 114, 118,

458 | Index

Xi Jinping (continued)
121, 148, 150, 153, 160, 172–73,
178, 191, 195, 196, 231, 241,
245, 248, 253, 254, 256, 263
on world order, 4, 75–76, 81,
89–90, 146, 149, 154, 169, 222,
275, 338n1
Thought, 75, 86, 88, 208, 228,
328n81
xiangchou (乡愁 homesickness),
168
Xinjiang (新疆), 33, 34, 36, 87,
88, 111, 112, 124, 147, 155,
184, 193, 199, 229, 230, 244,
306n188 & n190

Yang Jiechi (杨洁篪), 87, 250
Yellow Fever/Peril/ Promise, 228
Ying-shih Yu (余英時), 169
Yoon Suk Yeol (윤석열), 218
Yunnan (云南), 111, 306n188

Zambia, 98, 103
Zhou Enlai (周恩来), 91, 121, 301n81
Zimbabwe, 84, 99, 112, 118, 123,
124, 290n119